MW00855903

The Palgrave International Handbook of Animal Abuse Studies

Jennifer Maher • Harriet Pierpoint • Piers Beirne
Editors

The Palgrave International Handbook of Animal Abuse Studies

Editors
Jennifer Maher
Centre for Criminology
University of South Wales
Pontypridd, United Kingdom

Harriet Pierpoint
Centre for Criminology
University of South Wales
Pontypridd, United Kingdom

Piers Beirne
Criminology Department
University of Southern Maine
Portland, Maine, USA

ISBN 978-1-137-43182-0 ISBN 978-1-137-43183-7 (eBook)
DOI 10.1057/978-1-137-43183-7

Library of Congress Control Number: 2016949400

Cover illustration: Kat Cardy

Printed on acid-free paper

This Palgrave Macmillan imprint is published by Springer Nature
The registered company is Macmillan Publishers Ltd.
The registered company address is: The Campus, 4 Crinan Street, London, N1 9XW, United Kingdom

Acknowledgments

This *Handbook* has been quite a while in the making. Its origins can be traced to the UK International Symposium on Situating Animal Abuse in Criminology held in July 2010, in Cardiff, Wales. We are indebted to the generosity of the University of South Wales (formerly the University of Glamorgan) for funding the event. Many of the chapters in this book were written by symposium attendees.

As editors, our debts are legion. To all those who share our pro-animal passion for the advancement of animal abuse studies and who helped us complete the *Handbook*: thank you! We thank the many authors who contributed chapters and who in so doing helped advance this important field of enquiry. Your commitment has been invaluable. We also wish to acknowledge the contribution both of our immediate colleagues and of those further afield (our many colleagues and their networks, especially in green criminology); in different and important ways you have made this project possible.

Our gratitude must also be extended to the fine staff at Palgrave Macmillan, especially Julia Willan, Josephine Taylor, Dominic Walker and Stephanie Carey. Your enthusiasm and constructive engagement have been crucial.

The focus of the *Handbook* is the situation of animals who suffer death and other harms and abuses at the hands of humans. Because much animal abuse is intentionally and routinely rendered invisible, criminology, sociology and related disciplines have tended to ignore our fellow creatures. We wish to recognise and acknowledge these animals and the people and organisations who work so tirelessly on their behalf. As a small token of our support in this regard, our royalties from this

Handbook will be donated equally to the Animals and Society Institute and the Sea Shepherd Conservation Society.

Finally, we salute our family and friends for their love and support. The book is dedicated to a special few: To Harriet's Amelia, Tilly, Charlie and Mum. To Piers' Boz, Daisy, Lydia and late brother Nicholas. To Jennifer's Keith, Buffy and her many foster dog guests.

Contents

List of Figures

List of Tables

List of Boxes

Editors' Introduction

Jennifer Maher, Harriet Pierpoint and Piers Beirne

This Handbook tries to understand animal abuse and how we humans perceive it and respond to it. This is no easy task. The history of changing attitudes to animals and to our abuse of them indeed offers a sobering lesson about the limits of human compassion. What we give with one hand we take away with the other. So much of that history is ambiguous and of the sort 'on the one hand' *but* 'on the other.' For example, on the one hand, it has been and still is often claimed about early Judaeo-Christian texts, such as *Genesis*, that God has placed at our disposal all the animals that walk or crawl on the earth and those that swim in the sea and fly in the air—*all* animals other than humans, that is, for us to do with whatever we like and to do so without reservation. This was certainly the viewpoint of theologians such as St Augustine and Thomas Aquinas. On the other hand, however, especially as first seen in the writings of sixteenth-century essayists such as John Calvin and Michel de Montaigne and in the pleas for vegetarianism by the occasional eccentric, those very same early Christian texts have also been interpreted as obliging us to care for those (domesticated) animals under our control and to use them fairly and responsibly and without cruelty.

J. Maher (✉) · H. Pierpoint
Centre for Criminology, University of South Wales, Pontypridd, United Kingdom
e-mail: jenny.maher@southwales.ac.uk; harriet.pierpoint@southwales.ac.uk

P. Beirne
Criminology Department, University of Southern Maine, Portland, Maine, USA
e-mail: beirne@maine.edu

J. Maher et al. (eds.), *The Palgrave International Handbook of Animal Abuse Studies*, DOI 10.1057/978-1-137-43183-7_1

If early religious texts that pontificate on human–animal relationships are open to wildly different interpretations (which often result in harm to animals themselves), then much the same can be said about early legislative attempts to control and deter animal cruelty in Ireland, England and colonial America. Some of the most detestable forms of animal cruelty were outlawed by seventeenth-century parliamentary legislation. But both the motives of the reformers and the results of their activities were not part of some inevitable trajectory of humane progress.

Consider the three earliest 'animal protection' laws. The Irish *Act Against Plowing by the Tayle* (1635), first, attempted to ban the widespread practice of poor Irish tenant farmers attaching ploughs directly to horses' tails—rather than using more expensive 'horse furniture': saddle, reins, ropes and large plough. Seemingly an attempt to forbid cruelty to horses, the *Act* was more a mechanism to reinforce the dominance of English nationalism and culture in Ireland and to facilitate the private profiteering by English landlords and agricultural entrepreneurs and their allies. The practice of ploughing by tail did not disappear until well into the nineteenth century, and this as much because it was economically inefficient as it was perceived as injurious to horses.

The Puritans' *Of the Bruite Creature*, second, was enacted in 1641 as *Liberties* No 92 and No 93 in the newly-formed Massachusetts Bay Colony in colonial America. The ostensible aim of this enactment was to encourage pious and righteous sentiments towards domesticated animals, especially in respect of the obligation to provide them with fodder, shelter and care. Doubtless, some and perhaps, even, many of the Calvinist-inspired settlers embraced these humane sentiments. Just as much, however, *Of the Bruite Creature* was an artefact of economic necessity. It reflected, in other words, the importance of cattle, horses, pigs and sheep, in particular, to the politics of survival in a harsh and unforgiving frontier society.

Third and finally, the Cromwellian Protectorate's *Ordinance for Prohibiting Cock-Matches* (1654) was partly the result, on the one hand, of English puritanism's opposition to some bloodsports, such as enforced fighting between cocks and the baiting of bulls, bears and badgers. On the other hand, many Puritans enjoyed bloodsports because the opposition to them—as measured, for example, by the number of criminal prosecutions—was lukewarm and very small in number. It is very likely that in enacting the *Ordinance*, the members of the Protectorate had in mind not only a reduction in animal suffering, as such, but also an end to the drunkenness and public disturbances that such sports attracted. Bloodsports dishonoured God.

During the last 200 or so years, legislation on human–animal relationships has emerged at both the national and international levels. Its stated aim has been both to elevate animal welfare standards and to regulate our use of animals more effectively. Nowadays, some level of animal welfare is taken for granted, which perhaps suggests a change in the valoration of certain species (those appointed as animal companions, for example). However, as we have already alluded, motivations for protecting animals are varied, ranging from the positioning of animals as God-given-for-us, as sacred, as items for human survival (as food, clothing, labour and so on), as property, as profitable commodities, as objects of scientific research, as entertainment and as sport. The list is a lengthy one. Yet, even as animals have increasingly become valued to mankind—as companions or family members—only seldom have they been regarded as victims or individuals or persons.

Underlying the enhanced concern and compassion for animals is a long tradition of deliberate abuse. It is ironic, to say the least, that our efforts to imbue our use of animals with greater compassion has at the very same time been accompanied by a vast expansion in intensive rearing regimes and in the consumption of animals. In fact, the rendering of animals into edibles has led to unprecedented levels of needless cruelty. While current standards may allow some animals to be treated more humanely, the reality is markedly different for the billions of individual animals annually transformed into edibles by the meat, fish and dairy industries, for example, or used for scientific research and for entertainment. Animals killed inside the walls of a shuttered slaughterhouse, invisibly and en masse, nevertheless die as individuals, each suffering an artificially shortened life and a death that is of great consequence to him or to her.

To make sense of this paradox it is essential to understand the ideologies that favour and perpetuate the many ways that we use and dispose of animals and their bodies. In his enormously influential book *Animal Liberation*—which many followers still think of as the leading text in the modern animal rights movement—the moral philosopher Peter Singer argues that 'behind the mere momentary desire to eat meat on a particular occasion lie many years of habitual meat-eating which have conditioned our attitudes to animals' (1995, p. xiii). Singer's powerful insight also applies to the many uses that we make of animals as companions, as entertainment and so on. The mainstreaming of the welfare movement coupled with consistent, graphic campaigning by animal advocacy groups such as People for the Ethical Treatment of Animals and the Animal Liberation Front, have created a climate in which many people are sensitised to animal abuse and harm. Increasingly, these groups have adopted the role of exposing the harms concealed in everyday social practices (Samuel 2016, see also Singer 1995), which often results in the criminalisation of certain practices, such as the ban on fox hunting in the UK and a limited ban on the use of steel-jaw traps in the US.

Despite these advances, the legal status of animals remains essentially unchanged. Arguably, this is because the legitimate channels for protest and processes for change are protracted and unreliable. Changing mainstream ideologies 'not only of diet but also thought and language' (Singer 1995, p. xiv) are principal obstructions to any thoroughgoing or overall reduction in the level of harm inflicted on animals.

By the mid-nineteenth century, ever more efficient methods of rearing and killing animals have resulted in relatively less expensive 'product on the hoof'—as animal edibles or as clothing, for example. The commodification of the processes of transforming animals into edibles has resulted in more food being produced at lower costs. Spiralling upward demand for the flesh and skin of animals and the persistent entrepreneurial search for profit encourages producers to use evermore harmful procedures on animals. The result has been and can only have been a disastrous reduction in the extent of humane practices. In scientific research, moreover, the gross mistreatment of animals in the name of human health is financially and legally supported and thus condoned by the state, even when non-animal experimental procedures are available.

We have created and now live in an era of animal abuse that is unprecedented in its scale and severity. As this abuse has become normalised, expanded and entrenched into mainstream cultural and religious practices, in varying degrees we are all complicit in it. Even though the world's human population has doubled over the past 50 years, today's global production of meat—the flesh from cattle, pigs and chickens,—is projected to be twice that of 1986 and five times that of 1966 (Cook 2016). In the US, the meat and poultry industry generates $864.2 billion annually, or roughly 6 % of the entire GDP of the US economy (North American Meat Institute 2015).

Moral philosophy and animal rights theory have been central to recent academic discussions of animal abuse. As a result, while recognising the moral blindness of Descartes' assertion that animals are simple automata—unconscious machines with no ability to reason or feel pain—many of the authors in this book situate the ethical treatment of animals within the frameworks of utilitarianism, animal rights and feminist-vegetarian critical theory and ecofeminism. The development of animal rights theory is comparable to the philosophical probing of other liberation movements (such as those based on race, gender or sexual orientation). Singer (1995, p. xi) argues that a liberation movement demands:

> an expansion of our moral horizons. Practices that were previously regarded as natural and inevitable come to be seen as the result of an unjustifiable prejudice . . . If we wish to avoid being numbered among the oppressors, we must be prepared to rethink all our attitudes to other groups, including the most fundamental of them...

Though there has been somewhat of a movement from calls for better animal welfare, on the one hand, to animal liberation and to animal personhood and citizenship on the other, the tangible results have only applied to a few privileged species in select locations, two wildly discrepant examples of which include recent extensions of human rights to apes in Spain and elsewhere, and the use of the death penalty in China for offenders found guilty of killing pandas. The increased protection that favoured animals receive through legislation and changes in social attitudes tends to be directly linked to the intrinsic and extrinsic value that humans place on them. Paradoxically, the closer we move to viewing certain animals as valued individuals, the further away we seem to move from practices that respect and protect other individuals. For example: on the one hand, there has been a great reduction in the use of primates in scientific research; on the other hand, there has been a huge increase in the slaughter and consumption of cattle, pigs, sheep and chickens. Similarly, trophy hunting has been used to fund the protection of endangered species from poachers. Human–animal relationships continue to evolve on and in such paradoxes. Clearly, they demand more thought and consideration within criminology and related disciplines.

This book aims to identify and to disentangle some of the complicated relationships that exist at sites of animal abuse. It details some of the important sites—socially acceptable and unacceptable, legal and illegal—and attempts to explain what happens at those sites and how we respond to them. This detailed consideration of animal abuse is essential, first and foremost, *for the sake of animals themselves*. It is essential as well because of the tremendous damage that animal use and abuse inflicts on environments, including those that are animals' own habitats. This focus is surely long overdue. The ideologies and habits which facilitate the intensified use of animals, generation after generation, cannot exist alongside measures to enhance standards of animal welfare and a movement towards the securing of animals' rights. Furthermore, although there is widespread agreement with claims about 'the link'—that is, violence against animals is often an indicator of actual or potential interpersonal violence—our ability to fully comprehend the relationship between animal abuse and other forms of crime and violence is currently thwarted both by the complexities of defining animal abuse and by the absence of reliable research and appropriate remedies. Moreover, while recent attention to animal abuse has raised awareness and concern about its impact on humans, its effects on animals have received far less attention.

Thinking about animal abuse requires one to begin with and confront century-old issues in criminology about whether crime or harm should be the focus of study (criminology versus zemiology, that is). For our purposes, it matters little whether animal abuse is legal or illegal, intentional or unintentional, commonplace or infrequent, committed one-on-one or in large-scale institutions. However defined, all forms of animal abuse should be opened up for nonspeciesist scrutiny. This broader and deeper vision has already happened with other major forms of interpersonal and institutional violence such as sexism, racism and ageism. Criminology may have arrived late at the scene. But, as this book shows, it has arrived.

The Contents of This Book

This book was designed to fill three needs: (1) the need for an inclusive resource which would introduce the key concepts and issues in animal abuse studies; (2) the need for a research-based volume which would invite scholars, students and practitioners to think about a comprehensive range of animal abuse scenarios; and (3) the need for a useful platform for scholars of animal abuse to raise awareness of their own areas of expertise.

The central theme of the book is the use and abuse of animals. The wide range of human-animal relationships examined in the following 22 chapters include animals who live in close proximity to us (those whom we have domesticated and who live in our homes or those who are raised on farms and whom we slaughter as edibles); those animals collected and destroyed in 'the wild'; those animals whom we enlist as items of entertainment and sport; those animals sacrificed on the scientific altars of human health, human knowledge and human happiness; and those animals used and abused by political and military elites for our protection and by national and local states who decide certain animals are unwanted, dangerous, surplus to demand and otherwise expendable.

While we wish to consider animal abuse in its broadest sense and we recognise that all animal species are adversely affected by commonplace human behaviour, there is, inevitably, some bias in the Handbook's chapters in respect of what species are represented and what are ignored. There is a somewhat disproportionate representation of domesticated animals in the book, for example, but this is to be expected because it is these animals who are in the most immediate contact with people and who are consequently most commonly the focus of enquiry.

Some readers may find that some of the chapters do not address actual categories of crimes. As such, a central question weaving its way throughout this book, as one of us has previously asked, is:

> Why some harms to animals are defined as criminal, others as abusive but not criminal, and still others as neither criminal nor abusive? In exploring these questions, a narrow concept of crimes against animals would necessarily have to be rejected in favour of a more inclusive concept of harm. Without it, the meaning of animal abuse will be overwhelmingly confined to those harms that are regarded as socially unacceptable, one-on-one cases of animal cruelty. Certainly, those cases demand attention. But so, too, do those other and far more numerous institutionalized harms to animals, where abuse is routine, invisible, ubiquitous, and often defined as socially acceptable (Beirne 2009, p. 200)

That said, there are some forms of animal abuse that do not appear in this Handbook, either owing to limitation of space or because there is little or no current research on them. Prominent among these are the abuse of animals used in religious practices and in certain forms of entertainment, such as circuses and movies.

Much of the scholarly research and activist work on human–animal studies is conducted in the US, Europe, Canada and Australasia; regrettably, therefore, other regions appear here less often. Nonetheless, this book is international in scope: topics were selected and authors were invited to comment on the international context of animal abuse and, where possible, to recognise that many of the harms criss-cross national and cultural boundaries and are global in nature. Animals killed for food in the UK, for example, are increasingly likely to come from elsewhere: lamb from New Zealand, for example, makes up 30 % of lamb sales in the UK (worth $646 million NZD dollars), while the international trade in animals and their body parts is worth up to US $200 billion worldwide.

We asked that each chapter consider four key issues in the animal abuse that forms its subject matter: its basic characteristics; its incidence and prevalence; how it might be explained and the variety of social reactions and responses to it. We imposed no other restrictions on authors. Scholars and writers from a variety of disciplines and fields (criminology, sociology, law, psychology and science, for example) were invited to contribute original chapters to this volume. By design, we encouraged a multidisciplinary focus—conjoining lawyers, animal welfare/rights practitioners and journalists with academics—to discuss a particular type of animal abuse, writing, where possible, from a research-based and/or practitioner perspective. While the book was constructed with criminology and related subjects in mind, the selection of topics and construction of the book was deliberately chosen to make it accessible to a wide range of academic disciplines—including law, human–animal studies, forensics and environmental studies. It is our hope that this collaborative multidisciplinary approach opens new horizons and that it will enable new approaches to the understanding and prevention of animal abuse.

This Introduction sheds light on key issues in animal abuse studies. The Handbook has seven Parts. Chapter 1 provides an introduction to the book and to key issues in animal abuse studies. The following parts focus on specific harms and abuses experienced by animals within each of the areas identified above. Part I contains six chapters which redefine the abuse of domesticated animals. These chapters suggest that because domestic animals are wards under our control, they should receive an appropriate level of care and protection. That said, their closeness exposes them to specific harms, which are largely consistent with the continuum of abuse experienced in interpersonal domestic relationships—such as physical and psychological abuse, sexual abuse, cruelty and neglect. Consequently, 'the link' between animal abuse and interpersonal violence has received widespread recognition from both animal and human welfare groups, from social care, law, psychiatry, and so on, resulting in some types of animal abuse being recognised as serious harms and crimes (for example, animal sexual assault and status dogs ownership) and others as indicative of mental health disorders (for example, animal hoarding and neglect). However, each chapter highlights the ambivalence inherent in our responses to animal abuse and the importance of context to understand the motivation for, and problematic responses to, animal abuse.

Part II presents two accounts of the abuse experienced by animals in farming. The need for a harm-based definition of animal abuse is central to this discussion. The normative everyday practices of animal food production collectively result in the most widespread and systematic abuse of animals. Unlike the abuse of domesticated animals and the intense societal response, the abuse endemic in the farming of animals is normalised and contributes mightily to the cultural hegemony of meat production and to the general subjugation of animals.

Part III focuses on animal abuse that contributes to the decline of species who live in what we term 'the wild'. This abuse ranges from small-scale specialised egg collectors to the large-scale and organised poaching of millions of animals in the legal and illegal wildlife trade. The three chapters here demonstrate why animal abuse has found a home in the growing green criminology movement (Beirne and South 2007; Hall et al. 2016). Environmental destruction poses a real threat to biodiversity owing to the pollution and elimination of animals' habitat and the inadequate responses compromised by the complex relationship between legal and illegal behaviour. Specifically, those responsible for protecting wildlife are able to establish the thin line between legal and illegal acts and to profit from the harms towards wildlife.

In Part IV the focus shifts to animals used in entertainment. Three of the four chapters here ('Animal Racing', 'Hunting and Shooting' and 'Animal Fighting') discuss a variety of the changing practices, perceptions and attitudes associated with the use of animals in sport. They demonstrate the inherent conflict between rights and welfare responses to animal abuse, suggesting that the latter may have the paradoxical effect of tempering concern for animals, even as harm to animals remains very real. This part concludes by challenging the exclusive focus on terrestrial animals in animal abuse literature and highlights the plight of 'ornamental' animals used as entertainment. Although scientific evidence verifies that fish can feel pain and that they have feelings, this has not improved their legal standing or reduced their suffering. Rather, the failure to improve the welfare of fish emphasises a commonplace obstruction in animal abuse legislation, which exempts the great majority of animals from receiving protection, through an artfully or neglectfully chosen phrase in the legal definition of 'animal': all sentient beings? invertebrates? fish? birds? reptiles? 'vermin'?.

Part V looks at the use of animals in vivisection and scientific research. The two chapters here exemplify the contradictions in our approach to animal welfare and rights. The number of animals used in research continues to rise in large part due to outdated legal requirements, rampant scientific curiosity and widespread misinformation on the need for animal experiments rather than the use of non-animal alternatives. This is also often supported by government funding. The level of duplicity is highlighted in the extensive and secretive use and re-victimisation of shelter cats and dogs in experimentation. The harms these animals endure in the lab would be considered criminal in most parts of the developed world if they occurred in any other social situation or scenario.

Part VI addresses other state-sanctioned harms to animals. It focuses on the structural violence implicit in our use of animals—especially dogs and horses—in war and in criminal justice enforcement. The use of animals by the military and police, although well established, is seldom opened up for scrutiny. Centuries of untold exploitation, suffering and mass execution are hidden behind the caring, symbiotic relationship of human handler and animal. Similarly, alongside the veneer of management and care common-place in the conservation narrative, is the wide-scale and accepted destruction of animals who are deemed invasive alien species or insignificant species. Like the others, these chapters call attention to the inconsistencies and paradoxes in our treatment of animals.

Part VII—a concluding chapter—examines a range of interventions available for responding to animal abuse offenders. It sets out some possibilities for resolving the pervasive difficulties of responding to animal abusers that are identified in other chapters. In doing so, the chapter stresses that while many promising programmes exist which can be used to intervene with specific types of offenders, there is a need for extensive evaluation of their impact and effectiveness. Considerable work is still required in order to respond appropriately and effectively to all types of animal abusers. A chronological guess: this hard work will take two generations of extending humane education towards compassion and empathy.

A Note on Language and Production

In recognition of the natural variation in the use of language, the debates surrounding the harms perpetuated by anthropocentric and speciesist discourse and to facilitate effective communication, we have not imposed a common approach to language on authors and the result has been the use of a broad range of terms to refer to 'animal' (that is, non-human, other than human, more than human), 'pet' (for example, companion) and 'abuse' (for example, cruelty, harm), and so on. Inevitably, the acceptability and understanding of the terms used vary geographically, for example, when discussing the use of animals in scientific research 'vivisection' is commonly used in the US and also occasionally in the UK, while the term 'experimentation' is more common in Australian literature.

As editors, we three—Jen, Harriet and Piers—had hoped to be able to state definitively that 'no animals—*none*—were used and abused in the production of this book'. In this regard, however, animal abuse is regrettably present on every page—hidden, in plain sight, as it were—from the destruction of animals' habitat by the paper industry to the use of animals' bodies for glue for binding. This is a sad reminder of the seemingly, inescapable harm our everyday practices cause our fellow creatures.

References

Beirne, P. (2009). *Confronting animal abuse.* Lanham, MD: Rowman & Littlefield.

Beirne, P., & South, N. (2007). *Issues in green criminology: confronting harms against environments, humanity and other animals.* London: Willan.

Cook, R. (2016). *World meat production (1960–present).* Beef2Live. http://beef2live.com/story-world-meat-production-1960-present-0-111818. Accessed 23 May 2016.

Hall, M., Maher, J., Nurse, A. South, N., & Wyatt, T. (Eds.). (2016). *Greening criminology in the 21st century: Contemporary debates and future directions in the study of environmental harm.* London: Routledge.

North American Meat Institute. (2015). *The United States meat industry at a glance.* https://www.meatinstitute.org/index.php?ht=d/sp/i/47465/pid/47465. Accessed 23 May 2016.

Samuel, H. (2016). France's abattoirs to be inspected for animal cruelty after shock film. The Telegraph. Available at: http://www.telegraph.co.uk/news/2016/03/29/francesabattoirs-to-be-inspected-for-animal-cruelty-after-shock/. Accessed 20 April 2016.

Singer, P. (1995). *Animal liberation.* 2nd edition. London: Pimlico.

Dr Jennifer Maher is Senior Lecturer at the Centre for Criminology, University of South Wales. Her research interests include animal abuse, green criminology, human-animal studies, and youth and gang violence. She recently concluded a UK wildlife trafficking study for the FP7 (European Commission) EFFACE project which evaluated the impact of environmental crime in Europe and is currently researching puppy smuggling for the Scottish and English Governments. Her publications include co-editing *Greening Criminology in the 21st Century* (2016, Routledge, with M. Hall et al.) and the special journal issue 'Animal Abuse and Criminology' in *Crime, Law and Social Change* (2011 with P. Beirne).

Dr Harriet Pierpoint is a Reader in Criminology and Criminal Justice at the Centre for Criminology at University of South Wales. Her research interests relate to criminal process and vulnerable people, and, more recently, animal abuse. She has undertaken a number of funded research projects including for the Youth Justice Board, Home Office, Ministry of Justice and the National Offender Management

Service Cymru and has publications in internationally recognised, peer reviewed journals, such as *Policing and Society: An International Journal and Criminology and Criminal Justice: The International Journal.* She is a co-editor of the *Handbook on Crime*, for Willan Publishing. She has also presented her research at key national and international conferences and has been by invited by academics and practitioners to give guest lectures. She is a member of the Executive Committee of the British Society of Criminology (Chair, Regional Groups and Specialist Networks) and of the South Wales Police Independent Ethics Committee.

Professor Piers Beirne has taught sociology, law and criminology in England, Ireland and the United States, where he is currently Professor of Sociology and Legal Studies in the Department of Criminology at the University of Southern Maine. Among his books are *Hogarth's Art of Animal Cruelty* (2015, Palgrave Macmillan); *Criminology: A Sociological Approach* (2015, with James W. Messerschmidt, Oxford University Press, 6th edition); and *Confronting Animal Abuse* (2009, Rowman & Littlefield). Recent edited books include *Issues in Green Criminology* (2007, with Nigel South, Willan); a 6-volume reprint series, The Chicago School of Criminology 1914–1945 (2006, Routledge); and *Green Criminology* (2006, with Nigel South, Ashgate). He is the founding co-editor of the journal *Theoretical Criminology*.

Part I

The Abuse of Domesticated Animals

Breeding and Selling of Companion Animals

James Yeates and David Bowles

Introduction

This chapter considers the breeding, transportation and sale of pets and how criminals breed and trade in animals. The chapter uses data and insights from studies published largely by stakeholders (for example, non-government organisations [NGO]) and based on clinical and professional experience of working in a key UK animal welfare NGO with (separate) campaigning, legal enforcement and rehoming functions during the last two decades. This chapter focuses, as an example, on the breeding and sale of canine puppies in England and Wales.

This chapter describes the actions performed by breeders and dealers, starting with the nature of the activity and its consequences, then considering its prevalence, followed by explanations for those activities and possible responses in order to prevent or reduce their prevalence. This chapter provides a broader evaluation of harms than that currently defined in UK law. There is debate, for example, as to whether breeding animals to have (an unreasonable likelihood of) inherited disorders is illegal. Whether such harms are illegal will depend on the legal instruments

J. Yeates (✉)
RSPCA, Wilberforce Way, Southwater, United Kingdom
e-mail: james.yeates@rspca.org.uk

D. Bowles
RSPCA, Wilberforce Way, Southwater, West Sussex, United Kingdom
e-mail: david.bowles@rspca.org.uk

J. Maher et al. (eds.), *The Palgrave International Handbook of Animal Abuse Studies*, DOI 10.1057/978-1-137-43183-7_2

available and their interpretation in the relevant country. Some of the activities described here might, therefore, be considered legal (or at least unclear) in some countries.

Nature of the Abuse and Harm

This section looks at the key harms to animals involved in the puppy trade. It focuses on harmful breeding practices that impact on animals used as mates and their offspring, and how other processes within the trade may engender further harms, specifically intra- and inter-national transportation and sales. These harms, while clearly directly impacting on the animals involved, also result in secondary harm to the purchasers. This can include, for example, behavioural or health problems for the dogs that may mean owners spend considerable sums on remedial treatment or suffer significant disruption or potential personal risks (for example, from canine human-related aggression or some transferable diseases).

Breeding

The first key stage in the trade is the production of the product—that is, puppies. This involves both the breeding animals and their progeny. Deliberate breeding involves breeders selecting the mates from whom to breed, and who are under the breeders' management before, during and after the reproduction.

Care of Mates

The care of the breeding male and female can be problematic. These animals need care as other animals do, including a suitable diet, exercise and social interactions. These may not be provided by the breeders. For example, if a small number of staff are responsible for the care of a large number of bitches and their progeny, they will not have time to provide the required care. This, in turn, may affect how those dogs react (that is negatively) to humans (in front of the puppies).

Pregnancy and lactation place significant biological demands on the mother. They need to be fit and old enough to cope with the strain (and some breeds take several years to reach maturity). During pregnancy, good care—particularly good nutrition, hygiene and veterinary care—is imperative.

Thereafter, they need sufficient time to recover between litters: breeding bitches too frequently can place a cumulative demand on their internal resources. This can lead to weight-loss and poor immune responses, thereby making them more susceptible to diseases, especially if their hygiene and veterinary care is poor.

Harms arise as a result of a conflict between legal requirements and the economic commercial incentive to breed as many animals as cheaply as possible. For instance, in England, the legislation makes it illegal for bitches to be mated more than once a year, mated six times in their life time or mated before they are one year old (Breeding and Sale of dogs (Welfare) Act 1999). However, there may be greater profitability if bitches are mated as soon as they come into season and as often as they can.

Choice of Mates

Recent years have seen a number of reports into the prevalence of inherited health problems in pedigree and purebred dogs. The 50 most popular UK dog breeds, including labrador retriever, German shepherd, Alaskan malamute and pug, appear to have at least one conformation-related disorder, such as 'squashed' skulls and long backs (Asher et al. 2009). These can themselves cause suffering, make basic maintenance behaviours more difficult (such as breathing) and restrict the animal's abilities to perform other forms of natural behaviour. For example, dogs' abilities to give appropriate signals to other dogs requires adequate tail-length and muzzle length (Kerswell et al. 2010; Leaver and Reimchen 2008). Some breeds or lines also commonly need a caesarean section, because the anatomy of the mother (in particular her pelvis) is too small for that of the puppies (in particular their heads and shoulders). Inherited disorders are genetic disorders that predisposed dogs to certain conditions, such as hip dysplasia, or blood clotting disorders and, again, the 50 most popular UK dog breeds appear to have at least one of these inherited disorders (Summers et al. 2010).

A different issue is the production of hybrids, such as 'wolf dogs'. The legal position of these animals can be in dispute. For instance, any first- or second-generation wolf hybrids are deemed as needing a license under the Dangerous Wild Animals Act 1986, whereas subsequent generations (those with a greater proportion of dog genes) do not. Welfare concerns on keeping such animals arise as the needs of such hybrids may well be different to those of domestic animals, requiring specialist care. As it happens, many animals sold as hybrids are not genuine hybrids, but are instead just dogs that look like wolves. These issues can lead to a black market in such animals and issues around consumer protection (Cusdin and Greenwood 2000).

Raising of Offspring

Many breeding harms relate to the care of the progeny. In England, Scotland and Wales, there are licensing systems, conditional upon a veterinary surgeon or other inspector visiting the breeders to ensure their dogs:

- live in suitable accommodation
- receive adequate food, water and bedding
- get enough exercise
- are transported in safe and comfortable conditions
- are protected in case of fire or other emergency
- are protected from the spread of disease

Large scale commercial breeding establishments (often called 'puppy farms' or 'puppy mills') can be unsuitable environments for puppies (McMillan et al. 2011, 2013). Welfare problems can result from extremes of temperature, inadequate veterinary care or high levels of diseases. These diseases may not necessarily show themselves while the maternal antibodies (from the milk) are still active within the puppy, but may cause problems when they wear off. Stressors such as transport to a point of sale can also trigger diseases such as parvovirus, a reason why puppies succumb to illness in the week after being sold. For those illegal breeders and vendors, there is an increased incentive to sell or dispose of sick animals as quickly as possible and avoid being traceable to the purchaser.

Puppies and kittens need to spend long enough with their mother and littermates both to gain nutrition and to help them learn about the world and how to behave socially (e.g., Goodard and Beilharz 1986). Puppies and kittens also need to undergo experiences so they are familiar with what they will encounter later, such as meeting a range of other dogs (not just the mother and littermates); a variety of humans (that is, not just kennel staff); and household events and objects, so that they do not find those experiences stressful or fearful later (for example, see Bradshaw 2012; Defra 2009). Breeding dogs in 'intensive' conditions is unlikely to facilitate the required human interaction, due to the lack of time staff have to interact with the animals; similarly, breeding dogs in closed barn conditions restricts their range of experiences. In some cases, these conditions may directly violate legislation (for example, Animal Welfare (Breeding of Dogs) (Wales) Regulations 2014 sets a limit of 20 dogs per full-time member of staff or 10 per part-time), as there remains commercial incentives to avoid the legal requirements which could have welfare consequences.

An additional concern is that the 'victims' of this abuse may continue to suffer long-term harms and re-victimisation. For example, dogs that develop behavioural problems may be abandoned or neglected. Figures from a RSPCA study suggest that around one in five puppy buyers no longer have their pet two years later (University of Bristol 2011). Dogs showing defensive aggression may be relinquished for rehoming, but can be difficult or impossible for charities to rehome safely.

Trade

The puppies are then under the breeder's management until they are passed to transporters or dealers, or sold directly to consumers. This can involve transportation, in many cases across international borders, and their vending to consumers.

Transportation and Importation

As the largescale commercial breeders are not situated near the markets for puppies, the trade may often go through middlemen and dealers. Trade routes are uncertain, but it is clear puppies are being bred in West Wales, East Anglia, Lincolnshire and Northern Ireland, and imported from the Republic of Ireland and the European continent to the rest of the UK. Prior to 2012 Ireland was seen as the main exporting country for puppies to the UK. Trade patterns have changed markedly in the past five years, since the quarantine system was relaxed in 2012, with an apparent increase in movement from mainland Europe, specifically some parts of Eastern Europe, to the UK (RSPCA 2015a).

Moving young animals increases health risks to the puppy as they may have insufficient immune systems to deal with infections. In particular, young puppies may be too young to vaccinate against disease such as parvovirus or rabies. They also need regular food and fluids, which may be disrupted or stopped completely if they are transported without their mother. This may cause suffering during the period of transportation and also lead to ongoing welfare problems, for example, from diseases contracted and incubated during transportation. For example, of 39 puppies seized by the RSPCA from one commercial puppy dealer, six were so unwell they had to be euthanised immediately and 65 % had congenital defects. The extended duration of international transportation further exacerbates these welfare concerns.

In the UK, non-commercial importation of dogs is covered by the EU Pets Travel Regulations (576/2013) [PETS], however, commercial importers may illegally bring dogs in under this scheme. Puppies entering Great Britain under PETS must be microchipped, vaccinated against rabies at least 21 days earlier and treated for the tapeworm (*Echinococcus mulitlocularis)* between 24 hours and 5 days before arriving in the UK. They must have a 'pet passport' including the microchip number and details of vaccination. In comparison, there are stricter requirements for dogs transported commercially. As well as complying with the non-commercial PETS requirements, all dogs must come from a holding/business registered in the EU country of origin; have a health certificate (per group of over five dogs), listing each dog as having had a veterinary examination 24 hours before dispatch to ensure they are fit to travel under Council Regulation (EC) No 1/2005; and be registered on TRACES. While the PETS scheme limits the number of dogs imported per person, it remains a potential route for illicitly importing dogs (Dogs Trust 2014). Traders may provide false or invalid PETS scheme documents to potential buyers, which may inspire confidence, but not match the microchip and vaccination records to the puppy.

Sales and Marketing

The sale of animals provides additional opportunities for criminal activity, in particular in fraudulent representation to owners. First, there will be an economic incentive to get the puppy to its vender as quickly as possible. Puppies are at their most marketable between the ages of 6–15 weeks and as detailed above diseases such as parvovirus are more likely to arise once the puppy has been transported.

Second, in response to educational messages by charities on responsible dog purchasing and ownership, the vendor will try to put the buyer at ease. For example, members of the public have been encouraged to buy puppies from home 'non-commercial' breeders and advised to see the puppies with their mother. Consequently, illicit dealers may set up apparent 'homes' as a reassurance to potential buyers, making it look like the puppy comes from that home when in fact it has been transported in earlier. Dealers will also sometimes show an unrelated lactating bitch to reassure the potential buyer that it is being seen with its mother. Dealers will use different mobile numbers and aliases for different breeds in internet adverts to give the impression that this is a small-scale operation, when all the numbers will go back to one central address. In many cases the consumer is being misled into buying an animal that has had a poor quality of life and welfare. By hiding poor care, such deception removes the ability of consumers to make good purchasing decisions. This removes one barrier—consumer pressure—to poor breeding and sale, and thereby make it more likely puppies will be bred, transported and kept in harmful conditions. It also means that consumers inadvertently purchase animals who will cost them more financially and emotionally, in ways for which they may be unprepared (for example, not having the financial resources or expertise in dog care). Consequently, the dog may be passed on or abandoned, leading to further abuse.

Prevalence

This section focuses on how common the aforementioned harms and poor practices are. It focuses broadly on two areas: breeding and importation. However, whilst we know a lot about the health and welfare problems faced by puppies, to date there has been little information on where these animals are coming from, how they get to market and why prospective buyers continue to buy these animals, thereby perpetuating the trade.

There are no accurate figures available on the extent of the UK puppy market but estimates can be made. For example, in the UK, given an estimated population of 9 to 10 million dogs and an average life-span of 12 years, this would equate to just over 700,000 dogs needed to replace those deaths. The UK Government (Defra 2012) estimated that at least 560,000 puppies were born in England. The extent of the illegal trade is unknown, but a gauge can be made by taking away the numbers of puppies whose sources are known (around 500,000) from those that could be coming on to the market (between one and two million).

Another way to estimate prevalence of the trade is through its value, although many measures estimate the total trade, making it hard to differentiate legal and illegal trades. For example, all puppy breeding in Northern Ireland, alone, is worth £160 million pounds (BBC Scotland 2015). In England, one group of dealers, who were operating illegally (that is, without a sales license, without declaring their income, believed to be importing illegally and found guilty of animal welfare offences), were thought to be taking in £8,000 pounds per week. Another group of dealers were importing up to

70 puppies a week from Ireland, estimated to be earning them £35–40,000 pounds a week in cash. If extrapolated to the entire year, this would be a business turnover of around £2 million pounds. The financial incentive for the illicit trade in puppies is high.

Breeders

As it has only been mandatory to identify and register a puppy since April 2016, the numbers of puppies coming onto the market is still unknown. In 2010–2011, 149 unlicensed dog breeding centres were identified in Wales, of which 82 % were in the three counties of Pembrokeshire, Carmarthenshire and Ceredigion, areas reputed for large-scale commercial breeding (Welsh Government 2010/11).

The prevalence of unlicensed British breeders suggests that over half the puppies sold could originate from unlicensed breeders in the UK (RSPCA 2015a). Some of these may be legal, insofar as they are too small to require a licence: in 2011/12 there were believed to be around 2,000 breeders exempt from licensing in Wales. Note that breeding clubs are not usually statutory; they are membership organisations to serve its members (hence they may have few or no welfare criteria to basic registration) and its members are not necessarily licensed; indeed, as many members may breed less than one litter a year, so falling under the legislation's threshold, it seems plausible to assume that most kennel club registrations are from unlicensed breeding.

Importation

The numbers of illegally imported puppies are unknown. In the past year a number of high-profile investigations and prosecutions against breeding establishments in Ireland, and government enforcement on the trade has given a clearer picture of the trade from Ireland. Enforcement has improved including the closure of one large breeding farm (ISPCA 2016). But puppies continue to enter the UK through the western ports of Stranraer, Fishguard, Holyhead and Heysham. Some of this puppy trade is illegal (RSPCA 2015a), with some purportedly 'non-commercial' trade actually being for commercial reasons. In October 2015 three dealers were convicted of importing over 35,000 puppies annually from Ireland. These dealers concentrated on breeds commonly associated with the pedigree puppy trade such as pomeranians, shih tzus and Yorkshire terriers (RSPCA 2015b). There is also trade from other countries, for example the number of dogs recorded entering the UK under PETS from Lithuania increased by 780 % and from Hungary by 663 % between 2011 and 2013 (Dogs Trust 2014). This is evidenced by a recent successful prosecution of two Lithuanians importing puppies from Lithuania in 2016 for a number of offences under the Fraud, Animal Welfare and Pet Animals Acts.

Explanation for Harmful Behaviours

This section identifies the key drivers for the harms associated with the puppy trade. It begins by considering the attitudes, beliefs and behaviour of the people who purchase puppies, and thereby enable the legal and illegal trade. It then considers how this consumer behaviour can facilitate behaviours by breeders and traders, noting the drivers of those behaviours. Finally it considers how current legislation on trade and animal movement can also exacerbate these harmful behaviours.

Consumer Credulity

There is a huge demand for puppies, which has created a buoyant market economy, usually focused on a number of popular breeds. Purchasers are often strongly motivated to obtain a young puppy or kitten due to the 'cute factor'. Seemingly as a result, many breeds are bred to have large heads and eyes, intensifying cuteness—although these features can also increase the risks of some harms, such as brain problems in King Charles cavalier spaniels and eyes 'popping out' in breeds with very prominent eyes. Puppies and kittens are, therefore, at their most marketable at a very young age (between 6 and 16 weeks). Many people specifically want a purebred dog. Some consumers may still have the Victorian mindset that 'purebred' or 'pedigree' confer a mark of quality (whereas, in fact, at best, these descriptions are a mark of predictability —which includes predictable breed-specific diseases and inherited disorders). Some purchasers may also perceive an elevated status to be associated with pedigree ownership, either because purebreds may be more expensive than crossbred dogs, or because certain breeds confer a desirable social status.

More specifically, demand is often focused on certain breeds, as potential puppy owners usually want a certain breed or type of dog. The motivation for these breed choices may be dictated by:

- Personal experiences. Some owners have previously owned such a breed and want a 'replacement', anticipating that the new dog will be like the previous one (or that another breed would be dissimilar, and thus riskier). In particular, purchasers' childhood experiences may locate a type of dog in their template of a family unit.

- Influence of peers. There are notable trends in specific breeds among different social groups—often different breeds are associated with particular classes (for example, Staffordshire bull terriers, labradors, spaniels, pugs and corgis), often for spurious reasons. Ownership of these breeds can facilitate acceptance into and convey status within these social groups and classes (see also the chapter on Status Dogs herein).
- Celebrities. Role models or icons may be seen with particular breeds, and those who wish to emulate those celebrities may try to obtain similar dogs (not necessarily from the same sources). For instance, following President Obama's purchase of a Portuguese water dog in 2013, its popularity has risen from 60th most common breed in 2009 to 51st in 2014. The popularity of this breed even rose in the UK from 112 bred in 2014 to 155 by September 2015.
- Media. Occasionally films or other media may inspire a trend for certain popular breed. There is a direct relationship between the popularity of dog breeds and their appearance in films (Ghirlanda et al. 2014) For example, there was a 40 % increase in UK collie registration in the two years subsequent to the release of Lassie in 1943, a 400 % increase in the sales of Dalmatians after the release in 1985 of *101 Dalmatians* and the television show *Game of Thrones* has been linked to trends in the ownership of huskies and wolf-like dogs for status.

Breeder Cupidity

Consumer motivations, as detailed above, have several implications. First, there is likely to always be a demand for certain breeds or types of dog (especially those predisposed to certain features, such as, overly short faces that can make breathing more difficult, leading to respiratory distress); second, this demand can change rapidly (calling into question the sustainability of ownership of these breeds); third, breeders and dealers must respond promptly to raising demands for specific breeds; and fourth, existing registered breeders may be unable to respond to raising demand. Consequently, as the legitimate breeding market responds to these changing demands, so too the criminal element of the market. This is evidenced by the increase of certain breeds of dogs from other sources, such as imported puppies. Fundamentally, the motivation for abuse by offenders is financial, there is simply little consideration given towards the impact on the dogs.

There are a number of sources that prospective owners can choose when buying their puppy, and these range enormously in terms of the health of the puppy, the life that it has led and the welfare problems it has experienced prior to sale. Critically, these sources also vary in terms of how quickly they can provide these dogs. Where the motivation to obtain a puppy is strong, so will be the desire to reduce the time it takes to get the puppy. The internet enables impulse purchasing, in response to trends; puppies can be obtained in less than a day. This remote purchasing distances purchasers from vendors, and facilitates the sale of animals from imports or large scale commercial puppy breeding in England and Wales, thereby allowing consumers to support harmful practices. These breeders and dealers concentrate on a small number of sought-after breeds, such as pugs, bulldogs and spaniels, to satisfy demand and maximise profits.

Breed Standards

When producing particular breeds, especially for dog-showing success, there are strong incentives which drive breed-related health and behavioural problems. Simply put, breed standards and breeding practices cause breed-related welfare problems. Breed standards and their judging in shows can directly encourage the breeding of dogs with exaggerated features that can cause health problems. In order to breed dogs who conform most closely to that 'type', breeders have also inbred and 'line-bred' (which is effectively also 'inbreeding') those animals who have those features. These characteristics have been prioritised above breeding for health, temperament and welfare. In addition, many dog breeds were generally produced from a few founding animals and breeders have, inevitably, used particular animals (for example, champion males) disproportionately more than others, thereby making those few animals' genes common in the breed. This can lead to inherited health problems as described above. Breeders may also be motivated by non-financial incentives, in particular the prestige or status of breeding winning animals. The motivation for large-scale puppy breeders to breed dogs with these inherent disorders is financial, as they can charge higher prices for more fashionable breeds, thereby increasing revenue.

Trade and Movement Laws

The opportunity for breeders to act irresponsibly and/or criminally is dependent on what legislation is in place and how effectively this is enforced. Consequently, breeders' motivation to offend or harm their animals is likely increased by failures in the official response—whereby this issue is not recognised as a priority for enforcement bodies. Rational Choice Theory explains offenders' motivation as being encouraged by a lack of guardians (that is, people able to identify and help the dogs and to punish the offenders), the presence of suitable victims (that is, dogs are an easy target, unable to defend themselves and easy to cheaply breed and keep) and a motivated offender (such as a person motivated by the possible financial gain, as discussed above).

Current UK legislation is relevant to the problem of a lack of guardianship—a summary of which is provided in Table 1. Much of this legislation is old and outdated (for example, the legal definition of appropriate/criminal behaviour), and varies across each of the four nations that make up the UK, as certain policy areas are devolved to each of these four nations. The absence of a capable guardian is facilitated by inconsistencies and oversights in the current trade and movement laws and enforcement. For example, in England and in Wales, the licensing of commercial breeders (as detailed above) falls to local authorities to enforce and may not be a priority. Thereby, enforcers focus only on the most extreme harms—after they have occurred—rather than effectively preventing them by ensuring good breeding practices. Although pet dealers should have pet shop licences so they can sell the puppies commercially not all do so, largely because of the limited clarity and enforcement of the legislation. Additionally, some licensed dealers do not have physical premises but sell from a private address, which may not get inspected by the local authority when issuing the licence as it is not a commercial premises—making it difficult for local authorities to decide when renewing the licence if the business and its premises meets the conditions under the Pet Animals Act.

As a significant portion of the puppy trade is international in nature, this poses additional risks with regard to establishing a capable guardian. For example, the high rate of puppy exportation from Ireland to the UK was likely due to the combined opportunities provided by: EU/government subsidies given to Irish breeders, the availability of cheap land and geographical closeness to the UK market, and the lack of effective legislation and effective enforcement at the borders. In addition, puppies have been able to come from Ireland to Northern Ireland and Scotland, be mis-declared as

Table 1 Summary of main legislation relating to the trade, sale and breeding of dogs in the UK

Issue	Legislation	What it does	How effective is it at dealing with the trade?
Breeding of puppies	Breeding of Dogs Act 1973 (England and Scotland) Breeding and Sale of Dogs (Welfare) Act 1999 (England and Scotland) Animal Welfare (Breeding of Dogs) (Wales) Regulations 2014	Sets conditions for licensing of commercial dog breeding establishments; dogs cannot be sold before 8 weeks of age	Enforcement is a challenge; allows licensing of any dog breeders but it is only mandatory for those breeding over five (England) or three litters (Wales) a year
Identification of dogs	Dogs (Licensing and Identification) Regulations (Northern Ireland) 2012 Microchipping of Dogs (England) Regulations 2015 Microchipping of Dogs (Scotland) Regulations 2016 Microchipping of Dogs (Wales) Regulations 2015	Makes it compulsory to identify a dog from 8 weeks and ensure that its details are kept up to date	This is a relatively recent requirement in England and Wales and consequently is difficult to evaluate. Approximately 15 % of dogs are not yet microchipped and enforcement is expected to be challenging as, it will be difficult to ensure owner's details are updated and it is not seen as a priority area for local authorities (enforcers) and they have not been provided with any extra resources to do so

(*continued*)

Table 1 (continued)

Issue	Legislation	What it does	How effective is it at dealing with the trade?
International Trade	Commercial trade covered by Directive 92/65/EC Non-commercial by PETS Regulation 576/2013 OJ L178/1 28.6.2013	Sets rules on numbers, certification, age and vaccination of dogs traded between countries	Enforcement is a challenge; illegal trade occurring through PETS being used by commercial dealers and rescue organisations; fraudulent paperwork and illegal declaration of puppies' age
Sales of puppies/dogs	Pet Animals Act 1951 Licensing of Animal Dealers (Young cats and young dogs) (Scotland) Regulations 2009 Pet Shop Regulations (Northern Ireland) 2000	Sets up a licensing scheme for pet shops and sale of pet animals; the Scottish law aims to regulate the trade in young cats and dogs	Enforcement is a challenge; especially with regard to internet sales as updates under the Animal Welfare Act (see below) have been postponed.
Unnecessary suffering and animals' needs	Animal Welfare Act 2006 (England and Wales) Animal Health and Welfare Act (Scotland) 2006 Welfare of Animals Act (Northern Ireland) 2011	Defines animal welfare offences, including duties of persons responsible for animals	The law provides a good framework, however, it is identified as ineffective regarding regulating mate choices (required to avoid inherited disorders). Limited secondary adequate licensing regulations. Enforcement varies in effectiveness as it is done through the Police in Northern Ireland, Scottish Society for the Prevention of Cruelty to Animals [SSPCA] and Procurator Fiscal in Scotland and local authorities and the Royal Society for the Prevention of Cruelty to animals [RSPCA] in England and Wales (although the RSPCA do not have right of access to premises of commercial breeders)

British puppies and sold under false documentation. The recent reduction in the illegal trade from Ireland was achieved through new legislation—the Irish Dog Breeding Establishments Act (2010)—which regulates breeders by setting conditions on dog breeding and licensing. This legislation appears to have improved the conditions of breeding in Ireland which, coinciding with enhanced cross-border regulation of pets between Ireland and the UK, allowed something of a crackdown on this illegal trade route.

However, this coincided with changes in EU laws on the movement of puppies across Europe. The movement of puppies is one of the few dog laws covered by EU rules, particularly Regulation 576/2013. Pets can also be moved under European legislation intended to strike a balance between allowing free movement of peoples' pet dogs for holidays or dog shows and ensuring diseases such as rabies and *Echinococcus* are contained. In 2012, the UK law on non-commercial trade in dogs was changed to make it simpler for dog owners to move their animals around Europe. The PETS makes it easier for dog owners to travel throughout the EU but has checks in place to limit the spread of diseases being carried by dogs by vaccinating them before travel. The same law that allows for free movement of peoples' pets also creates the opportunities and loopholes that can be exploited by commercial dealers and criminal dealers to move puppies around (Dogs Trust 2014; RSPCA 2015a). As anyone can transport up to five dogs if they follow the rules, this opens the possibility for puppies to be moved as pets but then traded commercially in the UK. This often involves illicitly rebranding the puppies as British animals (BBC Scotland 2015). The RSPCA suspects this provides an opportunity for puppy dealers, including criminal networks, to exploit this new trade opportunity.

Responses to Reduce Harmful Behaviours

This section identifies the responses required to reduce the harms to pets in the trade and the practices that lead to these harms. There are a variety of possible responses which come from official and non-official agencies, both of which are discussed below.

Breeders

Breeders could be encouraged to improve their breeding practices to minimise harm to their animals and to pride themselves not on show or financial success, but on producing animals that are genuinely 'fit for purpose' as pets who will go on to have good lives free from suffering due to their breed or upbringing. Such breeders will need to be able to differentiate themselves as market leaders, which will require quality, well-recognised assurance schemes and prudent consumers (see below). It will also require steps to ensure good breeders are not 'tarred with the same brush' as less scrupulous breeders as a result of breed clubs denying there is a problem or defending pedigree breeding *en masse*, despite the existence of harmful practices. It is worth noting here that the UK's Kennel Club was recently publically critical of one breed club's practice after an outcry during their Crufts Dog Show.

In 2008, the RSPCA commissioned an independent study into the best methods to minimise harms involved in dog breeding (see Table 2). Breeders should avoid continuing poor practices and also try to remedy the current problems. In particular, breeders should avoid breeding dogs with exaggerated features or diseases that are suspected to be inherited (which necessarily includes all breed-related diseases). Breeders should use existing schemes to check for specific diseases in potential mates. These can be useful in removing some conditions (for example, UK Irish Setters breeders appear to have

Table 2 Priority recommendations to improve pedigree dog welfare (adapted from Rooney and Sargan 2010)

Rank	Action recommended
1	Systematic collection of morbidity and mortality data from all registered dogs
2	Revision of registration rule to prevent the registration of offspring of matings between 1st-degree and 2nd-degree relatives
3	Open stud books to allow more frequent introduction of new genetic material into established breeds
4	Setting up systems to monitor the effectiveness of any interventions and changes
5	Conducting a full ethical review of current breeds
6	Development of detailed management plans for each breed
7	Refinement of diagnostic tests and DNA markers for inherited disorders
8	Increase genetic diversity by encouraging importation and inter-country matings
9	Make registration of pedigree dogs conditional upon both parents undergoing compulsory screening tests
10	Introduction of codes of practice that encourage breeders to consider health, temperament and welfare
11	Training and accreditation of judges to prioritise heath, welfare and behaviour in the show ring
12	Creating and fostering the image of a happy and desirable dog being one that experiences high welfare
13	Formulation of an independent panel of experts from multiple disciplines
14	Development of schemes for calculating Estimated Breeding Values

reduced canine leucocyte adhesion deficiency through screening and selective breeding) but may be less effective for more complex genetic predisposition (for example, hip dysplasia). Ideally good practice should be enforced—through, for example, conditional registration on pedigree lists. At the very least, breeders should (be required to) inform purchasers of any significant potential genetic problems.

Consumers

Many efforts to improve breeding practices will require consumer action. One approach is to reduce the puppy trade altogether by encouraging rehoming. Rehoming organisations usually provide information to owners about that animal's needs, make reasonable checks that they will be able to care for the animals throughout their lives and take care in matching adopters with the right animals. However, rescue organisations usually have limited numbers of puppies and (except breed-specific organisations) may not have the breeds the consumers initially want. In addition, the checks done by rehoming organisations can make this a relatively long process and can span several weeks, which may be beyond the patience of some purchasers. While this helps prevent impulsive 'purchasing', some consumers are likely to choose the convenience of buying a puppy from a breeder or vendor.

Consumer decisions may be improved by accreditation schemes or through better consumer information. As examples, the UK Kennel Club runs an approved breeder scheme and the BVA AWF and RSPCA have created a 'puppy contract' by which purchasers can request, and breeders provide, information. At time of writing, this has been endorsed by a team of animal welfare charities, but the UK's Kennel Club have not yet agreed to endorse it. The Kennel Club Assured Breeder scheme also has limitations in the level of standards and lack of checks to ensure compliance—both of which can be remedied. There needs to be a robust and evidence-based assurance scheme which protects the health and welfare of the dog and potential owners.

Furthermore, potential owners require relevant advice on buying and owning puppies, for example, the RSPCA's Get Puppy Smart guidance, the Dogs Trust's 'think before you click' campaign and websites describing inherited disorders for different breeds.[1] These effectively allow consumers to

[1] For example, upei.ca/cidd; vetsci.usyd.edu.au/lida; vet.cam.ac.uk.idid; and ufaw.co.uk

include disease risks in their dog purchasing decisions—although one would hope consumers would try to choose puppies with minimal risks (which may require looking beyond some popular breeds). A strategy is required to ensure that consumers access the appropriate information (for example, by governmental and non-governmental organisations highlighting the problems) and in a timely fashion—that is, to interrupt consumers' desire to buy puppies immediately. This strategy also requires understanding of legal and illegal vendors, to prevent irresponsible breeders/dealers adapting their selling patterns to respond to these public information messages (see above).

Legal Controls: Breeding and Trade

Anyone who deliberately breeds for sale, or who trades, puppies should be licensed, whether or not they have physical commercial pet shops, so that local authorities can decide whether they meet the minimum legal standards even if they use a private address. In the UK, the Pet Animals Act 1951 needs to be updated (as acknowledged by the Government in 2006 and expected to be published in 2017) to ensure that any seller of dogs is licensed and evidence-based animal welfare standards are applied. This view is supported by the 2016 Government consultation on the review of animal establishments licensing in in England, which found that the majority of responses supported a generic licence for selling puppies attached to model licence conditions to improve the welfare conditions in this trade and drive out unscrupulous breeders and traders. Requiring every pet shop licence holder to have a designated business premises rather than conduct their business through a private house, so that that premise can be inspected according to the license welfare conditions, would close one loophole. At the same time, local authorities need to have the training and capacity to undertake inspections of breeding establishments and investigate complaints.

The development of a helpline would enable people to report anonymously any person they suspect of breeding or trading puppies illegally (including by not declaring the income). This system could perhaps work on the same lines as the National Benefit Fraud Hotline (https://www.gov.uk/national-benefit-fraud-hotline), Action Fraud (for any type of fraud: http://www.actionfraud.police.uk/fraud-az-tax-fraud) or Crimestoppers (which allows reporting of wildlife crime to the NWCU: http://www.nwcu.police.uk/crimestoppers/). Since councils (and NGOs) are ultimately responsible for cleaning up the long-term problems associated with irresponsible/illegal breeding/selling of dogs, this should provide an incentive to the authorities to set up such schemes and to act upon such information.

At the same time, the use of non-welfare laws may prevent future crime. Two recent successful prosecutions of puppy dealers using the Fraud Act in 2016 show the potential for using non-animal welfare-related laws as enforcement action against the illegal puppy trade. General trade regulations should apply to puppies as to other 'goods'. Where a dog is sold a contract is created and, therefore, the general law relating to contracts will apply, as will the Sale of Goods Act 1979. In some circumstances, a purchaser may have a claim against the seller for breach of contract and/or misrepresentation. However, the normal recourse of returning the product for a refund or a replacement is not an option that many puppy owners wish to take. More importantly, it is unlikely to be in the best interests of the puppy to be returned to the dealer/breeder. Thus, even if this approach is effective in deterring future welfare harms by the individual, it may not be the best outcome for the animals involved. There is also the potential to respond to some of the puppy trade as facilitated by or defined as serious and organised crime (see http://www.nationalcrimeagency.gov.uk/crime-threats/organised-crime-groups). This focus on serious and organised crime would enhance enforcement and offenders assets could be targeted as proceeds of crime (with the confiscated assets used to support enforcement and animal welfare (see http://www.nationalcrimeagency.gov.uk/news/88-nca-website/about-us/what-we-do/549-nca-approach-to-criminal-assets).

At the same time, internet sales need to be improved. This might partly come from voluntary standards—for example, some Internet sites such as Gumtree have proactive policies against sales of animals that could be illegal or have welfare concerns, resulting in tens of thousands of adverts being withdrawn since September 2013. This approach should be followed by all such sites. Sites should also be regulated effectively. For example, Internet sales should be allowed only when linked to a taxation reference number, to provide a link back to the breeder (Rapport au Président de la République 2015). Regulating the trade on the Internet might also parallel some of the methods used to tackle illegal wildlife trade—for example, sites may disallow the sale of particular species, have an automatic pop-up that advises buyers of legal requirements, or provide links to complaints or advice sites.

Legal Controls: Movement

Governments (for example, UK and Ireland) should meet to discuss and publish changes and trends in imports of dogs and puppies, particularly after changes in legislation (for example, PETS). Effective movement laws would require spot enforcement checks at the main entry points and prosecuting dealers who evade the rules. This responsibility should sit with the statutory border control agency.

Laws should prevent the sale or transportation of puppies until they are old enough and identifiable. A minimum age of at least 15 weeks may reduce international travel of earlyweaned or unvaccinated puppies, if enforcement agencies are trained to accurately estimate puppies' ages (which can be difficult between the ages of 6 and 24 weeks, until teeth are erupting) or transporters required to prove puppies' ages when contested. Recent legislation changes which require all puppies to be identifiable through a microchip registered to the owner should provide a link back to the breeder and any middle men. It should also give clearer information on the number of puppies sold every year in Britain. As there may remain some dogs unchipped (for example, around 15–25 % of dogs in England and 22 % in Wales: BVA 2015; Government of Wales 2015), this will need to be adequately enforced.

Conclusion

Harm is evident at each stage of the breeding and trade in animals—from the choice of mates, through the way in which mates and the young offspring are cared for, to their transportation and sale practices. These can coincide with animal owners suffering considerable financial and emotional harm—which is likely to further disadvantage and possibly victimise the animal. The harms identified are widespread in the puppy breeding industry—from individual breeders and traders who operate on a large scale, to low-level smaller 'hobby' breeders who may individually have low impact, but combined, may add up to a considerable number of parents, progeny and owners affected. This scale is driven by the popularity of dogs, more specifically purebred puppies of certain breeds. At a societal level, this popularity is unlikely to change, despite the best efforts of welfare charities, and so the demand is likely to continue. Consumers' motivation for puppies and their impulse buying behaviour account for a large amount of the demand for puppies that enables the harmful breeding trade.

For a minority of breeders and consumers, the motivation for specific breeds with inherited disorders is show success. This motivation can be difficult to distinguish from a motivation to develop the breed, which seems less selfish. Certainly, the motivation to perpetuate a breed unchanged is not worth any welfare harms of inbreeding or selection for exaggerated features. The motivation behind irresponsible and illegal breeding is, to a large extent, financial. These monetary opportunities can incentivise breeders and dealers risking the possible legal sanctions, especially when enforcement is insufficient. The risk of getting caught is low and even if caught the punishment is not a disincentive. Consequently, according to rational choice theory this facilitates crime being committed, as it may motivate offenders, present suitable targets and limit capable guardians. For instance a commercial puppy dealer could get through customs under the PETS with 20 puppies if they have four people in their vehicle. Sale of these dogs could result in profits of over £15,000, for one journey, in comparison to (if caught) their facing a maximum fine of £5,000.

This suggests that further legislative efforts are needed. Specifically, current regulations are limited by poor enforcement. Thereby current and future laws need to be effectively enforced to be affective. All breeders and vendors should be licensed and made responsible for causing unnecessary suffering through irresponsible mating decisions. Harms within puppy breeding are exacerbated by trade which requires the long-distance transportation of animals. Consequently, to remove loopholes that allow widespread suffering and disease risks to puppies, all commercial importation of puppies should be ended.

References

Asher, L., Diesel, G., Summers, J. F., McGreevy, P. D., & Collins, L. M. (2009). Inherited defects in pedigree dogs. Part 1: disorders related to breed standards. *The Veterinary Journal, 182*(3), 402–411.

BBC Scotland (2015). *Sellers using fake identities online to conceal illegal trade of puppies.* http://www.bbc.co.uk/news/uk-scotland-32305787. Accessed 14 June 2016.

Bradshaw, J. (2012). *In defence of dogs.* London, UK: Penguin.

British Veterinary Association [BVA]. (2015). *Still fishing for chips—a quarter of dogs not microchipped with less than a year to go.* http://www.bva.co.uk/News-campaigns-and-policy/Newsroom/News-releases/Quarter-dogs-not-microchipped-less-than-a-year-to-go/. Accessed 1 July 2015.

Cusdin, P. A., & Greenwood, A. G. (2000). *The keeping of wolf-hybrids in great Britain.* Keighley: International Zoo Veterinary Group

Defra [Department of Environment farming and Rural Affairs] (2009). *Code of practice for the welfare of dogs.* London, UK: Defra.

Defra (2012). *Micochipping of dogs impact assessment.* https://www.gov.uk/government/uploads/system/uploads/attachment_data/file/82470/dangerous-dogs-annexb-microchipping-ia-120423.pdf. Accessed 20 June 2016.

Dogs Trust (2014). *The puppy smuggling scandal.* https://www.dogstrust.org.uk/press-materials/dt_puppy_smuggling_report_v12_web(1).pdf. Accessed 14 June 2016.

Ghirlanda, S., Acerbi, A., & Herzog, H. (2014). Dog movie stars and dog breed popularity: a case study in media influence on choice. *PLoS ONE*, *9*(9), e106565.

Goddard, M. E., & Beilharz, R. G. (1986). Early prediction of adult behaviour in potential guide dogs. *Applied Animal Behaviour Science*, *15*(3), 247–260.

Government of Wales (2015). *National survey for Wales*. http://gov.wales/statistics-and-research/national-survey/?tab=el_home&topic=local_area__environment &lang=en. Accessed 14 June 2016.

ISPCA [Irish Society for the Prevention of Cruelty to Animals] (2016). *ISPCA, Gardaí and local authority shut down puppy farm in Carlow*. http://www.ispca.ie/rescue_cases/detail/ispca_gardai_and_local_authority_shut_down_puppy_farm_in_carlow. Accessed 14 June 2016.

Irish Statute Book (2016). *Dog breeding establishments act (2010)*. http://www.irishstatutebook.ie/eli/2010/act/29/enacted/en/html. Accessed 22 June 2016.

Kerswell, K. J., Butler, K. L., Bennett, P., & Hemsworth, P. H. (2010). The relationships between morphological features and social signalling behaviours in juvenile dogs: the effect of early experience with dogs of different morphotypes. *Behavioural Processes*, *85*(1), 1–7.

Leaver, S. D. A., & Reimchen, T. E. (2008). Behavioural responses of Canis familiaris to different tail lengths of a remotely-controlled life-size dog replica. *Behaviour*, *145*(3): 377–390.

McMillan, F. D., Duffy, D. L., & Serpell, J. A. (2011). Mental health of dogs formerly used as 'breeding stock' in commercial breeding establishments. *Applied Animal Behaviour Science*, *135*(1), 86–94.

McMillan, F. D., Serpell, J. A., Duffy, D. L., Masaoud, E., & Dohoo, I. R. (2013). Differences in behavioral characteristics between dogs obtained as puppies from pet stores and those obtained from noncommercial breeders. *Journal of the American Veterinary Medical Association*, *242*(10), 1359–1363.

The National Archives (2016). *Animal health and welfare act (Scotland) 2006*. http://www.legislation.gov.uk/asp/2006/11/contents. Accessed 22 June 2016.

The National Archives (2016). *Animal welfare act 2006 (England and Wales)*. http://www.legislation.gov.uk/ukpga/2006/45/contents. Accessed 22 June 2016.

The National Archives (2016). *Animal welfare (breeding of dogs) (Wales) regulations 2014*. http://www.legislation.gov.uk/wsi/2014/3266/contents/made. Accessed 22 June 2016.

The National Archives (2016). *Breeding of dogs act 1973*. http://www.legislation.gov.uk/ukpga/1973/60/contents. Accessed 22 June 2016.

The National Archives. (2016). *Breeding and sale of dogs (welfare) act 1999 (England and Scotland)*. http://www.legislation.gov.uk/ukpga/1999/11/contents. Accessed 22 June 2016.

The National Archives (2016). *Dogs (Licensing and Identification) Regulations (Northern Ireland) (2012)*. Available at: http://www.legislation.gov.uk/nisr/2012/132/contents/made. Accessed 22 June 2016.

The National Archives (2016). *Licensing of animal dealers (young cats and young dogs) (Scotland) regulations 2009*. http://www.legislation.gov.uk/ssi/2009/141/contents/made. Accessed 22 June 2016.

The National Archives (2016). *Microchipping of dogs (England) regulations 2014*. http://www.legislation.gov.uk/uksi/2015/108/contents/made. Accessed 22 June 2016.

The National Archives (2016). *Microchipping of dogs (Wales) regulations 2015*. http://www.legislation.gov.uk/wsi/2015/1990/contents/made. Accessed 22 June 2016.

The National Archives (2016). *Pet animals act 1951*. http://www.legislation.gov.uk/ukpga/Geo6/14-15/35/contents. Accessed 22 June 2016.

The National Archives (2016). *Sale of goods act 1979*. http://www.legislation.gov.uk/ukpga/1979/54/contents. Accessed 22 June 2016.

The National Archives. (2016). *Welfare of animals act (Northern Ireland) (2011)*. http://www.legislation.gov.uk/nia/2011/16/contents. Accessed 22 June 2016.

Rapport au Président de la République relatif à l'ordonnance n° 2015–1243 du 7 octobre 2015 relative au commerce et à la protection des animaux de compagnie. JORF n°0233 du 8 octobre 2015: page 18283 (texte n°30).

RSPCA [Royal Society for the Prevention of Cruelty to Animals] (2015a). *Pushing at an open door—how the present UK controls on rabies are failing*. Horsham: RSPCA

RSPCA (2015b). *Puppy dealers jailed after making £35,000 a week selling sick imported dogs*. http://www.politics.co.uk/opinion-formers/rspca-royal-society-for-the-prevention-of-cruelty-to-animals/article/puppy-dealers-jailed-after-making-35-000-a-week-selling-sick. Accessed 9 October 2015.

Summers, J. F., Diesel, G., Asher, L., McGreevy, P. D., & Collins, L. M. (2010). Inherited defects in pedigree dogs. Part 2: disorders that are not related to breed standards. *The Veterinary Journal, 183*(1), 39–45.

University of Bristol (2011). *One in five puppy buyers no longer have their pet two years later*. http://www.bristol.ac.uk/news/2011/7448.html. Accessed 14 June 2016.

Welsh Government (2010/11). *Companion animal welfare enhancement scheme*. http://gov.wales/docs/drah/publications/110915cawesbaselineen.pdf. Accessed 14 June 2016.

James Yeates is Chief Veterinary Officer of the RSPCA Fellow of the Royal College of Veterinary Surgeons, Honorary Lecturer at the University of Bristol, Visiting Fellow of the University of Surrey, Editor-in-Chief of the new *Journal of Animal Welfare Science, Ethics and Law*, previous chair of the British Veterinary Association's Ethics and Welfare Group and author of Animal Welfare in Veterinary Practice (UFAW/Wiley-Blackwell).

David Bowles is Assistant Director of Public Affairs and coordinates the RSPCA's political, local government and campaign work. David has worked for the RSPCA for 20 years, is a Board member of the Canine and Feline Sector Council, and the Association of Dog and Cat Homes, the umbrella organisation for organisations in the British Isles that run shelters. He has published over 20 papers on issues ranging from primate behaviour to the effect of free trade on animals.

Physical Cruelty of Companion Animals

Arnold Arluke and Leslie Irvine

Introduction

When incidents of animal cruelty appear in the media, they often evoke intense responses from the public. Most people express outrage (Levin et al. 2017). When the victim is a domestic dog or a cat, the abuse seems to represent a betrayal of the relationships we have with companion animals. If a perpetrator is charged, citizens often appeal for the strictest possible penalties. The online comments following coverage of two cruelty cases in 2015 reflect typical reactions. 'Prison sentence is a joke and a bullet through the head is too good for this guy', one reader wrote. Another said, 'This poor excuse for a human being should have received a much greater punishment', and one simply posted, 'rot in hell who ever [*sic*] is responsible' (Carey 2014; Vega 2015). Humane organisations make use of cruelty in fundraising efforts, selecting cases egregious enough to prompt donations and solidify support, but not so upsetting that donors will avoid their mail (Arluke 2006).

A. Arluke (✉)
Department of Sociology, Northeastern University, Boston, MA, USA
e-mail: aarluke@gmail.com

L. Irvine
Department of Sociology, University of Colorado at Boulder, Boulder, CO, USA

J. Maher et al. (eds.), *The Palgrave International Handbook of Animal Abuse Studies*, DOI 10.1057/978-1-137-43183-7_3

Not everyone responds sympathetically to animal cruelty, however. Some people consider the victims 'just' animals and the investigations a diversion of law enforcement's limited resources. Moreover, judging from common references to cruelty in popular culture, many people accept or selectively ignore it. They talk about 'killing two birds with one stone' and 'being a guinea pig', unaware of the suffering implied by the language of these sayings. In addition, people often find depictions of animal suffering humorous. Over a million websites offer jokes about animal abuse or cruelty. In the film There's Something about Mary, Matt Dillon's character gives Puffy—a dog—sedatives. He gives him too much, however, and Puffy passes out. In trying to revive the dog, Dillon's character takes the wires from a lamp and administers an electric shock that causes Puffy to catch fire. Many—if not all—of director Wes Anderson's films involve the killing of companion animals. In The Royal Tenenbaums, grandfather Royal runs over a dog while taking his grandchildren on an excursion. In The Grand Budapest Hotel, a character throws a cat out a window. The camera pans over the window ledge and down to the street to show the cat, dead on the cobblestones below. As Arluke (2002, p. 427) writes, 'humorous slants on cruelty are plentiful and can be seen in children's stories, cartoons, and comics, as well as in adult advertising, movies, and even occasional talk radio programs, that have long been known to make light of animals being harmed or even killed.'

These examples point out the ambiguity surrounding the meaning and significance of animal cruelty and the ambivalence that characterises our treatment of animals (Arluke 2006; Arluke and Sanders 1996). The contradictions in how we regard animals seem greatest when we look at our varied relationships with companion animals, ranging from complete devotion to indifference. Animal cruelty can constitute a crime against innocence and a sign of psychopathology. It can prompt collective sympathy and anger—or indifference. It can function as a marketing strategy, a metaphor, a joke or a cinematic device. Treatment considered abhorrent in one situation can become acceptable in another. An act intended to make a point in a movie or a cartoon takes on an entirely different meaning if inflicted on a living dog or cat.

In this chapter, we reveal how the ambiguous, conflicting nature of cruelty has shaped attempts to explain it, document its prevalence and determine appropriate ways of responding to it. Focusing on animals typically considered companions allows us to sift through some of the distortions and projections that surround dominant interpretations of cruelty. Using a symbolic interactionist perspective, we question the belief that cruelty has an objective definition, independent of context (Blumer 1986; Mead 1934). We also challenge the assumption that harming companion animals as well as other animals necessarily predicts future violent behaviour. Drawing on recent empirical research, largely in the USA, we specify the conditions under which cruelty to pets may signal, in particular, extreme forms of violence.

The Nature of Cruelty to Companion Animals

As Agnew pointed out, anyone attempting to understand cruelty to animals 'immediately confronts a definitional problem' (1998, p. 179). Because standards of acceptable treatment vary across species, discussions of the nature of cruelty must begin by determining which animals are under consideration. If the term 'pet' refers simply to a favoured animal, then any species can qualify, and would even include 'petted livestock' (Wilkie 2010). However, the cow, sheep or pig considered a companion animal typically holds that favoured status only temporarily. When the time comes to send the animal to market, he or she becomes a commodity. Thus, favour alone does not make an animal a companion animal, and nor does species. Some people know dogs solely as cherished companions. Others regard them as racing or fighting machines or research subjects (Arluke 1988; Jackson 2001; Kalof and Taylor 2007). Thus, what it means to 'be' a companion, or an animal, more generally, is 'less a matter of biology than it is an issue of human culture and consciousness' (Arluke and Sanders 1996, p. 9). Scholars of the practice of companion animal keeping limit the designation to those animals we (a) assign individual, personal names; (b) allow in the house; and most importantly, (c) would not eat (Thomas 1983). Consistent with this, we take 'pets' to include mostly dogs and cats but also the other species that meet these criteria. Some people prefer the term 'companion animal' to 'pet', suggesting that the latter designation trivialises the animal's role in the relationship, (Irvine 2004).

Even when limiting this discussion to companion animals, efforts to determine the nature of cruelty face further challenges. Legal definitions allow courts wide discretion by specifying cruelty as the infliction of *unnecessary* suffering. This recognises that physical existence might inevitably involve some suffering and that some might even occur legally. The question of how much suffering, if any, is 'necessary' depends on the setting and the aim of the activity (Arluke 2006; Regan 1980). While undergoing reasonable and ordinary treatment for an injury, a companion animal might endure pain, even to the extent of suffering. In providing such treatment, a licensed veterinarian does not engage in cruelty. A boy who sets a dog on fire to see what will happen inflicts unnecessary suffering; the researcher who burns the skin of a dog to study how burnt skin heals escapes charges of cruelty, whatever one might think of his actions (Favre 2009). Some methods of dog training include physical 'corrections', such as jerking, shocking and hanging or swinging the dog by a leash. Critics of these methods consider them cruel (Owens and Eckroate 2007). Concerned citizens who report the use of such methods have found that cruelty laws provide exemptions for training, and courts have ruled that 'a beating inflicted for corrective or disciplinary purposes without an evil motive is not a crime, even if painful and excessive' (State v. Fowler, 205 S.E.2d 749, N.C. Ct. App. 1974). Laws also provide exceptions for hunting and farming. Practices considered acceptable and necessary in agriculture, such as branding, castration and beak trimming, all done without anaesthetics or analgesics, would be considered inhumane and illegal if performed on a companion animal. The infliction of pain, even to the point of suffering, does not necessarily constitute cruelty. Thus, the nature of cruelty is situational, and the same treatment 'in one context can be regarded as cruel, while in another it can be considered culturally acceptable' (Arluke 2006, p. 184).

Some attempts to assess the nature of cruelty emphasise motive, specifying it as 'the wilful infliction of harm, injury, and intended pain' (Kellert and Felthous 1985, p. 1114), 'behavior that intentionally causes unnecessary pain, suffering, or distress' (Ascione 1993, p. 28), or the 'desire to gain satisfaction from the infliction of suffering, pain, or some other harm' (Rowan 1999, p. 330). Yet, sadism does not characterise all perpetrators of cruel acts. As Regan argues, 'some cruel people do not feel pleasure in making others suffer. Indeed, they seem not to feel anything' (1980, p. 534). *Insensitivity* to suffering, rather than sadistic enjoyment of it, can also count as cruelty. Consequently, many statutes include not only intention but also 'reckless indifference' to an animal's pain (Garner 2014, p. 303). Cruelty might result from ignorance, carelessness or neglect; indeed, these constitute the primary sources of suffering among companion animals (Patronek 1997; Solot 1997). Although some argue that the lack of 'deliberate maliciousness' makes the resulting abuse less serious (Rowan 1993, p. 218), statutes often use the term 'cruelty' 'generically to encompass both deliberate infliction of harm and harm that arises from neglect' (Patronek 1997, p. 277; see also Donley et al. 1999).

In sum, numerous challenges arise when attempting to characterise the nature of cruelty. Limiting the discussion to companion animals overlooks the suffering endured by the majority of animals, such as those involved in food production, through practices considered acceptable and legal. Determinations of cruelty depend not just on statutory language but also on context, situation, purported 'necessity', intention and motive.

The Prevalence of Cruelty to Companion Animals

Estimating the prevalence of cruelty to companion animals brings similar challenges. Researchers have assessed its prevalence through four sources of data, and each yields varying estimates. Some studies have examined reported and prosecuted cruelty cases. Vermeulen and Odendaal (1993) analysed the records of four Societies for the Prevention of Cruelty to Animals (SPCAs) in the Pretoria-Witwatersrand area of South Africa between March 1991 and February 1992. The authors found 1,863 reported cases of abuse and neglect towards any type of animal, including but not limited to companion animals. Investigators documented mistreatment in just over 25 % of the total reported cases, with only 3.4 % of abusers charged. The majority of cases involved issues related to husbandry or lack of medical care. An analysis of cases reported to the Massachusetts SPCA between 1975 and 1996 yielded similar results (Arluke and Luke 1997). Among 80,000 complaints of abuse and neglect, only 268 of these resulted in prosecution specifically for cruelty, amounting to only 0.3 % of all those investigated during the period studied. Courts found fewer than half of those prosecuted to be guilty. Another study randomly selected 200 of the 4,942 complaints of mistreatment made to the same SPCA in 1996 (Donley et al. 1999). Only 22 cases involved deliberate abuse, where the abuser intentionally sought to cause suffering or death. Of these, investigators found violations in only four cases, or 0.08 % of those studied, and just one case resulted in prosecution.

These low reported and prosecution estimates reveal more about the criminal justice system than about the prevalence of cruelty. As humane law enforcement agents attest, well-intentioned citizens often report animal welfare offenses where nothing prosecutable exists or there is insufficient evidence to pursue prosecution (Arluke 2004). This may change now that all 50 states have enacted a felony provision for animal cruelty; previously, criminal justice professionals, including police, district attorneys and judges, did not appear to consider animal abuse a serious or common crime (Arluke and Luke 1997; Vollum et al. 2004). Until 2015, the Federal Bureau of Investigation classified animal cruelty under 'other' crimes, among less serious offences including trespassing. From 2016, however, the US national Uniform Crime Reporting Program will list and track it as a distinct offence. Although this will provide more accurate information on animal cruelty, including its prevalence, low prosecution rates can persist if judges focus on cases they consider 'more important' (Arluke 2006, p. 1). The criminal justice system must address many serious human issues—such as homicide—that eclipse other concerns, including but not limited to animal cruelty. Moreover, many cruelty cases never advance to prosecution because of unknown perpetrators (Arluke and Luke 1997).

Researchers have also used data from veterinarians to estimate the prevalence of cruelty to companion animals. Veterinarians in Massachusetts (78.9 %), Indiana (87 %) and Michigan (88 %) claimed to have treated at least one animal deliberately injured by a client over the course of their careers (Donley et al. 1999; Landau 1999; Stolt et al. 1997). Nationally, American veterinarians reported a mean of less than one cruelty case per 100 total cases seen in the preceding year (Sharpe and Wittum 1999). In New Zealand, 63 % of veterinarians reported seeing cases of deliberate abuse in the five previous years, with most seeing one case per year (Williams et al. 2008). In Australia, 40 % of veterinarians saw between one and three cases of 'deliberate, physical maltreatment or neglect' per year (Green and Gullone 2005, p. 620). In Scotland, 48 % of veterinarians reported seeing 'non-accidental injuries' in their practices; the majority saw between one and three cases per year (Munro and Thrusfield 2008).

Although the reports of veterinarians also seem to suggest a low rate of companion animal abuse—about one case per year—Patronek (1997) points out that most 'victims of deliberate abuse will never be brought to a veterinarian for treatment by the abuser' (1997, p. 273). Moreover, many veterinarians report feeling inadequately prepared to recognise cruelty (Benetato et al. 2011; Landau 1999; Miller 2006; Patronek 1997; Sharpe and Wittum 1999). Recently, forensic veterinary pathology has begun establishing guidelines for distinguishing accidental and non-accidental injuries (Cooper and Cooper 2008; Merck 2012; Munro and Munro 2008). Still, some veterinarians said their fear of retaliation by clients would make them reluctant to report animal cruelty (Patronek 1997; Stolt et al. 1997).

Another source of data, Pet-abuse.com, has catalogued almost 20,000 documented court cases of animal abuse in the USA and several other countries in a searchable database. The 2013 annual US summary, the most recent one available, lists 132 cases. This represents an unexplained decline from previous years, when totals ranged from 559 in 2012 to 1,740 in 2008, with most attributed to neglect or to abandonment. Although many animal advocacy organisations report data from Pet-abuse.com on their websites, Pet-abuse.com itself notes, 'there is no real way of determining the true accuracy of the number of cases we have in the database for any given year versus the actual number of incidents (reported or unreported)'. Moreover, the data on Pet-abuse.com 'does not represent a random sample of abuse and cruelty cases. It is a form of convenience sample, and the ability to generalize from these data admittedly is suspect' (Gerbasi 2004, p. 362).

Finally, studies have also examined prevalence through the extent to which members of the public have witnessed or engaged in cruelty to companion and other animals. Much of this data comes from surveys of undergraduate students. Across seven such studies, the proportion of students who claimed to have ever engaged in or witnessed acts of cruelty varies from 17.6 % to 30 %, with an average of 18.2 % (DeGue and DiLillo 2009; Flynn 1999; Henry 2004a, 2004b; Henry and Sanders 2007; Miller and Knutson 1997). In studies of children and youth aged 12–17, the percentage reporting having abused various kinds of animals at least once in their lives ranges from 11 to 50, and averages 25.3 % (Baldry 2003, 2005; Lucia and Killias 2011; McVie 2007; Pagani et al. 2010). As Arluke points out, 'Because students are more likely to underreport than overreport their former cruelty, such estimates of frequency are likely on the low side. If this is true, then this phenomenon may be far more common than generally thought' (2002, pp. 408–409). Studies of adults reveal a greater variation. Kellert and Felthous (1985) found that 72 % of male respondents recalled engaging in one or more acts of cruelty to animals during childhood. Yet, a nationally representative survey of adults found that only 1.8 % of the respondents recalled intentionally harming an animal in their lifetimes (Vaughn et al. 2009).

Overall, these results vary too widely to make definitive claims about prevalence; between 1.8 and 72 % of the people have engaged in or witnessed cruelty to animals at some time in their lives. Issues of study design, especially the definitions of animal cruelty used and the specificity of acts described, likely account for some variation (Agnew 1998; Baldry 2003). For instance, the study by Kellert and Felthous (1985) included tearing wings off insects, an act many people might overlook when asked about cruelty to animals. Vaughn et al. simply asked participants, 'In your entire life, did you ever hurt or be cruel [*sic*] to an animal or pet on purpose?' (2009, p. 3).

Precisely because these studies provide such varying rates of animal cruelty, they reveal how its situational nature 'causes confusion over its meaning and significance' (Arluke 2006, p. 184). The judge facing a crowded dock or insufficient evidence dismisses a case. The veterinarian gives the benefit of the doubt to a client based on their longstanding relationship. The student completing an anonymous survey engages in 'impression management' (Goffman 1959) by denying involvement in behaviour that has always caused shame in recollection. In each instance, people make sense of cruelty through social and cultural filters, which influence whether and how much they appreciate the welfare of animals and perceive harm.

Explaining Cruelty to Companion Animals

The explanations offered for cruelty to companion animals reflect the priorities of the stakeholders in the issue, primarily criminal justice and mental health professionals, and animal welfare advocates. Mental health experts have long had a role in criminal justice, providing testimony, determining competence and conducting criminological research. This well-established symbiotic relationship, combined with the trend known as medicalisation, has secured the mental health profession's authority to account for many acts considered 'deviant' or criminal (see Conrad 1992; Conrad and Schneider 1992). From this perspective, animal cruelty constitutes an impulsive act indicative of psychopathological problems in the offender.

Until recently, some psychologists supported the therapeutic value of animal abuse as a 'healthy' form of displacement. In this paradigm, dogs, in particular, could provide children in need of power with satisfactory victims. For example, Bossard and Boll (1966, p. 128) write:

> The child who is commanded all day long may be commander over his dog.... The child who is full of resentment over what he believes is his bad treatment by adults may kick at his dog. Though this use of a dog, if carried to extremes, is not exactly commendable, there is some therapeutic effect for children when indulged in within reason.

Unlike the 'displacement' explanation, which depicts cruel acts as *reducing* the potential for further aggression, the 'graduation' hypothesis or 'progression thesis' (Beirne 2004) argues that cruelty represents early stages of a progression of aggressive responses that lead to future violence towards humans. Often referred to as the 'link', animal welfare organisations use this explanation to arouse public attention for crimes against animals that would otherwise go unpunished. Interest in the link increased during the 1960s, when criminologists and psychiatrists sought to predict who would commit murder. Forensic psychiatrist John MacDonald famously included animal cruelty among the warning signs of homicidal behaviour, along with firesetting and bed-wetting. Although MacDonald later acknowledged that he found no statistical support for the predictive power of his triad of behaviours, and subsequent studies found conflicting results (Felthous and Kellert 1987), the FBI's Behavioral Science Unit nevertheless incorporated the triad into the profile of the serial killer.

For every study linking animal abuse and subsequent violence (Felthous 1980; Hellman and Blackman 1966; Kellert and Felthous 1985; Verlinden et al. 2000;

Wright and Hensley 2003), another finds no association (Arluke et al. 1999; Climent and Ervin 1972; Miller and Knutson 1997; Goodney Lea 2007). Moreover, engaging in legal, socially acceptable forms of harm to animals, as in hunting and farming, does not increase one's propensity for violence (Flynn 2002; Richards et al. 2013). Research reporting high rates of violent crime in communities surrounding slaughterhouses suggests an exception (Fitzgerald et al. 2009), but none has studied workers directly. For centuries, there has been a perception that those who regularly kill animals are psychologically compromised, as exemplified by the exclusion of butchers from juries during the Middle Ages because they were assumed to lack compassion (Pattenden 1999). And although some studies claim to find a link between witnessing animal abuse and other forms of violence (Baldry 2005; Gullone and Robertson 2008; Henry 2004b; Tallichet and Hensley 2005; Thompson and Gullone 2006), others suggest that witnessing harm to animals can *promote* a sense of compassion (Arluke 2003; Atwood-Harvey 2007; Lewis 2007; Pallotta 2008).

The idea that cruelty to animals is necessarily 'indicative of something pathological and more sinister' (Piper 2003, p. 163) stems largely from psychologists' reliance on retrospective accounts of convicted criminals or violent psychiatric patients. In contrast, by comparing animal abusers with non-abusers, Arluke et al. (1999) found that, although abusers were more likely than non-abusers to have violent criminal records, they were also more likely to engage in other antisocial behaviour, including non-violent offenses. Thus, animal cruelty may correlate with antisocial behaviour generally, in addition to human violence. This supports a 'generalised deviance' hypothesis, in which cruelty to animals represents one manifestation of a tendency towards antisocial behaviour, rather than a step towards criminal violence (see also Goodney Lea 2007).

Some research even suggests that animal abusers desist, rather than advancing to, later violence or other forms of antisocial behaviour. For instance, in a survey of college students, Arluke (2002) found that 25 % admitted to having harmed or killed companion and other animals as children or adolescents (none were arrested for their acts). Arluke then interviewed a subset of these students to learn what significance their acts held for them and what their behaviour meant in the context of adolescent socialisation, recognising the subjectivity of these accounts, given the passage of time and the need to rationalise prior behaviour. Many students recalled their acts as just something kids did when they had nothing else to do. Some viewed their abuse as no different from other forms of play, alongside video games or skateboarding. Importantly, they recalled no feelings of violence or anger directing their acts, and they had not set out to harm or to kill animals but to toy with them.

One student explained that 'he did not "think about hurting" a rabbit when he and his friend shot it with a BB gun. Instead, the two of them focused on seeing the rabbit "flip"' (Arluke 2002, p. 412). The students recognised that their actions had 'a serious edge that distinguished it from everyday play in general or normal play with animals' (Arluke 2002, p. 411). This 'serious edge' gave their actions a social function of instructing them in adult knowledge, such as keeping secrets and establishing boundaries (Fine 1986). Among children, play of this sort is 'virtually inevitable. There are so many needs and traditions connected with the doing of these actions that we would be hard-pressed to visualize a serious program that would eradicate these behaviors' (Fine 1986, p. 67).

As children mature and their identities change, this kind of play loses its appeal. The students left the abusive behaviour in the past, along with the adolescent selves that had enacted it. They did not 'view their abuse as a serious and stigmatising form of deviance, but rather as a folkway violation or lapse in good judgment' (Arluke 2002, p. 409). Some felt guilt or regret, but most forgave themselves and understood that abusing animals was something they did to gain status or go along with their peers. The period during which their play had included abusing animals was 'more of a cultural "time out" than a lasting sign of incivility or anti social behavior' (Arluke 2002, p. 424). Despite acknowledging that they had harmed companion and other animals, the students did not identify themselves as abusers. They saw their acts as 'unrelated to their present selves and moral sensibilities' (Arluke 2002, p. 409).

These results emphasise that not all acts of cruelty have the same meaning and significance for those who engage in them and thus require differing explanations. Lumping together all instances of cruelty to companion animals as pathological precludes the possibility that the actions can be socially instrumental and normative, in the sense that those engaging in them may learn lessons about culture and values that the larger society supports and defines as essential. This does not suggest that parents and other authorities should simply disregard acts of cruelty. Rather, it emphasises that the context of the behaviour matters for how people make sense of cruelty, including the degree to which it represents a social problem or a predictor of subsequent crimes.

Responses to Cruelty

Responses to cases of cruelty to companion animals can involve law enforcement officers, mental health experts, humane organisations and activists, legislators, media, pet owners, veterinarians, educators, parents, peers and the public. The varying perspectives, values and priorities of these groups defy attempts to describe or recommend a particular response, or set of responses, to cruelty. Responses that meet the standards of one group exceed or fall short of the standards set by others, exemplifying 'society's confusion and conflict over cruelty', even in extreme cases (Arluke 2006, p. 186). For example, in May 2001, two boys, aged 16 and 17, set a tabby cat unknown to them on fire in Westminster, Colorado. A passing driver saw the event and called the police, who dispatched animal control officers to the scene. Veterinarians did not expect the cat, given the name 'Westy', to survive. Westy suffered severe burns. He endured five surgeries, including two skin grafts and the amputation of his tail, one hind leg and both ears. He required physical rehabilitation to regain mobility. The case received extensive media coverage. No owner claimed him. Donors sent more than $65,000 for his care, and potential adopters volunteered from around the world (Arluke 2006).

The boys surrendered to police a month later. They confessed that they had wanted to see what would happen if they set a cat's tail on fire, as they had seen in cartoons. After pleading guilty to misdemeanour charges—the maximum penalty for animal cruelty at the time—each boy spent two days in jail, paid fines of $500, and received 18 months of probation. Media coverage stressed the gratuitousness of adolescent male violence, suggesting that the brutality inflicted on Westy was no isolated prank but part of a larger pattern of unprovoked, egregious attacks on helpless animals and, eventually, on people. Angry citizens pressured Colorado politicians to change the designation of cruelty to a felony crime. In the ensuing debate, one politician argued that animal abusers would 'later go on to murder. These people really need to be put away. They need treatment, and they need to be taken off the streets'. A district attorney made his priorities clear by telling the press that, 'If lawmakers tell me I can have additional prison beds for those who are cruel to animals or for those who sexually assault children, I'm going to take the latter' (*Los Angeles Times* 2001). Eventually, a new law passed, but only after the still-recuperating Westy made a dramatic appearance at the state Capitol to persuade legislators. In the midst of intense media coverage, a cartoon satirising the veritable industry that had accompanied the crime appeared in a Denver newspaper. It featured the caption, 'A Full Line of Blazing Westy Souvenirs.' In the ensuring exchange, readers lashed out at what they understood as a tasteless trivialisation of Westy's suffering (Arluke 2006).

The Westy case illustrates the challenges of reaching consensus on appropriate responses to cruelty. The extent of people's concern or indifference has roots deeper than mere sympathy for or disinterest in animals. Behind the public's furore lies a sense of the vulnerability that permeates everyday life in modern societies. Many people believe that life is riskier than ever, and that unpredictable and senseless acts of violence, particularly by young males, threaten us all. Media coverage of incidents of animal cruelty feed into the public's fear that such violence might be redirected at them (Arluke 2010).

Conflicting responses to cruelty also give voice to anxieties about what it means to be human. Expressing outrage or dismissing its expression are two counterpoints in the enduring debate over the similarities between humans and other animals and, thus, over the significance of their suffering. Some responses draw on the culture's trivialisation of cruelty to companion animals, while others convey the increasing sensitivity to the humane treatment of animals and their moral and emotional importance. Responses to cases of cruelty to pets are thus not solely about the facts and circumstances surrounding the harm inflicted. Rather, they reflect wider concerns about how we differ—or do not differ—from other species. As long as these underlying anxieties and questions exist, we will continue to have ambiguous thoughts and feelings about the management of cruelty to pets (Arluke 2006).

It would be neither possible nor prudent for criminal justice authorities, mental health workers and others to make a significant response in terms of resources and personnel to every known incident of cruelty to companion animals. What is needed is a way of filtering cases to identify those abusers with some sort of psychopathology, while still addressing in some manner those cases that are less worrisome. One promising means to distinguish true red flags involves carefully focusing on types of animal cruelty that rarely appear in the general population, while not ignoring more everyday forms. Studies of repeat killers (Levin and Arluke 2009) and school shooters (Arluke and Mafdis 2013) suggest a way to do this. Analysis of the histories of repeat killers revealed that the majority had engaged in animal cruelty during childhood or adolescence, before they began committing murder. Over half had tortured animals. They often targeted dogs and cats, the most anthropomorphised species, the most common companion animals, and the animals highest on the 'sociozoologic scale', or the hierarchy of social value, relative to humans (Arluke and Sanders 1996; see also Felthous 1981). Moreover, the killers did not choose their own companion animals as targets, but instead chose strays and animals unfamiliar to them. The same applied to their human victims; the killers typically had a small circle of family and friends who were off limits as victims. The analysis of the histories of school shooters revealed similar results. Although less than half had engaged in animal cruelty, nearly all who did so had tortured their victims using up close and personal tactics. Most targeted dogs and cats unknown to them.

These results suggest that both the kind of animals chosen and the kind of abuse inflicted matters. The targeting of companion animals indicates a desire to insult what people consider socially good and valuable. The selection of pets also demeans the very idea of close connections with people. Moreover, harming unknown animals may provide a sense of superiority over the vulnerable. The hands-on approach involved in torture differs notably from the forms of cruelty often found in the population at-large. The torture of pets may allow killers to 'rehearse' a particular kind of subsequent human violence.

By finding that forms of cruelty rare among the general population more often constitute a red flag than does the 'everyday' cruelty commonly reported, this research shows how to reduce the false positive problem of labeling individuals who have only limited experience with animal abuse and might thus respond to education rather than punishment. Researchers have questioned the consequences of 'the attribution of transgressive acts to long-term personal traits' (Patterson-Kane and Piper 2009, p. 605). Although all acts of cruelty to companion animals merit some type of response, cases in which perpetrators harm unfamiliar pets, particularly in a hands-on manner, may deserve special attention. Identifying the kind of abuse that may predict dangerousness can spare individuals from stigmatising consequences and provide the conceptual clarity needed to develop responses tailored to individual offenders.

Conclusion

Recent sociological research refines the understanding of cruelty to companion animals in two important ways. First, it shows that cruelty is not necessarily a gateway to subsequent acts of violence. Many cases of cruelty to pets are terminal, not linked to later violent or antisocial behaviour. Because cruelty to animals, broadly defined, is pervasive, it does not necessarily predict subsequent acts of violence. Depending on the definition, virtually everyone who has swatted an insect has harmed animals, and most did not 'graduate' to other violence. Second, and related to this, the research indicates that cruelty does not necessarily signal psychopathology or moral degeneracy in the perpetrators. Not all acts of cruelty have the same significance to those who engage in them. The cultural ambivalence inherent in our treatment of animals means that even killing some species, such as rodents or snakes, may be considered acceptable. Indeed, this ambivalence no doubt also extends to the abuse of some 'higher' animals or pets that, for some people in certain circumstances, is viewed as normal.

In emphasising the ambiguous and conflicting meaning of cruelty to companion animals, we do not intend to underestimate its seriousness. Parents and other authorities should respond to and regard with importance all acts of cruelty. Rather, we point out that cruelty acquires meaning in the context in which it occurs. Various social and cultural filters will influence how people make sense of cruelty to pets, including the degree to which it represents a social problem or a predictor of subsequent crimes.

References

Agnew, R. (1998). The causes of animal abuse: a social-psychological analysis. *Theoretical Criminology, 2*, 177–209.

Arluke, A. (1988). Sacrificial symbolism in animal experimentation: object or pet? *Anthrozoös, 2*, 98–117.

Arluke, A. (2002). Animal abuse as dirty play. *Symbolic Interaction, 25*, 405–430.

Arluke, A. (2003). Childhood origins of supernurturance: the social context of early humane behavior. *Anthrozoös, 16*, 3–27.

Arluke, A. (2004). *Brute force: animal police and the challenge of cruelty.* West Lafayette IN: Purdue University Press.

Arluke, A. (2006). *Just a dog: understanding animal cruelty and ourselves*. Philadelpia: Temple University Press.

Arluke, A. (2010). Our animals ourselves. *Contexts, 9*, 34–39.

Arluke, A., Levin, J., Luke, C., & Ascione, F. (1999). The relationship of animal abuse to violence and other forms of antisocial behavior. *Journal of Interpersonal Violence, 14*, 963–975.

Arluke, A., & Luke, C. (1997). Physical cruelty toward animals in Massachusetts, 1975–1996. *Society & Animals, 5*, 195–204.

Arluke, A., & Madfis, M. (2013). Animal abuse as a warning sign of school massacres: a critique and refinement. *Homicide Studies, 18*, 7–22.

Arluke, A., & Sanders, C. (1996). *Regarding animals.* Philadelphia: Temple University Press.

Ascione, F. R. (1993). Children who are cruel to animals: a review of research and implications for developmental psychopathology. *Anthrozoös, 6*, 226–247.

Atwood-Harvey, D. (2007). From touchstone to tombstone: children's experiences with the abuse of their beloved pets. *Humanity & Society. 31*, 379–400.

Baldry, A. C. (2003). Animal abuse and exposure to interparental violence in Italian youth. *Journal of Interpersonal Violence, 18*, 258–281.

Baldry, A. C. (2005). Animal abuse among preadolescents directly and indirectly victimized at school and at home. *Criminal Behaviour and Mental Health, 15*, 97–110.

Beirne, P. (2004). From animal abuse to interhuman violence? A critical review of the progression thesis. *Society & Animals, 12*, 39–65.

Benetato, M. A., Reisman, R., & McCobb, E. (2011). The veterinarian's role in animal cruelty cases. *Journal of the American Veterinary Medical Association, 238*, 31–34.
Blumer, H. (1986). *Symbolic interactionism: perspective and method.* Berkeley: University of California Press.
Bossard, J., & Boll, E. (1966). *The sociology of child development.* 4th edition. New York: Harper and Row.
Carey, J. (2014). *West highland terrier takes witness stand in animal cruelty case.* http://www.nbcwashington.com/news/local/prince-william-county-ozzy-sharon-betts-hong-277284141.html. Accessed 26 October 2015.
Climent, C. E., & Ervin, F. (1972). Historical data in the evaluation of violent subjects: a hypothesis generating study. *Archives of General Psychiatry, 27*, 621–624.
Conrad, P. (1992). Medicalization and social control. *Annual Review of Sociology, 18*, 209–232.
Conrad, P., & Schneider, J. W. (1992). *Deviance and medicalization: from badness to sickness.* Philadelphia: Temple University Press.
Cooper, J. E., & Cooper, M. E. (2008). Forensic veterinary medicine: a rapidly evolving discipline. *Forensic Science, Medicine, and Pathology, 4*, 75–82.
DeGue, S., & DiLillo, D. (2009). Is animal cruelty a 'Red Flag' for family violence? Investigating co-occurring violence toward children, partners, and pets. *Journal of Interpersonal Violence, 24*, 1036–1056.
Donley, L., Patronek, G., & Luke, C. (1999). Animal abuse in Massachusetts: a summary of case reports at the MSPCA and attitudes of Massachusetts veterinarians. *Journal of Applied Animal Welfare Science, 2*, 59–73.
Favre, D. (2009). Living property: a new status for animals within the legal system. *Marquette Law Review, 93*, 1021–1071.
Felthous, A. R. (1980). Childhood antecedents of aggressive behaviors in male psychiatric patients. *The Bulletin of the American Academy of Psychiatry and the Law, 8*, 104–110.
Felthous, A. R. (1981). Childhood cruelty to cats, dogs and other animals. *Journal of the American Academy of Psychiatry and the Law Online, 9*, 48–53.
Felthous, A. R., & Kellert, S. R. (1987). Childhood cruelty to animals and later aggression against people: a review. *American Journal of Psychiatry, 144*, 710–717.
Fine, G. A. (1986). The dirty play of little boys. *Society, 24*, 63–67.
Fitzgerald, A. J., Kalof, L., & Dietz, T. (2009). Slaughterhouses and increased crime rates: an empirical analysis of the spillover from 'The Jungle' into the surrounding community. *Organization & Environment, 22*, 158–184.
Flynn, C. P. (1999). 'Animal abuse in childhood and later support for interpersonal violence in families. *Society & Animals, 7*, 61–172.
Flynn, C. P. (2002). Hunting and illegal violence against humans and other animals: exploring the relationship. *Society & Animals, 10*, 137–154.
Garner, B. A. (2014). *Black's law dictionary.* 10th edition. St. Paul, MN: Thomson Reuters West.

Gerbasi, K. (2004). Gender and nonhuman animal cruelty convictions: data from Pet-abuse.com. *Society & Animals, 12*, 359–365.

Goffman, E. (1959). *The presentation of self in everyday life*. New York: Anchor Books.

Goodney Lea, S. R. (2007). *Delinquency and animal cruelty: myths and realities about social pathology*. New York: LFB Scholarly Publishing.

Green, P. C., & Gullone, E. (2005). Knowledge and attitudes of Australian veterinarians to animal abuse and human interpersonal violence. *Australian Veterinary Journal, 83*, 619–625.

Gullone, E., & Robertson, N. (2008). The relationship between bullying and animal abuse behaviors in adolescents: the importance of witnessing animal abuse. *Journal of Applied Developmental Psychology, 29*, 371–379.

Hellman, D. S., & Blackman, N. (1966). Enuresis, firesetting and cruelty to animals: a triad predictive of adult crime. *American Journal of Psychiatry, 122*, 1431–1435.

Henry, B. (2004a). The relationship between animal cruelty, delinquency, and attitudes toward the treatment of animals. *Society & Animals, 12*, 185–207.

Henry, B. (2004b). Exposure to animal abuse and group context: two factors affecting participation in animal abuse. *Anthrozoös, 17*, 290–305.

Henry, B., & Sanders, C. (2007). Bullying and animal abuse: is there a connection? *Society & Animals, 15*(2), 107–126.

Irvine, L. (2004). *If you tame me: understanding our connection with animals*. Philadelphia: Temple University Press.

Jackson, E. N. (2001). Dead dog running: the cruelty of greyhound racing and the bases for its abolition in Massachusetts. *Animal Law, 7*, 175–219.

Kalof, L., & Taylor, C. (2007). The discourse of dog fighting. *Humanity & Society, 31*, 319–333.

Kellert, S. R., & Felthous, A. R. (1985). Childhood cruelty toward animals among criminals and noncriminals. *Human Relations, 38*, 1113–1129.

Landau, R. E. (1999). A survey of teaching and implementation: the veterinarian's role in recognizing and reporting abuse. *Journal of the American Veterinary Medical Association, 215*, 328–331.

Levin, J., & Arluke, A. (2009). Reducing the link's false positive problem. In A. Linzey (Ed.), *The Link between Animal Abuse and Human Violence* (pp. 163–171). Portland, OR: Sussex Academic Press.

Levin, J., Arluke, A., & Irvine, L. (2017). Are people more disturbed by dog or human suffering? Assessing the influence of victim's species and age on empathy. *Society & Animals*. In press

Lewis, J. E. (2007). The significant life experiences (SLEs) of humane educators. *Society & Animals, 15*, 285–298.

Los Angeles Times (2001, September 28). Cruelty to cat inspires push for stiffer penalties. http://articles.latimes.com/2001/sep/28/news/mn-50982. Accessed 22 November 2015.

Lucia, S., & Killias, M. (2011). Is animal cruelty a marker of interpersonal violence and delinquency? Results of a Swiss national self-report study. *Psychology of Violence, 1*, 93–105.

McVie, S. (2007). *Animal abuse amongst young people aged 13 to 17: trends, trajectories, and links with other offending*. Horsham: Royal Society for the Protection of Cruelty to Animals.

Mead, G. H. (1934). *Mind, self, and society: from the standpoint of a social behaviorist*. Chicago, IL: University of Chicago Press.

Merck, M. D. (2012). *Veterinary forensics: animal cruelty investigations*. 2nd edition. London: Wiley-Blackwell.

Miller, K. S., & Knutson, J. F. (1997). Reports of severe physical punishment and exposure to animal cruelty by inmates convicted of felonies and by university students. *Child Abuse and Neglect, 21*, 59–82.

Miller, L. (2006). *The recognition and documentation of animal abuse*. Salem, OR: Oregon Veterinary Medical Association.

Munro, H. M. C., & Munro, R. (2008). *Animal abuse and unlawful killing: forensic veterinary pathology*. London: Elsevier Health Sciences.

Munro, H. M. C., & Thrusfield, M. V. (2008). 'Battered Pets': features that raise suspicion of non-accidental injury. *Journal of Small Animal Practice, 42*, 218–226.

Owens, P., & Eckroate, N. (2007). *The dog whisperer: a compassionate, nonviolent approach to dog training*. Avon, MA: Adams Media.

Pagani, C., Robustelli, F., & Ascione, F. R. (2010). Investigating animal abuse: some theoretical and methodological issues. *Anthrozoös, 23*, 259–276.

Pallotta, N. R. (2008). Origin of adult animal rights lifestyle in childhood responsiveness to animal suffering. *Society & Animals, 16*, 149–170.

Patronek, G. J. (1997). Issues for veterinarians in recognizing and reporting animal neglect and abuse. *Society & Animals, 5*, 267–280.

Pattenden, R. (1999). The exclusion of the clergy from criminal trial juries: an historical perspective. *Ecclesiastical Law Journal, 5*, 151–163.

Patterson-Kane, E. G. & Piper, H. (2009). Animal abuse as a sentinel for human violence: a critique. *Journal of Social Issues, 65*, 589–614.

Piper, H. (2003). The linkage of animal abuse with interpersonal violence: a sheep in wolf's clothing? *Journal of Social Work, 3*, 161–77.

Regan, T. (1980). Cruelty, kindness, and unnecessary suffering. *Philosophy, 55*, 532–541.

Richards, E., Signal, T., & Taylor, N. (2013). A Different cut? Comparing attitudes toward animals and propensity for aggression within two primary industry cohorts—farmers and meatworkers. *Society & Animals, 21*, 395–413.

Rowan, A. N. (1993). Cruelty to animals. *Anthrozoös, 6*, 218–220.

Rowan, A. N. (1999). Cruelty and abuse to animals: a typology. In F. Ascione & P. Arkow (Eds.), *Child abuse, domestic violence, and animal abuse: linking the circles of compassion for prevention and intervention*. West Lafayette, IN: Purdue University Press.

Sharpe, M. S., & Wittum, T. E. (1999). Veterinarian involvement in the prevention and intervention of human violence and animal abuse: a survey of small animal practitioners. *Anthrozoös, 12*, 97–104.

Solot, D. (1997). Untangling the animal abuse web. *Society & Animals, 5*, 257–266.

Stolt, L. B., Johnson-Ifearulundu, Y. J., & Kaneene, J. B. (1997). Attitudes of veterinarians, animal control directors, and county prosecutors in Michigan regarding enforcement of state animal cruelty legislation. *Journal of the American Veterinary Medical Association, 211*, 1521–1523.

Tallichet, S. E., & Hensley, C. (2005). Rural and urban differences in the commission of animal cruelty. *International Journal of Offender Therapy and Comparative Criminology*, 49, 711–726.

Thomas, K. (1983). *Man and the natural world: changing attitudes in England 1500–1800*. London: Allen Lane.

Thompson, K., & Gullone, E. (2006). An investigation into the association between the witnessing of animal abuse and adolescents' behavior toward animals. *Society & Animals, 14*, 221–243.

Vaughn, M. G., Fu, Q., Bender, K., DeLisi, M., Beaver, K. M., Perron, B. E., et al. (2009). Correlates of cruelty to animals in the United States: results from the national epidemiologic survey on alcohol and related conditions. *Journal of Psychiatric Research, 43*, 1213–1218.

Vega, J. (2015). *Police need help with animal cruelty case in pup's death*. http://kxan.com/2015/04/08/police-need-help-with-animal-cruelty-case-in-pups-death/. Accessed 26 October 2015.

Verlinden, S., Hersen, M., & Thomas, J. (2000). Risk factors in school shootings. *Clinical Psychology Review, 20*, 3–56.

Vermeulen, H., & Odendaal, J. S. (1993). Proposed typology of companion animal abuse. *Anthrozoös, 6*, 248–257.

Vollum, S., Buffington-Vollum, J., & Longmire, D. R. (2004). Moral disengagement and attitudes about violence toward animals. *Society & Animals, 12*, 209–235.

Wilkie, R. M. (2010). *Livestock/deadstock: working with farm animals from birth to slaughter*. Philadelphia: Temple University Press.

Williams, V. M., Dale, A. R., Clarke, N., & Garrett, N. K. G. (2008). Animal abuse and family violence: survey on the recognition of animal abuse by veterinarians in New Zealand and their understanding of the correlation between animal abuse and human violence. *New Zealand Veterinary Journal, 56*, 21–28.

Wright, J., & Hensley, C. (2003). From animal cruelty to serial murder: applying the graduation hypothesis. *International Journal of Offender Therapy and Comparative Criminology, 47*, 71–88.

Arnold Arluke, Ph.D. is Professor of Sociology and Anthropology at Northeastern University, Vice President and Director of Research at Forensic Veterinary Investigations and a Visiting Scholar at the International Fund for Animal

Welfare. His research examines conflicts and contradictions in human-animal relationships. He has published over 100 articles and 12 books, including *Regarding Animals, Brute Force, Just a Dog, The Sacrifice, Between the Species, The Photographed Cat,* and *Beauty and the Beast.* His research has received awards from the American Sociological Association, the Society for the Study of Symbolic Interaction, the International Association for Human-Animal Interaction Organizations, and the Massachusetts Society for the Prevention of Cruelty to Animals.

Leslie Irvine is Professor of Sociology at the University of Colorado at Boulder. Her research has examined animal selfhood, animal sheltering, gender in veterinary medicine, animals in popular culture, animal abuse and animal welfare in disasters.

Animal Sexual Assault

Piers Beirne, Jennifer Maher and Harriet Pierpoint

Introduction

The focus of this chapter is 'animal sexual assault', though by way of a historical introduction, we need to begin with a discussion of 'bestiality'. A seventeenth-century English word, 'bestiality' derives from the Latin *bestialitas*, which was used severally to refer to primitive behaviour, to human–animal sexual intercourse and to the way in which animals copulate. Sometimes, bestiality has been classified as a crime against nature; in this it was a bedfellow of other crimes allegedly involving 'moral pollution' such as sodomy, buggery, masturbation and paedophilia. At other times, the terms 'sodomy' and 'buggery' were used interchangeably to describe bestiality, though they have also been employed to denote homosexuality. Each of these terms carries with it baggage of condemnation that varies in its moral sources, in its intensity and in the duration of its social censure. In some societies, such as in New England from the Puritan 1600s until the mid-nineteenth century, bestiality has been generally regarded with such trepidation that even the very mention of the word is censured. In legal and

J. Maher (✉) · H. Pierpoint
Centre for Criminology, University of South Wales, Pontypridd, United Kingdom
e-mail: jenny.maher@southwales.ac.uk; harriet.pierpoint@southwales.ac.uk

P. Beirne
Criminology Department, University of Southern Maine, Portland, Maine, USA
e-mail: beirne@maine.edu

J. Maher et al. (eds.), *The Palgrave International Handbook of Animal Abuse Studies*, DOI 10.1057/978-1-137-43183-7_4

religious documents and in polite company, accordingly, it has often been referred to as 'that unmentionable vice' or 'among Christians a crime not to be named'.

In what follows, we outline and discuss (1) the elements of animal sexual assault (henceforth, '*ASA*'); (2) the prevalence of *ASA* and the methodological issues involved in determining its incidence and prevalence; (3) several approaches to understanding the various forms of *ASA*; and (4) the societal reactions to *ASA*. In general, the focus of this chapter is on *ASA* in England and Wales.

The Elements of Animal Sexual Assault ('Bestiality')

From the outset Judaeo-Christianity applied austere standards and strict discipline to bestiality. According to the leading Judaic scholar Jacob Milgrom (2000), the motive behind the Mosaic ban on bestiality was that, if left unchecked, it would destroy the proper use of seed in the patriarchal family. *Exodus* (18:23), for example, stated: 'You shall not have sexual relations with any animal to defile yourself thereby; nor shall any woman give herself to an animal to mate with it; it is a perversion'. *Deuteronomy* (27:21) declared: 'Cursed be he that lieth with any manner of beast', while *Exodus* (22:19) commanded: 'Whosoever lieth with a beast shall surely be put to death' ('whosoever' here applying, at least in *Leviticus* (20:15–16), to both men and women). *Leviticus* mandated death for bestiality not only for guilty humans but also for offending animals. On conviction, both human and animal were usually put to death, often by burning at the stake but occasionally by beheading, by hanging or from blows to the head ('knocking'). The bodies of the condemned, both human and animal, were finally burned or butchered and buried together. Perhaps it was thought that offending animals needed to be put to death because, had they been allowed to live, then they would have served as an unwelcome reminder of shameful acts and thereby have tempted others to sin. Perhaps the burning of both guilty parties was a ritual purification and it was believed that a fiery death would deprive them both of a decent burial.

In her well-known historical analysis in the book *Purity and Danger*, the social anthropologist Mary Douglas demonstrates the important position occupied by the concept of 'holiness' is in the Mosaic commandments. As Douglas shows, to the ancient Hebrews holiness is exemplified by completeness, by keeping the categories of divine creation distinct and by defining the boundaries between them precisely. Prefaced by the general command 'Ye shall be holy: for I the Lord your God am holy' (*Leviticus* 19:2), holiness requires that individuals conform to the class to which they belong. This theme continues in *Leviticus* 19:19: 'Ye shall keep my statutes. Thou shalt not let Thy cattle gender with a diverse kind; thou shalt not sow thy field with mingled seed'. To the Mosaic lawmakers, if different classes of things should not be confused, then the mingling of humans and animals—bestiality—is confusion and should be harshly condemned. On this basis, the early Christian church regarded copulation with a Jew as a form of bestiality and penalised it with death. So, too, from the time of *Leviticus* onwards, bestiality has been regarded as sinful or criminal because it ruptures the natural order of the universe; it violates the procreative intent required of all sexual relations between Christians; and it produces monstrous offspring that are the Devil's work.

However, during and after the mid-nineteenth century, many non-reproductive sexual practices, including bestiality, were in effect decriminalised. Following the early lead of Jeremy Bentham and others, the social control of bestiality formally passed from religion and criminal law to a medico-psychiatric discourse at whose centre, it was thought, lie diseased individuals who are often simpletons or imbeciles with a variety of characteriological defects and/or psychopathic personalities. However, though fictional and quasi-autobiographical accounts of bestiality have occasionally appeared in serious works of literature, it is remarkable that a practice that has traditionally been viewed with moral, judicial and aesthetic outrage has been almost completely neglected by disciplines such as moral philosophy and the social sciences, including criminology. In higher education the discussion of human–animal sexual relations has until very recently been confined to lectures on criminal law given by professors who, with embarrassed chuckles, have referred to the declining volume of bestiality prosecutions as an example of the secularised tolerance and the supposed rationality of western law.

But how quickly times change! During and since the 1990s an unlikely coalition has emerged between ultra-conservatives (the 'moral majority') and animal rights groups. The ultra-conservatives wish to control sexual behaviour in the bedroom, their members believing bestiality to be immoral or unethical behaviour. Supporters of animal rights think that bestiality is a form of animal abuse. It can cause animals to suffer internal bleeding, ruptured anal passages, bruised vaginas, battered cloaca, psychological and emotional trauma and death (Beirne 2002). This coalition has resulted in the recriminalisation of human–animal sexual relations in many European societies (Maher 2015) and in about two-thirds of states in the USA (Beirne

2009). In most jurisdictions it is defined as that form of sexual intercourse when a human penis or digit enters the vagina, anus or cloaca of an animal. Nowadays the offending act has been renamed either as aggravated animal abuse or as *ASA* and is punishable by a term of imprisonment, often for up to five years (How often it is actually prosecuted, let alone punished, is quite another matter). The legal context in England and Wales is considered in more depth below.

Much of the impetus for these changes have come from the feminist movement. To feminists the first and most important issue to do with *ASA* is how we are to distinguish between a proper and an improper sexual relationship. At a minimum, however, proper sexual relations tend to be seen as those that involve genuine consent on the part of both parties. For consent to sexual relations to be genuine, both participants must be conscious, fully informed and positive in their desires. Carol Adams (1995, p. 65) was the first feminist to insist that sex between humans and animals can never be consensual, however, because animals are so thoroughly dependent on us for their very survival. Sometimes, one participant in a sexual encounter may appear to be consenting because she or he does not overtly resist. But lack of overt resistance does not, of course, mean that consent is actually present. Consent can be manufactured. Moreover, animals are incapable of saying 'yes' or 'no' to our sexual advances in forms that we can readily understand. If one party in a sexual encounter does not consent to sexual relations or lacks the ability to communicate consent to the other, then there can be no consent. In the same way, that the sexual assault of women by men differs from acceptable sex because the former is sex obtained by physical, economic, psychological or emotional coercion—any of which implies the impossibility of consent—so, too, coercion is a characteristic of most, if not all, human–animal sexual relations.

Moreover, in most situations, owing to their docile and often human-influenced natures, animals are incapable of resisting sexual assault in any meaningful way, especially when a human is determined to effect his or her purpose. Animals are even further disadvantaged because when they are subjected to sexual coercion and to sexual assault, it is impossible for them to communicate the facts of their abuse to authorities who might give them shelter and aid. They have no voice.

If it is right to regard unwanted sexual advances to women, to infants and to children as sexual assault, then sexual advances to animals should surely be viewed likewise. We therefore, begin this chapter with the warning that we have a duty to avoid harming animals if there is any possibility—however unintentional—of us inflicting it on them in the course of satisfying our sexual desires. For those animal rights activists who see animals as persons, as we do, then *ASA* may also be defined as rape (and see Beirne 2009, p. 13; and Cusack 2013). The legalistic definitions of *ASA* are considered in the sections below.

Issues in Measuring the Prevalence of *ASA*

Assessing the prevalence of *ASA* (that is, the proportion of a population who engage in it) is difficult for several reasons. As discussed above, there is no agreed-on definition either of how *ASA* should be named and defined or of what it is. Some definitions limit *ASA* to penetrative acts. Others are broader. Some studies only measure penetrative acts. Others also include touching an animal in a sexual way or even fantasising about sex with an animal. Some studies are not clear about what they are measuring. Similarly for most studies the motivation of the assault would have to be sexual gratification in order for it to be counted as sexual assault. However, there are common practices involving penetration (for example, artificial insemination) and stimulation (for example, induced ejaculation) of the genital area (albeit without pain or sexual motivation) which are not included in such studies. For some, there would certainly be an argument for counting all such acts within the figures regardless of whether the act is for sexual gratification or for the production of food, clothing or medicine. Moreover, there are different levels of sexual gratification ranging from adolescent sexual experimentation and aggravated cruelty (for example, sadistic sexual acts), as discussed in the section below on understanding *ASA*. Is it appropriate, when assessing the extent of *ASA* to count the numerous actions that result from these various motives irrespective either of how many times they occurred or of the seriousness of the harm suffered by the animal?

Notwithstanding the above, there are two sources of data on the prevalence of *ASA*—official statistics and scholarly research. Police and court statistics on *ASA* only focus on those acts deemed illegal (for example, not artificial insemination), they do not record all the offences which could be linked to *ASA*. Moreover, sometimes they conflate *ASA* offences with other offences against humans (for example, the 'unnatural sexual offences' category includes sex with an animal or a human corpse) and are not readily available (for example, the Ministry of Justice [MoJ] court statistics are only available via a freedom of information request). Moreover, it is accepted that these statistics will under-report the extent of *ASA* through non-reporting (clearly animals cannot report assaults) or non-detecting and non-recording (see Maher and Pierpoint 2012).

The scholarly literature which reports the extent of *ASA* is brief, often dated and methodologically problematic. Essentially, there are six categories of study in this field, as shown in Table 1 below:

Table 1 Categories of animal sexual assault studies

Case studies	This includes a small number of individual case studies (for example, Earls and Lalumiere 2009; Wilcox et al. 2005) which are not generalisable.
General population surveys	This comprises a very few self-report questionnaire surveys of the general population in the US (Hunt 1974; Kinsey et al. 1948, 1953). They depend on the adequacy of participants' knowledge, which is likely to have been strongly influenced—suppressed, even—by social condemnations of bestiality. This category is now considered outdated.
Specific population surveys	This, the largest category, comprises fairly recent studies that are based on very narrow samples such as male prison inmates (Hensley et al. 2006; Miller and Knutson 1997), college students (Flynn 1999), institutionalised young offenders (Fleming et al. 2002), young sex offenders (Abel et al. 1993) and psychiatric patients (Alvarez and Freinhar 1991) or urology and oncology patients (Zequi Sde et al. 2012). Gathering data from institutionalised populations has its own difficulties. For the most part, these studies have been conducted in the USA and may therefore have limited cross-cultural applicability.
Vet surveys	This, the smallest category, also comprises surveys but involved questioning vets about their caseloads including those cases in which their animal patients have sustained injuries that were sexual in nature (Munro and Thrusfield 2001a, 2001b).
Internet surveys	This includes studies which identified zoophiles through the internet (Beetz 2004; Miletski 2000, p. 2005; Williams and Weinberg 2003) and then went on to study their characteristics but did not identify their prevalence within the general population.
Internet content analysis	A few studies have examined the content of depictions of *ASA* on the Internet (e.g., Maher and Pierpoint 2012; Vermount Animal Cruelty Task Force 2005). Using the Internet to measure prevalence is problematic. For example, some sources may be posted for educational reasons rather than intended as pornography. Moreover, each image or video may represent an episode of *ASA* but may be distributed over more than one site and traffic to sites may represent users looking for information rather than for the purpose of engaging in, or viewing, the act itself.

Furthermore, it is generally accepted that many of these studies must underestimate *ASA*'s actual incidence. *ASA* is a crime in which the victim has no voice and, therefore, has a significant 'dark figure'. Maher (2015) maintains that a comparison to child abuse may be helpful: according to the UK National Society for the Prevention of Cruelty to Children (2013), one in 20 children have experienced sexual abuse and over a third (34 %) of those who had experienced 'contact sexual abuse', by an adult, did not tell anyone. Keeping these problems in mind, we now indicate what is known about the prevalence of *ASA* in official statistics and in the findings of academic studies.

Official Statistics

In respect of England and Wales, in brief for now, the offence of sexual intercourse with an animal is defined by the *Sexual Offences Act* (2003 s.69) as one which involves penetration of or by an animal. Possession of extreme pornographic images of a person performing an act of intercourse or oral sex with an animal (whether dead or alive) is also an offence under the *Criminal Justice and Immigration Act* (2008 s.63(1)(7)(d)). We will return to these definitions under the section below on societal responses to *ASA*.

The results from freedom of information requests (MoJ 2015a, 2015b) reveal that the numbers of offenders cautioned and sentenced for the offence of sexual intercourse with an animal are very small. Since the inception of the *Act* in 2004, between zero and four people have been cautioned each year and between zero and four people have been sentenced and only two of these offenders have been sent to prison. In terms of the number of people proceeded against, there was a jump to nine from the usual one to four people in 2010. It is not clear why this was. It does not appear to be an offence perpetrated by a group as a further freedom of information request revealed that the prosecutions came from across six police force areas. It could be explained by, for example, a slight increase in this type of offence in that year or an official 'push' by the Crown Prosecution Service or increased 'have a go mentality' (McConville et al. 1991) by prosecutors for this type of prosecution for that year. These offenders are predominately male: three females, compared with 28 males, have been found guilty of sexual intercourse with an animal since 2004.

Figure 1 shows further results from freedom of information requests (MoJ 2015a, 2015b). They reveal that the numbers of offenders cautioned, proceeded against and found guilty for the offence of possession of extreme pornographic images of a person performing an act of intercourse or oral sex with an animal sexual intercourse with an animal are higher than for the offence of sexual

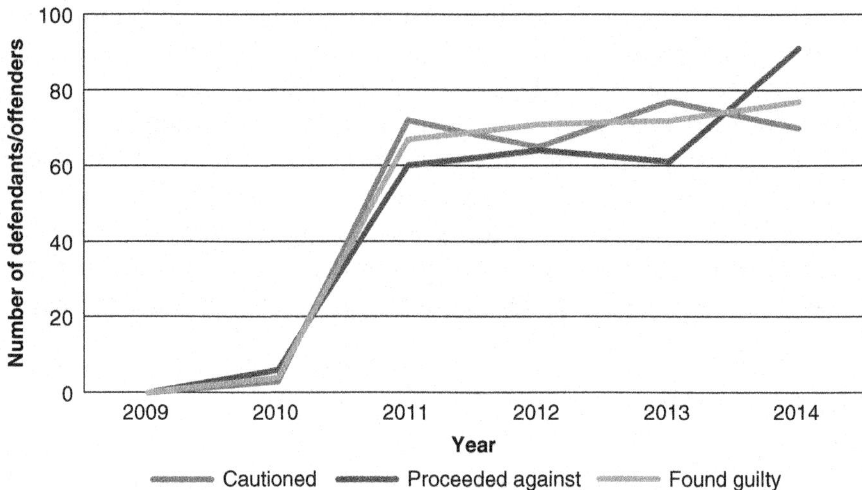

Fig. 1 Offenders cautioned and found guilty and defendants proceeded against for possession of extreme pornographic images – a person performing an act of intercourse or oral sex with an animal – in England and Wales
Source: Justice Statistics Analytical Services (MoJ 2015a, 2015b)

intercourse with an animal. Section 69 which makes possession of this type of pornography an offence came into force in January 2009. There were no offenders cautioned or proceeded against in the first year, but numbers have risen since then. In 2014, 70 offenders were cautioned, 91 defendants were proceeded against and 77 offenders were found guilty (MoJ 2015b). However, these figures undoubtedly represent a small portion of animal pornography being created and distributed (Maher and Pierpoint 2012). According to the Royal Society for the Prevention of Cruelty to Animals [RSPCA], the squish video industry is growing significantly—videos are constantly being found by customs, but are rarely prosecuted as they are videoed abroad (Personal correspondence with the RSPCA 2011).[1,2,3]

[1] Up to 8 April 2013, juveniles received reprimands and warnings instead of cautions. On 8 April 2013 these were replaced for juveniles by youth conditional cautions. The cautioned figure shown includes all of the categories of sentence

[2] The figures given relate to persons for whom these offences were the principal offences for which they were dealt with. When a defendant has been cautioned for or found guilty of two or more offences it is the offence for which the heaviest penalty is imposed. Where the same disposal is imposed for two or more offences, the offence selected is the offence for which the statutory maximum penalty is the most severe.

[3] The number of defendants found guilty in a particular year may exceed the number proceeded against in that year. For example, defendants may be found guilty at the Crown Court in the year following the magistrates' court proceedings or defendants may be found guilty of a different offence to that originally proceeded against.

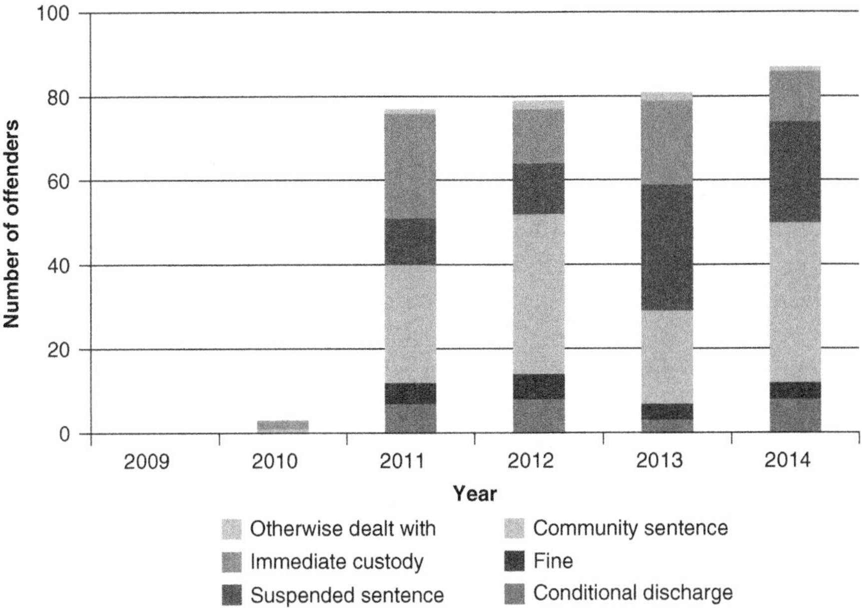

Fig. 2 Offenders sentenced for possession of extreme pornographic images – a person performing an act of intercourse or oral sex with an animal – in England and Wales
Source: Justice Statistics Analytical Services (MoJ 2015a, 2015b)

As shown in Fig. 2, the number of offenders sentenced for possession of extreme pornographic images of a person performing an act of intercourse or oral sex with an animal sexual intercourse has also risen (MoJ 2015b). However, the actual numbers still remain low. We now turn to the findings of the key academic studies on the prevalence of *ASA*.[4]

Academic Studies

Some of the earliest research by Kinsey et al. (1948, 1953), in which they conducted a survey with around 5,300 white male adults and 5,800 white female adults in the mid-western USA, reported that 8 % of the male population and 3 % of the female population had had sexual contact with

[4] The figures given relate to persons for whom these offences were the principal offences for which they were dealt with. When a defendant has been cautioned for or found guilty of two or more offences it is the offence for which the heaviest penalty is imposed. Where the same disposal is imposed for two or more offences, the offence selected is the offence for which the statutory maximum penalty is the most severe.

an animal at least once in their lifetime. Hunt's (1974) is the only other study to report on prevalence in the general population, wherein 5 % of the men and 2 % of the women in the study reported having engaged in bestiality. This decline between the two studies was explained by Beetz (2010) by urbanisation—the movement from rural to urban areas and the loss of access to animals, although this explanation fails to acknowledge the undoubted growth in sexual contact with 'pets' in urban areas.

More recent studies have focused on samples of selected populations rather than general populations. The key findings are the following:

- Flynn (1999) found very low rates of prevalence for sex with animals among his sample of 267 US college students—2 % of the male sample and 1 % of the female sample reported having engaged in sex with an animal.
- Zequi Sde et al. (2012) found much higher rates among men in Brazil. They investigated the behavioural characteristics of sex with animals and its associations with penile cancer patients in a case–control study. A questionnaire about personal and sexual habits was completed in interviews of 118 penile cancer patients and 374 controls (healthy men) recruited in 2009 and 2010 from 16 urology and oncology centres. Overall, sex with animals was reported by 35 % (n = 171) of subjects.
- Alvarez and Freinhar (1991) found that, of a sample of 20 psychiatric inpatients, six (30 %) reported having had sex with an animal, compared with none in similar groups of medical inpatients or psychiatric staff.
- Abel et al. (1993) found that 72 % of juvenile sex offenders in their study group also had an interest in bestial behaviours (n = 119).
- Miller and Knutson (1997) found that, in a sample of 314 prison inmates convicted of felonies, 9 (3 %) reported having had sex with an animal and 16 (5 %) having touched an animal sexually.
- Fleming et al. (2002) found that, of the 381 juvenile offenders who completed their survey, 6 % admitted to having done 'something sexual with an animal'. Similarly, Hensley et al. (2006) found that, of the 261 inmates who responded to the survey, 16 inmates (6 %) reported having engaged in bestiality.

Hence, there is little agreement over the extent of *ASA* (in its different forms in different studies)—ranging from 1 to 72 % of the populations studied (or 35 % excluding the population of juvenile sexual offenders). However, on the basis of such figures, a relationship has been claimed between bestiality and other types of offending, particularly violent and sex offending (Hensley et al. 2006), which is discussed below (see Understanding *ASA*). Unfortunately, none of the studies may accurately depict the current prevalence of bestial behaviour owing to their sampling techniques, the limitations of self-report studies and the age of the studies in some cases. Added to this, official statistics underestimate the extent of *ASA* (Maher and Pierpoint 2012). In trying to establish the extent of animal sexual assault, it may not be sufficient to consider only its prevalence. Some studies have also examined the frequency of assaults. For example, in Zequi Sde et al.'s (2012) study, of the 171 men who reported having had sex with an animal, 14 % reported a single episode, 15 % monthly episodes and 40 % weekly or more frequent episodes. A final approach to measuring *ASA* (unique, in that it focuses on the animal victim rather than offender), appears in Munro and Thrusfield's (2001a, 2001b) survey of 1,000 UK veterinarians, which found 448 reported cases of non-accidental injury, of which 6 % were sexual in nature. However, there will be many injuries which do not receive veterinary attention. There are no studies which assess the extent of the legal sexual assault of animals in the production of food, clothing or medicine. What we are left with is the sense that, while it is currently impossible to establish the true extent to which animals are victimised sexually, it is a problem that deserves our attempts to understand it and to respond to it.

Understanding *ASA*

Our understanding of *ASA* is remarkably limited, hampered by inconsistencies in how society has defined and anthropocentricised this behaviour, obscured through flawed measurements of prevalence, overlooked in the treatment of offenders and disjointed through fragmented claims on motivation of offenders by psychiatry, sexology and psychology studies. The condemnation of bestiality is largely entrenched in religious and in societal norms. Beirne, therefore, argues for cutting away these restraints to focus our criminological lens on animal rights and welfare. By doing so, the animal—the victim—becomes central to understanding the act; we loosen our grip on our need to study how the act impacts on people, letting go of the common approach. To follow Beirne's lead, two theoretical perspectives linking the denial of rights to animals with their victimisation will first be examined. The dominant speciesist attitude to animals—where animals are 'owned' by humans—makes acceptable many forms of animal abuse (flesh eating, hunting and experimentation, as examples) (Ryder 1975). In light of this, what is it about sexual acts with animals that is so unacceptable? In fact, given the dual role animals play in people's lives, as owned items and sources of emotional support, is it not easy to see how animals become victims of sexual abuse? Emotional congruence theory, used to explain why paedophiles are compellingly attracted to children, suggests that the immature psychosocial characteristics of the child (or animal, in this case) allow the adult's emotional needs to be met (Tingle et al. 1998, p. 213). Zoophiles are not alone in attributing human characteristics and emotions to animals; they are commonly anthropomorphised, with large segments of society viewing their pets as 'children', 'family' or 'friends'. Furthermore, the behaviour, anatomy and appearance of companion animals is increasingly moulded to the needs of their human owners, perhaps comparable to the human sexual selection of female partners (Serpell 2002). Consequently, despite absolute social condemnation of bestiality, it is not so difficult to see how someone could move from having an emotional attachment to an animal to perceiving them as a love object and even a sexual partner and rationalising that the animal's 'acceptance' of a sexual act is validation their behaviour is 'okay'. Of course, these animals are not seen as individuals, they are subject to the whims of their owners and society, and stripped of any dignity when it comes to their sexual rights. However this explanation does not tell us why presumably most pet owners refrain from engaging in sexual activities with their animals, and there is little research available to distinguish the relationship of those owners who offend to those that do not.

Affection is only one side of the human–animal relationship; indifference and control are also central. As 'much of the sexual victimisation takes place in such ways as to be invisible' (Adams 1998, p. 328), there are few repercussions for offenders. Fleming et al. (2002) suggest that youth animal sex offenders may identify their actions as deviant but victimless due to the lowly status offenders believed animals held in society. Ascione (1999) documented youthful sex offenders admitting to engaging in animal abuse and bestiality to 'elevate' their mood when bored or depressed. Thankfully some studies (such as Fleming et al. (2002), discussed below) counter the suggestion, as might be implied by these youth statements, that *ASA* should be considered 'normal or benign' when committed by a youth offender. That the suggestion exists is likely evidence that there is some level of cultural acceptance of this behaviour. Consequently, many comparisons have been drawn between the role of patriarchal norms in *ASA* and the rape and sexual assault of women and children. Beirne (1997) argues that the situation of animals as abused victims parallels that of women and, to some extent, that of children because: (1) human–animal sexual relations almost always involve coercion; (2) such practices often cause animals pain and even death; and (3) animals are unable either to communicate consent to us in a form that we can readily understand or to speak out about their abuse. *ASA* is also similar to rape in that it leads to the eroticisation of violence, control and exploitation. Evidence of the link between the objectification and sexualisation of animals with the sexualisation of women is commonplace in social norms. When examining distressing sexual images of animals online, it becomes easy to view *ASA* as part of the same malicious masculinity and patriarchal society that results in rape and sexual abuse of women and children (Maher and Pierpoint 2012). Language is also commonly used to demean and control both women and animals, with commonplace terminology used to objectify women as animals (dirty cow) and animals as sexual objects (beaver, pussy, tits, ass). Animals are also coerced into sex, like women and children, for financial gain, for example, in countries where 'animal brothels' are legal (Maher 2015). Within hunting and shooting culture the sexualisation of women, animals and weapons are intertwined, according to Kalof et al. (2004, p. 237) 'as if the three were interchangeable sexual bodies in narratives of traditional masculinity'. Historically, forced sex with animals has been used to demean Jewish women during the Holocaust and more recently against political prisoners in Chile (Grune 2008). This behaviour is also reported in domestic violence (Russell 1990; Walker 1979) where the batterers/rapist's control is amplified by requiring humiliating acts of his victim (Lovelace 1980 cited in Adams 1998). In these cases animals are denied individuality and rights. They are sexual puppets, made to perform sexual acts by force or by training. Animals make easy targets for sexual behaviour—whether motivated by 'love' or 'control'—due to their proximity to us and the mainstream social norms and values held towards animals.

More commonly explanations have looked at *ASA* from psychological and criminological perspectives which focus on the individual offender. Links have been made between victimisation and offending and animal abuse among young people. That is, children may engage in sexual acts with animals in response to their sexual victimisation by another person. In doing so, they may be trying to regain a sense of power and control by victimising something vulnerable. They may even use animals to 'practice' sexual acts before progressing to interpersonal sexual violence. More recently *ASA* is explained through the 'deviancy generalised hypothesis', which suggests that *ASA* is one of many manifestations of violence and deviance which have the same underlying causes (see Arluke et al. 1999). It must be noted that there are considerable methodological problems associated with studies on *ASA* and those that link animal abuse to interpersonal violence. This needs factoring in when considering the following studies.

Fleming et al.'s (2002, p. 31) study of young offenders found that those who reported animal sexual abuse came from families 'with less affirming and more incendiary communication, lower attachment, less adaptability and less positive environments'. They also reported more emotional abuse, neglect and a higher number of victimisation events than other offenders. This study suggests that *ASA* is an indicator of family dysfunction and co-occurring sexual victimisation. Duffield et al. (1998 cited in Hensley et al. 2010), in their study of juvenile sexual offenders, found that *ASA* was seldom an isolated paraphilia and that those involved in bestiality may in fact be more at risk of sexually abusing others in the future. Fleming et al.'s (2002) study supports the co-occurrence of animal and human sexual abuse. They identified that 96 % of those who reported *ASA* also admitted to sexual offences against humans (at a rate in excess of that perpetrated by non-animal sex offenders). Furthermore, the DSM-III-R (American Psychiatric Association [APA], (1987, p. 405) clinical diagnostic tool reclassified zoophilia as 'paraphilia not otherwise specified' in recognition that 'zoophilia is virtually never a clinically significant problem by itself'. In line with the deviance generalised hypothesis, sexual abuse of animals may be explained by Marshall and Barbaree's (1990) general theory of sexual offending (for example, rape, child abuse and other sexual deviance). They suggest a combination of influences can lead to the development of sexual deviance. First, psychological vulnerabilities, such as poor interpersonal skills, may lead to the development of intimacy deficits in childhood. Sexual offenders, according to Marshall (1989; Marshall et al. 2000), are more likely to have insecure attachment to parents, which makes it difficult to develop and maintain an intimate relationships with other adults. This rejection and detachment may lead to the development of deviant sexual behaviours. For example, a child living in a dysfunctional family may become overly attached to a companion animal, and this child may subsequently gratify its needs (sexual and other) without risking interpersonal involvement (Robin and Bensel 1998, p. 105).

As previously discussed pets may provide the warmth, love, closeness and acceptance desired. Second, Marshall and Barbaree suggest that feelings of aggression associated with rejection, may develop alongside this sexual interest, resulting in an increased likelihood of sexually aggressive behaviour. Merx-Perez and Heide (2004, p. 66) also identify that bestiality occurs when 'sexuality and aggression have become developmentally fused and the two are mutually inclusive in the psyche of the offender'. Cognitive distortions used to justify this behaviour can reinforce the behaviour, thus leading to further sex offending. Ward and Keenan (1999 cited in Hollin et al. 2010, p. 531) conceptualise these cognitive distortions into five implicit theories held by sex offenders (although they refer to offenders with child victims—animal could easily be substituted for child here): (1) victim as sexual being who enjoys and even seeks a sexual encounter; (2) nature of harm to victim is minimised; (3) the offender indicates uncontrollability of their emotions or urges; (4) offenders superiority to the victim confers entitlement to have needs met; and (5) the offender feels adult sexual encounters are a dangerous world, and victims may be identified as safe.

Evidently, the motivations for and causes of *ASA* vary considerably; sexual contact with animals may be youthful curiosity, misplaced affection, about establishing control, or evidence of an incipient psychopathology or sexual orientation. Consequently, the authors propose that any explanation of *ASA* must account for these variables. Singer (2001) and Adams (1995) introduce categories of abuse (deliberate cruelty versus non-physical injury) abusers (opportunistic/experimental, fixated/primary or domineering/sadistic) based on their motivation to abuse. Beirne (2009) produced a well-defined typology of *ASA* with four categories of offenders (see Table 2) based on their stated intentions in assaulting the animal.

This typology is useful for defining and responding to *ASA* as it considers the complexities of the human–animal sexual and emotional relationship. However, these categorisations are innately problematic. For example, there is clear overlap between the categories of aggravated cruelty and adolescent sexual experimentation. Additionally, it may be difficult to distinguish between malicious masculinity behind aggravated cruelty and other situations of adolescent sexual experimentation and exploration, but also between the latter and innocent and affective fondling. We have assessed the common explanations for *ASA*. In so doing, we offer Beirne's tentative typology of the motivations/intentions for *ASA*, including adolescent sexual experimentation, aggravated cruelty, commercial exploitation and zoophilia and argue for the animal victims to be central to any understanding of *ASA*.

Societal Reactions to *ASA*

We now examine societal reactions to *ASA*. Possibly the most influential societal reaction to *ASA* takes place *before* it occurs or is brought to the attention of authorities in the criminal justice system. Most will be

Table 2 Categories of animal sexual assault offenders

Commodification (commodity for sale/use)	This includes forced use of animals for sex by humans and coercion of animals to have sex with a human (for example, depictions of animals having sex with women in pornographic films, pornographic videos available on the Internet and animal brothels).
Adult sexual experimentation	This is arguably one of the most common forms of offending. The motivations and implications for this abuse varies depending on what the animal symbolises culturally and socially, may be individual or group, and motivated by opportunity, curiosity, insecurity, boredom, cruelty, reputation, or practice (for human partners). Many people grow out of this, while others become 'zoophiles'. It is acceptable to exploit and control animals for his/her own sexual gratification.
Aggravated cruelty	This refers to cruelty over and above that present in the other categories. These offenders derive enhanced sexual gratification from intentionally inflicting pain (and death) on their victims. Examples include partners using the animal for revenge in domestic violence situations or the desire to inflict pain and suffering on the animal, accompanied by mutilation (for example, horse ripping).
Zoophilia	This refers to a perceived consensual and loving relationship between an animal and a human (in the way that practitioners of paedophilia and incest justify their behaviour by claiming a genuine mutual relationship with their victim and identify as a minority discriminated against (that is, like homosexuals were). Zoophilia is identified as a mental health disorder in both the DSM-IV (APA 2000) and ICD-10 (World Health Organisation 1992) manuals.

deterred by the outrage and humour surrounding it. The most visible societal reaction to *ASA* is found in legislation aiming to punish, deter or rehabilitate offenders. This either prohibits specific sexual acts (for example, bestiality) or 'unnecessary harm' to animals or encourages treatment approaches for *ASA* offenders. Significantly, while legislation prohibiting specific sexual acts with animals is widely available in some countries (Maher 2015), data and literature on the enforcement of this legislation, on the treatment of *ASA* offenders and on the animal victims is scarce. Consequently, there are considerable limitations in evaluating the success of legislative responses to *ASA*.

Legislative Controls

ASA is currently criminalised in some countries, yet widely tolerated and ignored in others. Greatly influenced by religious beliefs, bestiality legislation has commonly focussed only on penetrative sexual acts (Maher 2015). However, a more complex legislative response is emerging, alongside animal welfare legislation, characterised by discussions around consent and evidentiary proof and influenced by tensions between civil liberties and animal protection groups. A few European countries notably employ a more animal-centred legislative approach. The Swiss Constitution of 1992 (s.80), for example, enshrines the protection of animals, including animals' dignity. Dignity includes the right to sexual integrity (Ethics Committee for Animal Experimentation of the Swiss Academies of Arts and Sciences 2010), thereby establishing a broader protection for animals from sexual assault (Maher 2015). Sadly, the majority of legislation in place is anthropocentric in nature, either emphasising human needs over animals' welfare or focused on reducing the impact on humans rather than the animal victims. An illustration of which is provided in the case study below on the UK legislative response to animal sexual assault, detailing the focus and nature of the legislation in place and the resulting limitations.

Legal Framework and Response in England and Wales

In England and Wales, the legal framework for responding to *ASA* includes the *Animal Welfare Act* (*AWA*) (2006), *Sexual Offences Act* (*SOA*) (2003) and the *Criminal Justice and Immigration Act* (*CJIA*) (2008). The *AWA* (2006) does not specifically name sexual abuse as a category of offending, however, s.4.1 may be used to prosecute offenders should the sexual act cause 'unnecessary suffering' to a vertebrate animal not living in the wild. Using this criteria, penetrative or non-penetrative acts (such as fondling or oral sex) are permitted while behaviour that causes injury and/or results in death—for example, squish videos—may be deemed criminal. The maximum possible penalty is 51 weeks imprisonment with a £20,000 fine.

Touched on above, Section 69 of the *SOA* (2003) prohibits intercourse (penetration that is 'vaginal or anal, either way') with a living animal, but does not recognise non-penetrative sexual acts as a crime. The maximum penalty is two years' imprisonment (prior to this, under the *Offences against the Person* Act (1861) offenders could receive life imprisonment).

Also referred to above, under Section 63 of the *CJIA* (2008) possession (but not the production or distribution) of images (including moving/still images or) detailing oral or penetrative sex with a (live or dead) animal is a criminal offence. Zoophilic pornography (the term used to describe erotic material depicting sexual acts with animals) is placed in the most serious category in the Oliver and COPINE scales used to classify the seriousness of pornographic materials. Zoophilic pornography makes up the significant majority of prosecutions under Section 63 (UK Citizens Online Democracy 2013). The maximum penalty is two years imprisonment with a fine.

Arguably, this legislative framework is inadequate, as it: (1) affords animals only minimal protection from inappropriate sexual behaviour; (2) excludes many categories of offender; and (3) is poorly enforced and punished. Each of these issues will now be considered in turn. The *AWA* requires proof of 'unnecessary suffering'—a complex and subjective measurement, especially as some sexual acts do not result in visible suffering. The *SOA* limits protection for animals to a handful of penetrative sexual acts, excluding many other harmful sexual behaviours. According to the UK Sex Offences Review Group (2000), Section 69 of the *SOA* was developed using the logic which governs other sexual offences: that is, the requirement of 'free agreement to sexual activity'. Thereby, as animals cannot freely consent to penetrative sex, they must be coerced. Following this logic, animals cannot agree to any sexual act, why then is the *SOA* unconcerned with the need for consent for other non-penetrative sexual acts? Equally, why are images of both penetrative and oral sexual acts prohibited under the *CJIA*, while the recently revised *SOA* is concerned with penetrative sexual acts alone? Furthermore, why is the punishment for the act of committing a sexual offence identical to the act of possessing inappropriate images—specifically, how can this be the case if the victim's welfare is of central concern?

The *SOA* narrowly identifies the offender as the person committing the sexual act, while the *CJIA* only concerns persons in possession of material depicting the sexual act. Omitted from these acts are those who coerce others to engage in the sexual act, those who offer their animals for sex (for example, animal brothels) and those who create and distribute sexual material depicting sexual behaviour. Examples can be found in other countries where the legislation prohibits the offering of animals for sexual activities (for example, Germany—Cottrell 2013), and/or the coercion of others to engage in sexual activity with animals (for example, Canada's Criminal Code (R.S.C. 1985, c. C-46) Government of Canada 2015). A Home Office (2000) review suggested that the latter should be legislated for, though this has not been enacted. Given the international and industrial nature of zoophilic pornography, Segura-Serrano (2006) argues for international legislation which prohibits the creation, distribution and possession of zoophilic material.

The *SOA* Section 69 is poorly enforced; as discussed previously, the official detection of these sexual offences is rare, with few offences resulting in arrest or referral to other services. As shown in Fig. 2 above, for the most part, offenders sentenced for possession of extreme pornographic images of a person performing an act of sexual intercourse or oral sex with an animal, under the CJIA, receive a community sentence. In 2014, 38 offenders received a community sentence, 24 a suspended sentence and 12 immediate custody (MoJ 2015b).

Boat (1999) suggests mandatory recording (using a standard questionnaire) and cross-reporting and training among law enforcement agencies, protective services and animal welfare services is necessary. Likewise, Monroe (2006) argues that veterinarians can play a pivotal role in detecting abuse because they are often the first point of contact for helping an animal and reporting a problem. Mandatory reporting by veterinarians may improve detection; however, it is important to recognise that many animal victims of sexual assault will never see a vet.

Punishment is also infrequent and relatively minor, when compared with that for the sexual assault of one human by another (that is, persons guilty of raping or sexual assaulting another person are liable to life imprisonment or a term not exceeding 10 years, respectively). According to a recent Sentencing Council (2012) consultation aimed at developing UK sexual offences sentencing guidelines, Section 69 was excluded from the guidelines due to it being a low volume offence—one conviction in 2011—with a low maximum sentence. As discussed above, only four people have been found guilty of sexual intercourse with an animal since 2004 (MoJ 2015b). The mere existence of legislation, therefore, is neither a good indicator of the seriousness with which the criminal justice system or society views and reacts to *ASA*, nor a useful measure of the protection afforded animals. With punishment less likely and less severe, offenders are unlikely to be deterred (assuming this is an aim of punishment); rather, the well-reasoning offender may even be encouraged to select non-human animals as victims.

Without clear measurement and recording of *ASA* offences in the criminal justice system and relevant non-governmental agencies, it is impossible to determine how effectively legislation protects animals or people. Failure to recognise the scale and complexity of *ASA*, results, in part, from the aforementioned discomfort sexual behaviour with animals causes officials and wider society. Also, a clearer understanding of the scale and complexity of *ASA* forces us to examine the structures of power in society (including the legislation) that promote or make more feasible the exploitation of these vulnerable animals. Limited understanding of *ASA* offences also reduces our understanding of the risks posed by, and the successful treatment of, offenders. English et al. (2003) suggest, effective treatment is essential in order to prevent further victimisation, which is discussed further below. For now, the legal responses available are limited, both in terms of victim protection and preventing future offences.

Treatment of Sexual Offenders

What follows is a brief critique of *ASA* offender treatment. Treatment is central to the social and official reaction to sexual offenders. With most sex offenders returning to their community (Greenfeld 1997), it is crucial that treatment can reduce recidivism (Yates 2013). However, according to Beetz (2010), there is almost a complete absence of prevention programmes and initiatives for *ASA* offenders. Perhaps because animals are marginalised as 'others', harms against animals are often not perceived as 'real crimes'—consequently *ASA* has been viewed as a victimless sexual offence. This perception of *ASA* will impact upon the treatment offenders receive—both in terms of their need for treatment and the level of treatment received based on the perceived risk the offender poses to society. For example, historically, offenders of *ASA* have been identified as having below normal intelligence and have received generic treatment with this in mind. Treatment would have included avoidance techniques, aversion therapy and relapse training, electroshock therapy, psychotherapy and neurosurgery (Earls and Lalumiere 2002, 2009), many now identified to be ineffective (Yates 2013). Furthermore, Vanstone previously documented that UK prison officers, embarrassed by sexual offenders' behaviour, have subsequently avoided them or failed to try to understand them. This mismanagement resulted in officers minimising offences and being unhelpful in terms of treatment and of managing risk (Brayford et al. 2012). Evidence of scholarly neglect of *ASA*, alongside society's humorous or outraged reaction to this behaviour, suggests that similar issues may compromise any treatment of *ASA* offenders. Howe (2003) for example, argues that care providers who view bestiality with disgust, induce shame in *ASA* patients, thereby limiting the effectiveness of the treatment. Wilcox et al (2015, p. 261) argue that due to the high risk and deviancy of *ASA* offenders, 'among all sexual offenders, these individuals [zoosexual offenders] require the most treatment'. They suggest the duration and intensity of existing treatment programmes are not sufficient for the acute risk associated with these offenders. Thereby, recommending long-term, individual and regular professional support which utilises a broad base of therapeutic and psychoeduational support.

In the absence of dedicated prevention programmes, managing offender risk and reducing recidivism is likely the most effective protection for animals. The containment approach is believed to manage this risk effectively (English et al. 2003). It involves a multidisciplinary and collaborate strategy based on full disclosure and verification of each individual offender's specific offending pattern. Focus on the individual is important; offenders and offender motivations clearly differ, suggesting responses must target offender types rather than using a broad-brush approach (Maher and Pierpoint 2012). Future treatment for *ASA* offenders could also follow in the footsteps of the AniCare Model currently available in the US for animal cruelty offenders. AniCare is the first professionally developed cognitive behavioural-based intervention programme for adult (and now youth) animal abusers (Shapiro et al. 2014), however, this programme is not currently tailored towards *ASA* abusers.

Conclusion

What is considered as *ASA* varies—ranging from the narrow, legal definitions of penetration of an animal to others which include touching an animal in a sexual way or using animal pornography. For us, the key issue is that animals cannot consent. Sexual acts with animals are coercive and harmful. As such, any form of *ASA* is rape. There is little consistency in the research findings on the prevalence of *ASA* (again in its different forms)—ranging from 1 to around 70 % of the populations studied. Moreover, the methodological limitations of these studies mean that many of the statistics are likely to be underestimations of the true extent of the crime. Official statistics will also underestimate the problem as *ASA* is a voiceless crime.

The existing literature furthers our understanding of *ASA*, proposing a number of explanations as to why individuals engage in this behaviour, as well as categorisations and typologies of the sexual acts and offenders motivations. For example, Beirne's typology includes adolescent sexual experimentation, aggravated cruelty, commercial exploitation and zoophilia, but we also recognise that categories proposed are never exhaustive nor mutually exclusive, and that they often neglect the impact on the animal victim. In terms of societal reactions, arguably an effective response to *ASA* is only possible if this behaviour is taken seriously. Due to the many myths and misconceptions and social attitudes towards *ASA*, it is not recognised by the general public or officials as a prevalent or serious offence. Without knowledge of how pervasive *ASA* is, and understanding the impact it has on victims and offenders, the importance of addressing it is lost. Since many sexual acts are not defined as animal sexual offences, and only a small percentage of those that are are ever recorded, it is critical that more is learned about the unrecorded cases and the victims who cannot report them. It is possible that through the development of reliable empirical research, animal-centred legislation and the adoption of multi-strategy responses, we can expand our knowledge of *ASA* and recognise its implications for both animals and humans. A necessary first step is the development of public education programmes to bring awareness of the prevalence of and motivations behind *ASA* to the public and officials responsible for responding to it (Fleming et al. 2002).

References

Abel, G. G., Osborn, C. A. & Twigg, D. A. (1993). Sexual assault through the lifespan: adult offenders with juvenile histories. In H. Barbee, W. Marshall, S. Hudson (Eds.), *The juvenile sex offender* (pp. 104–117). New York: Guilford Press.

Adams, J. C. (1995) Bestiality: the unmentioned abuse. *The Animals' Agenda, 15*(6), 29–31.

Adams, J. C. (1998). Bringing peace home: a feminist perspective on the Abuse of women, children and pet animals. In R. Lockwood & F. Ascione (Eds.), *Cruelty to animals and interpersonal violence: readings in research and application* (pp. 318–339). Indiana: Purdue University Press.

Alvarez, W. A., & Freinhar, J. P. (1991). A prevalence study of bestiality (zoophilia) in psychiatric patients, medical in-patients, and psychiatric staff. *International Journal of Psychosomantics, 38*, 1–4.

American Psychiatric Association. (1987). *Diagnostic and statistical manual of mental disorders*. 3rd edition. Washington, DC: American Psychiatric Association.

American Psychiatric Association. (2000). *Diagnostic and statistical manual of mental disorders*. 4th edition. Washington, DC: American Psychiatric Association.

Arluke, A., Levin, J., Luke, C., & Ascione, F. (1999). The relationship of animal abuse to violence and other forms of antisocial behavior. *Journal of Interpersonal Violence, 14*(9), 963–975.

Ascione, F. R. (1999). The abuse of animals and human interpersonal violence. In F. R. Ascione & P. Arkow (Eds.), *Child abuse, domestic violence and animal abuse:*

linking the circles of compassion for prevention and intervention (pp. 50–61). Indiana: Purdue University Press.

Beetz, A. M. (2004). Bestiality/zoophilia: a scarcely investigated phenomenon between crime, paraphilia, and love. *Journal of Forensic Psychology Practice, 4*, 1–36.

Beetz, A. M. (2010). Bestiality and zoophilia: a discussion of sexual contact with animals. In F. Ascione (Ed.), *The international handbook of animal abuse and cruelty: theory, research, and application* (pp. 201–220). West Lafayette, IN: Purdue University Press.

Beirne, P. (1997). Rethinking bestiality: towards a concept of interspecies sexual assault. *Theoretical Criminology, 1*(3), 317–340.

Beirne, P. (2002). On the sexual assault of animals: a sociological view. In A. Creager & W. Jordan (Eds.), *The animal/human boundary: historical perspectives*. Rochester, NY: Rochester University Press and Davis Center, Princeton University.

Beirne, P. (2009). *Confronting animal abuse: law, criminology and human-animal relations*. Lanham, MD: Rowman & Littlefield.

Boat, B. W. (1999). Abuse of children and abuse of animals: using the links to inform child assessment and protection. In F. R. Ascione & P. Arkow (Eds.), *Child abuse, domestic violence, and animal abuse: linking the circles of compassion for prevention and intervention* (pp. 83–100). West Lafayette, IN: Purdue University Press.

Brayford, J., Cowe, F., & Deering, J. (2012). *Sex offenders, punish, help, change or control? Theory, policy and practice explored*. London: Routledge.

Cottrell, C. (2013). German legislators vote to outlaw bestiality. *The New York Times*. http://www.nytimes.com/2013/02/02/world/europe/german-legislators-vote-to-outlaw-bestiality.html?_r=0. Accessed 13 November 2014.

Cusack, C. M. (2013). Feminism and husbandry: drawing the fine line between mine and bovine. *Journal for Critical Animal Studies Online-Only Journal, 11*(1), 24–45.

Earls, C. M., & Lalumiere, M. L. (2002). A case study of preferential bestiality (zoophilia). *Sexual Abuse: A Journal of Research and Treatment, 14*(1), 83–88.

Earls, C. M., & Lalumiere, M. L. (2009). A case study of preferential bestiality. *Archives of Sexual behaviour, 38*(4), 605–609.

English, K. Jones, L. Patrick, D., & Pasini-Hill, D. (2003). Sexual offender containment. *Annals of the New York Academy of Sciences, 989*(1), 411–427.

Ethics Committee for Animal Experimentation of the Swiss Academies of Arts and Sciences. (2010). *The dignity of animals and the evaluation of interests in the Swiss animal protection act*. http://www.akademien-schweiz.ch/en/index/Portrait/Kommissionen-AG/Ethikkommission-fuer-Tierversuche.html. Accessed 13 November 2014.

Fleming, W., Jory, B., & Burton, D. (2002). Characteristics of juvenile offenders admitting to sexual activity with nonhuman animals, *Society & Animals, 10*(1), 31–45.

Flynn, C. P. (1999). Animal abuse in childhood and later support for interpersonal violence in families. *Society & Animals, 7*(2), 161–172.

Government of Canada. (2015). *The criminal code (R.S.C., 1985, c. C-46).* http://laws-lois.justice.gc.ca/eng/acts/C-46/FullText.html. Accessed 30 August 2015.

Greenfeld, L. (1997). *Sex offenses and offenders: an analysis of data on rape and sexual assault.* Washington, DC: U.S. Department of Justice, Bureau of Justice Statistics.

Grune, K. (2008). *Changing perspectives of bestiality: breaking the human-animal distinction to violating animal rights.* http://www.stanford.edu/group/pwruab/cgi-bin/pwrofthepen/wp-content/uploads/2008/04/kerstin-grune1.pdf. Accessed 04 October 2011.

Hensley, C. Tallichet, S. E., & Dutkiewicz, E. L. (2010). Childhood bestiality: a potential precursor to adult interpersonal violence. *Journal of Interpersonal Violence, 25*(3), 557–567.

Hensley, C., Tallichet, S. E., & Singer, S. D. (2006). Exploring the possible link between childhood and adolescent bestiality and interpersonal violence. *Journal of Interpersonal Violence, 21*(7), 910–923.

Hollin, C. R., Palmer, E. J., & Hatcher, R. M. (2010). Sexual offences against children. In F. Brookman, M. Maguire, H. Pierpoint, & T. H. Bennett (Eds.), *Handbook on crime* (pp. 525–541). Uffculme, Devon: Willan.

Home Office. (2000). *Setting the boundaries: reforming the law on sexual offences.* http://webarchive.nationalarchives.gov.uk/+/http:/www.homeoffice.gov.uk/documents/vol1main.pdf?view=Binary. Accessed 11 December 2014.

Howe, E. (2003). Peter singer and bestiality. *The Journal of Clinical Ethics, 14*(4), 311–321.

Hunt, M. (1974). *Sexual behavior in the 1970s.* Chicago: Playboy Press.

Kalof, L., Fitzgerald, A., & Baralt, L. (2004) Animals, women and weapons: blurred sexual boundaries in the discourse of sport hunting. *Society and Animal, 12*(3), 237–251.

Kinsey, A. C., Pomeroy, W. B., Martin, C. E., & Gebhard, P. H. (1953). *Sexual behavior in the human female.* Philadelphia, PA: W. B. Saunders & Co.

Kinsey, A., Wardell, C., Pomeroy, B., & Martin, C. E. (1948). *Sexual behavior in the human male.* Philadelphia, PA: W. B. Saunders & Co.

Maher, J. (2015). Animal sexual assault. In A. Ackerman, & R. Furmanfor (Eds.), *Sexual crimes: transnational problems and global perspectives* (pp. 226–242). New York: Columbia University Press.

Maher, J., & Pierpoint, H. (2012). Animal abuse and sex offending. In J. Brayford, F. Cowe, & J. Deering (Eds.), *Sex offenders, punish, help, change or control? Theory, policy and practice explored.* London: Routledge.

Marshall, W. L. (1989). Invited essay: intimacy, loneliness and sexual offenders. *Behavior Research and Therapy, 27*, 491–503.

Marshall, W. L., & Barbaree, H. E. (1990). An integrated theory of the etiology of sexual offending. In W. L. Marshall, D. R. Laws, & H. E. Barbaree (Eds.),

Handbook of sexual assault: issues, theories, and treatment of the offender (pp. 257–275). New York: Plenum.

Marshall, W. L., Serran, G. A., & Cortoni, F. A. (2000). Childhood attachments, sexual abuse, and their relationship to adult coping in child molesters. *Sexual Abuse: A Journal of Research and Treatment, 12*, 17–26.

McConville, M., Sanders, A., & Leng, R. (1991). *The case for the prosecution.* London: Routledge.

Merz-Perez, L., & Heide, K. M. (2004). *Animal cruelty: pathway to violence against people.* Lanham, MD: Rowman and Littlefield.

Miletski, H. (2000). Bestiality/zoophilia: an exploratory study. *Scandinavian Journal of Sexology, 3*, 149–150.

Milgrom, J. (2000). *Leviticus 17–22.* New York: Doubleday.

Miller, K. S., & Knutson, J. F. (1997). Reports of severe physical punishment and exposure to animal cruelty by inmates convicted of felonies and by university students. *Child Abuse and Neglect, 21*(1), 59–82.

Ministry of Justice (MoJ). (2015a). Replies to Freedom of Information Requests 18 August (FOI 98889) and 16 June 2015 (FOI 97859). London: MoJ.

Ministry of Justice (MoJ). (2015b). Replies to Freedom of Information Requests 28 September (FOI 72179) and 6 Oct (FOI 72644). London: MoJ.

Monroe, H. (2006). Animal sexual abuse: a veterinary taboo? *The Veterinary Journal, 172*, 195–197.

Munro, H. M., & Thrusfield, M. V. (2001a). 'Battered pets': sexual abuse. *Journal of Small Animal Practice, 42*, 333–337.

Munro, H. M., & Thrusfield, M. V. (2001b). 'Battered pets': non-accidental physical injuries found in dogs and cats. *Journal of Small Animal Practice, 42*(6), 279–290.

National Society for the Prevention of Cruelty to Children. (2013). *Facts and figures about child abuse in the UK.* http://www.nspcc.org.uk/news-and-views/media-centre/key-information-for-journalists/facts-and-figures/Facts-and-figures_wda73664.html Accessed 12 December 2013.

Robin, M., & Bensel, R. (1998). Pets and socialisation of children. In R. Lockwood & F. Ascione (Eds.), *Cruelty to animals and interpersonal violence: reading in research and application* (pp. 211–224). West Lafayette: Purdue University Press.

Royal Society of Prevention of Cruelty to Animals [RSPCA]. (2011). *Personal correspondence between Harriet Pierpoint and Royal Society of Prevention of Cruelty to Animals.* Horsham: RSPCA.

Russell, D. E. H. (1990). Rape in marriage. New York: Macmillan Press.

Ryder, R. (1975). *Victims of science: the use of animals in research.* London: Davis-Poynter.

Segura-Serrano, A. (2006). Internet regulation and the role of international law. *Max Planck Yearbook of United Nations Law, 10*, 191–272.

Sentencing Council. (2012). *Sexual offences guideline consultation.* London: Sentencing Council.

Serpell, J. (2002). Anthropomorphism and anthropomorphic selection—beyond the 'Cute Response'. *Society & Animals, 10*(4), 437–449.

Sex Offences Review Group. (2000). *Setting the boundaries: reforming the law on sex offences.* Vol. 1. London: Home Office.

Shapiro, K., Randour, M. L., Krinsk, S., & Wolf, J. L. (2014). *The assessment and treatment of children who abuse animals: the AniCare child approach.* 2nd edition. New York: Springer.

Singer, P. (2001). *Heavy petting.* http://academics.eckerd.edu/instructor/grove/QM410-007/Singer/Heavy%20Petting,%20by%20Peter%20Singer.pdf Accessed 30 July 2011.

Tingle, D., Bernard, G., Robbins, L., Newman, G., & Hutchinson, D. (1998). Childhood and adolescent characteristics of paedophiles and rapists. In R. Lockwood & F. Ascione (Eds.), *Cruelty to animals and interpersonal violence: reading in research and application* (pp. 211–224). West Lafayette: Purdue University Press.

UK Citizens Online Democracy. (2013). *Prosecutions for possession of extreme pornographic images.* https://www.whatdotheyknow.com Accessed 13 Decemeber 2014.

Vermont Animal Cruelty Task Force. (2005). *FACT SHEET: animal sexual abuse.* http://www.vactf.com/pdfs/bestiality-factsheet.pdf Accessed 13 April 2011.

Walker, L. (1979). The Battered Woman. New York: Harper & Row.

Wilcox, D. T., Foss, C. M., & Donathy. M. L. (2005). A case study of a male sex offender with zoosexual interests and behaviours. *Journal of Sexual Aggression, 11*(3), 305–317.

Wilcox, D., Foss, C., & Donathy, M. (2015). Working with zoosexual offenders (addressing high levels of deviance). In D. Wilcox, T. Garrett, & L. Harkins (Eds.), *Sex offender treatment: a case study approach to issues and interventions* (pp. 242–266). Oxford: Wiley-Blackwell.

Williams, C. J., & Weinberg, M. S. (2003). Zoophilia in men: a study of sexual interests in animals. *Archives of Sexual Behavior, 32*, 523–535.

World Health Organisation. (1992). *The ICD-10 classification of mental and behavioural disorder.* Geneva: World Health Organisation.

Yates, P. M. (2013). Treatment of sexual offenders: research, best practices, and emerging models. *The International Journal of Behavioral Consultation and Therapy, 8*, 3–4.

Zequi Sde, C., Guimarães, G. C., da Fonseca, F. P., Ferreira, U, de Matheus, W. E., Reis, L. O., et al. (2012). Sex with animals (SWA): behavioral characteristics and possible association with penile cancer. A multicenter study. *Journal of Sex Medicine, 9*(7), 1860–1867.

Dr Jennifer Maher is Senior Lecturer at the Centre for Criminology, University of South Wales. Her research interests include animal abuse, green criminology, human-animal studies, and youth and gang violence. She recently concluded a UK wildlife trafficking study for the FP7 (European Commission) EFFACE project which evaluated the impact of environmental crime in Europe and is currently researching puppy smuggling for the Scottish and English Governments. Her publications include co-editing *Greening Criminology in the 21st Century* (2016, Routledge, with M. Hall et al.) and the special journal issue 'Animal Abuse and Criminology' in *Crime, Law and Social Change* (2011 with P. Beirne).

Professor Piers Beirne has taught sociology, law and criminology in England, Ireland and the USA, where he is currently Professor of Sociology and Legal Studies in the Department of Criminology at the University of Southern Maine. Among my books are *Hogarth's Art of Animal Cruelty* (2015, Palgrave Macmilan); *Criminology: A Sociological Approach* (2015, with James W. Messerschmidt, Oxford University Press, 6th edition) and *Confronting Animal Abuse* (2009, Rowman & Littlefield). Recently edited books include *Issues in Green Criminology* (2007, with Nigel South, Willan); a six-volume reprint series, The Chicago School of Criminology 1914–1945 (2006, Routledge); and *Green Criminology* (2006, with Nigel South, Ashgate). He is the founding co-editor of the journal *Theoretical Criminology*.

Dr Harriet Pierpoint is a Reader in Criminology and Criminal Justice at the Centre for Criminology at the University of South Wales. Her research interests relate to criminal process and vulnerable people, and, more recently, animal abuse. She has undertaken a number of funded research projects including for the Youth Justice Board, Home Office, Ministry of Justice and the National Offender Management Service Cymru and has publications in internationally recognised, peer-reviewed journals, such as *Policing and Society: An International Journal* and *Criminology and Criminal Justice: The International Journal.* She is a co-editor of the *Handbook on Crime*, for Willan Publishing. She has also presented her research at key national and international conferences and has been by invited by academics and practitioners to give guest lectures. She is a member of the Executive Committee of the British Society of Criminology (Chair, Regional Groups and Specialist Networks) and of the South Wales Police Independent Ethics Committee.

Animal Neglect

Angus Nurse

Introduction

As several chapters of this book identify, animal abuse is a varied concept incorporating multiple activities and behaviours occupying a spectrum from failure to adequately provide for a non-human companion's dietary and behavioural needs through to actual torture of non-human animals. The causes of animal abuse also vary; P`etersen and Farrington (2009, p. 28) identified animal cruelty as being rooted in ideas of strain, social learning and graduation theories. Particularly in respect of non-human animal harm in a domestic setting (the focus of this chapter), human behaviours and activities which constitute abuse are frequently prohibited by law and defined by specific conceptions of abuse or cruelty.[1] Nurse (2013) identifies mistreatment of domestic non-human animals as occurring for many reasons and can be either active or passive. *Active*

[1] This chapter mainly uses the terms 'non-human animals' and 'non-human companions' rather than the broader term 'animals' or 'pets'; the latter term being insufficient to reflect contemporary law's recognition of non-human companions as sentient beings with their own needs. Where the term 'animals' is used, this reflects its use within the relevant legislation and policy discourse.

A. Nurse (✉)
Middlesex University School of Law, London, United Kingdom
e-mail: a.nurse@mdx.ac.uk

J. Maher et al. (eds.), *The Palgrave International Handbook of Animal Abuse Studies*, DOI 10.1057/978-1-137-43183-7_5

mistreatment covers various deliberate acts and intended consequences that cause harm to non-human animals. *Passive* mistreatment can include neglect caused by 'failure to act' such that non-human animals are insufficiently cared for and harm is caused either as a result of misunderstanding an animal's needs or through deliberate neglect. This chapter's focus is neglect as animal abuse and looks specifically at neglect involving non-human (companion) animals (henceforth, non-human companions), examining neglect as both acts and omissions which inflict harm and cause unnecessary suffering to non-human companions whether deliberate or unintentional. This chapter's focus on non-human companion neglect reflects the reality that legal systems generally consider that a greater level of care is required in respect of non-human companions that share human homes (Nurse and Ryland 2014; Schaffner 2011). While neglect occurs in a range of settings, animal welfare and anti-cruelty laws arguably provide for a higher level of protection and redress in respect of non-human companions, although generally legal systems do not recognise non-human companions as crime 'victims'. This chapter also discusses the link between animal abuse and other offences arguing that much abuse of non-human companions is caused by a conception of animals as property and an anthropocentric view of animals which fails to adequately consider their status as sentient beings with specific needs (Wise 2000). Accordingly, this chapter argues that there is a necessity for a changed perception of animal abuse which includes accidental animal harm and neglect. However, via a case study of the UK Animal Welfare Act 2006, this chapter also argues that a contemporary conception on neglect as animal abuse already exists and could be adopted by other jurisdictions.[2]

Schaffner identifies animal law as 'legal doctrine in which the legal, social or biological nature of non-human animals is an important factor' (2011, p. 5), with animal law being socially constructed according to specific notions of animals' value and place within society—for example, different protections apply to wild animals than apply to non-human companions sharing a human home. Most individual jurisdictions (for example, countries) have animal protection laws codifying what constitutes animal abuse by defining abuse within their animal protection laws. Schaffner (2011) also identifies that

[2] I am indebted to my research partner Diane Ryland of Lincoln Law School with whom I worked on research commissioned by International Cat Care (iCatCare) into the implications of UK animal welfare law on feline companions. In particular, we examined the changes brought about by the UK Animal Welfare Act 2006 which redefined how non-human companion neglect is viewed by UK legal systems. Our joint work significantly informed this chapter and it is referred to throughout.

animal protection and anti-cruelty laws also specify the legal protections granted to non-human animals. But the extent to which animal protection, welfare and wildlife crime laws are embedded into civil and criminal justice systems varies across jurisdictions. This point notwithstanding, most countries have laws protecting domestic animals primarily through anti-cruelty laws codifying prohibited activities and criminalising actions inflicting pain or suffering on companion animals. In some jurisdictions, legal terminology defines cruelty and cruel activities primarily within the legal concept of causing 'unnecessary suffering', reflecting the fact that within domestic settings human harm to non-human animals frequently occurs, and the contemporary reality that much animal exploitation and harm remains legal. Indeed, some forms of accidental harm or harm that constitutes a 'necessary' part of human–companion animal relationships (such as neutering, spaying or castrating) may constitute legalised suffering. In effect, some laws argue that by keeping animals in captivity, through the process of domesticating certain species over a period of time, we have an obligation to ensure that they do not suffer harm. While animals are dependent on humans for food and shelter and unable to live independent lives, any suffering should be tightly controlled. The nature of such controls and specific definition of 'acceptable' suffering is socially constructed, so that neglect will often be classed as unacceptable suffering.

Defining Neglect

Benton suggests that 'it is widely recognized that members of other animal species and the rest of non-human nature urgently need to be protected from destructive human activities' (1998, p. 149). Animal protection legislation has developed in part to implement recognition of the prevalence of human harms to animals. Such laws provide a legal framework within which harms against animals are codified and defined, albeit animal protection laws generally fall short of providing animals with actual rights. Thus, 'animal protection legislation serves multiple purposes and is intended to address a variety of human activities considered harmful towards animals' (Nurse 2013, p. 6) while at the same time preserving anthropocentric interests in the continued exploitation of animals, for example, for food. Beirne defines animal abuse as 'those diverse human actions that contribute to the pain, suffering or death of animals or that otherwise adversely affect their welfare' (2007, p. 55). This conception encompasses various harmful activities including, but not necessarily always, those that result in non-human animal death. Given that much existing non-human animal harm is legal, criminologists, animal activists and policy-makers face challenges in precisely defining animal abuse and cruelty (Agnew 1998; Nurse 2013) and distinguishing between the lawful and unlawful. Consequently, defining neglect is problematic given that neglect encompasses a range of acts or omissions that adversely impact on non-human animals (with associated harms). As a result, there is no universally accepted offence of animal neglect. However, legal systems often define neglect within animal abuse discourse via the term unnecessary suffering, consistent with Ascione's definition of animal abuse and cruelty which contextualises animal abuse as being 'socially unacceptable behaviour that intentionally causes unnecessary pain, suffering, or distress to and/or death of an animal' (1993, p. 228). Thus, academic and policy discussions of animal abuse tend to concentrate either on *active* mistreatment or *deliberate* neglect where intent to cause animal harm is a significant factor and an indicator of either anti-social personality disorder, mental illness or of other forms of abuse, particularly within domestic contexts (Nurse 2013, p. 94). Animal abuse discourse predominantly considers direct harm caused to animals via deliberate action (even a deliberate omission such as intended failure to provide adequate care). In this respect, Agnew (1998) identifies that animal abuse is most likely when individuals (1) are unaware of the impact or consequences of their behaviour on non-human animals; (2) do not consider their behaviour to be wrong; and (3) benefit from their abusive behaviour (Agnew 1998, p. 182).

Ascione's definition importantly incorporates the concept of 'distress' which, broadly construed, includes non-physical harm, while Agnew's conception focuses on anthropocentric notions of human calculation and acceptance of the impact of their actions on non-human animals. However, the focus of each is still on *intentional* animal abuse, which this chapter contends is only one part of animal abuse and harm, albeit an important part. This chapter distinguishes between deliberate (intentional) neglect where harm to an animal is intended and arguably foreseeable, and neglect which is caused by omissions or failure to act. *Accidental* neglect, although receiving less attention in criminological study, is also a potent indicator of problems within a domestic setting (Linzey 2009) and of wider harm to animals. First, of considerable importance is the reality that accidental neglect frequently carries significant consequences for non-human companions. Accidental neglect can be serious where, for example, failure to take action or provide care is a byproduct of misunderstanding the appropriate care needs of a non-human companion. It can also include the process of non-human companion animals being bought for children who are unable to care for them adequately.

Children may also simply grow out of human-animal companionship as other priorities dominate. When dietary and mental health needs are not provided for, such that this constitutes abuse; even where such abuse is accidental, this neglect can have severe mental and physical consequences for a non-human companion. Secondly, accidental neglect can be indicative of an anthropogenic notion that non-human animal lives carry less importance than human lives and indeed of wider negative attitudes towards (all) other vulnerable members of a family including spouses or children (briefly discussed later). Thus neglect may be symptomatic of tolerance towards animal abuse which Nurse (2013) concluded includes inflicting cruelty either directly or indirectly, or failing to comply with statutory animal welfare standards such that a non-human animal incurs harm, injury, suffering or distress, either by human act or omission. Omission is central to neglect, but arguably whether the omission is deliberate or accidental is irrelevant; this chapter argues that neglect, in its various forms, constitutes animal abuse. Actions arising from well-meaning activity but which nevertheless result in neglect are also abuse.

This chapter considers both deliberate and accidental neglect and also examines how some neglect, in addition to being accidental, may arise from good intentions. Nathanson (2009, p. 307) and other researchers have also examined the phenomenon of animal hoarding, 'a deviant behaviour associated with extremely deleterious conditions of comorbid animal and self-neglect', where individuals attempt to take care of more animals than is practical and neglect is the result. While hoarding is covered in more detail in another chapter within this volume (see chapter on Animal Hoarding herein), Nurse (2013, pp. 92–93) identifies that the Royal Society for the Prevention of Cruelty to Animals (RSPCA) the Scottish Society for the Prevention of Cruelty to Animals (SSPCA) and environmental health agencies in the UK (and their respective organisations in other countries) frequently deal with these unlawful neglect cases. The American Society for the Prevention of Cruelty to Animals (ASPCA) also estimates 900–2,000 new cases of animal hoarding every year in the USA (ASPCA 2015). The Animal Legal Defense Fund (ALDF) has also identified that over a third of the thousands of cases on its animal cruelty database are of neglect. It states neglect as being among the most common animal abuse problems reported and one of the most significant animal cruelty problems in the USA today (Otto 2007, p. 4). Reliable UK figures on neglect are unavailable. Hoarding is, thus, a social problem and, represents neglect through omission where abuse is caused by a failure to adequately care for companions. The RSPCA defines a hoarder as somebody who has accumulated a large number of animals that 'have overwhelmed that person's ability to provide even minimal standards of nutrition, sanitation and veterinary care' (2010, p. 10). Although such neglect is sometimes driven by good intentions, for example, a desire to help and protect non-human animals, it nonetheless represents abuse where animals are kept in poor conditions which give rise to animal welfare and environmental health offences. However hoarding also represents a dysfunctional human–animal relationship where individuals may actively 'collect' animals as companions (see also the chapter on Collecting of Wildlife). Patronek and Nathanson (2009, p. 274) explained that animal hoarding is maladaptive, destructive behaviour where 'compulsive caregiving of animals can become the primary means of maintaining or building a sense of 'self''.

Neglect Legislation and Enforcement

At the heart of arguments supporting non-human animal welfare as a precursor to animal rights is the perception that society increasingly considers animal welfare to be important and that animals, as sentient beings adversely affected by human behaviour, require legal protection that can best be achieved by providing animals with legal rights (Regan 1983; Wise 2000). As this chapter indicates, animal welfare legislation primarily aims to protect animals from abuse whether intentional or unintentional (Nurse 2013), although 'animal welfare' and 'animal abuse' are often interchangeable terms in policy debates. Schaffner (2011) distinguishes between anti-cruelty and animal welfare laws noting that different types of law reflect different policy intentions. Anti-cruelty laws are usually negative, specifying prohibited acts, whereas animal welfare laws are generally positive, specifying required standards. However both types of law arguably define the precise nature of unlawful abuse and contextualise prohibited activity within legislative and public policy objectives which underpin legislative priorities. Thus, within anti-cruelty statutes 'laws protect animals from the intentional and gratuitous infliction of pain and suffering at the hands of humans' (Schaffner 2011, p. 22). Whereas animal welfare laws generally regulate humans use of animals and 'set standards beyond the mere prohibition of cruel practices already outlawed by the anti-cruelty laws' (Schaffner 2011, p. 70), notwithstanding the reality that exemptions generally exist allowing continued animal use for food or research purposes (subject to restrictions). While Ibrahim's (2006) notion of a welfarist approach and humane treatment for animals is primarily aimed at preventing or reducing suffering, animal welfare laws have increasingly sought to recognise and define minimum standards of care and comfort for animals. Welfare concerns are, however, generally separate from prohibitions on causing suffering that are the subjects of (pure) anti-cruelty statutes. Thus, while anti-cruelty statutes may prohibit certain deliberate animal abuse or 'harm' actions such as the kicking, crushing or stabbing of animals, animal welfare statutes may proactively provide for minimum welfare standards—for example, room or movement specifications for animals in factory farming operations and transport, or for food and water requirements. Such standards may, thus, acknowledge the necessity of a certain level of animal harm but seek to ensure its reduction rather than prohibition (for example, providing for a level of comfort prior to slaughter) (Nurse 2013). Animal abuse as contextualised by legislation may thus be physical, psychological or emotional and can involve active maltreatment, passive neglect (Beirne 2007, p. 55) or simple ignorance of the needs of animals such that their welfare needs are unmet or are actively ignored (Nurse 2013). Enforcement of such legislation also varies depending on whether the act or omission concerned is one subject to the negative contextualisation of an anti-cruelty statute or the 'positive' one of an animal welfare statute.

Francione (2007) argues that non-human animals' status as the property of humans dictates that laws which should require their humane treatment and prevent unnecessary suffering fail to provide any significant protection for animal interests. In reality, animals only receive protection commensurate with their value as human property or commodities. Historically, enforcement of animal protection legislation has largely been reactive rather than proactive falling outside of mainstream criminal justice activity (Nurse 2015; Wellsmith 2011). Instead, anti-cruelty laws are more commonly enforced by animal welfare agencies and NGOs such as the RSPCA and League Against Cruel Sports (LACS) in the UK and the ASPCA, Humane Society (HSUS) and state animal welfare enforcers in the USA. Thus, while abuse contextualised by anti-cruelty legislation is frequently part of the criminal law, its enforcement is socially constructed, varying according to jurisdictional practice and which state agency is allocated responsibility. For example, in the UK animal welfare is primarily the responsibility of the Department for Environment Food and Rural Affairs (DEFRA) and in the USA it is broadly within the remit of the US Department of Agriculture.

[3] There is country-specific legislation in Scotland and Northern Ireland; the Animal Health & Welfare (Scotland) Act 2006 and the Welfare of Animals Act (Northern Ireland) 2011 which have similar aims of preventing harm and promoting animal welfare.

However, UK legislation in the form of the Animal Welfare Act 2006 subtly shifts the anthropocentric position in respect of non-human companions by imposing a duty of care towards such companions. The UK Animal Welfare Acts[3] consider companion animals (non-human animals living in human homes such as dogs and cats) to be protected animals that are legally considered to be 'owned' or cared for by a 'responsible' person. This includes somebody who has accepted some form of obligation to look after them, even if that only means putting out food. The Animal Welfare Act 2006 is part of UK criminal law, creating new offences in respect of failure to adequately care for non-human companions (Nurse and Ryland 2014). Schaffner (2011) identifies the UK as having one of the strongest traditions of anti-cruelty laws although a duty of care towards non-human animals exists in various forms within US state anti-cruelty and welfare statutes. The Animal Welfare Act 2006, however, retains the offence of causing unnecessary suffering from previous legislation but considerably refines its scope to incorporate both the active and passive nature of an offence (discussed later).

Nurse and Ryland (2013) argue that contemporary law provides for a number of ways in which neglect caused by keeping too many animals or keeping animals in poor conditions is actionable. For example adverse animal conditions could constitute a nuisance subject to enforcement action by a local authority and/or the Magistrates court in the UK. The UK Environmental Protection Act 1990 (EPA) defines nuisance as an act or omission resulting in 'unacceptable interference with the personal comfort or amenity of neighbours or the nearby community' (Section 79 of the Act). Noise and odour can constitute a statutory nuisance, thus keeping too many animals with consequential noise or odour problems caused to neighbours would constitute enforceable environmental health problems. Local authorities have a duty to investigate and detect any statutory nuisances occurring within their jurisdiction as part of their environmental health obligations. UK legislation and case law also defines nuisance in particular contexts containing specific reference to 'any animal kept in such a place or manner as to be prejudicial to health or a nuisance' (Section 79 (1)(f) of the EPA 1990)[4]. Schaffner (2011, pp. 120–121) similarly notes the public health, safety and welfare concerns of animal neglect in US law, commenting on contrasting challenges to 'pet limit' laws in Pennsylvania and Minnesota.

[4] While the intention of the Act is likely to protect human health, it is worth noting that harm caused to the health of a non-human animal might constitute a nuisance on a strict reading of sections 78 and 79. Section 78 talks about harm in terms of harm to 'living organisms' and does not specifically refer to human harm.

Schaffner (2011) explains that a Pennsylvania law which limited owners to no more than five dogs or cats was successfully challenged by a woman cited for having 25 cats on the grounds that the limitation was arbitrary and unreasonable and the restriction violated due process rights (contrary to the 14th Amendment of the US Constitution). The matter was referred for trial and the Court was invited to consider the presumption that public health or safety was threatened by the mere presence of a large number of animals or whether the residence constituted a threat. In contrast a Minnesota court concluded that an ordinance which limited households to two dogs was not unreasonable and thus was constitutional. In this case, the burden of proof was held to be on the owner to demonstrate that limiting the number of dogs 'would not promote public well-being by reducing noise and odor' (Schaffner 2011, pp. 120–121). Nurse and Ryland (2013, p. 65) identify that, under UK law, for the keeping of animals to become actionable as a nuisance some 'extraordinary, non-natural or unreasonable action' is required (see *Peech v Best* [1931] 1 KB 1, 14). However, nuisances involving animals are not uncommon and the keeping of an excessive number of cats or dogs, for example, can give rise to nuisance complaints concerning odour, noise or relating to health concerns. The intent of the legislation is to improve human health and to protect humans from nuisances affecting peaceful enjoyment of their property (although in places the Act refers to wider harm caused to 'living organisms'). Analysing UK case law Nurse and Ryland (2013, pp. 65–66.) identified that in cases of insufficient care caused by neglect, a local authority might use Section 79(1)(f) of the *EPA 1990* to serve a specific notice requiring works to be carried out to improve the conditions under which animals are kept. In particular where the living conditions of non-human animals, including the number of animals produces problems such as excessive smell, noise or flies, action might be taken, although overcrowding by itself is not subject to action via this provision. However, where overcrowding causes the nuisance, for example, somebody keeps too many non-human companions and the number combined with the conditions causes a nuisance, then a local authority could impose restrictions on the number of animals kept thus addressing neglect issues.

The ALDF argues that comprehensive criminal prohibitions which include objective standards of care with well-defined neglect-related terms are essential to addressing neglect offences.[5] However, they also identify

[5] Such provisions exist in some animal welfare laws but the ALDF observation also amounts to a recommendation that there is a need for wider use of such provisions.

variance in (US) state laws on neglect, although failure to provide for an animal's basic needs constitute a common definition that can be arrived at by analysing state law. McMillan (2009, p. 75) identifies that 'of the cruelty statutes of the fifty United States and the District of Columbia, none include language specifically acknowledging or addressing emotional neglect, abuse, or suffering in their definition of cruelty'. Thus a definition of cruelty arguably exists in US law which sees abuse (including neglect) as solely being physical, active and direct harm inflicted on non-human animals. Yet, other jurisdictions have begun to recognise emotional distress, including that caused by neglect, as being integral factors in non-human animal abuse. The UK Animal Welfare Act 2006, for example, goes further by requiring a positive approach to animal welfare enshrined as a duty to provide a good standard of animal welfare, as illustrated by the following case study:

Case Study: The Animal Welfare Act 2006 and Neglect as Abuse

The Animal Welfare Act 2006 received Royal Assent on 8 November 2006 and became law in March 2007 in Wales and April 2007 in England making owners and keepers responsible for ensuring that the welfare needs of their non-human companions are met. Thus, a person who is cruel to an animal, or does not provide for its welfare needs, may be banned from owning or keeping animals, fined up to £20,000 and/or sent to prison. The government department, DEFRA, responsible for both animal welfare and wildlife crime has subsequently (2010) introduced Codes of Practice for the welfare of: cats (2009a); horses and other *equidae* (2009b); dogs (2009c); and privately kept non-human primates (January 2010). Contained within the legislation and the associated codes is the principle of recognising animals as sentient beings with individual needs. Thus, 'standard' approaches to companion welfare are no longer acceptable (Nurse and Ryland 2014, p. 6). The Animal Welfare Act 2006 consolidates much earlier legislation and both promotes animal welfare and provides an enforcement mechanism through which punishment may be pursued, by way of criminal sanctions, where there is a breach of animal welfare standards and the legally enforceable duty towards animals. By imposing this duty, the UK Animal Welfare Acts create the requirement for a 'responsible person' to ensure that a companion's needs are met. The duty of care is not solely one imposed on an animal's 'owner', recognising that ownership might be a contested concept, but also encompasses those for whom it might be possible to demonstrate legal ownership (i.e. through purchase of an animal) and those responsible for an animal by virtue of being the provider of food or shelter, even if only temporarily. Thus, those house-sitting for a non-human companion while owners are absent are temporarily bound by the requisite duty of care. The duty to ensure welfare enshrined in the Animal Welfare Acts requires that owners or those responsible for an animal should provide for: (1) a suitable environment, (2) a suitable diet, (3) the need to be able to exhibit normal behaviour patterns, (4) any need to be housed with or apart from other animals and (5) the need for protection from pain. The legislation thus departs from previous simplified prohibitions on unnecessary suffering which commonly defined this in practice as physical cruelty, to provide for a broader definition which includes mental distress and emotional harm linked to consideration of each non-human companion's individual needs. Donaldson and Kymlicka have argued for a change in the status of companion animals such that 'domesticated animals must be seen as members of our community' (2011, p. 101). They contend that a notion of animal citizenship should provide relational rights for animal citizens reflecting the preferences and desires of animals which includes freedom of movement and the sharing of public space, duties of protection and effective medical care tailored to the needs of the individual (animal) citizen (2011, pp. 126–142). Nurse and Ryland (2013, 2014) identify that under the Animal Welfare Act 2006 those responsible for non-human companions are required to do more than simply provide a home for their companion. In their assessment of the Act and DEFRA's Code of Practice for the Welfare of Cats they identify that owners and 'responsible persons' (those looking after a companion) are required to consider both the interior and exterior environment of their home and to ensure that, so far as is possible, it is suitable for the individual companion (Nurse and Ryland 2013, pp. 9–10). They identify that where owners and responsible persons fail to do so, they may commit an offence under the Animal Welfare Act 2006. Contemporary UK legislation therefore explicitly provides for a strong principle of animal welfare with prison sentences for 'general' offences.

While not fully achieving Donaldson and Kymlicka's (2011) notion of actual citizenship, this conception of the need to consider the individual characteristics of a companion arguably broadens the notion of companion animals as active participants in a home rather than the historical conception of non-human companions solely as 'pets'. Both the physical and psychological needs of the individual companion animal need to be considered as UK legislation on non-human companions has changed from its original conception of preventing 'unnecessary suffering' which historically meant avoiding cruelty to 'provide for a broader definition [of suffering] which includes mental distress and not just the physical discomfort or pain associated with cruelty offences under previous legislation' (Nurse and Ryland 2013, p. 9).

Unnecessary suffering can thus be caused either by taking action which causes unnecessary suffering or by failing to take appropriate steps to prevent suffering and being neglectful of an individual non-human companion. Inflicting pain, which may occur for example in cruelty cases, is not in itself sufficient to constitute unnecessary suffering even where extreme pain is caused, as the pain may be caused for allegedly 'beneficial' reasons such as in veterinary surgery to alleviate more serious harm caused to an animal. Pain may also be a by-product of other medical treatment where temporary pain or discomfort is caused with the aim of reducing overall suffering. It becomes necessary, therefore, to distinguish between *necessary* suffering caused to a non-human companion and *unnecessary* suffering; in effect, that which is excessive or avoidable. In making this distinction the courts are able to take into account a number of factors such as whether the suffering could have been avoided or whether it was incidental to a legitimate purpose. Factors to be considered include whether the suffering could have been reduced, was carried out in compliance with legislation, the conditions of a licence or a code of practice issued on a statutory basis. Nurse and Ryland (2014, p. 3) note, for example, that the Animal Welfare Act 2006 does not apply to any act lawfully carried out under the auspices of the Animals (Scientific Procedures) Act 1986 which provides authorisation for scientific use of non-human animals, notwithstanding the ethical and moral objections that may exist in respect of such procedures. The courts might also consider the purpose of the conduct, the proportionality of the suffering, and whether the conduct that caused the suffering was that of a reasonably competent and humane person.

Singer (1995, pp. 9–13) notes that the Committee on Cruelty to Animals set up in 1951 was satisfied that animals can suffer from acute fear and terror. UK animal welfare law has arguably incorporated utilitarian principles of 'equal' consideration for humans and non-human animals in respect of minimising pain and suffering so far as is practicable in order that we make our lives as free from cruelty as possible and avoid the infliction of pain and suffering on animals and humans. Radford (2001, pp. 198–199) argues that historical definitions of cruelty dating back to the UK 1911 and 1912 protection of animals acts, which included the concept of ill-treating or terrifying an animal, indicate 'that Parliament intended cruelty to encompass the infliction of both psychological and physical suffering'. The concept of unnecessary suffering is thus wide in scope and includes mental as well as physical suffering which incorporates both acts and omissions. Accordingly it is an offence to unnecessarily infuriate or terrify a protected animal in addition to, or instead of, causing physical pain. Nurse and Ryland (2013, p. 47) identify, for example, that while a police horse on riot control duty might suffer mental pain as a consequence of being in a stressful, violent environment, this is arguably 'necessary' for it to fulfil its legitimate purpose of protecting people or property and contributing to the maintenance of law and order (notwithstanding moral considerations about such animal use). However, a non-human companion such as a cat or dog which is tortured or suffers intense pain as a result of neglect before being humanely euthanised, has suffered excessively before its demise, and it is an offence for any person to cause unnecessary (physical or mental) suffering to a protected animal where the person committing the act knew or ought reasonably to have known, that the act would cause, or would be likely to cause, suffering. In addition, the law identifies that where a person is responsible for an animal, he would commit an offence if unnecessary suffering was caused to the animal by his failing to take some action. UK case law clarifies that this is the case where the person knew or ought reasonably to have known that any omission on their part would cause, or would be likely to cause, suffering. Nurse and Ryland highlight that it is not necessary to show that the person actually knew that his act or omission would cause suffering, but only that he ought to have known and is required to actively understand a specific non-human animal's needs (2014, p. 6). Thus neglect is linked to an objective standard of what constitutes reasonable behaviour. Radford (2001, p. 253) highlights this point in relation to a historical case—*RSPCA v Isaacs* [1994] Crim LR 517 where a defendant failed to seek veterinary care for her dog for 10 years fearing that it might be put down because of its condition. The Court in examining whether the suffering was unnecessary considered that an objective test could be applied as follows:

1. unreasonable conduct on the part of the defendant;
2. resulting in an animal suffering; and
3. that suffering being unnecessary. (Radford 2001, p. 251)

In respect of the omission or neglect on the *Isaacs* case, the Court thus posed the following questions:

1. Did the dog suffer? (Answer: yes)

2. Was the suffering necessary; which in this case means there was no reasonably practicable measure by which it could be terminated or alleviated? (Answer: no)
3. Would a reasonably caring and reasonably competent owner have made the same omission? (Answer: no) (Radford 2001, p. 253)

The objective test applied under (then) legislation relates to the potential for neglect to be avoided and both the 'knowledge' of an offender of the consequence of their actions and the 'intent' of the offender; that is, whether a competent and suitably caring non-human companion owner would make the same mistake of not seeking medical assistance. However, with the additional onus to provide a good standard of animal welfare contained within the Animal Welfare Act 2006, neglect is now contextualised as abuse, inextricably linked both to the concept of unnecessary suffering, and failure to comply with the positive obligation that now exists to provide for effective animal welfare.[6] Current UK law is thus arguably positive and proactive rather than negative and reactive. Nurse and Ryland (2014, 2013) contend that this is an important change in the law, of importance to those with non-human companions who are now responsible for ensuring that their companion's needs are properly considered in a way that effectively gives non-human companions legal protection from being kept in unsuitable conditions. While non-human companions such as cats and dogs technically remain 'property' as outlined earlier in this chapter, UK law now requires their individual needs to be considered and so anybody wishing to share their home with non-human companions need to have an awareness of their companion's individual characteristics. Failure to do so and neglect, whether by deliberate or accidental omission, now clearly constitutes abuse contextualised as failure to meet UK law requirement to provide good, individualised standards of animal welfare.

[6] See also *R (on the application of Gray and another) v Aylesbury Crown Court* [2013] EWHC 500 (Admin) where horse trader Gray argued that Sections 4 and 9 of the Animal Welfare Act 2006 Act required either actual knowledge or a form of constructive knowledge that an animal was showing signs of unnecessary suffering, and that negligence was not sufficient for him to be guilty of the alleged suffering. The court disagreed pointing out that section 4(1)(b) of the 2006 Act clearly aimed to impose criminal liability for unnecessary suffering caused to an animal either by an act or omission which the person responsible either had known or should have known was likely to cause unnecessary suffering whether by negligent act or omission. The court also pointed out that section 9(1) of the Act sets an objective standard of care which a person responsible for an animal is required to provide. This being the case, the distinction between Section 4 and 9 is whether the animal had suffered unnecessarily, not the mental state of the person concerned.

Neglect as a Factor in Other Harms

In addition to its importance as a form of animal abuse in its own right, non-human animal neglect can also be an indicator of other forms of abuse (and vice versa) particularly spousal and child abuse. Linzey (2009) identifies a link between animal abuse and human violence, building on the work of other commentators who identified that animal abuse and human violence are inextricably linked. Indeed non-human animal abuse can be used as a tool to effect human control (Linzey 2009; Nurse 2013). Accordingly, where one abuse occurs, the other is also likely to be present, although Beirne (2004) identifies that there is no absolute progression from animal to human abuse; thus the progression thesis often cited as indicating animal abuse as a human abuse precursor (Farrington 2002) is somewhat more complex than being a simple predictive link. Schaffner also identifies that the link between individualised animal abuse and human violence is an important factor in anti-cruelty legislation (2011, p. 28) and in enforcement perspectives. Nurse (2013, p. 104) argues that animal harm should not be seen in isolation but needs to be recognised 'as a form of abuse in its own right and as an indicator of antisocial behaviour or violent tendencies in both adults and children that may be associated with other forms of offending'. This being the case, neglect, where identified or observed by animal professionals, needs to be recognised as abuse, but also as indicative of other types of offending. For example, Montoya and Miller (2009, p. 276) identify that 'Colorado statutes dictate that any veterinarian, officer of the state bureau of animal protection, or animal control officer must report any situation in which he or she has reasonable cause to suspect that a child has been a victim of abuse or neglect, or who has observed situations or circumstances that the reporter believes would reasonably lead to abuse or neglect'.

Hawksworth and Balen (2009) recount the story of Family A, a case example drawn from their experiences as part of a health visiting practice in the UK. The family 'consisted of two school-age children, one child under five years, a mother, father, and uncle' (2009, p. 283). Concerns about the school-age children had been raised by educational staff because of their dirty appearance, the persistent presence of head lice and because they were becoming withdrawn. Health visitors, together with the school nurse, visited the property following unsuccessful attempts by school staff to gain entry. School staff had, however, noticed a pit bull terrier tied up outside the home in a small garden 'littered with animal faeces' (2009, p. 283). The health visitors and school nurse observed the same scene, noting that the dog also had no shelter or access to food and water. This indicated the possibility of neglect within the family and the interior of the property which contained a malnourished and frightened cat, the presence of animal faeces within the home, discarded used nappies and rotting food confirmed this. Animal neglect thus has importance not just in respect of its impact on animals as direct or indirect abuse causing animal harm, but also as an indicator of other forms of interpersonal abuse.

Conclusion: Re-contextualising Neglect as Abuse

This chapter identifies current animal protection law (both anti-cruelty and welfare) as making provision for neglect to be considered as animal abuse. While discussions of abuse primarily focus on deliberate acts of cruelty or maltreatment, failure to adequately consider non-human animal needs is recognised within some legal systems as a crime, notwithstanding the legal reality that animals are denied crime 'victim' status (Hall 2013; Wise 2000). Schaffner (2011) identifies flaws in contemporary law such that cruelty laws currently tend to address both abuse and neglect but with the unfortunate consequence that wild animals are exempt from both. Thus, she contends that 'the law must separately address abuse and neglect: laws against abuse should govern all animals, and neglect laws should govern only domestic animals (2011, p. 188). This chapter's discussion of non-human companion neglect identifies neglect as abuse, particularly, where specific legal responsibility is owed towards non-human companions.

The UK Animal Welfare Act 2006 falls short of providing animals with legal personhood and directly enforceable rights. However it does in part reflect Regan's (1983) distinction between legal rights and moral rights commensurate with arguments that animals should be granted the same (or similar) rights to humans because they have value. Tannenbaum has argued that anti-cruelty provisions in animal laws 'create legal duties to non-human animals. They therefore afford legal rights to non-human animals' (1995, p. 167) albeit these rights are not comparable with human rights and legal personhood. Arguably there are also problems with enforcing these rights within contemporary justice systems; numerous limitations and exemptions exist which provide for continued animal exploitation. As this chapter indicates, non-human animals continue to be exploited for food, for scientific purposes and in some 'entertainment' settings (for example, safari parks and zoos). Frasch (2000) explains that the principle behind much animal protection and welfare legislation is concern for the human actor and the wider community because denying animals rights and the subsequent cruelty and abuse that is permitted due to the absence of rights might lead to violence towards humans. UK law addresses many of these concerns by recognising animals as sentient beings capable of individual characteristics; explicitly making actions that inhibits these individualistic characteristics, whether direct or indirect, deliberate or unintentional, subject to criminal sanctions. Linzey (2009) has argued that the inability of non-human animals to give or withhold their consent, their inability to verbalise or represent their interests, their inability to comprehend, their moral innocence, and not least of all, their relative defencelessness and vulnerability—the core differences so often regarded as a basis for discriminating against them—are the very grounds for discriminating in favour of them (Nurse and Ryland 2013). The Animal Welfare Act 2006 addresses this principle by requiring those on whom companion animals are dependent for food, shelter and the opportunity to display their *own* normal behaviours to ensure that the conditions in which their companions live are sufficient for these needs to be met.

Arguably a new socially constructed notion of animal protection and respect for non-human animals' individualistic nature currently exists within UK law which now recognises animals living alongside humans as individual sentient beings. The law provides for their protection, respect and the punishment of those who infringe on their right to exhibit certain behaviours and live a particular lifestyle, even where done so via accidental neglect. Contemporary law recognises animals as sentient beings requiring not just protection from cruelty and mistreatment but also protection from psychological distress linked to suppression of an animal's individual characteristics. Thus, both deliberate and accidental mistreatment of non-human companions and abuse by means of neglect is punishable within the notion of a duty of care and a duty to provide welfare. While animals' status as human property remains problematic in addressing issues of animal rights, widening the principles of individualistic animal needs, inherent in contemporary UK law, provides a means through which the notion of animals as just things that can be neglected and ignored can be directly challenged.

References

Agnew, R. (1998). The causes of animal abuse: a social-psychological analysis. *Theoretical Criminology*, *2*(2), 177–209.

Ascione, F.R. (1993). Children who are cruel to animals: a review of research and implications for developmental psychopathology. *Anthrozoos*, *4*, 226–227.

American Society for the Prevention of Cruelty to Animals [ASPCA] (2015). *Frequently asked questions about animal hoarding.* http://www.aspca.org/faq-page#t273n1045. Accessed 20 June 2015.

Beirne, P. (2004). From animal abuse to interpersonal violence? A critical review of the progression thesis. *Society and Animals*, *12*(1), 39–65.

Beirne, P. (2007). Animal rights, animal abuse and green criminology. In P. Beirne, & N. South (Eds.), *Issues in green criminology: confronting harms against environments, humanity and other animals.* Devon: Willan Publishing.

Benton, T. (1998). Rights and justice on a shared planet: more rights or new relations? *Theoretical Criminology*, *2*(2), 149–175.

DEFRA [Department for Environment, Food and Rural Affairs]. (2009a). *Code of practice for the welfare of cats.* London: Department for Environment, Food and Rural Affairs.

DEFRA. (2009b). *Code of practice for the welfare of horses, ponies, donkeys and their hybrids.* London: DEFRA.

DEFRA. (2009c). *Code of practice for the welfare of dogs.* London: DEFRA.

DEFRA. (2010). *Code of practice for the welfare of privately kept non-human primates.* London: DEFRA.

Donaldson, S., & Kymlicka, W. (2011). *Zoopolis: a political theory of animal rights.* Oxford: Oxford University Press.

Farrington, D. P. (2002). Developmental criminology and risk—focussed prevention. In M. Maguire, R. Morgan, R. Reiner (Eds.), *The oxford handbook of criminology.* 3rd edition. Oxford: Clarendon Press.

Francione, G.L. (2007). *Animals, Property and the Law*, Philadelphia: Temple University Press.

Frasch, P.D. (2000). Addressing animal abuse: the complementary roles of religion, secular ethics, and the law. *Society & Animals*, *8*(3), 331–348.

Hall, M. (2013). Victims of environmental harm. In R. Walters, D. Westerhuis, T. Wyatt (Eds.), *Emerging issues in green criminology: exploring power, justice and harm.* Basingstoke: Palgrave Macmillan.

Hawksworth, D., & Balen, R. (2009). Animal cruelty and child welfare: the health visitor's perspective. In A. Linzey (Ed.), *The link between animal abuse and human violence* (pp. 281–294). Eastbourne: Sussex Academic Press.

Ibrahim, D.M. (2006). The anti-cruelty statute: a study in animal welfare. *Journal of Animal Law and Ethics*, *1*(1), 175–203.

Linzey, A. (Ed.). (2009). *The link between animal abuse and human violence*. Eastbourne: Sussex Academic Press.

McMillan, F. D. (2009). Emotional abuse of children and animals. In A. Linzey (Ed.), *The link between animal abuse and human violence* (pp. 75–92). Eastbourne: Sussex Academic Press.

Montoya, C., & Miller, C. (2009). The role of veterinarians in suspected child abuse. In A. Linzey (Ed.), *The link between animal abuse and human aiolence* (pp. 273–280). Eastbourne: Sussex Academic Press.

Nathanson, N.J. (2009). Animal hoarding: slipping into the darkness of comorbid animal and self-neglect. *Journal of Elder Abuse and Neglect, 21*(4), 307–324.

Nurse, A. (2013). *Animal harm perspectives on why people harm and kill animals*. Farnham: Ashgate.

Nurse, A. (2015). *Policing wildlife: perspectives on the enforcement of wildlife legislation*. Basingstoke: Palgrave Macmillan.

Nurse, A., & Ryland, D. (2013). *Cats and the law: a report for international cat care*. London & Lincoln: Middlesex University and University of Lincoln.

Nurse, A., & Ryland, D. (2014, December). Cats and the law: evolving protection for cats and owners. *Journal of Animal Welfare Law*, 1–6.

Otto, S.K. (2007). *Confronting animal neglect in America: current law and future possibilities*. Cotati, CA: Animal Legal Defense Fund.

Patronek G, J., & Nathanson, J.N. (2009). A theoretical perspective to inform assessment and treatment strategies for animal hoarders. *Clinical Psychology Review, 29*, 274–281.

Petersen, M.L., & Farrington, D.P. (2009). Types of cruelty: animals and childhood cruelty. In A. Linzey (Ed.), *The link between animal abuse and human violence* (pp. 25–37). Eastbourne: Sussex Academic Press.

Radford, M. (2001). *Animal welfare law in Britain: regulation and responsibility*. Oxford: Oxford University Press.

Royal Society for the Prevention of Cruelty to Animals [RSPCA]. (2010). *Prosecutions department annual report 2009*. Horsham: RSPCA.

Regan, T. (1983). *The case for animal rights*. Berkeley, CA: University of California Press.

Schaffner, J. (2011). *An introduction to animals and the law*. New York: Palgrave Macmillan.

Singer, P. (1995 [1975]). *Animal liberation*. London: Pimlico.

Tannenbaum, J. (1995). Nonhuman animals and the law: property, cruelty, rights. In A. Mack (Ed.), *Humans and other nonhuman animals* (pp. 125–193). Columbus, OH: Ohio State University Press.

Wellsmith, M. (2011). Wildlife crime: the problems of enforcement. *European Journal on Criminal Policy and Research, 17*(2), 125–148.

Wise, S. M. (2000). *Rattling the cage: towards legal rights for animals*. London: Profile Books.

Angus Nurse is Director of Criminology and Sociology Programmes at Middlesex University School of Law where he teaches and researches criminology and law and is Programme Leader for the MA Criminology and joint Programme Leader for the MA Environmental Law and Justice. Prior to becoming an academic Angus was Investigations co-ordinator for the Royal Society for the Protection of Birds (RSPB) and its Legal and Data Protection Officer. He was also an Investigator for the Local Government Ombudsman for eight years. Angus has research interests in green criminology, corporate environmental criminality, critical criminal justice, animal and human rights law and anti-social behaviour. He is particularly interested in animal law and its enforcement and the reasons why people commit environmental crimes and crimes against animals. Angus has also researched and published on the links between violence towards animals and human violence. His first book *Animal Harm: Perspectives on why People Harm and Kill Animals* was published by Ashgate in 2013, his second; *Policing Wildlife: Perspectives on the Enforcement of Wildlife Legislation* was published by Palgrave Macmillan in 2015.Angus is co-editor of Palgrave Macmillan's *Palgrave Studies in Green Criminology* book series (with Rob White from the University of Tasmania and Melissa Jarrell from Texas A & M University at Corpus Christi).

Animal Hoarding

Arnold Arluke, Gary Patronek, Randall Lockwood and Allison Cardona

Introduction

In the winter of 1875, the *New York Sun* published a profile of Rosalia Goodman, a woman living with over 80 cats in a dilapidated tenement on the Lower East Side of Manhattan. According to the article, she made up her mind to 'take care of all the cats I could when people turned them out in the cold to starve.' (Anonymous 1875, p. 4). The description of her home sounds like contemporary cases:

A. Arluke (✉)
Department of Sociology, Northeastern University, Boston, MAUSA
e-mail: aarluke@gmail.com

G. Patronek
Independent Consultant; Cummings School of Veterinary Medicine, Tufts University, MA, USA
e-mail: gary.patronek@tufts.edu

R. Lockwood
Forensic Sciences and Anti-Cruelty Projects, American Society for the Prevention of Cruelty to Animal, New York, NY, USA
e-mail: randall.lockwood@aspca.org

A. Cardona
Cruelty Intervention Advocacy (CIA) Program, American Society for the Prevention of Cruelty to Animal, New York, NY, USA
e-mail: allison.cardona@aspca.org

J. Maher et al. (eds.), *The Palgrave International Handbook of Animal Abuse Studies*, DOI 10.1057/978-1-137-43183-7_6

> . . . cats are perceptible on every hand . . . cats with eyes, without eyes, earless and cats of every description skulk in the black nooks or rush out and disappear in sudden panic. And all the time, from sunrise to sunrise, an aromatic and voluminous cloud of feline exhalation is rafted down the stairs into the street (Anonymous 1875, p. 4).

Such accounts occur in modern media on an almost daily basis (Arluke et al. 2002) yet the impact of the accumulation of large numbers of animals on human health and animal welfare has only recently been recognized as a serious concern. The issue was first described in the scientific/medical literature by Worth and Beck (1981), who characterized it as 'multiple animal ownership' in describing 31 case histories of problems presented to the New York City Department of Health and the American Society for the Prevention of Cruelty to Animals (ASPCA). Such individuals were later characterized as 'animal collectors' in publications aimed at animal welfare professionals (Lockwood and Cassidy 1988) and veterinarians (Lockwood 1994). Patronek (1999) and the Hoarding of Animals Research Consortium (HARC) introduced the term 'animal hoarding' as a designation that was more consistent with existing medical, psychological and psychiatric nomenclature since the term 'collecting' more appropriately described accumulations associated with benign hobbies (Frost et al. 2000; Nordsletten and Mataix-Cols 2012). Animal hoarding was formally defined by the following criteria (Patronek 1999; HARC 2002):

- Having more than the typical number of companion animals.
- Failing to provide even minimal standards of nutrition, sanitation, shelter and veterinary care, with this neglect often resulting in illness and death from starvation, spread of infectious disease, and untreated injury or medical condition.
- Denial of the inability to provide this minimum care and the impact of that failure on the animals, the household and human occupants of the dwelling.
- Persistence, despite this failure, in accumulating and controlling animals.

Subsequently, there was increased attention from other professional disciplines to the widespread problems caused by animal hoarding. These problems have been addressed by lawyers (Patronek 2001), social workers (Fleury 2007), adult protective service workers (Boat and Knight 2001; Lockwood 2002), firefighters (Merrill 2012) and others.

Nature of the Problem

Prevalence

There is currently no centralized record keeping for animal cruelty cases in the USA (Lockwood 2008). In 2015 the Federal Bureau of Investigation (FBI) added animal cruelty to the National Incident-Based Reporting System (NIBRS) which tracks incidence of severe animal neglect, including animal hoarding–but it is anticipated that it will rquire at least five years for useful data to be collected for analysis. Animal hoarding cases were once considered rare. The American Psychiatric Association (2013) indicates that hoarding disorder may affect 2–5 % of the adult population, a minimum of five million individuals in the USA (based on 2 % of adult US Census). Since about 68 % of US households have pets, that suggests a potential population of 3.4 million individuals with hoarding disorder who have close access to animals; how many of these live with multiple pets is unknown. Estimates based on actual caseloads handled by animal protection authorities are significantly lower. Original estimates suggested 2,000 to 3,000 new animal hoarding cases per year in the USA (Patronek 1999, 2006; Patronek and Nathanson 2009).

A survey of health officers in Massachusetts queried about reported cases of all types of hoarding (object and animal) estimated the five-year prevalence rate of 5.3 per 100,000 per year (Frost et al. 2000). The authors reported that animals were hoarded in roughly a third of these cases, which suggest about 1.75 cases per 100,000 per year that involved animals, although the authors indicated under-reporting was likely. Nevertheless, this figure, if extrapolated to the entire US population, would indicate a minimum of 5,100 reported cases per year. Presuming an average of 50 animals per case, it would not be unreasonable to suggest that nearly a quarter million animals are subjected to this form of abuse each year.

Another estimate can be based on informal inquiries of animal care and control agencies. Of the 13,000 animal sheltering organizations in the USA, approximately 2,500 have the responsibility to investigate reports of animal abuse or neglect. At animal hoarding workshops at national conferences for animal welfare or animal care and control agencies (including National Animal Care and Control Association and Animal Care Expo) one of us (RL) has regularly asked how many attendees have responded to an animal hoarding case in the last year. Virtually all agencies with investigation authority report that they have responded to at least one case and some report responding to 10 or more cases in the last year. This would suggest that the minimum of 5,100 cases per year calculated above is of the right order of magnitude, although it is possible that the actual number of cases is significantly higher.

Animal hoarding is not limited to any one culture or country. Reports have been published regarding cases in Alberta, Canada (Avery 2005); Manitoba, Canada (Refinish 2009); New South Wales, Australia (Joffe et al. 2014); Victoria, Australia (Ockenden et al. 2014); Belgrade, Serbia (Marijana and Dimitrijevic 2007) and Spain (Calvo et al. 2014).[1]

Severity

Animal cruelty in general has increasingly been viewed as a serious problem as evidenced by stronger anti-cruelty laws, increasing prosecutions and growing concern about the connection between some animal cruelty offenses and the potential for other forms of criminal activity and interpersonal violence (Phillips and Lockwood 2013). Animal hoarding is increasingly viewed as a serious problem by law enforcement and animal protection professionals. The first concern is the large number of animals involved. Cases involving hundreds of companion animals are common.

Another concern is the duration of suffering to which animals in hoarding situations may be exposed. Many live a life where their basic needs for food, water, shelter, a sanitary environment, safety, social interaction and veterinary care are rarely or inconsistently met, causing extended suffering before they eventually die a slow and lingering death from starvation or disease.

Hoarding can also have long-term behavioral effects on animals even after they are removed from the situation and placed in loving homes. McMillan (2013) surveyed 388 adopters of dogs from hoarding cases using the Canine Behavioral Assessment and Research Questionnaire (CBARQ) that had been used in earlier studies of rescued puppy mill dogs. (McMillan et al. 2011). At the time of removal from the hoarding environment, 88 % of the dogs were characterized as having behavioral, emotional or psychological problems. Upon follow-up several months later, 44 % were still reported to have moderate to severe behavior problems.

Yet another concern about animal hoarding cases is the enormous cost associated with responding. Housing, treating and caring for animals rescued from hoarding situations can be extremely expensive, particularly if they must be held as 'evidence' for a prolonged period (Bernstein and Wolf 2005).

[1] Although there are many press reports from the UK, the authors are unaware of any similar UK case summaries in the literature.

There are unique human problems associated with animal hoarding cases as well. In some animal-hoarding situations minor children, dependent elderly persons, or disabled adults are present and are also victims of this behavior. Serious unmet human health needs are commonly observed, and the conditions often meet the criteria for adult self-neglect, child neglect, or elder abuse (Nathanson 2009). Animal hoarding also creates risk of injury or zoonotic disease transmission to occupants of the property, as well as responders.

Demographics

Animal hoarders come from varied backgrounds, somewhat consistent with, the stereotype of the neighborhood 'cat lady' who is pictured as an older, single female, living alone. However, hoarding among men and younger women, as well as couples, is also often encountered. Worth and Beck (1981) reported that 70 % of the sample of 31 hoarders were unmarried women who had cats, while in another study (Patronek 1999) 76 % of the sample were women, 46 % were over 60 years of age, most were single, divorced, or widowed and cats were most commonly involved. In another study (HARC 2002), 83 % were women, with a median age of 55 years, and nearly three-quarters of the sample were single, widowed or divorced. In the review of animal hoarders in Australia (Joffe et al. 2014), most were female (72.4 %) and 79 % were 40–64 years of age at their first offence.

Animal hoarding behaviour cuts across all demographic and socio-economic boundaries. Hoarding behavior has been discovered among doctors, nurses, public officials, teachers, college professors, social workers and veterinarians, as well as among a broad spectrum of socio-economically disadvantaged individuals (Patronek et al. 2006).

Animals and Objects

Cats and dogs are the most commonly hoarded species, but wildlife, exotic animals and farm animals have been involved. One study of 71 animal hoarders (HARC 2002) found that approximately 82 % of the cases involved cats, 55 % dogs, 17 % birds, 6 % reptiles, 11 % small mammals, 6 % horses and 6 % cattle, sheep or goats. A review of 56 cases of animal hoarding involving prosecution of the hoarder noted that 46 % of cases involved dogs, 34 % involved cats, with the remainder of the cases evenly divided between birds, farm animals, rabbits and horses. The lower incidence of cat hoarding in this review suggests that cases involving dogs are more likely to attract prosecutorial attention, particularly if dead animals are found at the scene (Berry et al. 2005).

Animal hoarding frequently co-occurs with the hoarding of objects. Case reports indicate that between 31 % and 100 % of individuals who hoard animals also hoard inanimate possessions (Steketee et al. 2011). There are some notable differences between object and animal hoarding. Most animal-hoarding cases involved squalid living conditions, while only a minority of object-hoarding cases did so (Rasmussen et al. 2014). Men and women are evenly represented in cases of object hoarding, whereas animal hoarders are predominantly female (Steketee and Frost 2014). Although both conditions are characterized by poor insight, responding to animal hoarding cases is often complicated by animal hoarders' delusional beliefs about special abilities to communicate with, understand and/or provide care for animals (Frost and Steketee 2014).

Types of Hoarders

Animal hoarding appears to be more complex than object hoarding in the forms it can take and the range of underlying motivations. Several useful categories have been identified that go beyond the original basic definition (Frost et al. 2015; Patronek 1999; Patronek et al. 2006).

The *overwhelmed caregiver* minimizes rather than denies animal care problems that result from economic, social, medical or domestic changes, such as loss of job or health, but cannot remedy these problems. Despite their strong attachment to animals, the overwhelmed caregiver's compromised situation gradually leads to a deterioration of animal care.

The *rescue hoarder* often presents the largest and most costly problem to law enforcement and animal control agencies. Such cases often involve large numbers of animals, sometimes in excess of 500 cats or dogs. Virtually all of the large-scale animal hoarding cases responded to by the ASPCA involve 'rescue' situations. The rescue hoarder has a missionary zeal to save all animals. They also actively seek to acquire animals because they feel that only they can provide adequate care and because they oppose euthanasia. They view legitimate animal care and control agencies as the enemy and often disparage conventional veterinary medicine and make use of unconventional and ineffective approaches to medical care—if any. Several qualities differentiate rescue hoarders from individuals involved in legitimate animal rescue efforts (Lockwood 2011) including the failure of rescue hoarders to keep good records, have stable staff and dedicated veterinary services, and their failure to refuse new intake if overcrowded.

Finally, the *exploiter hoarder* is the most challenging type to manage. Considered to be sociopaths and/or to have severe personality disorders, their lack of empathy for people or animals means they are indifferent to harm they cause them. They may be motivated by financial gain from soliciting funds that are not used for animal care. Exploiter hoarders can be charismatic and articulate, presenting an appearance that suggests competence to the public, the media, officials and even the courts.

Diagnosis and Etiology

In the last 20 years, animal hoarding has gone from being largely ignored by mental health professionals to being considered a complex and potentially serious mental disorder. The DSM-5 added 'Hoarding Disorder (HD)' as an official diagnosis in 2013. Because animals are legally considered property the hoarding of animals would appear to qualify as HD, although this question is not yet resolved in the psychiatric literature (Frost et al. 2015). Since diagnosis of animal hoarding in the DSM is *descriptive* and does not account for etiology, we will explore various models that have been suggested for the development and expression of this behavior.

Addiction Models

When animal hoarding was first recognized as a problem for the animal welfare community, it was noted that parallels with addiction seem to fit the thinking and behavior of many hoarders (Lockwood 1994). Hoarders are preoccupied with animals, are in denial over their problems, have many excuses for their situation, may be socially isolated, claim to be persecuted and neglect themselves and their surroundings. Other evidence consistent with the addictions model is the similarity of hoarders to people suffering from impulse control problems, such as compulsive shopping (Frost 1998), compulsive gambling (Meagher et al. 1999) and significantly higher levels of smoking (Raines et al. 2014). Philip Flores, in his book *Addiction as an Attachment Disorder*, provides suggestions of how the addiction model is easily reconciled with attachment theory (discussed below).

Obsessive Compulsive Disorder

Hoarding was initially conceptualized as a variant of obsessive-compulsive disorder. However, additional research suggested a more complex pattern of overlap with attention deficit-hyperactivity disorder, organic brain disease, depression, anxiety and personality disorders, eventually leading to the designation of Hoarding Disorder as a distinct malady in DSM-5 (Bloch et al. 2014; Mataix et al. 2010; Pertusa et al. 2010; Tolin 2011; Tolin et al. 2011).

Attachment Theory

Animal hoarding is, by definition, associated with pathologically strong attachments to animals and is usually accompanied by a history of disordered or inadequate attachments to people. Refining what has been learned, Patronek and Nathanson (2009) and Nathanson and Patronek (2011) have woven these disparate models and approaches together, and rather than applying diagnostic labels to animal hoarders, have suggested that the problem is better understood by focusing on the thoughts and actions exhibited by hoarders. Animal hoarders often manifest traits such as suspiciousness, mistrust, fear of abandonment leading to unstable and intense interpersonal relationships, feelings of emptiness, difficulty with anger, and occasional paranoia. People having these traits often come from families where they had a history of unresolved grief due to tragic, untimely deaths or losses and emotional or physical abuse (Cassidy and Mohr 2001; Lyons-Ruth et al. 2006). Absence of nurturing relationships in childhood cause these people to have a deep sense of aloneness in adulthood that can never be filled.

Preliminary research (HARC 2002) suggested that hoarders grew up in households with inconsistent parenting, in which animals may have been the only stable feature. The vast majority report feelings of insecurity and disruptive experiences in early life, including frequent relocations, parental separation and divorce and isolation from peers.

Self-Psychology

Animal hoarders rely heavily on their connection to animals for their definition of self and self-worth, thus insights from the theoretical framework that focuses on that process can be helpful in understanding the disordered cognitive mechanisms that allow hoarding to rise to extreme levels of animal neglect coupled with lack of insight into the conditions by the hoarder. The process by which disordered attachments to people can develop into hoarding behavior in general and animal hoarding in particular is consistent with psychodynamic concepts such as self-psychology (Brown 2011).

Brown (2011) notes that animals can provide an ideal resource for building a strong, idealized but ultimately erroneous self-image. They cannot disagree with a human's interpretation of how they feel or what they want but the hoarder can believe that animals feel and think exactly like them and want what they want, whether or not they actually do.

Other Factors

Genetics

Family studies show that object hoarding is more common among first-degree relatives of people with hoarding when compared with non-hoarding controls. Pedigree and twin studies suggest that hoarding has a strong genetic component and complex pattern of inheritance. However, most of these studies have involved subjects with OCD or other disorders in addition to hoarding symptoms. Currently, there is a lack of replication of previous genetic studies (Hirschtritt and Mathews 2014). There have been no studies to date specifically looking at possible genetic contributors specific to animal hoarding.

Neurophysiology

Pathological hoarding behavior potentially involves disruption of brain mechanisms associated with decision-making, general cognitive function, impulsivity, assignment of emotional significance to possessions and anxiety associated with decision-making or separation from such objects or animals. The earliest studies of brain function in hoarding patients (Saxena et al. 2004) found that, compared to non-hoarding OCD patients, OCD patients with compulsive hoarding had significantly lower glucose metabolism in the dorsal anterior and posterior cingulate gyrus. Contemporary studies continue to elucidate other brain regions associated with hoarding symptoms, (Slyne and Tollin 2014), but there have, as yet, been no analyses specific to animal hoarding. Recent work has demonstrated how the pro-social hormone oxytocin increases in both dogs and people with certain forms of contact, so it is possible that there may eventually be a neurophysiological explanation for animal hoarding (Beetz et al. 2012; Nagasawa et al. 2015).

Infectious Disease/ Parasites

There have been periodic media reports drawing a potential connection between hoarding behavior and infection with the protozoan parasite *Toxoplasma gondii* commonly associated with cats and cat feces (Gibson 2015). The specific association of *Toxoplasmosis* with animal hoarding is questionable. The definitive hosts of *T. gondii*, and the only animals capable of spreading the parasite to humans or other warm-blooded animals are felines. However, many hoarding cases involve non-feline or non-mammalian species (for example dogs, birds, reptiles). It has been difficult to demonstrate *T. gondii* in the brain of patients with mental disorders, particularly schizophrenia, perhaps because the effect of the parasite, if real, is likely to be early in life at the neurodevelopmental stage rather than at the age of actual illness onset (Fekadu et al. 2010). To date, there have been no specific studies of *T. gondii* seroprevalence levels in animal hoarders.

Societal Factors

In many parts of America, abandoned and stray animals remain a big problem in part due to irresponsible breeding of pets that produces millions of unwanted animals (Benniston 2015). Euthanasia practiced by open-admission shelters became a way to manage this overpopulation problem, since not all of these unwanted animals could be adopted or kept indefinitely in their cages. However, there has been growing pressure to adopt a 'no-kill' philosophy which has contributed to the growing number of 'rescue hoarder' cases that are investigated (Benniston 2015).

People in the community, knowing the hoarder's reputation for wanting any animals, may drop off unwanted pets at the hoarder's home, thereby feeding their ever-growing collection. In this way, the neighborhood 'cat lady' or 'dog lady serve as a convenient, impromptu shelter where there will be no guilt imparted by staff members for dropping off unwanted animals (Frommer and Arluke 1999) and no risk of euthanasia.

The many factors that can be associated with animal hoarding are not mutually exclusive. Genetic predisposition and/or neurological impairment may interact with disrupted childhood attachments, abuse, trauma or other triggers which, coupled with societal reinforcement and reliance on interactions with animals to create a positive self-image, creates conditions conducive to animal hoarding.

Responses to Animal Hoarding

Discovery, Investigation and Documentation

The complex nature of hoarding cases makes them difficult to investigate and to resolve. Jurisdiction for these cases in the USA cross many state and local agencies and departments, including mental health, police, humane law enforcement, zoning, sanitation, fish and wildlife, child welfare, adult protective services, animal control, public health, building safety and social services.

Cases typically come to the attention of authorities because of complaints from neighbours or visitors. The primary problems reported about hoarders are unsanitary conditions, 'strong,' 'obnoxious' odours or 'stench,' and occasionally nuisance problems such as 'barking loudly' or observations of stray animals around the property. In the case of rescue hoarders, complaints often come from volunteers or local animal control organizations who may have been asked to transfer animals to the 'rescue' and become aware of deteriorating conditions (Lockwood and Eyre 2011).

Hoarders rarely voluntarily allow animal control or law enforcement officials to enter their premises and often take precautions to conceal conditions by covering windows with newspapers or foil. It is important to document such actions since it speaks to the hoarder's awareness that conditions were unacceptable and needed to be hidden. Several agencies have adopted checklists that allow a variety professionals to flag hoarding problems involving animals and the environment (for example, NYC Mayor's Alliance 2014).

The response to a hoarding situation should involve representatives from the various agencies mentioned above. In addition, veterinarians can play key roles in the investigation, documentation and prosecution of an animal hoarding case. A veterinarian may be called upon to provide triage decisions at the scene of a hoarding situation, deciding which animals require immediate treatment or euthanasia for humane reasons and which may be treated later. The veterinarian will play a central role in working with humane and law enforcement agents to document and testify to the condition of the animals, the nature and extent of illness and/or injury of each (Sinclair et al. 2006).

Seizing animals in hoarding cases is a complicated, expensive, labour intensive and emotionally upsetting process and potentially dangerous. The cost of managing these cases, including the seizure itself, can run into the tens or hundreds of thousands of dollars. If the animals are not immediately surrendered to a responding agency, there are a variety of proceedings that might take place to minimize the amount of time they need to be held prior to disposition including custody hearings or other civil procedures, guardianship or appointment of a 'special master' and posting of surety bonds. The common defense argument that animals should be held 'as evidence' until the case is resolved should be vigorously challenged. Any legal case will focus on the condition of the animals at the time of seizure. With proper care, both the physical and behavioral condition of animals rescued from a hoarding environment will change dramatically within days of removal. It should be argued that the detailed medical and behavioral evidence recorded regarding the initial conditions of the animals at the time of rescue can be reviewed by defense experts and that the condition of animals held for more than several weeks is of limited evidentiary value.

Alternatives to Prosecution

One therapeutic model that could serve as an alternative to prosecution is *relapse prevention*, a cognitive-behavioral approach with the goal of identifying and preventing high-risk situations that has generally been applied to substance abuse, obsessive-compulsive behavior and sexual offending (Witkiewitz and Marlatt 2004). However, animal hoarding presents significant challenges to this approach. In an analysis of relapse episodes obtained from clients with a variety of addictive behavior problems, three high-risk situations were associated with most of the relapses reported (Marlatt and Gordon 1985). They were negative emotional states, interpersonal conflict and social pressure, as well as cognitive distortions such as denial and rationalization. All of these obstacles are commonly encountered in dealing with animal hoarders.

Another intervention model that can be an appropriate response to animal hoarding cases is *harm reduction*, a range of policies designed to reduce the harmful consequences associated with various human behaviors, both legal and illegal. This approach accepts the fact that it may not be possible to stop the 'risky' behavior and instead attempts to prevent harm through close monitoring and 'wraparound' support services. In the case of animal hoarding, this would include frequent interaction with the client, spay/neuter assistance, veterinary care, environmental clean-up and connection to various social services, a model already used by many humane agencies.

Many communities have recognized the importance of an interdisciplinary approach to these situations and have established hoarding task forces that also include animal welfare professionals. Cooperation of a broad spectrum of municipal agencies and social service organizations can optimize the resolution of hoarding cases. Desirable members of such a task force would include representatives from animal control, public health and mental health agencies, child welfare and adult protective services, zoning and fire prevention officials, and veterinarians (Patronek 2001). This can be a very important step to overcome potential conflicts of interest and concerns about confidentiality (Clancy 2014; Patronek et al. 2006; Steketee et al. 2011). Over 85 hoarding task forces have been established in communities large and small, urban and rural in the USA, Canada, Australia and Europe (Bratiotis and Woody 2014).

In New York City, there has been a concerted effort to provide a coordinated response to hoarding cases. The American Society for the Prevention of Cruelty to Animals (ASPCA) has instituted a Cruelty Intervention Advocacy program that combines the talents of social workers, veterinary professionals, animal behaviorists, law enforcement agents, and others to work with a wide array of human and animal service agencies to respond to cases at the earliest possible stage and monitor them on a regular basis. In addition to the ASPCA, agencies involved in this collective effort have included the New York City Health Department, Animal Control, Environmental Affairs, Agriculture Department, Humane Law Enforcement, Mental Health Services, Child Protection, Adult Protective Services, Housing Authority, Department of Homeless Services, Human Resources Administration, Community Affairs Bureau, and many other social service agencies. Between 2010 and 2013 the ASPCA, working with these partners, handled more than 100 hoarding cases. Of these, 67 % involved women while 24 % involved male owners and 9 % were couples. Cats comprised 76 % of the cases while 13 % involved dogs (Colangelo 2013). This approach has proven to be an effective tool to respond to many hoarding cases without invoking the criminal justice system. The program employs a holistic approach to working with animal hoarders, engaging clients to build trust and voluntarily agree to services and/or relinquishment as appropriate. It also furthers the recognition that animal hoarding is a human welfare, animal welfare and community problem—not just an animal control issue.

Legal Actions

The goals of legal intervention into animal hoarding cases are to remove animals and dependent humans from harmful environments and provide treatment, to take steps that will reduce the likelihood of a recurrence of the problem, and to hold those responsible accountable for their actions and, where possible, seek restitution.

A major advantage of prosecution is that the criminal justice system may provide the leverage necessary to broker a wide variety of solutions, including those that do not involve conviction. However, this approach does not allow intervention before a provable crime has occurred, and until such evidence becomes available, the hoarding behavior may continue unabated (Patronek and Ayers 2014). Unlike child protection, there are currently no mechanisms in place to intervene at the earliest indications that caregiving may be deteriorating. Constitutional protections against unreasonable search and seizure often prevent intervention until environmental conditions and animal suffering are extreme.

The frustrations and difficulty of taking serious legal action against animal hoarders has led some jurisdictions to pass laws specifically creating the 'crime' of animal hoarding, based primarily on the definition used by HARC. Currently Hawaii and Illinois are the only states with such specific anti-hoarding laws, although similar legislation has been introduced in other states. There has been little support for such legislation among mental health and animal welfare advocates who see such laws as unnecessary and even counterproductive, given existing animal cruelty laws. In addition, such laws are viewed as criminalizing a mental health diagnosis. In reviewing the issue, Schwalm (2009) notes that such statutes employ arcane, subjective language that would likely be found unconstitutionally vague.

Many of the problems associated with hoarding may not rise to the level of criminal animal cruelty offenses but may be actionable as violations of local ordinances including sanitation codes, limits on animal ownership, licensing and vaccination requirements and housing codes. However, addressing only these superficial violations cannot accomplish the objectives of intervention and do nothing about the underlying mental health issues that may have initiated the problem. By definition, animal hoarding cases involve animal neglect thus almost always will include potential violations of misdemeanor animal cruelty laws. More serious felony level charges, which can carry significant fines, probation, and potential incarceration, usually require the presence of intent to cause harm or to torture (Arkow and Lockwood 2013). Animal hoarders almost always assert that they did not mean to harm the animals. Such purported lack of intent can make it hard to seek felony-level penalties, even if many animals have suffered or died. However, the presence of dead animals can increase the likelihood that felony charges may be filed (Berry et al. 2005). In cases involving rescue hoarders posing as legitimate charities or exploitative hoarders seeking to defraud people into providing money that never goes to animal care, the prosecution may use the financial aspects of these cases to add additional charges such as failure to pay taxes, misuse of funds or fraud (Sylvester and Baranyk 2011a, 2011b).

The recent inclusion of Hoarding Disorder in the DSM-5 may lead to greater use of 'mental health' or 'problem solving' courts to address the animal hoarding rather than conventional animal cruelty criminal proceedings. Such courts maintain a specialized docket established for defendants with mental illness that substitutes a problem-solving approach for the traditional adversarial criminal court processing. Participants are identified through mental health screening and assessments and voluntarily participate in a judicially supervised treatment plan developed jointly by a team of court staff and mental health professionals. This approach may be useful for some animal hoarding cases (Muller-Harris 2010), however, a therapeutically-oriented intervention or negotiation may not work with certain types of hoarders who are exploitative, irrational or uncooperative.

Sentencing

Animal protection and mental health professionals should advise the courts on the desired components of sentencing in animal hoarding cases. Without such guidance, some judges are inclined to make naïve recommendations, such as requiring a convicted hoarder to do community service at an animal shelter. A more egregious lapse in judgement is to order any apparently healthy animals returned to the offender, presumably under the assumption that because those animals have not yet shown obvious signs of physical harm, they are not suffering or at risk.

The first objective is to ensure that animals are safe and receive any needed medical or behavioral treatment, which is usually accomplished by removing animals from the harmful conditions in which they have been found, if this has not already been accomplished by a voluntary surrender or other pre-conviction court orders. Often courts will also issue a 'no-contact' order prohibiting the convicted hoarder from owning, possessing or being in proximity to animals for the duration of probation. It may be desirable to allow the hoarder to keep a small number of neutered animals that are subject to periodic inspection by animal control authorities. In the case of rescue hoarders posing as a formal organization, the courts may require the dissolution of the organization in addition to the surrender of the animals. Since hoarding cases places a great financial burden on responding agencies, it is desirable for courts to order reasonable restitution for these costs. However, even when ordered, such restitution is rarely paid (Berry et al. 2005).

Several dozen states have legislated mandatory or discretionary psychological evaluation of persons convicted of animal maltreatment, including animal hoarding (Phillips and Lockwood 2013). In principle, this seems to be a worthwhile step. In reality, although courts may order evaluation or counseling for animal hoarders, the goals of such an evaluation are not specified, and no validated therapy for animal-hoarding disorder is currently available. Furthermore, it is unknown what qualifications and skills the therapist or evaluator would need to have, what the expected outcomes of the process would be (for example, is a 'cure' even possible), how long the process might take, what should be done with the animal victims while a convicted offender would be in treatment, and whether convicted offenders could ever be trusted to provide a safe environment for animals in the future.

In addition, most individuals who have been adjudicated for animal hoarding are reluctant to participate in therapy and resistant to change, making this strategy difficult to enforce even if treatment were available (Frost et al. 2000; Nathanson 2009). This seems to be a case where laws are vague and far ahead of clinical mental health practice. Even if hoarders visit therapists, their cognitive distortions can complicate treatment and frustrate practitioners. A common characteristic of animal hoarders is their use of denial or other methods of justification for their situation and the refusal to acknowledge that a problem exists (Nathanson 2009; Patronek 1999). Vaca-Guzman and Arluke (2005) identified three types of justifications, including total denial, being a Good Samaritan, and being 'victims of the system.' In particular, saving animals from death is a recurrent theme used by hoarders to justify their behavior. Most cannot accept the concept of 'a life not worth living' even if that involves prolonged pain and suffering. This is a major philosophical divide between animal hoarders and conventional animal welfare and sheltering professionals who view euthanasia as an acceptable tool for the alleviation of suffering. This divide often leads animal hoarders to claim that officials and/or animal groups intervening in cases had personal vendettas against them, and that the whole 'system' was against them.

Since many studies of animal hoarding report extremely high rates of recidivism (McKay 2008), it is essential that an emphasis be placed on taking steps to limit the frequency with which people reacquire multiple animals after having animals legally removed (Steketee et al. 2011). Although progress continues to be made, object hoarding is still considered a very treatment-resistant condition requiring an experienced therapist. So any notion of a quick-fix for animal hoarding should be viewed with some skepticism.

As a widespread, severe and complex form of animal cruelty, there are no easy solutions to animal hoarding. Despite continued barriers to effective community coalitions to address hoarding there are many steps that can be taken to overcome these obstacles (Patronek et al. 2006). In addition, society's view of animal hoarding continues to evolve; it is promising that it is increasingly seen as a serious human and animal welfare issue that requires entire communities to respond effectively. Hopefully, the future will bring more information on the genetic, environmental, demographic, neurocognitive and neural substrates of animal hoarding leading to better informed interventions for the benefit of all involved—both human and non-human (Patronek and Ayers 2014).

References

American Psychiatric Association (2013). *Diagnostic and statistical manual of mental disorders*. Arlington, VA: American Psychiatric Publishing.

Anonymous (1875, February 12). A home for indigent cats. Eight mousers quartered in an east side tenement. *New York Sun*.

Arkow, P., & Lockwood, R. (2013). Defining animal cruelty. In C. L. Reyes & M. Brewster (Eds.), *Animal cruelty: a multidisciplinary approach to understanding* (pp. 3–24). Durham, NC: Carolina Academic Press.

Arluke, A., Frost, R., Steketee, G., Patronek, G., Luke, C., Messner, E., et al. (2002). Press reports of animal hoarding. *Society and Animals, 10*, 113–135.

Avery, L. (2005). From helping to hoarding to hurting: when the acts of 'good Samaritans' become felony animal cruelty. *Valparaiso University Law Review, 39*(4), 815–858.

Beetz A., Uvnäs-Moberg, K., Julius, H., & Kotrschal, K. (2012, July 9). Psychosocial and psychophysiological effects of human-animal interactions: the possible role of oxytocin. Front Psychology, *3*, 234. doi:10.3389/fpsyg.2012.00234. eCollection 2012.

Benniston, G. (2015, July 29). The state of sheltering. Forth Worth Magazine.

Bernstein, M., & Wolf, B. M. (2005). Time to feed the evidence: what to do with seized animals. *Environmental Law Reporter, 35*(10), 10679.

Berry, C., Patronek, G. J., & Lockwood, R. (2005). Animal hoarding: a study of 56 case outcomes. *Animal Law, 11*, 167–194.

Boat, B. W., & Knight, J. C. (2001). Experiences and needs of adult protective services case managers when assisting clients who have companion animals. *Journal of Elder Abuse and Neglect, 12*(3–4), 145–155.

Bloch, M. H., Bartley, C. A., Zipperer, L., Jakubovski, E., Landeros-Weisenberger, A., Pittenger, C., et al. (2014). Meta-analysis: hoarding symptoms associated with poor treatment outcome in obsessive–compulsive disorder. *Molecular Psychiatry*, *19*(9), 1025–1030.

Bratiotis, C., & Woody, S. (2014). Community interventions. In R. O. Frost & G. Steketee (Eds.), *The Oxford handbook of hoarding and acquiring* (p. 316). New York: Oxford University Press.

Brown, S. E. (2011). Theoretical concepts from self psychology applied to animal hoarding. *Society and Animals*, *19*, 175–193.

Calvo, P., Duarte, C., Bowen, J., Bulbena, A., & Fatjó, J. (2014). Characteristics of 24 cases of animal hoarding in Spain. *Animal Welfare*, *23*(2), 199–208.

Cassidy, J., & Mohr, J. (2001). Unsolvable fear, trauma, psychopathology: theory, research, and clinical considerations related to disorganized attachment across the lifespan. *Clinical Psychology: Science and Practice*, *8*, 275–298.

Clancy, E. (2014). Animals as community stakeholders: inclusion of pets in social policy and practice (occasional essay). *Families in Society: The Journal of Contemporary Social Services*, *95*(4), 285–289.

Colangelo, L. (2013, April 14). Intervention program helps pull animal hoarders from a downward spiral. *New York Daily News*.

Fekadu, A., Shibre, T., & Cleare, A. J. (2010). Toxoplasmosis as a cause for behaviour disorders–overview of evidence and mechanisms. *Folia Parasitol (Praha)*, *57*(2), 105–113.

Fleury, A. M. (2007). An overview of animal hoarding. *Praxis*, *7*, 58.

Frommer, S. S., & Arluke, A. (1999). Loving them to death: blame-displacing strategies of animal shelter workers and surrenderers. *Society and Animals*, *7*(1), 1–16.

Frost, R. O. (1998). Hoarding, compulsive buying and reasons for saving. *Behavioral Research and Therapy*, *36*, 657–664.

Frost, R. O., Patronek, G., Arluke, A., & Steketee, G. (2015). The hoarding of animals: an update. *Psychiatric Times*. http://www.psychiatrictimes.com/addiction/hoarding-animals-update. Accessed 5 May 2015.

Frost, R. O., Steketee, G., & Williams, L. (2000). Hoarding: a community health problem. *Health Soc Care Community*, *8*, 229–234.

Frost, R. O., & Steketee, G. (Eds.). (2014). *The Oxford handbook of hoarding and acquiring*. New York: Oxford University Press.

Gibson, M. (2015). *How Your Cat Could Make You Mentally Ill*. Retrieved June 1, 2015 from http://time.com/3912258/cats-parasite-mental-illness/

HARC (2002). Health implications of animal hoarding. *Health and Social Work*, *27*, 125–131.

Hirschtritt, M. E., & Mathews, C. A. (2014). Genetics and family models of hoarding disorder. In R. O. Frost & G. Steketee (Eds.), *The Oxford handbook of hoarding and acquiring* (p. 159). New York: Oxford University Press.

Joffe, M., O'Shannessy, D., Dhand, N., Westman, M., & Fawcett, A. (2014). Characteristics of persons convicted for offences relating to animal hoarding in New South Wales. *Australian Veterinary Journal*, *92*, 369–375.

Lockwood, R. (1994). The psychology of animal collectors. *American Animal Hospital Association Trends Magazine, 9*, 18–21.

Lockwood, R. (2002). Making the connection between animal cruelty and abuse and neglect of vulnerable adults. *The Latham Letter*, 23(1),10–11.

Lockwood, R. (2008). Counting cruelty: challenges and opportunities in assessing animal abuse and neglect in America. In Frank R. Ascione (Ed.), *International handbook of theory and research on animal abuse and cruelty* (pp. 87–110). W. Lafayette, IN: Purdue University Press.

Lockwood, R. (2011, November 3). Recognizing and responding to 'Rescue Hoarders'. *South Carolina Animal Care and Control Association.* Myrtle Beach, South Carolina.

Lockwood, R. & Cassidy, B. (1988). Killing with kindness? *The Humane Society News*, Summer, 1–5.

Lockwood, R., & Eyre, J. (2011, May 5). Recognizing and responding to 'rescue hoarders'. Paper presented at Animal Care Expo, Orlando, FL.

Lyons-Ruth, K., Dutra, L., Schuder, M., & Bianchi, I. (2006). From infant attachment disorganization to adult dissociation: relational adaptations or traumatic experiences? *Psychiatric Clinics of North America*, *29*, 63–86.

Marijana, V., & Dimitrijevic, I. (2007). Body condition and physical care scales in three cases of dog hoarding from Belgrade. *Acta Veterinaria (Beograd)*, *57*(5–6), 553–561.

Marlatt, G. A., & Gordon, J. R. (Eds.). (1985). *Relapse prevention: maintenance strategies in the treatment of addictive behaviors.* New York: Guilford Press.

Mataix-Cols, D., Frost, R. O., Pertusa, A., Clark, L. A., Saxena, S., Leckman, J. F., et al. (2010). Hoarding disorder: a new diagnosis for DSM-V? *Depression and Anxiety*, *27*(6), 556–572.

McKay, B. (2008). Animal hoarding: beyond the crazy cat lady. *Journal of Agricultural and Food Information*, *9*(4), 374–381.

McMillan, F. D. (2013). Long term erfects of hoarding and puppy mills on dogs. Paper presented at *International Veterinary Forensic Sciences Association*, Orlando, FL, 13 May 2013.

McMillan, F. D., Duffy, D. L., & Serpell, J. A. (2011). Mental health of dogs formerly used as 'breeding stock' in commercial breeding establishments. *Applied Animal Behaviour science*, *135*(1), 86–94.

Meagher, E., Frost, R., & Riskind, J. (1999, November). Compulsive lottery, scratch ticket, and keno gambling: Its relation to OCD, hoarding, impulsivity, and the urge to buy. Paper presented at the annual meeting of the Association for the Advancement of Behavior Therapy, Toronto.

Merrill, L. (2012, February 19). Firefighters train for hoarder homes. *Arizona Republic.*

Muller-Harris, D. L. (2010). Animal violence court: a therapeutic jurisprudence-based problem-solving court for the adjudication of animal cruelty cases involving juvenile offenders and animal hoarders. *Animal Law*, *17*, 313.

Nagasawa, M., Mitsui, S., En, S., Ohtani, N., Ohta, M., Sakuma, Y., et al. (2015, April 17). Social evolution. Oxytocin-gaze positive loop and the coevolution of human-dog bonds. Science, *348*(6232), 333–336. doi:10.1126/science.1261022. Epub 16 April 2015.

Nathanson, J. N. (2009). Animal hoarding: slipping into the darkness of comorbid animal and self-neglect. *Journal of Elder Abuse and Neglect, 21*(4), 307–324.

Nathanson, J., & Patronek, G. (2011). Animal hoarding: how the semblance of a benevolent mission becomes actualized as egoism and cruelty. In B. Oakley, A. Knafo, G. Madhavan, & D. Wilson (Eds.), *Pathological Altruism*, (pp.107–115). New York: Oxford University Press.

New York City Mayor's Alliance (2014). *Tips and tools: helping pets and people in crisis.* http://www.helpingpetsandpeoplenyc.org/animal-hoarding/. Accessed 3 June 2014.

Nordsletten, A. E., & Mataix-Cols, D. (2012). Hoarding versus collecting: where does pathology diverge from play? *Clinical Psychology Review, 32*(3), 165–176.

Ockenden, E. M., De Groef, B., & Marston, L. (2014). Animal hoarding in Victoria, Australia: an exploratory study. *Anthrozoos, 27*(1), 33–47.

Patronek, G. (1999). Hoarding of animals: an under-recognized public health problem in a difficult to study population. *Public Health Reports, 114*, 82–87.

Patronek, G. (2001). The problem of animal hoarding. *Municipal Lawyer, 42*, 6–19.

Patronek, G. (2006). Animal hoarding: its roots and recognition. *Veterinary Medicine, 101*(8), 520.

Patronek, G. J., & Ayers, C. R. (2014). Animal hoarding. In R. O. Frost & G. Steketee (Eds.), *The Oxford handbook of hoarding and acquiring.* New York: Oxford University Press.

Patronek, G., Loar, L., & Nathanson, J. (Eds.). (2006). *Animal hoarding: structuring interdisciplinary responses to help people, animals and communities at risk.* Hoarding of Animals Research Consortium. http://www.tufts.edu/vet/hoarding/pubs/AngellReport.pdf.

Patronek, G. J., & Nathanson, J. N. (2009). A theoretical perspective to inform assessment and treatment strategies for animal hoarders. *Clinical Psychology Review, 29*(3), 274–281.

Pertusa, A., Frost, R. O., Fullana, M. A., Samuels, J., Steketee, G., Tolin, D., … & Mataix-Cols, D. (2010). Refining the diagnostic boundaries of compulsive hoarding: a critical review. *Clinical Psychology Review, 30*(4), 371–386.

Phillips, A., & Lockwood, R. (2013). *Investigating and prosecuting animal abuse: a guidebook on safer communities, safer families and being an effective voice for animal victims.* Alexandria, VA: National District Attorneys Association.

Raines, A. M., Unruh, A. S., Zvolensky, M. J., & Schmidt, N. B. (2014). An initial investigation of the relationships between hoarding and smoking. *Psychiatry Research, 215*(3), 668–674.

Rasmussen, J. L., Steketee, G., Frost, R. O., Tolin, D. F., & Brown, T. A. (2014). Assessing squalor in hoarding: the home environment index. *Community Mental Health Journal, 50*(5), 591–596.

Saxena, S., Brody, A. L., Maidment, K. M., Smith, E. C., Zohrabi, N., Katz, E., et al. (2004). Cerebral glucose metabolism in obsessive compulsive hoarding. *American Journal of Psychiatry, 161*, 1038–1048.

Schwalm, J. (2009). Animal cruelty by another name: the redundancy of animal hoarding laws. *The Journal of Animal and Environmental Law, 1*(1), 32–60.

Sinclair, L., Merck, M., & R. Lockwood. (2006). *Forensic investigation of animal cruelty: a guide for veterinary and law enforcement professionals*. Washington, DC: Humane Society Press.

Slyne, K., & Tolin, D. F. (2014). The neurobiology of hoarding disorder. In R. O. Frost & G. Steketee (Eds.), *The Oxford handbook of hoarding and acquiring* (p. 177). New York: Oxford University Press.

Steketee, G., & Frost, R. (2010). *Stuff: compulsive hoarding and the meaning of things*. Boston: Houghton Mifflin Harcourt.

Steketee, G., – Frost, R. O. (2014). Phenomenology of hoarding. In R. O. Frost & G. Steketee (Eds.), *Handbook of hoarding and acquiring* (pp.19–32). New York: Oxford University Press.

Steketee, G., Gibson, A., Frost, R. O., Alabiso, J., Arluke, A., & Patronek, G. (2011). Characteristics and antecedents of people who hoard animals: an exploratory comparative interview study. *Review of General Psychology, 15*(2), 114.

Sylvester, S., & Baranyk, C. (2011a). When animal hoarding is warehousing for profit/part 1. *Tales of Justice, 1*(2), 1–3.

Sylvester, S., & Baranyk, C. (2011b). When animal hoarding is warehousing for profit/part 2. *Tales of Justice, 1*(3), 1–4.

Tolin, D. F. (2011). Understanding and treating hoarding: a biopsychosocial perspective. *Journal of Clinical Psychology, 67*(5), 517–526.

Tolin, D. F., Villavicencio, A., Umbach, A., & Kurtz, M. M. (2011). Neuropsychological functioning in hoarding disorder. *Psychiatry research, 189* (3), 413–418.

Vaca-Guzman, M., & Arluke, A. (2005). Normalizing passive cruelty: the excuses and justifications of animal hoarders. *Anthrozoos, 18*, 338–357.

Witkiewitz, K., & Marlatt, G. A. (2004). Relapse prevention for alcohol and drug problems. *American Psychologist, 59*(4), 224–235.

Worth, C., & Beck, A. (1981). Multiple ownership of animals in New York City. *Transactions and Studies of the College of Physicians of Philadelphia, 3*, 280–300

Arnold Arluke, Ph.D. is Professor of Sociology and Anthropology at Northeastern University, Vice President and Director of Research at Forensic Veterinary Investigations and a Visiting Scholar at the International Fund for Animal Welfare. His research examines conflicts and contradictions in human-animal relationships. He has published over 100 articles and 12 books, including *Regarding Animals, Brute Force, Just a Dog, The Sacrifice, Between the Species, The Photographed Cat*, and *Beauty and the Beast.* His research has received awards from the American Sociological Association, the Society for the Study of Symbolic Interaction, the International Association for Human-Animal Interaction Organizations, and the Massachusetts Society for the Prevention of Cruelty to Animals.

Dr Gary Patronek is a veterinarian and epidemiologist. He currently works as an independent consultant and is also Adjunct Professor at the Cummings School of Veterinary Medicine at Tufts. He founded the Hoarding of Animals Research Consortium (HARC), a multidisciplinary group of investigators who conducted much of the initial research concerning animal hoarding. The work of HARC was instrumental in the mention of animal hoarding in the new hoarding disorder included in DSM-5 in 2013. He has also been a shelter director, Vice President for Animal Welfare at the Animal Rescue League of Boston, and was formerly Director of the Tufts Center for Animals and Public Policy. Dr Patronek has published over 50 peer-reviewed papers and textbook chapters, many of which deal with animal welfare and shelter issues. He was one of the authors and editors of the *Guidelines for Standards of Care in Animal Shelters* put forth under the auspices of the Association of Shelter Veterinarians, and is one of three co-editors for the new book *Animal Maltreatment: Forensic Mental Health Issues and Evaluations* published by Oxford University Press in October 2015.

Randall Lockwood has degrees in psychology and biology from Wesleyan University in Connecticut and a doctorate in psychology from Washington University in St. Louis. In 2005 he joined the staff of the American Society for the Prevention of Cruelty to Animals where he is currently Senior Vice President for Forensic Sciences and Anti-Cruelty Projects. For over 30 years he has worked with law-enforcement agencies serving as an expert on the interactions between people and animals. He has testified in dozens of trials involving cruelty to animals or the treatment of animals in the context of other crimes, including dogfighting, child abuse, domestic violence and homicide. In 2008 he received a Public Service Award from the United State's Attorneys Office for his assistance in the Michael Vick dogfighting case. In 2014 he received an award from the American Academy of Forensic Sciences for outstanding contribution to forensic science.

He is co-author of Cruelty to Animals and Interpersonal Violence (1998), Forensic Investigation of Animal Cruelty: A Guide for Veterinary and Law Enforcement Professionals," (2006) and Animal Cruelty and Freedom of Speech: When Worlds Collide (2014). He is author of Prosecuting Animal Cruelty Cases: Opportunities for Early Response to Crime and Interpersonal Violence (2006) and Dogfighting Toolkit for Law Enforcement (2011).

Allison Cardona joined the ASPCA in 2003 and is currently the senior director of the organisation's Cruelty Intervention Advocacy (CIA) programme. The CIA programme, which launched in April 2010, aims to prevent animal cruelty in

New York City before it happens by addressing the root causes of animal suffering and providing long-term, sustainable change. To date, through this initiative, thousands of animals have been assisted that would likely have otherwise been at risk of neglect or ended up in a shelter. In 2014, the CIA programme expanded to also offer services on the West Coast, with a 'safety net' programme in Los Angeles that works to keep pets in their homes and out of shelters by providing services to low-income pet owners in need of resources.

Cardona was named Senior Director of the CIA programme in December 2012. In this role, Cardona oversees all facets of the CIA operation, focusing on continuing to build capacity to help many more animals in jeopardy of becoming cruelty victims through outreach, education and provision of vital services such as emergency veterinary care, spay/neuter and removal of and rehoming of hoarded animals. Cardona also oversees the ASPCA and Urban Resource Institute partnership in support of URIPALS, NYC's first-ever programme to house domestic violence victims with their pets.

Cardona is a member of the New York Women's Foundation Grants Advisory Committee and a volunteer mentor with Big Brothers Big Sisters of NYC. She received her Bachelor's degree of Science in Public Affairs from Empire State College and is currently enrolled in the National Urban Fellows Executive Leadership and Coaching Programme. She lives in Brooklyn, NY.

Status Dogs

Jennifer Maher, Harriet Pierpoint and Claire Lawson

Introduction

Historically 'status' dogs have taken many forms: as fashion items (toy or 'bag' dogs), national icons (English bulldog) and status symbols (such as the American pit bull terrier [pit bull] or Staffordshire bull terrier [sbt]). In previous decades, reference to 'status', 'accessory' or 'fashion' dogs implied association between some (usually) small dog breeds and rich and famous persons (that is, the Queen's corgi, Paris Hilton's chihuahua). These breeds then act as conduits for transferring the status and image of these iconic owners to other dog owners (Hirschman 2002).[1] The dog becomes inextricably linked to the owner's identity. This relationship commonly requires the dog to look and behave in a certain way, which often conflicts with their

[1] As is commonly promoted in the purchase of other status items such as cars, clothes and food.

J. Maher (✉) · H. Pierpoint
Centre for Criminology, University of South Wales, Pontypridd, United Kingdom
e-mail: jenny.maher@southwales.ac.uk; harriet.pierpoint@southwales.ac.uk

C. Lawson
Royal Society for the Prevention of Cruelty to Animals & Cardiff University, Cardiff, United Kingdom
e-mail: LawsonCE@cardiff.ac.uk

J. Maher et al. (eds.), *The Palgrave International Handbook of Animal Abuse Studies*, DOI 10.1057/978-1-137-43183-7_7

natural characteristics and behaviours. These dogs are harmed by an increase in breeding deformities, inherited disorders and behavioural abnormalities, being forced to live an unnatural existence, and the needless destruction of countless lives (due to over-breeding and/or a decline in popularity). Central to the harms experienced by these dogs is the fact that they are replaceable. Their value is linked to external, often changing factors.

Recent use in the UK of the term 'status dogs' has specifically referred to a trend amongst young people to own types of bull, illegal or other perceived to be aggressive breeds of dog. These dogs are used to confer an image of toughness, an air of aggression, and their use as an extension of UK youth gang violence (for example as weapons and in turf wars) has been documented (Harding 2012; Hughes et al. 2011). However, by treating these dogs as a commodity, status symbol, bodyguard or weapon, their owners subject them to behaviour frequently resulting in the torture and death of the dog and occasionally the injury and even death of a person. Additionally, the contributing factors to dog attacks—according to the experts—namely the history and temperament of the dog and the circumstances of how it is kept, including the welfare standards and type of training it is subjected to, appear irrelevant in media reports. Conversely, aggression is deemed to be entirely a derivative of breed—a conclusion that is thoroughly at odds with the findings of the scientific community (Newman 2012[2]). A US study (Duffy et al. 2008) of 6,000 dogs and their owners found that the most aggressive breed—that is, the dog most likely to bite strangers and their owners—was the Dachshund (the pit bull was eight on this list). In light of this it is encouraging to see in more recent times some evidence that dog owners are more aware that any dog is potentially dangerous (Oxley and Cheng 2014). Given the high levels of irresponsible dog ownership in the UK, as evidenced in Royal Society for the Prevention of Cruelty to Animals [RSPCA] and police statistics surrounding cruelty and dangerous dogs (see below), in addition to the high numbers of stray dogs (see below) and dog fouling (Keep Britain Tidy n/d), the connection between the way in which dogs are treated and the potential for this—albeit very rarely—to result in dog aggression, may not be widely understood. However, because of the implied risk to people, the official response further victimises these breeds and has unhelpfully placed other controversial labels onto them (for example, 'devil dogs').

[2] See also ongoing research which aims to evaluate this issue further: www.liverpool.ac.uk/dog-aggression/about-the-project/

The focus of this chapter is on the harms caused to dogs through their owner's behaviour and their being labelled as 'status' or 'dangerous' by their owners, the government and mainstream society. The chapter explores the nature of status dog ownership in the UK. The discussion is informed by four research projects conducted by the authors: (1) Pierpoint and Maher's (2010) analysis of convictions for animal abuse, (2) Maher and Pierpoint's (2011) small-scale qualitative research on the use of dogs by young people, involving interviews and observation of young people and youth justice and animal welfare professionals, (3) Hughes, Maher and Lawson's systematic literature review and qualitative fieldwork with young people variously involved with the status dogs problem (Hughes et al. 2011), and (4) Lawson's (forthcoming) 25 semi-structured expert interviews on anti-social and criminal use of dogs. We consider the nature of abuse, detailing harms ranging from the breeding, selling, training and habitation of the dog, to the subsequent abandonment and killing of these 'companions'. It must be noted that while the authors recognise there are considerable harms to humans, as a result of antisocial and aggressive dog behaviour in terms of intimidation and physical injury, and the links between status dog ownership and gang/criminal activity, the remit of this book is on the animal abuse and consequently these issues are not addressed here (see further Hughes et al. 2011 and Barnes et al. 2006).

Next, the prevalence of the status dog phenomenon in the UK and the problems with measurement are discussed. Thereafter, criminological theories—labelling theory, subcultural theory and differential association—are considered to explain the desire for, and harms experienced by, status dogs. Following this, societal reactions to the status dog phenomenon are considered, with particular focus on legislation and intervention approaches. We start with defining the key terms often used incorrectly and interchangeably.

Key Terms

Status Dogs

Although the term is rarely employed now by the RSPCA (Lawson, forthcoming), their briefing on status dogs referred to them as dogs

> used in an aggressive or intimidating way towards the public and other animals, often involving the fighting of these dogs...These dogs are traditionally, but not exclusively, associated with young people on inner city estates and those involved in criminal activity (RSPCA 2010, p. 1).

The terms 'bling', 'weapon', 'combat', 'devil' and 'antisocial' have been used interchangeably with 'status' by the media, politicians and animal welfare charities (O'Neill 2010; RSPCA 2010). Other dog breeds (for example, Rottweiler's, mastiffs and lurchers) have previously been described in this way (*The Sunday Times* 2006) although the term is now most commonly used to describe bull breeds and types (Gunter et al. 2016)—as described below—when owned by young people (Maher and Pierpoint 2011).[3]

Bull Breeds and Types

Bull breeds is the collective name for various breeds of dog of a particular type. Often, but not always, the word bull appears in the name, such as the English bulldog and the Staffordshire bull terrier. Bull types[4] are dogs either not recognised by the Kennel Club as a breed, such as the pit bull, or which include bull breeds in their parentage. While bull types are commonly associated with the status dog phenomenon, they are in fact owned by a cross-section of the public and there is no evidence to support the notion they are inherently problematic or dangerous. Although 'type' has a wider meaning than 'breed', for clarity and ease of use, the authors employ term 'breeds' to denote breeds, types' and their crosses.

Dangerous Dogs

The term 'dangerous dogs' is commonly used interchangeably with 'status dogs'. However, legally, the former refers to the definitions within the Dangerous Dogs Act [DDA] 1991, section one, which names four banned breeds—pit bull, Japanese tosa, dogo Argentino or fila Braziliero. Such dogs must be destroyed or placed on the list of exempted dogs, which requires the dog be, for example, neutered and kept on a lead and muzzled in public. There are a number of problems with the stereotyping of certain breeds as status dogs and breed-specific legislation, which are explored in the responses section (see also Associate Parlimentary Group for Animal Welfare 2008). Section 3 [DDA] describes the conditions whereby any breed of dog can be

[3] other breeds have more recently been identified as status enhancing for young people—the television show Game of Thrones is linked to a new trends in the ownership of huskies and wolf-like dogs for status and the subsequent abandonment of these breeds, which has tripled over the past four years (*Times*, 14 March 2015)

[4] For example, Pit Bull Terriers are not a recognised breed in the UK, they are a type (by definition a category broader than breed—see case law 'R v Knightsbridge Crown Court ex parte Dunne; Brock v DPP (1993)').

deemed dangerous. It is an offence for the person in charge of any dog (not just banned breeds) to allow it to be 'dangerously out of control' anywhere—in public or private space.[5]

Dog Fighting

Evans et al. (1998, p. 827) describe dog fighting as 'the act of baiting two dogs against one another for entertainment or gain' and is an offence under the Animal Welfare Act 2006. This is discussed in detail in the chapter on Animal Fighting, but, in brief, there are three types of dog fighting. The first is organised, which exists in the UK, but is more widespread in the USA (Ortiz 2010). The second form, more prevalent in the UK, is 'dog rolling' or 'chaining'. This is casual, impromptu fighting between status dogs with young owners in public places that may be filmed on mobile phones and is less likely to be motivated by significant financial gain (RSPCA 2009, 2010). The third type is cultural, which lies between the former two in terms of organisation. It has traditionally taken place in Pakistan and rural Punjab and Kashmir, but has been 'imported' to the UK by young Asians after they or their relatives have witnessed it in situ (Bassey 2009).

In sum, there is a lack of consensus around the definition of status dogs and associated terms, and consequently, a lack of clarity around the identification of these dogs. For example, are status dogs any bull breed accompanying a youth, any dog owned by a gang member, any dog out of control or used for dog fighting? What is clear is that the consequence of attributing the title of status dogs to select breeds has amplified the harm they experience, as discussed forthwith.

Irresponsible Ownership of Status Dogs: Nature of the Abuse

There are multiple harms caused by the irresponsible ownership of status dogs. This section will identify the nature of legal and illegal harms at each point of ownership: breeding, training, caring for, fighting, abandonment or killing of

[5] The DDA was amended again in 2014 and, under section 3, it is now a criminal offence for the person in charge of a dog to allow it to be 'dangerously out of control' anywhere—that is in a private place (e.g., a neighbour's house or garden) or in the owner's home, not just in a public space, as was the situation previously. This extension to the law was a response to dog attacks in the home and on private property. A dog is considered dangerously out of control if it injures someone or makes someone worried that it might injure them. The recent Anti-Social Behaviour, Crime and Policing Act 2014 also contained a number of clauses concerning dangerous dogs (see Bennett, 2016) including increased penalties.

dogs by their owners or by the state. It must be noted that a number of positive and negative behaviours and functions for the dog were identified by youths in Maher and Pierpoint (2011) and Hughes et al. (2011) studies. In other words, both intrinsic and extrinsic roles were evident (see Beverland et al. 2008). The intrinsic role—the dog as a loved companion—was commonly identified, though these dogs were still harmed by their owners. The extrinsic roles identified—the dog as protection, weapon, plaything, or commodity—resulted in harms such as irresponsible breeding and ownership/husbandry, injuries from dog fighting, abandonment and destruction resulting from difficulties in rehoming or if found to conform to an illegal 'breed'.

Irresponsible Breeding

At the height of the status dog trend, suitable puppies could fetch between £250 and £1000, making it a lucrative business for both the youth owners and the breeding sector as a whole. Harms related to breeding were identified within the (1) licensed and legitimate breeding sector, (2) the unlicensed (and as such) illegal sphere which is increasingly linked to other organised criminality (Winter and Gutteridge 2015), and (3) the non-licensable—meaning those falling outside the legal criteria requiring a licence. However, status dogs are predominately bred within the illegal and non-licensable sectors often referred to as backstreet and 'adhoc' breeders—where puppies, as a commodity, are only valued if they fetch a price. Breeding harms include:

- Puppies born and kept in unsanitary conditions associated with 'backstreet breeders'
- Puppies not provided with appropriate healthcare, for example, not vaccinated
- Puppies removed from their mother too early resulting in both health and behavioural issues
- Birthing problems as a result of a preference for larger cross-breeds—such as breeding small bitches with larger males which can result in suffering or death to the mother and puppies
- Breeding of 'banned' types and selling them as legitimate breeds or cross-breeds. When new owners or officials identify the breed, it often results in the dog being returned to the breeder, or the owner relinquishing or being required to relinquish them to officials.

- As a result of market saturation puppies were 'given away' (for example, sold for £50) to irresponsible owners or alternatively disposed of or abandoned
- Overbreeding dogs for puppies, where bitches are bred too many times in their lifetime and have more than one litter per year.
- Lack of adequate socialisation—which has been linked to behavioural problems in later life (including being relinquished by owners and/or destroyed as a result of aggression).
- Tail docking performed, despite being outlawed in most circumstances by the Animal Welfare Act 2006.[6]

Neglecting Dogs' Welfare Needs

The treatment of a status dog, as with any dog, will depend on its owner. In the case of a status dog owned by a (often young) person for its real or perceived aggression, its welfare needs can be ignored. Hughes et al. (2011) identified that while some owners exhibited knowledge and understanding of a dog's basic needs, these were reportedly not met by the majority of status dog owners. Youths' chaotic lifestyles impacted upon their dogs, for example, conflict with parents resulted in the dog being removed, providing attention and general care only when it was convenient to their owner. Problems involved:

- Lack of veterinary care (homemade or 'illegal' medicines used instead)
- Unsuitable living environment—that is, regular access to a bed, food, water and the outdoors
- Housed with or socialised with aggressive dogs (thus involved in fights)
- Limited positive socialisation with other dogs
- Lack of exercise
- Boredom and frustration (insufficient stimulation, left alone for long periods)
- Homelessness (dogs 'living rough' with their owners)
- Dogs permitted to illegally roam unsupervised (straying), resulting in injuries, malnourishment and/or death. This is different to abandonment (detailed below), whereby an owner 'relinquishes' their dog in an entirely irresponsible way (which is a specific welfare offence), thereby placing it in immediate danger.

---

[6] Domestic legislation has seen Scotland ban all tail docking, various exemptions are provided for in England, Northern Ireland and Wales. See http://www.bva-awf.org.uk/sites/bva-awf.org.uk/files/user/tail_docking_guidance.pdf

Punitive Training

Developments in understanding dog behaviour through positive training methods are not widely understood in society and this is perhaps more acute within status dog ownership. Without appropriate training, dog owners depend on unreliable advice from 'old-timers', their peers, or the internet. In Hughes et al. (2011) all youths indicated problems with basic behaviours such as toilet training and recall on command. Problems with training include:

- Training methods ordinarily involving physical and mental punishment (for example, hitting, kicking, starving, placing in solitary confinement for long periods) and the use of harsh paraphernalia (prong collars, electric collars)
- Training to enhance aggression and frustration (for example, encouraging aggression towards objects, people and other animals, by hanging dogs from branches by the mouth, pulling heavy objects, and putting irritants in their eyes)
- Physical punishment used in an attempt to stop the dog displaying natural behaviours (for example, not coming on command off-lead, chewing household items, urinating/defecating inside and fear of other dogs)
- Using the dog in an offence (for example, training to be aggressive in a robbery)

Dog Fighting

Hughes et al. (2011) found youths did not engage in traditional organised dog fighting, but rather 'rolling' dogs on chains, or releasing dogs in confinded public space as part of a bet, or fighting dogs as a way to resolve group conflict. Youths widely believed their dogs wanted and needed to fight and that it forms a natural part of their behaviour. When dog fighting resulted in injury veterinary treatment was unlikely to be provided.

Abandonment and Destruction

With youths' purchasing or acquiring dogs on a whim, it can place them in conflict with their parents or carers. Frequently youths identified themselves as the sole owner of their dog, although they were seldom able to provide the appropriate care for the animal. Hughes et al. (2011) noted the regularity with which dogs passed through the hands of young people, particularly as so little was known about the outcome for the dogs passed on. With status also comes competition with peers, sometimes resulting in a desire for a different (*better*) dog. These scenarios can lead to neglect of the animal and, ultimately, its abandonment. This issue is not just an owner's problem, but a policy, enforcement and social one. The status dog label is often a death sentence for dogs with irresponsible owners, as the dog is more likely to come to the attention of neighbours and local or housing authorities, thereby increasing the likeliness of abandonment. Abandoned dogs are also less likely to be returned to their owner and are likely to meet a natural or unnatural death:

- from malnourishment or injury when abandoned.
- resulting from the harmful effects of long-term kennelling (see also, Taylor and Mills 2007).
- due to limited space in kennels (council or charity) the dog is killed.
- due to injuring another person, assistance dog or other animals the dog is killed.
- due to being identified as a banned breed and must be destroyed
- when used as a bait dog and is killed.

Prevalence and Problems with Measurement

It is currently impossible to accurately identify the scale of the status dog problem. There is very little quantitative data available on the extent of status dog ownership and, even less so, on resulting harms. Compulsory microchipping and keeper registration has just been introduced in England, Scotland and Wales: from April 2016, it has been a legal requirement in Great Britain for all dogs to be microchipped with up-to-date contact details (for example see the Microchipping of Dogs (England) Regulations 2015). However, the accessibility and utility of the data that this will eventually yield is currently unquantifiable. Moreover, there is currently no centralised record keeping of dog breeding; this data is held by the (local) licensing authorities. The following information is available to provide some insight into the prevalence of the status dog problem:

1. The number of dangerous dogs seized and their outcomes (including their destruction) is recorded and published online monthly by the London Status Dog Unit (Metropolitan Police Service 2016). For example, in

March 2016, 74 dogs were seized in London boroughs of which 15 were destroyed. Other police forces in England and Wales release some of the same data sporadically, often as a result of a Freedom of Information (FOI) request (McCarthy 2016).

2. DEFRA maintains the Index of Exempted Dogs, which has been documented by the media as including 3,001 pit bulls, half a dozen dogo Argentinos and three Japanese tosas. A further 156 applications are being processed (Lyons 2015).
3. Local authorities record the number of stray dogs they collect and subsequently euthanise and this data should be available by FOI requests, but not centrally published. Each year the Dogs Trust surveys (via FOI) all local authorities throughout the UK to establish the state of the nation's stray dog problem. The last survey findings available are that in 2014–2015 there were 102,363 stray dogs collected by local authorities of which 5,142 were put to sleep. However, the breed is not identified.
4. Abandoned dog totals are recorded annually by the RSPCA using its own kennel data and data from local councils. They report on this annually, but again not detailing specific breeds. Other NGOs record and publish breeds specific data. For example, Battersea Dogs Home (Blunden 2014) reported that in 2014 bull breeds accounted for almost half of dogs entering their shelter. It is impossible to establish how many were 'status' dogs.
5. Dog fighting injuries have been recorded annually in the RSPCA London hospital, but not regularly published.
6. Court statistics and RSPCA data on convictions, calls, complaints and rescues on animal abuse more generally are available (see Pierpoint and Maher 2010), and the former identifies dogs as the most common animal victim, with neither recording offender characteristics.
7. Dog bite or strike statistics are available on human victims from the Royal Mail and NHS, however these do not record the dog breed or outcome for the dog involved (dogs are commonly reported in the media to have been destroyed). For example, according to the Royal Mail (2016), 2960 postmen and women were attacked between April 2014 and April 2015. The number of NHS consultations relating to dog bites/strikes are recorded annually, but such data, itself an incomplete picture, is only published periodically. A recent study in Wales identified an average of 114 child (aged under 18 years) admissions for dog bites/strikes per year, with an upwards trend in admissions over the past decade (from approximately 85 per year in 2003—Humphreys et al. 2014). Interestingly, they also indicate

that admissions are over three times higher amongst children from the most deprived areas as those from the least deprived. In this data the victim's details are recorded, but not the breed (but in any case this would be subjective as the victim may not have breed knowledge).

8. There is very limited data available on dog-on-dog or other animal attacks. The Guide Dogs for the Blind Association reported that between 2011 and 2013 there were an average of 10 attacks on guide dogs per month, with the largest proportion (35 %) of aggressors identified as bull breeds (Moxon 2013). The British Horse Society also collects reports of where horses have been attacked by dogs and an increase has been noted over a number of years (Mathieson 2015). They do not record the dog breed or outcome for the dog breeds involved.

In summation, there are many obstacles to accessing the already limited quantitative data on the status dog phenomenon and, even more so, harms to these dogs. One key barrier is the lack of consensus around the definition of status dogs and lack of clarity around their identification discussed above, and the general failure of the 'usual' sources to record breed and owner/keeper characteristics. We do know that there are substantial numbers of seizures of dangerous dogs and dogs on the index of exempt dogs. We also know that a considerable number of stray dogs and abandoned dogs are taken in by local authorities and shelters, and, in the case of the latter, these are most often bull breeds. This, along with the qualitative findings on the harms currently inflicted on dogs owing to their perceived status, calls for a consideration of explanations.

Explaining Harm towards Status Dogs

The motivations for animal companionship vary considerably; according to Beverland et al. (2008) these broadly fall into two categories—intrinsic and extrinsic ownership, the latter sometimes referred to as the 'dark side' of ownership. Ahuvia (2008) maintains these categories are consistent with the Bubarian (Buber 1923) 'Ich-Du' (I-Thou) and 'Ich-es' (I-It) perspectives on human interpersonal relationships. Intrinsic ownership fits with the 'Ich-Du' relationship where the owner sees their companion as intrinsically valuable: with an inherent value and with the relationship an end in itself. Extrinsic ownership fits with the Ich-es relationship, where the companion animal has no inherent value and is instead a means to an end—the owner 'constructs a mental idea of the other [animal] and relates only to that idea' (Ahuvia 2008,

p. 497). While both intrinsic and extrinsic dog ownership may result in harm, there are unique harms inherent in the nature of the extrinsic relationship between owner and companion animal (as detailed earlier). In terms of status dogs, extrinsic harms may be purposeful (intended) or consequential (a consequence of other behaviours) with both having similar, potentially fatal outcomes—for example, while dog fighting often results in a violent death (purposeful), abandonment and aggressive training commonly result in the death of the dog through euthanasia (consequential).

Evidence from many status dog owners interviewed by Hughes et al. (2011) suggested they were intrinsically motivated by a perceived companionship, loyalty, trust and special, emotional bond. However, they also identify their ownership, and that of the majority of peers, as being centrally motivated by enhanced status, profit, protection and entertainment (Hughes et al. 2011; see also Maher and Pierpoint 2011). In order words, while companionship is important for some, protection, money and peer acceptance are central motivations for status dog ownership. Consequently, status dogs are a form of social[7] and economic capital, whereby a youth's reputation is enhanced by, or even dependent upon, owning and/or breeding status dogs. Although enhanced social capital correlates with a decline in deviance (as offenders risk the loss of positive relationships—see Coleman 1988), this is dependent on the relationship being prosocial (Savage and Kanazawa 2002). In the same manner as prosocial relationships are believed to hinder criminality, the development of social capital amongst antisocial peers is likely to increase it. Sutherland et al. (1992) suggest 'differential association' with peers who hold antisocial or criminal values results in youths absorbing these values and behaviours. Through adopting these values youths can enhance their status, thereby avoiding ostracism and generating rewards (such as close relationships and social/financial opportunities). Furthermore, antisocial groups develop what subcultural theory terms 'oppositional culture', whereby their norms are consciously opposed to those of mainstream society—in this case, with regard to what is an acceptable breed, and the use and treatment of dogs.

In youth crime and gang literature, oppositional culture is commonly referred to as 'street culture' (Anderson 2000), at the centre of which is the need to enhance status and avoid disrespect. Status dogs, as the name suggests,

[7] Bourdieu (1980, 1986) and Coleman (1988) are commonly credited with the introduction of the concept of social capital—which generally describes the resources gained through social relationships with other humans. An absence or weakness in legitimate social relationships has been linked to increased criminality.

are a vehicle for enhancing status and can become an extension of their owner's status within social groups. In this culture a dog's worth to their owner is measured by their street value (or status). Failure to successfully engage in desirable 'street' behaviours (for example, protection, displays of toughness and aggression) diminishes this value. Consequently status dogs are required to live the same 'code of the street' (a set of unwritten rules that must be followed by those engaging in street culture—Anderson 2000) as their owners and are subjected to violent challenges by other youths and their dogs. According to Evans et al. (cited in Ortiz 2009), status dogs (through informal dog fighting—see also the chapter on Animal Fighting herein) reportedly help resolve US street/gang conflicts allowing youths to validate their masculinity while remaining on the periphery of actual interpersonal violence (Evans et al. cited in Ortiz)). Accordingly, it is not unusual to find that youths are profiling dogs (looking for specific 'status' characteristics, such as size, strength, aggression, toughness and resilience to pain) and then breeding for these characteristics (Hughes et al. 2011). Furthermore, harsh treatment by their owners is often required for the dogs to play their role. When they are no longer able to perform or their value plummets they are expendable and easily replaced. Using these theoretical perspectives, an explanation for the harm and abuse experienced by these dogs at the hands of their owners becomes discernible.

Status dogs are, arguably, one element of a 'unified phenomenon of antisocial and violent behaviour' (Arluke et al. 1999). This is consistent with the deviance generalisation hypothesis which maintains that animal abuse—especially amongst youths—is linked extensively to human interpersonal violence (Arluke et al. 1999; Ascione 1993, 2001) and criminality (Degenhardt 2005). Violence and harm towards animals may occur concurrently or separately to interpersonal violence and criminality. This is evidenced in Degenhardt's (2005) Chicago Police Department study, which identified animal abuse offenders were more likely to carry and use firearms and engage in the sale of drugs and with street gangs than non-animal abuse offenders. More specifically, in relation to status dogs, Barnes et al. (2006) found that US status dog owners had significantly more criminal convictions for serious crimes (that is crimes featuring aggression/violence or firearms, or involving drugs or children) than non-status dog owners. It is therefore reasonable to propose that status dog ownership, and its associated animal harms, occurs as part of a complex offending pattern exhibited by deviant youths.

To further the explanation of status dog ownership it is essential to ask the question—why do certain dog types provide status for youths? In line with the age-old proverb 'give a dog a bad name and hang him'[8] (Simpson and Speake 2000), the labelling of dogs as status giving, dangerous and aggressive thrusts these dogs into a vicious cycle of violence. The desire to own a status dog is linked to the label[9] placed upon them by society and youth peers as 'socially deviant' (or antisocial) companions, resulting in a harmful cycle where these dogs: (1) are labelled as aggressive, dangerous and linked to criminality (for example, dog fighting), (2) are established as valued amongst deviant youths; (3) become further associated with oppositional culture and are labelled as socially deviant and vilified by mainstream society, (4) have their status elevated amongst deviant youths and those pursuing anti-social or criminal activities (Ragatz et al. 2009 and Schenk et al. 2012), and (5) are abandoned, rejected and killed by mainstream society (including non-deviant bull-breed owners). Moreover, ownership of these dog breeds then becomes a tool with which society can label antisocial youth and other owners.[10]

Labelling theory, which focuses on the impact of social reactions to crime on the offender, has been extensively applied in criminological literature (Becker 1973). It can be understood as involving two main components, which help explain the harms experienced by status dogs. First, labels are imposed in part because of the status of those labelling differs to those being labelled. Second, as a result of the deviant label applied, secondary deviance occurs, as those labelled struggle to adjust to this new identity. Under certain conditions, this may lead the person labelled to greater involvement in crime and deviance. Notably, labelling is not always passive; as suggested earlier, status dog owners may actively seek out the deviant label rather than having it cast upon them by others (as indicated in Braginsky et al.'s theory of mental illness 1969).

While it is difficult to disentangle how and when the labelling process began, it is likely linked to the historical use of bull types in dog fighting, the spread of 'pit bull panic' from the USA in 2002 (Delise 2007) to the UK (and many other countries), the sensationalised media reporting of bull breed attacks on people, the association of these dogs with the working class and the aggressive measures used by the government to eradicate them. Status dogs are set apart from other breeds and labelled as inherently dangerous and aggressive. Society's insistence on labelling specific breeds gives rise to the most pervasive harm to status dogs—euthanasia. Many countries (for example, the UK, Ireland, USA) have introduced breed specific legislation [BSL]

[8] The proverb suggests that a person's plight is hopeless once his reputation has been blackened

[9] attaching a name or a signature to someone or some behaviour

[10] See for example the Policing and Crime Act 2009 prohibits 'status dogs' taken out in public by 'gang members'

effectively banning and requiring state sanctioned destruction of certain breeds. Control agencies (largely the media) have greatly influenced this approach, heightening public concern and anxiety (Cohen and Richardson 2002). Under the banner of 'protecting society' the routine killing of healthy dogs has become accepted and normalised, predicted and expected, guilt free and victimless animal abuse. While many stray and abandoned dogs are euthanised in the UK, there has been a significant increase in the number of status-type dogs who have met this fate at the hands of the state or NGOs. This response is consistent with other 'exaggerated' responses by control agencies identified by Cohen (1985) and Schur (1963) in reaction to homosexuality, abortion and drugs use, which they argue have generated more problems than were solved. These dogs are not inherently bad or dangerous, rather, their natural, positive, physical and personality traits are construed to be deviant: powerful becomes uncontrollable; confident becomes dominant; energetic becomes dangerous; resilient becomes unstoppable. The stark reality is that many status dogs are killed under the guise of being dangerous, when it is their conformity to a breed standard (such as the pit bull terrier) that seals their fate. The fact that existing dog behavioural literature and dog bite statistics evidence that dangerous dog behaviour is neither exclusive to, nor most prevalent in these breeds, is ignored or rebuked, even when organisations like the British Veterinary Association do not support BSL for these reasons. There is no scientific criterion yet identified to determine a dog is dangerous simply by virtue of its genetic or other physical parameters. As Humphreys et al. (2014, p. 5) confirm with regard to dog bites, 'Breed is not a good predictor of risk; other factors including the history of the dog, socialisation and context of the event are important'.

In terms of secondary deviance, evidently dogs do not themselves construct a deviant identity and turn to criminality; their owners do this via aggressive breeding and training. They shape a dog willing to protect and to fight other dogs and other perceived threats, often exposing them to negative welfare conditions, training and cruelty. To avoid rejection, these dogs learn to fulfil the deviant and dangerous label their owner assigns them.

Social Reactions to Status Dogs

As discussed, the reaction and responses to the status dog phenomenon has had serious consequences for dogs residing in the UK. Cultural developments, including society's disregard for 'dangerous' dogs can be seen within media reporting and imagery, while the path of legislation has been, and continues to be, a complex minefield, argued by many to be making the biggest contribution to the perpetuation of the problem.

Legislative Responses

A myriad of laws have been passed in the UK in relation to dogs, beginning with, in the context of this chapter, the Cruelty to Animals Act 1835 which prohibited dog fighting, and the 1839 Metropolitan Police Act, which lists an offence as 'to be at large any unmuzzled ferocious Dog, or set on or urge any Dog or other Animal to Attack, worry, or put in fear any Person, Horse, or other Animal'. Subsequent Acts have sought to improve standards of welfare and also the civil right of redress for a dog attack, but it was only in 1991 when dog fighting and dog attacks were deemed to be resolvable through BSL. Having initially declared such measures as 'manifest nonsense' (Home Office Minister Douglas Hogg MP, HC Deb 15 June 1989, c1187), the UK Government fast-tracked the DDA 1991 (Hallsworth 2011), an imported version of a US intervention which involved state-level measures designed to eradicate dogs of a certain breed, those deemed intrinsically dangerous, disregarding all other factors (possibly excusable within the context of what was known about dog behaviour 25 years ago, but now wholly without foundation). Whilst the international trend is now to repeal BSL (Bradley 2014, p. 13 and HSUS 2015), the UK does not look likely to follow—recent consultation exercises and developments which resulted in an expansion of offences to cover private property, amongst other things, omitted future scenarios where BSL could be repealed. Public debates thus far have been remiss in acknowledging the augmenting role BSL may have had on some breeds appearing more attractive to would-be owners looking for conferred status. The evidence on BSL strongly favours its abolition. Initial assessments of the DDA 1991 by Klaassen et al. (1996) determined there had been no significant reduction in dog bites, with 'dangerous' breeds contributing to only a small number. By retaining and even solidifying BSL on the UK statute books,[11] the government ignores the contribution this has made to the status dog problem, while also causing hysteria and myth-making

[11] The Dangerous Dogs Exemption Schemes [England and Wales] Order 2015 which came into force 3rd March 2015 closes the loophole for the transfer of ownership of a s1 prohibited dog. See https://www.gov.uk/government/publications/the-dangerous-dogs-exemption-schemes-order-2015

around links between status dog and the more serious criminal activities, including dog fighting and gangs.

By employing alternative methodologies Raghavan et al. (2013) appear to offer some evidence that BSL can reduce the incidence of dog bites, particularly bites on young people, however they do not examine in detail other contributing factors, such as a heightened public awareness—even a moral panic—which could itself cut opportunities for attacks. Success in terms of reducing dog bites may more likely be in the form of interventions through enforcement. Clarke and Fraser (2013) found that rather than BSL having any measurable effect, it was control notices or 'ticketing' issued by the local municipal authority that provided encouraging results. BSL penalises the dogs (covered in the legislation) and also responsible owners of those dogs for unproven *potentially* dangerous behaviour. If pre-emptive measures are to be utilised, better these centre around owners who have been identified as irresponsible or likely to misuse their dogs as this will also benefit 'the dogs themselves if it prevents them from being kept in situations contrary to good welfare' (Dobson 2011, p. 1). While the dog pays the ultimate price with its life, their owner is free to repeat these mistakes if they acquire a new dog, especially if the causes of the attack are not examined and addressed. Society rarely holds parents responsible for a dog attack on a child within the home, although there are increasing calls for alternative educational strategies which will require parental identification of the factors that led to an attack (Mannion et al. 2015). Furthermore, BSL could inadvertently be contributing to dog attacks and bites by falsely reassuring owners of non-prohibited breeds that their dog is not capable of being dangerous.

The prohibition of certain breeds has directly increased the allure of behaviourally similar, but marginally physically dissimilar breeds, in order to circumvent legislation. In addition to the direct consequences to the four banned breeds, there are clearly other substitute social harms arising from the DDA 1991 (Lawson forthcoming) such as the effect to these comparable breeds. Other measures have sought to address human behaviour, for example, the mandatory microchipping of dogs[12] provides a legal link between dog and owner. Other developments such as new dog breeding legislation[13]

[12] As previously stated, legislation has been passed by the UK Government for England (2015), the Welsh Government (2015) and Scottish Government (2016), all in force for April 2016. Northern Ireland has retained a dog licensing scheme which includes mandatory microchipping.

[13] Animal Welfare (Breeding of Dogs)(Wales) 2014 were passed by the Welsh Government and came into force in 2015. This is the first legislation in the UK which requires socialisation, enrichment and enhancement measures at licensed dog breeding establishments.

are designed in part to improve the standard of socialisation and, therefore, future (dog) behaviours. It is perhaps too early to determine the effect of new dog control measures within the Anti-social Behaviour, Crime and Policing Act (2014). Whilst its extension to cover private property and the increase in penalties for attacks on assistance dogs have been welcomed by the Communication Workers Union and Guide Dogs for the Blind Association respectively,[14] substantial trepidation exists elsewhere regarding the Act's preventative versus retributive nature and also the potential for innocent dogs and owners to get caught up in the new controls (RSPCA 2014). Rather than seeking to tackle the conditions in society that are leading to issues such as status dog ownership, these new measures apply to all dog owners. Dogs can be banned from certain public spaces or muzzled when not in the home; however, there is no requirement for the enforcer to seek behavioural or animal welfare knowledge or expertise when executing such controls. The danger may be that any early indications of aggressive behaviour, for which these restraints were intended to cure or control, could instead be exacerbated and this could lead to more, not less, dog attacks. The inclusion of attacks on private property, in the era of blame and litigation, is alarming for dog owners of all breeds as it essentially requires dogs to be able to tell the difference between 'safe' visitors and those who might cause harm. Any attack on the former could ultimately now result in the dog's destruction. Given the aforementioned lack of knowledge with regard to dog legislation and welfare amongst status dog owners, these new measures may well see their dogs disproportionately represented.

These new measures may also not be in force uniformly across the UK. In addition to the devolved nature of animal welfare and control[15] a number of police forces and local authorities have expressed concern regarding the requisite resources needed to execute associated duties, going as far as to say they will not enact the legislation within their jurisdiction. More local and regional disparity for dogs will arise from additional conditions levied by increasingly risk-averse housing providers keen to prohibit the keeping of dogs in their properties. Tenants may be unable to find alternative accommodation and rather than become

[14] http://www.cwu.org/media/campaigns/dangerous-dogs-bite-back/political-progress/ and https://www.guidedogs.org.uk/news/2014/may/new-law-protects-guide-dog-owners#.V1RiVvkrLIU

[15] The DDA, as amended, is in force in all three nations within GB, with the very similar Dangerous Dogs (Northern Ireland) Order 1991 in effect in the fourth nation of the UK. Additional dog welfare and control measures differ, however, as this policy area is devolved to each of those four nations. The respective administrations should be referred to for details of these.

homeless, may relinquish their dog to local shelters or animal welfare organisations or, worse, abandon them.

The cumulative effect of recent legislative developments may yet serve only to damage the human-dog bond and might exacerbate the status dog problem. For now we can rightly regard the dog as man's best friend: despite the large numbers of dogs kept and the high proportion of these living in cruel situations, dog attacks on people are rare.

Interventions

Calls for early intervention programmes emerged almost immediately after the rise of the status dog phenomenon in the UK. The Associate Parliamentary Group for Animal Welfare mini-report of 2008 reflected the growing recognition amongst animal welfare organisations of the value of education, training and awareness-raising as a means of preventing dog attacks and improving welfare standards. NGOs such as the RSPCA commissioned several research projects, including *Status dogs, young people and criminalisation: towards a preventative strategy (2011)*, to provide a platform on which to design such work. But whilst an understanding of the merits of intervention for ensuring prevention is widespread, the notion that the evaluation of such programmes is critical to success is perhaps not. Few of the main animal welfare organisations are able to provide a sound methodology or evidence-base for their programmes and whilst they claim to communicate and co-ordinate with each other to avoid duplication, in reality natural competition for supporters and donors has probably thwarted that. 'While there are an increasing number of projects providing information to young people, few are properly evaluated to determine their effectiveness' (RSPCA 2012).

Some models of intervention have been imported to the UK from the USA where they have since, however, been abandoned for being ineffective—as such the UK is perhaps trailing other nations. Clearly, it should be acknowledged that traditional methods of evaluation are impractical in these circumstances as it is impossible to know how many people would have gone on to be cruel to their dog or how many dogs would have gone on to attack. Also in defence of these programmes, it must be noted that there is no universally recognised method for evaluating intervention programmes in the animal welfare sphere. Any evaluation must feature practical knowledge of dog behaviour and training activities—and government patronage has thus far only amounted to an inadequately funded paper exercise. In practice therefore, intervention is most commonly dog control notices and out-of-court disposals, rather than programmes responding to the causes of the problem through education, training and awareness.

Conclusion

Data from the RSPCA and others demonstrates that all dogs can experience abuse at the hands of their owners. However, those dogs labelled as status dogs are victims of acute and specific abuses relating to their breeding, training and sometimes their roles (for example, fighting), all of which can lead to abandonment and even destruction. The data on the extent of the ownership of status dogs does not exist per se, but there are a number of indicators of the existence of this problem and the associated harms. In addition to qualitative academic research, there are substantial numbers of dangerous dog seizures, of dogs on the index of exempt dogs and of bull breeds taken in by local authorities and shelters. Status dogs are routinely abused by owners, breeders and government agencies. The form this abuse takes can be legal and illegal, with legislation and its enforcement being a key driver in the creation of the phenomenon as well as the dogs' suffering. Consequently, to explain the phenomenon it is crucial to explore both motivations for ownership and related abuses and the impact of societal reactions to these dogs.

Status dogs have become an extension of youths' reputation within hyper-masculine street subculture, wherein status is fragile and constantly challenged and in flux. Earning and maintaining status is a constant burden for youths, and requires harsh treatment of their dogs to ensure they perform their allocated role as a weapon, protection, a symbol of toughness, a badge of honour and social and economic capital. By labelling these dogs as dangerous, society unwittingly reinforces their value to these youths, endangering these animals by corralling them into a vicious cycle of violence. Contrary to the evidence available from the scientific community which contests the aims and efficacy of BSL, many status dogs are killed under the guise of being dangerous, when it is their conformity to a breed standard and association with interpersonal violence that determines their fate. Societal reactions (from the media, government and public), arguably, have generated more problems than they have solved.

Both formal and informal responses are documented as exacerbating the cultural norm to label and punish animals more than their irresponsible and abusive owners. In response, we the authors feel compelled to question the motivation behind these responses—are they a sincere response to legitimate animal welfare issues or simply more cost-effective means for government to address harms to people? Formal responses appear to demonstrate little concern for the dogs and the harms perpetrated by their owners and the state. And while informal intervention programmes with an emphasis on education, training and awareness-raising as a means of improving welfare standards and preventing irresponsible behaviour have emerged, there is, to their detriment, little in the way of evaluation of their impact and effectiveness, a sadly commonplace issue where animal-related interventions are concerned (see chapter on Interventions with animal abuse offenders herein).

> On the positive side, I find that dogs act as "tickets" for people to socialise and develop relationships, they facilitate the diversification of social networks, and they act as an avenue to political participation. On the negative side, dog ownership and dog breeds can become the basis for clique formation, stereotypes, and boundary formation, serving as grounds for exclusion. (Bueker 2013).

References

Ahuvia, A. C. (2008). Commentary on exploring the dark side of pet ownership: status and control-based pet consumption. A reinterpretation of the data. *Journal of Business Research, 61*(5), 497–499.

Anderson, E. (2000). *Code of the street: decency, violence, and the moral life of the inner city*. New York: W. W. Norton & Company.

Associate Parliamentary Group for Animal Welfare [APGAW] (2008). *Dangerous dogs—an APGAW* mini-report May *2008*. http://www.apgaw.org/Data/Sites/1/pdfs/apgaw-report-dangerous-dogs-may-2008.pdf. Accessed 25 May 2015.

Arluke, A., Levin, J., Luke, C., & Ascione F. (1999). The relationship of animal abuse to violence and other forms of deviant behaviour. *Journal of Interpersonal Violence, 9*, 963–975.

Ascione, F. R. (1993). Children who are cruel to animals: a review of research and implications for developmental psychopathology. *Anthrozoös, 6*(4), 226–247.

Ascione, F. R. (2001). Animal abuse and youth violence. In *Office of Juvenile Justice and Delinquency Prevention, Juvenile Justice Bulletin*. Washington, DC: US Department of Justice. https://www.ncjrs.gov/pdffiles1/ojjdp/188677.pdf. Accessed 13 October 2016.

Barnes, J. E., Boat, B. W., Putnam, F. W., Dates, H. F., & Mahlman, A. R. (2006). Ownership of high risk ('vicious') dogs as a marker for deviant behavior: implications for risk assessment. *Journal of Interpersonal Violence, 21*(12), 1616–1634.

Bassey, A. (2009). Inside the world of dog-fighting. *BBC News*. http://news.bbc.co.uk/1/hi/uk/8175047.stm. Accessed 30 May 2016.

Becker, H. S. (1973). *Outsiders*. New York: The Free Press.

Bennett, O. (2016). *Dangerous dogs*. Briefing Paper Number 4348. researchbriefings.files.parliament.uk/documents/SN04348/SN04348.pdf. Accessed 13 October 2016.

Beverland, M. B., Farrelly, F., & Lim, E. A. C. (2008). Exploring the dark side of pet ownership: Status and control-based pet consumption. *Journal of Business Research, 61*(5), 490–496.

Blunden, M. (2014). Battersea dogs home issues warning over 'danger breeds'. *The standard*. http://www.standard.co.uk/news/london/battersea-dogs-home-issues-warning-over-danger-breeds-9682575.html. Accessed 20 April 2016.

Bourdieu, P. (1980). *The logic of practice*. Stanford: Stanford University Press.

Bourdieu, P. (1986). The forms of capital. In Richardson, John G. (Ed.), *Handbook of theory and research for the sociology of education*. New York: Greenwood.

Bradley, J. (2014). *Dog bites, problems and solutions. policy paper: a contemporary perspective on incidence, risk factors and effective prevention*. Ann Arbor, MI: Animals and Society Institute.

Braginsky, B. M., Braginsky, D. D., & Ring, K. (1969). *Methods of madness: the mental hospital as a last resort*. New York: Holt.

Bueker, C. J. (2013). 'Leads' to expanded social networks, increased civic engagement and divisions within a community: the role of dogs. *Journal of Sociology & Social Welfare, XL*(4), 211–236.

Clarke, N. M., & Fraser, D. (2013). Animal control measures and their relationship to the reported incidence of dog bites in urban Canadian municipalities. *The Canadian Veterinary Journal, 54*(2), 145–149.

Cohen, J., & Richardson, J. (2002). Pit bull panic. *Journal of Popular Culture, 36*(2), 285–317.

Cohen, S. (1985). *Visions of social control*. Cambridge: Polity Press.

Coleman, J. S. (1988). Social capital in the creation of human capital. *The American Journal of Sociology Supplement: Organizations and Institutions: Sociological and Economic Approaches to the Analysis of Social Structure, 94*, 95–120.

Degenhardt, B. (2005). *Statistical summary of offenders charged with crimes against companion animals. July 2001–July 2004*. Animal Abuse Control Team. Chicago: Chicago Police Department.

Delise, K. (2007). *The pit bull placebo: the media, myths and politics of canine aggression*. New Jersey: Anubis Publishing.

Dobson, J. (2011, July 4). Do breed-specific traits exist and thus justify legislation? *Veterinary Times*.

Duffy, D., Hsu, Y., & Serpell, J. (2008). Breed differences in canine aggression. *Applied Animal Behaviour Science, 14*(3–4), 441–460.

Evans, R., Gauthier, D. K., & Forsyth, C. J. (1998). Dog fighting: expression and validation of masculinity. *Sex Roles, 39*(11/12), 825–838.

Gunter, L. M., Barber, R. T., & Wynne, C. D. L. (2016). What's in a name? Effect of breed perceptions & labeling on attractiveness, adoptions & length of stay for pit-bull-type dogs. *PLoS ONE. 11* (3). http://journals.plos.org/plosone/article?id=10.1371/journal.pone.0146857. Accessed 27 April 2016.

Hallsworth, S. (2011). And then they came for the dogs. *Crime, Law and Social Change, 55*(5), 391–403.

Harding, S. (2012). *Unleashed: the phenomena of status dogs and weapon dogs*. Bristol, UK: Policy Press.

Hirschman, E.C. (2002). Dogs as metaphors: meaning transfer in a complex product set. *Semiotica139*, 125–159.

HSUS (2015, March 24). *All dogs are equal: raise the bar for dogs, families and communities by fighting harmful breed-specific policies*. The Humane Society of the United States. http://www.humanesociety.org/issues/breed-specific-legislation/fact_sheets/breed-specific-legislation-all-dogs-are-equal.html?referrer=https://www.google.co.uk/. Accessed 11 June 2016.

Hughes, G., Maher, J., & Lawson, C. (2011). *Status dogs, young people and criminalisation: towards a preventative strategy*. Horsham: RSPCA.

Humphreys, C., Price, L., Heatman, B., & Ruggiero, B. (2014). *Child death review programme. Rapid review of deaths of children from dog bites or strikes*. NHS Wales. http://www.wales.nhs.uk/sitesplus/documents/888/20140811_CDR_RapidReview_DogBites_CH_v1_Final.pdf. Accessed 05 June 2016.

Keep Britain Tidy (n/d). *Dog fouling*. http://www.keepbritaintidy.org/dogfouling/573. Accessed 05 June 2016.

Klaassen, B., Buckley, J.R. & Esmail, A. (1996). Does the dangerous dogs act protect against animal attacks: A prospective study of mammalian bites in the accident and emergency department. *Injury-International Journal of the Care of the Injured, 27*(2), 89–91.

Lawson, C. (forthcoming). *'Hoodies', 'Hounds' and harm reduction: a criminological case study*. PhD Thesis, Cardiff University.

Lyons, J. (2015). Police and courts let 3,000 'devil dogs' go walkies. *The Sunday Times*. http://www.thesundaytimes.co.uk/sto/news/uk_news/Crime/article1539964.ece. Accessed 20 June 2016.

Maher, J., & Pierpoint, H. (2011). Friends, status symbols and weapons: the use of dogs youth groups and youth gangs. *Crime, Law and Social Change: Special Issue on Animal Abuse*, 55(5), 405–420.

Mannion, C. J., Graham, A., Shepherd, K., & Greenberg, D. (2015). Dog bites and maxillofacial surgery: what can we do? *British Journal of Oral and Maxillofacial Surgery, 53*(6), 522–525.

Mathieson, A. (2015). Dog attacks on horses at record high. *Horse & Hound*. http://www.horseandhound.co.uk/news/dog-attacks-on-horses-at-record-high-480154. Accessed 23 March 2016.

McCarthy, N. (2016, June 7). Cost of housing dangerous dogs doubles to £600,000. *Birmingham Mail*. http://www.birminghammail.co.uk/news/midlands-news/cost-housing-dangerous-dogs-doubles-11433690. Accessed 7 June 2016.

Metropolitan Police Service (2016). *Dangerous dogs seizure and disposal.* http://www.met.police.uk/foi/units/co11_public_order.htm. Accessed 13 June 2016.

Moxon, R. (2013). *A review of the reports from dog attacks on guide dogs between 2011 and 2013.* Guide Dogs Internal Report.

Newman, J. (2012). *Human-directed dog aggression; a systematic review.* Master of Philosophy Thesis, University of Liverpool. http://repository.liv.ac.uk/7753/1/NewmanJen_June2012_7753.pdf. Accessed 2 June 2016.

O'Neill, B. (2010). In defence of 'devil dogs'. *The spectator.* http://www.spectator.co.uk/2010/03/in-defence-of-devil-dogs/. Accessed 23 May 2016.

Ortiz, F. (2009). *Making the dogmen heel: recommendations for improving the effectiveness of dogfighting laws.* South Texas College of Law. http://works.bepress.com/cgi/viewcontent.cgi?article=1000andcontext=francesca_ortiz. Accessed 20 April 2016.

Ortiz, F. (2010). Making the dogman heel: recommendations for improving the effectiveness of dog fighting laws. *Stanford Journal of Animal Law and Policy, 3,* 1–75.

Oxley, J., & Cheng, J. (2014). Dog bites, treatment and prevention in New Zealand. *The New Zealand Medical Journal, 127*(1406), 93–94.

Pierpoint, H., & Maher, J. (2010). Animal abuse. In F. Brookman, M. Maguire, H. Pierpoint, T. Bennett (Eds.), *Handbook on crime* (pp.480–501). Uffculme: Willan Publishing.

Ragatz, L., Fremouw, W., Thomas, T., & McCoy, K. (2009). Vicious dogs: the antisocial behaviors and psychological characteristics of owners. *Journal of Forensic Sciences (American Academy of Forensic Sciences), 54*(3), 199–703.

Raghavan, M., Martens, P. J., Chateau, D., & Burchill, C. (2013). Effectiveness of breed-specific legislation in decreasing the incidence of dog-bite injury hospitalizations in people in the Canadian province of Manitoba. *Injury Prevention, 19,* 177–183.

Royal Mail. (2016). *Preventing dog attacks.* http://www.royalmailgroup.com/customers/customer-commitment/preventing-dog-attacks. Accessed 21 May 2016.

Royal Society for the Prevention of Cruelty to Animals [RSPCA]. (2009, May 21). New RSPCA figures show shocking rise in dog fighting on our streets. *News Bulletin.* http://www.rspca.org.uk/servlet/Satellite?blobcol=urlblob&blobheader=application%2Fpdf&blobkey=id&blobtable=RSPCABlob&blobwhere=1236788694832&ssbinary=true. Accessed 21 May 2009.

RSPCA (2010). *Briefing on status dogs.* RSPCA. http://www.rspca.org.uk/servlet/Satellite?blobcol=urlblob&blobheader=application%2Fpdf&blobkey=id&blobtable=RSPCABlob&blobwhere=1169720061490&ssbinary=true&Content-Type=application/pdf. Accessed 30 March 2016.

RSPCA (2012). *Dog control and welfare: written evidence submitted by the Royal Society for the Prevention of Cruelty to Animals to parliament.* http://www.publications.parliament.uk/pa/cm201213/cmselect/cmenvfru/writev/dogcontrol/dog24.htm. Accessed 27 May 2016.

RSPCA (2014). *Changes to dog control legislation: update paper for RSPCA staff, trustees and volunteers*. RSPCA. http://www.rspca.org.uk/ImageLocator/LocateAsset?asset=document&assetId=1232734882582&mode=prd. Accessed 03 June 2016.

Savage, J., & Kanazawa, S. (2002). Social capital, crime, and human nature. *Journal of Contemporary Criminal Justice, 18*(2), 188–211.

Schenk, A. M., Ragatz, L. L., & Fremouw, W. J. (2012). Vicious dogs part 2: criminal thinking, callousness, and personality styles of their owners. *Journal of Forensic Sciences (American Academy of Forensic Sciences), 57*(1), 152–159.

Schur, E. (1963). *Narcotic addiction in Britain and America*. London: Tavistock.

Simpson, J., & Speake, J. (2000). *The Oxford dictionary of proverbs*. 5th edition. Oxford: Oxford University Press.

The Sunday Times (2006). Criminals buy a bigger devil dog. *The Sunday Times*. http://www.thesundaytimes.co.uk/sto/news/uk_news/article201185.ece. Accessed 20 May 2016.

Sutherland, E. H., Cressey, D. R., & Luckenbill, D. F. (1992). *Principles of criminology*. Washington, DC: Rowman and Littlefield.

Taylor, K.D., & Mills, D.S. (2007). The effect of the kennel environment on canine welfare: a critical review of experimental studies. *Animal Welfare, 16*, 435–447.

Winter, S., & Gutteridge N. (2015). RSPCA smashes cruel puppy trading gang: sick dogs smuggled to UK and sold for huge profits. *Express*. http://www.express.co.uk/news/nature/595741/RSPCA-puppy-trading-gang-sick-dogs-smuggled-sold-profits. Accessed 05 June 2016.

Dr Jennifer Maher is Senior Lecturer at the Centre for Criminology, University of South Wales. Her research interests include animal abuse, green criminology, human-animal studies, and youth and gang violence. She recently concluded a UK wildlife trafficking study for the FP7 (European Commission) EFFACE project which evaluated the impact of environmental crime in Europe and is currently researching puppy smuggling for the Scottish and English Governments. Her publications include co-editing *Greening Criminology in the 21st Century* (2016, Routledge, with M. Hall et al.) and the special journal issue 'Animal Abuse and Criminology' in *Crime, Law and Social Change* (2011 with P. Beirne).

Dr Harriet Pierpoint is a Reader in Criminology and Criminal Justice at the Centre for Criminology at University of South Wales. Her research interests relate to criminal process and vulnerable people, and, more recently, animal abuse. She has undertaken a number of funded research projects including for the Youth Justice Board, Home Office, Ministry of Justice and the National Offender Management Service Cymru and has publications in internationally recognised, peer reviewed journals, such as Policing and Society: An International Journal and Criminology and Criminal Justice: The International Journal. She is a co-editor of the Handbook on Crime, for Willan Publishing. She has also presented her research at key national and international conferences and has been by invited by academics and practitioners to give guest lectures. She is a member of the Executive Committee of the British Society of Criminology (Chair, Regional Groups and Specialist Networks) and of the South Wales Police Independent Ethics Committee.

Claire Lawson is currently undertaking doctoral research at Cardiff University on the multi-agency responses to the 'dangerous' and 'status' dog phenomenon in England and Wales, following the publication of a joint research report on this issue in 2011. Her Master's Degree in Criminology and Criminal Justice focussed on the RSPCA and the criminology of control, a subject on which she has also published. Claire is an Assistant Director in External Relations for the RSPCA, where she has worked since 1999, and she has been Chair of the Animal Welfare Network for Wales since its inception in 2006.

Part II

The Abuse of Animals Used in Farming

Breeding and Rearing Farmed Animals

Erika Cudworth

Introduction

This chapter examines the mass breeding and raising of animals for meat and other 'animal products' (eggs, 'dairy' products). The most common relationship we have with domesticated non-human animals[1] is that we eat them, and this requires the routine breeding and raising of enormous populations. The farming of animals has long been the most significant social formation of human–animal relations and does not happen discreetly within national boundaries, but is a process that has been international in scope and is industrial in its scale of operation. While this chapter focuses on the breeding and rearing of the most commonly eaten domesticated land-dwelling animals

Throughout this chapter, the term 'farmed' rather than 'farm' animals will be used. This is consistent with critical approaches in animal studies which emphasise that the raising of non-human animals for food is something which is done to non-human animals rather than a neutral status which some kinds of domesticated species occupy.

[1] The term 'non-human animals' is used to make clear that the author knows that humans are animals! Where the term 'animal(s)' is used, it should be read as 'non-human animals' but has been shortened for ease of reading only.

E. Cudworth (✉)
School of Social Sciences, University of East London, UK,
London, United Kingdom
e-mail: E.Calvo@uel.ac.uk

J. Maher et al. (eds.), *The Palgrave International Handbook of Animal Abuse Studies*, DOI 10.1057/978-1-137-43183-7_8

in the West (cattle, sheep, pigs and chickens), there will be brief mention of less common farmed animals (such as rabbits) and those which are not clearly 'domesticated' (fishes in 'aquaculture', for example).

This chapter will suggest that the normative everyday practices of animal agriculture within which billions of animals are bred and raised are collectively part of the most widespread and systematic abuse of non-human animals. There are two senses in which this might be understood. Standard dictionary definitions of the term 'abuse' suggest that it is first, a misuse or misemployment; and second, that it is a cruel or violent treatment of a human or non-human animal with intent to harm. The breeding and rearing of farmed animals is naturalised in Western (and other) cultures but is unnecessary and involves the creation of artificial populations of creatures who live short and harsh lives—it is a misuse of non-human creatures. The processes of animal agriculture also involve systematic cruelties and violences towards the creatures who are farmed. The breeding and rearing (and killing, see Chapter on Slaughterhouses in this volume) of farmed animals is, in sum, an institutionalised site of animal abuse. Comparing contemporary animal agribusiness to other sites of institutionalised animal abuse, Erin Williams and Margot de Mello rightly argue that it is the most extreme and normative example of our exploitation of animals—globally, 99 % of all domesticated animals are commodities in animal agriculture (Williams and de Mello 2007, p. 14). This largest of animal populations, those used for 'food', are caught in relations of human dominion that involve their exploitation and oppression.

There are some who argue that we have seen some positive changes, for example in the UK or the European Union in terms of 'improvements' in farmed animal welfare and the mainstreaming of ideas about 'happy' and 'humane' farming associated with 'free-range' or 'ethically' produced animal-based food (Bock and Buller 2013). However, in terms of the global spread of intensive and industrial models of animal agriculture, the situation for farmed animals was worse (regarding the numbers raised and killed) in 2002 than in 1972, and numbers of animals to be killed for food is predicted to double in the next 50 years, overwhelmingly through the spread of Western intensive methods (Food and Agriculture Organisation 2002; Mitchell 2011). Such *prevalence* of intensive methods, associated with some of the most abusive practices and the transitions towards them internationally, is the focus for the first section of this chapter. The chapter then proceeds to examine the specific *nature* of the abuses which attend the breeding and raising of animals for food in more detail. The third section of the chapter is more theoretical, and focuses on *explanations* for the forms and degrees of abuse endemic in the breeding and raising of animals for food. Finally, the chapter considers *responses* to issues raised by the breeding and rearing of farmed animals in terms of policy changes adopted by national and international organisations of governance, the demands of different campaign organisations in civil society which expose and contest different kinds of abuses involved in the raising of non-human animals for food and the alterations in industry practices.

Prevalence

In this section of the chapter, I trace the development of the institutions and practices of breeding and rearing farmed animals, noting that the realisation of the global agribusiness industries of today emerged through entangled histories of colonialism and the development of capitalism.

From the thirteenth to the nineteenth century, the breeding and rearing of animals for food in Europe took place through small-scale farming which occurred on relatively sustainable pastures and was mixed with a range of species. There was regional difference in terms of the growing of different varieties of chickens, pigs, sheep and cattle and the production of different sorts of 'animal products'. While elements of this trend persist (Johnson 1991), the current scale of animal farming is both extensive and intense, and it has been growing rapidly since the 1950s. As a result, there has been a dramatic increase in the populations of farmed animals. In 2003, for example, the USA became the first country to raise over one billion farmed animals in a single year, and this was more than twice the number of animals raised for food in 1980 and 10 times the number raised in 1940 (Marcus 2005, p. 5). Since 1980, global meat production has more than doubled, but in the South (where levels of meat and dairy consumption are rising year on year), it has tripled. Sixty billion animals are currently used each year to provide meat and dairy products. On current trends, this figure could reach 120 billion by 2050 (MacDonald 2010, p. 34). The United Nations Food and Agriculture Organization predicts a dramatic rise in human population to 8.9 billion by 2050, and the rise in the food animal population, is promoted partly by this increase and also by heightened demand in both richer and poorer regions of the globe (Giles 2009).

The seeds of this contemporary globalised animal food system are to be found in the centuries prior to the industrialisation of agricultural production in the nineteenth century. The process of colonisation involved the development of an internationalised food system, which co-existed with the localised model in European regions outlined above. Extensive cattle ranching and sheep grazing was the farming system introduced by European colonisation of the Americas, Australasia and Africa from the sixteenth to the nineteenth centuries. This system involved particular forms of exploitative social relations such as the use of slave labour, displaced indigenous peoples and unwanted or exploited rural peasantries (Franklin 1999, pp. 128–129; also Nibert 2013). As colonised territories became increasingly independent, and many drew in burgeoning immigrant populations, the ranching system—exploitative of both land and labour became the model for an independent national system of production. In the seventeenth century, the Spanish and Portuguese imported their native cattle into South and Central America (Velten 2007). This model was adopted in much of the Southern USA from the late eighteenth to late nineteenth century, as ranchers were seeking to increase profits by serving the expanding markets in Europe.

Throughout the first half of the nineteenth century, the breeding methods pioneered in Britain were adopted elsewhere (Ritvo 1990). Animals were bred to gargantuan sizes, and fat-rich beef was a quintessential sign of status. This demand and the profits to be made from serving it, resulted in the 'cattelisation' of countries such as Argentina and Brazil, and the replacement of species type in the USA. The 'Great Bovine Switch' saw the replacement of buffalo with cattle through sponsoring the hunting of buffalo which led to their virtual and almost instantaneous elimination from the Western range lands after thousands of years of successful habitation (Nibert 2013, pp. 103–107; Rifkin 1994, pp. 74–76).

The colonial model of meat production was further enabled by the development of refrigerated shipping which made it possible to ship meat to Europe from the USA, South America and Australasia (Franklin 1999). In order to make best use of the potential market, the price had to be minimised by intensifying production and saving labour costs through increased mechanisation. By the 1920s, the USA was leading the way, and millions of diversified small family farms had been replaced by specialist, large, corporate enterprises (Nibert 2002). From the 1950s, one of the most important technological developments was the confinement of chickens for both eggs and meat. Such farming maximises land use through intensive housing and minimises labour time as animals are in situ and fed automatically. In the USA, one person may manage up to 150,000 laying hens (Mason and Finelli 2006), and the time taken to fatten a bird to slaughter weight declined from 60 to 39 days between 1966 and 1991, while the amount of feed needed fell from 9 lb to

7.75 lb. (Fine et al. 2006, pp. 207–208). While the bodies and minds of chickens endured intensely overcrowded, barren and polluted conditions, the post-war boom in the chicken business attracted the attention and investment of large pharmaceutical companies which developed treatments for diseases and 'unwanted' chicken behaviour.

Following the successful intensification of chicken-meat and chicken-egg production, the 1960s saw the development of intensified and highly automated systems for growing other birds, pigs, cattle and sheep. Key to success were automated feeding and watering systems, and for indoor raised animals, the elimination of bedding and litter through development of different kinds of food conveyance systems, cages, stalls, pens, forms of restraint and slatted floors over gutters or holding pits. Intensification has been applied to animals raised outdoors, and the cattle 'feedlot' of the USA is the strongest example of this. Feedlots are fenced in areas with a concrete feed trough along one side and were developed in the context of depleting soil through overgrazing and surplus corn production, from the early years of the twentieth century. With nothing else to do, and stimulated by growth promoting hormones, contemporary feedlot cattle eat corn and soya, which may be 'enhanced' with the addition of growth promoting additives such as cardboard, chicken manure, industrial sewage, cement or plastic feed pellets (Rifkin 1994, pp. 12–13). Slightly less barren and automated are the cattle 'stations' predominant in Australia and Central and South America (Nibert 2013, pp. 142–153). Increased demand for cheap meat (primarily for consumption by social elites) has also led to the establishment of indoor production systems in poorer countries. Battery systems for laying hens and the growing of chickens in broiler units are now widespread throughout the Indian sub-continent (Macdonald 2010).

Thus the breeding and raising of non-human animals has been an historical development exploitative of land and of both non-human animal and human labour and has been embedded in patterns of global inequality. The abusive treatment of non-human animals farmed for food has been a backdrop to this tale of global networks and practices thus far, and in the next section we turn to focus on the treatment of different kinds of farmed animal in the processes of breeding and rearing.

Nature

There is much evidence that the animals we breed and rear for food—sheep, goats, cattle, chickens, turkeys, ducks, geese and pigs—have complex emotional lives and are individuals with views about their worlds (Masson 2004).

Farmed animals are capable of experiencing physical pain and mental anguish. They may demonstrate 'stereotyped' (pointless, repetitive) and violent behaviours (killing young, attacking peers) when denied opportunity to engage in activities biologically normative to their species: caring for young, company of adults of the same species, adequate diet, exercise, play, sex and various species specific behaviour (dust-bathing for hens, swimming for ducks, foraging for pigs and so on). While this section will focus on the treatment of such non-human animals in intensive agricultural systems where animals are 'warehoused' and unable to engage in biologically normative species-appropriate behaviour, we will also consider the forms of violent and oppressive treatment animals experience in less intensive production systems. The data discussed here is drawn predominantly from UK sources, but the forms of abuse described here occur throughout more developed countries and as we have seen, are spreading across the globe.

In the West, the overwhelming proportion of the animal food we eat comes from intensive farming (Mason and Finelli 2006). The scale of contemporary industrial farming means that hundreds of millions of animals are 'grown' in conditions that leave them 'virtually immobilised' (Williams and de Mello 2007, p. 12). In intensive agriculture, the lives of animals are particularly 'nasty, brutish and short'. Most chickens are reared in large numbers (10–20,000 birds per unit in the UK, CIWF 2013a; considerably more in the US, Safran Foer 2009) in windowless sheds called broilers. They live for between four and seven weeks, fed on a high protein diet that rapidly multiplies their weight; putting strain on limbs and organs and leading to 60,000 dying daily from disease, deformity and stress (CIWF 2009a, 2013a).

Chickens in particular have paid a great price for advances in animal breeding technology which has genetically increased their metabolism to ensure quick fattening and a range of associated diseases and health problems (Marcus 2005). Towards the end of their lives, they are packed tightly, unable to move around on their contaminated litter which burns them when they rest, and in which rats, flies and maggots thrive. They are bred for passivity and kept in highly regulated conditions of heat and light in order to keep them calm. Laying hens in battery systems are kept five to a cage measuring 18 by 20 inches. They cannot spread their wings, their feet grow deformed from standing on wire mesh floors and lack of exercise means they suffer brittle bones, a fatty liver, prolapses and bronchitis (CIWF 2009a). The frustration associated with this environment may lead hens to pecking cage mates, and to prevent this, many are 'de-beaked' without the use of anaesthesia. 'Free range' describes a variety of systems and practices where hens have access to outside runs. These usually allow limited exercise, involve large groups and offer chickens no protective cover from the predators they fear, or at the other end of the spectrum may be smaller scale and on a woodland pastoral model. 'Free range' chickens are slaughtered within three to four months.

In non-intensive systems, where farmers may see the animals over some months, there may be some element of human compassion. Rhoda Wilkie (2010) found concern with physical welfare and mental health and stimulation amongst farmers she interviewed, although this was overwhelmingly concentrated amongst those breeding 'non-commercial' animal often in 'post-productivist' scenarios (small holdings for those with a hobby interest in farming, or in self-sufficiency). Here, she rightly notes there is ambiguity around the pet/livestock boundary, but only for those with very small numbers of animals. This concern with the quality of animals lives was a minority view amongst beef, dairy and sheep farmers who I spoke with in my research on animal agriculture, and, they suggested, was something absent from factory production models (Cudworth 2008). Interviews I have undertaken with commercial dairy farmers found some who were genuinely troubled that the animals they maintained had such 'boring lives', but this concern was framed in a narrative of animals as a source of food and animal farming as necessarily concerned with making an animal 'pay for itself'.

Pig farming in the UK is around 80 % highly intensive (in other countries less so and globally the average is 50 % intensive production, CIWF 2013b). In factory farms, pigs are routinely sedated and kept in the half dark to encourage them to eat and sleep. Most sows spend their time in metal crates, boars are kept in small pens, piglets fattened in pens and small runs with no bedding and nothing to do. The day after birth, piglets have teeth and tails 'clipped' to prevent 'vices' such as gnawing the mother's teats, and biting off tails of pen mates, caused by stress resultant from a barren, over-crowded environment. After two weeks, the piglets are separated from their mothers, packed into flat deck cages, hot rooms with slatted floors, graded according to sex and size. Once grown, the pigs are moved to fattening pens. In their short lives (of 18–24 weeks), these animals will see nothing outside the factory, have been deprived of exercise and had no opportunity to play (CIWF 2009b, 2013b). Pigs are gregarious and sociable animals with strong kin bonds who thrive on stimulation and affection (Masson 2004, pp. 22–24), yet in this system pigs are meat and can be nothing more.

Animals in less intensive systems still have radically foreshortened and difficult lives. Beef cattle in Britain are fattened quickly and slaughtered below 18 months; dairy cattle are usually slaughtered by 6 or 7 years of age when their productivity reduces and endure a life fraught with mastitis and lameness. The calves they must produce will be kept or sold for dairy production, sold for veal or beef production or often, simply shot (Stevenson 1993). Most beef and dairy cattle are reared on a 'free range' system, but some farmers are turning to semi-intensive housing and keep cattle inside over winter. Although there are battery lamb farms in Britain, most sheep live outside. This creates different problems, with estimates between three and four million lambs dying each year from cold or starvation (Gellatley 1994, p. 79). Most are five months old when slaughtered, although breeding females may be kept for up to five years, significantly less than their potential 12 or 14 year lifespan. There are, undoubtedly, examples of good practice, yet contemporary animal farming in a country such as the UK is overwhelmingly large scale and for some species (birds, pigs) operates predominantly on a warehouse model where disengagement rather than positive interaction with animals is a key feature of the organisation of labour. Jonathan Safran Foer's (2009) investigation of farming practices in the USA leads him to conclude that it is very difficult for small-scale producers to survive, or for animals to be raised with high welfare standards, such is the pressure towards intensive production and mechanisation that less than 1 % of farmed animals in the USA are raised outside an intensive and mechanised system.

There are other kinds of farming and farmed animal that have not been included here such as rabbits and deer, both growth areas in farming in Europe and in the case of rabbits, highly intensive in terms of production. Another important growth area has been the farming of fishes. Whereas in 1980 the proportion of intensively farmed 'fish' was negligible in terms of market share, it now constitutes 50 % of the market, and with depleting fish stokes, will likely expand. Like other intensive systems, fish in aquaculture have highly restricted mobility, are unable their ability to perform species-specific behaviours, and are subject to parasitic infestation and disease (CIWF 2009c).

My own research into the breeding and rearing of farmed animals has been particularly concerned with the ways forms of gender-based violence can be evidenced in terms of the treatment of chickens, pigs, sheep and cattle. In the egg industry, for example, laying hens, particularly in intensive conditions, are worth so little that any problems associated with laying (such as prolapsing of the uterus) are ignored and hens are simply left to die painfully and slowly from blood loss, infection or attacks from cage mates (CIWF 2012). Some species are also bred for characteristics which conform to patriarchal discourses of domesticated femininity. Cattle are selected via trade exhibitions, or through breed catalogues for weight gain, mothering instinct, reproductive ease and meat value and breeders map family trees of certain herds and determine the hereditability of each desirable trait. The gendered evaluation of cattle as potential meat is reflected at agricultural shows, where 'best of breeds' are groomed, paraded around a ring and judged on their appearance (Cudworth 2008).

Pork is one of the cheapest meats due to the 'efficiency' of an industry in which reproduction is incredibly intensive and controlled. In intensive systems, breeding sows are kept in stalls in which they are unable to turn round or exercise throughout their 16 and a half week pregnancies and often lapse into stereotyped behaviour, trying repeatedly to build a nest from nothing. They give birth in farrowing crates (with a concrete, plastic or perforated metal floor and no bedding). Once piglets are born, the mother cannot see them properly and this often results in sows becoming frightened of their young, or aggressive due to their biting. Piglets would properly be weaned at two months, but are taken away at two weeks, so good mothering is not an overwhelming breed requirement. When pigs are raised outdoors, the gendering of breed selection is stronger, as piglets need to be more 'durable', boars more highly sexed and gilts (young sows) docile and motherly, as unlike the factory farm, mothering on a free-range system is not fully deconstructed.

Gendering can further be seen in the human manipulation of female animals' fertility and reproduction, wherein animals are forced into constant reproduction. In some cases, the gendering of abuse is very clearly expressed. Reproductive violence includes forced intercourse between non-human animals (where farm workers for example, may force boars to mount sows, insert their penises by hand) or by inserting human hands, arms, instruments of various kinds to artificially inseminate. Some feminist scholarship has understood this as the rape of animals by humans (Alexis 2015; Cudworth 2008; see Chapter on Animal Sexual Assault).

The institutions of animal agriculture are constituted through forms of violence that are regularised and for the most part, legitimate. In intensive industrial systems in particular there is much evidence of cruelty—of animals beating beaten, killed (for example, 'unviable' piglets) or mutilated (for example, by tail docking or castration) as part of everyday encounters. Even in less-intensive production systems, there may be periods of forced confinement, the separation of social groups, and separation of mothers from young. There are also more ambiguous treatments which animals are subjected to, such as the inability to express species-life behaviours, which can be understood as forms of violence (Cudworth 2015). All animal lives in contemporary agricultural systems are drastically foreshortened and overwhelmingly, these short lives are barren and stressful. While there is much cruelty, this is not 'extreme' practice, rather it is inbuilt into the everyday operations of reproducing and growing animals for food.

Explanations

A number of explanations are advanced to explain the exploitation and abuse of animals in the processes of farming: first, the commoditisation of animals in capitalism and the demands of profit, second and relatedly, the development of industrial modes of production, third, the oppression originating in the early processes of domestication and finally, I will offer my own account which notes all of these processes but also emphasises the historical context of colonial relations and gendered power.

Some approaches emphasise the commoditisation of animals in agricultural production. David Nibert (2002, p. 7) explicitly uses the concept of oppression in relation to the historical development of human relations with non-human animals. He argues that social institutions such as those of animal agriculture are foundational for the oppression of animals. Nibert isolates three elements in his model of non-human animal oppression. First, we have economic exploitation where animals are exploited for human interests; second, power inequalities coded in law leave animals open to exploitation; and third, this is legitimated by an ideology—'speciesism'—which naturalises the oppression of animals in its many forms. Contemporary cultural processes and institutional arenas though which animals are exploited and oppressed—such as faming and food production are explained in terms of profit creation, corporate interest and the generation and sustaining of false commodity needs.

Bob Torres (2007) applies Nibert's model to the case of industrialised capital-intensive agriculture in the global north. Animals are largely understood by Torres as labourers, who labour by eating and breeding in producing commodities such as milk and eggs in dull, barren and stressful conditions. Animals are also property which enables their transformation into embodied commodities such as meat and leather (2007, pp. 36–58). Torres allows that the oppression of animals can exist before and beyond capitalism (2007, p. 156), but capitalism has 'deepened, extended and worsened our domination over animals and the natural world' (2007, p. 3). While human and non-human animals are exploited under capitalism, the forms of exploitation differ. The bodies of non-human animals are not only are exploited by working for us in order to produce animal food products, their bodies are *themselves* 'superexploited living commodities' (2007, p. 58). Animal lives and bodies are a means to profit creation within capitalism. In addition, animals are property, and this means that, in the case of animal agriculture, animals are 'sensate living machines' for the production of commodities (2007, p. 64). For Torres, as for Nibert, capitalism remains the key explanatory framework, and the analysis of human relations with non-human domesticate animals is conceptually underpinned by notions of property relations and commoditisation.

More recently, Nibert has made the case that the process of domestication is violent and abusive in and of itself. It involves the enslavement of species via their 'domesecration' (2013, pp. 24–30). Comparing practices of animal exploitation for food and resources in different societies over time, Nibert focuses on nomadic pastoralism and the development of commercial ranching, a practice that has been largely controlled by elite groups and expanded with the rise of capitalism. Beginning with the pastoral societies of the Eurasian steppe and continuing through to the contemporary exportation of Western, meat-centred eating habits, Nibert connects the domesecration of animals to the interests of powerful social elites and to mass violence, invasion, displacement and enslavement. Conquest and subjugation were the results of the need to appropriate land and water to maintain large groups of animals, and the amassing of military power has its roots in the economic benefits of the exploitation, exchange, and sale of animals. Nibert argues that the domesecration of animals was a precondition for the oppression of human populations, particularly indigenous peoples (2013, p. 4). Historically, the material interests of social, political and economic elites are inextricably linked to the exploitation of animals and this has been spread and deepened with the development of capitalism.

For other critics of industrial animal agriculture such as Jocelyne Porcher (2014), however, the history of domestication is not one of violence but of co-operation and shared working between human communities and the animal species they lived and worked alongside. Nibert would argue that relations with domesticates involved exploitation and abuse from the start, and might never by anything else. Porcher suggests, however, drawing on her experience as a small-scale farmer and her research on different farming practices and systems, that the problem is what industrial large-scale production for the profit motive has made of the breeding and rearing of farmed animals, rather than the processes of domestication itself. Our lives with farmed animals might be transformed back to a model of 'animal husbandry' wherein farmers have a work relationship with animals based on ties of community and of reciprocity wherein animals are not reduced to objects of production but understood as living and sensate co-producers (see 2014, pp. 10–15). In this model of domestication, there is reciprocity and recognition between humans and the domesticate species they work with. Porcher makes light of arguments for animal liberation and the end of the use of animals for food (2014, pp. 60–64), portraying a world of unnatural food and unnatural species separation and ultimately, the abolition of domesticate animals. This is a pity because she and those such as Nibert, Torres or Safran Foer share an analysis of the violences of industrial animal food production for the billions of animals bred and raised for killing and those humans working in such noxious systems.

Given that my own work is very much informed by feminist work in animal studies, I am very wary of seeking an original moment of fall (such as does Nibert with his conception of domesicration), or of return to the past which may (according to Porcher) involve collaborative rather than abusive relations between species. Feminist theory has much to say about the problems attending a search of origins of forms of abuse, such as gender domination, and same applies to a search for 'origins' in the domination and oppression of non-human animals. My own attempts to explain the abuse of farmed animals draws particularly the idea of intersectionalised oppressions (Cudworth 2011). This means I would look at the abuse of farmed animals in terms of various kinds of relational systems of power in addition to capitalism, gender, 'race' and so on as well as looking at the ways social hierarchies of species which privilege human beings are sustained and reproduced over time.

I use the term 'anthroparchy' to describe and explain a social system, a complex and relatively stable set of hierarchical relationships, in which the incredible diversity of non-human species are homogenised as 'animals', identified as part of 'nature' and dominated through formations of social organisation which privilege the human. Anthroparchy involves different degrees of dominatory power: oppression, exploitation and marginalisation. Different oppressive forms apply to different species due to their specific characteristics and normative behaviours such as the presence of sociality and the ways in which this presents itself. Thus for the active chicken or the gregarious pig, the terms 'dull', 'barren' or 'lonely' life are accurate descriptors of the lives of these farmed animals, whereas these terms would not be applicable descriptors for the lives of the bacteria living on the effluvia from pig and chicken farms. Exploitation refers to the use of some being as a resource for human ends, and we might speak of the exploitation of the properties of animal bodies, genetically altered to withstand intensive agricultural systems or the labour power of domesticated animals in agriculture (such as in breeding and lactation), for example. Marginalisation is most broadly applicable, referring to human centrism.

I have also suggested that five sets of social institutions and their related processes network to form the social system of relations I call anthroparchy. The first set of anthroparchal relations is production, wherein the breeding and raising of animals for food can be seen in the interlinked institutions and processes of breeding and growing which operate in a complex network of local, regional and global relations. The second relational arena is domestication which has characterised human engagements with other species for millennia through the selective breeding of certain kinds of plants and animals. The last two centuries have seen intensification of such processes, for example, in terms of reproductive interventions in animal food production. The third arena is political. States and international organisations can act as direct or indirect agents of anthroparchy; for example, by subsidising animal farming, or contest and change forms of abuse by making certain practices unlawful (such as the use of battery cages). Fourth, we have systemic violence, which as we have seen in the previous section, is embedded in the production systems of 'animal food'. Finally, anthroparchal social relations are characterised by cultures of exclusive humanism which may, for example, encourage certain practices such as animal food consumption.

The breeding and raising of farmed animals illustrates a specific site in which anthroparchal institutions, processes and practices may be evidenced. The case for the material intersections of class and race has been well made by those such as Nibert (2002) and Torres (2007). However, these material practices, can also be understood as co-constituted through gendered relations. The breeding and growth of non-human animals for 'meat' reflects the complex intersections of a range of relations of social power.

Responses

Given the prevalence of the abuse of animals in farming generally and in increasing degree and scale through intensive industrial modes of breeding and rearing, one might expect reactions from governing bodies, non-governmental and civil society organisations. This section will suggest that the most energetic responses to counter abuse in (and of) animal agriculture comes from civil society, but this has had a limited impact on national and international policy making primarily because agencies of governance have been implicated in the development and spread of some of the most highly abusive methods of raising and rearing creatures for food.

In the aftermath of the Second World War, European states and the USA set out to reduce malnutrition and hunger amongst their human populations with the promotion of cheap 'animal products'. Rising levels of 'meat' and 'dairy consumption became associated with social progress. This was promoted internationally by the United Nations, which, in the 1960s and 1970s, emphasised the necessity of increasing animal protein production and making such food increasingly available in poor countries (Rifkin 1994, p. 131). It is difficult not to conclude that such initiatives were strongly influenced by Western governments driven by the corporate interests of the multinational corporations based in their territories. In the 1980s and much of the 1990s, the Common Agricultural Policy of the European Community/European Union also encouraged intensive animal farming through systems of grants and subsidies which explicitly favoured equipment and buildings (Johnson 1991, p. 181).

More recently however, the UN Food and Agriculture Organization report, *Livestock's Long Shadow*, concluded that animal agriculture is a greater contributor to global warming than the combined effects of all forms of transportation (Steinfeld et al. 2006). The deployment of Western agricultural models and the spread of Western food practices have significant implications for the environment in terms of undermining bio-diversity, localised pollution, soil damage, rainforest depletion, and contributing 18 % of all greenhouse gases. It may be that with apparent concern about climate change demonstrated by international organisations and the incontrovertible evidence of the role of animal farming in contributing to environmental hazard, national and international policy proclivities will shift. We have also seen increased public awareness in the West about issues of farm animal welfare.

Certainly, there are a wide range of campaigning groups responding to the issues raised by the breeding and rearing of farmed animals. These involve conservative organisations such the Royal Society for the Prevention of Cruelty to Animals (RSPCA) in the UK exposing and investigating reported cruelty cases. The RSPCA advocates the production of 'Freedom Food' which is a labelling scheme and inspection system guaranteeing basic freedom for farmed animals (from fear, hunger and thirst, for example, and freedom to engage in certain species specific behaviours). This scheme was launched in 1994, with slow take up from businesses, and was relaunched in June 2015 as 'RSPCA Assured' (RSPCA 2015). Welfarist schemes have received significant boosts from television chefs such as Jamie Oliver and Hugh Fearnley-Whittingstall in the UK, who have campaigned on issues of animal welfare, environmental damage and human health resultant from intensive farming and aquaculture and have endorsed such food labelling (Fearnley-Whittingstall 2015; Oliver 2015). Other groups seeking reform of farming practices include Compassion in World Farming (CIWF) which campaigns for the abolition of certain methods (such as the use of sow stalls and tethering in intensive pig production, or the caging of rabbits and laying hens). More broadly, CIWF wishes to eventually abolish intensive farming methods, promoting smaller operations based on 'high' welfare standards. CIWF, established by a farmer appalled at the spread of intensive agriculture in 1967, has campaigned with success in the European Union, securing the recognition of animals as sentient beings, capable of feeling pain and suffering, and bans for battery cages for egg-laying hens and sow stalls (CIWF 2015). States, international organisations and even agribusiness corporations have deployed animal welfare arguments and combined them with ideas about meat quality in promoting 'ethical' branding of meat and other 'animal products'. However, research has indicated that there are limits to the welfare that might be secured through 'welfare quality' initiatives in the European Union, for example, and that any 'gains' in reducing cruelty towards animals are at best, partial and ambiguous (Miele and Lever 2013).

Other groups have more radical agendas that support the abolition of the breeding and rearing of non-human creatures for food and advocate for a vegetarian or vegan future. For example, the largest UK based animal rights group, Animal Aid, founded in 1977, 'promote[s] the adoption of an animal-free diet as the best single step anyone can take to stop cruelty to animals' (Animal Aid 2015) and seeks to raise public awareness about the cruelties involved in all forms of the raising of non-human animals for food. The largest animal rights organisation is People for the Ethical Treatment of Animals (PETA), founded in 1980. Its slogan is 'animals are not ours to eat, wear, experiment on, use for entertainment, or abuse in any other way', and PETA has a key focus on opposition to factory farming and eating meat and promoting a vegan diet (PETA 2015). Such organisations have been critiqued for the tactics they have deployed and for being either 'excessively' radical or not radical enough in supporting welfare reform as strategic in securing an agenda of the abolition of the use of animals for food. The work of such organisations has been significant in raising public awareness through investigative campaigns and causing pressure for change within the industry. The existence of such groups, their expanding memberships and the influence on national and international policy agendas may suggest possibilities for change.

Yet at this time of writing, two unsettling processes are at work. First, concerns for animal welfare or environmental damage by livestock farming appear insignificant in the face of development driven by multinational corporations. Thus we see that the feedlot system continues to be exported in beef farming, and intensive dairy farming pioneered in the US, where cattle are kept permanently inside, in small stalls has been adopted in European Union countries. Key targets for Western-based agricultural corporations in the near future however are parts of the Indian subcontinent and Africa.

Second, a very small but notable development in some Western countries (the Netherlands, Norway and Sweden) has been research and development activity around 'in vitro meat'. This involves the growth of muscle tissue in laboratories with the intention of developing it for consumption as food. Advocates, such as the 'In Vitro Meat Consortium' or the campaigning group 'New Harvest', promote IV meat as a solution to the problems of animal cruelty and environmental damage caused by meat production by animal farming. IV meat is promoted as a social good, able to reduce pollution, deforestation and greenhouse gas emissions associated with livestock production methods (Porcher 2014; Stephens 2010). Yet even the economic assessments undertaken for the In Vitro Meat Consortium suggest that this 'meat' will be intended for the high end niche market in Western countries, priced above free range organic meat products (Stephens 2010). As such, it seems an unlikely element of a solution to food poverty in developing countries. In addition, the production techniques suggest that IV meat production would place pressure on water resources, raising questions about the environmentalist credentials of this new technology.

Both these future scenarios suggest that the production and consumption of meat remains firmly within research, development and policy scenarios, despite the increasing presence of critical voices.

Conclusion

This chapter has described and critiqued the historical processes and current constitution of the global animal food industries involved with the breeding and raising of some domesticate animals for food. The development of animal breeding techniques and methods of animal raising which have resulted in intensive production systems are currently spreading apace across the globe. These processes have resulted in horrendous conditions for those species raised as 'meat', environmental degradation, food poverty in poorer counties, and reproduced and enhanced embedded inequities between human beings. In Britain, as elsewhere, legislative moves to limit violent practices against animals deal with the extreme instances of 'cruelty' in individual or corporate cases, rather than the regularised legitimated violent practices embedded in everyday human interactions with non-human animals. Whilst the articulation of claims for rights and welfare improvements may have been effectual in the last 70 years in ameliorating some of the extremes of violent behaviour, it cannot challenge the social domination of non-human species. Indeed, the articulation of political claims on behalf 'of' animals has proceeded alongside the global spread of Western intensive animal agriculture and an enormous increase in animal populations bred and grown for food.

References

Alexis, N. (2015). Beyond suffering: resisting patriarchy and reproductive control. In A. J. Nocella, R. While, E. Cudworth (Eds.), *Anarchism and animals: critical animal studies, intersectionality and total liberation*. Jefferson, NC: McFarland.

Animal Aid (2015). 'Campaigns' and 'About Us'. http://www.animalaid.org.uk/h/n/CAMPAIGNS/factory/ALL///. Accessed 1 July 2015.

Bock, B., & Buller, H. J. (2013). Healthy, happy and humane: evidence in farm animal welfare policy. *Sociologia Ruralis, 53*(3), 390–411.

Compassion in World Farming [CIWF] (2002). *Detrimental impacts of industrial animal agriculture*. CIWF: Godalming, Surrey.

Compassion in World Farming [CIWF] (2009a, March). *Factsheet: meat chicken*. Compassion in World Farming. www.ciwf.org.uk. Accessed 1 July 2015.

Compassion in World Farming [CIWF] (2009b, September). *Factsheet: pigs*. Compassion in World Farming. www.ciwf.org.uk. Accessed 1 July 2015.

Compassion in World Farming [CIWF] (2009c, July). *Farmed fish*. Compassion in World Farming. www.ciwf.org.uk. Accessed 1 July 2015.

Compassion in World Farming [CIWF] (2012, September). *The life of laying hens*. Compassion in World Farming. www.ciwf.org.uk. Accessed 1 July 2015.

Compassion in World Farming [CIWF] (2013a, May). *The life of broiler chickens*. Compassion in World Farming. www.ciwf.org.uk. Accessed 1 July 2015.

Compassion in World Farming [CIWF] (2013b, May). *The life of pigs*. May 2010. Compassion in World Farming. www.ciwf.org.uk. Accessed 1 July 2015.

Compassion in World Farming [CIWF] (2015). Available from: http://www.ciwf.org.uk/about-us/. Accessed 1st July 2015.

Cudworth, E. (2008). Most farmers prefer blondes' – Dynamics of Anthroparchy in Animals' Becoming Meat. *The Journal for Critical Animal Studies, 6*(1), 32–45.

Cudworth, E. (2011). *Social lives with other animals: tales of sex, death and love.* Basingstoke: Palgrave.

Cudworth, E. (2015). Killing animals: sociology, species relations and institutionalised violence. *The Sociological Review, 63*(1), 1–18.

Fearnley-Whittingstall, H. (2015). https://www.rivercottage.net/hugh-fearnley-whittingstall Accessed 4 July 2015.

Fine, B., Heasman, M., & Wright, J. (2006). *Consumption in the age of affluence: the world of food.* London, Routledge.

Food and Agriculture Organization of the United Nations (2002). *World agriculture: towards 2015/2030: summary report.* ftp://ftp.fao.org/docrep/fao/004/y3557e/y3557e.pdf Accessed 1 July 2015.

Franklin, A. (1999). *Animals and modern cultures: a sociology of human-animal relations in modernity.* Sage: London.

Gellatley, J. (1994). *The silent ark: a chilling expose of meat – the global killer.* London: Thorsons.

Giles, J. (2009, February 10). Eating less meat could cut climate costs. *New Scientist.*

Johnson, A. (1991). *Factory farming.* Oxford: Blackwell.

MacDonald, M. (2010, March/April). Eat like it matters, footprints in the future of food. Special issue of *Resurgence, 259,* 32–33.

Marcus, E. (2005). *Meat market: animals, ethics and money.* Boston: Brio Press.

Mason, J., & Finelli, M., (2006). Brave new farm? In P. Singer (Ed.), *In defense of animals: the second wave.* Oxford: Blackwell.

Masson, J.M. (2004). *The pig who sang to the moon: the emotional world of farm animals.* London: Jonathan Cape.

Miele, M., & Lever, J. (2013). Civilizing the market for welfare friendly products in Europe? The techno-ethics of the Welfare Quality assessment. *Geoforum, 48,* 63–72.

Mitchell, L. (2011). Moral disengagement and support for non-human animal farming *Society and Animals, 19,* 38–58.

Nibert, D. (2002). *Animal rights/human rights: entanglements of oppression and liberation.* Lanham, MD: Rowman and Littlefield.

Nibert, D. (2013). *Animal oppression and human violence: domesecration, capitalism and global conflict.* New York: Colombia University Press.

Oliver, J. (2015). *Milk, farming and nutrition – what to avoid.* http://www.jamieoliver.com/news-and-features/features/milk-farming-nutrition-what-to-avoid/#oXfzZAraXEDkTEjv.97. Accessed 2 July 2015.

People for the Ethical Treatment of Animals [PETA] (2015). http://www.peta.org.uk/. Accessed 1 July 2015.

Porcher, J. (2014). *Vivre Avec Les Animeaux: Une Utopie Pour le XXI Sciècle (Living with animals: a Utopia for the 21st century).* Paris: Editions La Découverte.

Rifkin, J. (1994). *Beyond beef: the rise and fall of cattle culture.* London: Thorsons.

Ritvo, H. (1990). *The animal estate: the English and other creatures in the victorian age*. Harmondsworth: Penguin.

Royal Society for the Prevention of Cruelty to Animals (RSPCA) (2015). RSPCA assured is the new name for freedom food. http://www.freedomfood.co.uk/news/2015/05/rspca-assured-is-the-new-name-for-freedom-food. Accessed 2 July 2015.

Safran Foer, J. (2009). *Eating animals*. London: Hamish Hamilton.

Steinfeld, H., Gerber, P., Wassemaar, T., Castel, V., Rosales, M., & de Haan, C. (2006). *Livestock's long shadow: environmental issues and options*. Rome: United Nations Food and Agriculture Organisation.

Stephens, N. (2010). *In vitro meat: zombies on the menu?*, *7*, 2 *SCRIPTed* 394. http://www.law.ed.ac.uk/ahrc/script-ed/vol7.2/stephens.asp. Accessed 12 June 2012.

Stevenson, P. (1993). *Report: the welfare of pigs, cattle and sheep at slaughter*. Compassion in World Farming. www.ciwf.org.uk. Accessed 1 July 2015.

Torres, B. (2007). *Making a killing: the political economy of animal rights*. Oakland, CA: AK Press.

Velten, H., (2007). *Cow*. London: Reaktion Books.

Wilkie, R. (2010). *Livestock/deadstock: working with farm animals from birth to slaughter*. Philadelphia: Temple University Press.

Williams, E. E. & De Mello, M. (2007). *Why animals matter: the case for animal protection*. Amherst: Prometheus Books.

Erika Cudworth is Professor of Feminist Animal Studies in the School of Social Sciences at the University of East London, UK. Her research interests include complexity theory, gender and human relations with nonhuman animals, particularly theoretical and political challenges to exclusive humanism. She is author of *Environment and Society* (2003), *Developing Ecofeminist Theory: The Complexity of Difference* (2005) and *Social Lives with Other Animals: Tales of Sex, Death and Love* (2011); co-author of *The Modern State: Theories and Ideologies* (2007) and *Posthuman International Relations: Complexity, Ecologism and International Politics* (2011); and co-editor of *Technology, Society and Inequality: New Horizons and Contested Futures* (2013) and *Anarchism and Animal Liberation: Essays on Complementary Elements of Total Liberation* (2015). Erika's current empirical projects are on animal companions and animals and war. Her theoretical work involves looking at posthuman emancipation and undertaking a critical reappraisal of the legacy of classical social theory for posthumanist scholarship.

Slaughterhouses: *The Language of Life, the Discourse of Death*

Nik Taylor and Heather Fraser

Introduction

To some it might sound counterintuitive to include a chapter on animal slaughter in a book about animal abuse. To others, it will be a welcome addition. This disjunct reflects the paradoxical ways our society approaches the slaughter of animals for human food.[1] This slaughter happens in numbers so large as to be almost incomprehensible for the vast numbers of humans who prefer not to know where their meat comes from, with the foreshortened and often miserable lives of 'livestock' and their likely horrific deaths ignored if not made entirely invisible. The cultural erasure of the violence to 'farmed' and butchered animals occurs when social systems render such violence normative.

[1] Unwanted companion animals are also routinely slaughtered; albeit this is usually referred to euphemistically as euthanasia. While the focus of this chapter is on animals farmed for human food, the numbers of companion animals killed are substantial. While our relationships with companion animals are a form of speciesism, it is sobering to note that even the animals that we hold dear and seek to protect are subject to poor treatment and early death due to human actions. McHugh (2004, p. 9) points out that 'the dangers for contemporary dogs are real: destroyed by the millions every year as unwanted pets, strays and research subjects'.

N. Taylor (✉) · H. Fraser
School of Social and Policy Studies, Flinders University, South Australia, Australia
e-mail: nik.taylor@flinders.edu.au

J. Maher et al. (eds.), *The Palgrave International Handbook of Animal Abuse Studies*, DOI 10.1057/978-1-137-43183-7_9

Uncovering how this normativity is expressed and embedded is crucial to understanding and countering institutionalised animal abuse.

This chapter explores *condoned* animal abuse in and beyond the slaughterhouse. We begin with the argument that cultural beliefs towards meat are tied to attitudes towards animals. After all, one cannot have meat without first killing an animal. From there we seek to assess the ways in which the killing of nonhuman animals for meat becomes normalised through various institutional and cultural practices which, in large part through the operation of the Animal Industrial Complex (AIC), work to maintain the cultural invisibility of animal killing for food. We focus on the most common form of research done within slaughterhouses—ethnographic research. We argue that one finding common to much of this research is the constant and consistent separation of humans and animals into discrete categories. This 'purification' of categories occurs at a symbolic level by ensuring animals are considered as objects instead of subjects.

Through an analysis of the mechanisms whereby animal slaughter and death are normalised, this chapter addresses the ways in which the cultural hegemony of meat and the normalisation of institutional animal abuse are interconnected and can meaningfully be challenged. We do this by considering the prevalence and nature of violence done in slaughterhouses, followed by a discussion of explanations for the acceptance and normalisation of such violence. We conclude with a consideration of how we might respond to such violence.

Prevalence

Condoned violence is violence that is commonly accepted, overlooked, ignored, dismissed, trivialised and/or minimised. Systemic violence is violence that is organised, institutionalised and/or embedded in social systems. In slaughterhouses animals are butchered for food, providing a good example of both systemic and condoned violence.

Increasing Slaughterhouse Violence

The number of animals killed for slaughter is staggering. It is so large that it is virtually incomprehensible. According to the Animal Kill Counter (AKC), more than 150 billion animals are slaughtered each year across the world. The AKC counts from a composite of industry and popular media sites. Original data used came from the Food and Agriculture

Organization of the United Nations for 2003, which conservatively estimated that 53 billion land animals were slaughtered annually worldwide. According to the AKC site:

> These numbers do NOT include the many millions of animals killed each year in vivisection laboratories. They do NOT include the millions of dogs and cats killed in animal shelters every year. They do NOT include the animals who died while held captive in the animal-slavery enterprises of circuses, rodeos, zoos, and marine parks. They do NOT include the animals killed while pressed into such blood sports as bullfighting, cockfighting, dogfighting, and bear-baiting, nor do they include horses and greyhounds who were exterminated after they were no longer deemed suitable for racing. (AKC n.d.)

Slaughterhouse violence is rising. According to the FAO (2002, p. 19):

> Between 1964–66 and 1997–99, per capita meat consumption in developing countries rose by 150 percent, and that of milk and dairy products by 60 percent. By 2030, per capita consumption of livestock products could rise by a further 44 percent. As in the past, poultry consumption will grow fastest.

The report also notes 'An increasing share of livestock production will probably come from industrial enterprises. In recent years production from this sector has grown twice as fast as that from more traditional mixed farming systems and more than six times faster than from grazing systems' (p. 6). In a report by the Australian Institute of Health and Welfare (AIHW 2012), for example, the rate of Australian meat consumption is estimated to be almost three times higher than the rest of the world. This is not likely to decrease given the official endorsement of meat-eating by governments who still advise that the daily recommended intake for adults and children includes 'lean meat, fish, poultry and/or alternatives' (AIHW 2012, p. 139).

Ironically, it is the prevalence—or commonness—of the institutionally sanctioned slaughter of animals that poses one of the most important challenges to ending the killing. Rather than compel people to take the issue more seriously, the scale of the violence complicates matters, making it for many too large and confronting to face. This is even more confronting if other forms of socially sanctioned slaughter were included, such as the culling of animals in the name of animal management, such as sharks (see for instance, Small 2014), the 'commercial harvesting' of kangaroos (see Ben-Ami et al. 2014), the international exchange of animals and their body parts, whether for bushmeat (see Bowen-Jones 2003), for medicine, fashion or ornamental reasons (see chapter on the International Trade in Animal Parts herein).

Nature

While it is tempting to polarise the issues, explaining the nature and extent of animal slaughter is far more complex in some ways. Not all readers will, for example, accept the argument that slaughter is institutionalised animal abuse. This is because *intent* to harm is (usually) missing and because there are several layers of welfare statutes in place to ostensibly 'protect' animals whose sole purpose is to be farmed for human consumption. However, the reality is that this welfare framework serves to turn attention away from the systemic and institutionalised nature of slaughterhouse violence by perpetuating the idea that animal welfare is paramount in the food chain. As Regan (2001, p. 34) argues, 'it should not be surprising that the loudest, most powerful voices speaking in the name of animal welfare today are those of individuals who have an interest in perpetuating institutionalized utilization of nonhuman animals. By this I mean that those who identify themselves with the cause of animal welfare increasingly are those who speak for the commercial animal agriculture community.' This goes some way to explaining the ongoing existence and acceptance of slaughterhouses despite widespread claims to take animal welfare seriously, that is, that welfare legislation regarding the rearing and slaughtering of animals is developed within, and broadly supports, the animal industrial complex (AIC); a concept we turn to shortly.

Carnistic Defenses

Slaughterhouse violence to animals is predominantly hidden (see for example, Pachirat 2011; Wicks 2011) and generally accepted. While these two points are connected, it is simplistic to assume that it is accepted *only* because it is out of sight. Rather, while removing slaughterhouses and the work that goes on in them from sight is a prerequisite to the acceptance of them, this is but one part of a much larger ideological whole that supports the rearing, breeding, killing and consuming of animals as food. As Vialles (1994, p. 66) points out, modern cultural sensibilities (see Elias 2000) dictated a need to 'render invisible what used to be a bloody spectacle', which allows their activity to continue largely unfettered and unquestioned. However, there are other cultural and social mechanisms at play that support the rearing and slaughter of animals for food. Weitzenfeld and Joy (2014, p. 21) refer to these as 'carnistic defences' that 'enable gross cognitive and affective distortions in order for human consumers to support the system'. It is our contention that these various mechanisms work to normalise the animal abuses that occur in the slaughterhouse (and in society more generally) and that the concept of the animal industrial complex is a useful way of making such mechanisms visible.

The Animal Industrial Complex

First discussed by Barbara Noske (1997) in a prescient book, *Beyond Boundaries: Humans and Animals*, the term AIC picks up on the original idea of a military-industrial complex, which was first used in a speech by Eisenhower in 1961 to highlight the increasing problem of the connections between government force and industry (Twine 2011). Throughout the 1970s, and beyond, this concept of interlocking institutions was extended and is now commonly used to understand the prison-industrial complex, the entertainment-industrial complex, and the pharmaceutical-industrial complex. The terminology is intended to problematise the overlapping interests of capital accumulation and particular industries.

Specifically, the AIC is

> a partly opaque and multiple set of networks and relationships between the corporate (agricultural) sector, governments, and public and private science. With economic, cultural, social and affective dimensions it encompasses an extensive range of practices, technologies, images, identities and markets and seeing it as a complex, integrated ideological system then opens the door to us asking, for example 'What networks are at play? How do they interconnect? How are particular speciesist norms naturalised, carried and circulated? Why are such norms so successful at recruiting adherents? (Twine 2011, p. 23)

Attempting to answer such questions allows us to highlight the complexity of the systems of animal rearing and slaughter and to demonstrate the ideological support they have—support which renders them normative and thus powerful.

The AIC and our related poor treatment of nonhuman animal species both rest upon the idea that animals are 'other' to our humanity. They are not only different, but categorically inferior. Binary worldviews invoke hierarchical thinking which leads to animals being cast as inferior to humans. They are mere animals to our cultured humanity, barbarians to our civility and nature to our culture. This gives humans license to see themselves at the top of the food chain, presiding over all other animals who are enslaved and objectified.

Ecofeminist scholars have long chronicled the damage that has arisen from such binary worldviews, and it is a damage that affects both other species and groups of disenfranchised humans (for example, Gruen 1993). It is an outlook that justifies the oppression of those considered to be other and, to many, it is the foundation of multiple harms. As Will Tuttle (2014, pp. 20–21) argues,

> ... the underlying mentality causing our problems is injected into us via our cultural programming, and that it is not innate. It's animal agriculture. Besides being the driving force behind global climate disruption, rainforest destruction, air and water pollution, soil erosion, desertification, collapse of ocean ecosystems, species extinction, world hunger, chronic disease, economic inequality, and war, animal agriculture is also the driving force in creating the inner mentality that drives conflict, injustice, competition, and the various forms of social injustice that plague our world.... we are injected with a cultural program of violence toward defenceless and enslaved animals, and the ripples of that radiate as exclusivism, speciesism, and the many forms of separateness and entitlement that we see around us.

Here Tuttle points to the ways in which the AIC is embroiled within, and often creates, systems of oppression that damage humans, animals and the environment. Recognising these links takes some courage as it involves stepping outside the usual, human preoccupation. Understanding the ideological underpinnings of the AIC is crucial to understanding how it is that the systematic and publicly endorsed slaughter of billions of animals can be accepted by the vast majority of people. In particular, it sheds light on understanding this acceptance by people who are not otherwise particularly violent or cruel; people who may often demonstrate compassion for others, including other animals, such as their companion dogs or cats. The AIC helps us to understand why animal abuse is accepted as normative.

Explanations

When many people in the West consider themselves to be 'animal lovers', it may seem contentious to claim that slaughterhouse abuse is a legitimate category of abuse and that animal abuse is normative. Similarly, it may seem contentious to draw links between slaughterhouse abuse and the attempted genocide of people during the Holocaust, or between the overlapping poor treatment of women and animals. Yet these are our explanations, which we expand on below, along with our earlier emphasis on animal abuse as a condoned and socially sanctioned industrial complex.

Animal Abuse as Normative

The use of animals underpins our very existence and is inextricably tied to capitalist relations of production, including those of profit and exploitation. As Murray (2011, p. 95) argues, 'rather than appearing as an anomaly opposite the capitalist system, the enslavement of non-human animals has become embedded in and an intrinsic component of the capitalist economy'. This is especially the case for the billions of 'farm' animals bred, reared and slaughtered for food who, according to Torres (2007, p. 11) are destined to become 'nothing more than living machines, transformed from beings who live for themselves into beings that live for capital. Capital has literally imprinted itself upon the bodies of animals' (Torres 2007, p. 11).

Earlier we mentioned that a rich body of ecofeminist work has examined how animal slaughter is normalised in male and human-dominated societies (see for example, Adams and Donovan 1995). Ecofeminists have helped to establish that by humans placing them/ourselves at 'the top of the food chain' (other) animals are transformed into consumable *things;* things that no longer have any sense of agency, individuality or (potential) personhood (see for example, Cudworth 2014). This neatly separates humans from animals and, crucially for the current debate, allows them to be seen as 'walking larders'. Quite simply they become objects and potential food sources, as opposed to emotional individual subjects with any rights or entitlements. In effect, any potential connection that humans may feel with other (consumable) animals is removed through a series of cultural sleights of hand that deny empathising with their plight. It is also why great efforts are made to separate meat products from their sources.

Meat eating has become so normalised that it need not be explained or seriously defended. Rather than stand by their/our decision to eat meat and face how this 'meat' is produced, treated and dismembered, most people subscribe to dominant discourses that have a variety of techniques for explaining away the inherent abuse of animals in meat production and consumption. In the *Doing and the Being*, Girshick (2014, p. 57) explains that,

> . . . our society is founded upon animal consumption and use, and people are blinded to the horror of this. Packaging meat in a way that does not look like an animal separates the consumer from the fact the product contains what was once a living creature with feelings, family, and a community. This encourages a mental and emotional disconnect, and creates enormous alienation both from the self and from nature.

Yet, the idea that animal abuse is normative and institutionalised through animal slaughter can be difficult to fully grasp as it forces us to look at such abuse not as an aberration but as constitutive of modern society. Digging underneath the human respectability afforded modern societal life can feel destabilising. Even members of the committed left, outside human–animal studies circles, might find it hard to comprehend the crude barbarism that lies behind our human lives of fast-paced work and travel, our lust for electronic devices and pride in high-tech health products. Rather than face the slaughter of animals the argument might be that such a focus is an indulgence, given the scale of problems facing humans across the world.

Recognising (Animal) Abuse beyond Individual Acts of Intended Cruelty

As humans, especially those of us in the West, we are encouraged to think about violence predominantly as an individual and intentional, if not psychotic affair. We see this in the media reports that concentrate on the individual perpetrator, his psyche, childhood and more recently, the possible triggers to the outburst. This lone psychotic focus occurs even when there are mass killings, such as gunmen opening fire on people in cinemas, shopping centres or schools (Kimmel 2013). Less frequently, attention is given to groups of people involved in violence. Sometimes, blame for this violence is attributed to the entire group, irrespective of perpetrators or victims, as in theories about cultures of violence, sometimes attributed to racially profiled groups (see Birzer 2012); groups that have a history of being likened to animals.

Seriously facing the scale and extent of animal slaughter takes us into some difficult and uncomfortable terrain. For example, Cantor (2014, p. 29) draws parallels between mass animal slaughter and human genocide when he argues that 'Such institutionalized atrocities as the American Holocaust and human slavery derive from the logic inherent in humanism that any kind of animal, including human animals, can be less than human'. This idea picks up on ecofeminist scholarship (for example, Griffin 1978; Ruether 1975) that demonstrates the intersections between the oppression of women and of nature; intersections that challenge binary and dualistic thought that 'allows for the continued conceptualization of hierarchies in which a theoretically privileged group or way of thinking is superior' (Gruen in Gaard 1993, p. 80).

Slaughterhouse Violence as Gendered

Drawing attention to the epistemologies that underpin current knowledge systems, ecofeminists have pointed out the co-occurrence of the subjection of women and animals. Cudworth (2011, pp. 163–169) underlines the fact that it is female animals who are mostly used in the AIC (although this should not be read as meaning male animals are not harmed by the AIC; bobby calves and male chicks are routinely slaughtered shortly after birth as they are an unwanted 'by-product' in an industry that relies on female reproductive capacity):

> . . . agricultural animals are gendered in two ways. First, farmed animals tend to be female—being the most useful profit maximizers as they produce feminized protein (eggs and dairy products) and reproduce young, as well as becoming meat themselves. . . . Second, farmed animals are constructed in ways resembling human gender dichotomies. Breed journals, for instance, indicate that genetics are manipulated to produce attractive, docile 'good mothers', and 'virile', strong, 'promiscuous' males.

Cudworth notes the circularity that pervades the AIC, pointing out that factory farming and slaughter are 'patriarchally closed' systems complete with gender segregated work and the masculinisation of work cultures (p. 166). Focusing on the British meat industry, Cudworth explains that the AIC sits at 'the intersection of capitalist and patriarchal relations . . . [where] . . . the object of domination in the manufacture of meat is patriarchally constituted' (p. 170; see further Cudworth's chapter in this volume).

It is worth reflecting on the notion that patriarchy not only underlies ongoing gender relations but it sits behind the manufacture of meat. Many will balk at these ideas, either because they refuse to consider the slaughter of animals as violence, and/or they refute the relevance of patriarchy as an analysis of contemporary gender relations. Well educated, progressive intellectuals might even mock protest messages such as 'meat is murder' or otherwise poke fun at people concerned about the widespread, socially sanctioned enslavement and slaughtering of animals. The irony here is how easily the barbaric practices of domination and slaughter are pushed away through laughter and scorn under the guise of intellectual and even ethical supremacy. It is made possible by the associations of men with (trusted) reason and women with (unruly) emotions.

Most western post-Enlightenment discourses still need to 'civilise' or otherwise 'discipline' and control beings constructed as unruly and closer to nature, classifications long attributed to women and other animals. The same works in reverse with the assumption that nature is something 'out there' to be 'mastered' by human practice, usually through technological means, and this is evident in slaughterhouse work where the technology is something to be proud of (Hamilton and Taylor 2013), something we will return to later. The need to dominate and control nature—and anything and anyone associated with it— is not only old but it is so deeply embedded within modern thought as to be one of its constitutive paradigms. Far from being considered an aberration, it is instead a belief system whereby oppression is considered a legitimate, and indeed necessary starting point. Murray (2011), for example, points out that speciesist relations have been constitutive of capitalism, rather than an effect of it, in the same way that other scholars argue that the very roots of modern capitalist practices have been dependent upon the subjugation of women. This analytical approach allows us to see the interconnected nature and consequences of animal and human abuse and oppression. Cantor (2014, p. 30) succinctly summarises it: 'animal abuse is a root cause of even human miseries that do not appear linked at first glance'.

Accepting that such violences are linked is challenging as it encourages a different view of the role of violence—and specific violent events—in society. Bauman (2001, pp. 4–5), for example, argued that traditional thinking and scholarship that regard the holocaust through a 'theoretical framework of malfunction are misplaced, and possibly even dangerous', as they can only lead to a conception of '. . . the Holocaust as a unique yet fully determined product of a particular concatenation of social and psychological factors, which led to a temporary suspension of the civilizational grip in which human behaviour is normally held.' This traditional understanding, Bauman argued, offers an odd sense of comfort because the alternative is to accept that such violence is endemic, normative and constitutive of our current social organisation:

> We suspect (even if we refuse to admit it) that the Holocaust could merely have uncovered another face of the same modern society, whose other, more

> familiar, face we so admire. And that the two faces are perfectly comfortably attached to the same body. What we perhaps fear most, is that each of the two faces can no more exist without the other than can the two sides of a coin (2001, p. 7).

If we strip away that comfort and confront the Holocaust on Bauman's terms we are left with the uncomfortable idea that 'the Holocaust was not an irrational outflow of the not-yet-fully-eradicated residues of pre-modern barbarity. It was a legitimate resident in the house of modernity; indeed one who would not be at home in any other house' (2001, p. 17). The crucial point for this discussion is that the mass slaughter of living, sentient beings is not an aberration. Rather, it is woven into and a direct consequence of modernist social relations.

It is essential, albeit confronting, coming to terms with the violent not just refined face of modernity. Arendt (2006) explained how it is that violence and atrocities are normalised and routinised; how they come to be accepted by many—otherwise 'good' or compassionate—people. The strength of such a view that is an inherently sociological one is that it moves away from binary thinking of (individual) good versus evil and instead allows us to acknowledge the way violence and abuse are embedded in and often justified by social systems and their authorities. Identifying the ideological mechanisms used to uphold socially sanctioned regimes of power is important if we are to have any hope of untangling and dismantling them.

In the next section, we consider some of the recent ethnographic work done in slaughterhouses and discuss the specific ideological mechanisms that contribute to the normalisation and acceptance of the immense scale of the slaughter of animals. We start with a discussion of the use of technology for large-scale violence.

Responses

While there has been considerable multidisciplinary work focussing on the slaughterhouse, attention has tended to focussed on labour conditions, public health implications and the economics of meat processing and consumption as opposed to the animals themselves (for example, Gouveia and Juska 2002; LeDuff 2003; Young Lee 2008). In part this is because such foci reflect the interests of the AIC and/or reflect the anthropocentrism common to the vast majority of scholarship in the west. However, it is also worth noting that gaining access to slaughterhouses, their workers and their animals, is often difficult. Coupled with the fact that human–animal studies is still a relatively recent development, this might explain why there are so few empirical studies of slaughterhouses that attempt to centralise the experience of the animals.

Developing Knowledge from Ethnographies of the Slaughterhouse

Ethnography can also be used to expose slaughterhouse abuse perpetrated against animals, including acts that abide by slaughterhouse processing protocols. In other words, it is not simply a question of ensuring slaughterhouse workers do not enact unusually cruel behaviours but of questioning the legitimacy of the very nature of their work. Ethnographies can help bring to the surface some of the finer details of abuse. With other forms of publicly exposing otherwise hidden and normalised issues, including a variety methods of video-based activism, these documents can help integrate reasons with emotions for a more holistic witnessing to violence. This is important because humans can hide behind technologies, from factory farming and mass human genocide.

In *Working undercover in a Slaughterhouse*, (Soloman 2012) Timothy Pachirat explains what he hoped to learn by becoming a meat processer in a North American slaughterhouse,

> **Pachirat:** I wanted to understand how massive processes of violence become normalized in modern society, and I wanted to do so from the perspective of those who work in the slaughterhouse. My hunch was that close attention to how the work of industrialized killing is performed might illuminate not only how the realities of industrialized animal slaughter are made tolerable, but also the way distance and concealment operate in analogous social processes: war executed by volunteer armies; the subcontracting of organized terror to mercenaries; and the violence underlying the manufacturing of thousands of items and components we make contact with in our everyday lives.

Rather than ethics of use, an emphasis may also be placed on training people in the efficient use of the chosen machine, such as how to best use a gas chamber, or in the case of 'meat processing', a bolt gun, a hock cutter or a hide puller.

> **Pachirat:** Working in the chutes took me out of the sterilized environment of the cooler and forced a confrontation with the pain and fear of each individual animal as they were driven up the serpentine line into the knocking box. Working as a quality control worker forced me to master a set of technical and bureaucratic requirements even as it made me complicit in surveillance and disciplining my former coworkers on the line (Solomon 2012).

Such instrumental rationality and compliance to what become bureaucratic processes distract and overwhelm any lingering moral questions. As Pachirat notes, 'at the rate of one cow, steer, or heifer slaughtered every twelve seconds per nine-hour working day, the reality that the work of the slaughterhouse centers around *killing* evaporates into a routinized, almost hallucinatory blur' (2011, p. 138).

Hamilton and Taylor (2013, pp. 78–80), based on their ethnographic work in UK slaughterhouses, demonstrate how violence to animals in the slaughterhouse is normalised through a 'reverence for the efficiency of the machine and of the technology housed within it'. Considering how slaughterhouse workers refer to animals as 'units' and their deaths as 'processing', they argue that language and pride in technology combine to contribute to 'the ideological obfuscation of them [animals] as embodied subjects.... Language is used here to sanitise and justify their deaths' (p. 79). This reverence for efficiency and technology, seen for example in the pride taken to kill animals 'every twelve seconds' (Pachirat 2011), is part and parcel of the ways in which animal deaths in the slaughterhouse are made palatable.

Justifying Slaughterhouse Violence: The Roles of Language and Technology

Technology can be used to perpetrate but also sanitise violence. It can be used to extend the magnitude of violence, allowing humans to execute violence much more efficiently than if perpetrated manually. Because machines, devices and 'innovative methodologies' can all be used for violent purposes and ends, documenting their use is a helpful step to recognising slaughterhouse violence. For example, Roe (2010) provides an excellent and detailed analysis of the treatment of pigs, sheep and other livestock from the farm to the slaughterhouse.

As we have indicated above, knowledge from other hidden, state-sanctioned and approved violent practices can be very instructive as they can help us to see beneath taken for granted ideas and practices; beneath automated processes and persuasive ideological rationalisations. With reference to the Holocaust, Bauman (2001) points out that instrumental rationality and technology were the very linchpins that allowed violence to occur on such a large scale,

> ..... the bureaucratic culture, which prompts us to view society as an object of administration, as a collection of so many 'problems' to be solved, as 'nature' to be 'controlled', 'mastered' and 'improved' or 'remade', as a legitimate target for 'social engineering', and in general a garden to be designed and kept in the planned shape by force (the gardening posture divides vegetation into 'cultured plants' to be taken care of, and weeds to be exterminated), was the very atmosphere in which the idea of the Holocaust could be conceived, slowly yet consistently developed, and brought to its conclusion.... [this] made the holocaust-style solutions not only possible, but 'eminently reasonable'(p. 18).

Animals become things in a system that prides itself on its efficiency much as Bauman, quoting Feingold (2001, p. 8) described how Auschwitz was, '... a mundane extension of the modern factory system. Rather than producing goods, the raw material was human beings and the end-product was death, so many units per day marked up carefully on the manager's production charts'. Quoting Rubenstein's (p. 9) argument that the Holocaust 'bore witness to the *advance of civilization*', Bauman adds that:

> 'It was an advance... in a double sense. In the Final Solution, the industrial potential and technological know-how boasted by our civilization has scaled new heights in coping successfully with a task of unprecedented magnitude.... Taught to respect and admire technical efficiency and good design, we cannot but admit that, in the praise of material progress which our civilization has brought, we have sorely underestimated its true potential.'

Here, then, we have argued that technology and attendant pride in efficiency, which are taken to be hallmarks of modernity and human civilisation and superiority, work to numb the reality of slaughterhouse violence. Implicit is the use of specific language. Technologies of violence rely on language, which is itself a powerful tool in the depersonalisation and objectification of those subordinated as Others, whether they are human or animal (see Dunayer 2001).

Questioning the Language of Life and Death Used for 'livestock'

We share Jepson's (2008, p. 129) interest in the question, 'In what ways does the use of language support the assumption that humans have the right to take the lives of animals?' We also accept Nibert's (2002, p. 150) argument that, '... language is a powerful tool in rationalizing and naturalizing injustice'. Humans use language, often expressed through dominant discourses, to make them/ourselves superior to (other) animals. We define *language* as a system of communication, *discourse* as the human mobilisation of language, particularly words, and *dominant discourses* as those that are common, popular, socially acceptable, 'normal' and 'natural' prescriptions for living. For example, when applied to people, *butchery* describes macabre and grotesque acts of violence. However, animal abuse is so normative that when applied to animals, butchery is a term that manages to be emptied of violence. Butcher shop signs are proudly displayed and being a butcher is still a relatively esteemed occupation. Sleights of hand work in the slaughterhouse too. As Pachirat (2011, p. 30) outs it, 'Here there occurs both linguistic and material manufacturing: the fabrication department is a site of production, a hidden workshop floor where the linguistic leap from *steer* to *steak*, from *heifer* to *hamburger* is enacted'.

The seemingly simple act of naming a being helps to constitute individual uniqueness, whereas allocating them only a number does the opposite. Naming and individualising helps to recognise sentience and suffering. In 'Othering' animals and viewing them not as individuals but as groups (of cattle for instance) we deny them grievability. As Butler (2004) points out, to ensure that someone is considered grievable they have to, first, be seen as irreplaceable. One of the most basic linguistic manoeuvres is to turn individual animals into 'livestock' and 'cattle'. Always interchangeable 'cattle' 'sheep' and 'chicken' become nameless, faceless and indistinct from each other. This helps translate cattle into meat, if not the further de-identified 'protein'. As Piazza et al. (2015) argue, this is then further embedded culturally as seen in the 4 Ns— necessary, natural, normal, nice—that rationalise discomfort around meat consumption.

Challenging the Injunction that Humans are Meant to Eat Meat

Mainstream media plays an important role in the promulgation of shared language, which is used to constitute normality and determine the existence of violence. Commercial advertisers who use outlets such as television, radio and web programs to reach mass audiences, are usually well aware of the leverage language, in particular, engaging turns of phrase or memorable sound bites can have for how products are perceived, thus whether they are purchased and consumed. Consider for instance, the language 'meat producers' use to reach mass audiences during prime time viewing; how their language can be used to deny and erase violence perpetrated against 'livestock'. This can be done in covert ways, for instance, where cooking and consuming meat (or 'protein') is central to popular Australian cooking programs such as *Master Chef, My Kitchen Rules, Hot Plate* or the *Restaurant Revolution*.

Yet, the injunction to eat meat can also be done in explicit, if not belligerently celebratory ways, as in the many advertising campaigns for red meat, pork and lamb. In many meat advertising campaigns, the old adage 'feed the man meat' is expanded to assert that humans (women included) are *meant* to eat meat; that it is essential to good health and an important part of human interactions, from steak dinners, to spit roasts and barbeques. Well-known Australian actor Sam Neill's promotion of red meat illustrates this perfectly. Standing in front of a barbeque and being the envy of his neighbours, Sam reiterates the dominant discourse of red meat eating being 'instinctive', before chanting the slogan is, *'Red meat, we were meant to eat it'* (https://www.youtube.com/watch?v=hNWB6Vq18xc). The more recent 2014 advert by Sam Kekovich, a former Australian footballer renowned for his hypermasculinity, goes further, shouting at parents to induct their children into meat eating early, including the toddler wearing a T-shirt emblazoned, 'Vegan and Proud'. In this discourse, it is so normal to eat meat that to not do so is to be 'unAustralian' (https://www.youtube.com/watch?v=v9Xo0v63wMA). Such a position underlies the 2015 Meat and Livestock Australia (MLA) advertisement, 'You're better on Beef' with the executive creative director asserting that, 'The chance to reframe an Aussie icon like Beef as the *ultimate life fuel* is one of our proudest moments' (http://www.campaignbrief.com/2015/03/youre-better-on-beef-the-messa.html, emphasis added).

Exposing the Happy Meat Illusion

The call to eat meat as an act of patriotism, health and history denies the importance of life and discourse of death for slaughtered animals. To quote Young Lee (2008, p. 3),

> ... that the early human diet included (rotten, raw) meat does not make meat-eating 'natural'. Rather, that inheritance exposes the extent to which meat-

eating in the modern world has been narrated through ideology rather than physiology.

With meat eating so normalised, the focus slides away from the question of whether it is ethical to eat meat towards other questions about how to 'harvest' meat more humanely. Rather than consider the most obvious effects on the animals of producing meat, that is their death, attention is placed on the lead up to and method of death. Contemporary efforts to promote humane farming and processing practices do just this: use language to sanitise and naturalise their practices (Fitzgerald and Taylor 2014). As Pilgrim (2013, p. 123) in her analysis of three popular books that consider the notion of 'happy meat',[2] 'As texts calling for ethical meat consumption, the overarching fate of the animals they describe is ultimately to pass from a state of happy animal to 'happy meat'; this is central to the tracts of these authors, and the ethical meat movement overall, in that animals that are raised in more naturalized settings are therefore well cared for . . . The insistence on happy meat serves the twofold purpose of justifying the consumption of the animals' flesh, since the animal is a beneficiary of this supposed happiness, and furthermore making the animal taste better' (see also, Smith 2002).

Concluding Comments

Concluding this discussion is not easy. Traditional academic formats usually call for suggestions for further research. It is difficult for us to suggest that more research should be done into slaughterhouses because it begs the question, for what purpose? While there may be merit in discovering more about the mechanisms of slaughterhouses and their impacts on the humans who work in them or even their impacts on the communities and environment around them (for example, Fitzgerald et al. 2009), their impact on the animals who travel through them needs no such research as, in one way, their impact is simple—animals come here alive and leave dead. Calling for more research into how this is done and its effects seems superfluous and in some ways complicit in the AIC as it has the potential to stall action. Similarly, we could call here, for new methods of oversight in slaughterhouses—stricter policies and frameworks, more abilities to actually ascertain that welfare

[2] The books are Michael Pollan's *The Omnivore's Dilemma*, Susan Bourette's *Meat, a Love Story*, and Scott Gold's *The Shameless Carnivore*.

policies are being applied or even the installation of CCTV in all slaughterhouses. While all of these have their merits, they do not stop the violence done to animals in slaughterhouses. They may prevent the 'incidental' acts of cruelty that are commonly exposed in the media, but if one accepts that the taking of animal lives is abusive and violent then no measures will stop this as it is the very raison d'être of the slaughterhouse.

With that in mind, the only real call we are left with, then, at the end of this chapter is for a cessation of meat eating and the promulgation of vegan lifestyles (and by this we mean ideological outlooks, not simply dietary choice). This is no simple solution, as it necessitates a wholesale revision of how we see ourselves, other animals, the earth we live on and the relationships between all three. It requires us to move beyond anthropocentrism, beyond bastardised, neoliberal reformulations of rights that stress the individual over the communal and give rise to claims of personal freedom and choice regarding *who* we eat. As Jenkins and Twine (2014, pp. 230–231) note, assuming that 'the choices of the individual are somehow sovereign and free from much in the way of social and ecological consequence' is a corollary of our belief in our inalienable right to a freedom of choice. What this misses, however, as we have aimed to show throughout this chapter, is that 'consuming animals is a dominant cultural practice, and so it is part of the set of normalised values and ontological distinctions of the culture we are born into . . . Discourses of choice de-socialise and personalise eating practice as a means of attempting to remove them from the political.' Politicising slaughterhouses and attendant meat eating practices is a crucial first step, and one to which we hope to have contributed.

References

Adams, C., & Donovan, J. (Eds.) (1995). *Animals and women: feminist theoretical explorations*. Durham and London: Duke University Press.

AKC (n.d.). *Animal kill counter*. http://www.adaptt.org/killcounter.html. Accessed 20 November 2015.

Arendt, H. (2006). *Eichmann in Jerusalem: a report on the banality of evil*. New York: Penguin.

Australian Institute of Health and Welfare (2012). *Australia's food and nutrition 2012*, Australian Government, Canberra. http://www.aihw.gov.au/publication-detail/?id=10737422319. Accessed 13 October 2015.

Bauman, Z. (2001). *Modernity and the holocaust*. New York: Cornell University Press.

Ben-Ami, D., Boom, K., Boronyak, L., Townend, C., Ramp, D., Croft, D., et al. (2014). The welfare ethics of the commercial killing of free-ranging kangaroos: an evaluation of the benefits and costs of the industry. *Animal Welfare*, *23*(1), 1–10.

Birzer, S. (2012). *Racial profiling, they stopped me because I'm________*. Boca Raton: Taylor & Francis.

Bowen-Jones, E. (2003). Bushmeat: traditional regulation or adaptation to market forces. In S. Oldfield (Ed.), *Trade in Wildlife: Regulation for Conservation*, 132–145. London: Earthscan.

Butler, J. (2004). *Precarious life: the powers of mourning and violence*. London: Verso.

Cantor, D. (2014). Beyond humanism, toward a new animalism. In W. Tuttle (Ed.), *Circles of compassion: essays connecting issues of justice* (pp. 22–36). Danvers, MA: Vegan Publishers.

Cudworth, E. (2011). 'Most Farmers prefer Blondes': social intersectionality and species relations. In B. Charles & N. Carter (Eds.), *Humans and other animals: critical perspectives* (pp. 153–172). Basingstoke and New York: Palgrave Macmillan.

Cudworth, E. (2014). Beyond speciesism: intersectionality, critical sociology and the human domination of other animals. In N. Taylor & R. Twine (Eds.), *The rise of critical animal studies: from the margins to the centre* (pp. 19–35). London: Routledge.

Dunayer, J. (2001). *Animal equality: language and liberation*. Maryland: Ryce Publishing.

Elias, N. (2000). *The civilizing process. sociogenetic and psychogenetic investigations*. Oxford: Blackwell.

Fitzgerald, A., Kalof, L., & Dietz, T. (2009). Slaughterhouses and increased crime rates: an empirical analysis of the spillover from 'The Jungle' into the surrounding community. *Organization and Environment*, *22*(2), 1–27.

Fitzgerald, A., & Taylor, N. (2014). The cultural hegemony of meat and the animal industrial complex. In N. Taylor & R. Twine (Eds.), *The rise of critical animal studies: from the margin to the centre* (pp. 165–182). London: Routledge.

Food and Agriculture Organization of the United Nations (2002). *World agriculture: towards 2015/2030: summary report*. ftp://ftp.fao.org/docrep/fao/004/y3557e/y3557e.pdf. Accessed 12 July 2015.

Girshick, L. (2014). In the doing and the being. In W. Tuttle (Ed.), *Circles of compassion: essays connecting issues of justice* (pp. 54–62). Danvers, MA: Vegan Publishers.

Griffin, S. (1978). *Woman and nature: the roaring inside her*. New York: Harper and Row.

Gouveia, L., & Juska, A. (2002). Taming nature, taming workers: constructing the separation between meat consumption and meat production in the U.S. *Sociologia Ruralis*, *42*(4), 370–390.

Gruen, L. (1993). Dismantling oppression: an analysis of the connection between women and animals. In G. Gaard (Ed.), *Ecofeminism: women, animals, nature* (pp. 60–90). Philadelphia: Temple University Press.

Hamilton, L., & Taylor, N. (2013). *Animals at work: identity, politics and culture in work with animals*. Boston and Leiden: Brill.

Jenkins, S., & Twine, R. (2014). On the limits of food autonomy—rethinking choice and privacy. In N. Taylor & R. Twine (Eds.), *The rise of critical animal studies: from the margins to the centre* (pp. 225–240). London: Routledge.

Jepson, J. (2008). A linguistic analysis of discourse on the killing of nonhuman animals. *Society & Animals, 16*(2), 127–148.

Kimmel, M. (2013). *Angry white men, American masculinity at the end of an era*. New York: Nation Books.

Le Duff, C. (2003). At a slaughterhouse, some things never die. In C. Wolfe (Ed.), *Zoontologies*. Minneapolis: University of Minnesota Press.

McHugh, S. (2004). *Dog*. London: Reaktion Books.

Meat and Livestock Australia (MLA) (2015). 'You're better on Beef' the message behind MLA's latest marketing campaign via BMF. http://www.campaignbrief.com/2015/03/youre-better-on-beef-the-messa.html. Accessed 13 October 2015.

Murray, M. (2011). The underdog in history: serfdom, slavery and species in the creation and development of capitalism. In N. Taylor & T. Signal (Eds.), *Theorizing animals: re-thinking human animal relations* (pp. 85–106). Boston and Leiden: Brill.

Nibert, D. (2002). *Animal rights/human rights. Entanglements of oppression and liberation*. Lanham, MD: Rowman and Littlefield.

Noske, B. (1997). *Beyond boundaries: humans and animals*. New York: Black Rose Books.

Pachirat, T. (2011). *Every twelve seconds: industrialized slaughter and the politics of sight*. New Haven and London: Yale University Press.

Piazza, J., Ruby, M., Loughnan, S., Luong, M., Kulik, J., Watkins, H., et al. (2015). Rationalizing meat consumption. The 4 Ns. *Appetite, 91*, 114–128.

Pilgrim, K. (2013). 'Happy Cows,' 'Happy Beef': a critique of the rationales for ethical meat. *Environmental Humanities, 3*, 111–127.

Regan, T. (2001). *Defending animal rights*. Chicago: University of Illinois Press.

Roe, E. (2010). Ethics and the non-human: the matterings of animal sentience in the meat industry. In B Anderson & P Harrison (Eds.), *Taking place: non-representational theories and geography* (pp. 261–280)). Aldershot: Ashgate.

Ruether, R. (1975). *New heaven/New earth: sexist ideology and human liberation*. New York: Seabury.

Small, S. (2014, October 24). *Nearly 700 sharks killed in Queensland's cull program but conservationists say no evidence it works*. ABC News. http://www.abc.net.au/news/2014-10-24/nearly-700-sharks-killed-in-queensland-this-year/5839188. Accessed 21 November 2015.

Smith, M. (2002). The 'Ethical' space of the Abbatoir: on the (in)human(E) slaughter of other animals. *Human Ecology Forum, 9*(2), 49–58.
Soloman, A. (2012). Working undercover in a slaughterhouse: an interview with Timothy Pachirat. http://boingboing.net/2012/03/08/working-undercover-in-a-slaugh.html. Accessed 13 October 2015.
Torres, B. (2007). *Making a killing. The political economy of animal rights.* Oakland: AK Press.
Tuttle, W. (2014). Introduction: the circles of compassion vision. In W. Tuttle (Ed.), *Circles of compassion: essays connecting issues of justice.* Danvers, MA: Vegan Publishers.
Twine, R. (2011). Revealing the 'Animal Industrial Complex'—a concept and method for critical animal studies? *Journal for Critical Animal Studies, 10*(1), 12–39.
Vialles, N. (1994). *Animal to edible* (trans. J.A. Underwood). Cambridge: Cambridge University Press.
Wicks, D. (2011). Silence and denial in everyday life: the case of animal suffering. *Animals, 1*, 196–199.
Weitzenfeld, A., & Joy, M. (2014). An overview of anthropocentrism, humanism, and speciesism in critical animal theory. In A. Nocella, J. Sorenson, K. Socha, & A. Matsuoka (Eds.), *Defining critical animal studies: an intersectional social justice approach for liberation* (pp. 3–27). New York: Peter Lang.
Young L., P. (Ed.) (2008). *Meat, modernity and the rise of the slaughterhouse.* Durham, NH: University of New Hampshire Press.

Nik Taylor is a sociologist who has been researching human-animal relations for over 15 years, after spending years running an animal shelter. Nik has published four books and over 40 journal articles and book chapters on the human-pet bond; treatment of animals and animal welfare; links between human aggression and animal cruelty including those between domestic violence, animal abuse and child abuse; slaughterhouses; meat-eating and animal shelter work. She has written for diverse audiences including, *The Guardian*, *The Drum*, *The Conversation* as well as numerous blogs and websites. Her most recent books include *The Rise of Critical Animal Studies* (ed., with Richard Twine, Routledge, 2014), *Humans, Animals and Society* (Lantern Books, 2013) and *Animals at Work* (with Lindsay Hamilton, Brill Academic, 2013). More information can be found at https://animalsinsocietygroup.wordpress.com/

Dr Heather Fraser is a social work academic who started her career three decades ago in shelters for women, young people and children fleeing from domestic violence and/or child abuse. Feminist intersectional perspectives that include concerns about species are her theoretical orientations and care work and emotional labour are related interests. She is the author of *In the Name of Love, Women's Narratives of Love and Abuse* (Women's Press, 2008). With Nik Taylor, she is working on several human-animal projects and they are the co-convenor of the Animals in Society Working Group at Flinders University.

Part III

The Abuse of Animals in the Wild

Collecting Wildlife

Angus Nurse

Introduction

Animal abuse is often characterised as intentional cruelty and direct harm caused to live animals (Ascione 1993; Conboy-Hill 2000; Daugherty 2005; Schaffner 2011), particularly in respect of unnecessary suffering and the illegal exploitation of animals. The ecological justice and species justice perspectives of green criminology (Beirne 2007; Benton 1998; White 2008) contend that justice systems need to do more than just consider anthropocentric notions of detection, apprehension and punishment; they should also consider how effective justice systems can provide protection and redress for other species (Benton 1998; White 2008). Green criminological scholarship has, thus, already paid attention to theoretical questions of whether, how and to what extent justice systems deal with crimes against animals and has begun to conceptualise policy perspectives that can provide effective contemporary species justice alongside mainstream criminal justice. This chapter considers these issues but is primarily concerned with explanations for crimes against animals. In particular it examines collecting as animal abuse and activity encompassing both direct and indirect harm.

Animal abuse is significantly influenced by masculinities (Groombridge 1998), often involving the exercise of male power (frequently patriarchal) over

A. Nurse (✉)
Middlesex University School of Law, London, United Kingdom
e-mail: a.nurse@mdx.ac.uk

J. Maher et al. (eds.), *The Palgrave International Handbook of Animal Abuse Studies*, DOI 10.1057/978-1-137-43183-7_10

other less powerful members of a family or a community. Calvo (2008, pp. 32–33) identifies that human–animal relations are dominated by 'relations of human dominion that involve their exploitation and oppression'. Thus animal lives are largely subservient to human conceptions of animals as potential food or as exploitable resource for clothing, labour or entertainment (see the chapters on this in this volume). The cruelty inflicted on animals, whether physical or psychological, often illustrates stereotypical male behaviour such as the exercise of control through physical force, intimidation and coercion employed in other areas such as domestic abuse, spousal control or the disciplining of children (Arkow 1996; Browne 1993). Many animal crimes (such as trophy hunting and illegal taking of wildlife) also involve recognised male behaviours such as aggression, thrill-seeking or the exercise of an adventurous nature (Nurse 2011). Recklessness, thrill-seeking and assertiveness are also applicable to animal abuse activities which are sometimes committed in difficult and dangerous conditions, with a requirement to negotiate aggressive animals, and evade the attentions of law enforcement, NGOs and conservation and game management staff. Sport and trophy hunting linked to the collection of animal trophies, such as antlers, tusks and skins, is inextricably linked to power and masculinities within a deviant recreational culture. Such hunting enthusiasts are predominantly male and tend to target larger nonhuman animal males for shooting (Palazy et al. 2012; Short and Balaban 1994) thus overtly exercising masculine power over less powerful males; those animals selected for hunting purposes.

This chapter examines collecting as a form of animal abuse, examining the collection of both live and dead non-human animal specimens, and non-human animal parts and derivatives as forms of animal abuse. Some collecting activities are difficult to quantify due to their covert nature and the lack of any official monitoring. Egg collecting, for example, is an underground activity that encompasses a range of unlawful activities in the taking and possession of eggs (see Case Study 1 later in this chapter). But no formal market exists for wild birds' eggs (Nurse 2013a) and its basis in collecting for personal possession contributes to the difficulties in assessing its prevalence although Table 1 identifies recent reported levels of offending in the UK. However, activities like trophy hunting form part of a legitimised industry worth considerable sums to some African countries (Lindsey et al. 2012; Palazy et al. 2012; Baker 1997). Thus, collecting linked to sporting activity is widespread in some states and is discussed later in this chapter (see Case Study 2). Anthropocentric notions of animals as human 'property' and available primarily for human exploitation, are central to animal collecting. Unhealthy or deviant attitudes towards animals are ingrained in some aspects of Western society where masculinities and the social acceptance of male power influence the extent to which male violence and perspectives on male dominance are generally accepted as social norms. But excessive use of violence is criminalised, remaining socially unacceptable and subject to sanction. However within such societal constructs, certain males will naturally be attracted to activities which emphasise the expression of male power and male behaviours (Harland et al. 2005; Kimmel et al. 2005). Big game hunting, for example, sometimes places the hunter at personal risk and incorporates a range of stereotypical male behaviours relating to aggression, dominance and the thrill of chasing after an animal in its natural environment where nominally, at least, it should have the upper hand (Nurse 2013a). Contemporary environmental and wildlife protection legislation has criminalised activities such as egg collecting (illegal in the UK since 1954) and strictly regulates the possession of dead animals, parts and derivatives via both international legislation such as the Convention on International Trade in Endangered Species of wild fauna and flora (CITES) and domestic (national) conservation and animal protection policies. Accordingly, those wishing to continue with such activities engage in stereotypical male activities via their resistance to control.

Understanding the psychology of offenders, the socio-economic pressures that affect them and the sociological and cultural issues that impact on behaviour greatly aids understanding of what needs to be done to address criminal and deviant behaviours (Becker 1963) and the conditions that lead to animal abuse. Previous research (Nurse 2013a) identifies that animal offenders are not a homogenous group and that a range of offender types and offending behaviour exist in the area of animal harm. Thus, some animal harm offences are motivated by purely financial considerations, some by economic or employment constraints (Roberts et al. 2001, p. 27). Others are motivated by predisposition towards some elements of the activity such as collecting; or exercising power over animals or the need to control others via the threat of harm to animals (Nurse 2013a). Via case studies of egg collecting and taxidermy and trophy collection this chapter examines anthropogenic commodification of animal parts and derivates and looks both at the causes of animal collecting and the nature of collecting as animal abuse. It also examines some issues concerning the prevalence of collecting activity and societal and law enforcement responses. But in doing so, notes that collecting as animal abuse is very much on the fringes of policing animal abuse and is poorly monitored, although this chapter argues that collecting is a direct form of animal abuse given that its consequence is termination of a nonhuman animal life.

The Nature of Animal Collecting

The focus of this chapter is deliberate, intentional collecting as a form of animal abuse. Thus this chapter distinguishes between hoarders, who may well collect animals through 'good' intentions but will inadvertently commit animal abuse, and those whose intent is collection of an animal with disregard for animal life or an active intent to cause animal abuse via killing.

Hoarding and neglect are dealt with elsewhere in this volume and so are only briefly referred to in this chapter. Previous research (Nathanson 2009, p. 307; Nurse 2013a, p. 93) identifies hoarding as an extreme form of *passive* animal harm which may initially be the result of good intentions gone awry, albeit indicating the serious consequences of collecting and neglect. By contrast, *active* animal harm consists of deliberate and intentional harm caused to animals (Daugherty 2005). In the case of collecting activity, such active cruelty indicates elements of malicious intent towards nonhuman animals on the part of the offender. This activity may be an indicator of psychological factors such as a predisposition towards cruelty (Ascione 1993; Boat 1995) and may also indicate that an abuser commits other forms of abuse within the home such as spousal or child abuse (Schleuter 1999; Turner 2000). Active animal collection, of the kind typified by the compulsive egg collector or acquirer of taxidermy specimens and sport trophies, represents a different kind of behaviour from hoarding or passive neglect. Here, the end result and arguably the *intent* of collecting activity is the death of a nonhuman animal to serve the collecting need. Thus egg collectors, quite literally flush away an animal life in order to acquire their 'trophy' (discussed further below), while taxidermy and sport hunting trophy collectors employ speciesism (Beirne 2007; Sollund 2008) objectifying animals in order to suit their collecting needs and neutralise the cruelty inherent in their actions. Animal life is thus simply a barrier to their obtaining the object of their desire and abusing animals becomes a tool to facilitate their trophy acquisition. Collecting activity thus requires negating the animal abuse and harm involved as offenders take an anthropocentric view of nonhuman animals as existing only to serve human needs or desires.

Previous research (Nurse 2013a, 2011) identified a typology of wildlife offenders concluding that five main types of offender existed as follows:

A. Traditional Criminals
B. Economic Criminals
C. Masculinities Criminals
D. Hobby Criminals
E. Stress Offenders

Utilising this typology (Nurse 2013a, 2011), animal collectors predominantly fall within Model D (Hobby Offenders) and Model C (Masculinities Criminals). Collecting where there is no direct benefit or financial gain to the offender (for example, egg collecting) is primarily driven by the collecting behaviour as a hobby or personal interest. Egg collectors, for example, primarily collect wild birds eggs for personal use and gratification (see case study below). There is no concrete evidence of any market for wild birds' eggs; except where viable eggs are being taken primarily for illegal bird breeding purposes. However the theft of viable wild birds' eggs is distinct from egg collecting *per se*, where the end result is for a collector to obtain egg shells for their own private collections, similar to other acquisitive activities such as stamp collecting. Thus egg collectors and those engaged in large scale taxidermy (as collectors), but who do not operate mainly as traders or dealers in dead wildlife specimens, are involved in an activity largely situated within personal gratification discourse rather than the profit-driven activity which drives much wildlife trafficking (Schneider 2008; Wyatt 2013).

Collecting in this context can be more readily likened to a hobby or obsession, and the collection or acquisition of items is a primary motivator rather than the activity being driven by business imperatives. In the case of egg collecting, for example, offences are rarely committed by those directly employed within the countryside (Nurse 2013a). Instead, the offences are often committed by those employed (or unemployed) elsewhere and who may travel specifically to commit their offences. This element of *mens rea* on the part of the offender might account for the seriousness with which these offences are considered by NGOs and the criminal justice agencies. Collecting activities arguably attract disproportionate attention and response by, for example, continuous enforcement activity aimed at collecting activity that has limited impact in conservation terms and considerable adverse publicity for an activity that is at the lower end of animal abuse criminality (Nurse 2013a, 2013b).

Case Study 1: Egg Collecting

Egg collecting is primarily a UK (and arguably English) pursuit with some origins in schoolboy nature and natural history studies. Richards (1914, p. 4) wrote 'probably there is no natural history pursuit which has had more active and enthusiastic devotees than that which involves the collection of birds' eggs and the study of nidification in general'. The Royal Society for the Protection of Birds (RSPB) identifies that 'collectors can devote their life to the pursuit of eggs and can become obsessed with the practice. They usually take the whole clutch of eggs, and may return for a second clutch. Rare species of birds are often targeted. An egg will rot if the contents are left inside, so eggs must be 'blown'. Collectors will take eggs at every stage of incubation, although freshly laid eggs are preferred as it is easier to blow out the yolk and the white of the egg' (RSPB 2009). As this description illustrates, viable eggs must first be deprived of the yolk, usually carried out by drilling a small hole in one end and then either flushing out the contents by blowing them out through a tube, or by inserting a caustic substance into the shell which dissolves the contents yet leaves the shell intact. Eggs can then be retained for private display, often in custom-made cabinets.

Egg collecting thus represents destruction of wildlife with its associated abuse on wildlife populations and the natural lifecycle and breeding success of wild birds. Sutherland's (1973) differential association theory helps to explain the situation that occurs when potential animal abusers and wildlife offenders learn their activities from others in their community or social group (Sutherland 1973). For example, mature egg collectors in the UK argue that there is no harm in continuing an activity that they commenced legitimately as schoolboys, as typified by Richards' (1914) writings. Examination of case files and newspaper reports on egg collecting confirm that new collectors continue to be attracted to the 'hobby' and learn its ways through interaction with more established collectors (Nurse 2013a, 2011). Research has identified that communities of egg collectors exist where collecting techniques and knowledge are shared (Nurse 2013a, pp. 79–80). For example, the demonstration of climbing or egg blowing techniques, identification of bird breeding sites and discussion of display techniques all help novice collectors to learn their craft. Thus, Sutherland's (1973) differential association theory provides a partial explanation for the emergence of new egg collectors who develop an understanding and appreciation of the activity from those older and more established egg collectors who impart knowledge and experience of the activity. Hobby criminals such as egg collectors (Nurse 2013a) are obsessive and the pursuit of their hobby can cost them thousands of pounds each year. Egg collectors have been known to travel all over Europe in pursuit of eggs and some individuals involved in (illegal) taxidermy have been found in possession of species taken globally (Huffington Post 2012; National Crime Agency 2015). There is some similarity with other forms of offender who obsessively collect banned rare or expensive items such as rare books, pornography and stolen paintings (Burk 2001; Taylor and Quayle 2003, and discussed below). The desire not just to obtain items but also to catalogue and categorise them is a factor in the offending behaviour. Examination of case records and prosecution evidence as well as the author's past knowledge of casework indicates that egg collectors are exclusively male as no records could be found of any female egg collectors in the UK.[1] Hobby criminals thus typify specific male activity and while issues of masculinities should be considered in examining hobby crimes these crimes are not primarily of the distinctly masculine type identified in Model C but instead are often driven by obsessive-compulsive needs as discussed below. Recidivism is a particular issue in animal collecting offences where investigators regularly encounter the same repeat offenders and evidence exists that even those offenders who are repeatedly caught convicted and fined are not deterred (Nurse 2013a). English egg collector Colin Watson for example was caught and convicted six times; had paid fines of thousands of pounds and had his collection of eggs confiscated. Despite the fact that he was known to police and staff involved in protecting rare birds' nests he was suspected of still being involved in an egg collecting expedition when he fell to his death in May 2006 (Wainwright 2006).

Collecting as Prohibited Activity

Much animal collecting activity is prohibited by law, partially reflecting a species justice approach to protecting nonhuman animals from human persecution (Benton 1998; White 2008). Within the UK, for example, possession of wild birds' eggs is an offence of strict liability by virtue of provisions within the Wildlife and Countryside Act 1981 making it an offence merely to possess wild birds' eggs. Possessors of wild birds' eggs are obliged to show, on a balance of probabilities, that their possession is lawful;

[1] Nurse (2013a, 2011) conducted analysis of RSPB statistics, annual reports, case reports and newspaper reports on egg collecting cases.

Table 1 UK reported collecting offences by year

Offence	2008	2009	2010	2011	2012	2013
Possession of dead wild birds or taxidermy	5	15	12	13	6	7
Egg Collecting and Egg Thefts	39	65	43	33	25	14
Total	**44**	**80**	**55**	**46**	**31**	**21**

Source: RSPB Annual Reports on Wild Bird Crime

albeit the taking of wild birds' eggs has been unlawful in the UK since the introduction of the Protection of Birds Act 1954. For persons found guilty of possession offences, Magistrates have the power to impose maximum sentences of £5,000 fine and/or six month's imprisonment per egg.[2]

The prevalence of egg collecting is difficult to ascertain but in the UK relates to a small but persistent group of offenders. In 2013 (at time of writing the most recent year for which figures are available), the RSPB recorded 14 reported incidents' of egg collecting and egg thefts; a significant reduction on previous years as shown in Table 1.

This also compares with 41 reports received in 2007, and an average number of 66 reports received between 2003 and 2007. The RSPB argues that the introduction of custodial sentences by the Countryside and Rights of Way Act 2000 has had a 'positive effect in reducing egg-collecting activity in the UK' (RSPB 2009) although recidivism remains a significant issue. In England and Wales, the law also creates a strict liability offence in respect of possessing a dead wild bird or any part of a dead wild bird (Section 1(2)(a) of the Wildlife and Countryside Act 1981) and creates offences in relation to selling dead wild birds (Section 6(2)(a) of the Wildlife and Countryside Act 1981). The law also makes it an offence, under Section 1(3) of the Protection of Badgers Act 1992, for a person to possess a dead badger, or part of a dead badger, unless he can prove that the badger had not been killed in contravention of either the Protection of Badgers Act 1992, or its predecessor, the Badgers Act 1973.

While space does not permit a detailed discussion of the UK, the USA or international law concerning the possession of live or dead animals, these examples illustrate how wildlife protection law addresses some aspects of collecting activity, classifying them as undesirable and prohibited activities. Schaffner (2011, p. 189) argues that generally current law 'allows humans to use animals for a variety of purposes including breeding and confining

[2] Sentencing information correct at the time of writing.

huge numbers of animals so that we can then kill them and eat their bodies'. Thus animal protection laws do not entirely outlaw collecting activities, for example, battery farming arguably consists of 'collecting' a large number of animals for food production purposes. But within the confines of specifying prohibited activities, commensurate with animal welfare and sustainable use perspectives (Schaffner 2011; Stallworthy 2008) collecting activities are prohibited under current laws which determine such actions as deviant.

Collecting as Deviance

The acquisitional imperative typified by collecting illustrates varied aspects of deviant behaviour directed at nonhuman animals. Roberts, Cook, Jones and Lowther (2001) assessing wildlife crime in a report for the Department for Environment Food and Rural Affairs (DEFRA) acknowledged that:

> The offenders who commit wildlife crime are driven by a range of motivations, some of which are associated with the nature of the market for the products of the crimes—whether those products be the animals or plants themselves, by-products (such as shahtoosh), or events and gambling opportunities such as badger-baitings. (Roberts et al. 2001, p. 27)

Analysis of collecting activity illustrates varied notions of deviance, the idea that the individual involved in crime breaks away from the norm or ideal to act in an abnormal manner (i.e. the commission of a crime). Muncie and Fitzgerald (1994) explain that the deviant is one to whom the label of deviant is applied according to the rules of the society. Deviance is not, therefore, defined by the quality of the act the person commits but is a consequence of the application of the rules and sanctions to an offender (Becker 1963). Theoretically, then, for crime to exist there must be not just deviance but also a social reaction. In the classification of animal abuse and harm, there are many acts of deviance that will not be classified as crimes or may be classified as low level crimes not requiring official sanction. These classifications change over time and vary across cultures. Certainly egg collecting defined as wildlife crime in respect of its unlawful exploitation of animals (Nurse 2013a; Schaffner 2011; Wyatt 2013) was a popular schoolboy pursuit during much of the twentieth century but today is considered to be crime, attracting the attention of law enforcement professionals and action in the courts.

White (2007, p. 41) explains that 'when it comes to environmental harm, what actually gets criminalised by and large reflects an anthropocentric perspective on the nature of the harm in question'. The way in which environmental 'rights' are framed in law is determined by a range of strategic interests (political, cultural and even the interests of industry) and depends on which of a series of conflicting rights achieves prominence. School children are now taught the value of wildlife and an environmentalist perspective, thus egg collecting is no longer a socially condoned activity. Until recently hunting with dogs (and in particular fox hunting) was also legal in the UK, demonstrating that while it may have been the subject of deeply polarised debate between enthusiasts and opponents, what was considered to be deviant behaviour by one group of people was viewed as perfectly normal by another group. Whether or not a person is considered to be deviant can, therefore, depend on the legal and cultural conditions of a society. The social reaction to deviant behaviour also differs from group to group, and evidence exists that anthropocentric notions of animals as property to be exploited are implicit if not explicit in collecting activity. Collectors may, therefore, deny that their actions are a crime explaining them away as legitimate use of natural resources or as an 'error of judgement' but not a criminal act. Matza (1964) developed drift theory to explain how delinquents often accept a moral obligation to be bound by the law but can drift in and out of delinquency. He suggested that people live their lives fluctuating between total freedom and total restraint, drifting from one extreme of behaviour to another. While they may accept the norms of society they develop a special set of justifications for their behaviour which allows them to justify behaviour that violates social norms. These techniques of neutralisation (Eliason 2003; Sykes and Matza 1957) allow delinquents to express guilt over their illegal acts but also to rationalise between those whom they can victimise and those they cannot. This means that offenders are not immune to the demands of conformity but can find a way to rationalise when and where they should conform and when it may be acceptable to break the law. As an example, for those offenders whose activities have only recently been the subject of legislation, the legitimacy of the law itself may be questioned allowing for unlawful activities to be justified. Many fox hunting enthusiasts, for example, strongly opposed the (UK) *Hunting Bill* as being an unjust and unnecessary interference with their existing activity and so their continued hunting with dogs is seen as legitimate protest against an unjust law (The Hunting Act 2004) and is denied as being criminal. Similarly egg collectors, taxidermists and trophy hunters neutralise condemnation of their activities citing the past legitimacy of the activity and the imposition of sanctions as being the misguided preserve of urban elites.

Lemert (1951) argued that there are two types of deviance—*primary* and *secondary*. Primary deviance occurs when offenders do not recognise themselves as deviant, rationalise their behaviour or see it as part of a socially acceptable role. By contrast secondary deviance becomes a means of defence or attack against societal reaction. Lemert explained that:

> When a person begins to employ his deviant behaviour or a role based upon it as a means of defense, attack, or adjustment to the overt and covert problems created by the consequent societal reaction to him, his deviation is secondary. Objective evidence of this change will be found in the symbolic appurtenances of the new role, in clothes, speech, posture, and mannerisms, which in some cases heighten social visibility, and which in some cases serve as symbolic cues to professionalization. (Lemert 1951, p. 76)

Lemert argued that as a result of societal reactions the original causes of the deviation receded and gave way to the importance of the disapproving, degradational, and isolating reactions of society. In this way criminal careers (discussed later in this chapter) are created. Attitudes towards regulation are also an important factor in identifying the nature of wildlife offending and collecting activity. Eliason's (2001) assessment of poachers in Kentucky consisted of a mail survey to individuals cited and convicted for wildlife violations in Kentucky during 1999 with a follow-up survey to conservation officers in Kentucky during 2001. The second phase of his research consisted of in-depth interviews with offenders and conservation officers. Eliason's work identified that neutralisation techniques are often employed by those convicted of poaching offences. These techniques included; denial of responsibility, claim of entitlement, denial of the necessity of the law, defence of necessity and recreation and excitement, again reflecting the research of Sykes and Matza (1957) which identified that individuals involved in crime use these techniques both before and after engaging in illegal activity. Significant numbers of those interviewed by Eliason were aware that they were contravening regulations but considered that their breaches were minor or technical infringements and that they should not have been the subject of law enforcement attention. They often also denied the right of law enforcement officers to take action against them or contended that there were better uses of officers' time and that enforcement action should be directed towards the 'real' criminals (a rationalisation also used where collecting is viewed by its participants as being minor offending at best). In addition, some offenders argued that it was necessary for them to kill wildlife in order to feed themselves or their families, although this latter excuse is not an issue in collecting activity.

The justice system's response to egg collecting is primarily reactive, dependent on reports of egg collections in private possession or observation of egg collecting activity by field wardens and members of the public. In relation to animal abuse, the involvement of NGOs without which offenders might not be apprehended provides an additional motivation for some individuals to commit crime. For example, in a Channel Four Documentary entitled *The Egg Detectives* (1991); egg collector Colin Watson blamed the RSPB for his continued offending citing the destruction of his egg collection by the RSPB as a primary cause. A complete list of possible neutralisations employed by wildlife offenders (as with some other offenders) can be outlined as follows:

1. The denial of responsibility
2. The denial of injury
3. The condemnation of the condemners
4. The appeal to higher loyalties
5. The defence of necessity
6. The denial of the necessity of the law
7. The claim of entitlement

Different offenders may use different neutralisations and may also be subject to different motivations (Nurse 2013a). Awareness of the illegal nature of their actions leads to the justifications outlined by Sykes and Matza (1957) but the association with other offenders, the economic (and employment related) pressures to commit offences and the personal consequences for them should they fail are strong motivations to commit offences (Merton 1968). Evidence (Nurse 2013a, 2011) shows that egg collectors use the following rationalisations to explain their activities:

1. It is not harming anybody, the eggs are not fertile so why shouldn't they be collected;
2. Everybody did it when I was a boy it's ridiculous that it's considered to be criminal;
3. The NGO needs to make the problem appear to be serious to keep raising money;
4. It's not a job for the police they should be out catching real criminals;
5. We're not criminals, we're bird enthusiasts.

The techniques of denial, avoidance and attacks on the legitimacy of the enforcement agency (in the UK this means the RSPB in the USA the (state)

Department of Fish and Game or US Fish and Wildlife Service) are all present. In addition, claims for the legitimacy of *oology* as valuable scientific study have been made, by for example the Jourdain Society, an oological society that promoted the collection of eggs for scientific study (Braid 1994), highlighting the fact that the study of eggs and eggshell thinning in the 1950s highlighted the harm being caused to wildlife by pesticides such as DDT. Egg collecting has been likened to a form of kleptomania where offenders' compulsive behaviour drives them to commit crimes and experience the adventure involved in doing so. Rather like a collector of stolen paintings, some of whom pay large sums of money for stolen works, egg collectors may in part be driven by the acquisition of an item that cannot be obtained legitimately. Pleasure is also derived by the act of possession with the acquired item serving as a reminder of the adventure gained in its acquisition. Some stolen works of art, many of which are recognisable cannot be traded on the open market but are acquired for private collectors to appreciate. Burke (2001) suggested that the trade in ancient manuscripts and historic books in the UK was worth millions of pounds with criminal gangs turning to trafficking for private collectors and with thefts of works by Copernicus and Ptolemy being commissioned by private collectors. Although there is evidence of some stolen works being traded (Burke 2001), the drive to obtain items for personal use and which cannot be publicly exhibited is a primary factor of the obsessive collector. Taylor and Quayle (2003) explain that 'the emotional intensity that is part of collecting behaviour' (2003, p. 48) is a significant factor with the collector interacting with others who share his interests and often being driven to have a bigger, better and more comprehensive collection than others. The competitive drive and the obsessive need to acquire items can turn a hobby interest in certain items into a passionate desire to collect (Belk 1995; Taylor and Quayle 2003).

The obsessive nature of animal collecting offences is confirmed by egg collectors themselves. Egg collector Derek Lee confirmed this to *The Guardian* stating that many egg collectors are consumed by their habit and simply cannot stop. He explains that:

> There are quite a few who are obsessed with it. Every single spring and summer they can't wait to get out. If you put a child in a chocolate factory their eyes light up with excitement. It's like that. When spring and summer come, the eggers are on edge. They're like big kids. (Barkham 2006)

The obsessive-compulsive nature of offending is a factor, and the meticulous notes retained by collectors is, in fact, used by investigators as evidence of their offences (Barkham 2006; Wood 2008). The UK legislation also allows for charges to be laid in respect of items used to commit an offence such as cars or maps of bird breeding sites. While the obsession of offenders gives some clue to their behaviour, egg collecting is a peculiar activity that defies ready explanation. In these times of environmental awareness it seems odd that a form of crime from which the offender derives no financial benefit should continue.

Case Study 2: Taxidermy and Trophy Collection

While taxidermy and trophy hunting are arguably distinct activities; they share a common 'interest' in the collection of dead animal species and classification as hobby-related activities (Nurse 2013a, 2011). Neither taxidermy nor sport and trophy hunting are inherently unlawful, albeit they are regulated activities. Yet research indicates that illegality and corruption are endemic in the sport and trophy hunting industries and, separate from the lawful killing of small numbers of animals carried out under permit and quota systems, a wider problem of the illegal killing of protected animals and collection or harvesting of their parts for trophies or animal products exists (see for example Bever 2015 and Crowley 2015 and discussions of the recent Cecil the Lion case). Trophy hunting thus contributes to other illegal trades and has implications beyond its immediate animal harm activities. Trophy hunting in African countries also represents continued dominance by western societies over the developing world. Although African hunting is not exclusively carried out by white male hunters, this group makes up a significant proportion of hunters in part because of the socio-economic considerations that are determining factors in hunting. Kotler et al. (2008) identified that the price fixed by hunting companies is determined by market rules and that while prices need to be adjusted to meet demand, the perceived value of the trophy is a significant factor in determining price. Palazy et al. (2012) identified that human attraction to rarity is a pricing factor, thus inevitably the rarer and more challenging species are more expensive to hunt and attract hunters from more affluent backgrounds willing and able to pay a 'rarity' premium. Sport and trophy hunting inevitably attract those individuals disposed towards direct animal harm and for whom the notion of animal rights and species justice is, at best, secondary to their own interests (Nurse 2013a). The animal abuse associated with sport and trophy hunting consists of deliberately exercising power over an animal by consciously taking its life. However, sport hunting, aimed at smaller species, perhaps lays more claims to being a recreational activity than trophy hunting which is more closely associated with the hunting experience and dominion over animals and wild places. Yet, while in principle legal trophy hunting is regulated and monitored by law enforcement and conservation authorities, the large sums of money involved dictate that illegal activity is closely associated with trophy hunting which in reality is poorly regulated, subject to weak enforcement, lacklustre prosecutorial efforts and provides opportunities for corruption (Lindsey et al. 2006). Thus regulatory and legislative frameworks that govern the trophy hunting industry require improvement (Lindsey et al. 2006) and also need dedicated resources to be in place, not only aimed at ensuring that the 'legal' trophy hunting industry is effectively monitored and its regulations complied with, but that the illegal aspects of trophy hunting are properly enforced. Seemingly 'minor' breaches of sport and trophy hunting regulations indicated by illegal activities carried out as part of legal trophy hunting show a disregard for animals that leads to them being considered only in respect of their value as trophies and subjects of the hunt. The more serious illegal poaching and trophy hunting that takes place, also illustrates how illegal commercial activity firmly views animals as disposable. Thus it becomes a form of animal abuse that ignores the conservation imperatives of legal sport and trophy hunting which is intended to represent sustainable use of wildlife and ignores the species conservation imperative of preserving rare and threatened animals for future generations.

Collecting as Animal Abuse: Some Preliminary Conclusions

Debates in theology, criminology and the study of animal law concerning the rights of animals and the moral wrong of inflicting harm on other sentient beings have explored the relationship between man and non-human animals, the need for legal rights for animals and issues of animal abuse and the need for increased standards of animal welfare (see Ascione 2008; Scruton 2006; Sunstein and Nussbaum 2006 and Wise 2000). Green scholars have exposed ecological and species injustice as well as identifying areas where mainstream criminal justice will benefit from a green perspective while 'general' criminal justice techniques can be applied to green crimes. Species justice concerns mean consideration of both direct and indirect harms to nonhuman animals and the rejection of speciesist notions of justice that may contextualise some forms of animal abuse as victimless crime. Within green criminology, considerable attention has been paid to the topics of animal abuse and cruelty and the study of animal abusers (Beirne 2007; Nurse 2013a; Sollund 2012). Green criminology also provides a mechanism for rethinking the study of criminal laws, ethics, crime and criminal behaviour (Lynch and Stretesky 2003; Situ and Emmons 2000). Much animal abuse discourse is concerned with direct abuse in the form of physical cruelty caused to animals and the links between domestic animal abuse, domestic violence and more 'serious' forms of offending such as serial killing (Linzey 2009). Collecting, however, must be seen in the context of its harm or impact on animal populations and species survival but also in respect of its links to anthropocentric notions of nonhuman animals as property to be disposed of as humans see fit and whose lives are inherently worth less than human lives. Animals generally do not have legal personhood that would confer victim status (Kean 1998; Regan 2004; Wise 2000). Sollund (2008) identifies such discrepancy as speciesism, reflecting the construction of animals as 'others' and which emphasises the difference between humans and animals.

This chapter argues that various forms of collecting constitute animal abuse; reflecting both anthropocentric notions of what constitutes crime, and ideological perceptions about the value of nonhuman animal life. One important rationalisation provided by the Hobby Criminal (Nurse 2013a, 2011) is that of their offences being 'victimless' crimes and thus, their activities should not be the target of law enforcement activity. An example can be found in the case of egg collector Richard Pearson, jailed in 2008 for possessing more than 7,000 eggs (Wood 2008) whose defence solicitor argued at court that:

> It is of some significance that this defendant is not a dangerous man to the public. He is simply a working man who had an overwhelming fascination for eggs. In reality what he has been experiencing over the last months and years is an unlawful habit. (Wood 2008)

Such denial of criminality; avoidance of responsibility and attempt to minimise the severity of collecting offences as a 'habit' or 'hobby' is integral to an offender's rationalisation. While egg collecting and large-scale taxidermy possession cases are routinely prosecuted, in the UK at least, these activities have limited negative impact on species' populations. Yet in the case of rarer species such as big game, illegal trophy hunting risks impacting negatively on carefully constructed conservation plans and can risk species survival. Hobby criminals, particularly collectors, do not readily accept that their activities amount to criminal behaviour and use techniques of avoidance, denial, displacement of blame and challenges to the legitimacy of enforcers to explain away their actions. Much like those who are caught speeding by traffic enforcement cameras challenge the legitimacy of the cameras, the fines imposed or argue that cameras are simply a revenue raising device, hobby wildlife offenders dispute that their activities fall within the remit of the criminal law. In the case of the hobby wildlife offender, the fact that wildlife legislation does not fall within the remit of the criminal law and mainstream criminal justice responses is a factor that allows offenders to classify their activities as minor crime. In the case of egg collecting, for example, it is only with the introduction of the *Countryside and Rights of Way Act 2000* that offences have carried a limited option for prison sentences. However, the existence of laws prohibiting taking of wild birds' eggs for more than 50 years indicates that such activities have been socially constructed as unacceptable within contemporary morality. Undoubtedly, animal collecting both legally and morally is a form of animal abuse.

References

Arkow, P. (1996). The relationship between animal abuse and other forms of family violence. *Family Violence & Sexual Assault Bulletin, 12*(1–2), 29–34.

Ascione, F. R. (1993). Children who are cruel to animals: a review of research and implications for developmental psychopathology. *Anthrozoos, 4*, 226–227.

Baker, J. (1997). Trophy hunting as a sustainable use of wildlife resources in southern and Eastern Africa. *Journal of Sustainable Tourism, 5*, 306–321.

Barkham, P. (2006, December 11). The egg snatchers. *The Guardian*. http://www.theguardian.com/environment/2006/dec/11/g2.ruralaffairs. Accessed 10 January 2015.

Becker, H. (1963). *Outsiders: studies in sociology of deviance*. New York: Free Press of Glencoe.

Beirne, P. (2007). Animal rights, animal abuse and green criminology. In P. Beirne & N. South (Eds.), *Issues in green criminology: confronting harms against environments, humanity and other animals* Cullompton: Willan.

Beirne, P., & South, N. (eds.) (2007). *Issues in green criminology: confronting harms against environments, humanity and other animals*. Devon: Willan Publishing.

Belk, R. W. (1995). *Collecting in a consumer society*. London: Routledge.

Benton, T. (1998). Rights and justice on a shared planet: more rights or new relations? *Theoretical Criminology, 2*(2), 149–175.

Bever, L. (2015). The death of cecil the lion and the big business of big game trophy hunting. *Washington Post*. http://www.washingtonpost.com/news/morning-mix/wp/2015/07/29/how-the-death-of-cecil-the-lion-at-the-hands-of-american-walter-palmer-has-shed-light-on-the-big-business-of-big-game/. Accessed 10 January 2015.

Boat, B. (1995). The relationship between violence to children and violence to animals: an ignored link? *Journal of Interpersonal Violence, 10*(4), 229–235.

Braid, M. (1994). Egg society denies aiding nest thefts: an obscure group named after a Victorian clergyman is accused of acting as a front for illegal collectors who damage rare species. *The Independent*. http://www.independent.co.uk/news/uk/home-news/egg-society-denies-aiding-nest-thefts-an-obscure-group-named-after-a-victorian-clergyman-is-accused-1440402.html. Accessed 20 September 2015.

Browne, A. (1993). Violence against women by male partners: prevalence, outcomes, and policy implications. *American Psychologist, 48*, 1077–1087.

Burke, J. (2001, Sunday June 10). Britain leads illicit trade in rare books. *The Observer*.

Calvo, E. (2008). 'Most farmers prefer Blondes': the dynamics of anthroparchy in animals' becoming meat. *Journal for Critical Animal Studies, 6*(1), 32–45.

Conboy-Hill, S. (2000). *Animal abuse and interpersonal violence*. Lincoln: The Companion Animal Behaviour Therapy Study Group.

Cudworth, E. (2003). *Environment and society*. London: Routledge.

Daugherty, P. (2005). *Animal abusers may be warming up for more*. Los Angeles: Community Policing. http://www.lacp.org/2005-Articles-Main/LAPDsDedicatedAnimalCrueltyUnit.html. Accessed 20 January 2012.

Harland, K., Beattie, K., & McCready, S. (2005). *Young men and the squeeze of masculinity: the inaugural paper for the centre for young men's studies*. Ulster: Cenre for Young Men's Studies.

Howard, B. C. (2015). Killing of cecil the lion sparks debate over trophy hunts. *National Geographic*. http://news.nationalgeographic.com/2015/07/150728-cecil-lion-killing-trophy-hunting-conservation-animals/. Accessed 15 August 2015.

Huffington Post (2012). *Artist enrique gomez de molina sentenced to prison for wildlife smuggling*. http://www.huffingtonpost.com/2012/03/02/artist-enrique-gomez-de-molina-sentenced-wildlife_n_1316807.html. Accessed 2 February 2016.

Kean, H. (1998). *Animal rights: political and social change in Britain since 1800*. London: Reaktion Books.

Kimmell, M., Hearn, J., & Connell, R. W. (2005). *Handbook of studies on men & masculinities*. London: Sage.

Lemert, E. M. (1951). *Social pathology: systematic approaches to the study of sociopathic behaviour*. New York: McGraw-Hill.

Merton, R. K. (1968). *Social theory and social structure*. New York: Free Press.

Nathanson, N. J. (2009). Animal hoarding: slipping into the darkness of comorbid animal and self-neglect. *Journal of Elder Abuse and Neglect, 21*(4), 307–324.

National Crime Agency (2015). *Taxidermy haul seized as man arrested over illegal import*. London: NCA. http://www.nationalcrimeagency.gov.uk/news/623-taxidermy-haul-seized-as-man-arrested-over-illegal-import. Accessed 02 February 2016.

Nurse, A. (2011). Policing wildlife: perspectives on criminality in wildlife crime. *Papers from the British Criminology Conference, 11*, 38–53.
Nurse, A. (2013a). *Animal harm perspectives on why people harm and kill animals.* Farnham: Ashgate.
Nurse, A. (2013b). Privatising the green police: the role of NGOS in wildlife law enforcement. *Crime Law and Social Change, 59*(3), 305–318.
Palazy, L., Bonenfant, C., Gailard, J. M., & Courchamp, F. (2012). Rarity, trophy hunting and ungulates. *Animal Conservation, 15*, 4–11.
Palazy, L., Bonenfant, C., Gailard, J. M., & Courchamp, F. (2012). The significance of African lions for the financial viability of trophy hunting and the maintenance of wild land. *PLoS ONE, 7*(1), e29332. doi: 10.1371/journal.pone.0029332
Patronek, G. J., & Nathanson, J. N. (2009). A theoretical perspective to inform assessment and treatment strategies for animal hoarders. *Clinical Psychology Review, 29*, 274–281.
Regan, T. (2004). *The case for animal rights.* Berkeley: University of California Press.
Richards, T.W. (1914). A plea for comparative oology. *The Condor, 16*(4), 161–167.
Roberts, M, Cook, D, Jones, P., & Lowther, D. (2001). *Wildlife crime in the UK: towards a national crime unit.* Wolverhampton: Department for the Environment, Food & Rural Affairs/Centre for Applied Social Research (University of Wolverhampton).
RSPB (2009). Wild *birds and the law: egg collecting*, Sandy: RSPB. http://www.rspb.org.uk/forprofessionals/policy/wildbirdslaw/wildbirdcrime/egg_collection.aspx. Accessed 14 August 2015.
RSPCA (2010). *Prosecutions department annual report 2009.* Horsham: RSPCA.
Schaffner, J. (2011). *An introduction to animals and the law.* Basingstoke: Palgrave Macmillan.
Schleuter, S. (1999). Animal abuse and law enforcement. In F. R. Ascione & P. Arkow (Eds.), *Child abuse, domestic violence, and animal abuse: linking the circles of compassion for prevention and intervention* (pp. 316–27). West Lafayette, IN: Purdue University Press.
Schneider, J. L. (2008). Reducing the illicit trade in endangered wildlife: the market reduction approach. *Journal of Contemporary Criminal Justice, 24*(3), 274–295.
Short, R. V., & Balaban, E. (1994). *The differences between the sexes.* Cambridge: Cambridge University Press.
Sollund, R. (2008). Causes for speciesism: difference, distance and denial. In R. Sollund (Ed.), *Global harms: ecological crime and speciesism.* New York: Nova Science Publishers.
Sutherland, E. H. (1973). *On analysing crime* (edited by K. Schuessler). Chicago: University of Chicago Press (original work published 1942).
Sykes, G. M., & Matza, D. (1957). Techniques of neutralization: a theory of delinquency. *American Sociological Review, 22*, 664–673.

Taylor, M., & Quayle, E. (2003). *Child pornography an internet crime*. London: Brunner-Routledge.

The Hunting Act. 2004. *Crown Prosecution Service*. http://www.cps.gov.uk/legal/h_to_k/hunting_act/. Accessed 15 November 2016.

Turner, N. (2000). Animal abuse and the link to domestic violence. *The Police Chief, 67*, 28–30.

Wainwright, M. (2006. May 27). The day Britain's most notorious egg collector climbed his last tree: birder falls to his death from larch tree while checking out unusual nest. *The Guardian*. http://www.guardian.co.uk/uk/2006/may/27/topstories3.mainsection. Accessed 10 June 2015.

White, R. (2007). Green criminology and the pursuit of social and ecological justice. In P. Beirne & N. South (Eds.), *Issues in green criminology: confronting harms against environments, humanity and other animals*. Cullompton: Willan Publishing.

White, R. (2008). *Crimes against nature: environmental criminology and ecological justice*. Devon: Willan.

Wood, A. (2008). 'Evil' thief is jailed over haul of 7,000 bird eggs. *Yorkshire Post*. Accessed 4 June 2008.

Wyatt, T. (2013). *Wildlife trafficking: a deconstruction of the crime, the victims and the offenders*. Basingstoke: Palgrave Macmillan.

Angus Nurse is Director of Criminology and Sociology Programmes at Middlesex University School of Law where he teaches and researches criminology and law and is Programme Leader for the MA Criminology and joint Programme Leader for the MA Environmental Law and Justice. Prior to becoming an academic, Angus was Investigations Co-ordinator for the Royal Society for the Protection of Birds (RSPB) and its Legal and Data Protection Officer. He was also an Investigator for the Local Government Ombudsman for eight years. Angus has research interests in green criminology, corporate environmental criminality, critical criminal justice, animal and human rights law, and anti-social behaviour. He is particularly interested in animal law and its enforcement and the reasons why people commit environmental crimes and crimes against animals. Angus has also researched and published on the links between violence towards animals and human violence. His first book *Animal Harm: Perspectives on why People Harm and Kill Animals* was published by Ashgate in 2013; his second, *Policing Wildlife: Perspectives on the Enforcement of Wildlife Legislation*, was published by Palgrave Macmillan in 2015.

Angus is a co-editor of Palgrave Macmillan's *Palgrave Studies in Green Criminology* book series (with Rob White from the University of Tasmania and Melissa Jarrell from Texas A and M University at Corpus Christi).

International Trade in Animals and Animal Parts

Jennifer Maher and Tanya Wyatt

Introduction

Societies have always consumed wildlife, making it a part of markets and trade between people. Whereas trade of wildlife typically reflects the monetary value attached to their instrumental worth (to people), this chapter also recognises the intrinsic value of wildlife. Our exploration of the welfare of wildlife in trade is thereby underpinned by green criminology, specifically a species justice framework where wildlife have the right to live free from suffering and harm. With that in mind, our chapter not only investigates the abuse inflicted upon wildlife smuggled to fill the demand for illegal wildlife trade (IWT) but also touches upon the abuse that is inherent in the *legal* trade as well.

The language used to discuss both the legal and illegal trade in wildlife can reflect the instrumental nature of people's relationship with wildlife and where possible we try to avoid this. Consequently, we do not use some common phrases such as 'harvesting' or 'collecting' as these commodify wildlife rather than recognising them as individuals. Furthermore, we recognise the anthropomorphic nature of categories such as 'wildlife' and 'animals', however, for clarity and stylistic purposes, we use these terms.

J. Maher (✉)
Centre for Criminology, University of South Wales, Pontypridd, United Kingdom
e-mail: jenny.maher@southwales.ac.uk

T. Wyatt
Northumbria University, Newcastle, United Kingdom

J. Maher et al. (eds.), *The Palgrave International Handbook of Animal Abuse Studies*, DOI 10.1057/978-1-137-43183-7_11

In referring to wildlife as 'animals' we specifically mean 'non-human animals' in this context, because clearly humans are also animals.

Our discussion is informed by data taken from the Convention on the International Trade in Endangered Species of Wild Fauna and Flora (CITES) online trade database and also by data collected for the European Union EFFACE project[1] (Sollund and Maher 2015). The chapter begins with an overview of the prevalence of legal and illegal wildlife trade providing an insight into the regions of the world involved. This is followed by details of the abuse that is endured by the wildlife in either case. We then explore the motivations for engaging in the wildlife trade, using two criminological theories to help explain offenders' behaviour in the illegal trade. This is followed by an evaluation of current responses to the illegal wildlife trade, with a particular focus on the official UK response.

Prevalence

Due to the scale and global and complicated nature of the legal and illegal trade, accurate data is scarce and estimates are often relied upon. Some information is available in the form of which species of animals are protected and in which capacity by CITES. As of October 2013 there are 5,592 species listed in the CITES appendices—630 in Appendix I, 4,827 in Appendix II, and 135 in Appendix III (CITES 2015). The animals traded are amphibians, birds, fish, invertebrates, mammals and reptiles. The legal trade in CITES species is worth billions of dollars annually and includes millions of individual animals. It is important to note that the CITES database only records trade in protected species; many more species fall outside the CITES remit and are thus traded legally without regulation or measurement. (Thereby, these estimates do not include the billions of additional dollars generated from non-regulated animal trade, such as from non-protected fish species). The World Wildlife Fund (WWF) (n.d.) estimates a yearly total of USD 160 billion. As indicated above, a portion of this trade is live animals and plants. These fill the demand by zoos, circuses and laboratories as well as for private collections, gardens,

[1] The EFFACE project contained four case study locations—UK, Norway, Brazil, Columbia—where qualitative data was collected by means of 28 semi-structured expert interviews (UK: 11, Norway: 12 and five offenders) and five observations (UK: 4, Norway 1) and documentary analysis on 46 customs confiscation reports. Professor Ragnhild Sollund, co-researcher on the EFFACE project, compiled the data from Norway and South America.

and as companion animals. There are also derivatives or processed goods made from wildlife. This is incredibly diverse, ranging from food to medicine to clothing to decorative objects. CITES keeps track of 104 different forms in which wildlife is traded. This includes alive (animals, eggs and raw coral) and in parts such as baleen, bark, bones, carapaces, claws, feathers, flowers, fruit, gall bladders, genitalia, scales, shells, skins, skulls, tails, teeth and tusks. Additionally, there are products simply labelled as derivatives and extracts. Belts, leather products (small and large), handbags, carvings, ivory carvings and pieces, trophies, garments and rugs are some of the products that could be decorative items or souvenirs. The WWF (2002) has estimated that 25,000–30,000 primates, 2–5 million birds, 10 million reptile skins, 7–8 million cacti and 500 million tropical fish are traded each year. There is no indication that after more than a decade quantities have decreased. Also, these figures are just a snapshot of an immense legal trade.

The legal trade thereby takes place on a massive scale and is difficult to measure and track not only due to its size but also the inconsistencies in how the trade is measured. As is evident from looking through the CITES trade database, when quantities of animals (and plants) are recorded this may be by weight, volume or individuals. Practically then, it is not possible to generate one accurate measurement of the scale of the legal trade. With the IWT estimations become even more problematic due to the clandestine nature of trafficking and the victims not being able to speak out against their suffering and abuse. Due to the latter in particular, it has been argued that the dark figure of undetected and unreported IWT is particularly high (Wyatt 2013c). Furthermore, most offences go unnoticed due to problems in the enforcement of the trade, which is often identified as low-priority, with inadequate resources and sanctions (Maher and Sollund 2016). That being said, attempts are made to estimate the profits earned from this black market. Estimates, omitting illegal fishing and timber trafficking, range from between USD 10 and USD 20 billion (CAWT n.d.; Fison 2011; McMurray 2008; Wyler and Sheikh 2008).

As mentioned, part of the challenge in tracking the amount of wildlife traded both legally and illegally is that it is a vast market. This is in part because the black market involves all regions of the world. Countries may act as the source or origin of wildlife, as a point of transit or smuggling, as the final destination where the wildlife is consumed, or any combination thereof. Vietnam, for instance, is both a source of wildlife and a transit country where wildlife passes through on its way to China (Cao and Wyatt 2013). In contrast, the EU is a consumer, a transit and to a lesser degree, a source for the IWT (Sollund and Maher 2015). Whereas often the source countries are those which are 'hotspots' or 'mega diverse' in biodiversity, this is not always the case. Russia, Canada, and the US, for example, have lower levels of diversity, but still are the source of some wildlife fuelling the black market (Wyatt 2013c).

China, the USA and the EU are thought to be the largest consumers of illegal wildlife (McMurray 2008). The demand in China is for traditional medicines, whereas in the USA and the EU consumers buy a diverse range of wildlife from exotic companion animals and bird eggs to traditional medicines and bushmeat (McMurray 2008). Using the CITES online trade database, Wyatt (2013c) found that North America was responsible for 64 % of the illegal imports reported to CITES in 2012. In contrast, the region only accounted for 18 % of the illegal exports. Most illegal exports (28 % of the total) originated in Asia, but surprisingly this region only accounted for 2 % of the illegal imports reported to CITES—this clearly contradicts with the reports from NGOs and academics. Europe's illegal imports and exports were nearly the same—21 % and 20 % respectively. Oceania and the Pacific (Australia, New Zealand and the Pacific Island countries) are responsible for much smaller portions—12 % of the illegal imports and 5 % of the illegal exports. Central and South America including the Caribbean countries who are Parties to CITES only had 1 % of illegal imports and then 12 % of illegal exports. Finally, Africa illegally imported very little 1 %, but accounted for 17 % of illegal exports. To reiterate, these can only be considered estimations due to the secretive nature of the IWT and inconsistencies with measuring and recording what is traded and confiscated. It is evidence though that every region of the world is involved as both sources of and destinations for wildlife. Given these estimations, questions must be raised over the sustainability of both the legal and illegal trade? Additionally, how can the welfare of these animals be adequately monitored and protected?

Wildlife, whilst being traded legally and illegally, is often subjected to suffering and harm. The abuse that takes place occurs on two levels. As Beirne (2007) has explored, human abuse of animals happens not only on an individual basis but also on an institutionalised level. This is evident in many contexts of human–animal relations such as instances of abuse of companion animals as an example of individual level abuse and also at the institutional level with the normalised legal abuse of 'pets' in government-funded scientific experimentation (see chapters on 'Physical Abuse' and 'The use of animals in Medical Research') Both levels of abuse are evident in the legal and illegal trade as will be detailed in the next section, though it is impossible to estimate the actual extent of harm the animals experience. First though, a discussion follows on the organised nature of wildlife trafficking, which arguably enables the abuse of a greater number of animal victims than the legal trade.

IWT can be conceptualised as consisting of three basic stages—poaching/collecting/harvesting; smuggling; selling. Admittedly, in some cases, there is also a processing or manufacturing stage that takes place. Whereas the first stage has some element of opportunity to it—a person happens upon wildlife which they kill or kidnap for profit—the other stages need to be more organised to ensure success. This is fulfilled by both structured or organised criminal actors and also organised crime groups (Wyatt 2013c). The latter are drawn to IWT in increasing numbers because of a variety of factors.

Profit entices organised criminals into particular black markets. Certain wildlife markets are very profitable, and in turn, there is evidence that organised crime plays a role here. For example, organised crime is documented in the smuggling of caviar and whale meat, as well as rhino horn—all of which are highly profitable (Wyatt 2013c). Other factors which are favourable for organised crime are the scarcity or abundance of the wildlife. Endangered or rare wildlife are typically worth more, and therefore, offer more profit for organised crime groups who have the resources to access these species—the trade in rhinos exemplifies this. In contrast, other more prevalent wildlife markets, like that in fur-bearing mammals or pangolins, may be organised in the sense the trafficking is structured, but this is not necessarily facilitated by organised crime groups (Wyatt 2013c). Another factor affecting the involvement of organised crime is the location of the wildlife habitat in relation to the location of the consumer. If the two are in close proximity, the smuggling is fairly straightforward and handled by local people. In contrast, if there is a considerable distance between the two—as in the rhino in Africa and the use of the horn in Asia—smuggling is much more organised and risky. Wyatt (2013c) argues this more complicated dangerous trafficking is undertaken by organised crime groups who are experienced and sophisticated enough to be successful. Since organised crime's primary objective is profit presumably animal welfare is not taken into consideration during capture or smuggling as discussed further below. Also to ensure profit, if possible it makes sense to smuggle large quantities of wildlife to guarantee some survive to be sold. This might mean increased numbers of victimised animals. This victimisation is outlined below.

Nature

Each stage of trade potentially harms and/or injures the wildlife victim. This section will explore such harm and injury during capture, smuggling and killing. It should be noted that even farmed or captive wildlife bred for the trade face abuse and that abuse and suffering extends beyond transportation or smuggling for much wildlife. For instance, ENDCAP (2012) reports that 60 % of wildlife kept as companion animals die within one month of purchase and that 70 % of wildlife living in pet stores die within six weeks. The harms experienced are similar to those reported in the farming of domesticated animals—who are subjected to brutal practices and living conditions (Wyatt 2013a). Here, though, the exploration is of those wildlife taken from the wild and forced to endure being traded, smuggled and/or killed to be made into products for human consumption.

Capture

Those animals kidnapped alive for legal and illegal wildlife trades are captured with nets, snares, pits and leg-traps (Wyatt 2013c). Each of these methods is stressful in its own way to the animals subjected to it. In addition to the obvious mental and emotional trauma of being captured, each method also has the potential to cause physical injury. The fur trade clearly demonstrates the type of physical injury to which wildlife is subjected. For capturing fur-bearing mammals, some countries still allow the use of steel-jawed leg-traps (Wyatt 2014). As Harrop (2000) has noted, these traps can cause fractures, tissue damage, amputations, lacerations and dislocations of all of the limbs as well as the skull. Clearly, all these injuries cause significant pain and suffering. None of these methods for capturing animals alive is short-term in that the animal is trapped for indeterminate amounts of time until the poacher returns to check the net, snare, pit or trap. Whereas in the EU, this is supposed to be no longer than five minutes (Harrop 2000) (arguably still a long time), in other countries where fur-bearing mammals are captured, such as Russia and China, there is no such animal welfare legislation. This clearly causes further suffering and the potential for injury as animals attempt to free themselves. Wildlife have been known to self-mutilate and become unresponsive due to the injury caused by leg-traps (Harrop 2000). Additionally, the wildlife has no access to food or water and may be exposed to severe weather conditions while confined to the trap. For some species captured alive, such as great apes, there is additional injury and death to the other individuals who are not being captured. For instance, adult great apes are killed when poachers come to kidnap the babies (Great Ape Survival Project [GRASP] 2012). Experts estimate that for every live great ape taken one to 15 others have been murdered (Nellemann et al. 2010; Nijman 2009). Once wildlife are kidnapped, they must endure being used to produce a product, being smuggled to a market or other place to be sold or killed.

In terms of being used to create products, one of the clearest examples of animal abuse is the farming of bears for bile. To collect bile, the bears on these farms are kept alive. They live in small cages just big enough for them to stand up. Metal shunts puncture their skin and are inserted directly into their gallbladders. The bile is then collected by dripping down the shunt into pans (World Society for the Protection of Animals [WSPA] n.d.). The live, unanaesthetised bear then lives with an open wound being 'milked' for its gall. Another example of animal abuse inflicted to obtain a single product is the act of shark finning. Fishing vessels catch sharks, only to chop off their fins. The sharks, still alive, are then thrown back into the ocean where they slowly die a painful death (Humane Society International 2013). Both of these examples demonstrate that the abuse occurring in legal and illegal wildlife trade is at the individual level—a single bear or shark enduring injury—and at an institutional level—entire species are subjected to commercialisation and industrial- scale consumption with little or no regard for welfare. At the next stage of the trade or trafficking journey, a significant portion of wildlife that makes up the legal and the black market are kept alive during transportation or smuggling and this has its own welfare implications.

Transportation and/or Smuggling

Transportation of live animals, be it legally or illegally, is unavoidably stressful and most likely emotionally and physically traumatic for the wildlife. Arguably, to avoid detection, smugglers need to employ covert transportation, which increases the likelihood that the animals experience suffering and/or injury (Wyatt 2013c). There are instances where illegal wildlife are trafficked 'openly'—laundered—with permits and documentation used in the legal trade. Yet even when wildlife is laundered or legal, there are potential harms endured during transportation. For example, legal shipments of reptiles and other live animals are packed into containers to be flown around the world. These containers may be unsuitable—either too small and cramped or overcrowded with too many individuals in any one container (Wyatt 2013b). Even though CITES parties must enforce the International Air Transport Association [IATA] (2004) Live Animal Regulations [LAR] which are applied to animals in air transit, requiring a minimum standard of space and welfare conditions and involving a maximum period in transit—as established through scientific research—not all legal shipments meet this standard (Wyatt 2013b). Flights and boat journeys may take many hours or several days. During these long journeys, animals may be kept outside or in areas where they are subjected to extreme fluctuations in temperatures. Often they are not able to eat or drink, and the spaces they are in are very dark and filled with loud noise (Wyatt 2013b). To reiterate, these are minimum welfare standards when the trade is legal—so stress and potential suffering will always be a factor in the wildlife trade.

In the IWT, where there are no protective measures, it is likely the conditions are much worse, particularly when live animals must be kept hidden. The wildlife must somehow be made to be calm, which most likely involves tranquilising drugs or physical methods to subdue them. In the case of endangered birds such as raptors, this may mean sewing their eyelids shut and being tightly swaddled, so they can fit in tubes or other containers to hide them (Wyatt 2011). Wildlife are then carried on people's bodies or in suitcases to be smuggled across borders. The survival rate for raptors smuggled in this way is very low—it is estimated only around 10 % survive the journey (Lyapustin 2006). This is also true of reptiles and mammals, who are subjected to similar circumstances while being smuggled (Maher and Sollund 2016). Landais (2008) estimates 10 great apes have died enroute to Egypt for every one of the great apes in captivity. Smuggling is thus particularly harmful to great apes (GRASP 2012), but causes significant suffering and loss of life to all wildlife targeted by this black market. Many of these live animals are fuelling the legal demand for pets, entertainment at zoos and circuses and for scientific experimentation. Some wildlife captured alive will be killed to make legal and illegal wildlife products and the methods used for killing are also abusive.

Killing

Animals can be killed in straightforward ways with the use of weapons like guns and bows and arrows. This may be the case when hunting rhino, elephants or game animals. Animals that are captured with traps and so forth, as mentioned above, may be killed in other ways like bludgeoning or having their throats slit. Fur-bearing mammals and wildlife consumed as bushmeat are often killed in these ways. Consumption of some wildlife products entails even more suffering whilst the wildlife is being killed. For instance, pangolins, which are in high demand as an exotic meat and as an ingredient in traditional medicines, are boiled alive when made into soup (Pantel and Anak 2010). In another example, not all rhinos are simply shot and killed and then their horn removed; some are tranquilised with their horns sewn off while they are still alive. These rhinos later die from blood loss or shock (Milliken and Shaw 2012). Again, there are both individual and institutional degrees of abuse in the methods of killing. Obviously, individuals suffer from being shot, bludgeoned, stabbed, cooked or mutilated, but equally important is the systematic use of these methods to routinely inflict injury and death in order to sate human demand for consumption. There is little consideration for using the most humane methods possible, which arguably should be the case if humans insist on using wildlife. Why the abuse happens is explored in the next section.

Explanations

No single theory can effectively explain the variety and extent of animal abuse evidenced in the legal and IWT. While it is likely that active, intentional and malicious abuse occurs in both (for example, when an animal is specifically injured to satisfy anger or frustration), this is not commonly identified or discussed in the wildlife trade literature, and so will not be discussed here. Rather, given the scale of the wildlife trade and the norms associated with the capture, consumption and use of wildlife, this section focuses on explaining the commonplace abuses inflicted on wildlife as a consequence of trade, as discussed above. Specifically, two notable criminolgical theories are utilised—Rational Choice Theory and Techniques of Neutralisation—to help explain how broader societal factors influence offenders to engage in IWT. These theories are often used to explain criminal behaviour, but they can also help to understand why people also engage in the abuses common to the legal trade. As noted earlier, there is a fine line between legal and illegal harm in the trade; the behaviour and motivations are often the same, only the context changes as a result of limitations placed on the offender. A useful starting point is to consider the people who engage in IWT and why.

IWT Offenders and Motivations for Offending

There is no recognised profile of the IWT offender. A diverse assortment of actors are motivated to offend: from deprived women and men who hunt, capture and kill native wildlife, to corrupt officials taking bribes to turn a blind eye, to organised crime groups who kill, capture, purchase and distribute wildlife to order, to collectors or consumers of wildlife products in the general public (Hubschle 2014). Consumer demand is recognised as the most significant driver of IWT, and financial gain is therefore the most common motivation for offending. Nonetheless, motivating factors are many and complicated; they extend beyond profit to cultural practices (religion or traditions), status, entertainment and fashion (see Cowdrey 2002). Increasingly animals are captured, killed and forced to endure many kinds of abuses motivated by fascination with the latest pet trend or fashion or health craze. The motivations of traders, hunters and consumers can differ significantly. Organised crime groups may be motivated by financial gain, political ideologies or instability. Native hunters may be motivated by status or poverty. Consumers are motivated by desire rather than need wildlife trade mainly involves luxury goods.

Theoretical Explanations for Abuses in the IWT

As noted earlier, the wildlife trade considerably impacts the animal victims. Whether this trade is legal or illegal matters not to the wildlife; harms result from both because these animals are individuals who have intrinsic value and interest in living unharmed (see Regan's (1983) 'subjects-of-a-life'). Thus, the harms approach taken in green criminology (South et al. 2013) is a helpful place to begin explaining abuses in the trade. The idea of species justice (Beirne and South 2007; White 2013) is particularly useful, both in highlighting the difficulty in explaining harm in the trade and also for understanding why offenders are motivated to harm. Human interests, being anthropocentric and speciesist (Beirne 1999), usually override those of non-human species, creating prejudice leading to the exploitation and harm of wildlife in ways that are often deemed legal. Essentially, as long as wildlife are identified as 'property', 'commodity', 'product' or 'natural resource', their needs and interests are ignored, and they will experience abuse. Within the illegal trade, this is exacerbated as consideration for the animal's welfare is unlikely to benefit the offender. Sadly, offenders are less likely to percieve individual animals to be victims of illegal abuse if those animals can be harmed by legal means; their actions are more easily justified and rationalised. Sustained by human interests manifest in capitalism and consumerism, (White 2013) arguably, both economics and speciesism must be central to any explanation of abuse.

Rational Choice Theory

As the IWT is regarded to be the third largest black market in the world, explanations often focus on rational choice and opportunity theories. Rational choice theory (Cornish and Clarke 1986) has been used repeatedly to explain how and why offenders chose certain species and processes to engage in IWT (Pettrossian and Clarke 2014; Pires and Clarke 2011, 2012). This research persuasively argues that acceleration in the collection and killing of wildife is mainly explained by market forces. Put simply, substantial economic gain is increasingly likely as more wildlife is labelled 'endangered' and 'scarce', leading to intensified demand, higher prices and thereby a stronger motivation to offend. The resale value of rhino horn, for example, is estimated at around €40,000/kilo (comparatively gold is approximately €31,000/kilo), while tiger bones sell for up to €900/kilo and raw ivory prices can reach €620/kilo (European Commission [EC] 2014, p. 2). Where individual wildlife does not command such large financial sums—Regueira and Bernard (2012), for example, have recorded the sale of song birds for as little as $1 in South American markets—animals are traded in their millions to ensure profit. Although most of these live animals may die enroute, this is deemed acceptable collateral damage. Self-interested rational offenders are only concerned with the instrumental value of wildlife—any harms or abuses inflicted on animals happen as an indirect consequence of trade activities—a simple cost benefit analysis.

The 'rational' choice to engage in legal or illegal trade can be influenced by a combination of push and pull factors which help inform decision making. IWT is frequently linked to the socio-economic and political characteristics of countries and regions, typically facilitated in countries characterised by poverty, economic development, new trade borders, governance challenges, organised crime, violent conflicts and corruption (De Greef and Raemaekers 2014; Lemieux and Clarke 2009; Nellemann et al. 2014). In countries, such as Brazil, with high biodiversity and social inequality, poachers and smugglers without legitimate means to achieve their financial goals, use the IWT to subsidise their earnings. Frequently, there are few obstacles in the path of would-be offenders as these countries are also often characterised by their remoteness and poorly managed and monitored trade systems, challenges that are exacerbated by bureaucracy, corruption (Sollund and Maher 2015; Wyatt 2014), conflict (Lemieux and Clarke 2009) and, more recently, organised crime groups. Rapid economic and population growth can also provide the perfect conditions in which IWT can flourish.

Seidensticker's (2010) study in 13 Asian tiger range countries found human population growth (which doubled over 40 years) alongside significant economic growth influenced tiger population decline and increased all types of IWT offenders—poachers, smugglers and consumers. Consumers, increasingly encouraged to own wildlife as status symbols, health remedies and more, could look to a ready and accessible IWT market. Offenders, willing to meet this demand, were substantially rewarded for tapping into the IWT market in order to meet the needs of these new, wealthy consumers. While economic motivations clearly influence the rational choice offender, this is only one of a number of factors which can explain the abuse, as discussed next.

Techniques of Neutralisation

In their study on poaching (not specifically for the IWT), Von Essen et al. (2014) suggest offenders are motivated by a combination of livelihood (for example, economic factors), folk (for example, custom and continuity) and social (for example, political stance on regulation) factors. They suggest neutralisation theory (Sykes and Matza 1957) is potentially the most holistic explanation when looking beyond economically motivated factors in understanding the abuse of wildlife. Neutralisation theory suggests five ways in which offenders defend their behaviour and thereby minimise the impact and consequences of their actions (Sykes and Matza 1957)—denial of the victim, denial of injury, denial of responsibility, condemnation of the condemners and appeal to higher loyalties—each of which is evident in the legal and IWT.

Animals are seldom given victim status due to their inferior status in society (Beirne 2009), furthermore, by focusing on 'species', the individual animal victim is seldom recognised. The status conferred to wildlife (most commonly as commodities, pests, products and objects of beauty/wonder) is anthropocentric, fluid and often conflicting. For example, according to CITES, elephants are an iconic species deserving of the greatest protection, yet to indigenous farmers elephants are pests which require elimination (Fernando et al. 2008). Even as protected species, their status is largely linked to their commodified use as ivory. Sollund (2012) argues the denial of injury to wildlife in the illegal trade is possible due to the accepted systematic abuse in the legal trade, which is perceived to be *necessary suffering*. Consequently, denial of responsibility for the harm caused by the trade is also facilitated by the perception that *some* suffering is acceptable and thereby outside the offender's control. This, in turn, helps offenders in the IWT to condemn the condemners—it is not their behaviour (others can, after all, engage in these acts legally), but the unreasonable rules and legislators at fault. Von Essen et al. (2014) recognise poachers' offences as a form of social defiance in reaction to disillusionment and distrust of authority, legislation and processes. Finally, in terms of appealing to higher loyalties, Sollund (2012) suggests offenders legitimise their actions by claiming the use of animals serves a higher need. For example, the need to cure serious human illnesses is central to the demand in traditional medicine; as evidenced by exponential growth in demand for rhino horn linked to uncorroborated claims that rhino horn medicine cured cancer (UNODC 2013). Accordingly, the commonplace harms inflicted on wildlife are an indirect consequence of trade activities, as offenders use techniques of neutralisation to routinely permit or ignore this abuse.

Responses to the IWT

Responses to the wildlife trade, while diverse, broadly fall into official (political mobilisation, legislation, enforcement and prosecution) and unofficial responses (non-governmental prevention and intervention), both are discussed below with a particular focus on UK data from the EFFACE project. The official response to abuse in the wildlife trade primarily focuses on regulating the trade, while the unofficial response engages with both regulation and animal welfare. What follows is a brief description of the official and unofficial responses to the wildlife trade. In so doing, we detail the nature of these responses and consider how effective they are in preventing harm to wildlife.

The Official Response

Maher and Sollund's (2016) evaluation of the UK and Norwegian responses to the IWT supports existing literature in identifying shortfalls in the regulation of the wildlife trade. Fundamentally, animal welfare does not underpin the official response, resulting in inadequate prevention of harm to wildlife. Their research found that legislation, policy and the enforcement, prosecution and sentencing of offences not only fails to adequately consider animal welfare but also causes further harm through, for example, the euthanasia of healthy animals. This is not to say animal welfare has not influenced these responses but, crucially, that it is seldom the central focus. In practical terms, these responses aim to reduce IWT offences and protect species rather than individual wildlife victims. Consequently, enforcement agencies are commonly 'fire-fighting'; responding after significant harms occur, many of which will be irreversible.

Political Mobilisation and Support

The 1975 CITES convention, a flagship international wildlife agreement, united governments worldwide in regulating the wildlife trade and protecting threatened species. Subsequently, however, limited political mobilisation has impeded their response (impacting negatively on legislation, enforcement, prosecution, sentencing and societies response). It is only in recent years, with growing concerns over biodiversity loss and the widespread consequences of the trade, that political mobilisation involving global and international entities and consortiums, national governments and civil society (for example, Bangkok 16 CITES and London IWT Conference), through international declarations, resolutions and operations, has renewed political momentum and enhanced policy responses. The scale and nature of problems associated with the IWT are now widely recognised, however, the focus remains anthropocentric, regarding the harms—such as the loss of iconic species—as affecting humans, rather than the individual animals. Political support for protecting wildlife is thus limited until this focus expands to include the environmental costs to ecosystems and the animals themselves (Maher and Sollund 2016).

Legislation

The CITES convention requires the 180 Member State parties to monitor and regulate the wildlife trade through dedicated domestic legislation based on the three aforementioned lists—Appendix I, II and III—which respectively ban, regulate and monitor trade. However, member states do not share common domestic IWT legislation, creating opportunities for fractures and loopholes which impact upon the effectiveness of CITES. The UK, for example, under the EU Council Regulations (338/97), provides a more robust national implementation of CITES through the Control of Trade in Endangered Species [COTES] (1997). The CITES appendices are expanded to include additional banned, regulated and monitored species, divided among four Annexes (A, B, C, D) (EC 2010). However, this approach is not shared with most EU member states. Disparities in the enforcement and sanctioning levels among member states weaken the responses of all member states. In recognition of the problems in the enforcement of CITES, the EU has recently become party to CITES and is currently developing an EU IWT Action Plan.

There are many limitations documented in terms of how effectively CITES regulates the wildlife trade and deters IWT. Reeve (2002) suggests CITES has been compromised by (a) being a self-policed system with no global enforcement agency to oversee compliance, (b) the dissolution of borders making the permit system irrelevant, and (c) chronic underfunding. Additionally, both Yury Fedotov, the Director of the UNODC, and John E. Scanlon, Secretary General of CITES, noted deficiencies in the official response to organised offences, particularly with regard to legislation, law enforcement, prosecution and punishment, criminal analysis and international cooperation (CITES 2013).

As the chief aim of CITES and related national legislation is to protect the economic sustainability of the wildlife trade, trade is banned in only a few critically endangered species, and the majority of wildlife are neither listed nor protected (Sollund 2011). Non-CITES animals are an even lower priority and thus even more vulnerable (Regueira and Bernard 2012) with only minimal protection through generic animal welfare laws and transport requirements. No specific legislation exists to provide international protection for the welfare of animals in the trade. As it stands, legislative protection for wildlife from abuse is deficient. To send a clear message to poachers, traders and consumers legislative changes are essential. Both the wildlife trade and the related harms could be reduced through legislation which exerts pressure on source countries to prevent, capture and remove the trade in illegal products from local marketplaces, and on demand countries to develop a clear message and response to reducing demand (Wyatt 2014).

Enforcement

Through monitoring only certain species and regulating, rather than banning, the wildlife trade, loopholes arise, creating opportunities for fraud and corruption. Warchol et al. (2003), among others (Hubschle 2014; UNODC 2012; Wyatt 2009), have identified forgery, fraud and corruption in the enforcement of CITES. Consequently, CITES (and related legislation) is not easy to enforce. In the UK, for example, it requires the cooperation and coordination of numerous government agencies, non-ministerial departments, criminal justice agencies, government advisory groups and multi-agency groups (Maher and Sollund 2016). Prioritising the IWT as a serious and organised crime in the UK coincided with the development of specialised enforcement units, training for non-specialist enforcers, a commitment to the collection of intelligence and intelligence-led enforcement, and the development of partnership work with other enforcement agencies and key stakeholders. Transnational enforcement displaying effective co-operation, communication and data-sharing (for example, EU-TWIX—an online forum and database) has also resulted in successful operations targeting organised crime groups, (for example, Operation Charm) and has, albeit rarely, facilitated the return of endangered wildlife to their native habitat (Border Force 2014).

Animal welfare must also be considered during enforcement. CITES requires Member States to provide for the welfare of seized and confiscated wildlife (for example, the UK Heathrow Animal Reception Centre [HARC]), and includes the IATA LAR, as discussed above, as part of its compliance expectation. In the UK, these regulations can simplify prosecution in IWT abuse cases as 'suffering' need not be 'proved' (as is required by the UK Animal Welfare Act 2006). Nonetheless, even with these conditions in place, as previously discussed, animals will suffer harm in transit/trade. The protection provided for wildlife through LAR, is limited by EU Regulations that employ old standards (2004)—although the new Memorandum of Understanding signed between CITES and IATA June 8, 2015, may go some way to rectify this (IATA 2015). Additionally, CITES (and related legislation) fails to adequately consider the welfare of seized/confiscated wildlife by not stipulating rehoming requirements. Few individuals are returned to the wild—most, thereby, require costly long-term care and rehoming. Consequently, countries like Norway, which have limited funding and capacity for caring for or rehoming these animals, resort to euthanasia (Maher and Sollund 2016). In other cases (UK), wildlife may also be returned to the offending owners or rehomed to unregulated collectors. It is impossible to determine how prevalent these practices are as CITES does not require Member States to publicly record outcomes.

Given the difficulty in enforcing CITES and protecting animal's welfare in the wildlife trade, there have been calls to ban the trade in many species (and their derivatives). Although consideration has previously been given by the EC to ban the ownership and trade of reptiles, Norway (alongside Iceland) is unique in enforcing such a ban. Maher and Sollund (2016) suggest this makes the enforcement of CITES for reptile species in Norway more effective. The ban is also likely to eliminate many of the harms reptiles would expect to suffer as part of the legal trade. However, caution is required as bans are not necessarily effective in all locations and circumstances (see Lemieux and Clarke's (2009) evaluation of the 1989 CITES ban on ivory) and may have unexpected and unacceptable consequences (Rivalan et al. 2007). Bans may inflate the value, and thereby the incentive to kill, certain species (Low 2003, in Sollund 2011, p. 445) and increase the domestic trade of these species (Guzman et al. 2007; Lemieux and Clark 2009; Moyle 2003).

Prosecution and Punishment

Effective detection and enforcement deters would-be offenders and benefits animal victims by reducing harm and removing them from the trade. However, these efforts are diminished by failures to prosecute or punish offenders. Sollund and Maher (2015) argue IWT offenders are unlikely to be deterred as few offences are prosecuted and, if prosecuted, offenders commonly only receive fines and are seldom punished to the law's full extent. Notably, UK penalties are significantly lower for killing or injuring wildlife (AWA 2006—a fine and/or six months custody) than for incorrectly trading or paying duty on wildlife (CEMA—seven years custody and/or an unlimited fine), raising further concerns about sentencing policy and practice and emphasising the limited consideration for animal welfare (see also UK Environmental Audit Committee 2012).

The Unofficial Response

NGOs are central to the official and unofficial response, particularly with regard to prioritising the interests of the animal victims. In the UK, NGOs provide financial support to enforcement agencies, scientific and welfare evidence and advice to government agencies, and facilitate public and political education and awareness (see TRAFFIC, WWF, World Animal Protection [WAP]). More importantly, perhaps, NGOs have provided prevention and intervention strategies aimed to help animal victims. In doing so, NGOs prevent the removal of animals from the wild and, where possible, facilitate their return. Technology has altered the nature of the IWT trade, removing barriers, facilitating communication and trade between offenders and increasing opportunities for harm. In response, NGOs have embraced the internet and new technology and scientific advancements to prevent and monitor (IFAW 2008) the wildlife trade, protecting both animal and human victims. UNEP (2014, p. 2) confirmed the benefits of technology—such as 'acoustic traps, mobile technology, UAVs, radio frequency identification tags, encrypted data digital networks, camera traps, DNA testing, radio collars, metal scanners, and satellite imagery'—for rangers in source countries. Protection is enhanced through increasing the effort needed to target the animal victims and their habitat and enabling surveillance across larger areas with fewer resources. Importantly, this approach may prevent, rather than just respond to, the harm. Prosecutions are also enabled through the evidence gathered. According to Sonricker et al. (2012), for example, the development of the HealthMap Wildlife Trade website, a digital surveillance system, is the most comprehensive and freely accessible monitoring tool available to support enforcement agencies. The website augments traditional approaches by combining both official and unofficial (for example, social networks) data generated by an automated web-crawling surveillance system. NGOs also work in source countries (WAP), offering alternative livelihoods to indigenous people to reduce the need to poach wildlife and to strengthen their participation in the conservation of animals (see also REDD in Brazil). Of the responses taken to IWT, this is the most likely to reduce abuse and directly impact the lives of animals.

The remit of NGOs varies considerably with regard to the prevention of abuse; while some organisations call for an end to all abuse (animal rights perspective), others aim to improve animal welfare or conservation of specific species and their environment. Most commonly, responses aim to improve welfare and conservation—their focus is therefore on preventing 'unnecessary suffering' (see arguments against this approach in Beirne 2009). Consequently, there is little protection for individual trafficked victims. There are also concerns over the effectiveness of conservation programmes. Seidensticker (2010) argues that ongoing habitat destruction and poaching may simply make tiger conservation unsustainable. The problem is more complex than simply providing funding for conservation. Rather a multifaceted and multiagency response is required that is internationally focused on suppressing demand by changing anthropocentric attitudes towards the consumption of wildlife. Furthermore, some strategies unhelpfully substitute the killing or harm of one animal for another. For example, trophy hunting—highlighted in the controversial killing of 'Cecil the Lion' (Guardian 2015)—has been used extensively as a management tool to protect wildlife in South Africa (Department of

Justice 2015). Likewise, the farming of captive-bred tigers and bears, as discussed above, is practiced as a contentious alternative to killing wild populations (IFAW 2006).

Conclusion

Clearly, IWT threatens the survival of some species. Yet, perhaps more significantly, in terms of the focus of this chapter, the wildlife 'utilised' in both the legal and illegal trade are forced to endure individual and institutionalised abuse. Though estimates of scale have been provided here, these must be considered with caution as they are highly imprecise and difficult to measure, as Regueira and Bernard (2012) note. We do know that the IWT happens essentially everywhere and that it costs numerous animals their lives: for each wild animal traded alive, 3 (Redford 1992) to 10 (RENCTAS 2001) others may have died. Illegal trade conditions are frequently degrading: animals are caged in overcrowded compartments, without water and food, and suffer stress, fights, mutilations and death (RENCTAS 2001) or a significant reduction in life expectancy (Vanstreels et al. 2010). The interconnected nature of this damage makes this a transnational crime in that it harms more than the individuals directly in contact with it. For example, the removal of such a high number of individuals from their habitat can lead to species extinctions and compromise several ecological services (for example, pollination, seed dispersal, and control of populations of other animals) (Regueira and Bernard 2012). The routine abuse, suffering and death all provide profound evidence of the victimisation of animals within the legal and illegal wildlife trade. Wyatt (2013c) argues there is not a single case of wildlife trade where an animal has not suffered in some fashion. Being captured, smuggled, possibly dying, or living a life in pain and/or confinement (even possibly after being 'rescued' from the trade) are all forms of animal abuse.

As with other types of animal abuse, offenders in the IWT vary considerably in terms of demographics and background, and there is no simple or definitive answer as to what motivates them (Wyatt 2013c). Offender types and motivations are rarely discrete; typically, they overlap and are influenced by both macro and micro factors. Rational choice theory highlights that IWT offenders motivated to secure significant financial reward can do so with little cost, risk or concern for welfare. However, it is also crucial to understand the broader social norms (Von Essen et al. 2014), facilitated by speciesism and anthropocentric interests, which allow individuals to ignore or reject the harms evident in the wildlife trade. The techniques of neutralisation evident among actors in both the legal and illegal trade reflect the complexity of offender motivations and the multiplicity of factors influencing these.

Despite growing concerns and seemingly positive international political will, particularly from consumer nations who often lead the political charge, the wildlife trade continues to grow. Arguably, any attempt to reduce the illegal trade and the associated suffering is compromised by a booming, culturally legitimised trade, which involves wide-scale abuse of wildlife. The current response is limited, partly due to existing loopholes in regulations and limitations in the political, enforcement and judicial response, but also, and perhaps more importantly, it is our inability to reduce demand and move beyond catching offenders to preventing the killing/capture in the first place. What is urgently needed is a long-term strategy which might evoke a sea change in attitudes towards the use and abuse of wildlife.

References

Beirne, P. (1999). For a nonspeciesiest criminology. Animal abuse as an object of study. *Criminology An interdisciplinary Journal, 37*(1), 117–149.

Beirne, P. (2007). Animal rights, animal abuse and green criminology. In P. Beirne & N. South (Eds.), *Issues in green criminology: confronting harms against the environment, humanity and other animals* (pp. 55–86). Cullompton: Willan Publishing.

Beirne, P. (2009). *Confronting animal abuse: law, criminology, and human-animal relationships*. Maryland: Rowman & Littlefield Publishers.

Beirne, P., & South, N. (Eds.). (2007). *Issues in green criminology: confronting harms against environments, humanity and other animals*. Devon: Willan Publishing.

Border Force. (2014). *Smuggled iguanas returned home by border force*. https://www.gov.uk/government/news/smuggled-iguanas-returned-home-by-border-force. Accessed 12 August 2015.

Cao, A., & Wyatt, T. (2013). The illegal wildlife trade in Vietnam. *Asian Journal of Criminology, 8*(2), 129–142.

Coalition Against Wildlife Trafficking [CAWT] (n.d.). *Illegal wildlife trade*. http://www.cawtglobal.org/wildlife-crime/. Accessed 6 July 2012.

Convention on the International Trade in Endangered Species of Wild Fauna and Flora [CITES] (2015). *The CITES species*. http://cites.org/eng/disc/species.php. Accessed 28 April 2015.

CITES Secretariat (2013). *Heads of UNODC and CITES urge wildlife and forest offences to be treated as serious transnational organised crimes*. http://www.cites.org/eng/news/pr/2013/20130423_CCPCJ.php. Accessed 14 October 2014.

Cornish, D. B., & Clarke, R. V. (Eds.) (1986). *The reasoning criminal: Rational choice perspectives on offending*. New York: Springer-Verlag.

Cowdrey, D. (2002). *Switching channels: wildlife trade routes into Europe and the UK. A WWF/TRAFFIC Report December 2002*. http://www.wwf.org.uk/filelibrary/pdf/switchingchannels.pdf. Accessed 14 October 2014).

Department of Justice (2015). *Owners of safari company indicted for illegal rhino hunts*. http://www.justice.gov/opa/pr/owners-safari-company-indicted-illegal-rhino-hunts. Accessed 12 August 2015.

ENDCAP (2012). Wild Pets in the European Union. http://endcap.eu/wp-content/uploads/2013/02/Report-Wild-Pets-in-the-European-Union.pdf. Accessed 14 August 2015.

European Commission (2014). *Communication from the commission to the council and the European parliament on the EU approach against wildlife trafficking*. Brussels: European Commission.

Fernando, P., Kumar, M. A., Williams, A. C., Wikramanayake, E., Aziz, T., & Singh, S. M. (2008). *Review of human-elephant conflict mitigation measures practiced in South Asia*. Gland, Switzerland: WWF.

Fison, M. (2011). The £6bn trade in animal smuggling. *The Independent*. http://www.independent.co.uk/environment/nature/the-1636bn-trade-in-animal-smuggling-2233608.html#. Accessed 11 February 2013.

Guzmán, J., Saldaña, M., Teyeliz, A., Grosselet, M., & Gamez, J. (2007). *The illegal parrot trade in Mexico. Defenders of wildlife*. www.defenders.org/mexicanparrot. Accessed 25 June 2014.

Great Ape Survival Project [GRASP] (2012). *Home*. http://www.un-grasp.org/. Accessed 13 March 2013.

De Greef, K., & Raemaekers, S. (2014). *South Africa's Illicit Abalone trade: an updated overview and knowledge gap analysis*. Cambridge: TRAFFIC International.

Harrop, S. (2000). The international regulation of animal welfare and conservation issues through standards dealing with the trapping of wild mammals. *Journal of Environmental Law, 12*(3), 333–360.

House of Commons (2012). *Environmental audit committee: wildlife crime. Third report of session 2012–13*. London: Stationary Office.

Hubschle, A. (2014). Of bogus hunters, queen pins and mules: the varied roles of women in transnational organized crime in Southern Africa. *Trends Organised Crime, 17*, 31–51.

Humane Society International (2013). *Shark finning*. http://www.hsi.org/issues/shark_finning/. Accessed 26 February 2013.

International Fund for Animal Welfare [IFAW] (2008). *Killing with keystrokes. An investigation of the Illegal wildlife Trade on the World Wide Web*. http://www.ifaw.org/Publications/Program_Publications/Wildlife_Trade/Campaign_Scientific_Publications/asset_upload_file64_12456.pdf. Accessed 14 June 2011.

IFAW (2006). *Selling out the tiger won't save it.* http://www.ifaw.org/sites/default/files/Fact%20Sheet%202006%20Selling%20out%20the%20tiger%20wont%20save%20it.pdf. Accessed 12 August 2015.

International Air Transport Association [IATA] (2004). *Live animals regulations (LAR) the global standard for the transportation of live animals by air.* http://www.iata.org/publications/pages/live-animals.aspx. Accessed 18 August 2015.

IATA (2015). *IATA & CITES against illegal wildlife trade.* http://www.iata.org/publications/tracker/jul-2015/Pages/illegal-wildlife-trade.aspx. Accessed 18 August 2015.

Kassam, A., & Glenza, J. (2015). Killer of Cecil the lion was dentist from Minnesota, claim Zimbabwe officials. *The Guardian.* http://www.theguardian.com/environment/2015/jul/28/killer-of-cecil-the-lion-was-american-zimbabwe-officials-claim. Accessed 18 August 2015.

Landais, E. (2008, September 19). Unheeded call of Africa's apes. *Gulf News.*

Lemieux, A., & Clarke, R. (2009). The international ban on ivory sales and its effects on elephant poaching in Africa. *British Journal of Criminology, 49*(4), 451–471.

Lyapustin, S. (2006, March). The smuggling of falcons of the far east—a threat to the existence of rare birds. *Preservation of Bioresources*, 89–100. In Russian.

Maher, J., & Sollund, R. (2016). Strengths, weaknesses, opportunities and threats in law enforcement of the illegal wildlife trade: a comparative case-study on the illegal wildlife trade in the UK and Norway. *Journal of Trafficking, Organized Crime and Security—Special Issue on Illicit Trafficking in Wildlife and Forest Resources, 2*(1), 82–99.

Moyle, B. (2003). Regulation, conservation and incentives. In S. Oldfield (Ed.). *The trade in wildlife. Regulation for conservation.* London: Earthscan.

McMurray, C. (2008). *Illegal trade in wildlife and world environment.* http://2001-2009.state.gov/g/oes/rls/rm/106259.htm. Accessed 9 July 2012.

Milliken, T., & Shaw, J. (2012). The South Africa—Viet Nam rhino horn trade nexus: a deadly combination of institutional lapses, corrupt wildlife industry professionals and Asian crime syndicates. *A TRAFFIC Report.* Southeast Asia: TRAFFIC.

Nellemann, C., Redmond, I., & Refisch, J. (2010). *The last stand of the gorilla—environmental crime and conflict in the Congo basin. A rapid response assessment.* United Nations Environment Programme, GRID-Arendal: Arendal, Norway.

Nellemann, C., Henriksen, R., Raxter, P., Ash, N., & Mrema, E. (Eds.) (2014). *The environmental crime crisis—threats to sustainable development from illegal exploitation and trade in wildlife and forest resources. A UNEP rapid response assessment.* United Nations Environment Programme and GRID-Arendal, Nairobi and Arendal.

Nijman, V. (2009). *An assessment of trade in gibbons and Orang-utans in Sumatra, Indonesia.* TRAFFIC Southeast Asia, Petaling Jaya, Selangor, Malaysia.

Pantel, S., & Anak, N. A. (2010). A preliminary assessment of sunda pangolin trade in sabah. *A TRAFFIC Report.* Southeast Asia: TRAFFIC.

Pettrossian, G., & Clarke, R. (2014). Explaining and controlling illegal commercial fishing: an application of the CRAVED theft model. *The British Journal of Criminology*, *54*, 73–90.

Pires, S., & Clarke, R. (2011). Are parrots CRAVED? An analysis of parrot poaching in Mexico. *Journal of Research in Crime and Delinquency*, *49*(1), 122–146.

Redford, K. H. (1992). The empty forest. *Bioscience*, *42*(6), 412–423.

Reeve, R. (2002). *Policing international trade in endangered species. The CITES treaty and compliance*. London: Earthscan.

Regan, T. (1983). *The case for animal rights*. Berkeley: University of California Press.

Regueira, R. F. S., & Bernard E. (2012). Wildlife sinks: quantifying the impact of illegal bird trade in street markets in Brazil. *Biological Conservation*, *149*(1), 16–22.

RENCTAS (2001). *1st national report on the traffic of wild animals*. http://www.renctas.org.br/wp-content/uploads/2014/02/RELATORIO-INGLES_final.pdf. Accessed 5 December 2014.

Rivalan, P., Delmas, V., Angulo, E., Bull, L., Hall, R., Courchamp, F., et al. (2007). Can bans stimulate wildlife trade? *Nature*, *447*, 529–530.

Seidensticker, J. (2010). Saving wild tigers: a case study in biodiversity loss and challenges to be met for recovery beyond 2010. *Integrative Zoology*, *5*, 285–299.

Sollund, R. (2012). Speciesism as doxic practice, or valuing plurality and difference. In R. Ellefsen, R. Sollund, & G. Larsen (Eds.), *Eco-global crimes. Contemporary problems and future challenges* (pp. 91–115). Aldershot: Ashgate.

Sollund, R. (2011). Expressions of speciesism: the effects of keeping companion animals on animal abuse, animal trafficking and species decline. *Crime, Law and Social Change*, *55*(5), 437–451.

Sollund, R., & Maher, J. (2015). *Illegal wildlife trade: a case study report on the illegal wildlife trade in the* United Kingdom, Norway, Colombia and *Brazil*. EFFACE Project WP 4. http://efface.eu/sites/default/files/EFFACE_Illegal%20Wildlife%20Trade_revised.pdf. Accessed 15 August 2015.

Sonricker Hansen, A. L., Li, A., Joly, D., Mekaru, S., & Brownstein, J. S. (2012). Digital surveillance: A novel approach to monitoring the illegal wildlife trade. *PLoS ONE*, *7*(12), e51156.

South, N., Brisman, A., & Beirne, P. (2013). A guide to a green criminology. In N. South & A. Brisman (Eds.), *Routledge international handbook in green criminology* (pp. 27–42). London and New York: Routledge.

Sykes, G., & Matza, D. (1957). Techniques of neutralization: a theory of delinquency. *American Sociological Review*, *22*, 664–670.

United Nations Environment Programme [UNEP] (2014). *Thematic focus: environmental governance Emerging Technologies: smarter ways to fight wildlife crime*. http://na.unep.net/geas/getUNEPPageWithArticleIDScript.php?article_id=113. Accessed 15 August 2015.

United Nations Office on Drugs and Crime [UNODC] (2012). *ICCWC launches wildlife and forest crime toolkit*. https://www.unodc.org/unodc/en/frontpage/2012/July/iccwc-launches-wildlife-and-forest-crime-toolkit.html. Accessed 15 August 2015.

UNODC (2013). *Transnational organized crime in East Asia and the pacific: a threat assessment*. https://www.unodc.org/unodc/en/data-and-analysis/TOC-threat-assessments.html. Accessed 15 August 2015.

Vanstreels, E.T., Teixeira, R.H.F., Camargo, L.C., Nunes, A.L.V., & Matushima, E.R. (2010). Impacts of animal traffic on the Brazilian amazon parrots (Amazona species) collection of the Quinzinho de Barros Municipal Zoological Park, Brazil, 1986–2007. *Zoo Biology, 29*, 600–614.

Von Essen, E., Hansen, H. P., Nordstrom Kallstrom, H., Peterson, M. N., & Peters, T. R. (2014). Deconstructing the poaching phenomenon: a review of typologies for understanding illegal hunting. *British Journal of Criminology, 54* (4), 632–651.

Warchol, G., Zupan, L., & Clarke W. (2003). Transnational criminality: an analysis of the illegal wildlife market in Southern Africa. *International Criminal Justice Review, 13*(1), 1–26.

White, R. (2013). *Environmental harm. An eco-justice perspective*. University of Bristol: Polity Press.

World Society for the Protection of Animals [WSPA] (n.d.). *Bear bile industry*. http://www.wspa-international.org/wspaswork/bears/bearfarming/default.aspx. Accessed 26 February 2013.

World Wildlife Fund [WWF] (n.d.). *Unsustainable and illegal wildlife trade*. http://wwf.panda.org/about_our_earth/species/problems/illegal_trade/. Accessed 6 July 2012.

WWF (2002). One million illegal wildlife items seized at UK ports and airports. http://forests.org/articles/reader.asp?linkid=7936. Accessed 8 October 2005.

Wyatt, T. (2009). Exploring the organization in Russia far East's illegal wildlife trade: two case studies of the illegal fur and illegal falcon trades. *Global Crime, 10* (1 & 2), 144–154.

Wyatt, T. (2011). The illegal raptor trade in the Russian federation. *Contemporary Justice Review, 14*(2),103–123.

Wyatt, T. (2013a). A criminological exploration of the industrialisation of pig farming. *International Journal of Criminology*, 12–28. Special Issue on Green Criminology. www.internetjournalofcriminology.com. Accessed 11 October 2015.

Wyatt, T. (2013b). The local context of wildlife trafficking: the Heathrow animal reception centre. In D. Westerhuis, R. Walters, & T. Wyatt (Eds.), *Emerging issues in green criminology: exploring power, justice and harm* (pp. 142–162). Basingstoke: Palgrave Macmillan.

Wyatt, T. (2013c). *Wildlife trafficking: a deconstruction of the crime, victims and offenders*. Basingstoke: Palgrave Macmillan.

Wyatt, T. (2014). The Russian Far East's illegal timber trade: an organized crime? *Crime, Law and Social Change, 61*(1), 15–35.

Wyler, L., & Sheikh, P. (2008). *International illegal trade in wildlife: threats and U.S. policy*. http://fpc.state.gov/documents/organization/110404.pdf. Accessed 6 July 2012.

Dr Jennifer Maher is Senior Lecturer at the Centre for Criminology, University of South Wales. Her research interests include animal abuse, green criminology, human-animal studies, and youth and gang violence. She recently concluded a UK wildlife trafficking study for the FP7 (European Commission) EFFACE project which evaluated the impact of environmental crime in Europe and is currently researching puppy smuggling for the Scottish and English Governments. Her publications include co-editing *Greening Criminology in the 21st Century* (2016, Routledge, with M. Hall et al.) and the special journal issue 'Animal Abuse and Criminology' in Crime, Law and Social Change (2011 with P. Beirne).

Tanya Wyatt is Reader in Criminology at Northumbria University in Newcastle, UK. She has numerous publications on wildlife trafficking and is currently the co-investigator on a British Academy funded project exploring Mexico's role in wildlife trade and trafficking with the European Union. Tanya was recently the rapporteur for the Defra, OECD, FCO and US State Department sponsored 'Wildlife Crime and International Security: Strengthening Law Enforcement' workshop at Wilton Park, UK. She also is currently an advisor to the USAID funded Wildlife Crime Technology Challenge.

Animal Abuse Resulting from Wildlife Habitat Destruction

Rob White

Introduction

Animal abuse occurs in different forms and takes place in diverse locations. It is ubiquitous although there are important qualitative differences in regard to the nature, dynamics and seriousness of the harm as these pertain to particular nonhuman animal species. The focus of this chapter is on the destruction of wildlife habitat and how this impinges upon the health and well-being of nonhuman animals. Without a home in which to live or to which to migrate to, suffering and death is inevitable for nonhuman animals. Destroying species homelands, therefore, is a profoundly harmful activity that intrinsically constitutes a form of animal abuse.

In this scenario, humans have a major role to play both as perpetrators of wildlife habitat destruction *and* as moral agents with the capacity to intervene in instances where habitat destruction originates from nonhuman sources. The issue of who or what, precisely, causes certain habitat damage is an important consideration in the discussions below. From the point of view of human causation, matters of power and profit tend to come to the fore in explanations of wide scale habitat destruction. Human agency is also linked to decisions about whether or not to intervene to 'save' particular species from the competitive pressures generated by other nonhuman species

R. White (✉)
School of Social Sciences, University of Tasmania, Hobart, Tasmania, Australia
e-mail: r.d.white@utas.edu.au

J. Maher et al. (eds.), *The Palgrave International Handbook of Animal Abuse Studies*, DOI 10.1057/978-1-137-43183-7_12

'invading' or occupying the same terrain (see chapter Violent Love: Conservation and Invasive Alien Species herein). As demonstrated in this chapter, animal abuse resulting from wildlife habitat destruction is not solely about human action. It also encompasses human inaction as well, including the decision to 'do nothing'.

For the purposes of illustration, the chapter initially focuses on de-forestation and its impacts on nonhuman animals, before briefly considering pollution-related harms. Later, the chapter turns to matters of habitat change due to competing nonhuman species, and the choices foisted upon humans regarding suitable intervention strategies. In the first two instances, wildlife habitat is literally destroyed, to be replaced by new forms of vegetation and/or mining operations. In the latter, wildlife habitat is transformed or denuded, not by human action *per se*, but by the migration and (re)settlement of non-endemic species in new territories and/or population explosion of particular species relative to others. The chapter thus considers the nature, prevalence, explanations and responses to habitat loss from the point of view of harms to nonhuman animals, and does so by highlighting the specific role of human agency in regards to these issues.

Biodiversity, Deforestation and Habitat Loss

The loss of biodiversity in all three of its main components—genes, species and ecosystems—continues at a rapid pace today and the principal pressures directly driving biodiversity loss (habitat change, overexploitation, pollution, invasive alien species and climate change) are either constant or increasing in intensity (Secretariat of the Convention on Biological Diversity 2010). Biodiversity is generally defined as the variety of all species on earth. It refers to the different plants, animals and micro-organisms, and their genes, that together make up life on the planet. It also includes reference to the terrestrial (land), marine (ocean) and freshwater (inland water systems) ecosystems of which they are a part.

With biodiversity, the key ecological message is the greater the number of species the greater the resilience of the system as a whole to potential catastrophe, whether this is fire, drought or climate change. Any particular ecosystem is made up of both abiotic components (air, water, soils, atoms and molecules) and biotic components (plants, animals, bacteria and fungi). Changes to an ecosystem through human intervention may occur through manipulation, contamination or destruction of these components (for example, through mining or land clearance or use of pesticides), although it is not only human intervention that can lead to change (for example, the spread of invasive species can transform local ecologies—although this, too, can be caused by human interventions directly [by purposefully transferring species] or indirectly [through human-caused climate changes that induce migration of species]).

Many environmental harms can be characterised as natural resource crimes (for example, illegal trafficking of wildlife, illegal logging and illegal fishing) or pollution crimes (for example, illegal movement and disposal of hazardous wastes). Even when legal, such activities can nonetheless be harmful, even if subject to regulation and permit conditions. Certain activities, such as both legal and illegal land grabs for the purpose of transforming forests into monoculture 'flex crops' (crops that can be used for food, feed, fuel or industrial material), also cause considerable environmental harm (pollution, land degradation and contribution to carbon emissions). All of these, in turn, can be linked to wider ecological threats to the planetary environment and, in the present context, threats to specific nonhuman animal species.

According to the United Nations there are five principle threats to biodiversity (United Nations Environment Programme 2013). These are:

1. the unsustainable harvesting of natural resources, including plants, animals and marine species;
2. the loss, degradation or fragmentation of ecosystems through land conversion for agriculture, forest clearing, etc.;
3. invasive non-native or 'alien' species being introduced to ecosystems to which they are not adapted, i.e. where they have no, or not enough, predators to maintain an ecological balance;
4. pollution; and
5. climate change.

There are complex reasons why these threats emerge as they do, and they are interlinked in a variety of ways. Reduction in species includes both animals and plants. This is significant insofar as complex ecosystems depend upon the interaction between all species, and any change will impact upon overall functioning. This is particularly apparent with respect to forest ecosystems.

About 13 % of the world's total forest area is under formal protection and almost 75 % is covered by national forest programs. Yet, despite progress in the regulatory sphere and net gains in forest areas in Europe and Asia, total loss of forest cover during the last decade still averaged around 13 million hectares per year. Most deforestation is occurring in tropical forests, many located in Asian countries such as Indonesia, Malaysia, Thailand and Myanmar, with substantial biodiversity impacts:

> Although the global rate of net forest cover loss has slowed, partly due to the expansion of plantations and to natural forest restoration, forest biodiversity loss continues to occur disproportionately since the highest levels of deforestation and of forest degradation are reported for biodiversity-rich natural forests in developing countries. (United Nations Environment Programme 2011, p. 48)

Net losses are especially significant in South America and Africa.

Factors affecting deforestation, and reduction in forest biodiversity, include unsustainable harvesting of forest products for industrial use and livelihood needs, deforestation for agriculture, and severe drought and forest fires. Every year some 10 million hectares of forest are destroyed, industrial timber exports total around US$150 billion per year, and estimates of illegal logging account for about 25 % of removals worldwide (Setiono 2007, p. 27). Much of this illegal logging occurs with the involvement of corrupt government officials, including law enforcement officers, financial institutions and backers, and business people who import timber or wood-base products. Bribery and 'goodwill' payments, smuggling, illicit trafficking, money laundering and forging of documents are all part of the illegal logging industry (Bisschop 2015; Setiono 2007).

Deforestation and species reduction are not only solely the outcome of logging. Land clearance is also due to agricultural exploitation, cattle farming, mining, oil and gas installations, and hydroelectric dams (see Boekhout van Solinge 2008a, b, 2010a, b; Boekhout van Solinge and Kuijpers 2013; Khagram 2004). There is also the phenomenon of 'conflict timber', associated with West Africa, for example, in which deforestation is linked to the funding of civil wars and armed conflicts (Boekhout van Solinge 2008a; Brisman and South 2013; Brisman et al. 2015). In these contexts, the ecological impact of logging and land clearance transcends the legal-illegal divide insofar as vast amounts of forest are destroyed in many different locations—from Peru and Brazil, Liberia and Sierra Leone, to Indonesia and Australia. The motivations, objectives and practices may vary depending upon the social context and specific industry interests, but the result is further depletion of many different kinds of trees and variety of forests.

Another reason for deforestation and biodiversity reduction is the increasing reliance on energy from organic sources, especially in the global North (see Burrell et al. 2012; Charles et al. 2013). For example, global vegetable oil supplies used for biodiesel production are on the increase because of European and North American demand, with Indonesia and Malaysia major producers in the Asian region (Mitchell 2008). This translates into massive shifts in land use. Indeed, the profitability of biofuel production is leading to large-scale plantations in places such as Indonesia, Brazil and Colombia. This has resulted in the clearing of rainforests and in some instances forcing Indigenous people off their lands. The latter is important insofar as those living on and with the land have traditionally done so in ecologically sustainable ways (Caughley et al. 1996; Robyn 2002). Mol (2013, p. 254) critically observes that in Colombia:

> The gift of palm oil to the world leaves the people and the environment of the tropics with contaminated soils, groundwater, and rivers; habitat destruction; ecosystem disturbances; the loss of flora and aquatic and animal species; and processes of displacement and emplacement that inflect a whole range of physical, psychological, social, and cultural consequences upon local communities.

Cutting down trees also has a direct bearing on global warming. For instance, it has been estimated that by 2022, biofuel plantations could destroy 98 % of Indonesia's rainforests and that 'Every ton of palm oil used as biofuel releases 30 tons of CO_2 into the atmosphere, ten times as much as petroleum does' (Shiva 2008, p. 79). Overall, it has been estimated that deforestation accounts globally for about 12 % of total human-caused greenhouse gas emissions (Greenpeace 2014; Intergovernmental Panel on Climate Change 2013). This deforestation not only involves the cutting down of trees but also frequently the burning of forests as part of converting land for other uses such as agriculture and biofuel plantations (see Box 1).

Box 1 Indonesian Peat Blaze Affects Orangutans

2015 saw the worst ever smoke haze over Indonesia, Malaysia and Singapore, extending to Thailand and the Philippines. This was caused by illegal fires started in peatland and forest on Indonesia's Sumatra Island and the Indonesian part of Borneo. The fires were started in order to cheaply clear land for palm oil and pulp and paper plantations (ABC news 19 October 2015). It was claimed by the World Resources Institute that the Indonesian forest and agricultural fires cloaking South-East Asia in acrid haze were spewing more greenhouse gases into the atmosphere each day that all United States economic activity (ABC news 22 October 2015). The already threatened orangutans living in Borneo suffered greatly from exposure to the smoke and fire, especially the young who, as with humans, were most at risk. The orangutans experienced malnutrition, dehydration and hunger as a direct consequence of the fires burning up and in their habitat (ABC news 2 November 2015).

The rise of 'flex crops and commodities' are also having a major impact on biodiversity (Borras et al. 2013). These refer to a single crop/commodity that is highly valuable precisely because of its multiple characteristics and uses. Typically, a flex crop straddles multiple commodity sectors (food, feed, fuel, other industrial commodities); geographical spaces (for example, North-South); and international political economy categories (for example, OECD countries, non-OECD countries). This makes flex crops very attractive to growers and buyers around the world insofar as everyone it seems can find a place in the market. The four key flex crops today are maize, oil palm, soybean and sugarcane. Important producers and exporters of flex crops and commodities include, for example, Argentina for soya, Malaysia and Indonesia for palm oil, and Vietnam for fast-growing trees (Borras et al. 2013). One type of crop, such as fast-growing trees, can be sold as a commodity in respect to diverse markets, including in this case timber products, biofuel and/or carbon offsets.

Multi-purpose crops exacerbate the push towards fewer varieties. Species reduction is also associated with ease of production, distribution and marketing. For instance, there is also a trend towards monoculture since uniformity means ease of cultivation and harvest, translating into higher profits. New agricultural and pastoral technologies reinforce this broad tendency towards simplification. The global political economy of genetically modified organisms (GMOs) provides a case in point. Countries that have been reluctant to adopt genetically modified (GM) crops have been subjected to intense pressures to do so (Walters 2005, 2011). Ironically, given political claims that GM crops are vital in order to feed the world, GMO invasion of endemic species and crops is nonetheless seen to be capable of destroying unique genotypes, thereby creating the potential to threaten food security (i.e., diminishing diverse genetic material) (see Engdahl 2007).

The potential size of the problem is considerable as the use of GM crops has rapidly increased over the past decade.

> In 2007, transgenic crops (90 percent of which, it should be recalled, have genetic traits patented by Monsanto) covered about 250 million acres: more than half were located in the United States (136.5 million acres), followed by Argentina (45 million), Brazil (28.8 million), Canada (15.3 million), India (9.5 million), China (8.8 million), Paraguay (5 million), and South Africa (3.5 million). (Robin 2010, p. 4).

Almost all of these crops were 'legally' planted, but the genetic and species consequences of transfer are potentially of a huge scale especially in terms of negative ecological impact.

Also of concern are those crops which have not been distributed through legitimate and legal means. For instance, in Mexico traditional corn has been found to be contaminated by GM corn, despite the fact that in 1998 Mexico declared a moratorium on transgenic corn crops in order to preserve the extraordinary biodiversity of the plant. Meanwhile, in Paraguay, where (as of 2007) no law authorised the cultivation of GMOs: 'From 1996 to 2006, surfaces devoted to soybean cultivation went from less than 2.5 million acres to 5 million acres, an increase of 10 % a year' (Robin 2010, p. 275). To avoid losing markets and by ensuring proper labelling of crops for markets such as the European Union, the Paraguayan government ended up simply legalising the illegal crops. Much the same thing happened in Brazil and Poland (Engdahl 2007), and for much the same reasons (namely EU rules on traceability and labelling of GM foods intended for human and animal consumption) (Robin 2010).

The lucrative market for biofuels and GM crops has been linked to the forced takeover of communal lands, using armed men and bulldozers, as well as fraudulent claims of land title (see Robin 2010). Moreover, given that the focus of the UN mechanism for Reducing Emissions from Deforestation and Forest Degradation (REDD) is on minimising carbon emissions caused by the destruction of living forest biomass, there will be greater pressures to convert or modify other ecosystems, especially savannahs and wetlands, for food or biofuel (Sutherland et al. 2009). In other words, forests are privileged over other types of ecosystems, and the result could well be the loss of biodiversity associated with destruction or conversion of these 'less valued' non-forested ecosystems. Again, compulsory take-over of biodiversity-rich land of any type is not uncommon. Recent land grabs in Cambodia and Laos by Vietnamese companies and the subsequent clear-felling of intact forests for the purposes of rubber plantations involves corrupt decision-making processes at elite levels and systematic contravention of existing environmental laws (Global Witness 2013).

The conversion of land for commercial purposes is entirely relevant to the wellbeing and survival of nonhuman animals. For example, the native woodlands demolished for cash crops such as GM soybeans in Argentina have a major impact on the habitats of animals such as pumas, jaguars, Andean cats and tapirs, which cannot survive outside this particular ecosystem (Robin 2010, p. 271). Similar events are happening in places such as Indonesia, where deforestation is putting pressure on the Sumatran tiger and the orangutan (Boekhout van Solinge 2008b).

Simultaneously, GMO technologies are also being applied to animals, including fish, with potentially dire consequences. To put this into context it is useful to consider several other interrelated factors that are putting pressures on animal species around the world. One of these is the relationship between pollution and endangerment. For example, PCBs (polychlorinated biphenyl) have been found in whales, seals and polar bears. Moreover, sea mammals, such as killer whales, are threatened with extinction caused by PCBs (Robin 2010). Building resilience is part of the agenda of GMO animal production. But this, in turn, can generate a 'Frankenstein effect'—the construction of super species that pose dangers to those around them. Shiva (2000), for example, tells the story of GM fish which, as invasive species, have had a devastatingly negative impact on endemic fish species; similar concerns plus health and ecological considerations have also been raised in regards to approval of GM salmon for sale in the USA from 2015 (Park 2015).

As the above discussions demonstrate, harm to animals results from major shifts in land use driven by the pursuit of profit. The threats to biodiversity, and thus to specific species of nonhuman animal, are primarily related to deforestation, which in turn is associated with multiple alternative uses of existing forest spaces. From mining to cattle farming, building of dams through to planting of monoculture flex crops, the net result is diminishment of habitat for many creatures and subsequently their death, impairment and/or potential extinction.

Pollution of Air, Land and Water Habitats

Air, land and water pollution is now reaching every part of the planet and is evident across many different types of terrain. Even though specific acts of pollution may not be illegal and/or be allowed to occur under license, the harms of pollution are nonetheless important to consider. The problem of air pollution, for example, basically impacts upon humans in ways that fundamentally undermine their health and wellbeing, and is associated with millions of premature deaths worldwide each year (Walters 2010). Smog in the industrial cities of China is a well-known phenomenon, as are pollution events stemming from intentionally lit forest fires in Indonesia. In the latter case, deforestation associated with the planting of flex crops and the subsequent smoke haze periodically affects people living in Malaysia, Singapore, Brunei, Cambodia, The Philippines, Vietnam and Thailand (Varkkey 2013) and of course the nonhuman animals with whom they share these places (see Box 1).

Land (or soil) pollution occurs when chemicals are released into the soil, including heavy metals such as lead and cadmium and pesticides, which can kill living bacteria in the earth or contaminate all life within the soil (including plants and tiny creatures). Agriculture and mining stand out as two of the most polluting activities here, along with the burgeoning extractive and resources industries and the use of chemicals. Corporations are increasingly mining ever deeper into the earth to extract mineral reserves and burying some of the world's most hazardous waste deep in the ground (e.g., radioactive waste) (White and Heckenberg 2014; see also Stretesky et al. 2014) (see Box 2).

Box 2 Catchment Run-Offs Affect the Great Barrier Reef

Pollution from mining and agricultural activities can have devastating impacts on marine environments, which are also habitats to many diverse species. Catchment run-off is having major negative effects on the Great Barrier Reef, situated off the coast of Queensland, Australia. As water runs towards the ocean, it collects farm fertiliser, pesticides and soil and flushes these pollutants onto the Reef: 'The impact on corals and seagrass, and the species that rely on them for food and shelter, is immense' (WWF 2014, p. 119). A recent study pointed out that reef coral cover had halved since 1985 and that more than 40 % of this loss was due to outbreaks of the coral-eating crown of thorns starfish, which are fuelled by fertiliser run-off from farms (WWF 2014, p. 119). The consequences of pollution, therefore, are not only demolition of habitat, but provision of an avenue for the advancement of invasive species (see discussions below).

Water pollution occurs when contaminants, such as untreated sewerage waste and agricultural runoff containing chemical fertilisers, poison and alter existing surface and ground waters. Surface run-off transfers contaminants from one place to another and harmful chemicals which are suspended in the air get dissolved in rainwater and pollute the soil when they come to the earth's surface in the form of acid rain (Naik 2010). The scope of water pollution extends from small-scale ponds, to inland waterways, estuaries, to lakes and rivers, to the world's oceans. Sea currents transfer pollutants and wastes around the globe. Of particular concern is the accumulation of plastics in the world's oceans (see White 2013).

Plastics have been found on beaches, in coastal waters and their sediments, and in the open ocean on the surface as well as in seabeds including the continental shelf. Debris has been found in deep water canyons, at abyssal depths. The environmental harm stemming from plastics in the ocean varies according to size and composition of the material. Threats to biodiversity and individuals manifest in physical damage through ingestion and entanglement in plastic and other debris, and through chemical contamination by ingestion. The importation of alien species can also alter endemic community structures of animals. In general, 'potential chemical effects are likely to increase with a reduction in the size of plastic particles while physical effects, such as the entanglement of seals and other animals in drift plastic, increase with the size and complexity of the debris' (United Nations Environment Programme 2011, p. 25). Fish, seabirds, sea turtles and marine mammals have all been affected by ingestion of plastics.

A key concern is the biochemical and physiological response of organisms to ingested plastics contaminated with PBTs (Persistent, Bioaccumulative and Toxic chemicals). Not only are there issues associated with the potential impacts of the releases of chemical additives that were part of the plastics' original formulation, but as plastic breaks down into fragments (plastic particles of small size), it accumulates PBTs that are already present in seawater and sediments. Many of these specific pollutants cause chronic effects such as endocrine disruption affecting reproduction, increases in the frequency of genetic mutations (mutagenicity) and a tendency to cause cancer (carcinogeniticy). According to the United Nations Environment Programme (2011, p. 28):

> We know that microplastics are ubiquitous in the ocean, contain a wide range of chemical contaminants, and can be ingested by marine organisms. However, the lack of certainly about the possible role of microplastics, as an additional vector for contaminants taken up by organisms, calls for caution and further research.

Compounding these continuous processes of contamination by plastics are other types of contamination, some of which are systemic (for example, related to agricultural practices), others the outcome of extraordinary events (such as the BP oilrig disaster).

For instance, there is evidence that the nitrogen-based fertiliser used in (the increasing) corn production is causing environmental harm in its own right. Millions of kilograms/pounds of those nitrates end up in the Gulf of Mexico each year, where it is causing a massive algae bloom. This bloom negatively impacts the ecology of the Gulf: 'When the algae dies it sinks to the bottom, where it absorbs oxygen as it decays. In recent years that oxygen depletion has created an aquatic "dead zone" covering about 8,000 square miles in which shrimp, fish, oysters and crabs cannot survive' (Reliable Plant 2007).

The main causes of pollution are human-made and directly linked to existing techniques and processes of production (for example, agriculture, mining, manufacturing), consumption (for example, waste disposal), transportation (for example, internal combustion engine of cars, trucks and buses) and war (for example, use of depleted uranium in armaments). Pollution is therefore generally ingrained in everyday practices and systems, although these, in turn, are frequently subject to regulation. That is, industry and citizens are generally free to pollute, but the law stipulates under what conditions and to what extent. Chemicals and other toxic waste such as persistent organic pollutants (POPs) have proliferated over the past 60 years (Pellow 2007). Specifically, the rise of the chemical industries means that many different types of toxic waste are produced, gathered up and put together into the same dump sites (for example, rivers and lakes and ocean outlets, landfills). This has both immediate and longer-term impacts on nonhuman animal species as their habitats are denuded, destroyed and diminished.

The destruction of wildlife habitat as a result of war and social conflict also warrants mention. The continuing impacts and legacy of war are evident, for example, in the ongoing efforts in Vietnam to recuperate from the horrors of Agent Orange, with its legacy of deforestation and toxicity. The militarised uses of natural resources as funding sources not only includes direct exploitation of vulnerable species and their use as 'bush meat' in places such as West Africa, but the unregulated demolition of countryside in pursuit of minerals and the like (Brisman et al. 2015). The intentional destruction of the environment during warfare remains a social and ecological problem of major proportions, one that has still not been adequately addressed in international legal forums (Freeland 2015).

Resource extraction industries are the economic lifeblood of many countries around the world. Mining, forestry and petroleum (involving drilling at sea as well as on land) constitute major sources of revenue and profit for states and corporations alike. They employ many people, across a broad range of occupations and types of paid work. They also demand huge expenditure from the point of view of investment, exploration, operations and rehabilitation. Resource extraction is not cheap. It also has its environmental and social costs.

The harms resulting from extractive industries like mining are concerning (Carrington et al. 2011; Ruggerio and South 2013). These include harms stemming from environmental degradation and contamination. In some circumstances, mining ventures create toxic sites, and thus produce the conditions for contaminated communities, with significant detrimental consequences for local habitats and human residents. There are huge questions surrounding the environmental and social consequences of mining, particularly the huge large-scale open-cut mining projects, mountaintop mining, and new forms of mining such as coal-seam fracking (Munro 2012; Stretesky et al. 2014).

Air, land and water are directly affected by the extraction (mining) and processing (smelting) of mined substances. So, too, the world's climate is being altered by the emission of greenhouse gases to which mining is a major contributor. Recent developments, such as mega-mines and coal-seam fracking will exacerbate these harms due to the scale and nature of the methods used. It is notable in this regard that scientists are now reporting the wide scale movement of many species towards the world's poles due to a warming climate. It has also been observed that changes in sea temperatures are impacting upon fish and kelp habitat, and that bird migration patterns and breeding grounds are being disrupted and/or changing as a result of changing climatic parameters (Macaulay 2016).

This section has briefly reviewed how the pollution of air, land and water habitats is creating harm to nonhuman animals. Pollution has direct effects, as in the case of catchment run-off draining into the sea and the prevalence of plastics in the ocean. It also has indirect effects, as evidenced in how carbon emissions, the main contributor to accelerated global warming, eventually translates into fundamental transformations of habitat. For fish in the sea, birds in the air, and bears on the ice, the ramifications are profound.

Preservation and Conservation of Habitat

Responding to the issues identified in this chapter is not as straightforward as may first appear. Specific responses might include introduction and better enforcement of environmental laws that prevent land clearing, stricter controls on or abolition of polluting industries (especially those most contributing to carbon emissions), and banning of the planting of GM crops. These strategies depend entirely upon the balance of political forces at the local through to the international levels. There are other factors and dilemmas that impinge upon the question of how best to respond to habitat destruction and subsequent harm to animals as well.

The reverence for and privileging of nonhuman nature sometimes translates into a concern for the 'righteous management' of nature, and manifests in an agenda that advocates for the mass preservation of wilderness, protection of endangered nonhuman species and restoration of disturbed areas towards a *pristine nature* or pristine condition (Devalleand Sessions 1985). There are two immediate problems with this view. First, it implies a separation of humanity and nature as if this was and always has, empirically, been the case. The notion of 'pristine nature' implies precisely this kind of rigid separation, yet historical and cross-cultural study indicates exactly the opposite—namely, constant and continuous living in nature by humans (Merchant 2005; Plumwood 2004; Tsing 2005), including within the most inhospitable environments possible from a human perspective (Robyn 2002).

Second, the notion of 'pristine nature' implies immutable or unchanging conditions. Yet, nature is inherently changeable. If we re-cast the issue into the language of 'harm', then it becomes even more complicated. To protect against intrinsic harm to the environment requires an understanding of what the environment is and how it can be harmed. If 'environment' refers to the natural world, and if the source of value in the natural world is its self-maintaining sustaining properties, then harm to the environment involves setbacks to these self-maintaining properties. Harm to the environment, in other words, might be defined as a change from the environment's 'natural', self-maintaining state. The problem with this view is that the environment is not in static equilibrium; rather, it is a dynamic entity undergoing constant change. Preserving the environment in its natural state is likely an impossible, and perhaps undesirable, mission (Lin 2006, p. 981).

So, too, when it comes to the relationship between particular kinds of habitat and particular species of animal difficult choices frequently present themselves. For instance, debates presently occur over which animals are valued over others when it comes to survival dilemmas. Human intervention in the lives of both wild and domesticated animals has major ramifications for species survival and biodiversity. Consider, for example, the phenomenon of assisted colonisation, which involves the moving of species to sites where they do not currently occur or have not been known to occur in recent history. This is happening in response to climate change, and usually is directed at species in the wild. 'In the UK, two native species of butterfly were recently translocated approximately 65 km northward into areas identified by modelling as climatically suitable for occupancy by the butterflies' (Sutherland et al. 2009).

The problem is that non-native species moving into new ecosystems are already recognised as a major conservation problem (see Secretariat of the Convention on Biological Diversity 2010). This is evidenced, for example, by the rapid expansion in the numbers of Indo-Pacific lionfish along the east coast of the USA and in the Caribbean to the detriment of native coral reef fish (Sutherland et al. 2009). Assisted colonists could be viewed as invasive and as constituting a potential danger to existing ecosystems and their inhabitants. Classic cases where considerable damage has resulted include the introduction of the cane toad into Australia. Its subsequent spread has had colossal impacts on native species. With no or few natural predators, it has proliferated and continues to take over more and more territories previously held by other endemic species.

The debates over the ways in which 'feral' and 'invasive' animals are approached provide a useful summary of conflicting views pertaining to human intervention. Invasive species are seen as a threat to local species in the same way that ill animals are seen as a threat to local animal populations. More generally, from the perspective of humans, certain creatures are by their very nature hostile to human interests. As such, they demand action to eradicate or control them in order to protect humans from harm. This applies to 'vermin, pests and parasites' that cannot adjust their behaviour and with which there is no possibility of communication or compromise. If left unchecked, they would create ecological havoc and harm to humans—and to other species (Anderson 2004).

Animals have rights, but which and how these are enforced are variable depending upon natural and social contexts (Anderson 2004; White 2013). As has been observed by some writers (Cazaux 1999), consideration of human practices that are detrimental to the well-being of animals, such as loss and fragmentation of habitat, tend to focus on the effects regarding *animal populations* of a certain species (matters pertaining to the threat of extinction). Less attention is paid to the consequences of broad trends to the well-being of animals as *individual subjects* (see Sollund 2012).

Ethical and moral dilemmas involving animals—in life and death situations—also extend to instances where individual animals of one species are sacrificed for the sake of the preservation of an entire other species, which can be either plant or animal.

> In a 1996 case, the US Fish and Wildlife Service moved to poison 6,000 gulls at Monomoy National Wildlife Refuge off Cape Cod, in order to save 35 piping plovers, an endangered species. … San Clemente Island, off the coast of California, has both endemic plant species and a population of feral goats, introduced by Spanish sailors two centuries ago. To protect plants numbering in the few hundreds, the Fish and Wildlife Service and the US Navy have shot tens of thousands of feral goats. (Rolston 2010, pp. 605–606).

This represents cases where the so-called ethic of species has triumphed. The death of individual creatures has been weighed up against the potential demise of whole species. While objectionable from the point of view of killing animals, unless suitable alternatives for relocation are possible or available, there is a moral justification for such acts insofar as they allow future and more diverse life to flourish. Likewise, threats to those habitats that service a wide variety of species may mean human intervention to 'cull' the 'offending' creatures—as in the case of expanding populations of kangaroo in Canberra that promised to completely denude the landscape and thereby ruin the survival chances of all species in the same vicinity.

The way in which animals are valued is complicated and depends upon circumstance and behaviours (of both animals and humans). There are often distinctions made between 'good' and 'bad' invasive/native species, as illustrated by the welcome and protection afforded to (introduced) trout to the lakes of Tasmania, to the detriment of their local cousins, the galaxia fish. How they are defined, and what is valued, when it comes to animals is highly variable and subject to ongoing contestation at the level of philosophy as well as at the level of legislative practice (see Beirne 2009; Sankoffand White 2009). This has important consequences for the way in which harm against different species of animal is socially constructed. Built into this equation is also consideration of what kind of environment or habitat best suits which species, and how this particular habitat might be preserved or conserved to support the most privileged species.

Fundamentally, it would seem that the 'value' of a species is shaped by its utility in regard to human needs and services, and its relative abundance as a species. For example, certain types of fish, and elephants, may be assessed in terms of their value as a resource. The central issues are those of scarcity and appropriate regulation of trade. The problem is construed in terms of illegal (or unreported or unregulated) use of the species as a resource (for example, as a food, as an ornament). In other cases, the status of the species is defined in terms of biodiversity. For example, for polar bears the key issue is that of extinction or diminishment of habitation, associated with climate change (for example, the melting of Arctic ice in ways that affect the environment of the polar bear).

There are a number of issues relevant to consideration of how to respond to habitat destruction and harm to animals. Specific circumstances dictate particular responses, and it is clear that a 'one size fits all' strategy is not suitable or appropriate. Yet, habitat destruction due to climate change, pollution and exploitation of the environment is rapidly changing the policy and moral context within which human decision-making about animal welfare and survival is taking place. Mass migrations of nonhuman animals are happening in the here and now, and exceptional events such as a 'marine heatwave' are already dramatically affecting many diverse species living in the ocean (Macaulay 2016). How and when to intervene remain questions that are highly political, contentious—and urgent.

Conclusion

As illustrated in this chapter, the demise of habitat is occurring both on land and in the sea and is largely associated with economic imperatives. Thus, animal abuse resulting from wildlife habitat destruction needs to be located conceptually and empirically within the context of a political economy that privileges particular sectoral interests—and anthropocentric interests—over and above others, including the interests of nonhuman animals. This overarching type of analysis is essential in comprehending the scale, dynamics and consequences of the problem and in understanding the ways in which the processes and pressures of global capitalism are constitutive in its making (see also Lynch et al. 2015).

Yet there are interesting and important moral elements to this story that require thoughtful reflection on who is doing what to whom and why. Destruction of wildlife habitat is not all the same, everywhere. Nor is it interpreted the same by different stakeholders and participants. There is a significant difference, for example, between fire burning carried out by Indigenous people in northern Australia (part of traditional methods of landscape management and reverence for country) and burning of fires in Borneo and Sumatra (which are largely for commercial purposes even if performed by local villagers). The rejuvenation of the land sometimes requires actions that superficially appear destructive and damaging to wildlife habitat and the creatures living therein. This is very different from the sorts of exploitative efforts generally driving wildlife habitat destruction in most parts of the world today. In a similar vein, it is important to acknowledge that how humans, and specific agencies, intervene to manage habitat likewise has nuances and choices built into them. This is seen in the way in which some habitats, and some species, are protected ahead of others and sometimes to the detriment of others.

Animal abuse is thus, as ever, a complex social phenomenon. It necessarily involves value judgement and scientific expertise, a willingness to learn from the nonhuman Other and a commitment to act in good faith rather than mean spirit or ideological pureness. Whose habitat we 'save' (or for that matter, destroy) and why and how we do so is implicated in precisely these sorts of issues and conundrums.

References

Anderson, E. (2004). Animal rights and the values of nonhuman life. In C. Sustein & M. Nussbaum (Eds.), *Animal rights: current debates and new directions*. Oxford: Oxford University Press.

Australian Broadcasting Corporation [ABC] (2015, October 19). Southeast Asia's haze: find out what is behind the choking smoke covering Indonesia, Malaysia and Singapore. *ABC News*.

Australian Broadcasting Corporation [ABC] (2015, October 22). South-East Asian haze strikes the Pacific as fires exceed greenhouse gas output of the US'. *ABC News.*

Australian Broadcasting Corporation [ABC] (2015, November 2). Borneo's orangutans forced out of habitat by haze from Indonesian peat blaze. *ABC News.*

Beirne, P. (2009). *Confronting animal abuse: law, criminology, and human-animal relationships.* New York: Rowman and Littlefield Publishers.

Bisschop, L. (2015). *Governance of the illegal trade in e-waste and tropical timber: case studies on transnational environmental crime.* Farnham, Surrey: Ashgate.

Boekhout van Solinge, T. (2008a). Crime, conflicts and ecology in Africa. In R. Sullund (Ed.), *Global harms: ecological crime and speciesism.* New York: Nova Science Publishers.

Boekhout van Solinge, T. (2008b). The land of the orangutan and the bird of paradise under threat. In R. Sullund (Ed.), *Global harms: ecological crime and speciesism.* New York: Nova Science Publishers.

Boekhout van Solinge, T. (2010a). Equatorial deforestation as a harmful practice and a criminological issue. In R. White (Ed.), *Global environmental harm: criminological perspectives.* Devon: Willan Publishing.

Boekhout van Solinge, T. (2010b). Deforestation crimes and conflicts in the amazon. *Critical Criminology, 18,* 263–277.

Boekhout van Solinge, T. & Kuijpers, K. (2013). The amazon rainforest: a green criminological perspective. In N. South & A. Brisman (Eds.), *Routledgeinternational handbook of green criminology.* New York: Routledge.

Borras Jr., S., Franco, J., & Wang, C. (2013). The challenge of global governance of land grabbing: changing international agricultural context and competing political views and strategies. *Globalizations, 10*(1), 161–179.

Brisman, A., & South, N. (2013). Resources, wealth, power, crime and conflict. In R. Walters, D. Westerhuis, T. Wyatt (Eds.), *Emerging issues in green criminology.* Basingstoke: Palgrave Macmillan.

Brisman, A., South, N., & White, R. (Eds.) (2015). *Environmental crime and social conflict: contemporary and emerging issues.* Farnham, Surrey: Ashgate.

Burrell, A., Gay, S., & Kavallari, A. (2012). The compatibility of EU biofuel policies with global sustainability and the WTO. *The World Economy, 35*(6), 784–798.

Carrington, K., Hogg, R., & McIntosh, A. (2011). Resource boom underbelly: the criminological impact of mining development. *Australian and New Zealand Journal of Criminology, 44*(3), 335–354.

Caughley, J., Bomford, M., & McNee, A. (1996). Use of wildlife by indigenous Australians: issues and concepts. In M. Bomford & J. Caughley (Eds.), *Sustainable use of wildlife by aboriginal peoples and Torres strait islanders.* Canberra: Bureau of Resource Sciences, Australian Government Publishing Service.

Cazaux, G. (1999). Beauty and the beast: animal abuse from a non-speciesist criminological perspective. *Crime, Law and Social Change, 31,* 105–126.

Charles, C., Gerasimchuk, I., Birdle, R., Moerenhout, T., Asmelash, E., & Laan, T. (2013). *Biofuels—at what cost? A review of costs and benefits of EU biofuels policies.* Manitoba: International Institute for Sustainable Development.

Devalle, B., & Sessions, G. (1985). *Deep ecology: living as if nature mattered.* Layton, UT: Gibbs Smith.

Engdahl, F. (2007). *Seeds of destruction: the hidden agenda of genetic manipulation.* Montreal: Global Research.

Freeland, S. (2015). *Addressing the intentional destruction of the environment during warfare under the Rome statute of the international criminal court.* Cambridge: Intersentia.

Global Witness (2013). *Rubber Barons: how Vietnamese companies and international financiers are driving a land grabbing crisis in Cambodia and Laos.* London: Global Witness.

Greenpeace (2014, March 31). What does the IPCC WGII report say on forests? *Greenpeace briefing.* greenpeace.org.

Hay, D. 1975. Property, authority and the criminal law. In D. Hay, P. Linebaugh, J. G. Rule. E.P. Thompson and C. Winslow, (Eds.), *Albion's Fatal Tree: Crime and Society in Eighteenth Century England.* Harmondsworth: Allen Lane.

Intergovernmental Panel on Climate Change (2013, September 27). *Working group I contribution to the IPCC fifth assessment report climate change 2013: the physical science basis: summary for policymakers.*

Khagram, S. (2004). *Dams and development: transnational struggles for water and power.* Ithaca, NY: Cornell University Press.

Lin, A. (2006). The unifying role of harm in environmental law. *Wisconsin Law Review, 3*, 898–985.

Lynch, M., Long, M., & Stretesky, P. (2015). Anthropogenic development drives species to be endangered: capitalism and the decline of species. In R. Sollund (Ed.), *Green harms and crimes: critical criminology in a changing world.* Basingstoke: Palgrave Macmillan.

Macaulay, C. (2016). Species on the move worldwide. *The Mercury*, Hobart, pp.14–15.

McKenna, K. 2013. Scotland has the most inequitable land ownership in the West. Why? *The Guardian*, 10 August 2016.

Merchant, C. (2005). *Radical ecology: the search for a liveable world.* New York: Routledge.

Mitchell, D. (2008, July). A note on rising food prices. *World* Bank *policy research working paper no. 4682.* The World Bank, Development Prospects Group.

Mol, H. (2013). 'A Gift from the Tropics to the World': power, harm, and palm oil. In R. Walters, D. Westerhuis, T. Wyatt (Eds.), *Emergingissues in green criminology.* Basingstoke: Palgrave Macmillan.

Munro, S. (2012). *Rich land, wasteland—how coal is killing Australia.* Sydney: Pan Macmillan Australia.

Naik, A. (2010). Causes of pollution. *Buzzle*, 22 October 2010. http://www.buzzle.com/articles/causes-of-pollution.html. Accessed 13 January 2012.

Park, A. (2015, November 19). 7 things you need to know about GMO Salmon. *Time Magazine*.

Pellow, D. (2007). *Resisting global toxics: transnational movements for environmental justice*. Cambridge, MA: The MIT Press.

Plumwood, V. (2004). Gender, eco-feminism and the environment. In R. White (Ed.), *Controversies in environmental sociology*. Melbourne: Cambridge University Press.

Reliable Plant (2007, November/December). *New study favors tree over corn as biofuel source*. Accessed 21 January 2008.

Robin, M.-M. (2010). *The world according to monsanto: pollution, corruption and the control of our food supply*. New York: The New Press.

Robyn, L. (2002). Indigenous knowledge and technology. *American Indian Quarterly*, *26*(2), 198–220.

Rolston, H. (2010). Wild animals and ethical perspectives. In M. Bekoff (Ed.), *Encyclopaedia of animal rights and animal welfare*, Volume 2. Santa Barbara, CA: Greenwood Press.

Ruggiero, V., & South, N. (2013). Toxic state–corporate crimes, neo-liberalism and green criminology: the hazards and legacies of the oil, chemical and mineral industries. *International Journal for Crime, Justice and Social Democracy*, *2*(2), 12–26.

Sankoff, P., & White, S. (Eds.) (2009). *Animal law in Australasia: a new dialogue*. Sydney: The Federation Press.

Secretariat of the Convention on Biological Diversity (2010). *Global biodiversity outlook 3*. Montreal: SCBD.

Setiono, B. (2007). Fighting illegal logging and forest-related financial crimes: the anti-money laundering approach. In L. Elliot (Ed.), *Transnational environmental crime in the Asia-pacific: a workshop report*. Canberra: Australian National University.

Shiva, V. (2000). *Stolen harvest: the hijacking of the global food supply*. London: Zed Books.

Shiva, V. (2008). *Soil not oil: environmental justice in an age of climate crisis*. Brooklyn: South End Press.

Sollund, R. (2012). Speciesism as doxic practice versus valuing difference and plurality. In R. Ellefsen, R. Sollund, & G. Larsen (Eds.), *Eco-global crimes: contemporary problems and future challenges*. Farnham, Surrey: Ashgate.

Stretesky, P., Long, M., & Lynch, M. (2014). *The treadmill of crime: political economy and green criminology*. London: Routledge.

Sutherland, W.J., Clout, M., Cote, I., Daszak, P., Depledges, M.H., Fellman, L., et al. (2009). A horizon scan of global conservation issues for 2010. *Trends in Ecology and Evolution*, *25*(1), 1–7.

Tsing, A. (2005). *Friction: an ethnography of global connection*. Princeton: Princeton University Press.

United Nations Environment Programme (2011). *UNEP year book: emerging issues in our global environment 2011*. Nairobi, Kenya: UNEP.

United Nations Environment Programme (UNEP) (2013). *Threats to biodiversity*. http://www.unep-wcmc.org/threats-to-biodiversity_52.html. Accessed 4 September 2013.

Varkkey, H. (2013). Oil palm plantations and transboundary haze: patronage networks and land licensing in Indonesia's peatlands. *Wetland, 33*, 679–690.

Walters, R. (2005). Crime, bio-agriculture and the exploitation of hunger. *British Journal of Criminology, 46*(1), 26–45.

Walters, R. (2010). Toxic atmospheres: air pollution, trade and the politics of regulation. *Critical Criminology, 18*, 307–323.

Walters, R. (2011). *Eco crime and genetically modified food*. New York: Routledge.

White, R. (2013). *Environmental harm: an eco-justice perspective*. Bristol: Policy Press.

White, R., & Heckenberg, D. (2014). *Green criminology: an introduction to the study of environmental harm*. London: Routledge.

World Wide Fund for Nature [WWF] (2014). *Living planet report 2014: species and spaces, people and places*. (Eds. R. McLellan, L. Iyengar, B. Jeffries, N. Oerlemans). Gland, Switzerland: WWF.

Rob White is Professor of Criminology in the School of Social Sciences at the University of Tasmania, Australia. He has published widely in the areas of youth studies and green criminology. Among his recent books are *Environmental Crime and Collaborative State Intervention* (with Grant Pink, eds); *Environmental Harm: An Eco-Justice Perspective*; and *Environmental Crime and Social Conflict* (with Avi Brisman and Nigel South, eds).

Part IV

The Abuse of Animals Used in Entertainment

Animal Racing: Shifting Codes of Canadian Social Tolerance

Kevin Young

Introduction

As public and official concern with the ethics of animal treatment reaches new heights in many countries (DeGrazia 2002), as inquiries into institutionalized corruption in equine sports gather pace (Drape et al. 2012), as drivers of racing horse wagons begin to be punished over animal deaths (*CBC News* 2015b), and as the first criminal prosecution related to horse doping heads to the Supreme Court of Canada (*Calgary Herald* 2015 October 13, p. B1), the time seems right to reconsider the question of racing animals for public 'entertainment' and 'sport'.

The term 'animal racing' likely conjures up images of horses competing at high speed over set distances, over obstacles, or propelling wagons and carriages of various dimensions (Scott 2005; Gerber and Young 2013; Young and Gerber 2014). However, horses are not the only animals to be 'raced'. In fact, the range of racing animals is surprisingly diverse and often imbued with deep historical and cultural significance. It includes, but is not limited to: dogs (for example, Hsinchun 1994; Kemp 1999; Grundlingh 2003; Atkinson and Young 2005), camels (for example, Khalaf 1999), yaks (for example, Bhutan 1996), buffalo (for example,

K. Young (✉)
Department of Sociology, University of Calgary, Calgary, Canada
e-mail: kyoung@ucalgary.ca

J. Maher et al. (eds.), *The Palgrave International Handbook of Animal Abuse Studies*, DOI 10.1057/978-1-137-43183-7_13

Chaudhari and Chaudhari 2005), bulls (for example, Lamoureux 2003), elephants (for example, Delaney and Madigan 2009), and even mice (for example, Bancroft 1978), hamsters (for example, Gardiner 2001; Phillips 2004), and turtles (for example, Ryan 1974). Further, numerous types of birds (notably pigeons) have featured centrally in the racing traditions of many societies (for example, Walcott 1996). Threaded through all of these traditions are rituals, often very colourful and flamboyant, of spectacle, betting[1] and masculinity. Needless to say, one might also add rituals of risk and injury both to animal and human participants. More than anything else, it is changing social sensibilities to questions of risk, and who/what is and is not able to consent to such risk that increasingly projects animals used for public entertainment and sports into the limelight. The Calgary Stampede represents one forum for examining the nature and prevalence of, as well as the response to, animal treatment in racing sports. This chapter undertakes such an examination using the figurational approach of Norbert Elias.

Nature

The Calgary Exhibition and Stampede is an annual 10-day-long event in Calgary, Alberta, that takes place every July. The Stampede itself features a world-famous parade, midway entertainment, agrarian style competitions, a major trade show, world class concerts, a daily rodeo and the Rangeland Derby Chuckwagon races. These elements of what can be called the 'Stampede proper' occur at Stampede Park, a 200-acre site on the south-eastern edge of Calgary's downtown core (Beniot 2012, p. 23).

In addition to events on the Stampede grounds, the city itself is transformed from a modern metropolis and one of Western Canada's foremost business hubs into a place of boisterous celebration and spectacle. Each day, pancake breakfasts take place all around the city with some breakfasts at major shopping malls attracting upwards of 100,000 people. Many citizens participate in parties and social events, often claiming a connection to Western (that is, cowboy, ranching, etc.) heritage. The Stampede even transforms corporate Calgary as dozens of shops and businesses have their storefronts decorated in Western themes,

[1] Whilst it is generally very difficult to find reliable statistics on those who bet and/or attend animal racing, at least in the UK horseracing overwhelmingly makes up the majority of betting (http://www.gamblingcommission.gov.uk/Gambling-data-analysis/statistics/Industry-statistics.aspx).

companies host Stampede parties, and many workplaces allow and even encourage staff to wear Western attire for the duration of the festivities. It is common for businesses to slow and even close down, allowing employees time to attend events. The Stampede generates millions of dollars in direct and indirect spending for the local economy and is perhaps the single most important annual event for the local economy (Hirsch 2010).[2]

The Calgary Stampede is organized and managed by the Calgary Stampede Board, an entity comprising well-known and well-connected Calgarians. The Mayor of Calgary and two sitting counsellors also occupy positions on the Board. As a corporate event, the Stampede presents a commercial opportunity that many Calgary businesses simply cannot afford to pass up. Many companies engage in campaigns that relate their brand to the Stampede and associated Western themes (Hirsch 2010). In addition to corporate connections, the Stampede receives various forms of assistance from all three levels of government (municipal, provincial and federal) and many have argued that the line separating local politics from local businesses has become extremely blurred (Foran 2008, p. 150).

The Stampede has become closely entwined with the city of Calgary's image, identity, governance and economy. As Foran argues in *Icon, Brand, Myth: The Calgary Stampede*, some central aspects of the Stampede and its image—including whether the Stampede accurately reflects historical practices—are amplified by myth and legend (2008, pp. 148–149).Together, all of these aforementioned elements form a unique phenomenon encompassing much more than an innocuous municipal festival. The Calgary Stampede brashly brands itself as 'The Greatest Outdoor Show on Earth'. However, all is not as well as it seems, and for some time storm clouds have been gathering over the Stampede.

Indeed, the Stampede has become a hub of controversy locally, nationally and internationally. While a variety of elements related to the Stampede have drawn critical consideration, and in some cases, condemnation, nowhere has criticism been more pronounced than in relation to the treatment of animals for public entertainment—in particular, the impact to horses in the Rangeland Derby Chuckwagon racing. Criticism takes many forms, and

[2] Annually, the Calgary Stampede brings in an estimated $250 million for the city of Calgary (Hirsch 2010).This is a 2010 figure based off the total economic impact derived by the community including hotels, restaurants, tourism companies, in addition to the revenue generated on the Stampede grounds. The Calgary Stampede's 2014 consolidated financial statements (http://corporate.calgarystampede.com/ar2014/ar2014.pdf) reveal that the Stampede Board (between the Stampede itself, facility rentals, Cowboys Casino and other activities) made $137 million in gross revenue.

often focuses on the injuries to and fatalities of horses that occur before, during and after competition. For many years, in the lead-up to July, local newspaper editorials have been replete with impassioned letters of both support for and condemnation of the Stampede, and particularly, the chuckwagon racing. As the following examples show, just a cursory glance through local and national newspapers reveals the newsworthiness of serious accidents at the Stampede 'chucks': 'Two horses die during race on first night of Stampede' (*Globe and Mail* 2006 July 10, p. A8); 'Horse put down at derby' (*Calgary Sun* 2011 July 9, p. 6); 'Second horse put down at Calgary Stampede; Broken leg discovered after chuckwagon race' (Stone and Ho 2011, p. A2); and '4 Calgary Stampede horses die in 2015 chuckwagon races' (*CBC News* 2015a).

In addition to the public discourse often aired in the media, several animal rights and animal welfare organizations such as People for the Ethical Treatment of Animals (PETA), the Vancouver Humane Society (VHS), and the Calgary Humane Society (CHS) have run provocative public awareness campaigns opposing the inclusion of animals in Stampede events. As described by Gerber and Young (2013), emotive headlines and graphic images broadcast in the news media related to injured or dying animals sometimes being dragged off the track by tractors during high-profile Stampede events have become commonplace in recent years.

The increasingly contested nature of the Calgary Stampede and its use of horses lend itself particularly well to analysis using figurational or 'process' sociology. Assessing the Stampede and controversies surrounding it with conceptual tools such as 'thresholds of repugnance', 'civilization/de-civilization' and 'sportization', represents an illuminating line of inquiry. But it is first necessary to consider the prevalence of the problem increasingly at the centre of public concern.

Prevalence

Much, although certainly not all, of the controversy related to animal use and animal care in the context of the Stampede relates to the daily rodeo and chuckwagon races. The Rangeland Derby (chuckwagon racing) in particular is subject to the most media scrutiny and public opposition because of its high-profile nature, its often very violent crashes, and the harm incurred by its equine 'athletes'.

Chuckwagon racing concludes each day's competition. It is also the event perhaps most entwined with both corporate Calgary and what is viewed as the Stampede's 'Western values' (van Herk 2008). In the annual build-up to the Stampede, local companies including many high-profile oil and gas firms, law firms, car dealerships, and the like bid on 'tarp rights' for the competing drivers in a televised 'tarp sale' (van Herk 2008; Fisher 2016[3]). Tarpaulins cover each team's wagon and are colourfully adorned with the logos and advertisements of Calgary's most prestigious businesses, some of which pay upwards of $200,000 in order to sponsor top flight drivers (van Herk 2008, p. 247). In addition to these corporate links, in Stampede marketing material and advertisements, 'the chucks' are purported to be closely associated with 'western values' and notions of the 'traditional cowboy'. As van Herk (2008, p. 247) describes, corporate sponsorship of the chucks goes beyond marketing; it weaves together a 'tapestry of competition and cooperation'. Sponsoring chuckwagon racing simultaneously allows regional companies to situate their brand in a very public space and also foster the impression of connectivity to, and respect for, local history and culture.

However, despite what many locals are brought up to believe and often aggressively defend, the Rangeland Derby has little actual connection to authentic Cowboy culture or the region's history (van Herk 2008). Rather, chuckwagon racing at the Calgary Stampede owes its genesis to the Stampede's first major promoter, Guy Weadick. As van Herk notes, 'the chucks' were introduced first and foremost to add a thrilling spectacle to conclude the Stampede and to attract larger audiences: 'In search of an exciting event to cap his hyperbolic rodeo, Guy Weadick figured that some kind of wagon race would be crazy and chaotic enough to guarantee audience interest' (2008, p. 242). The first chuckwagon racing competition occurred during the 1923 Stampede (11 years after the inaugural Stampede in 1912), and since that time, has evolved into the massively popular event it is today.

Chuckwagon racing has indeed become the Stampede 'crown jewel' and is aggressively promoted by the Stampede Board itself and by thousands of locals who actively endorse the festival. Many of those who support both the rodeo and the chucks see criticism based on injury to animals as attacks on Calgary's identity or Western ways of life per se—as though either of these things were homogeneous wholes. As noted above, however, these responses are largely misplaced, as chuckwagon racing is not based on any material or factual connection to Calgary (or Western) history; instead, the sport was

[3] In what is widely considered "an annual litmus test for the local economy" (Fisher 2016, p. A1), the 2016 Rangeland Derby canvas auction brought in $2.29 m.

introduced solely to titillate audiences and enhance economic value. Promotion of the chucks heavily underscores the bravado, adrenaline and risk imbued in all rodeo events (Mikklesen 2008; van Herk 2008) and is amply demonstrated by the way the Stampede's own website publicizes itself in unambiguously spectacular ways: 'You'll witness all the heart-stopping action as 36 drivers, 216 horses and the teams vie for over $1.15 million in prize money.'

The principal controversy underlying much of the debate surrounding the chuckwagon racing relates to the prevalence of (often gruesome) injuries and fatalities that occur as a direct result of racing. Countering its success as a hugely popular attraction (thousands of spectators pour into the Stampede grounds every night) and the undeniably popular view that 'the chucks' are exciting to watch, is the Stampede's equally undeniable—and clearly discouraging—report card where animal safety is concerned.

Reliable statistics on horse racing accidents, injuries and deaths at the Stampede are both difficult to find and rationalized at every turn. To provide some depth to the question of the prevalence of horse injuries and deaths, there are, of course, innumerable news articles posted online describing individual cases of horse injuries and deaths, as well as social responses to such cases raising critical questions about the legitimacy, responsibility, and viability of such obviously high-risk 'sports' (for both human and animal participants) (for example, *CBC News* 2010; *CBC News* 2012). While news of such individual cases is not hard to find, locating reliable quantitative data on horse deaths at the Calgary Stampede, related either to chuckwagon racing or the cluster of other equine activities that the Stampede sanctions, is a different matter altogether. Certainly, sites and lists exist (for example, *Global News* 2012; Ban Chuckwagon Racing 2013; Vancouver Humane Society 2010), but their reliability is again debatable. In all cases, it is not difficult to see that such lists are posted by groups with interests to defend and ideological positions to advance. Similarly, several organizations beyond Calgary and indeed Canada maintain and publish records of equine injuries and fatalities in the form of 'data bases' in racing sports. Within Canada, for instance, Woodbine Racetrack in Ontario, fully accredited by the National Thoroughbred Racing Association, posts current and past archives (e.g., Woodbine Entertainment 2010). Beyond Canada, the British Horseracing Authority, for example, regularly updates racetrack reports (for example, British Horseracing Authority 2014). And finally, organizations such as *Animal Aid* maintain and release a 'Race Horse Death watch' (Animal Aid

2015). A so-called 'Racehorse Memorial Wall Worldwide' is also illuminating (Racehorse Memorial 2016). Needless to say, none of these sites cast a flattering light on the question of racing horses at high risk, though many of their findings remain vague and questionable.

These measurement problems, notwithstanding, there are strong indicators that chuckwagon racing and equine health are not natural partners. According to the VHS (2011), over 50 chuckwagon horses were fatally injured or had to be euthanized between 1986 and 2011. As noted generally by McBane and Douglas-Coope (2005), and more specifically by the CHS (2011), horses involved in, and being trained for rodeo, face regular physical discomfort and mental distress. Accidents, injuries and fatalities are simply a routine feature of the annual chuckwagon races at the Calgary Stampede. More troubling is the fact that unknown numbers of injuries and fatalities take place behind the scenes in preparation for competition—that is, in situations where the public normally has no access and where injury tolls go unreported. According to both media reports (for example, Ban Chuckwagon Racing 2013) and the aforementioned VHS (2011) report, in 2005, at least nine horses died while being transported to Stampede Park. In 2006, two horses died as a result of chuckwagon races, in 2007 three died, and in 2008, one more horse died. In 2009, two horses died, and in 2010 six horses died (four in chuckwagon racing competitions, and the other two in other rodeo events). Despite well-publicized rule changes to chuckwagon racing in 2011, intended to facilitate enhanced animal welfare on the track, two more horses perished during the 2011 competition, and in 2012, three more died. One horse died in both 2013 and 2014.[4] Most recently, four more horse deaths in 2015 led the Stampede to finally acknowledge its embarrassing safety record ("Calgary Stampede 'Not Proud' of its Animal safety Record as Fourth Horse Dies in Chuckwagon Races," *National Post* 2015). Almost all of these deaths took place on the chuckwagon track, several due to driver error. The GMC Rangeland Derby is perhaps suitably known as the 'Half Mile of Hell'.

In some cases horses involved in crashes have had to be euthanized on site in front of spectators before being removed from the track using heavy machinery. However, other instances of abuse related to overtraining or overuse are far removed from the cameras and glare of the public eye (Gerber and Young 2013, p. 537). As viewed through the lens of symbolic

[4] http://www.vancouverhumanesociety.bc.ca/wp-content/uploads/2010/08/Deaths-at-the-Calgary-Stampede-1986-to-July-2015.pdf

interactionism (such as the work of Goffman 1959), much of the harm sustained by horses at the Stampede occurs not in the visible 'front regions' of public sensibilities but in the 'back regions'—away from competition, common sight and public consideration.

Theoretical Considerations

The contested nature of the Calgary Stampede and chuckwagon racing conceived of as 'sport' or public entertainment contains obvious potential for critical reflection and sociological analysis. As mentioned above, figurational sociology offers real promise because it allows for the critical study of dynamic structures, processes and meanings that occur in a given setting. Further, figurational approaches are effective in the study of violence (for example, animal abuse) because they can be used to consider the relationship between specific actions and the 'civility' of the wider society. Clearly, the Stampede does not occur in a vacuum. Far from it; it is closely tied to the governance, identity, economy and cultural history of the city of Calgary, and indeed the province of Alberta more generally. As such, several figurational tools may be used to throw explanatory light on harmful Stampede practices and social responses.

Referring to the conceptually central processes of 'civilization', Morrow (2009) acknowledges that sport has always operated as a social barometer of 'civility'. This theme has been developed in many figurational analyses of sport—particularly the social-historical evaluation of violence in the evolution of activities such as soccer, foxhunting and rugby (Elias and Dunning 1986). From this point of view, links have been drawn between violence reduction initiatives in certain sports and broader civilizing processes in society (Morrow 2009, p. 216).

Within the sociology of sport subdiscipline, the study of sports violence has not systematically considered the role of animals, despite the fact that animal cruelty and violence may certainly be seen as one manifestation of sport-related violence (Young 2012). As argued by Gerber and Young (2013) and Young (2014), the study of animal treatment, including equine treatment, has also rarely been at the forefront of sociological research per se. Instead, when equine events have been considered, the focus is often on how participants operate within subcultural frameworks or how they derive benefit from horse use in specific contexts (cf., Scott 2005).

Elias argues that as 'ill-mannered' and violent societies increasingly find mechanisms to reform their laws, values and mores, a process occurs whereby various practices which increasingly offend public sensibilities become less and less acceptable. The collective taste for viewing or participating in certain violent acts, even indirectly as spectators, has been referred to by Elias (2000) as a 'threshold of repugnance'. For Elias, such a 'threshold' is not dormant or stagnant but, rather, shifts dynamically over time in keeping with other social changes.

For Elias (1986b), people in increasingly 'civilized' societies are expected to control aggressive impulses toward other humans and other living things. As such, as wider civilizing occurs at a macro-societal level, forms of entertainment previously found to be acceptable face increased scrutiny and possible rejection. Elias cites examples from the past of public torture and executions as acts viewed to be increasingly displeasureable, and Pinker (2011) shows how public cruelty toward animals (such as the public burning of cats to exorcise what was seen as the physical incarnation of evil) has changed massively over time. Elias explains how in an overall trend toward civilization societies are prone to both 'spurts' of civilization *and* de-civilization (Elias and Dunning 1986; Dunning 1999; Elias 2000). In the latter case, an event, process, practice or institution may hold out as a bastion of a form of once accepted but now contested behaviour.

Changing views in Canadian society vis-à-vis the appropriate treatment of animals and placing animals at risk for public entertainment and economic profit fall in line with what Eliasian scholars would deem to be a 'civilizing spurt'. The debate over rodeo and chuckwagon racing may well fit with a broader civilizing spurt, but the actual rodeo and chuckwagon events themselves are consistent with what Elias would term 'modern barbarism' (van Krieken 1998, p. 112), what Elias and Dunning (1986, 1999) would deem instances of *de-civilization*. Evidence of de-civilization related to modern chuckwagon races at the Stampede can be found in progressions of the sport itself. Van Herk explains how chuckwagon racing has become faster, riskier and more entertaining for spectators; once heavily set horses have been replaced by hyper-fit, lightweight thoroughbreds that now pull lighter wagons at far greater speeds (2008, p. 243). The audience desire to witness riskier behaviour and experience more excitement with increased risk to driver and horse alike fits within the Eliasian definitions of de-civilizing spurts.

The figurationalist notions of 'civilizing' and 'de-civilizing' are hardly linear in their real world examples. The Calgary Stampede Rangeland Derby is evidence of this. The (de-civilizing) increase of risk and injury in order to build tension and excitement occurs within a broader (and civilizing) societal rejection of, or at least concern with, exposing animals to unnecessary risk for mere entertainment. Even within what could be termed a de-civilizing process a civilizing spurt can be observed. In recent years, the CHS has been granted increased access to behind-the-scene areas outside of the public view and has made several recommendations to mitigate risks associated with rodeo. The way these processes occur is influenced by broader patterns of morality, ethics and tolerance in society manifested in all social institutions.[5] Where the Stampede is concerned, despite an evident growth in public disdain over gruesome accidents as summarized above, the local government and its provincial and federal counterparts have assumed a largely passive posture. The Stampede Board, as previously demonstrated the benefactor of millions of dollars in revenue from the rodeo and chucks, has started to show signs of responding to public pressure with attempts to increase safety and better manage risk to animals.

The Stampede's shifting use of rationalizing strategies, or what sociologists Sykes and Matza (1989) would call 'techniques of neutralization' can be analyzed and explained through a further figurational lens. Dunning links the civilizing process in sport with a process of what he calls 'sportization' whereby stricter rules and greater levels of supervision and surveillance of a sporting environment are created, indeed necessary, for an activity to survive in a wider process of growing sensitivity (1999, p. 48). Through the evolution in public sensibility, sport related regulations and their supervision become more efficient and surveilling:

> A central part of this 'sportization' process involved the development of a stricter framework of rules governing sporting competition. Thus rules became more precise, more explicit and more differentiated while, at the same time, supervision of the observance of those rules became more efficient... (1999, p. 48).

The link between 'sportization' and the civilizing process is exemplified by the fact that the level of tolerated violence in a sporting pursuit adjusts over time to match the level of violence tolerated by the broader community. As society becomes more repulsed by violence and its outcomes, the level of combative or risky behaviour permitted in sporting events also decreases. Elias argues that sports which are excessively violent by normal social standards are often discredited as 'illegitimate' sports; in many ways this seems to be the growing reputation of chuckwagon racing in some quarters. Why else would the

[5] Such shifts co-exist with broader developments in philosophical debates on animal welfare/rights which demonstrate notions of civilizing process and no doubt impact on welfare standards in the Stampede. Arguably, there are similarities in the conflict between welfare and rights approach and the civilizing/de-civilizing approach.

Calgary Stampede go so far out of its way to convince the public that it is responsibly and consistently tightening up its rules and regulations?

Finally, figurationalists contend that the pacification of societies associated with 'civilizing trends' creates a need to find alternative sources of excitement and intrigue (Elias and Dunning 1986). Expansions of regulatory frameworks and policing regimens restrain people's ability to behave emotionally or exuberantly. Van Krieken (1998) describes sport as an example of emotional management in modern societies whereby a tension is created within controlled frameworks (p. 136). Therefore, sport can and indeed often does function as a place where a 'controlled de-controlling' of emotions takes place. Elias (1986) also discusses problems associated with this such as managing the risk of harm to participants while maintaining an enjoyable level of competition. The spectacle and pageantry associated with Calgary Stampede chuckwagon racing encapsulates a space for such a 'managed de-controlling' of emotions. In the nine decades since its induction, chuckwagon racing has become one of the most prestigious and richest sports in the entire province of Alberta (van Herk 2008, p. 241). In excess of 180,000 people attend the 'chucks' every Stampede and many more watch on television. Although some are likely drawn to the more technical aspects of the sport, there seems little denying that many are drawn to the sheer speed, danger and excitement of chuckwagon racing (van Herk 2008).

Response

Of the aforementioned theoretical constructs providing illumination on the treatment of chuckwagon racing horses at Calgary Stampede, perhaps the most tangible and visible is the figurational notion of sportization. A chuckwagon 'sportization' process can be seen in: the introduction of new rules and policies to make the sport safer for both horse and rider; the use of increasing sanctions in the form of fines and penalties for violators; increasingly collegial collaboration with animal welfare groups such as the CHS and the Alberta Society for the Prevention of Cruelty to Animals (ASPCA); and the creation of various commissions and groups, such as the Animal Care Advisory Panel (ACAP) and the Chuckwagon Safety Commission (CSC).

As part of the Stampede's stated commitment to 'animal care', such commissions, programs and partnerships are expanding and forms of both internal and external surveillance are becoming more and more obvious. The Stampede has partnered and worked collaboratively with various organizations in Alberta to ensure that its practices are acceptable in terms of animal welfare, including two animal welfare organizations—the CHS and the ASPCA. These groups consult with the Calgary Stampede throughout the year, and also regulate the Alberta Animal Protection Act (2010)[6] throughout the duration of the annual Stampede. A number of publicly available sources explain the changing role that the CHS has played in implementing these rule changes. For example, *Thirty-six Ways We've Improved Treatment of Stampede's Animals* (Cameron 2011) explains the role that the CHS has played in enhancing animal welfare in this context. The author, Patricia Cameron, Director of the CHS, explains the goals of the 'partnership' between the two organizations in the following way: '. . . to engage in long-term relationship building, to foster dialogue, to mutually seek solutions and understanding, to conduct solid research, to educate and to provide evidence-based recommendations' (Cameron 2011, p. A11). Ultimately, this might further legitimize the rules put forward by the Calgary Stampede because they have been collaboratively and visibly agreed upon by an animal welfare organization. In addition to partnering with animal welfare organizations, the Calgary Stampede has also partnered with Moore and Co., an equine veterinary practice, which monitors the care and health of animals throughout the Stampede. Of course, one of the paradoxical consequences of *appearing* to respond to animal welfare is that concerns can be disregarded or put aside even when harm to animals remains very real (see Beirne and South 2007).

Further, the Calgary Stampede has created two independent groups in its pursuit of a more transparent and animal-friendly mandate—the ACAP and the CSC. As outlined on the Calgary Stampede website, the role of such groups is to 'ensure we set the highest standards for proper animal care.' The CSC was developed in 2008, just two years after the Calgary Stampede opted to develop its own rodeo format (as opposed to continuing as a more broadly sanctioned rodeo event). In an article written for *Canadian Geographic*, Dixon (2011) explains that this group '. . . developed a code of conduct and set stiff fines and penalties for dangerous conduct jeopardizing the horses or drivers.' The purpose of such fines and penalties was to decrease (ideally eliminate) horse deaths which result from avoidable accidents, such as those caused by driver error or track conditions. The ACAP, made up of independent experts from various disciplinary backgrounds, was developed in 2010, and was charged with ensuring that the Calgary Stampede maintains robust animal care practices (see Calgary Stampede 2015a).

The so-called 'Fitness to Compete' program illustrates another level of codification through which the health and well-being of the horse is more formally surveilled; this plays a crucial role in minimizing the danger faced by

[6] http://www.qp.alberta.ca/documents/Acts/a41.pdf

Stampede horses. Specifically, it allows veterinarians to police the health of horses, and to regulate the frequency of their participation. Through a microchip inserted under the animal's skin, regulators can ensure that competitors are not 'stretching' or breaking the rules that have been implemented to protect horses (such as the rules that prevent over-use of a horse and preventing unhealthy or unfit horses from competing—discussed below).

In addition to such partnerships and commissions, all clearly indicative of an ongoing, and importantly, surveilled sportization process, in 2011 the Calgary Stampede undertook a number of significant rule and safety changes to chuckwagon racing, making that year particularly interesting to look at through the lens of sportization. These rules include limiting the use of horses in chuckwagon racing to four consecutive days (to lower the risk of injury and accidents from fatigue or over-use), requiring that horses used in a race be identified 'pre-race' so that they can be examined by a veterinarian before running (to prevent an unfit horse from racing), reducing the number of outriders from four to two (to decrease the number of horses on the track during a race), and increasing track maintenance by harrowing the track after every second race (to improve footing, and therefore safety, for the horses) (Calgary Stampede 2015b). These rule changes persist as the focus of media attention and debate, so much so that one news article suggested that the 2011 Stampede '. . . will likely be remembered as the year new animal care rules were instituted and declared a tentative success even in the wake of two horse deaths' (Stone and Tetley 2011, p. A1). It is also important to note that not only has the Stampede implemented these rules, but that it has also widely publicized these changes throughout the local and national media. The sheer number of articles which reference the rule changes illustrate the important role that rules and regulations play in the debate over horse-use. These examples suggest that the Calgary Stampede has attempted to legitimize the continued existence of chuckwagon racing as 'sport' by implementing and publicizing a variety of rules aimed at minimizing the violence (by way of injuries and fatalities), so as to fall within a socially acceptable level. Clearly, what is at stake in programs such as 'Fitness to Compete' is as much about marketing and public image as it is about animal safety, especially in the face of ongoing harm to horses.

Conclusion

As an example of how modern societies are increasingly reconciling questions of humanity against common practices that harm animals, this chapter examines a cultural institution of the Canadian West—the Calgary Stampede. Using chuckwagon racing as a case study, and couching the high-risk use of horses in the figurational language of Elias, Dunning and others, it considers shifting views toward the 'civility' of the self-proclaimed 'Greatest Outdoor Show on Earth'. As just one site in the broader debate regarding animal rights and social justice, the Calgary Stampede represents a fascinating setting for the assessment of a changing social climate regarding the use of animals in all aspects of life, from factory farming to pharmaceutical testing to sport, games and play for popular entertainment. The use of horses (and animals more broadly) at the Calgary Stampede has become extremely contentious and there now exists a clear struggle between supporters or traditionalists and proponents of change. At the center of this debate is the thorny question of how humans should treat what Brandt called our 'equine companions' (2009, p. 315), and whether the 'techniques of neutralization' that have been used to rationalize risk, pain and death in this century-old tradition are as compelling as they once were.

With specific respect to equine welfare in chuckwagon racing at the Calgary Stampede, and in conclusion, this chapter makes four essential arguments: (i) chuckwagon racing provides clear evidence of changing social perceptions toward the use/abuse of animals in entertainment/sport; (ii) there are obvious and acknowledged examples of harm/abuse toward the animals involved, although it is difficult to provide an accurate account of this due to limited data/research/transparency; (iii) the figurational approach (and especially its core concepts of civilization/de-civilization and sportization) are helpful for understanding these shifts in social perceptions and how they are linked concretely to changing practices; and (iv) although it is questionable as to whether current social responses are enough (in terms of preventing harm to animals), the appearance of more caring approaches to animal welfare may have the paradoxical effect of softening concern even as potential harm to animals remains very real, and injury continues.

References

Animal Aid (2015). *1371 deaths in 3309 days*. http://www.horsedeathwatch.com. Accessed 2 April 2016.

Atkinson, M., & Young, K. (2005). Reservoir dogs: greyhound racing, mimesis and sports-related violence. *International Review for the Sociology of Sport*, *40*(3), 335–356.

Ban Chuckwagon Racing (2013). *Comments*. http://www.banchuckwagonracing.ca/wagon/calgary-stampede. Accessed 2 April 2016.

Bancroft, N. (1978). Of mouse and man. *Psychological Perspectives*, *9*(2), 115–124.

Beirne, P., & South, N. (Eds.). (2007). *Issues in green criminology: confronting harms against environments, humanity and other animals*. Devon: Willan Publishing.

Beniot, A. (2012). Stampede Park: origins of a gathering place. *Alberta History, 60*(3), 23.

BBC News (2015). *Calgary Stampede: why horses die on the 'Half Mile of Hell'. BHA Injuries of racehorses in Britain*. http://www.bbc.com/news/world-us-canada-33511970. Accessed 2 April 2016.

Bhutan, D. (1996). *Tibet handbook*. New York: Footprint Handbooks, pp. 436–437.

Brandt, K. (2009). Human-horse communication. In A. Arluke & C. Sanders (Eds.), *Between the species: readings in human-animal relations* (pp. 315–320). New York: Pearson.

British Horseracing Authority (2014). *Injuries of racehorses in the UK*. http://www.britishhorseracing.com/wp-content/uploads/2014/03/Injuries-of-Racehorses-in-the-UK.pdf. Accessed 2 April 2016.

Calgary Herald. (2015, October 13). *Doping Racehorses is Wrong—But is it Criminal?*, p. B1

Calgary Humane Society (2011). *Calgary Humane Society's position statement: animals in entertainment*. http://www.calgaryhumane.ca. Accessed 28 January 2011.

Calgary Sun. (2011, July 9). *Horse put down at derby*, p. 6.

Calgary Stampede (2010). *GMC rangeland derby history*. http://cs.calgarystampede.com/events/chuckwagon-races/history.html. Accessed 29 January 2011.

Calgary Stampede (2012–2013). *GMC rangeland derby*. http://cs.calgarystampede.com/events/gmc-rangeland-derby. Accessed 2 April 2016.

Calgary Stampede (2015a). *Calgary stampede 2015 report to the community*. http://news.calgarystampede.com. Accessed 2 April 2016.

Calgary Stampede (2015b). *2014 animal care practices*. http://corporate.calgarystampede.com/animal-care/rule-and-format-changes-2012.html. Accessed 2 April 2016.

Cameron, P. (2011, July 10). Thirty-six ways we've improved treatment of Stampede's animals. *Calgary Herald*, p. A11.

CBC News (2010, July 8). *Calgary rodeo condemned by UK MPs, activists*. http://www.cbc.ca. Accessed 2 April 2016.

CBC News (2010, July 16). *6th Stampede horse dies after fall*. http://www.cbc.ca/news/canada/calgary/6th-stampede-horse-dies-after-fall-1.930628. Accessed 2 April 2016.

CBC News (2012, July 14). *Chuckwagon racing days numbered*. http://www.cbc.ca/news/canada/are-chuckwagon-racing-s-days-numbered-1.1176200. Accessed 2 April 2016.

CBC News (2015a). *4 Calgary Stampede horses die in 2015 chuckwagon races*. http://www.cbc.ca/news/canada/calgary/4-calgary-stampede-horses-die-in-2015-chuckwagon-races-1.3149106. Accessed 2 April 2016.

CBC News (2015b). *Calgary Stampede chuckwagon drivers fined over horse death*. http://www.cbc.ca/news/canada/calgary/calgary-stampede-chuckwagon-drivers-fined-over-horse-death-1.3142676. Accessed 2 April 2016.

Chaudhari, S., & Chaudhari, S. (2005). *Primitive tribes in contemporary india: concept, ethnography and demography*. New Delhi: Mittal Publications.

DeGrazia, D. (2002). *Animal rights: a very short introduction*. Oxford: Oxford University Press.

Delaney, T., & Madigan, T. (2009). *The sociology of sports: an introduction*. Jefferson, NC: McFarland and Co.

Dixon, J. (2011, December). Rodeo renewal: new animal-care practices are changing perceptions of the century-old Stampede. *Canadian Geographic*, 46–52.

Drape, J., Bogdanich, W., Ruiz, R. R., & Griffin, P. (2012, April 30). Big purses, sore horses, and death. *New York Times*. http://www.nytimes.com/2012/04/30/us/casino-cash-fuels-use-of-injured-horses-at-racetracks.html?pagewanted=all&_r=0. Accessed 2 April 2016.

Dunning, E. (1999). *Sport matters: sociological studies of sport, violence and civilization*. New York: Routledge.

Elias, N. (1986a). Introduction. In N. Elias & E. Dunning (Eds.), *Quest for excitement: sport and leisure in the civilizing process* (pp. 19–62). New York: Basil Blackwell.

Elias, N. (1986b). The genesis of sport as a sociological problem. In N. Elias & E. Dunning (Eds.), *Quest for excitement: sport and leisure in the civilizing process* (pp. 126–149). New York: Basil Blackwell.

Elias, N. (2000). *The civilizing process (revised edition)*. In E. Dunning, J. Goudsblom, S. Mennell (Eds.), (trans. E. Jephcott). Oxford, UK: Blackwell Publishing.

Elias, N., & Dunning, E. (1986). *Quest for excitement: sport and leisure in the civilizing process*. New York: Basil Blackwell.

Fisher, S. (2016, March 18). Rangeland Derby canvas auction brings in $2.29 m. *Calgary Herald*, pp. A1–A2.

Foran, M. (Ed.). (2008). *Icon, brand, myth: the Calgary Stampede*. Edmonton, AB: Athabasca University Press.

Gandia, R. (2011, July 17). HUGE FINE: Chuckwagon crash and horse's death lead to record $12,500 penalty. *Calgary Sun*, p. 4.

Gardiner, B. (2001). Hamster races soothe restless bettors as foot-and-mouth slows action. In *Boston Globe*. Boston: Globe Electric Publishing.

Gerber, B., & Young, K. (2013). Horse play in the Canadian West: the emergence of the Calgary Stampede as contested terrain. *Society and Animals*, *21*(6), 523–545.

Globe and Mail (2006, July 10). Two horses die during race on first night of Stampede. *Globe and Mail*, p. A8.

Global News (2012, July 13). *By the numbers: animal deaths at the Calgary Stampede*. http://globalnews.ca/news/266118/by-the-numbers-animal-deaths-at-the-calgary-stampede. Accessed 2 April 2016.

Goffman, E. (1959). *The presentation of self in everyday life*. Garden City, NY: Doubleday-Anchor.

Griffin, E. (2007). *Blood sport: hunting in Britain since 1066*. New Haven: Yale University Press.

Grundlingh, A. (2003). 'Gone to the Dog': the cultural politics of gambling- the rise and fall of British greyhound racing on the Witwatersrand, 1932–1949. *South African Historical Journal, 48*(1), 174–189.

Hirsch, T. (2010, July 21). What's the real value of the Calgary Stampede? *Vegreville Observer*, p.3.

Hsinchun, C. (1994). *Expert prediction, symbolic learning, and neural networks: an experiment on greyhound racing*. Tucson, AZ: Arizona University *Press*.

Kemp, S. F. (1999). Sled dog racing: the celebration of co-operation in a competitive sport. *Ethnology, 38*(1), 81–95.

Khalaf, S. (1999). Camel racing in the gulf. notes on the evolution of a traditional cultural sport. *Anthropos, 94*, 85–106.

Lamoureux, F. (2003). *Indonesia: a global studies handbook*. Santa Barbara, CA: ABC-CLIO.

McBane, S., & Douglas-Coope, H. (2005). *Horse facts*. London: Quantum Publishing.

Mikkelsen, G. (2008). A spurring soul: a tenderfoot's guide to the Calgary Stampede. In M. Foran (Ed.), *The Calgary Stampede: icon, brand, myth* (pp. 203–235). Edmonton, AB: Athabasca University Press.

Morrow, R. (2009). Review essays—Norbert Elias and figurational sociology: the comeback of the century. *Contemporary Sociology, 38*(3), 215–219.

National Post (2015). *Calgary Stampede 'Not Proud' of its animal safety record as fourth horse dies in chuckwagon races*. http://news.nationalpost.com/news/canada/calgary-stampede-not-proud-of-its-animal-safety-record-after-fourth-horse-dies-in-chuckwagon-races. Accessed 2 April 2016.

Phillips, K. (2004). Homing: Hamster style. *Journal of Experimental Biology, 207*(9), 1–3.

Pinker, S. (2011). *The better angels of our nature: why violence has declined*. New York: Penguin.

Racehorse Memorial (2016). *Racehorse memorial wall worldwide*. https://docs.google.com/spreadsheets/d/1g1H393sQMp2OzXPYDjyZLSyo_8EsDldV8_vpLngXB4A/pub?output=html. Accessed 2 April 2016.

Renfrow, S. (2011, July 17). Record fine in chuck horse's death: Collision during race costs driver $12,500. *Calgary Herald*, p. B5.

Ryan, P. (1974). The last word on turtle racing. *New Scientist, 64*, 597–598.

Rollin, B. (1996). Rodeo and recollection—applied ethics and Western philosophy. *Journal of the Philosophy of Sport, XXIII*, 1–9.

Scott, M. (2005). *The racing game*. New Brunswick: Transaction Publishers.

Stone, L., & Ho, C. (2011, July 16). Second horse put down at Calgary Stampede; broken leg discovered after chuckwagon race. *Calgary Herald*, p. A2.

Stone, L., & Tetley, D. (2011, July 18). Cochrane cowboy wins $100,000 rodeo payday; Stampede enjoys resurgent year. *Calgary Herald*, p. A1.

Sykes, G., & Matza, D. (1989). Techniques of neutralization: a theory of delinquency. In D. Kelly (Ed.), *Deviant behavior: a text-reader in the sociology of deviance* (pp. 104–111). New York:St. Martin's Press.

Vancouver Humane Society (2010). *Animal deaths at the Calgary Stampede and rodeo & chuckwagonraces*. http://www.vancouverhumanesociety.bc.ca/wp-content/uploads/2010/08/Deaths-at-the-Calgary-Stampede-1986-to-July-20151.pdf. Accessed 2 April 2016.

Vancouver Humane Society (2011). *The Calgary Stampede*. http://www.vancouverhumanesociety.bc.ca/. Accessed 1 March 2016.

van Herk, A. (2008). The half a mile of heaven's gate. In M. Foran (Ed.), *The Calgary Stampede: icon, brand, myth* (pp. 235–251). Edmonton, AB: Athabasca University Press.

van Krieken, R. (1998). *Norbert Elias*. New York: Routledge.

Walcott, C. (1996). Pigeon homing: observations, experiments and confusions. *Journal of Experimental Biology*, *199*, 1, 21–27.

Woodbine Entertainment (2010). *Racetrack safety*. http://www.woodbineentertainment.com/Woodbine/Racing/Thoroughbred/Pages/RacetrackSafety.aspx. Accessed 2 April 2016.

Young, K. (2012). *Sport, violence and society*. Abingdon, UK: Routledge.

Young, K. (2014). Toward a less speciesist sociology of sport. *Sociology of Sport Journal*, *31*(4): 387–401.

Young, K., & B. Gerber (2014). Necropsian nights: animal sport, civility and the Calgary Stampede. In J. Gillett & M. Gilbert (Eds.), *Sport, society and animals* (pp. 154–169). London: Routledge.

Kevin Young is Professor of Sociology at the University of Calgary. His research interests bridge Criminology and the Sociology of Sport.

His most recent books include *Sport, Violence and Society* (Routledge, 2012) and *Sport, Social Development and Peace* (Emerald, 2014).

Hunting and Shooting: The Ambiguities of 'Country Sports'

Peter Squires

Introduction

This chapter discusses live animal shooting as a 'country sport' and the attitudes and practices associated with it. It begins by discussing recent cases of gratuitous 'trophy hunting' and the controversies these have generated before moving on to consider the cultural and historical changes which have shaped the development of shooting as an elite country sport and the changing sensibilities towards it. The chapter discusses the character, or 'nature', of this form of shooting and, in particular, challenges some of the justifications advanced for the 'sport shooting' of live animals, especially those arguments which claim that hunting and shooting engender a distinctive sense of respect or 'communion' with the natural world (Kheel 1995). By way of contrast, the chapter then turns to consider the substantially non-natural prevalence of intensive grouse shooting, especially in Scotland, where a highly concentrated and unaccountable pattern of private estate ownership, geared primarily to shooting activities, has generated significant collateral harms for local environments whilst also resulting in much illegal persecution (poisoning) of indigenous predators, especially rare birds of prey and protected species. A body of recent research

P. Squires (✉)
Professor of Criminology and Public Policy, School of Applied Social Science, University of Brighton, Brighton, United Kingdom
e-mail: p.a.squires@brighton.ac.uk

J. Maher et al. (eds.), *The Palgrave International Handbook of Animal Abuse Studies*, DOI 10.1057/978-1-137-43183-7_14

on the conflicts between the social, economic and environmental priorities of landowners, shooters, walkers and naturalists, employees, residents and nature conservation lobbies is considered, including suggestions for how some of the worst harms associated with shooting might be ameliorated. Finally, the chapter turns to the most troubling, extreme, 'industrial' and inglorious form of wildlife slaughter, driven shooting, to question its ethical, traditional and 'environmental' credentials.

Bad-Faith Hunting

Just as this chapter was nearing completion, an international media storm erupted following news that an American 'big game hunter' (Walter Palmer, a dentist) had shot a lion using a high-tech crossbow in Zimbabwe. Unfortunately, whether due to the incompetence of the hunter or his arrogance in using such an unsuitable weapon, the crossbow had only wounded the lion, which was then tracked for almost two days before being finished off by a rifle shot. The story gradually emerged that the wealthy American had paid two local men the equivalent of £32,000 to 'find' him a lion to shoot. Keen to honour their side of the bargain and claim the money, the men had left a trail of meat intending to entice a lion from Zimbabwe's Hwange National Park. Unfortunately, 'Cecil the lion', wearing a GPS tracking collar, had been part of a research study since 2008 undertaken by the Wildlife Conservation Research Unit at the University of Oxford and was well known to the research community. One of the researchers on the project remarked that Cecil had become popular because he had become relatively accustomed to humans, sometimes allowing vehicles to approach as close as 10 metres 'making it easy for tourists and researchers to photograph and observe him' (Bittel 2015). But this also made him a trusting and easy target. A similar fate befell the so-called 'Emperor of Exmoor' in 2010, a large red stag, which had been pictured in the national press. Such notoriety simply increased the willingness of private hunters, in what was described as a 'supreme act of selfishness', to pay a four-figure sum for the right to kill the animal (Mathews 2010).

In the wake of Cecil's killing, the media commentaries traversed a wide range of issues covering, in turn, the strange, perhaps 'psychotic', tendency of smiling hunters to relish their post-kill photo-opportunity, posing with their majestic, now dead, prey and the sophisticated hunting rifles with which they had killed. Of these new age hunters, few have incited the *Facebook* outrage achieved by 19-year-old Texan cheerleader, Kendall Jones, who posted several beaming pictures of herself—the 'hot hunter'—alongside a host of dead animals she had killed. Her ambition, she claimed, was to shoot one each of Africa's 'big 5' game animals (rhino, elephant, Cape buffalo, leopard and lion), but she was also pictured peering over a dead hippopotamus and, rifle raised, beside a dead zebra. Commentaries accompanying the photographs referred to her love of nature and wildlife, hunting only in 'legal areas', the importance of predator control, the role of the safari economy in areas with few other commercial opportunities, and donating the kill meat to local people. She also spoke of respecting the dignity of animal life, although this claim cut little ice with critics as it accompanied a smugly grinning picture of herself sitting astride a dead lion and pulling on its mane to raise its head for the camera. In due course, Facebook removed several of the images. But what especially appeared to drive the contempt of critics, which pictures of men in similar poses have seldom occasioned (although the pictures of men, which are pretty standard fare in hunting publications,[1] hardly ever made it to *Facebook*) was not so much the killing as the utterly banal and disingenuous justifications offered up for the slaughter. Cohn and Linzey (2009) have discussed the 'morally suspect' and 'anti-social' character of 'trophy hunting' which Jones' *Facebook* entries appeared to represent, for behind the wafer-thin justifications offered up for an activity she clearly enjoyed, was a claim about the right to kill for nothing more than fun, an attitude seemingly out of touch with modern sentiments. Yet what such an attitude shared with the far more common representations of *masculine* delight in the right to slaughter—and the *rites of slaughter*, more routinely published in hunting magazines—was the uncomfortable juxtaposition of high powered weaponry in the absence of any moral accountability regarding its use. This is an issue discussed elsewhere (Squires 2014, p. 321) and to which I will return later.

After a number of airlines announced they would no longer be willing to transport 'trophy' animal carcasses (Cummings 2015), the University of Oxford's Wildlife Conservation Research Unit itself came under fire for apparently accepting funding from two companies which advocated 'sustainable trophy hunting'. The complaint direct at the Oxford researchers appeared to be that, having accepted such donations for their research, the researchers, some of whom had made the early running in the chorus of condemnation against the lion killing, ought not to criticise the killing of any

[1] An Animal Aid campaign against the display of hunting magazines featuring proud hunters and dead animals on their front covers excited some activity amongst the shooting fraternity and wider media when it referred to such magazines as 'shooting porn': see Tyler (2012) http://www.animalaid.org.uk/images/pdf/booklets/gunningforchildrenreport.pdf, and reactions to it.

particular animal, in any circumstances (Hutton 2015). The heated and often emotive arguments surfacing are indicative of the issues which regularly arise when hunting is debated in the national media. While many such arguments will include well honed 'neutralisation strategies' (Sykes and Matza 1957), others involve rather more fundamental claims, such as questions of culture, tradition, land use and management, sustainability, conservation and biodiversity, predator control as well as economics and morality, and cannot be so easily dismissed. Compromise on such complex issues, however necessary, can be hard to find especially when independent evidence is in short supply and the debates are animated by moral absolutes, critiques of privilege and the complaints of social class. Although, as we shall see later, only an evidence-based approach is likely to foster effective solutions, yielding appropriate policies and fostering much needed reforms.

Wider Questions of History and Culture

The furore over the death of Cecil the lion subsided as July, 2015, moved into August. Yet as the so-called 'Glorious 12th' (the 'traditional' date for the commencement of the grouse shooting season in the Scottish uplands) drew closer, the *Times* published an article noting the establishment of a new hunting lobby group, *You Forgot the Birds*, established to attack the Royal Society for the Protection of Birds (RSPB), and financed by Crispin Odey, a billionaire hedge-fund manager (Webster 2015). Odey's specific complaint concerned his opposition to RSPB lobbying in favour of the licensing of grouse shooting estates, a policy the RSPB hoped would bring greater quality control to the management of estates and help bring pressure to bear to prevent gamekeepers killing birds of prey commonly found on and around grouse moors. Odey's more general complaint was that the RSPB was using the plight of certain endangered raptor species, the hen harrier in particular, to fight a 'class war' by proxy against country landowners and the shooting fraternity.

Allegations concerning class and privilege are never far away when issues of hunting and land rights are considered, even as far back as the 1671 Game Act which established a property qualification for the right to hunt and thereby effectively criminalised the subsistence economy of the rural poor (Hay 1975). By the 1820s, Horn notes, fully one seventh of the criminal convictions in England were for offences against the Game laws (Horn 1980). Yet there are undoubtedly wider and deeper cultural and historical changes influencing public sentiments towards the hunting and killing of animals that the remaining forms of 'sports shooting' continue to encounter—and indeed, as we have seen, which they also appear to provoke.

As part of the wider transcultural civilisation thesis, Elias (1939) has both depicted the decline of—and the growing opposition to—such popular entertainments as cat-burning and bear baiting while acknowledging something of a corresponding desire for 'exciting' or even visceral encounters with 'real nature' (Elias 1986). Thomas (1983) has similarly outlined the changing human/animal relations, specifically the retreat from anthropocentric thinking (and later, increasing urbanisation), within which human attitudes towards and treatments of animals were reconstituted. Tester (1991), likewise, addresses the moral and ideological discourses within which contemporary notions of 'animal rights' are positioned in respect of latter day 'green' thinking and notions of environmental justice. As, during the late nineteenth and twentieth century, animal cruelty came to be increasingly regulated and, even more recently, when activities such as hare coursing and foxhunting with dogs have become prohibited, field sports shooting (stalking and shooting) remain to bear the brunt of a popular animosity that is rooted, in part, in a hostility to the notion of killing for pleasure.[2] Of course, although somewhat in the face of the photographic evidence referred to earlier, shooters often tend to deny the 'pleasurable' or 'exciting' aspects of their shooting (such as alluded to by Elias, above), preferring to present shooting as if shooting were a necessary component of environmental conservation, bio-diversity, sustainable rural economies and estate management—or at least, as the economic foundation for these more wholesome priorities. In this sense, the popular juxtaposed portraits of proud hunter and vanquished 'game'[3] convey, as Kheel has argued (1995), such a combination of achievement, entitlement and domination—the thrill of the chase, the visceral challenge of the wild—as may be plausibly sustained by any hunter with a high-powered and precision engineered rifle. More fundamentally, Kalof et al. (2004) regard hunting as an 'aggressive, powerful and violent' performance of masculinity. Popular cultural images celebrating hunting, glorifying weapons,

[2] As Fukuda has argued, although here specifically in respect of fox-hunting, although the point applies equally to field sports shooting: 'The actual and evident reason for people's participation in fox-hunting is that they enjoy it, although the content of [this] enjoyment has not been well discussed in public' (Fukuda 1997, p. 3)

[3] Also perpetuating the egalitarian myth that the hunt has been a game – although really, sport for the one, survival for the other.

killing and violence 'perpetuate attitudes of domination, power and control over others' and, crucially, over nature (Kalof et al. 2004, p. 247).

Lately, as we have seen, these controversies have become subsumed within deeper urban/rural ideological conflicts (witness, for example, the politics of the Countryside Alliance) which, even as the viability of rural economies is further imperilled by global economic developments, serve most obviously as a tweed and worsted fig-leaf for a set of affluent urban-class interests with rural week-ender aspirations. Much like the campaigning billionaire hedge-fund manager, referred to already, their hearts may be on the grouse moors but their money is firmly rooted in Canary Wharf—or, more likely, distant tax havens.

Consistent with this pattern, Thomas has argued that, historically, debate about the use and abuse of animals has seldom been free from the distracting and conflicting perceptions 'imposed by social class' even as he acknowledges that modern attitudes appear underpinned by a distaste for 'the warlike traditions of the aristocracy' whose enthusiasm for hunting appeared to be founded upon 'wanton slaughter and the domination of nature' (Thomas 1983, p. 184). Cooper, likewise, detects in hunting a masculine and proprietorial attitude, wrapped around with doubtful myths regarding tradition, the status quo, culture and cherished ways of life (Cooper 2009). Horn's historical focus is more directly upon the vital years when patterns of rural land-ownership, country pursuits and elite fashions began to assume a distinctly modern form. As she has shown for the landed classes of the early nineteenth-century England, 'hunting, shooting and fishing were *the* major leisure activities' with the popularity of shooting increasing dramatically with the perfection of the flintlock double-barrelled shotgun. Amongst such well-armed sportsmen, she argues, 'mass slaughter was the order of the day', well-equipped hunting parties were achieving such large numbers of kills that some even drew unfavourable comment in the press (Horn 1980, p. 172).

Despite the claims of 'tradition', it was technological development in the form of the breech-loading shotgun, invented in the 1860s, and the expansion of the railways which really cemented the elite hunting way of life. Just as the enclosures and Highland clearances before them had turned small proprietor and croft farming over to sheep (Richards 2013) so, in turn, the shotgun and shooting became a more profitable land use on the more remote estates than sheep-farming, thereby establishing a pattern of land-use management that is still with us. During his celebrated walks through the remote landscapes of coastal East Anglia, W.G. Sebald likewise described the several factors which combined to fabricate this modern hunting 'tradition' as it emerged in rural Suffolk. 'The hunting of small game' he argued,

> had become fashionable in the Victorian age. Men of middle class background who had achieved great wealth through industrial enterprise, wanting to establish a legitimate position in higher society, acquired large country mansions and estates where they abandoned the utilitarian principles they had always upheld in favour of hunting and shooting, which, although it was quite useless and bent on destruction, was not considered by anyone as an aberration' (Sebald 2002, p. 222).

In the past, he suggested, hunting had been the especial privilege of royalty and aristocracy, but now, thanks to new money, technological changes making shooting simpler and the accessibility provided by transportation improvements, anyone who wanted to translate their new wealth into status and reputation 'would hold hunting parties at their estates, several times a season, with as much ostentation as possible' (Ibid.). Aside from the lavish display, the scale of entertainments provided and the number and rank of the invited guests enjoying the sport, the respect achieved by the host of such parties lay 'in direct proportion to the number of creatures that were killed'. It followed that the land management principles adopted by the estate were henceforth governed 'by considerations of what was necessary to maintain and increase the stocks of game'. Accordingly many thousands of pheasants were reared each year in pens, subsequently released while, still scarcely able to fly, to be driven towards the lines of guns. The lands on which the shoots took place were henceforth lost to farming. Furthermore, the rural population not engaged in the new estate-based activities such as rearing pheasants, breeding and training gun dogs, or working as gamekeepers or in any other capacity connected with shooting, were forced to leave. According to Sebald, the Suffolk pheasant craze was at its height in the decades before the First World War. At this time, one particular estate (Sudbourne Hall, near Orford) employed fully two-dozen gamekeepers. On some occasions up to six thousand pheasants were blasted from the sky in a single day's shooting, not to mention many other examples of local wildlife, including birds, hares and rabbits which found themselves at the wrong end of a shotgun. Sebald concluded his overview of this culture of casual rural slaughter, and perhaps in prescient anticipation of different forms of slaughter and another kind of list, by noting 'the staggering scores were punctiliously recorded in the game books of the rival estates' (Sebald 2002, p. 223).

Bal-morality and the Inglorious 12th?

In Scotland, the debate about stalking and shooting are invariably tied closely to questions of Scottish landownership, patterns of landownership that have evolved since the mid-nineteenth-century 'hunting revival' and which have given rise to particular forms of land management and the creation of a 'triumphant new cultural formation'—the Highland Sporting Estate. These new elite recreational destinations, 'formed the centrepiece of the social calendar for the upper classes who would head north on the new railways to shoot grouse, stalk deer and fish for salmon' (Wightman 2004, p. 4). Now such estates are said to form a sports shooting tourist economy that is claimed to bring substantial economic benefits to Scotland as a whole. Grouse-shooting alone is said to earn the Scottish economy £30 m while some even estimate that country sports as a whole bring some £350 m annually to the nation's account. Unfortunately, the final destinations of much of this income are seldom so clearly accounted for (McKenna 2013). For instance, Wightman and Higgins show that, despite their homespun tartan veneer, sports estates are, first and foremost, economic and business assets making predictable use of off-shore tax-havens (Wightman and Higgins 2000). On the other side of the coin, a report commissioned in 2012 by the Scottish Government, the Scottish Land Reform Review Group, estimated that, as one legacy of the Highland Clearances, today just 432 people owned 50 % of Scotland's private rural land (LRRG 2014). Wightman argues that 'the development of hunting estates was merely the next stage in the transition to a capitalist system of landholding, [and that] the emotions that the Clearances had evoked were in many senses rekindled by the spread of the hunting estates' (Wightman 2004, p. 7).

The Land Reform Review Group went on to propose limits to individual landholding and a system of licensing for shooting estates. Jim Hunter a former member of the Review Group remarked that: 'Scotland continues to be stuck with the most concentrated, most inequitable, most unreformed and most undemocratic land ownership system in the entire developed world' (quoted in McKenna 2013). The *Field* magazine, true to its mission of promoting the interests of the world of hunting and shooting classes, said something similar, but put it rather differently: Scotland, it claimed, 'is the last place in Europe where a rich man can buy a large chunk of wilderness to act out his dreams of owning a kingdom as well as enjoying a wide diversity of sport' (cited in Wightman et al. 2002, p. 64). Perhaps this is what it is really all about: personal autonomy, dominion over nature and a power over life and death.

The core dilemmas deriving from this inequitable distribution of land have concerned the extent to which issues of public interest, bio-diversity and sustainability were being served by such concentrated patterns of land-ownership. The Review Group Report catalogued a number of instances where the land management practices of the shooting estates had impinged negatively upon local communities, public amenities and, in particular, other animal species and their habitats. Evidence from the Grampian Fire and Rescue Service to the LRRG, in particular, confirmed that during 2011–2013 a third of the wildfires attended by the Service resulted from supposedly 'controlled' grouse moor burnings which had got out of control (LRRG 2014, p. 171). In other areas, the over-breeding of deer for shooting has caused problems for farmers and other land users. Yet, above all, it has been the impact of the large grouse shooting estates which have attracted the most enduring criticisms. Even from the late nineteenth-century, the rapid expansion of the shooting estates was considered to be primarily responsible for the widespread persecution of a range of bird species (especially birds of prey) as well as a variety of mammals thought to be a threat to game bird populations (Lister-Kaye 1994). In more recent years, the management of land for high-density game-bird yields, especially on grouse moors has been blamed for the continuing practice of gamekeepers poisoning rare birds of prey (RSPB 2003), even though this practice was outlawed in 1912.[4] As Whitfield et al. have concluded, 'illegal poisoning in the uplands of Scotland occurs disproportionately on land actively managed as grouse moor' (2003, p. 162).

In Scotland, between 1989 and 2008, some 450 birds of prey were killed by illegal poisoning, and a further 320 were shot or trapped and their nests destroyed in what RSPB Scotland have referred to as 'twenty years of relentless human killing of Scotland's protected bird of prey species' (RSPB Scotland 2009). The fact that the Scottish grouse moors, where a majority of these killings occurred, comprise some of the more remote and under-populated areas of mainland Britain and that most only came to light almost by accident when reported by walkers or birdwatchers, strongly suggests that the *known* incidents are but a small proportion of a much larger total. According to the Scottish Raptor Study Group (1997), confirmed incidents reflect just the tip of an iceberg; a view supported by the findings of a recent study which compared unpublished 'vermin' destruction records from one estate in Perthshire with incidents for the whole of Scotland as recorded by the authorities. 'The results showed that over a

[4] The setting of poison baits in the open was first prohibited in 1912, under the Protection of Animals (Scotland) Act in 1912. The legislation did not include specific legal protection for birds which only came in 1954 when the persecution of raptors (including poisoning, trapping and shooting) was prohibited by the Protection of Birds Act. Despite this, populations of many birds of prey are significantly constrained in parts of Scotland as a result of continuing illegal persecution. See http://www.scottishraptorstudygroup.org/persecution.html

period of years, the number of raptors illegally killed on just one estate far exceeded the number of 'official' incidents recorded across the whole of Scotland' (McMillan 2011).

Whole areas of suitable habitat are thought to be devoid of breeding birds of prey, either directly exterminated or driven out by illegal activities. In 2009, the number of confirmed illegal raptor poisonings hit a 20-year high, with 46 incidents. Reported poisoning incidents show a regular annual pattern with a significant peak in the spring, followed by a smaller peak in the autumn.

The incidents depicted in Fig. 1 comprised the confirmed killing of 64 red kites, 24 golden eagles, six white tailed eagles, 344 buzzards, 24 peregrine falcons and four hen harriers. Additionally, 313 other bird species were recorded as killed by carbofuran poisoning, and 104 other animals. Part of the problem with poisoning as a means of killing is precisely its indiscriminate nature when left as bait.

Fully 85 % of persons convicted of illegal poisonings worked in a gamekeeping or estate management capacity. Between 2003 and 2008, 157 cases were brought but only 24 made it to court. Of these 21 resulted in a guilty verdict for at least one of the charges listed. Many charges related to the possession of the banned pesticide carbofuran which, although prohibited in 2001, featured in 61 % of the confirmed poisoning incidents during 2009. Data gathered for the UK as a whole compiled through the Wildlife

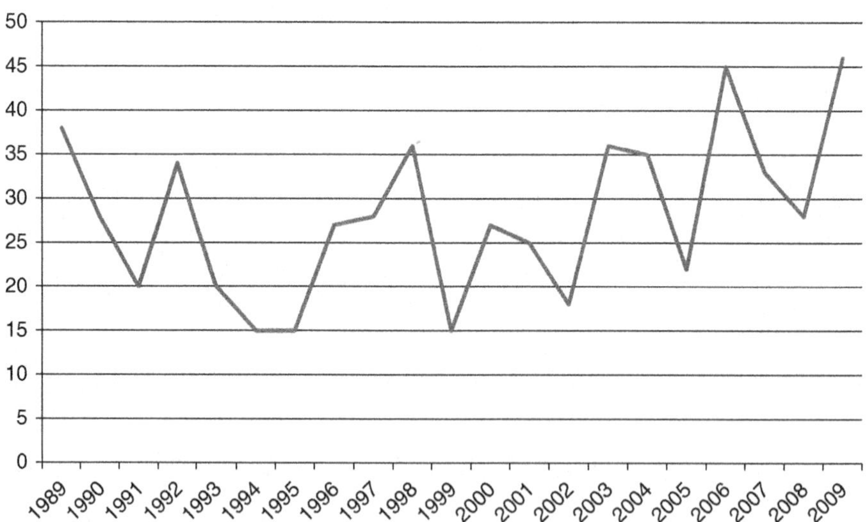

Fig. 1 Confirmed Bird of Prey Poisoning Incidents in Scotland, 1988-2009 (RSPB Scotland 2009)

Incident Investigation Scheme (WIIS), during the 10-year period 2002-2011, since the use and storage of carbofuran was made illegal, shows that there have been 643 bird poisoning incidents where birds were poisoned following the abuse of pesticides. Of these, 317, or just under a half (49 %) involved carbofuran. A significant proportion of crime intelligence reports to the police National Wildlife Crime Unit (NWCU) related to raptor poisonings in Scotland, most of these involving carbofuran. Further, police intelligence suggested that supplies of the pesticide were being accessed from outside the UK. The NWCU have reaffirmed the continuing seriousness of the issue by identifying raptor persecution as one of six key wildlife crime priorities in the UK. The conclusion, published in their 2013 Strategic Assessment, was that, 'Intelligence continues to indicate a strong association between raptor persecution and grouse moor management' (NWCU 2013, p. 25).

The issue of raptor poisoning was twice discussed by the House of Commons Environmental Audit Select Committee (2004, 2013) considered environmental and wildlife crime in both 2004 and 2012–2013. The committee noted, in its 2013 report, the particular difficulties associated with the remote locations in which the majority of offences occurred: this hampered developing an accurate assessment of the extent of the problem, hindered the gathering of evidence and made bringing prosecutions difficult. As Akella and Cannon (2004) have argued, uncertainties regarding the 'dark figure' of wildlife crime represents one of the major difficulties in addressing the problem. Noting that the worst problems appeared to be related to some of the less well-managed estates, it went on to recommend the adoption of a multi-agency approach for working with major landowners and rural interests and tough action to control pesticides (HoC: EASC 2013, pp. 15–19).

In Scotland, in addition to the poisoning incidents depicted in Fig. 2 and wider habitat loss or destruction, 322 further birds of prey were known to have been shot, trapped and killed or subjected to nest destruction, in the 20 years leading to 2009. These included, five red kites, 17 golden eagles, one white-tailed eagle, 137 buzzards, 60 peregrine falcons, 49 hen harriers, 11 goshawks, 13 sparrow hawks, 26 kestrels, one osprey and one tawny owl. Of particular concern to RSPB investigators has been the apparent disinclination of the courts to pass more than 'moderate' sentences on those found guilty. Indeed, in 17 % of cases, the accused were merely 'admonished' or given an absolute discharge. Such sentencing contrasts significantly with the pattern of sentencing of persons found guilty of egg theft (see section on Egg Collecting), despite the fact that poisoning, shooting and otherwise killing birds has a far greater detrimental effect on the overall raptor populations.

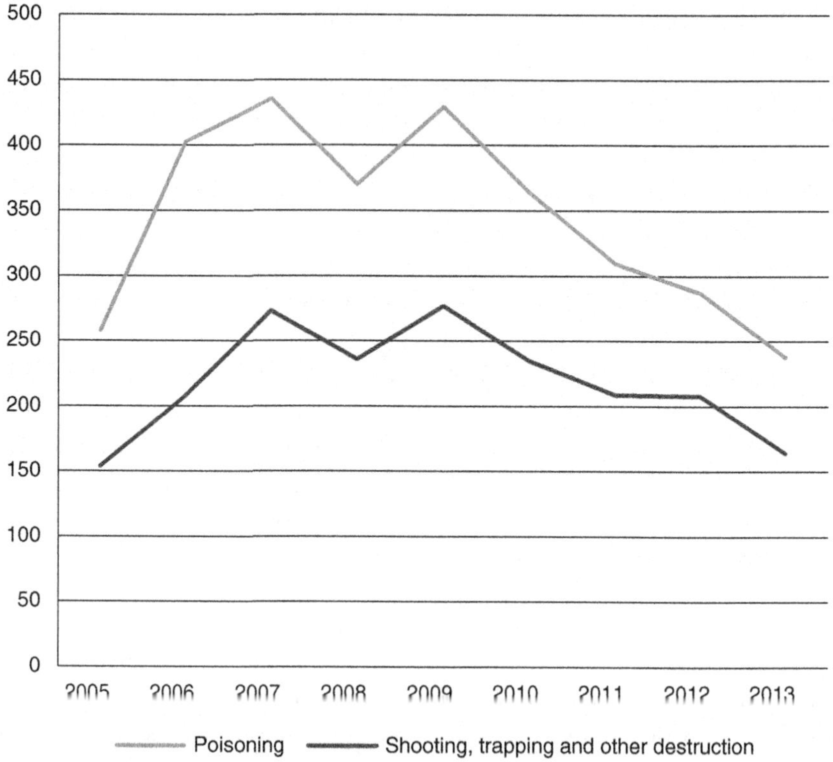

500 450 400 350 300 250 200 150 100 50 0

2005 2006 2007 2008 2009 2010 2011 2012 2013

Poisoning — Shooting, trapping and other destruction

Fig. 2 Combined Reports of Illegal Killing of Birds of Prey in the UK, 2005–2013. (Data before and after 2008 are not strictly comparable because of changes in the ways they have been collected)
Source: RSPB, Bird Crime report Series: Annual Reports 2010-2013

At present the maximum fine for offences tried in Magistrates' Courts under the Wildlife and Countryside Act 1981 is £5,000 and/or up to six months imprisonment. Despite this, the wildlife lobby acknowledges that fines of this order, even if they were more consistently imposed, would be unlikely to act as an effective deterrent. The RSPB argues that penalties for the killing of birds of prey should be increased to a maximum £50,000 fine and/or up to 12 months in prison in the Magistrates' Court, with unlimited fines and/or up to five years imprisonment available in the Crown Court. Fines alone, however, are seldom regarded as an effective strategy, especially where there is evidence of landowners apparently paying fines on behalf of their staff (Nurse 2011, p. 42). However, the RSPB Scotland report (2009) notes many instances of landowners, upon whose land the killing occurs, being deducted many tens of thousands of pounds from their agricultural subsidy payments. The practice of deducting payments goes some way towards the 'vicarious liability' principle recently adopted in Scotland,[5] but not in the rest of the UK. The principle entails that where, for example, a land-owner's agent or gamekeeper is found to be guilty of killing birds of prey then criminal responsibility also extends to the land-owner considered to have either encouraged or required or otherwise facilitated from the illegal killing.[6] The House of Commons Environmental Audit Select Committee recommended in 2012 that the Government should review the impact of the vicarious liability principle in Scotland, and report back with a view to implementing a similar measure in England and in Wales. The Government, however, disagreed, wanting a longer review of the new process in Scotland. Police intelligence reported by the Police National Wildlife Crime Unit in 2013 indicated that some land agents in Scotland have been 'changing their business practices by setting up management companies' in order to distance themselves from any investigation under vicarious liability principles (NWCU 2013).

In the same year, the Law Commission (2012), in its *Wildlife Law: Consultation Paper* also considered the vicarious liability measures operating in Scotland but, with the exception of recommending the extension of liability to landowners who 'knowingly permit' their employees to commit wildlife offences, declined to recommend the adoption of a similar principle in England and in Wales. The RSPB was relatively unimpressed, noting that 'such provisions already exist in parts of the Wildlife and Countryside Act 1981 [but] have proved ineffective' (RSPB 2013, p. 10). For its part, the Law Commission consultation document acknowledged that the seriousness of some wildlife- related crime was not reflected in the penalties available in the Magistrates' Courts (a perception reflected in Lowther et al. 2002). The Commission recommended that some wildlife offences might in future be tried on indictment at Crown Courts (with access to higher penalties, especially where the harms were greatest and species viability might be at stake). However, it was reluctant to pursue a strategy that relied upon criminalisation *alone* as a remedy, especially in light of the often complex

[5] Section 24 of the Wildlife and Natural Environment (Scotland) Act 2011

[6] As Nurse (2011) acknowledges, many gamekeepers may be placed in a quite invidious position with their jobs, livelihood and family homes (tied cottages) tied to the performance of a range game-keeping duties, all this might be in jeopardy should they choose to manage their estates contrary to the expectations of their employers.

social, economic and environmental considerations—which we will consider later—in play (Law Commission 2012).

The Developing Research and Policy Picture

A substantial body of research has drawn attention to the continued persecution of birds of prey and other predatory animals on the grouse shooting estate. Studies of a range of iconic bird species—golden eagles, hen harriers, peregrines, goshawks and red kites have confirmed time and again that the illegal persecution persists, that the major forms it takes still include poisoning, shooting, trapping and nest destruction and that it has significant deleterious effects upon the population, breeding habits and viability of various species in the vicinity of certain estates (see inter alia, Whitfield et al. 2004, 2007; Etheridge et al. 1997; Fielding et al. 2011; Hardey et al. 2003; Smart et al. 2010 and Amar et al. 2012).

The picture seems pretty clear, but the policy options may be less straightforward. While advocates of the enforcement approach may well argue that sufficient efforts have not yet been devoted to effective enforcement, there are, as we have seen, many impediments to an enforcement-led strategy. As Amar et al. (2012, p. 8), have argued, 'at present considerable sums of money are being spent by conservation NGOs and government agencies, and considerable time invested by dedicated volunteers in trying to shield protected raptors from persecution, and by the police in trying to enforce existing legislation, with relatively little effect'. This conclusion is suggestive of the need for other approaches. Thirgood and Redpath (2008) have argued for a sensitive evidence-based approach to mitigating the conflict between the various stakeholders involved—including land management interests, conservationists and political interests. They acknowledge that the research evidence thus far assembled demonstrates: '(i) there is widespread illegal killing of raptors; (ii) raptor predation can limit grouse populations and reduce hunting revenues; and (iii) mitigation techniques are available but are either unacceptable to stakeholders or unproven in the field' (Thirgood and Redpath 2008, p. 1550). They argue that viable and sustainable solutions require more than just the presentation of evidence but also attention to its implications for key stakeholders dependent upon the rural economy. In other words, understanding the barriers to the reception and internalisation of scientific evidence and the uses to which it is put are as critical as the production of the evidence in the first place.

Redpath and his colleagues (Redpath et al. 2010) have shown that particular forms of grouse shooting, notably *driven* grouse shooting, where birds are flushed out and driven by beaters to over-fly a line of waiting guns,[7] requires very high densities of birds to be economically viable. It appears to be a form of shooting—and related land management practice—especially associated with the illegal killing and disturbance of birds of prey. On the one hand, high-density grouse rearing may be particularly attractive to predators but, while predator levels remain relatively low, predation is unlikely to significantly impact grouse production. On the other hand, low-density grouse rearing may be more seriously impacted by predation. Different balances, perhaps including further strategies such as supplementary feeding, management of other predators (such as foxes), ceilings on the numbers of resident raptors and habitat variation, might be achieved at different game bird and predator densities and in different contexts, without necessarily incentivising the game-keeper's resort to illegal solutions, namely, their killing of birds of prey. Scientific work has attempted to model these relationships with some degree of success given the variety of factors and multiple predator activities potentially involved (Redpath and Thirgood 1999). Some researchers have expressed doubt about such an approach, shifting to lower intensity grouse production—the availability of fewer birds to shoot—could make estates uneconomic: less birds to shoot might translate into less tourists paying to shoot them, resulting in diminishing income levels. After all, they suggest, 'much of the conflict between red grouse and hen harriers arises from the need to produce high grouse densities to justify the large investment made by moor owners in moorland management' (Sotherton et al. 2009, p. 956). The diminishing profitability of the estate, resulting from declining numbers of grouse to shoot, could lead to lower employment levels, ultimately producing a less intensively or effectively managed environment. Essentially, similar claims have been made regarding the commercial viability of African trophy hunting.

More positively, Baines and Richardson (2013) have produced evidence attempting to show how changes in habitat and predator management might bring both conservation and economic benefits. Their research involved a two-stage project based upon a shooting estate in Scotland. During the first research phase, the estate was legally managed for *both* grouse and hen harriers. The hen harriers increased significantly in number, eventually rendering intensive grouse

[7] Driven shooting, as described, is contrasted with 'walked-up' shooting where a group of shooters, spaced at intervals in line abreast, preceded by dogs, walks across the land shooting at birds which break cover and fly up in front of them. Kills are generally fewer in number and this activity, in contrast to driven shooting, requires higher levels of fitness and stamina. Two reasons, perhaps, for its diminished popularity.

shooting no-longer commercially viable. Land management and gamekeeping then ceased, and during this second research phase hen harrier numbers fell significantly as other predators (foxes and crows) began to their toll of harrier nests. Hen harrier survival rates and population levels were higher when the estate was properly (and legally) managed. Baines and Richardson (2013, p. 1402) concluded 'we consider this study to be the first that quantifies how control of generalist predators as part of grouse moor management can benefit harrier productivity'. They argue that the research points to the importance of finding ways to ensure grouse moors are effectively managed for a diversity of wildlife, while remaining economically viable. 'If techniques can be devised and put in place to reduce the impact of harriers on grouse, then the control of generalist predators may be viewed as a more acceptable component of conservation management for ground-nesting birds' (2013, p. 1365). If this seemingly *'win-win* situation' could be deployed in other contexts and cases, thereby 'reducing the motivation behind the persecution of [rare bird] species' (Amar et al. 2012, p. 93), it might also herald the development of more considered or consensual strategies for land management. But that would be a much bigger issue.

It has to be said, such 'strategies' are unlikely to find favour amongst those fundamentally opposed to all manner of field sports shooting, but it may have particular implications for driven shooting: the particular form of live animal shooting comprising the most high volume slaughter. Furthermore, if, as Thompson et al. (2009, p. 950) have suggested, driven grouse shooting is 'only viable when birds of prey are routinely disturbed and killed' then it becomes appropriate to question 'the legitimacy of driven grouse shooting as a sustainable land use'. And they conclude, 'Moorland owners need to consider more broadly sustainable shooting practices for the 21st century' (Thompson et al. 2009, p. 950). The argument they make here becomes especially compelling where the shooting estates in question receive public subsidies for their land management; greater accountability here may bring a range of social and environmental benefits.

Driven To It?

As we have seen, driven shooting, involves beaters driving birds towards a line of eight to ten guns, the birds being shot as they fly high over the shooting line. Safety and etiquette, apparently, demand that the shooters fire only upwards and forwards of the line. Driven grouse shooting is said to be the 'sport of kings', the 'most exclusive' form of shooting today, although, in reality today, this is largely a question of price. Driven shooting is also the most expensive, labour-intensive and 'industrial' form of shooting, resulting, as we have seen, in the greatest collateral damage to the countryside. It also yields the greater number of kills, the shooters simply wait for the birds to fly over and blast away. These are some of the reasons behind a recent RSPB-supported proposal to license 'shooting estates'. The idea is strongly resisted by shooting interests who welcome the idea of regulation with no more enthusiasm than they welcome publicity, a reaction which rather calls into question the confident bluster with which shooting lobbyists invariably veneer their sport and its claimed benefits.

A film posted on the League Against Cruel Sports (LACS) website depicts a driven hare shoot in Norfolk during 2011 in which one of the shooters threatened and physically assaulted the camera operator until he was diplomatically led away by one of his colleagues.[8] Watching the short film, one can appreciate his concern. Hares were driven right to left across a field, having to run a de facto gauntlet of a line of guns; shot hares cart-wheeled into the grass as they were hit, others sat dazed and wounded, still others struggled to crawl away, dragging shattered bodies and limbs behind them. The League commentary notes that the shoot is an annual event, for participation in which many shooters paid large sums of money. The event filmed (one of many) took place on land owned by Sir Nicholas Bacon, a former president of the Norfolk Wildlife Trust who was forced to resign when his sponsorship of this gratuitous ritual of killing for pleasure was publicly exposed. Photographs on the League website show dozens of dead hares although it is not made clear what was to become of them. Perhaps they would have been eaten, although consumption of animals killed by lead shot is generally not recommended. Perhaps this slaughter was primarily an exercise in pest control, and the carcasses would be dumped in a landfill, a fate which befalls many a victim of driven shooting—simply because far too many carcasses are produced than could ever be sensibly consumed by the game gourmands who desire them (even if they were all safely edible). The British Association for Shooting and Conservation (BASC) document *The Value of Shooting* asserts that 'ninety-seven percent of all edible quarry shot was destined for human consumption; with 62 % consumed by those who shoot or provide shooting, and 35 % used

[8] League Against Cruel Sports, The Hidden Reality of Shooting. http://www.league.org.uk/our-campaigns/shooting/hidden-reality-of-shooting.

elsewhere' (BASC 2014, p. 25), and goes on to detail survey data findings about how many people eat game. But this claim is quite meaningless without data indicating how much of what was shot was indeed 'edible', as opposed to just shot for sport.

Shooting is an expensive business, a two-hour training package with a venue's instructors will cost around £200; out on the moor itself, it will be double that. If you want a mid-August day's shooting for a full team of 10 shooters on the Yorkshire Moors, this will set you back £33,000 (at the time of writing). For this you can expect to 'bag' 200-plus brace of grouse (that is 400 birds), and the same for the rest of the month. Across the country immense numbers of game birds—grouse, pheasant and partridge—are reared simply to be released and shot, the League Against Cruel Sports estimating that some 47 million birds a year are reared specifically to be shot,[9] with driven shooting representing the most basic, 'industrial' version of this supposedly 'traditional' country sport. A householder in the West Country describes, on her *Common Decency* website,[10] the year-round workload and the constant intrusion associated with rearing pheasants to shoot following a driven shooting range being established adjacent to her home. During the shooting season itself, men with guns routinely patrol the borders of her property her garden spent shot falls from the sky and dead and dying birds plummet to her lawn. In keeping with this 'industrial' characterisation, a sizeable scientific literature has now accumulated, which the shooting fraternity seems keen to ignore, detailing the consequences of lead shot use: the build-up of poisonous lead toxins in birds of prey and other wildlife, the contamination of watercourses and the poisoning of fish and water-fowl (see for example: Mudge 1983; Pain et al. 1995 and Fisher et al. 2006). Despite clear evidence of the contaminating effects of lead shot, the shooting fraternity are reluctant to shift to steel shot, citing the superior ballistic qualities of lead.

Such a brief comment about lead shot seems a good point on which to close for, as we have seen throughout this review of sports shooting, hunting and shooting advocates and practitioners appear especially unwilling to hold themselves morally or environmentally accountable for their actions and the consequences of their actions. There may indeed be something here that resonates with the idea of the 'sport of kings': personal autonomy, some lack of accountability, a claimed dominion over nature, but which, in an age of

[9] http://www.league.org.uk/our-campaigns/shooting/gunsmoke-and-mirrors.

[10] http://www.commondecency.co.uk.

rising inequality and neo-liberal marketisation, has simply become the pricey exclusivity of a right to kill. Shooting enthusiasts often assert the dignity of nature and wax spiritual about the transcendent character of the hunting and shooting experience, but protest that they are misunderstood when they pose, grinning, with an animal carcass, having employed a sophisticated modern firearm to kill that animal. They wrap their 'sport' with sometimes questionable social, economic and conservation purposes and benefits as if to conceal the fact that they do this for pleasure. This is the debate we never have. Furthermore, game shooting in the UK, like the slaughter of migrating songbirds in Southern Europe,[11] or trophy hunting in Africa is manifestly not about essential food production. The briefest glimpse of hunting parties in the elite shooting magazines confirms that the hunting fraternity are far from undernourished.

A particularly telling recent article explores the social etiquette of, following a shoot, participants accepting a brace of dead birds to take home to pluck, cook and eat (cited in Squires 2013). Apparently, it was not the 'done thing' to 'refuse your pair', although the article left a distinct impression of a practice more honoured in the breach and, even when the dead birds were accepted by a rather nonplussed shooter (after all, filling up the freezer with pheasants was manifestly *not* why they were there), one suspects, that a significant number end up as landfill, in the nearest bin or in a convenient ditch. Nevertheless, the article went on to explain how 'at one time dressing a bird was second nature to guns'. But now, apparently, this was no longer the case. Shooting is, above all, about killing for fun—anything else gets in the way of the champagne. A residual purpose for these post-shooting 'dressing' activities seems to be that, 'plucking is a great way to eradicate fear of blood and guts' (in Squires 2013, p. 5). The ironies multiply; today's shooters seem bold enough to pull the trigger, but rather too squeamish to cope with the consequences. Another rather revealing insight to the shooting mind-set might be found in a blog on a shooting society website. A recently inducted member of a 'Sloane ranger' shooting set wittered on about her rising anxieties as the day of her first shoot approached; just how would she feel about 'actually killing something'. Afterwards she reassuringly reflected, 'you know, it didn't bother me a bit' (ibid, p. 6). Lack of remorse is not always such an endearing quality.

---

[11] A recent referendum in Malta in April 2015 resulted in a narrow victory (51 %) for the hunting lobby, which will continue to shoot migrating birds in their thousands before they breed. The future of many already endangered species is further imperilled by this result (Barkham 2014).

Conclusion

This chapter has explored the animal abuse associated with the 'country sport' of live animal shooting and the widespread collateral harms this involves. It began with a critical discussion of the gratuitously offensive practice of 'trophy hunting', the attitudes and economics sustaining it and the controversies surrounding it, before moving on to examine changing popular sensibilities towards sport shooting of live animals. Taking a particular focus upon intensive game shooting on Scottish Highland estates, the chapter then sought to demonstrate how this was embedded within a highly concentrated and unaccountable pattern of private estate ownership, resulting in significant social and environmental harms and, not least, resulting in much illegal persecution (poisoning) of indigenous predators, especially rare birds of prey and protected species. A body of recent research, drawing upon the Scottish context, explored the ways in which conflicts between the social, economic and environmental priorities of land-owners, shooters, walkers and naturalists, employees, residents and nature conservation lobbies might be ameliorated, more sustainable land management practices developed, and the worst excesses of animal abuse associated with shooting prevented. By way of conclusion, however, the chapter closed by acknowledging that, driven shooting, perhaps the most extreme and ignoble, form taken by wildlife slaughter, sustained by an unhealthy veneer of social exclusivity, short term financial ethics and a toxic disdain for the natural world, remained the dominant form of this so-called sport.

References

Akella, A.S., & Cannon J.B. (2004). *Strengthening the weakest links: strategies for improving the enforcement of Environmental Laws.* Washington, DC: Conservation International Centre.

Amar, A., Court, I. R., Davison, M., Downing, S., Grimshaw, T., Pickford, T., & Raw, D. (2012). Linking nest histories, remotely sensed land use data and wildlife crime records to explore the impact of grouse moor management on peregrine falcon populations. *Biological Conservation, 145*(1), 86–94.

Baines, D., & Richardson, M. (2013). Hen harriers on a Scottish grouse moor: multiple factors predict breeding density and productivity. *Journal of Applied Ecology, 50*, 1397–1405.

Barkham, P. (2014, April 20). Conservationists and marksmen of Malta battle over annual bird hunt. *The Guardian.*

Bittel, J. (2015, July 30). Why Cecil the lion was so popular with people. *National Geographic Magazine.*

British Association for Shooting and Conservation [BASC] (2014). *The value of shooting.* BASC. http://basc.org.uk

Cohn, P.N., & Linzey, A. (2009). Hunting as a morally suspect activity. In A. Linzey (Ed.), *The link between animal abuse and human violence.* Brighton: Sussex Academic Press.

Cooper, J. (2009). Hunting as an abusive subculture. In A. Linzey (Ed.) *The link between animal abuse and human violence.* Brighton: Sussex Academic Press.

Cummings, W. (2015, August 4). Airlines ban hunters' big-game 'trophies' after uproar over Cecil the lion. *USA Today.*

Elias, N. (1939/1969). *The civilizing process.* Oxford: Blackwell.

Elias, N. (1986). An essay on sport and violence. In N. Elias & E. Dunning (Eds.), *Quest for excitement: sport and leisure in the civilizing process* (pp. 150–74.). Basil: Blackwell.

Etheridge, B., Summers, R.W., & Green, R.E. (1997). The effects of illegal killing and destruction of nests by humans on the population dynamics of the hen harrier *Circus cyaneus* in Scotland. *Journal of Applied Ecology, 34,* 1081–1105.

Fielding, A. H., Haworth, P. F., Whitfield, D. P., McLeod, D. R. A., & Riley, H. (2011). *A conservation framework for Hen Harriers in the UK.* Peterborough: Joint Nature Conservation Committee (JNCC).

Fisher, I. J., Pain, D. J., & Thomas, V. G. (2006). A review of lead poisoning from ammunition sources in terrestrial birds. *Biological Conservation, 131*(3), 421–432.

Fukuda, K. (1997). Different views of animals and cruelty to animals: cases in fox-hunting and pet keeping in Britain. *Anthropology Today, 13*(5), 2–6.

Hardey, J., Rollie, C. J. & Stirling-Aird, P. K. (2003). Variation in breeding success of inland peregrine falcon in three regions of Scotland 1991–2000. In D.B.A. Thompson, S.M. Redpath, A.H. Fielding, M. Marquiss, C.A. Galbraith (Eds.), *Birds of prey in a changing environment* (pp. 99–109). Edinburgh: The Stationery Office.

Horn, P. (1980). *The rural world: 1780–1850. Social change in the English country-side.* London: Hutchinson University Press.

House of Commons Environmental Audit Select Committee (2004, September). *Environmental crime/wildlife crime,* 12th Report of Session 2003–04. The Stationery Office. HC 605

House of Commons Environmental Audit Select Committee (2013). *Wildlife crime* 3rd Report of Session 2012–13. The Stationery Office HC 140.

Hutton, A. (2015, August 5). Oxford under fire for taking pro-hunting cash. *The Times.*

Kalof, L., Fitzgerald, A., & Baralt, L. (2004). Animals, women and weapons: blurred sexual boundaries in the discourse of sport hunting. *Animals and Society, 12*(3): 237–251.

Kheel, M. (1995). Licence to kill: an ecofeminist critique on hunters' discourse. In C. Adams & J. Donovan (Eds.), *Animals and women: feminist theoretical explorations*. Durham & London: Duke University Press.

Law Commission. 2012. Wildlife law: A consultation paper. LCCP No. 206. London: the Stationery office.

Lister-Kaye, J. (1994). *Ill fares the land. A sustainable land ethic for the sporting estates of the highlands and islands* (p. 13). Edinburgh: Scottish Natural Heritage.

Lowther, J., Cook, D., & Roberts, M. (2002). *Crime and punishment in the wildlife trade*. Wolverhampton: WWF/TRAFFIC/ Regional Research Institute.

Mathews, J. (2010, October 26). Emperor of Exmoor shot dead by hunter. *Daily Express*.

McMillan, R.L. (2011). Raptor persecution on a large Perthshire estate: a historical study. *Scottish Birds 31*, 195–205.

Mudge, G. P. (1983). The incidence and significance of ingested lead pellet poisoning in British wildfowl. *Biological Conservation*, *27*(4), 333–372.

Nurse, A. (2011). Policing wildlife: perspectives on criminality in wildlife crime. In *Proceedings from the British Criminology Conference*, *11*, 35–53. The British Society for Criminology.

NWCU [National Wildlife Crime Unit] (2013). Strategic Assessment 2013. www.nwcu.police.uk/wpcontent/uploads/2014/04/NWCU-strategic-assessment-2013-final-v2.pdf.

Pain, D. J., Sears, J., & Newton, I. (1995). Lead concentrations in birds of prey in Britain. *Environmental Pollution*, *87*(2), 173–180.

Royal Society for the Protection of Birds [RSPB] (2005–2013). *Bird crime report series: annual reports 2005–2013*. RSPB.

Redpath, S., & Thirgood, S. (1999). Numerical and functional responses in generalist predators: hen harriers and peregrines on Scottish grouse moors. *Journal of Animal Ecology*, 68(5),879–892.

Redpath, S., Amar, A., Smith, A., Thompson, D., & Thirgood, S. (2010). People and nature in conflict: can we reconcile raptor conservation and game management? In J. Baxter & C.A. Galbraith (Eds.), *Species management: challenges and solutions for the 21st century*. Edinburgh: The Stationery office.

Richards, E. (2013). *The highland clearances*. Edinburgh: Birlinn.

RSPB Scotland (2009). *The illegal killing of birds of prey in Scotland in 2009*. Edinburgh: RSPB.

Scottish Land Reform Review Group [LRRG] (2014). *The land of Scotland and the common good*. Edinburgh: The Scottish Government.

Scottish Raptor Study Group (1997). The illegal persecution of raptors in Scotland. *Scottish Birds*, *19*, 65–85.

Sebald, W.G. (2002). *The rings of Saturn*. Vintage Books.

Smart, J., Amar, A., Sim, I.M.W., Etheridge, B., Cameron, D., Christie, G., et al. (2010). Illegal killing slows population recovery of a re-introduced raptor of high conservation concern—the red kite *Milvus milvus*. Biological Conservation, *143*, 1278–1286.

Sotherton, N., Tapper, S., & Smith, A. (2009). Hen harriers and red grouse: economic aspects of red grouse shooting and the implications for moorland conservation. *Journal of Applied Ecology*, *46*, 955–960.

Squires, P. (2013). Bang! . . . goes the countryside: from criminology to cruelty. *Protect Magazine*, (4), 3–6, The League Against Cruel Sports.

Squires, P. (2014). *Gun crime in global contexts*. Abingdon: Routledge.

Sykes, G., & Matza, D. (1957). Techniques of neutralization: a theory of delinquency. *American Sociological Review*, *22*(6), 664–673.

Tester, K. (1991). *Animals and society: the humanity of animal rights*. London: Routledge.

Thirgood, S., & Redpath, S. (2008). Hen harriers and red grouse: science, politics and human–wildlife conflict. *Journal of Applied Ecology*, *45*, 1550–1554.

Thomas, K. (1983). *Man and the natural world: changing attitudes in England 1500–1800*. Harmondsworth: Allen Lane.

Thompson, P. S., Amar, A., Hoccom, D. G., Knott, J., & Wilson, J. D. (2009). Resolving the conflict between driven-grouse shooting and conservation of hen harriers. *Journal of Applied Ecology*, *46*(5), 950–954.

Tyler, A. (2012). *Gunning for children: how the gun lobby recruits young blood*. Tonbridge: Animal Aid. www.animalaid.org.uk

Webster, B. (2015, August 5). Billionaire takes aim at RSPB class warriors. *The Times*.

Whitfield, D. P., Fielding, A. H., McLeod, D. R., & Haworth, P. F. (2004). Modelling the effects of persecution on the population dynamics of golden eagles in Scotland. *Biological Conservation*, *118*, 319–333.

Whitfield, D. P., Fielding, A. H., McLeod, D. R. A., Morton, K., Stirling-Aird, P., & Eaton, M. A. (2007). Factors constraining the distribution of golden eagles *Aquila chrysaetos* in Scotland. *Bird Study*, *54*, 199–211

Whitfield, D. P., Macleod, D., Watson, J., Fielding, A. H., & Haworth, P. F. (2003). The association of grouse moor in Scotland with the illegal use of poisons to control predators. *Biological Conservation*, 114(2),157–163.

Wightman, A. (2004, September). *Hunting and hegemony in the highlands of Scotland: a study in the ideology of landscapes and landownership*. Agricultural University of Norway, Noragric Working Paper No. 36.

Wightman, A., & Higgins, P. (2000). 'Sporting estates and the recreational economy in the Highlands and islands of Scotland'. *Scottish Affairs*, (31), 18–36.

Wightman, A., Higgins, P., Jarvie, G., & Nicol, R. (2002). The cultural politics of hunting: Sporting estates and recreational land use in the highlands and islands of Scotland. *Culture, Sport, Society*, *5*(1): 53–70.

Peter Squires is Professor of Criminology and Public Policy at the University of Brighton. His work covers areas such as gun crime, policing and anti-social behaviour. His most recent book was *Gun crime in Global Contexts* (Routledge, 2014). He is currently working on a book about gender and firearms.

Fish used in Aquariums: Nemo's Plight

Jordan E. Mazurek

Introduction

'The sea is everything! . . . On the surface, they can still exercise their iniquitous laws, fight, devour each other, and indulge in all their earthly horrors. But thirty feet below its surface their power ceases, their influence fades, and their dominion vanishes! Ah, monsieur, to live in the bosom of the sea! Only there can independence be found! There I recognize no master! There I am free!' (Captain Nemo in Verne 1962, pp. 73–74). A century-and-a-half of anthropocentric capitalist expansion later, one can only wonder with what horror the avowed anti-imperialist, expert marine biologist, and intrepid Captain of the *Nautilus* might look upon the state of his beloved ocean. Evidence of human domination of the surface and depths of Earth's oceans is pronounced and profound: from rising ocean acidification and temperature due to anthropogenic global warming to rampant overfishing and species collapse to the spreading of oxygen-deprived 'dead zones' to the accumulation of hundreds of millions of tons of plastic and other debris in vast gyres to the rapidly increasing destruction of coral reefs and corresponding decline of ocean biodiversity. While Captain Nemo would no doubt be troubled by the state of the world's oceans, he might find little solace in

J.E. Mazurek (✉)
School of Social Policy, Sociology and Social Research (SSPSSR),
University of Kent, Canterbury, United Kingdom

Institute for Criminological Research (IKS), University of Hamburg,
Hamburg, Germany
e-mail: jem63@kent.ac.uk

J. Maher et al. (eds.), *The Palgrave International Handbook of Animal Abuse Studies*, DOI 10.1057/978-1-137-43183-7_15

the non-speciesist criminological literature of animal abuse. Indeed, he might well ask, 'What about the fish?' This chapter takes steps toward addressing this question by focusing on the practice and conditions of keeping aquatic species—specifically, fish—in captivity. Its main argument is that such acts constitute *animal abuse*—a classification of harm that heretofore has been applied almost exclusively to terrestrial animals.

This chapter begins by situating the treatment of fish within Singer's (1990) utilitarianism and Regan's (1983) intrinsic 'subjects-of-a-life' animal rights framework. By incorporating research in the fields of marine biology and animal cognition into the debate around the extension of moral consideration to fish, this chapter contends that not only do fish meet the utilitarian threshold of having a capacity to suffer, but they are complex and intelligent social creatures, on par with mammals, to fall squarely within Regan's (1983) understanding of 'subjects-of-a-life.' Next, this chapter develops an intertwined political-economic and green-cultural criminological framework with which to critique public aquariums as sites of important capitalist ideological work that serve to maintain dominant anthropocentric conceptions of marine life—abuse that results, as such, through utilitarian discourses of 'conservation' and 'animal welfare.' This chapter concludes by applying this political economic/green cultural criminological framework to those fish held captive in the US marine aquarium fish trade, and describes the layers of abuse and theriocide necessary to maintain such consumption.

Fish as Sufferers and 'Subjects-of-a-Life'

Within the broader green criminological literature, fish are treated anthropocentrically—as resources ('fisheries') for human consumption (see, e.g., Croall 2007, pp. 211–212; Hauck 2007; Hauck and Sweijd 1999; McMullan and Perrier 2002; Tailby and Gant 2002). Within the green criminological literature that focuses on animal abuse from a non-speciesist perspective, fish are mentioned in passing, if mentioned at all, with a great deal more focus placed on their mammalian or avian counterparts. These mammals and birds are implicitly or explicitly deemed to be of superior sentience to fish; that is, beings with complex mental lives marked by feelings, self-consciousness, memory, intention and the like. The reason for such a slanted focus on mammals and birds may arguably be a 'thoroughgoing speciesist' (Beirne 1999) prejudice against fish inherent in the anthropocentric biases of Singer's (1975) utilitarianism and Regan's (1983) 'subjects-of-a-life' animal rights frameworks so integral to the early non-speciesist works of Beirne (1999), Benton (1998), Cazaux (1999) and others.

That is, whether fish are capable of experiencing pain or suffering, much less sentience—basic prerequisites in Singer's and Regan's moral frameworks—has long been the subject of debate. Let us first turn to Singer's utilitarianism.

Building off Bentham's eighteenth-century application of utilitarianism to animals—'The question is not, Can they reason? nor Can they talk? but, Can they suffer?' (Bentham 2005, p. 283)—Singer (1975) argues against various forms of anthropocentric speciesism that cause unnecessary suffering to other sentient creatures capable of feeling pain or pleasure (see Beirne 1999 for an overview). In order to act morally in Singer's utilitarian framework, humans are obligated to give equal consideration to all beings capable of suffering. This consideration is not an extension of *rights* to the individual being (see Brisman 2014 for a discussion), but a *moral calculus*—one which holds that if a nonhuman animal species can *suffer*, he/she (see Sollund 2015 on the use of 'he/she' rather than 'it' to move away from speciesist language) is worthy of such consideration that will lessen that suffering (although balanced in regards to the benefits that may be derived from said suffering for the typically anthropocentric, followed by species, majority). This focus on suffering in the utilitarian framework can be understood as a fundamental stumbling block in the extension of moral consideration to fish. It has long been assumed—in both marine biology literature and popular culture—that fish possess neither the necessary nerve pathways nor brain structures capable of turning external stimuli that may damage their physical being into pain, a perspective perhaps most vehemently defended by Rose (2002; see also Rose et al. 2014). In turn, this inability to feel pain and to suffer physically has been used as a basis to assert that fish also lack the capacity for intelligence and sentience (Rose et al. 2014). Without the establishment of such capacity for suffering and in turn sentience within fish, there is certainly little argument to be made that a utilitarian framework applies to them, rendering them little more than Cartesian automaton.

Regan (1983) argues that humans and nonhuman animals contain intrinsic value (instead of having value ascribed to them, such as in Singer's utilitarian framework) if they are 'subjects-of-a-life':

> Individuals are subjects-of-a-life if they have beliefs and desires, perceptions, memory and a sense of the future, including their own future; an emotional life together with feelings of pleasure and pain; preference- and welfare-interests; the ability to initiate action in pursuit of their desires and goals; a psychophysical identity over time; and an individual welfare in the sense that their experiential life fares well or ill for them (Regan 1983, p. 243).

Such 'subjects-of-a-life' are 'moral agents' who have the capacity to be held accountable for their own behavior and a duty to uphold the intrinsic rights of other 'subjects-of-a-life,' namely 'moral patients' (Beirne 1999). 'Moral patients' differ from 'moral agents' in that the former cannot be held morally accountable for their behavior because they are unable to control said behavior. Nevertheless, 'they have inherent value and one is required to respect them no less than one respects moral agents. To respect a moral patient means not only to revere her life but also to defend her from harm' (Beirne 1999, pp. 133–134). In his critique of the extension of a rights framework to non-human animals, Benton (1998) seeks to problematize Regan's (1983) concept of a 'subject-of-a-life' by deploying fish as an illustrative example of the 'species boundary' of 'moral patients,' echoing other critiques of Regan's moral framework for being mammalian-centric and thus 'super-speciesist' (Kappeler 1995). As Benton (1998, p. 161) argues, 'It may be open to dispute whether . . . fish are subjects of a life in the relevant respects, but this can be addressed by a generous application of the necessary criteria, just in case they are.' Benton reasons that one means by which to overcome the arbitrary cut-off line between those nonhuman entities considered 'subjects-of-a-life' and those who are not could be to simply 'extend the moral purchase of rights and justice beyond psychologically complex mammalian relatives to include other forms of animal and plant life and even non living beings' (1998, p. 161). As Benton notes, though, the danger with this approach is dissolution of the very criteria of the application of rights in the first place.

Given this chapter's focus on fish, the alternative strategy of keeping in place the requisite criteria that Regan has laid out as qualifying animals as 'subjects-of-a-life' will be adopted. The following argument will endeavour to demonstrate how research in the biological sciences has shown fish to meet said criteria.

In order to establish the capacity of fish to suffer—and thus satisfy Singer's utilitarian moral framework—Rose and colleagues' (2014, p. 104; see also Rose 2002) core argument must first be addressed which centers around the lack of a human-like neocortex in fish: '[t]he conscious experience of pain most likely requires highly developed and regionally specialized forebrain neocortex (and associated limbic cortex), which fishes do not have.' Brown (2014, p. 123) argues that Rose's (2002; Rose et al. 2014) 'central argument is both anthropocentric and anthropomorphic' in that 'this argument is contingent on Rose's erroneous belief that the neocortex is the center of consciousness in humans and that fish lack any comparable structure.' Brown (2014, p. 123) then undermines Rose's (2002) argument by pointing to recent research that indicates that there is little reason to suspect the human neocortex is involved in consciousness and research showing that fish 'effectively have analogous [brain] structures and functions to other vertebrates.'

In addition, there is a host of experimental research indicating the capacity of fish to respond to physical stimuli with behaviors indicative of experiencing pain (Braithwaite 2010; Braithwaite and Huntingford 2004; Chandroo et al. 2004a, 2004b; Sneddon 2003; Sneddon et al. 2003a; Sneddon et al. 2003b).[1] While it cannot be said definitively whether fish are capable of experiencing physical pain as suffering, the preponderance of the evidence laid out in the above studies lend credence to the argument that they can—at least, insofar as, any other nonhuman animal can. Even hypothetically conceding, however, that fish are incapable of suffering from physical pain would still not completely disqualify them from moral consideration under a utilitarian framework or 'subjects-of-a-life' moral framework. Reducing these frameworks to the capacity for physical suffering, after all, would automatically disqualify those humans inflicted with congenital analgesia or congenital insensitivity to pain with anhidrosis (CIPA) (also called hereditary sensory and autonomic neuropathy type IV)—conditions that render individuals unable to feel physical pain.

But, what of fish as 'subjects-of-a-life' or as 'moral patients'? As Beirne (1999, p. 134) says of Regan's (1983) criteria for claims for 'subjects-of-a-life': 'among the leading attributes of the mental life of many animals, especially normal mammalians aged one or more, are perception, memory, desire, belief, self-consciousness, intention, and a sense of the future.' Bekoff (2007, p. 89), also bypassing the problematic utilitarian stumbling block of suffering, states in regard to fish that 'intelligence and suffering are not necessarily correlated and clever animals do not suffer more than less clever individuals.' Establishing such intelligence, such sentience, is an issue that Brown (2014, p. 123) takes head on, compiling a comprehensive literature review of the relevant marine biology and animal cognition research that shows:

> Fish have very good memories, live in complex social communities where they keep track of individuals and can learn from one another; a process that leads to the development of stable cultural traditions. They recognize themselves and others. They cooperate with one another and show signs of Machiavellian intelligence such as cooperation and reconciliation. They build complex structures, are capable of tool use and use the same methods for keeping track of

[1] It should be noted that such experimentation conducted to determine the pain capacity of fish are forms of animal abuse in and of themselves. The experimenters utilize a utilitarian scientific rationale that justifies the harming of a few fish to primarily advance the body of scientific knowledge, and in some cases with a secondary objective of showing that fish should fall under our current rights frameworks due to their capacity to suffer (see Bekoff 2007 for discussion).

> quantities as [humans] do. For the most part, their primary senses are just as good, and in many cases better, than our own. When comparing their behavior to primates, one finds very few differences... One must conclude, therefore, that the level of cognitive complexity displayed by fishes is on a par with most other vertebrates, and that if any animals are sentient then one must conclude that fish are too.

In other words, Brown's (2014) systematic approach establishes that fish fall squarely within Regan's (1983) conceptualization of 'subjects-of-a-life' and thus qualify as moral patients deserving protection due to their intrinsic value. Additionally, Kappeler's (1995) argument that Regan's 'subjects-of-a-life' framework is 'super-speciesist' is partially undercut by Brown's (2014) findings that serve to greatly expand the range of species the framework covers beyond solely mammals. Having firmly situated fish within the two rationalistic moral pillars at the base of the nonspeciesist animal abuse literature, this chapter can now interrogate how the discourse of utilitarianism as expressed through calls for 'conservation' and 'animal welfare' by zoos and aquariums serves to actually perpetuate conditions conducive to animal abuse.

The Ideological Work of Public Aquariums and Zoos

As a theoretical tool, Lynch and colleagues' (2013) use of the political economic concept of the 'treadmill of production' to illuminate the capitalistic crime of ecological disorganization has significant bearing on the expansion of the animal abuse literature. The 'treadmill of production' focuses on capitalism's imperative to expand and transform ever wider swaths of nature from, as White (2002, p. 85) puts it, 'previously unproductive or noncapitalist forms of activity into sites of productive labor.' Importantly, the 'treadmill of production' also incorporates an understanding of ecological additions (pollutants) and withdrawals ('raw material input into the treadmill and the forms of ecological damage created in accessing those materials' (Lynch et al. 2013, p. 1003)) that contribute further to ecological disorganization and destruction. Such a framework is powerful in making theoretical sense of individual instances and wider processes of environmental destruction; its mechanistic metaphor, however, is lacking an explanation of the lubricating grease that keeps the gears of the treadmill turning. A more holistic theoretical framework is one that incorporates an understanding of how the consumption of nature is culturally constructed, and how ideological narratives perpetuate such consumption. This incorporation of 'cultural grease' into the 'treadmill of production' framework furthers Brisman and South's (2014, p. 6; see also Brisman and South 2012; Brisman et al. 2014) argument for an overlapping green-cultural criminology in which 'green criminology must attend to . . . the commodification and marketing of nature and the construction of the insatiable consumption that underpins this.'

Having established the political economic treadmill and its cultural grease, the argument presented here is primed for a green criminology capable of theoretically situating 'the sources of animal abuse' not only in individual acts 'but also in various institutionalised social practices where animal abuse is seen as socially acceptable' (Beirne 2007, p. 55). Such an articulation of animal abuse establishes a base from which a critique of the various sites of ideological work that undergird such socially acceptable practices can be developed, in which 'denial is ingrained in the hegemonic dominance of anthropocentric, and specifically capitalist, conceptions of the relationship between human beings and nature' (White 2002, p. 83). Having established the moral standing of fish, whether utilitarian or intrinsic, this chapter will now interrogate one of the predominant sites of such anthropocentric ideological work that influences our collective relation to marine life in general and fish in particular: the public aquarium.

The non-profit Association of Zoos and Aquariums (AZA), established in 1924, remains the predominant accreditation agency in the USA with 230 member zoos and aquariums and over 181 million annual visitors. Organizationally, the AZA is 'committed to being a global leader in promoting species conservation and animal welfare by leveraging the size, scope, expertise, and public trust of its member institutions' (AZA 2015, p. 1). While this may sound innocuous—and perhaps even *noble*—the terms 'species conservation' and 'animal welfare' reveal problematic orientations to fish and other animals.

In making a distinction between those working from an 'animal rights' perspective and those focusing on 'animal welfare,' Bekoff (2007) identifies 'animal rights' as consistent with Regan's 'subjects-of-a life' framework; the 'animal welfare' perspective, adopted by zoos and aquariums, views animals in primarily utilitarian terms. Thus, 'animal welfarists,' according to Bekoff (2007, p. 89), 'believe that while humans should not abuse or exploit animals, as long as we make the animals' lives comfortable, physically and psychologically, we are taking care of them and respecting their welfare' and that 'it is permissible to use animals if the relationship between the costs to the animals and the benefits to the humans is such that the costs are less than the benefits.' Such a utilitarian rational represents the philosophical justifications of modern zoos and aquariums, as evidenced by the discourses of 'species conservation' and 'animal welfare' (to be read: cultural grease) running throughout the AZA's publications and website. Operating from a 'subjects-of-a-life' framework, on the other hand, would necessarily preclude the caging of complex social creatures, such as fish or other sentient animals, even if their basic biological needs were met, because:

> To place animals with such [social] desires in situations in which these desires cannot be fulfilled—as is done by caging wolves in, say, roadside zoos—is to cause them *prima facie* harm, whether they suffer or not, because it is to deny them the opportunity to satisfy their desires for companionship or physical freedom of movement (Regan 1983, p. 98).

With Regan's perspective in mind, it is clear that while on the surface AZA 'species conservation' and 'animal welfarism' discourses support a potential ecocentric view of nature and the animals within it (see Halsey and White 1998; White 2013), a closer read of the activities of the AZA-member institutions points to the anthropocentric ideological work at play.

In 2014, an AZA-estimated 81.9 million people participated in some form of their member's 'conservation education' programs, however, the '5 most frequently reported conservation actions' advocated to participants were to:

> Learn about the issue and teach others/Encourage collective action; Make informed purchasing decisions/Be a conscious consumer; Support conservation efforts and organizations; Create safe environments for wildlife; [and] Reduce/Reuse/Recycle [efforts] (AZA 2014, p. 6).

It is arguable whether certain forms of collective action are conducive to the generation of positive environmental effects. More important, for the purposes of this chapter, is that the primary focus on 'conservation' through pathways of 'action' that involve individualistic changes in consumption habits leaves the environmentally-destructive contradictions of capitalism unaddressed. In addition, the very spatial arrangements of zoos and aquariums are worrisome in that they perpetuate an attitude of an *I* to an *It*, to borrow from Buber (1970)—one separated by discrete bounds—an exceptionally anthropocentric view of nature paralleling Louis XIV's menagerie for viewing exotic animals as 'the metaphorical expression of His Majesty's absolutism' (Beirne 2014, p. 51; see Halsey 1999 on how an Australian marine park reinforced a division between discrete understandings of 'human' and 'nature').

While the prior discussion is applicable to both zoos and aquariums, this chapter will now focus on a rather explicit example of the ideological work performed by public aquariums: the AZA-accredited Audubon Aquarium of the America's 'Gulf of Mexico' exhibit in New Orleans. As per its website description, the Gulf of Mexico exhibit 'measures 17 feet deep and holds 400,000 gallons of man-made saltwater. It is packed with sharks, schools of fish, sting rays, and sea turtles- including King Mydas an endangered green sea turtle' (Audobon 2015). At the center of the tank sits the crown-ideological jewel, 'a quarter-scale replica of an offshore oil rig' designed to let individuals 'meet the aquatic animals that thrive around its barnacled pilings.' This exhibit is sponsored by five oil companies with vested interest in maintaining green(washed)[2] images and drilling operations in the Gulf: BP, Shell, ExxonMobil, Chevron, and Kerr McGee.

While visiting the Audubon Aquarium's 'Gulf of Mexico' exhibit in 2013, I could not help but observe the distinct lack of 'conservation education' related to the environmental destruction wrought by the 152-day BP Deepwater Horizon oil disaster that poured 210 million gallons of oil into the Gulf in 2010 (Beirne 2014, p. 59). Nor was there any aquarium sponsored education related to the effect of BP's use of 1.84 million gallons of toxic Corexit 9500A and 9527A chemical dispersants that were injected directly into the Deepwater Horizon wellhead and sprayed over the surface of the ocean—a figure that makes the 5,500 gallons of dispersant used in the Exxon Valdez spill pale in comparison (Bradshaw 2014, p. 170). Typically, chemical dispersants are used to sink and disperse oil throughout the water column, thus preventing the spilled oil from reaching and affecting shore ecosystems—a measure that comes at the expense of offshore ecosystems and one guided by a utilitarian calculus of 'net environmental impact.' BP, in collusion with the US Coast Guard, completely disbanded any veneer of a utilitarian environmental calculus, however, and deployed copious amounts of the dispersant in a strategic attempt to conceal the damage of the spill from the media—an effort that also included blocking of beaches and harassing journalists (Bradshaw 2014; see documentary *Dirty Energy* by Hopkins and Stencel 2012). All the while, BP deployed a 'no harm'

[2] 'Greenwashing' typically refers to the utilization of green imagery, token-gestures (e.g., small donations to 'conservation' organizations), and other public relations efforts that corporations use to mislead the public about the true environmental consequences of their company or industry's practices and products, thus providing a false or over-inflated impression of 'environmental friendliness' (See Simon 2000, p. 642). For an example of the Chevron Corporation's greenwashing practices see Lynch and Stretesky (2003), pp. 220–222.

technique of neutralization—neutralizing *the public*, that is—claiming that the Gulf of Mexico was so large that the amount of oil and dispersants pouring into it was negligible (Bradshaw 2014, p. 170).

At the height of the disaster the National Oceanic and Atmospheric Administration (NOAA) banned fishing in 37 % of federal waters in the Gulf spanning an 88,522 square miles (229,270 square kilometers) area (NOAA 2016). The maximum size of the oil slick itself extended an estimated 28,958 square miles (75,000 square kilometers) with 'the extent and location of the slick changing from day to day depending on weather conditions' (Cleveland 2010). BP's actions in the immediate aftermath of the disaster and in the Audubon Aquarium's 'Gulf of Mexico' exhibit—a cheap, greenwashed token gesture to the public—reflect the extent to which oil companies are truly concerned with aquatic life. Perhaps more revealing is the AZA's complicity, through public news releases, in BP's efforts to help rehabilitate its image by using the language of 'spill' and focusing solely on the importance of AZA-accredited zoos and aquariums in research and rehabilitation efforts related to preserving impacted wildlife. Not a single word in these news releases criticized BP's negligent role in the production of this particular instance of widespread ecological disaster. As producers of ideological work the Audubon Aquarium of the America's exhibition and the AZA's official responses to the oil 'spill' serve to reify a 'cultural silence' in which our global reliance on fossil fuels, and the associated environmental disaster this reliance produces, remain unquestioned (see Websdale and Ferrell 1999, pp. 349–350 on cultural silence; see Brisman 2012, pp. 61–63 for the cultural silence produced by climate change contrarianism).

The utilitarian discourses of welfarism and conservation displayed here and deployed elsewhere by the AZA and member aquariums thus serve as mere logs in a voracious treadmill of production where 'the aim of such development is to operate within the context of global capitalist markets, rather than to challenge the logic of these forms of production and consumption' (Halsey and White 1998, p. 351). By encouraging 'conservation action' behaviors primarily centered around minor shifts in individualistic acts of conspicuous consumption, the AZA and aquariums merely reinforce the capitalistic political economy of consumption where, drawing inspiration from White (2002, p. 86), the issue ultimately becomes the conservation of a particular speciesist, anthropocentric social order, rather than conservation as such.

It may be argued that the AZA and member institutions still do important conservation work and research (see, for example, South et al. 2013, p. 34), even while being sites of ideological work supporting capitalism. Nevertheless, the speciesist mammalian-bias of this work must not be lost sight of. When it comes to species-specific field conservation projects, an estimated $154 million was spent by AZA member institutions in 2014, however only 4 % of these projects focused on fish—the lowest of any category in comparison to 55 % of projects focused on mammals and 14 % each on birds and reptiles (AZA 2014, p. 5). Such mammalian-bias is even more pronounced when looking at *research* conducted by AZA member institutions: of approximately $21 million spent on research projects on over 700 species in 2014, 69 % of these projects focused on mammals, compared to 4 % on fish; birds and reptiles had 11 % and 8 % of the pie respectively (AZA 2014, p. 13).

The Impact of the Private Marine Aquarium Trade

Having explored the ways in which public aquariums perpetuate the hegemonic anthropocentrism of capitalism, this chapter will now focus on the means whereby the treadmill of production facilitates the commodification of nature, particularly both coral and fish, through the private US marine aquarium trade. Sollund (2011, p. 442) identifies the use of cages on companion animals as undermining that very companionship through the enforcement of captivity, with the cage itself 'establish[ing] a solid physical and mental barrier to nearness,' resulting in speciesist objectification of the animal as property. Fish are unique in that they cannot survive without the 'cage,' perhaps establishing an inherent material basis within their companion animal status that predisposes them to treatment as property which 'may in turn legitimate other abuse, just as the abuse and death of animals destined for material use is "legitimated" by their property status (Beirne 1999)' (Sollund 2011, p. 443). Such psychological barriers and property classification of fish may also serve to further fuel the marine aquarium fish trade in particular, in that if a fish, understood as *object*, dies within an owner's aquarium one need simply purchase another with little emotional involvement. This is evident in the ways that many stores that sell fish offer various forms of money-back guarantees. For example, the Red and White Ryukin Goldfish, Item 36-4032756, which retails at PetSmart for $12.47, comes with the following 'Vet Assured™ Promise':

> All pets purchased at PetSmart are raised under our exclusive Vet Assured program and come with a 14-day satisfaction guarantee. Vet Assured is a program designed by PetSmart veterinarians to improve the health and well-being of our pets. The program sets standards for the care of our pets by our live animal partners and store associates and establishes strict standards for the monitoring and prevention of common illnesses found in pets. PetSmart makes a significant investment in the care of our pets and it is apparent in the quality

> and comfort of the pets in our stores. However, if your pet becomes ill during this initial 14-day period, or if you're not satisfied with your pet for any reason, PetSmart will gladly replace the pet or refund the purchase price. Please keep your sales receipt and return the pet to the store where it was purchased if needed. (Petsmart 2015).

Overall, the US demand for marine aquarium pets is fuelled by approximately one million hobbyists in a trade wrought with systematic instances of individual animal abuse as well as major environmental destruction and ecological disorganization. At the individual level, given the relative inability to distinguish recognizable cues of potential suffering in individual fish, it is important to illustrate types of abuse that may easily be overlooked. Table 1, adapted from Huntingford and colleagues (2006, pp. 356–358), indicates a range of specific instances of potential animal abuse throughout the treadmill of production inherent in not only the marine aquarium trade, but also applicable to those fish stored in public aquariums.

At the level of ecological disorganization, over the past two decades, the consumption preferences of aquarium hobbyists have increasingly moved toward ecosystems mimicking the aesthetic of full reefs, versus fish-only tanks. This consumption pattern has resulted in the commodification and abduction of both fish and the coral habitat in which they live, 'with a premium on both biodiversity and scarcity [where] critical ecological roles are particularly vulnerable' (Rhyne et al. 2012, p. 1; see also Rhyne et al. 2009). Both coral and fish specimens are primarily extracted in Southeast Asia with a significant amount of coral being extracted from China and the vast majority of both coral and fish extracted from the Coral Triangle area (primarily from Indonesia and the Philippines but including Malaysia, Papua New Guinea, the Solomon Islands, and Timor Leste). The Coral Triangle is the most biologically diverse marine ecosystem in the world and 'the most seriously threatened, with 40 % of reefs effectively lost, 45 % under threat, and 15 % at low threat' due to a combination of local and global environmental factors (Hoegh-Guldberg et al 2009, pp. 5–6).

Coral habitat broadly serves in the most critical ecological role for countless marine species including fish, but the trade in coral has been profoundly

[3] The Convention on International Trade in Endangered Species of Wild Fauna and Flora (CITES) is an international trade agreement between 181 nations designed to regulate the trade in plant and animal species so that such trade does not result in extinction. CITES covers 5,600 animal and 30,000 plant species through three Appendices: Appendix I species are threatened by extinction (international trade in such species is prohibited, but there are exemptions); Appendix II species are not yet threatened by extinction but 'may become so unless trade is closely monitored'; and Appendix III species are protected by at least one CITES member country that asks other member countries to help control the international trade in that species (CITES 2015).

Table 1 Examples of sources of abuse, morbidity, and mortality in ornamental fish keeping practices (adapted from Huntingford et al. [2006])*

Practice	Some demonstrated effects on the health of fish
Capture	The usual process of capturing marine tropical fish in Indonesia and the Philippines through the use of sodium cyanide results in very high mortality rates for several weeks after capture (Hignette 1984), with estimates ranging up to 80 % (WWF 2013). Clove oil is a better alternative (Erdmann 1999). Mortality during capture of ornamental fish from South America ranges may be as high as 30 % (Ferrez de Olivera 1995).
Transportation	In South America a further 5–10 % mortality is estimated to occur during transportation and at the holding facilities (Ferrez de Olivera 1995). During the acclimation period following importation, mortality rates can be up to 30 % (FitzGibon 1993). Shipping of zebra fish (*Brachydanio rerio*) by road in oxygenated bags causes elevated cortisol levels but recovery is rapid on transfer to aquaria (Pottinger and Calder 1995). Elevated cortisol and glucose levels are used as a measure of stress in fish and high levels of cortisol can result in immunosuppression and derivative health deterioration (Weyts et al. 1999).
Handling	Physical disturbance evokes a neuroendocrine stress response in many species of farmed fish (reviewed by Pickering 1998) and reduces disease resistance (Strangeland et al. 1996). Handling stress increases vulnerability to whitespot disease in channel catfish (Davis et al. 2002).
Constraint in a confined space	Physical confinement in otherwise favourable conditions increases cortisol and glucose levels and alters immunological activity in various species (Garcia-Garbi 1998). Carp (*Cyprinus carpio*) show a mild, physiological stress response to crowding that decline as the fish adapts, but crowded fish are more sensitive to additional stressors (e.g., confinement in a net) (Ruane et al. 2002). Crowding during grading (the process of sorting fish based on size) increases cortisol levels for up to 48 hours in Greenback flounder *Rhombosolea tapirinia*, Gunther (Barnett and Pankhurst 1998).

(*continued*)

Table 1 (continued)

Practice	Some demonstrated effects on the health of fish
Poor water quality	81 % of ornamental fish are held outside the optimal pH range, 36 % at inappropriate temperatures (Etscheidt and Manz 1992). Poor water quality is the most common cause of mortality in ornamental fish (Schunk 1980).
Inappropriate food levels	Inappropriate range and types of food can cause poor health in ornamental fish (Etscheidt 1995). Inappropriate feeding is not usually a direct cause of mortality in ornamental fish, but can be a contributory factor (Schunck 1980).
Health treatment	There is evidence therapeutic treatments themselves may be stressful to fish (e.g., Yildiz and Pulatsu 1999; Griffin et al. 1999, 2002; Thorburn et al. 2001; Sørum and Damsgard 2003).
Deprivation of social contact	Angelfish transferred singly to a new tank take longer to resume feeding than those transferred in groups of three or five (Gomez-Laplaza and Morgan 1993).
Inappropriate species combinations/Unavoidable contact with predators	Lack of appropriate social environment (wrong species or inappropriate numbers) is an important cause of poor health in ornamental fish (Estcheidt 1995). In 19 % of ornamental tanks, prey were housed in small tanks in direct contact with predators (Etscheidt and Manz 1992; Foggitt 1997). Brief exposure to a predator causes increased cortisol levels and ventilation rate and suppressed feeding (*e.g.*, Metcalfe et al. 1987).

*The research compiled in this table is primarily based on studies of individual species in the field of marine and fish biology. The categories and examples provided are derived from a broad overview of the literature by Huntingford et al. (2006) and are thus illustrative and not exhaustive. A more holistic and exhaustive review would undoubtedly contribute to the animal abuse literature, but such an endeavour is outside the scope of this chapter.

shaped by the marine aquarium fish trade itself. Utilizing the CITES[3] Trade Database, which monitors the trade in threatened and endangered species including over 2,000 species of coral, Green and Shirley (1999, p. 1) analysed the legal global trade in coral from 1985 to 1997 calculating that the USA imported 56 % (just under 10,800 tonnes) of the total global market. For this time period Green and Shirley (1999, p. 21) estimate that 76 % of all coral reef trade by weight was 'for commercial purposes, presumably with dead corals supplying the ornamental trade and the live aquarium industry.' While the majority of coral during this period was traded dead (86 % by weight), by 1997 the trade in live coral had rapidly increased to dominate between 53–56 % of total global trade due primarily to the growth in popularity and changing aesthetic-based consumption habits of the marine aquarium fish trade enthusiasts in North America and Europe (1999, pp. 26–27). Between 1986 and 1997, 96 % of all coral traded globally originated in the wild with Indonesia dominating exports (41 % of global exports; followed by China at 24 % and the Philippines at 18 %) (1999, p. 11). In 1973, 1977, and 1980 the Philippines government took measures to completely ban the harvesting and export of coral due to environmental concerns, however, until the late 1980s the Philippines and Indonesia, which had no bans, still exported approximately the same amount of coral annually. Philippine collectors and poachers (using similar tactics to others across the region) have historically taken advantage of loopholes, mislabelling of wares, forged permits, confusion between governments, and lack of oversight (all exacerbated by temporary lifts in export bans in 1986 and 1992 meant to allow traders to clear old stock) to continue the illegal export of new coral (see Mulliken and Nash 1993; Elliott 2007). When the Philippines 1992 export ban was restored all legal trade in coral rapidly dropped off prompting a rise in legal exports from Indonesia to meet global demand (Green and Shirley 1999, p. 12).

The size of the illegal coral market (and broader illegal marine trade) in Indonesia, China, the Philippines and elsewhere is unknown but likely significant in the context of East Asia and the Pacific where an estimated USD $2.5 billion is generated annually from the illegal trade in wildlife (Elliott 2007; UNODC 2013; see also the chapter on International Trade in Animals and Animal Parts). The proliferation of the marine aquarium fish trade and corresponding increase in demand for live coral in the 1990s provided lucrative economic incentives for legal and illegal trade alike with 'the retail value of the international trade in live corals [quadrupling] during the 1990s . . . and generat[ing] between $27–78 million in sales in 1997' (Green and Shirley 1999, p. 50). These high sales prices in importing nations translated to approximately $5 million in legal revenue for exporting nations in 1997, a significant revenue stream for coral gatherers who, for example, in Cebu, Philippines 'were paid US $0.20 per piece of coral in 1983 (Ross 1984)' (Green and Shirley 1999, p. 51). Indeed, a tonne of living coral is estimated to be worth USD $7,000 while a tonne of coral harvested to produce limestone only fetches around USD $60 (Wabnitz et al. 2003, p. 9). Trade in endangered and threatened coral species is even more lucrative with CITES Appendix-II protected black coral, almost exclusively used in the ornamental and jewellery trade, fetching as much as USD $350,000 per tonne.[4] While the demand for black coral is not directly linked to the marine aquarium fish trade like the demand for living coral is, both types of coral collection and commodification can and do take place on both the legal and black market. It stands to reason that both trades may utilize very similar if not the same human pathways along the treadmills of production that connect the coral and marine aquarium fish trade: starting with impoverished coral and fish gatherers attempting to make a living, traveling through various middlemen making significantly more profit moving product out of the country, and onto the markets of developed countries (see Elliott 2007; UNODC 2013, pp. 75–86; Green and Shirley 1999, p. 51; Mulliken and Nash 1993). To more fully integrate this argument though this chapter will now turn to the side of the treadmill dealing with marine fish in particular.

Rhyne and colleagues (2012) attempted to estimate the size and biodiversity of the virtually unregulated (and thus un-tracked) non-CITES US marine aquarium fish trade; they compared shipment declarations, which must be produced for the USA before the importation of fish and other animals, with commercial invoices for each shipment between May 2004 and May 2005. Their findings indicate a grand importation total of nearly 10.5 million fish of over 1,800 species with 'the Philippines and Indonesia account[ing] for 86.6% of [USA] imports 5,774,579 (55%) and 3,288,434 (31%) individuals, respectively'—a total of over 990 species represented between the two countries (Rhyne et al. 2012, p. 7). This is necessarily an underestimation of the total fish impacted by the US market given that: it does not include CITES species

[4] Toward the end of the treadmill encompassing black coral, the figure of $350,000 per tonne of black coral was calculated from the U.S. Department of Justice's [DOJ] largest ever indictment of a U.S. company knowingly trading in falsely-labelled black coral supplied by a Taiwanese company operating through China. On top of a USD $1.8 million criminal fine the jewelry company GEM Manufacturing LLC 'was also ordered to forfeit dozens of jewelry items, 10 artistic sculptures and over 13,655 pounds of raw black coral, the total value of which, at current prices, exceeds $2.17 million' (see U.S. Department of Justice 2011). An example closer to the beginning of the treadmill comes from Manila, Philippines where in 2011 poachers harvested at least 21,000 black coral specimens and killed at least 161 endangered sea turtles. The specimens were packed in two vans destined for exports, both falsely labelled as containing 'rubber' when the Philippines Bureau of Customs intercepted them. The harvesting of these black coral specimens is estimated to have destroyed as much as 191 square kilometers of habitat (five times the size of Manila) that supported thousands of other species (see more at Tubeza 2011a, 2011b).

(see Sollund 2011 on the anthropocentric limitations of CITES); it does not account for illegal trafficking (see Elliott 2007; UNODC 2013, pp. 75–86); it does not reflect the number of marine fish traded within the USA that derive primarily from Hawaii (see Tissot and Hallacher 2003 on the environmental impacts of the marine aquarium trade in Hawaii); and it does not include the number of fish that died during or after capture (but before export). This considered, it is clear there is a significant amount of individual cases of animal 'abduction' (see Sollund 2011, p. 438 on the use of the word 'abduction', instead of poaching, 'to emphasise that birds and animals are born free and do not belong to anyone'), as well as ecological withdrawals and potential ecological disorganization in terms of the quantity and biodiversity of fish affected along this treadmill of production (see Lynch et al. 2013).

To illustrate further the ways in which the US marine aquarium fish trade contributes to the death of individual fish, as well as to their coral reef habitat (beyond the harvesting of living and dead coral specimens outlined above), consider how the death of coral reef fish are widely facilitated in the Philippines and Indonesia through attempted capture using poisons (primarily sodium cyanide) that are squirted directly into coral reefs in order to stun the fish. Aside from extremely high fish mortality due to toxic poisons, this process produces ecological withdrawals in the form of coral destruction because '[t]he application of dilute solutions of cyanide will disrupt photosynthesis and cause corals to bleach and die . . . and if applied at higher concentrations will kill entire communities of corals' (Hoegh-Guldberg et al. 2009, p. 57). The World Wildlife Fund-Philippines (2013) estimates that, due to such destructive extraction practices and other environmental stressors involved, up to 80 % of marine fish captured for the marine aquarium trade die before ever being sold, with an overall estimation of 98 % of wild-caught fish dying within the first year. With this figure in mind, it stands to reason that the roughly 9.06 million live marine fish, abducted, sold, and imported to the USA in 2005 (Rhyne et al. 2012) is indicative of a much larger 36.3 million fish who were victims of abduction and subsequent theriocide.

The massive scale of death and ecological disorganization caused by the marine aquarium fish trade's treadmill of production receives at least partial direct support from public aquariums, despite those greasy discourses of 'conservation' and 'animal welfare'. Rhyne and colleagues (2012, p. 7) found that '[p]ublic aquariums significantly overlap with the home hobbyist aquarium trade, as 54% of the species held in public aquariums were imported into the USA in 2005 . . . [with] many [public aquariums] sourc [ing] fish from commercial retail sources.' It is difficult to estimate the exact number of marine fish that public aquariums obtain from treadmills of production that start in wild reefs, however it is likely significant due to the extremely limited amount of breeding of marine ornamental fish in captivity (Tlusty 2002). Whether perpetrated by the ideological anthropocentrism of the public aquarium or the seemingly benign private hobbyist, within the intertwined treadmill of production of the marine aquarium fish trade, encompassing fish and coral alike, there exists the intersection of four of the seven major sites of theriocide that Beirne (2014, pp. 58–59) lays out: fishing, trafficking, and pollution as explicit components in the foreground; and the support of discourses that facilitate climate change in the background, thus further acidifying oceans, bleaching coral reefs, and leading to the death of countless marine species (Hoegh-Guldberg et al. 2009).

Conclusion

This chapter has situated fish as worthy of inclusion within Singer's (1975) utilitarian and Regan's (1983) 'subjects-of-a-life' moral frameworks, and, in so doing, has called for heightened attention to their place within the animal abuse literature. In addition, this chapter has proposed utilizing an integrated 'treadmill of production' and green cultural criminology of consumption framework in order to improve our understanding of the various specific, dispersed, and intertwined instances and sources of animal abuse as perpetuated in ideological and political economic dimensions. To better illustrate this framework, this chapter has explored the anthropocentric and speciesist ideological work of public aquariums that, through utilitarian discourses of 'conservation' and 'welfarism,' serve as cultural grease for an anthropocentric worldview necessary to perpetuate the specific abuses and widespread ecological disorganization perpetrated in the treadmill of marine aquarium fish production, against fish and coral reefs alike.

References

Association of Zoos & Aquariums (2014). 2014 annual report on conservation and science: highlights. *Silver Spring, MD: Association of Zoos & Aquariums*. https://www.aza.org/uploadedFiles/Conservation/Commitments_and_Impacts/AZA_ARCSHighlights_2014_web.pdf. Accessed 20 November 2015.

Association of Zoos & Aquariums (2015). DRAFT: strategic plan review and update (3/2/15): 2015–2017. *Silver Spring, MD: Association of Zoos & Aquariums*. https://www.aza.org/uploadedFiles/About_Us/AZA-Strategic-Plan-2015-2017.pdf. Accessed 20 November 2015.

Audubon (2015). *Audubon nature institute*. http://audubonnatureinstitute.org/aquarium/explore-aquarium/aquarium-exhibits/386-gulf-of-mexico-exhibit. Accessed 18 November 2015.

Barnett, C. W., & Pankhurst, N. W. (1998). The effects of common laboratory and husbandry practices on the stress response of greenback flounder (*Rhombosolea tapirinia*, Gunther 1862). *Aquaculture, 162*, 113–329.

Beirne, P. (1999) For a nonspeciesist criminology: animal abuse as an object of study. *Criminology, 37*(1), 117–147.

Beirne, P. (2007). Animal rights, animal abuse and green criminology. In P. Beirnes & N. South (Eds.), *Issues in green criminology: confronting harms against environments, humanity and other animals*. London: Routledge.

Beirne, P. (2014). Theriocide: naming animal killing. *International Journal for Crime, Justice and Social Democracy, 3*(2), 50–67.

Bekoff, M. (2007). Aquatic animals, cognitive ethology, and ethics: questions about sentience and other troubling issues that lurk in turbid waters. *Diseases of Aquatic Organisms, 75*(2), 87–98.

Bentham, J. (2005). *Introduction to the principles of morals and legislation*. Oxford: Oxford University Press. (First published, 1789).

Benton, T. (1998). Rights and justice on a shared planet: more rights or new relations? *Theoretical Criminology, 2*(2), 149–175.

Bradshaw, L. (2014). State-corporate environmental cover-up: the response to the 2010 Gulf of Mexico oil spill. *State Crime Journal, 3*(2), 163–181.

Braithwaite, V. (2010). *Do fish feel pain?* Oxford: Oxford University Press.

Braithwaite, V., & Huntingford, F. (2004). Fish and welfare: do fish have the capacity for pain perception and suffering? *Animal Welfare, 13*, s87–s92.

Briefing prepared by TRAFFIC for the European Commission TRAFFIC. 2015. http://ec.europa.eu/environment/cites/pdf/Overview%20significant%20seizures%202014.pdf

Brisman, A. (2012). The cultural silence of climate change contrarianism. In R. White (Ed.), *Climate change from a criminological perspective* (pp. p. 41–70). New York: Springer.

Brisman, A. (2014). Environmental and human rights. In G. Bruinsma & D. Weisburd (Eds.), *Encyclopedia of criminology and criminal justice* (Vol. 3, pp. 1344–1345). New York: Springer Verlag.

Brisman, A., McClanahan, & B., South, N. (2014). Toward a green-cultural criminology of 'the Rural'. *Critical Criminology, 22*, 479–494.

Brisman, A., & South, N. (2012). A green-cultural criminology: an exploratory outline. *Crime Media Culture, 9*(2), 115–135.

Brisman, A., & South, N. (2014). *Green cultural criminology: construction of environmental harm, consumerism, and resistance to ecocide*. London: Routledge.

Brown, C. (2014). Fish intelligence, sentience and ethics. *Animal Cognition, 18*(1), 1–17.

Buber, M. (1970). *I and Thou* (trans. W. Kaufman). New York: Touchstone.

Cazaux, G. (1999). Beauty and the beast: animal abuse from a non-speciesist criminological perspective. *Crime, Law & Social Change, 31*(2), 105–126.

Chandroo, K. P., Duncan, I. J. H., & Moccia, R. D. (2004a). Can fish suffer? Perspectives on sentience, pain, fear and stress. *Applied Animal Behaviour Science, 86*(3–4), 225–250.

Chandroo, K. P., Yue, S., & Moccia, R. D. (2004b). An evaluation of current perspectives on consciousness and pain in fishes. *Fish and Fisheries, 5*(4), 281–295.

CITES (2015). The convention on international trade in endangered species of wild fauna and flora appendices. https://www.cites.org/eng/app/index.php. Accessed 18 November 2015.

Cleveland, C. (2010). *Deep water horizon oil spill.* http://www.eoearth.org/view/article/161185/. Accessed 27 January 2016.

Croall, H. (2007). Food crime. In P. Beirnes & N. South (Eds.), *Issues in green criminology: confronting harms against environments, humanity and other animals.* London: Routledge.

Davis, K. B., Griffin, B. R., & Gray, W. L. (2002). Effect of handling stress on susceptibility of cannel catfish *Ictalurus punctatus* to *Ichthyophthirius multifiliis* and channel catfish virus infection. *Aquaculture, 214*, 55–66.

Elliott, L. (2007). Transnational environmental crime in the Asia Pacific: an 'un(der) securitized' security problem? *The Pacific Review, 20*(4), 499–522.

Erdmann, M. V. (1999). 'Clove oil: an 'eco-friendly' alternative to cyanide use in the live reef fish industry? *SPC Live Reef Fish Bulletin, 5*, 4–7.

Etscheidt, J. (1995). Kriterien zur Beurteilung der Haltung von Susswasseraquarienfischen im Zoohandel. *Tierarztl Prax, 50*, 196–199.

Etscheidt, J., & Manz, D. (1992). Suswasseraquaristik und tierarzliche Praxis. Teil 2: Untersuchungen zur artgerechten Haltung von Zierfuschen. *Tierarztl Prax, 20*, 221–226.

Ferrez de Olivera, E. (1995). Studies on parasites of ornamental fish from South America with potential for transfaunation. *PhD Thesis*, University of Stirling.

FitzGibon, D. (1993). UK restriction proposals. *Ornamental Fish International Journal, 10*, 12–14.

Foggitt, R. (1997). Fish health in a new aquarium. *Aquarist and Pondkeeper, 61*, 34–36.

Garcia-Garbi, N., Inglis, V., & Turnbull, J. F. (1998). Assessment of phagocytosis by flourchrome acridine orange. In A. Barnes (Ed.), *Methodology in fish disease research* (pp. 91–96). Aberdeen: Fish Research Services.

Gomez-Laplaze, L. M., & Morgan, E. (1993). Transfer and isolation effects on the feeding behavior of the angelfish (*Pterophyllum scalare*). *Experiementia, 49*, 817–819.

Green, E., & Shirley, F. (1999). *The global trade in coral* Cambridge: UNEP World Conservation Monitoring Center.

Griffin, B. R., Davis, K. B., & Schlenk, D. (1999). Effects of simulated copper sulphate on stress indicators in channel catfish. *Journal of Aquatic Animal Health, 11*, 231–236.

Griffin, B. R., Davis, K. B., Darwish, A., & Straus, D. L. (2002). Effect of exposure to potassium permanganate on stress indicators in channel catfish. *Journal of the World Aquaculture Society, 33*, 1–9.

Halsey, M., & White, R. (1998). Crime, ecophilosophy and environmental harm. *Theoretical Criminology, 2*(3), 345–371.

Halsey, M. (1999). Environmental discontinuities: the production and regulation of an eco-experience. *Criminal Justice Policy Review, 10*(2), 213–255.

Hauck, M. (2007). Non-compliance in small-scale fisheries: a threat to security? In P. Beirnes & N. South (Eds.), *Issues in green criminology: confronting harms against environments, humanity and other animals*. London: Routledge.

Hauck, M., & Sweijd, N. A. (1999). A case study of abalone poaching in South Africa and its impact on fisheries management. *ICES Journal of Marine Society, 56*, 1024–1032.

Hignette, M. (1984). Utilisation du cyanure pour la capture des poisons tropicaux marins destnes a l'aquariologie: methods de diagnostic. *Oceanis, 10*, 585–591.

Hoegh-Guldberg, O., Hoegh-Guldberg, H., Vernon, J. E. N., Green, A., Gomez, E. D., Lough, J., et al. (2009). *The coral triangle and climate change: ecosystems, people and societies at risk*. Brisbane: WWF Australia.

Hopkins, B. D., Stencel, E. (Producers), & Hopkins, B. D. (Director). (2012). *Dirty energy* [motion picture]. United States of America: Cinema Libre Studio.

Huntingford, F. A., Adams, C., Braithwaite, V. A., Kadri, S., Pottinger, T. G., Sandoe, P., et al. (2006). Review paper: current issues in fish welfare. *Journal of Fish Biology*, 68, 332–372.

Kappeler, S. (1995). Speciesism, racism, nationalism . . . or the power of scientific subjectivity. In C. Adams & J. Donovan (Eds.), *Animals and women: feminist theoretical explorations*. Durham, N.C.: Duke University Press.

Lynch, M., Long, M., Barrett, K., & Stretesky, P. (2013). Is it a crime to produce ecological disorganization? Why green criminology and political economy matter in the analysis of global ecological harms. *British Journal of Criminology, 53*, 997–1016.

Lynch, M., & Stretesky, P. (2003). The meaning of green: contrasting criminological perspectives. *Theoretical Criminology, 7*(2), 217–238.

McMullan, J. L., & Perrier, D. C. (2002). Lobster poaching and the ironies of law enforcement. *Law & Society Review, 36*(4), 679–720.

Metcalfe, N.B., Huntingford, F. A., & Thorpe, J.E. (1987). The influence of predation risk on the feeding motivation and foraging strategy of juvenile Atlantic salmon. *Animal Behaviour, 35*, 901–911.

Mulliken, T., & Nash, S. (1993). The recent trade in Philippine corals. *TRAFFIC Bulletin, 13*(3), 97–105.

NOAA (2016). *National oceanic and atmospheric administration- deepwater horizon/ BP oil spill: closure information.* http://sero.nmfs.noaa.gov/deepwater_horizon/closure_info/. Accessed 27 January 2016.

Petsmart (2015). *Petsmart live fish.* http://www.petsmart.com/live-pet/live-fish/red-and-whiteryukin-goldfish-zid36-15292/cat-36-catid-700002?var_id=36-15292&_t=pfm%3Dcategory. Accessed 2 December 2015.

Pickering, A. D. (1998). Stress responses in farmed fish. In K. D. Black. & A.D. Pickering (Eds.), *Biology of farmed fish* (pp. 222–255). Sheffield: Sheffield Academic Press.

Pottinger, T. G., & Calder, G. M. (1995). Physiological stress in fish during toxicological procedures: A potentially confounding factor. *Environmental Toxicology and Water Quality, 10,* 135–146.

Regan, T. (1983). *The case for animal rights.* Berkeley: University of California Press.

Rhyne, A., Rotjan, R., Bruckner, A., & Tlusty, M. (2009). Crawling to collapse: ecologically unsound ornamental invertebrate fisheries. *PloS ONE, 4,* e8413.

Rhyne, A., Tlusty, M., Schofield, P., Kaufman, L., Morris Jr., J., & Bruckner, A. (2012). Revealing the appetite of the marine aquarium fish trade: the volume and biodiversity of fish imported into the United States. *PLoS ONE, 7*(5), e35808.

Rose, J. D. (2002). The neurobehavioral nature of fishes and the question of awareness and pain. *Reviews in Fisheries Science, 10,* 1–38.

Rose, J. D., Arlinghaus, R., Cooke, S. J., Diggles, B. K., Sawynok, W., Stevens, E. D. et al. (2014). Can fish really feel pain? *Fish & Fisheries, 15*(1), 97–133.

Ross, M. A. (1984). A quantitative study of the stony coral fishery in Cebu, Philippines. *Marine Ecology, 5*(1), 75–91.

Ruane, N. M., Carballo, E. C., & Komen, J. (2002). Increased stocking density influences the acute physiological stress response of common carp (*Cyprinus carpio* L.). *Aquaculture Research, 33,* 777–784.

Schunk, O. (1980). Ergebnisse aus der Zier- und Versuchsfischpraxis. *Kleintier Ptaxis, 25,* 1–56.

Simon, D. (2000). Corporate environmental crimes and social inequality: new directions for environmental justice research. *American Behavioral Scientist, 43*(4), 633–645.

Singer, P. (1975). *Animal liberation.* New York: Random House.

Singer, P. (1990). *Animal liberation.* 2nd edition. New York: Avon.

Sneddon, L. U. (2003). The evidence for pain in fish: the use of morphine as an analgesic. *Applied Animal Behaviour Science, 83*(2), 153–162.

Sneddon, L. U., Braithwaite, V., & Gentle, M. (2003a). Do fish have nociceptors? Evidence for the evolution of a vertebrate sensory system. *Proceedings of the Royal Society London B, 270,* 1115–1121.

Sneddon, L. U., Braithwaite, V., & Gentle, M. (2003b). Novel object test: examining nonciception and fear in the rainbow trout *Proceedings of the Royal Society, 270,* 1115–1121.

Sollund, R. (2011). Expressions of speciesism: the effects of keeping companion animals on animal abuse, animal trafficking and species decline. *Crime, Law & Social Change, 55*(5), 437–451.

Sollund, R. (2015). With our without a license to kill: human-predator conflicts and theriocide in Norway. In A. Brisman, N. South, & R. White (Eds.), *Environmental crime and social conflict: contemporary and emerging issues* (pp. 95–121). Surrey, UK: Ashgate.

Sørum U., & Damsgard, B. (2003). Effects of anaesthisation and vaccination on feed intake and growth of Atlantic salmon (*Salmo salar* L.). *Aquaculture, 232*, 333–341.

South, N., Brisman, A., & Beirne, P. (2013). A guide to a green criminology. In N. South & A. Brisman (Eds.), *Routledge international handbook of green criminology* (pp. 27–42). London & New York: Routledge.

Strangeland, K., Hoie, S., & Taksdal, T. (1996). Experimental induction of infectious pancreatic necrosis in Atlantic salmon (*Salmo salar* L.) post-smolts. *Journal of Fish Diseases, 19*, 323–327.

Tailby, R., & Gant, F. (2002). The illegal market in Australian abalone. *Trends & Issues in Crime and Criminal Justice, 225*, 1–6. http://www.aic.gov.au/media_library/publications/tandi_pdf/tandi225.pdf. Reprinted in White, R. (ed.) (2009). *Environmental crime: a reader* (pp. 399–411). Cullompton, Devon: Willan.

Tissot, B. N., & Hallacher, L. E. (2003). Effects of aquarium collectors on coral reef fishes in Kona, Hawaii. *Conservation Biology, 17*(6), 1759–1768.

Thorburn, M. A., Teare, G. F., Martin, S. W., & Moccia, R. D. (2001). Group-level factors associated with chemotherapeutic treatment regiments in land-based trout farms in Ontario, Canada. *Preventative Veterinary Medicine, 50*, 451–466.

Tlusty, M. (2002). The benefits and risks of aquacultural production for the aquarium trade. *Aquaculture, 205*, 203–219.

Tubeza, P. [Newspaper Article] (2011a). Coral reefs twice size of Manila destroyed: poachers 'rape' sease off Cotabato. Manila, Philippines: Philippine Daily Inquirer. http://newsinfo.inquirer.net/8892/coral-reefs-twice-size-of-manila-destroyed. Accessed 19 February 2016.

Tubeza, P. [Newspaper Article] (2011b). Damaged coral area much bigger. Manila, Philippines: Philippine Daily Inquirer. http://newsinfo.inquirer.net/10121/damaged-Coral-area-much-bigger. Accessed 19 February 2016.

United Nations Office on Drugs and Crime (2013). *Transnational organized crime in East Asia and the pacific: a threat assessment.* Bangkok, Thailand: United Nations Office on Drugs and Crime, Regional Office for Southeast Asia and the Pacific. https://www.unodc.org/documents/data-and-analysis/Studies/TOCTA_EAP_web.pdf. Accessed 20 November 2016.

U.S. Department of Justice [Press Release] (2011) U.S. Virgin Islands company sentenced for illegal trade of protected coral: gem manufacturing sentenced to highest financial penalty for illegal coral trade. Washington, DC: U.S. D.O.J. Environment and Natural Resources Division. https://www.justice.gov/opa/pr/us-virgin-islands-Company-sentenced-illegal-trade-protected-coral. Accessed 20 February 2016.

Verne, J. (1962). *20,000 Leagues Under the Sea* (trans. A. Bonner). New York: Bantam.

Wabnitz, C., Taylor, M., Green, E., & Razak, T. (2003). *From oceans to aquarium.* Cambridge: UNEP World Conservation Monitoring Center.

Websdale, N., & Ferrell, J. (1999). Taking the trouble: concluding remarks and future directions. In J. Ferrell & N. Websdale (Eds.), *Making trouble: cultural constructions of crime, deviance, and control.* Aldine de Gruyter: Hawthorne, NY.

Weyts, F., Cohen, N., Flik, G., & Verburg-van Kemenade, B. (1999). Interactions between the immune system and the hypothalamo-pituitary-interrenal axis in fish. *Fish & Shellfish Immunology, 9,* 1–20.

White, R. (2002). Environmental Harm and the Political Economy of Consumption. *Social Justice, 29*(1–2), 82–102.

White, R. (2013). The conceptual contours of Green Criminology. In R. Walters, D. Westerhuis, and T. Wyatt (Eds.), *Emerging issues in Green Criminology: Exploring power, justice and harm.* London: Palgrave/Macmillan.

World Wildlife Fund-Philippines (2013). *Saving Nemo: transforming the marine aquarium industry.* Quezon City, Philippines: WWF-Philippines.

Yildiz, H. Y., & Pulatsu, S. (1999). Evaluation of the secondary stress response in healthy Nile tilapia (*Oreochromis niloticus* L.) after treatment with a mixture of formalin, malachite green and methylene blue. *Aquaculture Research, 30,* 379–383.

Jordan E. Mazurek is an Erasmus Mundus Joint Doctoral fellow pursing a Doctorate in Cultural and Global Criminology at the University of Kent and University of Hamburg. His primary areas of study are green criminology, cultural criminology and visual theory.

Animal Fighting

Claire Lawson

Introduction

This chapter begins with a brief introduction to the subject of animal fighting generally before focusing specifically on dog fighting which, unlike many other forms of baiting animals, would appear to have remained popular, despite being illegal in most of the developed world. Evidence, which, in this chapter, focuses specifically on the UK and the USA, suggests that dog fighting is the most popular form of illegal animal fighting, and it has also received the most attention from researchers and civil society (Pet-Abuse.com 2016). It is, subsequently, presented, as a case study in the remainder of the chapter to illustrate the nature, prevalence, explanations of, and responses to animal fighting. Initially, an outline of the characteristics of dog fighting, its prevalence and the categorisation of dog fighters is presented, followed by an evaluation of the harms experienced by the dogs and the difficulties of measurement. The different forms of dog fighting such as the informal and the formal, as well as the rise of a cultural element imported to the UK from Pakistan, will be discussed. Thereafter, the subculture of dogmen (a term

C. Lawson (✉)
Royal Society for the Prevention of Cruelty to Animals & Cardiff University, Cardiff, United Kingdom
e-mail: LawsonCE@cardiff.ac.uk

J. Maher et al. (eds.), *The Palgrave International Handbook of Animal Abuse Studies*, DOI 10.1057/978-1-137-43183-7_16

used for dog handlers in dog fighting) and the process of neutralisation is considered by way of theoretical explanation for the participation of offenders in dog fighting. The final section examines the various responses to this offence, namely education, legislation and enforcement. These issues will be discussed in the context of both the USA and the UK, although the data available is limited and does not yet allow for a direct comparison. In addition to drawing on relevant academic, official and non-governmental organisation [NGO] literature, the chapter is informed by 25 semi-structured interviews[1] conducted by the author with a group of UK experts directly related to the issue of antisocial and criminal use of dogs in society (Lawson forthcoming). This group comprised police, animal welfare NGOs including the RSPCA, local authorities, and vets, amongst others—many of whom have directly worked on investigating and prosecuting dog fighting in the UK over several decades.

Animal Fighting

Animal fighting is a violent contest where humans encourage or goad two or more animals to fight for the purposes of entertainment, and more often, gambling. Depending on the country and species involved there are different legal definitions of animal fighting and its related offences, of which elements can include: spectating; making or accepting bets; publicising fights; supplying or showing video footage; and possessing the paraphernalia associated with preparing and training animals to fight.

A comprehensive analysis of historical texts that focuses specifically on animals, may be absent within academic literature although there would appear to be a consensus from commentators on many aspects such as the Roman and ancient Greek traditions of animal fighting, as for instance discussed by Harding and Nurse (2015). Animal fighting is also often absorbed into the collective terminology for blood sports (see also chapter on hunting and shooting). The mounted pursuits of coursing, hunting and the chasing of wild species such as boar, developed initially from a need for food to, later, a legitimate sport. These are collectively referred to as 'blood sports' due to the entertainment being centred on the likely drawing of the blood of its participants (Atkinson and Young 2008, p. 76). However, fighting has much earlier roots and a long history within many

[1] Each interview lasted between 60 and 180 minutes and all were conducted face-to-face between June 2014 and September 2015

cultures, with some of its most obscure forms, such as the little-known camel wrestling for instance, dating back more than 2,400 years (Robehmed 2014).

'Baiting'[2], an alternative term for fighting, is applied to any activity where forced, often inter-species, combat occurs. It can take many forms but most, such as bear-baiting, badger-baiting and bull-baiting will involve one or more dogs trained to torment and attack the other animal (Atkinson and Young 2008). In the case of bear-baiting the teeth and claws of the bear would usually be filed down and the animal often chained up by the neck or leg before one or more dogs attacked. If a dog should become injured or be killed, a replacement dog would be sent into the pit. In the UK, the very similar activity of lion-baiting was popular from the times of James 1 in the 1600s until public outrage saw the last of this sport in 1825 (Hone 1826, p. 499; Waters 2013). Bull-baiting too enjoyed widespread popularity in Britain during the same period. Many of these sports would attract royal patronage and dedicated amphitheatres, pits or arenas called 'bear-gardens' (Elmes 1831).

Cockfighting is also considered to date from antiquity, being possibly one of the more global of the animal fighting sports. Some reports claim it has roots before 2000 BC but certainly the first recorded cockfight in China dates back to 517BC (Dundes 1994, p. 242). This 'sport' sees two roosters or 'gamecocks', bred for their stamina, strength and natural aggression to other males, pitted against each other in a ring or 'cockpit'. For increased entertainment the birds are sometimes fitted with metal spurs, called 'gaffs', upon their natural spurs to ensure blood is drawn, although that is often the outcome without such additional aids. Not every fight will result in the death of a bird but they will usually sustain significant physical trauma. The breeding, housing and training of these birds is highly structured and can even involve the use of performance enhancing or illegal drugs to aid their capacity to fight in the pit (Merck 2013, p. 250).

In the UK, cockfighting should not be dismissed as an obsolete sport, rather, the Royal Society for the Prevention of Cruelty to Animals' (RSPCA) database reveals an increase in reports on cockfighting from

---

[2] In the UK the term was specified in law as an offence within section 1.1 of the 1911 Protection of Animals Act, see http://www.legislation.gov.uk/ukpga/Geo5/1-2/27 This was then superseded by the Animal Welfare Act 2006 which does not employ this term. Elsewhere baiting is defined in more detail within legislation, see https://www.animallaw.info/statute/sc-dogfighting-chapter-27-animal-fighting-and-baiting-act

29 in 2010 to 55 in 2015.[3] For the 10 years between 2006 and 2015 the RSPCA received a total of 440 reports of organised fighting involving a total of 2,847 farm birds, almost all of which are referencing cockfighting.[4] In 2012, the RSPCA secured in court suspended prison sentences against a father and son who had one of the largest and most sophisticated breeding and cockfighting operations ever discovered which included 500 poultry, 96 of which were mature fighting cocks. Prosecutions for animal fighting, however, are uncommon, making it impossible to determine from the number of complaints to the RSPCA, alone, how prevalent cockfighting is in the UK.

Trainers of fighting animals will often consider their husbandry and animal care skills to be of a very high standard so as to produce the finest specimen able to withstand the rigours of the ring. In reality, and with few exceptions, these animals are kept and fought in a way that is contrary to their behavioural and welfare needs.[5] Ultimately they will at the very least sustain painful and debilitating injuries during the course of their fighting career. Even where such injuries heal, the animal will likely still have a much shortened life expectancy, either succumbing to a stronger animal in the ring or being cast aside by their keeper when their gambling odds lengthen.

It was the advent of social reformers, during the early Victorian era, which saw the plight of fighting animals first highlighted, with legislation to outlaw barbaric sports following in the UK in 1835 (Cruelty to Animals Act 1835) and then later in many other developed nations. It is notable, however, that as recently as 2007, Louisiana (USA) banned cockfighting, and it remains legal within the unincorporated territories such as the US Virgin Islands and Puerto Rico. Dog fighting, although banned in the UK and USA, has remained popular, an unfortunate outcome of the ban on animal fighting, in that it was more portable and easier to operate and conceal (compared to fights involving bulls and bears). To this day, some forms of animal fighting, in particular dog and cock fighting remain legal, mostly in developing nations. They also retain sufficient underground popularity, in nations

[3] Caution must be taken when using RSPCA data on reported animal abuse as each report does not necessarily equate to an actual fight (e.g offence) or to separate incidents (http://news.bbc.co.uk/1/hi/uk/731514.stm)

[4] On rare occasions quail fighting has been reported to the RSPCA, such as a case in 2000 which led to the prosecution of a man who had been keeping 75 quail for the purposes of fighting, some of which had sustained injuries from fighting

[5] As defined by s9 of the UK's Animal Welfare Act 2006

where a ban does exist, as to often qualify as organised crime.[6] In the USA, for example, in addition to an active online community, numerous animal fighting magazines still circulate nationally promoting and advertising these cruel sports (US Congress 2007).

Animal fighting is often associated with other serious criminality such as illegal weapons and drug dealing, and of course it is intrinsically linked to illegal gambling (Lockwood 2012). In addition, although there are no figures, certainly within the UK, to support such claims, there is also growing concern that pets, usually dogs, are stolen to provide a regular supply of bait animals. The sole purpose of these bait animals is to test and train endurance and aggression ('gameness') into the fighting animal. Their teeth may be broken, their mouths taped shut or they may be chained up, so that their own ability to fight back and defend themselves is suppressed, resulting in an agonising and terrifying death.

Traditional animal fighting is universally recognised by investigators, campaigners and enforcers to be a secretive and clandestine industry which few, other than those involved in its activities, would know it exists. As a result it is notoriously difficult to identify, investigate or prosecute. In many nations it would be extremely rare for law enforcers to discover a fight in progress, often only the immediate perpetrators implicated by the evidence discovered at a crime scene (perhaps the home of an animal breeder/fighter) are identified, allowing the wider criminal network and its associated spectators to evade capture. Despite the secretive nature of animal fighting, in some countries such as the USA, the size of the criminal operation can be very significant. In the case of a dog fighting ring which included, at its very heart the NFL professional star football player Michael Vick, many millions of dollars is thought to have changed hands through gambling and on the dog fighting business itself (see below).

Dog Fighting

Dog fighting, as with many forms of animal 'sports', has a long history and has been recorded across a number of cultures, possibly existing since dogs were first domesticated. Certainly 'man's best friend' was bred specifically for its

[6] According to the UK National Crime Agency, organised crime can be defined as serious crime planned, coordinated and conducted by people working together on a continuing basis. Their motivation is often, but not always, financial gain—see: http://www.nationalcrimeagency.gov.uk/crime-threats/organised-crime-groups.

strength and demeanour. Their ability to protect and fight successfully for their keeper as well as in large-scale military campaigns (see also chapter on Animals in War) and competitive entertainment made them very attractive (Fleig 1996). This resulted in selective breeding for the anatomical traits perceived to provide the best performance in the ring, married with the aim to produce a dog that was human-friendly but aggressive to its own species and often other animals. The USA imported dog fighting from the UK in the early 1800s and through selective breeding created the American pit bull terrier, although the Staffordshire bull terrier and other related bull terriers also continued to be used. These dogs were attractive, and remain so, to dog fighters for their compact size, agility, 'gameness', strength and lack of threat-displays. But despite these breeds being carefully bred for docility towards humans—perhaps further than that, a strong social bond with humans (McMillan and Reid 2009)—their use in fighting led to many US states, followed by other countries, including the UK (s1 of the Dangerous Dogs Act 1991), introducing breed specific legislation to ban ownership across the whole of society. The intention to eradicate the various breeds banned under this type of legislation—most famously the pit bull terrier—has rather conspicuously failed, nevertheless, there has, undoubtedly, been consequences for these types of dog. This is discussed further in the chapter on Status Dogs (herein).

The offences related to dog fighting and indeed all animal fighting in the UK are now contained within s8 of the Animal Welfare Act (2006). Harding and Nurse (2015) suggest that the lack of a separate offence for dog fighting is problematic primarily because dog fighting is indiscernible from other animal fighting offences and the variation which exists in the level of offending and the type of offender is invisible in data recorded under s8. While there is no corresponding reference to such a problem made by investigators and enforcers (Lawson forthcoming), there is consensus that the problem of identifying and recording dog fighting is inherently linked to the legislation, and the offences contained within, which does not provide for a clear data set. This issue is as much to do with the fact, however, that the majority of enforcement is conducted by the RSPCA, and the UK Government is not required to record and report on these private prosecutions. In the USA, dog fighting was not made illegal in all states until 1976 and it was not a felony in all states (and at a federal level) until the last decade. In addition some states still regard spectating as a mere misdemeanour (Gibson 2014). In most states the situation can be considered to be similar to that of the UK whereby the offences relating to dog fighting are contained within a broader category of animal fighting (and indeed wider still as part of animal protection statutes), with no standard data collection requirements or procedures.

Characteristics of Dog Fighting

Many of the characteristics of dog fighting can be revealed by discussing the Michael Vick case in more detail. Vick and his fellow dog fighters were breeding, training, selling and fighting dogs over a number of years and were suspected to be connected to the uppermost elite network of dog fighters in the USA. Their Badd Newz Kennels was a major operation involving extensive land, outbuildings, training equipment, illegal veterinary supplies and a total of nearly 60 dogs, all housed on site (Strouse 2009, pp. 23–28).

Only a small number of dogs in the Vick case were euthanised for their injuries or their extreme aggression, most required specialist evaluation, rehabilitation and care. The scale of the case and the money involved were actually of benefit in this regard as it encouraged the court to reserve nearly $1million in escrow to be used for the ongoing care of the dogs. This would be unusual, if unheard of, elsewhere in the world. Indeed, in the UK if a pit bull, the same breed of dog as in the Vick case, is seized as part of a successfully prosecuted dog fighting case, the law will require it to be euthanised as it is of a prohibited type under the Dangerous Dogs Act (1991) and ownership is only allowed under very strict conditions.

There are many online and non-academic texts describing the finite detail—from the terminology to the rules—of dog fighting, its essence though is defined by Evans et al. (1998, p. 827) as 'the act of baiting two dogs against one another for entertainment or gain. It involves placing two dogs in a pit until one either quits or dies'. A pit of enclosed low walls, perhaps up to a metre high, will span a space of no more than four to six metres. Dogs will be weighed before a fight to ensure parity, and handlers may be allowed to wash their opponent's dog to ensure no subterfuge in the form of a toxic substance has been placed on the dog's coat to harm or inhibit the other dog (Gibson 2005). Those who directly handle the dogs and are permitted to enter the ring in the USA are referred to as 'dogmen' by Forsyth and Evans (1998, p. 202), a term that until recently has been used far less in the UK.

In its most extreme and organised form, dog fights will last until one dog fails to scratch (charge over their corner 'scratch line', into the centre of the pit to engage with the other dog); jumps out of the pit; dies; or is declared the winner, which can take anything from just a few minutes up to a few hours. The losing dog, unless kept for breeding based on its bloodlines and past performance, may often be beaten, drowned, shot or strangled to death, sometimes on the night as entertainment for the other participants.

Prevalence

In the USA, dog fighting has been estimated to be an industry worth in excess of half a billion dollars, and involves approximately 40,000 dogmen who can be categorised as professionals (Gibson 2005); up to $500,000 seized at one fight (Lockwood 2012, p. 8); and perhaps 2000 fights being held per year[7] (Strouse 2009, p. 17). Due to no standardised law enforcement data collection across the 50 states, the number of offences (both state and federal), and the range of agencies involved, the tracking of dog fighting cases has been problematic. Many have relied upon pet-abuse.com which catalogues press reports of fighting cases. This may change as the FBI re-categorised animal cruelty and began tracking data from 2016.

In the UK, dog fighting is predominantly investigated and prosecuted in England and Wales by the animal welfare charity the RSPCA. The police will sometimes investigate alone but they are far more likely to assist with RSPCA investigations, whose own officers possess no power of entry or arrest. With only two agencies involved, reporting could be expected to be clearer than the USA. The nature of the way in which the UK Government collates its own Crown Prosecution Service and court data suggests that RSPCA prosecutions are not always recorded by the Ministry of Justice. For example, Table 1 details the official prosecution and conviction rates for dog fighting, declared by the Government in 2015.[8,9]

This data does not reveal how many separate instances or cases of dog fighting to which these prosecutions relate. It is perhaps symptomatic of one of the problems of recording and tracking criminality in this sphere, that the official data, in Table 1 above, and also the RSPCA's data, in Table 2 below, does not tally with those reported by Harding and Nurse (2015, pp. 49–50).

[7] Strouse (2009) cites figures reported by the now-defunct *Sporting Dog Journal* to which dog fighters submitted fight reports and applied for certificates of championship. Note the SDJ had, despite strict conditions, 6,000 subscribers in its heyday. The publishers were arrested in 2004 and the SDJ ceased to exist apart from one further edition in 2007.

[8] Response in answer to Parliamentary Questions 223989 and 9486 answered on the 23rd March and 16 th September 2015 respectively.

[9] http://www.parliament.uk/business/publications/written-questions-answers-statements/written-question/Commons/2015-09-08/9486.

Table 1 Total dog fighting prosecutions and convictions recorded by the Ministry of Justice, 2009–2014

Outcome	2009	2010	2011	2012	2013	2014
Proceeded Against	8	2	13	7	17	10
Found guilty	4	1	7	4	7	5

Although they had sourced previous reports from the RSPCA, no commentary has been supplied as to whether the figures year on year are comparable. Furthermore, Harding and Nurse (2015, p. 43) contend that a range of organisations, such as the League Against Cruel Sports, are involved in compiling animal fighting figures, but this is somewhat misleading. While many organisations may comment from a distance on crimes against animals and indeed discuss unrecorded or under-reported crimes of this nature, the detection, investigation and prosecution is largely left to the RSPCA in England and Wales and far less frequently, the police, who often have little or no resource with which to act alone.

The RSPCA's data would suggest that in fact dog fighting has remained relatively consistent over a 10 year period. However, the figures for convictions do not reveal the number of defendants. In many cases, one defendant will receive several fighting convictions. It is also not possible to determine the breakdown for informal and formal classifications of dog fighting within these figures or thereby, if there has been an increase in one category corresponding to a decrease in another. Evidence is emerging that the phenomenon of status dogs may have had an impact on the reporting of street dog fighting. Local authorities in the UK, such as those in inner city London may sometimes collect reports from within their own managed housing estates or in other areas where they operate or participate in responsible dog ownership schemes. Some of these councils who have previously received a number of dog fighting complaints are now reporting fewer concerns from residents. Their own research has revealed that these reports were often from people who had been influenced by the media and succumbed to the associated moral panic. When they observed dogs hanging by their jaws from tree branches, they had assumed they were witnessing the preparation for a dog fight. In reality there was very little to support the notion of actual dog fighting. (Lawson forthcoming).

There is an innate difficulty in determining the extent of professional dog fighting in the UK, given its clandestine and impregnable networks. When offences have been detected it can still be a challenge to secure a successful conviction given the seemingly innocent way in which dogs can be kept and their injuries and minor paraphernalia explained away in court. One of the

Table 2 Total dog fighting complaints and convictions recorded by the RSPCA from 2006–2015

	2006	2007	2008	2009	2010	2011	2012	2013	2014	2015	Total
No of complaints of special type 'organised fighting' involving a dog[(a),(b)]	493	601	461	435	421	495	440	491	512	506	**4,855**
Total numbers of dogs involved in complaints reported[(b)]	1,335	1,418	979	1,092	1,068	1,205	1,201	1,136	1,390	1,389	**12,213**
Total number of convictions secured in court by the RSPCA under s8 of the Animal Welfare Act 2006[(c)]	n/a	0	10	28	8	18	23	9	13	28	**137**

[(a)] These are the number of complaints from the public to the RSPCA national call centre. The RSPCA makes every effort to ensure the accuracy of data but it is acknowledged that due to reporting and updating methods some of these reports of dog fighting may very occasionally relate to organised fighting of other species, such as cockfighting or badger baiting. Some incidents involving dog fighting may also be omitted from the figures if for example they were reported direct from the police to the RSPCA Special Operations Unit and not from the public via the national call line. In addition, where others have sought to publish RSPCA data they may have failed to appreciate the difference between numbers of offenders and numbers of convictions, or they may inadvertently be including other fighting offences.

[(b)] 'Complaints reported' can have any number of outcomes including prosecution and welfare advice, but may also include those where, upon looking into them, the RSPCA could not find evidence to take further action, or where there was no cause for concern.

[(c)] The Animal Welfare Act 2006 came into force in March (Wales) and April (England) 2007 and as such offences occurring before that date may have been prosecuted under previous legislation. This data is not currently available. These convictions also relate to the possession of dog fighting paraphernalia and associated equipment.

UK's top and longest serving dog fighting experts places a figure of somewhere between 50 and 100 top dog fighters (formal) in current operation and perhaps thousands for the street or ad hoc (informal) fighting category (Lawson forthcoming). Again this contrasts starkly with the USA. Additionally, UK events do not see spectator levels equivalent to what is reported in the USA, most attending the fight will be directly connected, will know each other and will perhaps be fighting their own dog within that network arranged for another occasion.

Towards a Typology of Dog Fighting

Objective descriptions of the world of dog fighting may not be in abundance, due to the abhorrent and underground nature of this criminal activity, but those that do exist provide a detailed insight into its nature. Most notably, Ortiz (2010, pp. 14–18) describes three categories of dog fighter: (a) street-fighter, (b) hobbyist and (c) professional;

a) The **streetfighters** are considered to conduct impromptu dog fights, with a younger-profile dog owner who may associate with gangs (Randour and Hardiman 2007). There will be no fight rules employed and little or no money will change hands. They may breed their dogs, but with less knowledge of bloodlines and gameness, they will simply seek dogs of size and menacing appearance. The dogs may also be used for other criminal activity such as the protection of their handlers or their illegal merchandise. Dog fights will be more about bragging rights or the protection of territory than any form of income, and dead or dying dogs will be found abandoned. Although conducting this on the streets and public parks may make them more susceptible to detection, the spontaneity and ability to disperse quickly allows many perpetrators to avoid arrest. These dog fighters are generally more likely to have interaction with the police and as a result their dogs are more likely to be seized and euthanised.
b) The **hobbyists** are defined as very similar to streetfighters but with some notable variables. They are deemed to be marginally more organised by locating fights in abandoned buildings or garages and while they operate across a wider area than streetfighters, this will remain relatively local. They also pay greater attention to their dogs' welfare, but they will own fewer dogs than the professional category below. Hobbyists also employ some structured gambling as a supplemental income stream.

c) The **professional** category may be the most notorious for its national and international networks and its highly organised covert operations. As in the Vick case, these dog fighters are very well equipped both in the training of their own dogs—of which they may have very many—and in the provision of a formal pit, as detailed earlier. There will normally be a significant number of spectators and perhaps a referee to officiate. This sophistication extends to the financials, with very substantial sums of money being exchanged, not just from fighting and gambling but also from stud fees. The prized lineage of the dogs may go back many generations and equally the knowledge is handed down from father to son, with children often reported present at such fights. There is a comprehensive set of rules; a code amongst dog fighters; essential handbooks; and even very successful trade journals. In recent times this has all been aided by the existence of the internet. With such a wide network of participants there is an increased risk of discovery and as such veterinary treatment will be forgone in favour of amateur, often barbaric, treatments including surgery.

Evans and Forsyth (1998, p. 63), who immersed themselves in the world of dog fighting in the USA's deep south, interviewing dog fighters and even attending fights, report only two forms of dog fight—the informal and the formal—observing no differentiation between hobbyists and streetfighters. Harding (2012, p. 168) initially found inconclusive evidence for the three classifications, as described by Ortiz (2010), in a UK context and then later argued there is merit in their use (Harding and Nurse 2015, p. 15). However, the only empirical research employing this typology is based in the USA, and as such there may be an over-reliance by Harding and Nurse (2015) in their analysis on its applicability to the UK. A typology is of course useful when designing responses to a problem; however, where the data exists in the UK to support the use of these classifications, is not made clear.

The RSPCA, as the main enforcer of dog fighting legislation in England and Wales, has itself employed an amended classification of dog fighting but again this differs to Ortiz in that the category of hobbyist is replaced by 'cultural' following observations of a new element of British-born men with Pakistani origins forming their own dog rings (Robinson et al. 2015). Despite being illegal, dog fighting enjoys widespread support in Pakistan (Hafeez 2014) where large crowds regularly come out to watch lengthy and brutal battles in public spaces. Given that dog fighting falls within the traditions of the prophet that are considered *haram*—that which is forbidden or proscribed by Islamic law (Foreword and Alam 2003, p. 235)—this cultural element and its transposition to the UK context warrants further study.

There is evidence emerging, constructed from first-hand accounts of those responding to the problem (Lawson forthcoming), that the UK may have its own typology, which employs just the two labels of informal and formal. In the UK, the informal category incorporates the lower strata of streetfighter and those involved with status dogs (Hughes *et al* 2011, p. 14; see also chapter on Status Dogs). They are more likely to breed and train dogs to be human-aggressive either through intention or through a general ignorance of animal behaviour. Furthermore, they are more likely to engage in ad hoc fights in public. Consequently, society is fearful of these dogs, because fault, via erroneous reporting, has been transferred from owners to certain breeds of dog. Status and danger are also transferred from dog to fighter—this category has been enhanced by the reputation of certain breeds of dog, amplified by the media's sensationalist accounts and the prohibition of some types of dog, '*Whenever pit bulls are outlawed, the ownership of the breed and association with dog fighting can become an "outlaw" status symbol.*' (Lockwood 2012, p. 8). 'Hobbyists' also perhaps fall into this category because although the gambling stakes are a little higher, they remain opportunists very much on the outside of the elite dog fighting network, not least because organised dog fighters would not tolerate poor breed standards, bloodlines and human-aggressive dogs (Lawson forthcoming).

The formal dog fighting sphere in the UK, although as organised and as brutal, bears no relation to the USA in terms of scale of operation. As an account from a lead investigator with 30 years' experience of dog fighting across the UK notes '*numbers in the UK, are anything, you know, 5, 6, up to 10 people there but it's the exception where we've found up to 27 people there—that's the largest number at one fight*' (Lawson, forthcoming).

The scale of the money involved in the UK also contrasts starkly with the USA. Smith (2011) rightly contends that dog fighting is also a financial crime due to the illegal profits made from their entrepreneurial operations. This research further confirms the difficulty in quantifying the financial aspects, and by extension the scale of the dog fighting in the UK, because as the same frontline investigator stated, '*Money is an element of it but it's not the be-all and end-all. The purse for a fight, if it's organised, will be about £5k to £10k on a reasonable fight on the night, [the gambling] is not that organised. There are no touts or anything like that*' (Lawson forthcoming).

There is a third element, as referred to in the RSPCA typology, of an Asian contingent of dog fighters who are thought to be importing and breeding the Bully Kutta, popular in Pakistan, as well as utilising the dog of choice for UK dog fighters, the pit bull (Robinson et al 2015, p. 2). The evidence suggests that this 'cultural' classification is not a standalone category, however, but is in fact, a subset of both informal and formal categories with the almost unique feature of graduation occurring from informal to formal. As is seen here further into the testimony from the front line investigator:

> [My] experience of dog fighting up until the late 90s, early 2000s, we were dealing with the old traditional, old white, English dog fighter. They are very, very proud of their bloodlines, so they breed the gameness into the dog. That changed really with the Asian population becoming involved in dog fighting from the early 2000s onwards and they didn't give a damn about the breeding lines, they were just going to fight the thing, if it died, it died. They'd go and buy another one from Ireland. So there were two distinct fractions there. White, traditional dog fighters are probably more 30s onwards, anything up to 50s. Their clandestine activities are much more closely guarded than perhaps the Asian communities where it would be very much word of mouth, bringing mates in off the street. Whereas the traditional fighters . . . you would need to know someone in there and go through some form of, I won't say initiation, but checking out of their status before they are let anywhere near. You've pretty much got to have a dog and want to fight it too or demonstrate that's your interest. The Asians have a much younger bracket with a few 30/40 year olds but mostly 20-somethings. In terms of moving from one group to another, this is more so in the Asian community, it has become more of a natural progression—the status dogs being used by potentially young, drug users, dealers, becoming involved in—I'm still never sure if it's their history from their roots in Pakistan or whether it is just a progression of the street culture really—but that is how it started, it's status dogs, then moving on to chain fighting or fighting in parks and then to becoming more organised and mingling with the old traditional dog fighters, if you like, who I think in the first place were just selling them their cast off dogs. One operation in 2003 looking at dog fighters in the West Midlands, that then knocked on to another dog fighting case 6 months later, was 27 Asians arrested at a venue. I'm not sure if that's when it started but that's certainly when we became aware of it. Since then there is more inter-racial, as it were, fighting. Occasionally the higher levels of the Asian fighters might meet with the English fighters although they are still fairly separate. (Lawson forthcoming).

Harding and Nurse (2015, p. 30) contend that graduation from streetfighter to hobbyist or from hobbyist to professional occurs in some circumstances within the UK. The evidence for this is based on Harding's earlier research (2012) conducted with dogfighters who self-reported their progression from streetfighter to a more organised category. As such these accounts may be unreliable as they can be vulnerable to the same issues around machismo and status (such as embellishment or magnification) that intrinsically interests dogfighters. Such accounts also remain contentious as there is no substantiating testimony from within the field of responders. These frontline investigators report that organised dog fighters in the UK, while content to deal with the new immigrant and cultural element of fighting—by way of supplying dogs and meeting for occasional organised fights—do not associate with streetfighters, who they consider to be sullying the sport.

Nature of Abuse

Consideration must also be given to the range and complexity of the harms experienced by the fighting dogs. Evans and Forsyth (1998) report that despite an understanding that gambling and animal protection laws have been flouted, dogmen still regard fighting as a victimless crime. The relatively low profile of dog fighting in the media, in official enforcement and the academic sphere at the time that research was conducted, may well have contributed to that view. The years following, however, saw several high-profile convictions in the USA, including that of Vick, and the associated public outcry at the plight of the animals being used and abused. It is perhaps to be expected that as attention to this sphere increased, researchers such as Kalof and Taylor (2007) emerged to contend that the issue of dog fighting warrants examination from the perspective of the most abused, that of the dog and other animal victims of the dog fighting world (for example, bait animals).

The fight itself is not the only sadistic treatment a fighting dog will endure. The training of fighting dogs has the potential to put their bodies in top physical shape, however, the regime and negative reinforcement they are subject to are also likely to cause significant pain and behavioural issues. The following harms to fighting dogs have been identified (Lockwood 2012 and Strouse 2009):

- use of a breeding stand, often referred to by dogmen as a 'rape stand' to produce off-spring
- use as a bait animal if they refuse to fight or if they are born 'cold' (considered not to have the instinct) to train the fighting dogs. As previously discussed, dogs (and other domestic animals) may also be stolen to order to supply this need
- inability to act naturally or socialise due to the desire to create aggression towards other dogs and animals

- docked ears and tail—usually by the dogmen—to prevent the other dog gaining purchase and causing damage and also to make the dog harder to read as it will inhibit normal body signals related to aggression
- filed teeth—to make them sharper and more dangerous
- drug misuse—steroids, amphetamines or other illegal drugs are used to enhance size and aggression and to relieve pain to enable dogs to fight longer
- starvation, beating and torture (for example, cigarettes burned into their skin) to increase aggression
- forced training routines on treadmills and with increasing weights to develop strength
- amateur veterinary treatment, such as IV or subcutaneous fluids, drugs to combat swelling and diuretics so that the dogs will empty themselves to make the necessary weight
- multiple physical injuries including bites that puncture, loss of blood, shock, dehydration and bone fractures during the fight, frequently resulting in death from trauma or infection some time after the event.
- being drowned, shot and/or hung when they lose a fight or come to the end of their fighting career. When a dog that Vick had hung by a nylon cord refused to die, it was lifted into the air and slammed into the ground in order to kill it.

In the process of enhancing the dog's aggression, dogmen abuse their dogs in unthinkable ways. This inhumane treatment can make fighting dogs, and indeed any breed of dog, aggressive and dangerous. Consequently, the reputation and life of all so-called 'bull breeds', identified with dog fighting, are negatively impacted, 'thereby driving the pit bull's negative media image and fuelling support for breed-specific bans' and compulsory euthanasia of these breeds (Medlin 2007, pp. 1298–1299). Boucher (2011) details the problems that pit bulls encounter, particularly in the USA where there is wider ownership in society and a mixed response across the 50 states regarding breed specific legislation. Delise (2007) tackles similar issues and also places the myths surrounding this much maligned type/breed in the context of society's response to other breeds of dog. Both these monographs lay out a very convincing argument as to why pit bulls should no more be singled out than any other type of dog and why they are so attractive to those with criminal intentions. People with criminal intentions desire bigger and more aggressive bull breeds, thereby, fuelling the myths and perceptions of this type of dog, resulting in an increasing number of temperamentally and physically 'unsound'[10] dogs (Hughes et al. 2011).

Explaining Involvement and Harm in Dog Fighting: The Sub-culture of Dogmen and Neutralisation

Contemporary dog fighting, as previously noted, can be professional, informal or cultural in nature, operating at the street level or internationally across highly secretive networks (Boucher 2011). What unites all types of dog fighters is the cultural norms of masculinity and status commonplace in what is a heavily male-dominated sport; women are usually only ever recorded as spectators. Consequently, this section explains the involvement of offenders through a subcultural lens (Cohen 1955) and the related harms through neutralisation theory (Sykes and Matza 1957). With scarce testimony from within the dog fighting fraternity (in particular, culturally motivated dog fighters), little is known about the values systems employed which help explain their involvement in the associated criminal and violent behaviour, accordingly Clure and Lum (2011) rightly argue more research is needed to expand on these theories.

Subcultural theories (Cohen 1955; Wolfgang and Ferracuti's 1967), originally referring to urban working class youth, argue that offenders create an oppositional (sub)culture in reaction to social inequality and exclusion, facilitating shared antisocial values and behaviours. Evans and Forsyth (1998) note a loyalty hierarchy among dogmen, whereby attachments to their dog fighting fraternity eclipse all allegiances to wider society, with the subcultural values of this smaller group underpinned by a system of rationalisation and neutralisation (discussed further below). In the UK, at least, dog fighting is deemed to be within only the lower social classes, as explained by the front line investigator (Lawson forthcoming):

> [Dog fighting] doesn't relate to professional, well educated people involved in it, and the reason for specifying that is that we actually do see that in other cruel sports, cock-fighting for instance, that does go right across the strata of society—traveller community, farming community, titled gentry even, are

[10] The pit bull's once-revered characteristics of loyalty and tenacity have been manipulated, through breeding, by those looking for large and aggressive dogs to ruthlessly defend their homes or make them rich by fighting to the death in dog fighting matches.

> involved in cockfighting and we can prove that. In dog fighting it does tend to be more working class and unemployed.

In the USA, Ortiz (2009) linked an increase in street-based dog fighting to the proliferation of US youth gangs. Among interviewed dog fighters and youths (aged 9–16 years), dog fighting was so imbedded in the subculture, it was used to help resolve street/gang conflicts (Evans et al. cited in Ortiz 2009). While dog fighters subscribe to pro-criminal values, they are not necessarily in complete conflict with mainstream society. Among professional dog fighters, Evans and Forsyth (1998, p. 214) observed that although their lives appear to be otherwise conventional 'Dogmen are committed to the unconventional values associated with dog fighting'.

Distinct subcultures of violence exist in which members embrace values that are more permissive of the use of violence (Wolfgang and Ferracuti's 1967). Implicit within these subcultures is the use of violence as a means of social control and status. Dog fighting culture is historically status driven and based on values of masculinity and honour (Gibson 2005; Drabble 1948)—values central to the subculture of violence theory (Anderson 1999). The pit bull—and similar types—are the epitome of such masculinity and consequently are the prime choice for dog fighters. The decades of breeding for gameness in the pit bull and the valued bloodlines, ensures they remain the first choice of the professional dog fighter; a prize dog can also bestow great social status on its owner due to the transition of sexual virility, masculinity and aggression from the dogs to their handlers (Kalof and Taylor 2007). Furthermore, legislation prohibiting these breeds/types extends to them the label of 'dangerous', making them more attractive to informal dog fighters who wish to intimidate, threaten and occasionally fight. *'They want a dog that matches their reputation. It's a show of strength and aggression, it is a sidearm really'* (The front line dog fighting investigator—Lawson forthcoming; see also "Status Dog" chapter herein). Both formal and informal dog fighters are thought to identify with the fearlessness, loyalty and courage they perceive their dogs to possess—supporting the notion that the dogs in the ring are merely an extension of their owner's bravado. As Ortiz (2009) indicates, gang rivalries can be resolved through dog fighting as the dogs represent the male owners themselves fighting in the ring; arguably this explains why status rather than financial gain is the key motivation for informal dog fighting. As status is not fixed, but must be constantly tested and proved, the subculture requires fighting dogs be discarded and easily replaced when they no longer bestow status.

In order to justify their violent behaviour, Forsyth and Evans (1998, p. 203) discern four recurring techniques that dogmen use: '(a) denial of injury; (b) condemnation of the condemners; (c) appeal to higher loyalties; and (d) a defence that says dogmen are good people (their deviance-dog fighting expunged by their good character)'. These conditions are consistent with neutralisation theory (Sykes and Matza 1957), which suggests offenders drift between conventional and deviant behaviour using five techniques to neutralise their feelings of guilt and shame (that is: denial of responsibility, denial of injury, denial of victims, appeal to higher loyalties, and condemnation of condemners). According to neutralisation theory, offenders dispute the conventional meaning attached to their anti-social behaviour or try to evade moral blame. However, unlike subcultural theory where offenders oppose mainstream values, Cohen (2013) proposes pro-social values remain salient for the offender even when violated. Each of these techniques were evident in Hughes et al. (2011) study with informal UK dog fighters: for example, that the dog needed to fight; was doing what was natural; and was fighting for their group/gang, were common street narratives. Furthermore, attention was deflected from their own behaviour to those who reportedly 'incorrectly' fought and mistreated their dog, or did it 'only' for the money. Consequently, those dog fighters who identify themselves as good owners, simultaneously rationalise and minimise the harm they cause to their dogs. Arguably, some dog fighters, such as the new informal street fighters criticised by professional fighters, may not require any neutralisation as their abusive behaviour is morally legitimate within their group and thereby free from troubling guilt.

Responses to the Problem

In their investigation into what methods of prevention work, or could work, to suppress dog fighting, Clure and Lum (2011) discuss the various responses to the problem and divide these into the three sections namely (a) education, reformation and redirection programmes, (b) the creation of legislation, and (c) the enforcement of legislation. These categories are considered and developed further below:

Education Programmes

A number of projects that fall within this category in the USA are listed by Clure and Lum (2011), who also identify the absence of thorough evaluation. Harding and Nurse (2015, Appendix 4) take a brief tour of some intervention programmes in both the UK and USA. There is an important omission in their analysis of the ultimate learning outcomes of the Humane Society of the United States (HSUS)'s failed 'End Dog Fighting Campaign'. The initial project, started in 2006, had targeted dog fighters with very little success. By specifically focusing on potential dog fighters they had labelled and alienated their target market. The project, thereafter, was transformed into the successful programme, 'Pets for Life', which is both community and service based, and open to all dog owners. This approach has fostered understanding between owners of different breeds and encouraged some pit bull owners to access the scheme and avoid a path to dog fighting. This outreach scheme is unlikely to identify and attract the professional dog fighter, who is invested financially and culturally in dog fighting, and thereby not so easily thwarted.

In addition to discussing the limitations of the HSUS's original project in more detail, a recent report has highlighted the lack of critical assessment of any such intervention programmes either in theory or practice and has urged caution in their applicability to a UK setting (RSPCA 2015).

Legislation

Much of the issues surrounding legislation surrounding dog fighting and associated offences has been outlined earlier in this chapter. Lockwood (2012) further discusses the legislation that is now in place in the USA which culminated in February 2014 with President Obama signing the Farm Bill, containing the Animal Fighting Spectator Prohibition Act, making it a federal crime to attend or bring a child under the age of 16 to an animal fighting event. As such, since that time, there have been no calls for further legislation in the USA. The UK is in the same situation in this regard as no law enforcement body has identified any deficiencies in the legislative framework. Harding and Nurse (2015), however, have highlighted the need for accurate and species-specific data within the offence of animal fighting.

Enforcement

> [T]he lack of emphasis in training police to detect dog fighting and the failure of communities to conduct sensitivity and outreach training, thus allowing children to be exposed to cruelty which in turn results in a belief that this inhumane treatment of animals is acceptable, are the predominant reasons why dog fighting is growing in popularity (Searle 2008, p. 3).

In the USA there have been a number of recent developments in this area. The ASPCA has created a community guide and a law enforcer's toolkit.[11] From 2016 the FBI also began classifying animal cruelty as a significant crime and it is now using the National Incident-Based Reporting System (NIBRS) for tracking purposes.[12] This will allow, for the first time in the USA, for the creation of some basic statistics regarding the incidents of crimes involving cruelty to animals and provide information on the offenders involved. The recording of not just arrests, but also incidents where no case proceeds will also allow for developments around crime mapping in this sector.

While there is no clear evidence that dog fighting—or a specific sub-category of it—is increasing (see Table 2 above), in the UK at least, poor detection and poor animal welfare standards may well be allowing dog fighting to continue. Harding and Nurse (2015) discuss the issues around reporting which is inherently linked to detection. The nature of spontaneous fights is such that unless they are overheard and reported, and immediately responded to while the fight is still taking place, there is little chance of apprehending the perpetrators. It had been thought that formal dog fighting was in decline but in reality the advent of the internet may just have enabled it to become even more hidden. Not only can the network of dog fighters communicate very effectively using social media and secure email (Strouse 2009, p. 19), they can also locate viable fighting venues far more easily.

Police forces in most parts the UK are required to prioritise public safety over animal welfare and public safety would include enforcing the Dangerous Dog Act (1991 as amended). Interviews with serving and ex-police officers specialising in dogs, offered very little insight into dog fighting. Specialist Dog Legislation Officers (DLOs) may only often work on dog fighting as part of an RSPCA investigation, to provide the necessary legal warrants and determine if any other non-animal related offences have occurred.

There was once widespread concern regarding the skilled enforcement of the relevant legislation in the USA. Ortiz (2010) provides an analysis of the varied detection and prosecution issues and inconsistencies across the states. Often police were not able to identify items of paraphernalia at a crime scene and indeed Strouse noted how some of the first responders to Vick's property postulated they were merely witnessing a low standard breeding

[11] http://aspcapro.org/resource/disaster-cruelty-animal-cruelty-animal-fighting/dogfighting-tool-kit-law-enforcement.

[12] https://www.fbi.gov/news/stories/2016/february/tracking-animal-cruelty/tracking-animal-cruelty.

establishment (2009, p. 28). Lockwood (2012, p. 4) notes an awakening, fuelled by the very high-profile conviction and incarceration of Vick, with new successful, multi-state, interagency operations resulting in large numbers of arrests and dogs seized.

Such interagency collaboration is beginning to be employed in the UK, with one animal fighting case resulting in £25k being seized under the Proceeds of Crime Act (2002). Smith suggests the inclusion of 'financial crime investigators and asset confiscation officers would be a valuable and welcome innovation' (2011, p. 343), which is entirely feasible given this is already happening in the detection of puppy breeding and trafficking offences. The RSPCA's Special Operation Unit are not able to mirror US enforcement tactics, due to the moral aspects of not being able to participate or even watch a dog fight take place or indeed watch several and perhaps fight a dog themselves in order to infiltrate the ring. Such tactics may also not please the courts of England and Wales and put into question the admissibility of evidence. Lengthy and sustained surveillance is, therefore, crucial in the detection of this crime. The dog fighters have learned not to keep their dogs at home in case the RSPCA come to the door and so only careful and thorough observation with intelligence-led work can determine where the dogs are being kept to enable the best chance of conviction.

This aspect could, however, be addressed through the introduction of specific recording practices to include the police, RSPCA and the courts, which would crucially involve the details of the species and the level of organisation involved.

Perhaps related to both categories above of education and enforcement is that of the awareness campaign aimed at those with no formal relationship to dog fighting. These are utilised in the USA to aid in the detection and reporting of dog fighting, such as the ASPCA's community guides (above) and the HSUS's public service announcements detailing a $5,000 reward for information that leads to a conviction. In the UK, the League Against Cruel Sports has adopted a similar role, running conferences and public campaigns to raise awareness of the problem and operating an 'Animal Crimewatch' hotline for the reporting of dog fighting—although details surrounding actions taken in connection with any such reports, are relatively vague, with the suggestion they may be simply passed to another organisation.[13] Clearly all such press and awareness campaigns have an important role in reminding the public that this barbaric 'sport' has not yet been confined to

[13] http://www.league.org.uk/get-involved/help-put-an-end-to-animal-cruelty.

the history books, as the frontline investigator concluded the interview 'People see a big dog fighting case in the media every couple of years and then it disappears again but what they don't appreciate is it's going on every weekend somewhere in the country. There is a league of dog fighters out there doing what they do' (Lawson forthcoming).

Conclusion

This chapter has sought to provide an overview of animal fighting through a specific focus on dog fighting and in the process evaluate the extreme abuse experienced by fighting and bait animals. While both frontline accounts and the collection of complaints and prosecutions provide a compelling case for the existence of a problem, legal and enforcement complexities in the UK and USA, such as the difficulties in detecting such crimes via covert means, significantly inhibits an accurate picture of the scale of dog fighting in either country. While the prevalence of dog fighting, and the use of other species in animal fighting, would appear to be higher in the USA than the UK, it is clearly a thriving and active sport in both nations, which warrants further empirical study, not least of all to produce more accurate estimates on how many animals may be falling victim to this abuse. The nature of these abhorrent crimes also presents obstacles for researching the motivations of dogmen who operate in utmost secrecy and would only accept and trust other active dogmen into the fold. Dog fighting culture is recognised as status driven and based on values of masculinity and honour—suggesting a distinct subculture of violence exists which encourages members to embrace values permitting the use of violence and which provides justification for their harmful violent behaviour. Without further and detailed evidence of prevalence and scale, all such challenges may hinder the development and appraisal of the suggested typology of dog fighting in the UK and as a result the efficacy of any intervention or prevention programmes designed to eliminate such acts of animal cruelty.

References

Anderson, E. (1999). *The code of the streets: decency, violence and the moral life of the inner city*. New York: WW Norton.

Atkinson, M., & Young, K. (2008). *Deviance and social control in sport*. Leeds: Human Kinetics.

Boucher, B. G. (2011). *Pit bulls: villains or victims? underscoring actual causes of societal violence*. USA: Puffa and Co.

Clure, D., & Lum, C. (2011). *Developing an evidence-base for the understanding and prevention of dog fighting crimes*. Washington, DC: Association of Prosecuting Attorneys

Cohen A. (1955). *Delinquent boys: the culture of the gang*. Glencoe: The Free Press.

Cohen, S. (2013). *States of Denial: knowing about atrocities and suffering*. London: Polity Press

Delise, K. (2007). *The pit bull placebo: the media, myths and politics of canine aggression*. Ramsey, NJ: Anubis Publishing.

Drabble, P. (1948). Staffords and baiting sports. In B. Vesey-Fitzgerald (Ed.), *The book of the dog*. London: Nicholson and Watson.

Dundes, A. (1994). *The cockfight: a casebook*. Madison: University of Wisconsin Press.

Elmes, J. (1831). *A topographical dictionary of London and its environs*. London: Whittaker, Treacher and Arnot.

Evans, R. D., & Forsyth, C. J. (1998). The social milieu of dogmen and dog fights. *Deviant Behavior, 19*(1), 51–71.

Evans, R., Gauthier, D. K., Forsyth, & Craig J. (1998). Dog fighting: expression and validation of masculinity. *Sex Roles, 39*(11/12), 825–838.

Fleig, D. (1996). *The history of the fighting dogs* (trans. William Charlton). Neptune City, NJ: TFH Publications.

Forsyth, C. J., & Evans, R. D. (1998). Dogmen: the rationalization of deviance. *Society and Animals, 6*(3), 203–218.

Forward, M., & Alam, M. (2003). Islam. In S. J. Armstrong, G. Richard, R.G. Botzler (Eds.), *The animal ethics reader* (pp. 235–237). London: Routledge.

Gibson, H. (2005). *Dog fighting detailed discussion*. Animal Legal and Historical Centre, Michigan State University, College of Law. https://www.animallaw.info/article/detailed-discussion-dog-fighting. Accessed 10 April 2010.

Gibson, H. (2014). *Chart of state dog fighting laws*. Animal Legal and Historical Centre, Michigan State University, College of Law. https://www.animallaw.info/article/chart-state-dogfighting-laws. Accessed 23 March 2016.

Hafeez, Z. (2014). The bloody world of dog fighting: Victory or death, there is no mercy. *The Express Tribune Blogs*. http://blogs.tribune.com.pk/story/22043/the-bloody-world-of-dog-fighting-victory-or-death-there-is-no-mercy/. Accessed 2 February 2016.

Harding, S. (2012). *Unleashed: the phenomena of status dogs and weapon dogs*. Bristol, UK: Policy Press.

Harding, S., & Nurse, A. (2015). *Analysis of UK dog fighting, laws and offences*. Middlesex University Working Paper for the League Against Cruel Sports. http://www.league.org.uk/~/media/Files/LACS/Publications/Dog-Fighting-Report-2015.pdf. Accessed 3 February 2015

Hone, W. (1826). *The every day book, or, a guide to the year: describing the popular amusements sports, ceremonies, manners customs and events incident to the three hundred and sixty-five days, in past and present times*. Vol. 1. London: Hunt and Clarke.

Hughes, G., Maher, J., & Lawson, C. (2011). *Status dogs, young people and criminalisation: towards a preventative strategy*. Cardiff: Cardiff University and also Horsham: Royal Society for the Prevention of Cruelty to Animals.

ITV. (2012). Cockfighting duo avoid jail. *ITV News*. http://www.itv.com/news/meridian/story/2012-10-17/cockfighting-sentences-today/. Accessed 20 February 2010.

James, B. (2012). Cockfighting father and son avoid jail after Brighton court conviction. *The Argus*. http://www.theargus.co.uk/news/9993457.Cockfighting_father_and_son_avoid_jail/. Accessed 20 February 2010.

Kalof, L., & Taylor, C. (2007). The discourse of dog fighting. *Human and Society*. *31*(4), 319–333.

Lawson, C. (forthcoming). *'Hoodies', 'Hounds' and harm reduction: a criminological case study*. PhD Thesis, Cardiff University.

Lockwood, R. (2012). *Dog fighting: A guide to community action*. ASPCA. http://www.aspcapro.org/sites/pro/files/aspca_cruelty_dogfighting_action.pdf. Accessed 8 February 2016.

McMillan, F. D., & Reid, P. J. (2009, June 22–23). Selective breeding in fighting dogs: what have we created? *Presented at the UFAW International Symposium: Darwinian Selection, Selective Breeding and the Welfare of Animals*. Bristol, UK: University of Bristol.

Medlin, J. (2007). Pit bull bans and the human factors affecting canine behavior. *DePaul L. Rev.*, *56*, 1285–1320.

Merck, M. D. (2013). Animal Fighting. In *Veterinary Forensics: Animal Cruelty Investigations*. 2nd edition. West Sussex, UK: John Wiley and Sons, Inc.

Ortiz, F. (2009). *Making the Dogmen Heel: recommendations for improving the effectiveness of dogfighting laws*. South Texas College of Law. http://works.bepress.com/cgi/viewcontent.cgi?article=1000andcontext=francesca_ortiz. Accessed 20 April 2016.

Ortiz, F. (2010). Making the dogman heel: recommendations for improving the effectiveness of dog fighting laws. *Stanford Journal of Animal Law and Policy*, *3*, 1–75.

Randour, M. L., & Hardiman, T. (2007). Creating synergy for gang prevention: taking a look at animal fighting and gangs. The Humane Society of the United States. *Proceedings of Persistently Safe Schools: The 2007 National Conference on Safe Schools*. http://gwired.gwu.edu/hamfish/merlin-cgi/p/downloadFile/d/19160/n/off/other/1/name/030pdf/. Accessed 20 February 2010.

Robehmed, S. (2014). Do the participants of Turkey's annual Camel Wrestling festival enjoy it as much as the audience?. *The Independent*. http://www.independent.co.uk/news/world/europe/do-the-participants-of-turkeys-annual-camel-wrestling-festival-enjoy-it-as-much-as-the-audience-9065497.html. Accessed 23 March 2016.

Robinson, C., Briggs, I., & Flower, M. (2015). *RSPCA: dog fighting understanding the issue and tackling the Cruelty*. http://politicalanimal.org.uk/wp-content/uploads/2015/12/Dogfighting.pdf. Accessed 23 January 2016.

Royal Society for the Prevention of Cruelty to Animals (2015). *Review of responsible dog ownership in wales: a report submitted to the Welsh Government*. http://politicalanimal.org.uk/wp-content/uploads/2016/03/Responsible-Dog-Ownership-Review-March-2016.pdf. Accessed 4 March 2016.

Searle, A. M. (2008). *Release the dogs: creating a social remedy to the dog fighting epidemic*. http://works.bepress.com/amanda_searle/4/. Accessed 23 March 2011.

Smith, R. (2011). Investigating financial aspects of dog-fighting in the UK. *Journal of Financial Crime, 18*(4), 336—346.

Strouse, K., & Dog Angel (2009). *Badd Newz: the untold story of the Michael Vick dog fighting case*. Charleston, South Carolina: BookSurge.

Sykes, G., & Matza, D. (1957). Techniques of neutralization: a theory of delinquency. *American Sociological Review, 22*(6), 664–670.

US Congress (2007). *Animal fighting prohibition enforcement act of 2007: report together with dissenting views*. House of Representatives: 110th Congress, 1st Session. Washington, DC: U.S. G.P.O.

Waters, N. (2013). *Surviving the Warwick lion fight*. http://www.dogworld.co.uk/product.php/103107/1/surviving_the_warwick_lion_fight_by_nick_waters. Accessed 22 February 2016.

Wolfgang, M., & Ferracuti, F. (1967). *The subculture of violence*. London: Tavistock.

Claire Lawson is currently undertaking doctoral research at Cardiff University on the multi-agency responses to the 'dangerous' and 'status' dog phenomenon in England and Wales, following the publication of a joint research report on this issue in 2011. Her Master's Degree in Criminology and Criminal Justice focused on the RSPCA and the criminology of control, a subject on which she has also published. Claire is an Assistant Director in External Relations for the RSPCA, where she has worked since 1999, and she has been Chair of the Animal Welfare Network for Wales since its inception in 2006.

Part V

The Abuse of Animals in Vivisection and Scientific Research

Shelter Animals in Laboratory Experimentation

Allie Phillips and Anthony Bellotti

Introduction

The central question considered in this chapter: *Is pound seizure (the sale or giving of shelter cats and dogs for experimentation) government-sanctioned and government-funded animal abuse?* This chapter will explore the body of evidence on the harms inflicted on shelter pets that lead us to the conclusion that it does (PCRM 2012).

Vivisection, or the use of animals in experimentation for education, medical, cosmetic, biological and other testing, has divided our culture in recent years. In 1975, Peter Singer discussed the morality of vivisection in his book *Animal Liberation* where he exposed the treatment of animals in experimentation. Singer analyzed how animals feel pain and have feelings similar to humans, an approach which was not supported within the vivisection community then and to an extent today. Singer's position has been debated and in 2006 was called into question when it appeared he was supporting experimentation on monkeys.

A. Phillips (✉)
Michigan and Maryland, USA
e-mail: alliephillips10@gmail.com

A. Bellotti
White Coat Waste Movement, Washington, DC, USA
e-mail: ab@whitecoatwaste.com

J. Maher et al. (eds.), *The Palgrave International Handbook of Animal Abuse Studies*, DOI 10.1057/978-1-137-43183-7_17

Tom Regan has also published on the benefits and harm of vivisection and how there are insufficient legal protections for the animals:

> The very best that can be said for vivisection (and it is very little) is that some people sometimes benefit from using some medicines or some procedures that were first either given to or used on animals. And for this hundreds of billions of dollars are spent; hundreds of millions of animals are denied their freedom, are subjected to debilitating physical injury, are made to suffer, only to be killed in the end; and uncounted millions of human beings are harmed in ways both minor and major, even to the point of death. Vivisection as it is practiced today is not the panecea for the world's ills its champions would have us believe; it poses a very serious threat both to humans and animals. (Regan 2016)

Regan has called for the criminalization of vivisection.

Those in favor of animal experimentation (even on shelter cats and dogs) focus on advances in medical research, product safety, and training future doctors, veterinarians, and clinicians. Those who oppose focus on advances in science to more accurate non-animal models, that animals are not good models for human illnesses, and the welfare and humane treatment of the animal subjects.

By some estimates, upwards of 500 million animals are killed in US laboratories every year (APHIS 2000). While the use of cats and dogs (particularly shelter cats and dogs) in experimentation has declined drastically in recent years (NAS 2009), we think it has been primarily due to advocacy and pressure from citizens and communities rather than from laboratories concluding that their animal-based experiments have not been successful.

It is unknown how many shelter animals are sold into the world of experimentation because most states do not track shelter intake and disposition records. These once-family pets are subjected to experimentation that often ends in death. The experimentation can be for cosmetic testing, human or animal drug testing, medical technique or tool testing, biochemical testing, and much more.

The USA and other countries still allow, promote, fund, and incentivize the harm to animals, including shelter pets and former family pets, all in the name of scientific research and education. As taxpayers and voters become more aware of the consequences and pitfalls of animal experiments, particularly on those cats and dogs found in animal shelters, advocacy for change has increased. This chapter will outline how shelter cats and dogs are used in research, the prevalence of animals (including shelter pets) used in research, laws attempting to protect animals in research, the controversy of Class B dealers brokering shelter animals for research, government funding of animal research, and advocacy to end this practice for the wellbeing of human and animal health.

Shelter Pet Experimentation (Aka Pound Seizure)

History and Past Practice in the USA

> In the 1940s, pound seizure became a common practice in taxpayer-funded animal shelters across the country and resulted in numerous state laws requiring the practice. Pound seizure, or pound release, involves a shelter selling or giving away cats and dogs to Class B Dealers, random source animal brokers licensed by the U.S. Department of Agriculture, who then resell the animals for research and experimentation. It also involves shelters providing animals directly to research laboratories or university training programs. (Phillips 2010, p. 14)

The theft of a Dalmatian dog named Pepper from her front yard in Pennsylvania created the US Laboratory Animal Welfare Act of 1966 (7 U.S.C. 2131, et seq.), now called the Animal Welfare Act, a law that provides some protection to cats and dogs in research laboratories. After Pepper's theft, she was transferred several times until she died during a pacemaker research study at a New York hospital. Her family searched for her, but found her too late. Pepper's heartbreaking story and the Life Magazine exposé *Concentration Camp for Dogs* (4 February 1966) quickly led to a grassroots uprising in which voters bombarded Congress with outrage. The volume and intensity of this letter-writing campaign briefly surpassed even those surrounding the civil rights movement and the Vietnam War.

Decades later, the controversy of using former family pets in experimentation resulted in The Atlantic magazine, in July 2000, publishing an exposé called *From the Leash to the Laboratory* on the animal experimentation industry using family pets that had been stolen and brokered on the black market (Reitman 2000). The Animal Welfare Act was created to stop the theft of pets being brokered into research, but there are still enough anecdotal stories that cause concern in knowledgeable pet owners in the USA. Yet, the practice continues to this day with one primary argument from advocates for the practice: the shelter cats and dogs sold into research would have otherwise been euthanized. The justification from proponents is to allow the cat and dog to be useful and contribute in the efforts to solve human and animal diseases through research experimentation. Opponents to the practice argue that using animal shelters in this manner is a betrayal of trust to communities, to the animals involved, that animals are not an effective model when it comes to human health research, and the practice involves the unconsented use of American taxpayer dollars to fund the research projects.

US Federal Laws

The Animal Welfare Act (AWA) and AWA regulations (7 CFR 2.22, 2.80, and 371.7) were intended to protect and provide humane treatment of animals used in experimentation. However, rats, birds, and mice used in experimentation are specifically excluded from AWA protection, yet comprise up to 95 % of all research animals (7 U.S.C. 2132(g)). Farm animals used in research are also excluded and have been used in military training exercises by Canada, Denmark, Norway, Poland, the UK and the USA (Gala et al. 2012). The purpose of the AWA is:

(1) to insure that animals intended for use in research facilities or for exhibition purposes or for use as pets are provided humane care and treatment;
(2) to assure the humane treatment of animals during transportation in commerce; and
(3) to protect the owners of animals from the theft of their animals by preventing the sale or use of animals which have been stolen. (7 U.S.C. 2131)

Section 2135 of the AWA specifically requires dealers to hold cats and dogs at their facilities for at least five business days before re-selling to research. This section was enacted to help people locate their lost pets. Section 2143 outlines the 'humane treatment' of cats and dogs in research facilities but has a provision about surgical procedures that states 'that no animal is used in more than one major operative experiment from which it is allowed to recover except in cases of—(i) scientific necessity.' Section 2158 is entitled 'protection of pets' and provides a five-day hold for cats and dogs at animal shelters or animal experimentation laboratories before they can be transferred to a dealer and then resold for experimentation.

The 1985 AWA Amendment mandates exercise requirements for dogs in experimentation laboratories 'as determined by an attending veterinarian in accordance with general standards promulgated by the Secretary,' but even this modest welfare enhancement was opposed by the taxpayer-funded animal experimentation lobby. For example, Frankie Trull, an animal experimentation lobbyist for the National Association for Biomedical Research (NABR), even argued that laboratory dogs confined to cages their entire lives will live just as well as dogs permitted limited exercise. As quoted by the *Associated Press*, Trull asserted: 'There are no scientific data which say any minimum exercise per day, or per week, is physiologically better. You just sleep better at night because you think if exercise is good for you, it must be good for the dog.' (Drinkard 1986).

The subsequent gaps in the AWA and regulations have resulted in harm to animals in laboratories. For example, a cat or dog can be subject to multiple surgeries if it is of scientific necessity. Scientific necessity is not defined and is simply the subjective rationalization of the experimenter. The same goes for withholding pain medication if deemed scientifically necessary. While the protection to cats and dogs in experimentation laboratories is minimal, the extent of harm to unprotected animals is unknown.

US State Laws

Minnesota was the first state to pass a law requiring pound seizure in 1949. The law allowed licensed research facilities free access to shelter pets for experimentation from publicly funded animal shelters and if the shelter denied access then the shelter would lose funding. Minnesota revoked that law in 2012. As of early 2015, there are 19 states that ban pound seizures: California (only bans for abandoned pets), Connecticut, District of Columbia, Delaware, Hawaii, Illinois, Maine, Maryland, Massachusetts, Minnesota, New Hampshire, New Jersey, New York, Pennsylvania (ban for dogs only) Rhode Island, South Carolina, Vermont, Virginia, and West Virginia. There are 10 states with laws addressing pound seizure that allow the animal shelter discretion in whether they participate in pound seizure: Arizona, California (only allowed for owner-surrendered pets), Colorado, Iowa, Michigan, Ohio, Tennessee, Washington (only for non-owner surrendered dogs), Wisconsin, and Utah. And one state, Oklahoma, mandates pound seizure. That means that if a dealer or research facility goes to a shelter looking for animals to broker into experimentation, the shelter cannot turn the dealer or facility away and they are allowed to take any animal that is available. All other states are without laws that address pound seizure, and thus, are vulnerable. A listing of current pound seizure laws in the USA can be found at http://alliephillips.com/wp-content/uploads/2010/07/Pound-Seizure-Laws-by-State-Oct-2013.pdf.

In all US state animal anti-cruelty laws, animal experimentation practices are exempted from punishment. Going back to the scenario at the beginning of this chapter, if the abuse of a cat or dog were performed by a citizen, that person should be charged with felony animal cruelty; if committed by an experimenter on the NIH payroll, however, he/she will collect a check from the government and remains exempt from prosecution.

International Law

As of March 2013, there is a complete ban on animal testing in cosmetics in the European Union (HSI 2014). As of 2014, India no longer allows animal-tested cosmetics. Brazil's animal testing regulatory agency recognized 17 non-animal cosmetic testing alternatives in 2014 but put a slow five-year implementation phase into effect (HSI 2014). However, other countries such as Australia, Brazil, Canada, China, Japan, New Zealand, South Korea, Taiwan, and the USA still allow or require testing of animals for purposes of beauty products. While this is not an exhaustive list, more countries are starting to phase out and modernize the testing of cosmetics on animals. With advances being made in science, including newer testing models that do not involve animals, most people do not understand why the cosmetic and other experimentation industries have not kept up with those advances in science.

The Problem with USDA Class B Dealers

The majority of cats and dogs that are used in experimentation are purpose-bred by USDA Class A dealers who then resell them to medical and educational laboratories, and other testing facilities. However, there is still one class of dealer that is obtaining cats and dogs from animal shelters in the USA. Those are USDA random-source Class B dealers. USDA Class B Dealers, in general, are licensed by the US Department of Agriculture to buy, sell or transport any animal that they did not breed or raise themselves. They are only allowed to obtain animals from other dealers, from animal shelters, or from people who breed and raise animals on their property. It is illegal for them to obtain a stray animal or an animal that cannot be traced back to one of the three allowable sources listed above. Stray and untraceable animals are the problems that lie with random-source Class B dealers.

While there are thousands of USDA licensed Class B dealers in the USA currently the USA only has three 'random source' Class B dealers, those who obtain and resell animals that are not purpose-bred and come from random sources, such as animal shelters. Random source animals are most often family pets that lost their way and were unfortunate to arrive at a shelter that practices pound seizure. Random source animals also include pets that have been taken to animal shelters due to financial reasons, the death of their owner, or were removed from abusive or neglectful homes, puppy mills, dog fighting rings, or hoarding situations. These are companion animals that were unlucky to end up in a pound seizure shelter, often unbeknownst to the person surrendering the animal. And for those animals who were rescued from abuse and neglect situations, they are betrayed again when they are sold into the research industry.

Class B dealers are legally protected and regulated under the Animal Welfare Act, with strict laws on how Class B dealers can obtain animals. USDA is expending many resources on a very small number of random-source Class B dealer licensees, such as quarterly on-site inspections to insure that animals are obtained properly and conducting trace backs on the animals in an effort to identify any stolen animals. Changes to the oversight of this small number of Class B dealers occurred in September 2008 as a result of chronic inspection violations, inhumane housing conditions for the cats and dogs, improper obtainment of cats and dogs, and criminal indictments and convictions for some Class B dealers (NAS 2009). The requirement for in-person trace backs on cats and dogs in the possession of a Class B dealer requires that the USDA inspector review documentation that tracks the animal back to its original source of sale, and that the animal was received from a proper source under the Animal Welfare Act.

'Bunchers', on the other hand, may have a Class B dealer license, but are generally unlicensed by the USDA and their activities are difficult to trace. Their activities may also be illegal if it involves theft or fraud. They are commonly known to be people who obtain pets from a variety of unapproved random sources including 'free to good home' pet advertisements, pets wandering the streets, and even some accounts of pets being stolen. The buncher has been linked to improperly reselling the pets to Class B dealers. This is their profit-driven career because random-source animals are a lucrative business because some experimentation laboratories are looking for older pets to study arthritis, cardio vascular health, diseases associated with aging that cannot come from a young purpose-bred cat or dog.

The business of Class B dealers and bunchers often involves the transport the animals across US state lines to experimentation laboratories and institutions requesting animals, thus making it difficult for owners to locate their pets. Therefore, no companion cat and dog is safe in the USA so long as experimentation and educational laboratories are paying for random-source cats and dogs from Class B dealers and bunchers.

As outlined in *From the Leash to the Laboratory* published in The Atlantic magazine in July 2000 (Reitman 2000), some Class B dealers were caught obtaining animals from large-scale auctions (which is not permitted under the Animal Welfare Act) and caught with stolen pets in their possession. In recent years, there have been a few criminal prosecutions and convictions of Class B dealers. For example, large-scale dealer C.C. Baird from Arkansas (who was detailed in the HBO (2006) documentary *Dealing Dogs*) pled guilty to federal money laundering charges in 2005 and forfeited 700 acres of property, paid $200,000 in criminal forfeiture, and was sentenced to three years of federal probation. He was also sanctioned in a civil lawsuit under the Animal Welfare Act where all of his Class A and B licenses were revoked and he paid over $262,000 US in a civil penalty (see, Last Chance for Animals). Floyd and Susan Martin from Pennsylvania were criminally charged, pled guilty to mail fraud involving the fraudulent sale of animals into research and had their businesses shut down for illegally acquiring animals from bunchers, along with a host of other crimes. Floyd Martin was sentenced to six months in prison, while Susan Floyd received three year's probation (Worden 2013).

Allie Phillips, co-author of this chapter, volunteered in a pound seizure shelter in Michigan and successfully advocated to remove the Class B dealer after years of push-back from county leaders and the shelter director. She has had interactions with Class B Dealers in attempts to save shelter pets from experimentation and has listened to why they believe that former family cats and dogs are perfect research specimens. In a speech before the Montcalm County (Michigan) County Commissioners on January 26, 2009, a Class B dealer provided the following written statement in defense of why he should maintain his pound seizure contract with the county shelter.

> Why release animals for research? Animals at the pound must be held for a period of 4 to 7 days. Animals released for research, must be held according to Federal law a minimum of 7 days. In addition, R & R Research must hold the animal another 7 days to allow the owner to reclaim the animal. This allows families who have lost an animal an additional l day to acquire the animal which would have been euthanized, at no additional cost to the county. Animals used in medical research provide training in surgical techniques, development of new medicines and procedures. Dogs are primarily used for cardiovascular procedures and devices, bone, knee, joint and hip replacement, and older dogs are used for prostate research.
>
> Cats are primarily used in neurological, AIDS, and Sudden Infant Death Syndrome research. Also consider the vaccines, wormers, cancer treatments, and, heartworm medications for your animals. None of these would be available WITHOUT medical research. Can anyone name just one medical

> advance which was developed without the use of animals? It is a fact that animals are raised exclusively for use in research, however, the cost to raise a dog or cat from birth is prohibitively more expensive than acquiring an animal which would otherwise be euthanized. Given the limited amount of financial resources and the fact that two animals will die instead of one, it simply makes sense to use pound animals. An animal is no longer considered a 'pet' once ownership is relinquished, has not been properly cared for, or has failed to be reclaimed, rescued, or adopted. (Written statement by James Woudenberg to the Montcalm (Mich.) County Commissioners (26 Jan. 2009)).

The Pet Safety and Protection Act has not been enacted despite being introduced every session to the US Congress since the mid-1990s as a means to prevent the use of federal funds for the purchase of random-source animals. Consequently Class B dealers continue to profit by turning former family pets into subjects for experimentation laboratories.

On a positive note, the number of random-source Class B dealers has dramatically decreased over the past 15 years through advocacy of animal rescue groups, citizens and communities, and animal shelters prohibiting pound seizure. The winning message is that animal shelters should not be the shopping ground and bargain bin for taxpayer-funded animal experimenters. They should, as their name suggests, offer shelter to animals that have been abused, neglected, abandoned, and are awaiting new homes. With the decline and hopeful elimination of the Class B dealer classification and pound seizure, advancement in medical research and education will not be impacted due to increasing use of high-tech, 21st century non-animal models.

Current Practice in the USA

The most recent report from the USDA on the number of cats and dogs used in research comes from the 2014 Fiscal Year Animal Care Annual Report of Activities. (USDA 2014) The total number of dogs and cats used in research in 2014 was 5,795 dogs and 1,315 cats. Comparatively, in 2007 there were 72,037 dogs and 22,687 cats (USDA 2007:38) (these numbers do not differentiate between random source shelter cats and dogs and cats and dogs bred for research). In 2014, there were a total of 166,274 animals used in research, with approximately 4 % being cats and dogs (USDA 2014). This number excludes birds, rats and mice which are not protected by the Animal Welfare Act or tracked. In 2007, there were a total of 1,027,450 animals used in research (USDA 2007, p. 46), excluding birds, rats and mice; thus only 9 % of research animals were cats and dogs. In contrast to 1979 where 211,104 dogs and 69,103 cats were used in research, comprising of more than 15 % of research animals. (USDA 2007, p. 45) This suggests a decline in the use of cats and dogs in experimentation.

In a report from 2009 from the National Academies of Science, at the request of the US Congress, the committee found that less than 1 % of laboratory animals are cats and dogs, and most cats and dogs are specifically bred in research colonies or by Class A dealers. For dogs, 48.8 % came from individuals, 30.8 % from other Class B licensees, and 20.4 % from shelters. For cats, 60.9 % came from shelters, 21.4 % came from other Class B licenses, and 17.7 % came from individuals. (NAS 2009)

In Michigan, which is currently home to two of the three remaining random source Class B dealers in the USA, and numerous university and biomedical experimentation companies, the battle to end the practice has been hard fought, but still there is no law prohibiting pound seizure. But as a result of consistent and effective advocacy, there are no known Michigan animal shelters engaging in pound seizure as of 2016. But this could change if a Class B dealer gains entry into a financially struggling shelter and offers to pay to take cats and dogs otherwise slated for euthanasia.

Table 1 outlines the decline in shelter cats and dogs in Michigan shelters being given or sold to Class B dealers for experimentation.

Since 2000, co-author Allie Phillips has worked with citizens, animal shelters, and animal rescue organizations to successfully ban Class B dealers and pound seizure from Michigan animal shelters. She became aware of the secretive practice while volunteering at an animal shelter that was engaging in pound seizure. Through advocacy in the face of significant opposition from community leaders, a ban on the Class B dealer was eventually obtained in 2003 in the shelter where Ms. Phillips volunteered. In 2003, there were 15 animal shelters known in Michigan that allowed a Class B dealer to take cats and dogs for resale to research. One by one, advocates worked to end the practice in their communities and as of 2015 there are no known animal shelters selling or giving shelter cats and dogs to B dealers. However, knowing that pound seizure is a secretive practice that is not advertised, it would require obtaining disposition records on all shelter animals in all animal shelters in the state to validate this claim. This is why efforts are on-going to pass an anti-pound seizure law in Michigan.

In recent years, the authors have observed that pound seizure has been on the decline as community awareness increases, experimentation

Table 1 Michigan department of agriculture annual shelter reports of shelter cats and dogs sold to research or class B dealers, 2005–2013

Shelter	2013 Dogs	2013 Cats	2012 Dogs	2012 Cats	2011 Dogs	2011 Cats	2010 Dogs	2010 Cats	2009 Dogs	2009 Cats	2008 Dogs	2008 Cats	2007 Dogs	2007 Cats	2006 Dogs	2006 Cats	2005 Dogs	2005 Cats
Eaton county animal control					1	38	7	23	0	0	44	22	164	69	127	103	144	52
Gratiot county animal control					114	0	61	0	40	131	170	176	146	141	162	206	165	215
Mecosta county animal control									114	0	158	0	161	0	173	0	198	0
Montcalm county animal control									33	11	120	31	187	67	178	87	192	49
Oseeola county animal control													10	21	53	35	80	1
TOTAL	0	0	0	0	115	38	68	23	187	142	492	229	668	298	693	431	779	317

Sections that are blank demonstrate the shelter ceasing the practice of pound seizure facilities opt to not work with Class B dealers, and non-animal models grow in popularity and effectiveness. Although the process has been slow, progress is being made to protect shelter cats and dogs from being used in experimentation. On December 17, 2013, the US National Institutes of Health (the largest funder of animal experimentation in the country) issued a press release that it would transition away from using dogs (no mention of cats) from Class B dealers as of October 1, 2014. Dogs now may only be obtained from 'other legal sources include[ing] Class A vendors, privately owned colonies (for example, NCI-supported intra-institutional existing colonies, or colonies established by donations from breeders or owners because of genetic defects such as bleeding disorders) or client owned animals (e.g., animals participating in veterinary clinical trials.)' (NIH 2013)

Cat and Dog Experimentation in Medical Schools

It was commonplace for university medical schools to require students to experiment on live animals, including cats and dogs. As of 2014, 173 USA and Canadian medical schools have ceased the practice of using live animals to train medical students (but the schools may still use animals in other experimentation capacities). Only four medical schools in the USA still use live animals. (PCRM 2014)

However, there have been incidents that have been made public where dogs have been sacrificed as part of a medical experiment. One noteworthy example occurred in January 2007 at the Cleveland Clinic, a prestigious medical facility, where a dog was abused during a medical device sales demonstration where an aneurysm was induced and the dog killed. (Grens 2007) The salesman went ahead with the sales demonstration of the medical device before receiving approval to kill the dog, which likely would not have been approved. The community was outraged, and the Cleveland Clinic issued a public statement that the salesman violated Clinic policies, but there were no sanctions.

Medical schools are evolving their educational practices for a variety of reasons, one of which is the emergence of non-animal training models that are as, if not more effective, than experimenting on live animals. The claim that animal experimentation is essential to medical development is not supported by advancements in scientific studies, but rather by opinion and anecdote. Systematic reviews of its effectiveness do not support the claims made on its behalf. (Pound 2004)

Cat and Dog Research in Veterinary Schools

There are 30 accredited veterinary schools in the USA, as well as 5 in Canada and 14 other international veterinary schools. (AVMA 2015) Like their human medical school counterparts, veterinary schools have traditionally used live animals in their training curriculum and for experimentation. Most people agree that veterinarians should work with live animals; after all, live animals will be their future clients. Where the veterinary school industry has come under fire is the experimentation and study of live animals resulting in euthanasia when euthanasia is unnecessary. These 'terminal labs' have occurred in settings such as teaching the students how to conduct spaying and neutering where euthanasia at the conclusion is unwarranted (Veterinary Practice News 2009).

Many veterinary schools have traditionally obtained their animal test subjects from local animal shelters, thus engaging in pound seizure. Communities and animal advocates have been vocal that veterinary schools should provide the beneficial practice of spaying and neutering unsterilized shelter pets; but instead of euthanizing the animal after practicing the surgery, return the animal to the shelter where they would have a greater likelihood at adoption as a result of the surgery.

Currently, veterinary schools are increasingly moving towards non-animal models for certain training courses to avoid the ethical and moral concerns of the terminal labs. After all, veterinary schools should be teaching the students to save lives and should not ask them to end the life of a pet simply because the teaching was completed. As of 2015, 21 veterinary schools offer dissection alternatives. (Animalearn 2015)

Some veterinary schools have switched to ethically sourced cadavers, shelter medicine programs (where people can bring their pet in for treatment as part of a research study) and simulators. Tufts University School of Veterinary Medicine was the first US vet school to eliminate all terminal labs in all species. Instead, Tufts is providing hands-on experience through their spay/neuter clinic where animals are helped and later placed for adoption, rather than being euthanized. Tufts, also has an Educational Memorial Program where people can donate the remains of their deceased animal.

Michigan State University Veterinary School has The Elmo Model and silicone stomachs to give students the chance to practice surgical procedures and syringe techniques on something that feels similar to skin. 'A recent study demonstrated that using models of animals is as effective as using live animals for training clinicians in neonatal intubation skills.' (Andreatta 2015)

Cats and Dogs in Biomedical and Biochemical Research

According to the government's official USDA statistics, nearly 60,000 dogs (mostly beagles) are used in animal experimentation laboratories. (USDA 2014) Significant debate has occurred for years between researchers, medical/veterinary doctors, and concerned citizens as to whether animals (cats, dogs, rats, mice) are appropriate models when it comes to creating safe human drugs. While that discussion and debate continues, even the US Food and Drug Administration has admitted that 'a stunning 9 out of every 10 candidate new medicines that appear safe and effective in 'animal models' fail in human trials due to unforeseen toxicity or lack of effectiveness.' (HSUS and USDA 2004) The latest data shows a 96 % failure rate. (Pippin 2013)

Dogs, especially beagles, are not chosen for experimental protocols because they are good models for human disease. They are selected because they are *cooperative* test subjects; 'the size, biologic features, and cooperative, docile nature of the well-socialized dog make it the model of choice for a variety of scientific inquiries.' (Johnson 2010, p. 4)

The biomedical and biochemical experimentation industry is cloaked in secrecy. Data detailing the types, numbers and source of animals used in experimentation has been difficult to obtain, despite the fact that it is largely funded by public tax money. A 2015 investigative TV exposé in Boston found 1299 dogs (primarily beagles) in 12 Massachusetts research laboratories. Charles River Labs was the largest facility and The Wilmington Company had 750 dogs. Veterinary schools and hospitals were also found to be using dogs in research. Yet, when the reporter reached out to visit the facilities and see the condition of the dogs, not one institution agreed. (Leamanczyk 2015).

While is it believed that an overwhelming number of cats and dogs in research are purposefully bred for experimentation (via USDA Class A dealers), there are former family pet from shelters that have been sold into biomedical and biochemical laboratories. Robert's story is a rare example with a happy ending.

An investigation of Utah's pound seizure practices by the People for Ethical Treatment of Animals in 2009, along with advocacy from local rescue groups and citizens, resulted in overturning Utah's mandatory pound seizure law in 2010. Part of the campaign to end pound seizure involved shelter cats being used in experimentation at the University of Utah. Documents from the University showed that cats from Utah animal shelters were being used in non-survival experimentation studies. The live cats had electrodes implanted in an attempt to treat traumatic injuries and other neurological pathologies in humans. Thirty cats and 60 rats were part of this particular study that occurred from September 2006 through September 2009.

In documents filed to justify the use of cats, the experimenters stated, 'the major reason for using cats is that they are one of the lowest phylogenic species that is gyrencephalic and has a cortical thickness that is similar to humans. This allows for a more realistic extrapolation of biocompatibility to humans than performing the study in a lisencephalic species such as the rat. Since immunological responses are similar across mammals, we will use rats to examine the response of neural tissue to implantation of micro-electrode arrays.' (IACUC Approval application 06-09015, University of Utah, C 3.0)

Without detailing whether cats, especially former family pets, are appropriate for research for the benefit of humans, the above paragraph indicated that rats were not appropriate for the study, yet 60 rats were approved for use.

The application to conduct this study further described what would happen to the cats during experimentation: 'The cats will be made accustomed to resting in the shielded experimental chamber through prolonged exposure and positive reinforcement prior to beginning experiments. If necessary a cat restraint bag, a zippered bag which encloses the cat's body and limbs but not the cat's head, will be employed.' (IACUC Approval application 06-09015, University of Utah, C 4.0) Further, 'We will implant [electrode arrays] into the hind-limb region of the primary motor cortex in up to 10 cats for each type of EA tested.' (IACUC Approval application 06-09015, University of Utah, C 4.0) The EAs stayed in place up to 180 days.

An orange tabby cat named Robert was one of the abused cats in the above study. According to public records, Robert was taken from an animal shelter under pound seizure in Utah on March 13, 2009 and sent to the laboratory at the University of Utah in exchange for $15. Robert was subsequently renamed 'F09-017' where experimenters made an incision in his skull and forcibly implanted electrodes into his brain. The electrodes were fired up causing Robert's legs to move involuntarily. In a letter dated December 7, 2009, PETA requested the University of Utah president retire Robert and allow him to be adopted. The letter states, 'Laboratory "life" has taken a physical and psychological toll on Robert. He vomits repeatedly in his cage, and through his nearly nine months at the U, this once-affectionate cat has become skittish and withdrawn.' (PETA 2009)

Of concern regarding the information contained in PETA's letter is the physical and behavioral distress of Robert as the experiment continued contrary to the written assertions of the University that assured the animals would be monitored and treated if distressed. Specifically the University stated 'The animals will be observed every day during experimentation, usually for several hours. The animals' behavior will be carefully observed for signs of distress. Any signs of distressed behavior or weight loss will trigger further assessment of the animal's health.... The success of our research program demands and depends on the preservation of the state of their wellbeing.' (IACUC Approval application 06-09015, University of Utah, C 5.0). The safeguards in place did not appear to be safeguarding Robert.

What happened to Robert, if done outside of a laboratory, would be deemed animal cruelty in violation of US laws. Instead, the University of Utah cashed cheques, courtesy of the NIH, while cats like Robert remain locked up in college basements. In an uncommon conclusion, Robert was released from the laboratory and adopted into a loving home in December 2009. Robert's plight helped to amend Utah's mandatory pound seizure into a discretionary law in 2010, thus putting the decision in the hands of shelters.

As discussed in the National Academies of Science 2009 report, there continues to be a debate of whether dogs purposefully bred for experimentation make better test subjects as compared to former family pets who ended up at a shelter. The argument being that the former family pet would be overly stressed due to the unfamiliarity of the experimentation setting. But with the growth of organizations like the Beagle Freedom Project, an organization that works with research laboratories to rescue dogs (and sometimes cats, horses and other animals) after the research study concludes, the former research animals once placed in an adoptive home begin to have the same personalities and characteristics as animals not bred for research. So this has broadened the debate as to whether any dog and cat, purpose-bred or random-sourced, is appropriate in a laboratory setting.

Whether bred for experimentation or to live as a companion pet, studies have been clear that all animals feel pain, have feelings, and therefore would not make good research subjects. (Kluger 2014) Yet the minimal legal safeguarding in place for experimentation animals are not recognizing the sentient nature of animals and are continuing to treat animals as property that do not feel.

For example, in 2013, Melanie Kaplan adopted a purpose-bred beagle now named Alexander Hamilton from a taxpayer-funded animal experimentation laboratory. As she told *U.S. News and World Report*, 'The whole ride home he was just drooling like crazy, shaking,' she explained. She covered the entire downstairs of her home in newspaper in case Hammy's stomach reacted to eating better dog food. The beagle, who spent the first three years of his life in a cage, did not know at first what to do with his squishy dog bed. 'And then he was on it and he curled up and he just basically did not want to move for the first several weeks,' Kaplan said. It took about six weeks for him to start acting like a typical dog. 'It was never that he didn't trust people, it was just all of the uncertain things in the real world that he had never seen before,' Kaplan said. (Schwab 2014).

How the Government is Funding US Animal Research

In January 2015, overall top-line public opinion for animal experimentation in the USA reached a new low. For the first time, as reported by the non-partisan Pew study, 'citizens are closely divided over animal research: 47 percent favor and 50 percent oppose the use of animals in scientific research.' (Funk 2015)

Earlier studies confirm this trend. The Star Tribune reported that from 2000 to 2008, the number of Americans that support using animals in research shrank from 70 % to 54 %. (Spencer 2009) And a close examination of the underlying demographics within the topline polling data shows even greater drips among key audiences, including women (52.2 %), and younger voters 18–24 (55 %), who outright oppose animal experimentation. (Wilke 2013) This declining support is even more interesting in light of the fact that these surveys did not specify the species used in laboratories—such as dogs and cats or their status—e.g., former pet, who would presumably garner even more support.

Yet, the overall number of animals abused in laboratories continues to climb. In February 2015, a new PETA study identified that taxpayer-funded animal experimentation is up 73 %, and 'the number of animals tested rose from 1,566,994 in 1997 to 2,705,772 in 2012 in testing by the top 25 institutional recipients of National Institute of Health grants.' (Casey 2015)

How does one explain the disconnect between falling public support for animal experimentation and rising numbers of animals experimented on? Part of the answer can be traced back to the US government's role in federally funding laboratory animal experimentation. Nobody knows for sure how much the US government spends on animal experimentation but there is documentation regarding baseline minimum spend from NIH data.

According to NIH, approximately 47 % of all NIH grant funding is spent on animal experiments, which is consistent with spending over the past decade. (Pankevich et al. 2012) With a 2015 federal NIH budget of $31 billion, 80 % of which is spent on grants, this roughly equates to $12 billion NIH spends on animal experimentation. This figure does not include intramural NIH spending (i.e. spending within internal NIH government campuses versus grants to colleges and universities), and thereby excludes USDA, Pentagon, Environmental Protection Agency, any other US federal spending on animal experiments. 'Conservative estimates, however, put it into the tens of billions annually. ' (Greek and Shanks 2009, p. 8). Since 1995 Congress has tripled the NIH budget thereby becoming the primary market maker for animal experimentation in the USA.

Moreover, there is evidence that government subsidies for animal experimentation have incentivized the problem. In another widely criticized NIH-funded experiment on cats, professors at the University of Wisconsin received millions in federal grant money to cut into the brains of cats, drill holes in their skulls, place wire coils in their eyes, deafen them, and then starve them to death. (Hansen 2012) These Wisconsin experimenters did not even justify the cat deafening based on its benefits to humans. (Hansen 2012) (FOIA records)

Pound Seizure is a Declining Practice

While the occurrence of using shelter cats and dogs in research is reported to be rapidly declining, there is in fact no mechanism to truly assess whether it is (without obtaining shelter disposition records of every animal from every animal shelter). Animal shelter staff, volunteers, animal rescue volunteers and communities are relied upon as watchdogs to ensure that Class B dealers and pound seizure do not take hold in a shelter. Until every state bans pound seizures, and the USDA eliminates the license classification for random source Class B dealers, all pets are at risk and could inadvertently become a victim of pound seizure.

To advance the abolition of animal experimentation, including on former family pets, the World Congress on Alternatives and Animal Use in the Life Sciences is held every three years. The 10th World Congress is scheduled for 2017 in Seattle, Washington. Moreover, organizations such as the American Anti-Vivisection Society and the Physicians Committee for Responsible Medicine are working with product testing, research, and educational facilities to change to non-animal testing models. For the numerous non-animal models available, visit www.aavs.org/alternatives/.

Successful arguments against pound seizure have included:

- Pound seizure is a betrayal of trust because shelters mostly keep the practice secret.

- Citizens in some localities are obligated to take strays to the shelter and are expected to be Good Samaritans and call in abuse and neglect complaints. Turning those pets over to shelters engaging in pound seizure undermines these laws and ordinances.
- People who surrender their beloved pet due to job loss and homelessness should not worry that their pet will be an experiment.
- The hold period at some shelters is not sufficient time if a family is looking for their lost pet.
- Pets that are taken by a Class B dealer are often transferred to other state laboratories thus making it difficult for families to reclaim them.
- Family pets are not good experimentation subjects as they may not be accustomed to being handled by strangers, being in a cage, being poked, being denied affection and the comforts of home. These pets often stop eating, become depressed, develop stress-related ailments and this impacts the validity of research.
- All national animal protection organizations, including the National Animal Care and Control Association, object to pound seizure.
- A vast majority of shelters have rejected the practice as it is contrary to the purpose of an animal shelter.
- There are too many concerns regarding the conduct and secrecy by the Class B dealers, including the expensive oversight by the USDA.

Conclusion

The issue of animal experimentation, especially on shelter cats and dogs, evokes heightened emotions in those that find the practice to be barbaric and abusive. It also evokes a defensive response from those that support the practice as providing relevant life-saving measures for people. No matter where you fall in this continuing debate, an objective look at US animal anti-cruelty laws demonstrate that the conduct in experimentations would be deemed animal cruelty in any other setting, which is why animal experimentation is specifically exempted from all US animal cruelty laws.

The positive step in fixing this problem is to recognize that laboratory animal abuse is not only an ethical or scientific issue but is also a US Congressional budget appropriations problem that requires a fiscal solution. A top to bottom audit of the NIH's spending on animal experimentation is sorely needed and must be done before Congress appropriates another blank check or budget increase. So long as taxpayers are footing the bill for most laboratory animal abuse, greater transparency is needed from NIH. Continued awareness of how cats and dogs are used in animal experimentation laboratories will also help move this issue into the light and into elimination.

References

American Anti-Vivisection Society. (2015). *Class B dealers*. http://aavs.org/our-work/campaigns/class-b-dealers/. Accessed 8 July 2015.

American Veterinary Medical Association. (2015). *Accredited colleges of veterinary medicine*. https://www.avma.org/ProfessionalDevelopment/Education/Accreditation/Colleges/Documents/colleges_accredited.pdf. Accessed 8 July 2015.

Andreatta, P. B., Klotz, J. J., Dooley-Hash, S. L., Hauptman, J. G., Biddinger, B., & House, J. B. (2015). Performance-based comparison of neonatal intubation training outcomes: simulator and live animal. *Advanced Neonatal Care, 15*(1), 56–64.

Animalearn. (2015). *Schools offering dissection alternatives*. http://www.animalearn.org/vetSchools.php#.VWNGTc76Ylo. Accessed 8 July 2015.

Animal Freedom. (2016). *Is peter singer backing animal testing?*. http://animalfreedom.org/english/column/peter_singer.html. Accessed 9 March 2016.

APHIS. (2000). *Rats/mice/and birds database: researchers, breeders, transporters, and exhibitors*. A Database Prepared by the Federal Research Division, Library of Congress under an Interagency Agreement with the United States Department of Agriculture's Animal Plant Health Inspection Service, Washington, DC.

Casey, M. (2015, February 26). Animal experimentation up 73 percent, study says'. *CBS News*. http://www.cbsnews.com/news/peta-study-finds-animal-testing-in-federal-labs-on-the-increase/. Accessed 8 July 2015.

Drinkard, J. (1986, April 27). Animal research critics pin hopes on new law for more humane care. *Associated Press*. http://articles.latimes.com/1986-04-27/news/mn-24114_1_animal-research. Accessed 20 November 2015.

Funk, C., & Raine, L. (2015, January 29). Public and scientists' views on science and society. *Pew Research Center*. http://www.pewinternet.org/2015/01/29/public-and-scientists-views-on-science-and-society/. Accessed 13 July 2015.

Gala, S. G., Goodman, J. R., Murphy, M. P., & Balsam, M. J. (2012). Use of animals by nato countries in military medical training exercises: an international survey. *Military Medicine, 177*(8), 907.

Greek, R., & Shanks, N. (2009). *FAQs about the use of animals in science: a handbook for the scientifically perplexed*. New York: University Press of America, Inc.

Grens, K. (2007, January 18). Dog sacrificed for sales demonstration. *The Scientist*. http://www.the-scientist.com/?articles.view/articleNo/24669/title/Dog-sacrificed-for-sales-demonstration/. Accessed 8 July 2015.

Hansen, L. (2012, September 15). Cruel cat experiments unnecessary. *Madison.* http://host.madison.com/news/opinion/column/guest/dr-lawrence-hansen-cruel-cat-experiments-unnecessary/article_d06988ea-fea7-11e1-84e6-001a4bcf887a.html. Accessed 8 July 2015.

Humane Society International. (2014). *HSI welcomes Brazil's recognition of 17 alternative tests for cosmetics and chemicals but five-year delay is unsatisfactory.* http://www.hsi.org/news/press_releases/2014/09/brazil-concea-animal-testing-090814.html. Accessed 8 July 2015.

Humane Society of the United States. (2015). *Biomedical research.* http://www.hsi.org/issues/biomedical_research/ and http://www.hsi.org/issues/advancing_science/research/horizon2020report.pdf. Accessed 8 July 2015.

Institute for Laboratory Animal Research Division on Earth and Life Studies, National Research Council of the National Academies of Science. (2009). Scientific and humane issues in the use of random source dogs and cats. *The National Academies Press.* www.nap.edu/catalog/12641.html. Accessed 8 July 2015.

Johnson, P. (2010). *Dogs in biomedical research.* University Of Arizona, Tucson. http://www.readbag.com/uac-arizona-vsc443-dogmodel-10-dog-as-models-lect. Accessed 8 July 2015.

Kluger, J. (2014, August 25). What are animals thinking? *Time Magazine.* http://time.com/3173937/what-are-animals-thinking-hint-more-that-you-suspect/. Accessed 8 July 2015.

Last Chance for Animals. (2006). *Dealing Dogs.* http://www.lcanimal.org/index.php/campaigns/class-b-dealers-and-pet-theft/dealing-dogs-class-b-dealer-cc-baird-investigation. Accessed 8 July 2015.

Leamanczyk, L. (2015, February 16). I-team: dogs used for medical research may never go outside. *CBS NEWS.* http://boston.cbslocal.com/2015/02/16/i-team-dogs-used-for-medical-research-may-never-go-outside/. Accessed 8 July 2015.

National Institutes of Health. (2013, December 17). Notice regarding NIH plan to transition from use of USDA class B dogs to other legal sources. http://grants.nih.gov/grants/guide/notice-files/NOT-OD-14-034.html. Accessed 8 July 2015.

Pankevich, D. E., Wizemann, T. M., Mazza, A., & Altevogt, B. M. (2012). International animal research regulations: impact on neuroscience research: workshop summary. *The National Academy Press.* http://www.nap.edu/read/13322/chapter/1. Accessed 21 November 2015.

People for the Ethical Treatment of Animals. (2009, December 7). *Letter to university president Michael K. Young.*

Phillips, A. (2010). *How shelter pets are brokered for experimentation: understanding pound seizure.* Lanham, MD: Rowman & Littlefield.

Physicians Committee for Responsible Medicine. (2012). *Good Medicine Magazine,* pp. 6–7. http://issuu.com/physicianscommittee/docs/good_medicine_-_winter_2012. Accessed 8 July 2015.

Physicians Committee for Responsible Medicine. (2014). *2014 progress report.* http://www.pcrm.org/pdfs/media/2014ProgressReport.pdf. Accessed 8 July 2015.

Pippin, J. (2013). Animal research in medical sciences: seeking a convergence of science, medicine, and animal law. *South Texas Law Review, 54*, 469–498.

Pound, P., Ebrahim, S., Sandercock, P., Bracken, M.B., & Roberts, I. (2004). Where is the evidence that animal research benefits humans? *British Medical Journal, 328*, 514–517.

Regan, T. (2016). *Criminalizing vivisection.* http://tomregan.info/criminalizing-vivisection/. Accessed 9 March 2016.

Reitman, J. (2000, July). From the leash to the laboratory. *The Atlantic.* http://www.theatlantic.com/magazine/archive/2000/07/from-the-leash-to-the-laboratory/378269/. Accessed 8 July 2015.

Schwab, N. (2014, July 9). Beagles 'Lobby' against taxpayer-funded animal experiments a watchdog group counts $12 billion in federal funds going annually toward animal experimentation. *US News and World Report.* http://www.usnews.com/news/blogs/washington-whispers/2014/07/09/beagles-lobby-against-taxpayer-funded-animal-experiments. Accessed 20 November 2015.

Spencer, J. (2009, November 10). Researchers defend merits of animal testing in a new campaign. *The Spokesman-Review.* http://www.spokesman.com/stories/2009/nov/10/critical-research/. Accessed 13 July 2015.

United States Department of Agriculture Animal and Plant Health Inspection Service. (2008, September). Fiscal year 2007 animal care annual report of activities. http://www.aphis.usda.gov/publications/animal_welfare/content/printable_version/2007_AC_Report.pdf. Accessed 8 July 2015.

United States Department of Agriculture. (2014). Annual report animal usage by Fiscal year 2014. http://www.aphis.usda.gov/animal_welfare/downloads/7023/Animals%20Used%20In%20Research%202014.pdf. Accessed 13 July 2015.

University of Utah. (2006). *IACUC approval application 06–09015.*

University of Wisconsin-Madison. (2013). *Freedom of information act (FOIA) records.* http://grants.nih.gov/grants/olaw/foia-uwm-2013/r_Exhibit%201.pdf. Accessed 13 July 2015.

U.S. Food and Drug Administration Report. (2004). Innovation or stagnation: challenge and opportunity on the critical path to new medical products. http://www.fda.gov/downloads/ScienceResearch/SpecialTopics/CriticalPathInitiative/CriticalPathOpportunitiesReports/UCM113411.pdf. Accessed 8 July 2015.

(2015, April 17). Are live terminal labs necessary? *Veterinary Practice News.* http://www.veterinarypracticenews.com/April-2009/Are-Live-Terminal-Laboratories-Necessary/. Accessed 20 November 2015.

Wilke, J., & Saad, L. (2013, June 3). Older Americans' moral attitudes changing. *Gallup.* http://www.gallup.com/poll/162881/older-americans-moral-attitudes-changing.aspx. Accessed 13 July 2015.

Worden, A. (2013, August 28). Pa. man gets 6-month term in research scheme. *The Philadelphia Inquirer*. http://articles.philly.com/2013-08-28/news/41500820_1_random-source-dogs-martins-chestnut-grove-kennel. Accessed 20 November 2015.

Allie Phillips is a former prosecuting attorney, founder of the National Center for Prosecution of Animal Abuse at the National District Attorneys Association and was named one of the top Animal Defenders of 2015. She is an expert on the topic of pound seizure (selling and giving shelter pets to research) and is the author of *How Shelter Pets are Brokered for Experimentation: Understanding Pound Seizure* (2010) and *Defending the Defenceless: A Guide to Protecting and Advocating for Pets* (2011).

Anthony Bellotti is the founder and National Campaign Manager of the White Coat Waste Movement. For over a decade, Bellotti has consulted for national GOP candidates, ballot initiatives, and public affairs campaigns. He's been honoured as one of the 40 'best and brightest' campaign professionals under 40 by the American Association of Political Consultants and as a 'Rising Star of Politics' by the magazine *Campaigns & Elections*.

Animals in Scientific Research

André Menache

Introduction: Historical Origins of Animal Abuse in Science

Animal suffering and animal abuse in science are as old as science itself. The earliest recorded experiments and observations involving animals date back to a period of Egyptian medicine from around 3000 to 400 BC, and in particular the Ebers papyrus of 1500 BC discovered at Thebes (Bryan 1930 cited in Cox 2002). Roman physicians achieved fame through their medical discoveries, with Galen (Galenus of Pergamon, AD 129 to 200) among the most prolific of animal experimenters of his day (Kuhn 1821 – 1833 in Cox 2002). Galen was well known for his dissections of nerves and muscles in animals such as pigs and goats and has been variably described as the founder of experimental physiology (Crawford 2013) and the somewhat less flattering 'Father of Vivisection' (Watson 2009, p. 11). Indeed, many of Galen's views held sway for centuries, in particular his observation that blood was produced by the liver and did not circulate through the body. His distorted views were finally put to rest in 1628 by the Englishman William Harvey, based on the latter's meticulous study of human anatomy at a time when the Renaissance in Italy paved the way for physicians to

A. Menache (✉)
Antidote Europe, Strasbourg, France
e-mail: andre.menache@gmail.com

J. Maher et al. (eds.), *The Palgrave International Handbook of Animal Abuse Studies*, DOI 10.1057/978-1-137-43183-7_18

dissect human cadavers (Aird 2011). Andreas Vesalius (1514 – 1564) was also a staunch critic of Galen and concluded that Galen in his anatomical works had relied too much on animal dissections (Joutsivio 1997).

An examination of the contextual role of animals in the more recent history of medicine is equally helpful in explaining the culture of animal abuse in science today. A logical place to begin is the 1865 publication, 'An Introduction to the Study of Experimental Medicine' by Frenchman Claude Bernard (Bernard and Greene 1957). This treatise firmly established animal experimentation as a scientific method in which the similarities between animals and people were considered by far to outweigh the differences. Bernard put scientific medicine on a new foundation, namely the animal laboratory, where hypotheses could be rigorously tested. Indeed, he placed laboratory study above clinical and epidemiological findings and rejected evolution and evolutionary biology in favour of creationism (Lafollette 1997). A pupil of Descartes, Bernard promoted Cartesian reductionism in the form of 'hypothetico-deductivism' whereby species differences are merely quantitative. In other words, although a dog liver was visibly smaller than that of a human, both nevertheless, functioned in exactly the same way. Considered a genius by many in his day, Bernard could be forgiven today for not knowing that there are significant physiological differences between the liver of a human and a dog. In the modern era, this species difference is evidenced by the fact that drug-induced liver damage in people is the most frequent reason cited for the withdrawal from the market of an approved drug, despite extensive preclinical animal testing, and accounts for more than 50 % of acute liver failure in the USA (Lee 2003).

The Legal Basis for Animal Abuse in Science

The Nuremberg Code

A major influence on the legal requirement that animals be used in research and testing was formalised in the Nuremberg Code, which came out of a second trial in post-war Germany in December, 1946 (Greek 2012). Most of the defendants on trial were medical doctors charged with conspiracy to commit war crimes against humanity. The Nuremberg Code subsequently emerged from these proceedings, laying the groundwork for safeguarding the rights of human subjects in clinical trials. During the course of the legal proceedings, the advisor to the prosecutor for *US v. Brandt,* Dr Andrew C Ivy was responsible for authoring the manuscript the prosecutors used to evaluate the scientific aspects of the charges (American Medical Association 1946a). The manuscript included the following:

> The [human] experiment to be performed must be so designed and based on the results of animal experimentation and a knowledge of the natural history of the disease under study that the anticipated results will justify the performance of the [human] experiment... (American Medical Association 1946b; Ivy 1946).

These and other guidelines were subsequently adopted in the final version of the Nuremberg Code as well as in the World Medical Association Declaration of Helsinki (World Medical Association 1964) with the result that regulatory bodies such as the US Food and Drug Administration and the European Medicines Agency require animal testing on a rodent and non-rodent species in order to determine safe dose levels for human subjects taking part in clinical trials (US Food and Drug Administration 2010; European Medicines Agency 2008).

Directive 2010/63/EU

In addition to the pivotal role played by the Nuremberg code, European Directive 2010/63/EU provides a legal framework regarding the general use of animals in scientific procedures. In terms of legislation, the focus of this chapter will be on the European Union (EU) in general and the UK in particular, whose national statistics are arguably among the most accurate and up to date on animal experiments, compared with the rest of the world. For example, in the USA, the many millions of birds, rats and mice bred for scientific research purposes are not included in national statistics (United States Department of Agriculture, Animal Welfare Act 2013).

Whereas animal based research was loosely regulated during the first half of the twentieth century, either through general animal protection laws or by a voluntary institutional code of ethics, the latter half of the twentieth century began to see the formulation of laws specifically covering animal experimentation. An important contribution to the subject was the publication in 1959 of 'The Principles of Humane Experimental Technique' by two UK scientists, Russell and Burch, which enunciated the concept of the 3Rs: 'reduction' (the use of fewer animals, wherever possible), 'refinement' (the greater use of analgesics or the use of 'lower' organisms) and 'replacement' (the replacement of live animals with other methods) (Russell and Burch 1959).

Thus, in the EU, Directive 86/609/EEC on the protection of animals used for experimental and other scientific purposes was adopted in 1986, the chief aim of which was to harmonise the laws of EU Member States to ensure that:

> the number of animals used for experimental or other scientific purposes is reduced to a minimum, that such animals are adequately cared for, that no pain, suffering, distress or lasting harm are inflicted unnecessarily and ensure that, where unavoidable, these shall be kept to the minimum; in particular, unnecessary duplication of experiments should be avoided. (European Economic Community 1986—Council Directive of 24 November 1986 on the approximation of laws, regulations and administrative provisions of the Member States regarding the protection of animals used for experimental and other scientific purposes).

Prior to 1986 in the UK, the use of animals in scientific procedures was regulated by the Cruelty to Animals Act 1876, which enforced a licensing and inspection system for animal experiments. Although both the UK Animal Welfare Act 2006 and the Animals (Scientific Procedures) Act 1986 currently outlaw the causing of 'unnecessary suffering' the major difference between these two pieces of legislation is that specific exemptions apply to animal experiments licensed under the 1986 Act (Select Committee on Animals in Scientific Procedures Report 2001). As will become evident later on in the chapter, identical acts of deliberate animal cruelty potentially punishable by custodial sentencing under the Animal Welfare Act 2006 are essentially immune from prosecution under the Animals (Scientific Procedures) Act 1986. The 1986 Act effectively enshrines animal suffering by means of legal definitions, whereby an animal experiment becomes a 'regulated procedure' licensed to potentially cause pain, suffering, distress or lasting harm to a 'protected animal', which encompasses all living vertebrates other than humans, under the responsibility of humans.

The 1986 legislation (Directive 86/609/EEC) was amended and subsequently replaced by Directive 2010/63/EU (European Commission 2010—Directive 2010/63/EU of the European Parliament and of the Council of 22 September 2010 on the protection of animals used for scientific purposes). The revised directive sets down guidelines on the general care and use of live animals. In addition, methods of killing animals are described in Annex IV. These include cervical dislocation without prior sedation in birds, rodents and rabbits below a given weight. Killing by concussion or percussive blow to the head without prior sedation is permitted in larger birds, rodents and rabbits, in addition to dogs, cats, ferrets and foxes.

Decapitation without prior sedation is permissible in birds and rodents. Electrical stunning without prior sedation is permissible in fish, amphibians, birds, rabbits, dogs, cats, ferrets, foxes as well as larger mammals (sheep, for example).

Annex VIII of the directive provides a classification of the severity of an experiment, based on the degree of pain, suffering, distress or lasting harm expected to be experienced by an individual animal during the course of the procedure. Four categories are recognised:

Non-recovery

'Procedures which are performed entirely under general anaesthesia from which the animal shall not recover consciousness shall be classified as "non-recovery"'.

Example: an animal is anaesthetised and subjected to a series of invasive procedures, after which it receives a lethal overdose of anaesthetic agent and is killed without first regaining consciousness.

Mild:

'Procedures on animals, as a result of which the animals are likely to experience short-term mild pain, suffering or distress, as well as procedures with no significant impairment of the well-being or general condition of the animals shall be classified as " mild"'.

Example: an experiment of this sort may involve a small or a large number of animals (from as few as 25 animals in a pilot study to a few thousand animals in an experimental vaccine study). The procedures in this category may include repeated injections of substances by subcutaneous, intramuscular, intravenous or intraperitoneal routes on a regular basis for a period of days, weeks or months. The use of gavage (where a tube is passed directly into the stomach of the animal without anaesthesia or pain relief) is also included in the 'mild' category. In addition to the aforementioned procedures these same animals can expect to be forcibly restrained to provide blood samples at regular intervals throughout the study. At the end of the study all of the animals will be killed and their tissues examined.

Moderate:

'Procedures on animals as a result of which the animals are likely to experience short-term moderate pain, suffering or distress, or long-lasting mild pain, suffering or distress as well as procedures that are likely to cause moderate impairment of the well-being or general condition of the animals shall be classified as "moderate"'.

Example: major surgery under general anaesthesia, such as organ transplantation, where the animal is allowed to recover and subsequently subjected to multiple additional procedures associated with such surgery. Such experiments may last from a few weeks to several months. The animals will be killed at the end of the study and their organs and tissues examined.

Severe:
'Procedures on animals as a result of which the animals are likely to experience severe pain, suffering or distress, or long-lasting moderate pain, suffering or distress as well as procedures, that are likely to cause severe impairment of the well-being or general condition of the animals shall be classified as "severe"'.
Example: the experimental induction of inflammation of the brain in a group of animals in order to test a new drug against a human disease. The animals are expected to suffer severely as a result of the inflammation of the nervous system, including paralysis, and some may die in extremis before the end of the study. Although researchers may choose to euthanase animals that are moribund, animals that are moribund 'out of hours' will not be euthanased at night nor possibly during weekends due to reduced human supervision on those occasions.

It should be noted that the above classification does not take into account the psychological stress and fear imposed on an animal as a result of its incarceration in a cage (in some cases, in solitary confinement), its inability to move freely, to express normal behaviour and separation from family groups. Studies have shown that routine laboratory procedures, including handling and blood collection, are an additional source of increased stress to the animals (Balcombe 2004). It should also be noted that the killing of an animal in a 'non-recovery' procedure is de facto less significant than using a live animal in a 'mild' procedure, in the context of the severity classification. In other words, taking away an animal's life counts for less than, subjecting an animal to a mild procedure. Finally, the severity classification largely ignores cumulative suffering. For example, a monkey may require several months of forced training in order to correctly perform a cognitive task. The training regimen will entail several hours of restraint in a primate chair five days a week for a period of weeks to months, in combination with periodic food and water deprivation. Once the monkey has completed the training regimen the actual experiment will begin. This could involve invasive brain surgery, either to deliberately destroy selected parts of the brain or else to permanently implant brain electrodes, after which the monkey will spend a few more weeks watching objects on a screen and pushing a button or pressing a lever in order to obtain a reward of a few drops of water or fruit juice. This sort of experiment could be classified as 'moderate' rather than 'severe' by the researcher, if the training regimen and the actual experiment are seen as consecutive, rather than cumulative events.

The distinction between mild and moderate or moderate and severe categories may be blurred. A subjective assessment by an animal researcher to 'down grade' an animal experiment into a lesser category of suffering will in turn increase the likelihood of ethical approval by the institutional Animal Welfare and Ethical Review Body.

The Nature and Prevalence of Animal Abuse in Science

Although there are at least nine different ways in which animals are used in science (Shanks 2009) this section will focus on what are arguably the two biggest categories, which together account for the vast majority of animal experiments, namely fundamental research (aka basic or 'curiosity driven' research) and regulatory toxicology. In 2014, the EU produced its Seventh statistical report detailing the number of animals used in research by EU member states in 2011 (with the exception of France, which provided 2010 statistics), which totalled nearly 12 million animals (European Commission 2013). Fundamental research collectively accounted for 64.9 % of the total while regulatory toxicology and quality control collectively accounted for 22.7 % of the total (see Fig. 1).

Regulatory Toxicology

While the use of animals to test pharmaceutical drugs is regulated by the US FDA and the EU EMA, the safety of other substances, such as pesticides and industrial chemicals is regulated by the Organisation for Economic Co-operation and Development [OECD]. Their Test Guidelines represent a collection of internationally agreed test methods used by government, industry and independent laboratories (OECD 2015a). These test guidelines were developed in 1981 and serve all OECD member and partner countries. Section 4 of the list of test guidelines describes the actual animal procedures. These include acute poisoning tests (oral, dermal and

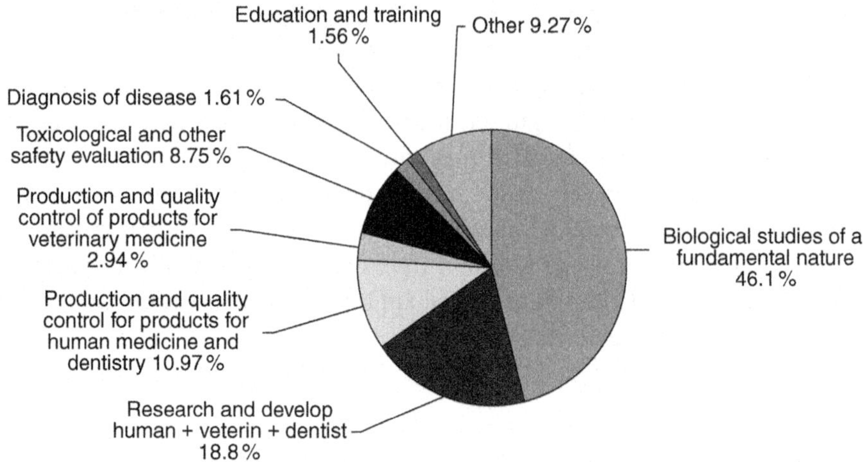

Fig. 1 Purpose of animal experiments in 2011, as reported to the EU in 2014

inhalation toxicity that may last from several hours up to 14 days), chronic (repeated dose) poisoning tests that last 90 days, as well as tests to establish skin irritancy, skin sensitisation, eye irritation, reproductive toxicity studies, carcinogenicity studies and more.

As an example, Test Guideline 423 (Section 4 - one of the Acute Oral toxicity methods) requires administering the test substance to female rats in a single dose by gavage using a stomach tube:

> Three animals are used for each step. The dose level to be used as the starting dose is selected from one of four fixed levels, 5, 50, 300 and 2000 mg/kg body weight. The starting dose level should be that which is most likely to produce mortality in some of the dosed animals. Animals are observed individually after dosing at least once during the first 30 minutes, periodically during the first 24 hours, with special attention given during the first four hours, and daily thereafter, for a total of 14 days, except where they need to be removed from the study and humanely killed for animal welfare reasons or are found dead. (OECD 2015b).

The above Test Guideline is one of a series of toxicity tests aimed at reducing the number of animals used per procedure and was developed to help replace the 'median lethal dose' or LD50 for a substance, which is the dose required to kill half the number of a test population after a specified time (Gribaldo et al. 2005). This policy is in line with Directive 2010/63/EU, which promotes the 3Rs concept of 'replacement, reduction, refinement' of animal experiments wherever possible. Although the directive stipulates that non-animal replacement methods should be used whenever possible, in reality this is almost impossible to enforce, for several reasons. The first is that the European Commission relies on industry to voluntarily adopt approved non-animal replacement methods. For commercial reasons it is often easier for industry to continue to submit 'tried and trusted' animal data to the regulatory authorities, rather than change old habits or develop new methods. The second reason is that national governments have no real incentive, to oblige industry to adopt non-animal replacement methods. The third reason is that animal protection organisations generally lack the resources to challenge industry in the courtroom.

Despite these seemingly insurmountable obstacles, an exceptional success story illustrates the formula required to motivate industry to replace animal experiments. The LD50 test traditionally used in the potency testing of Botox by its manufacturer, Allergan, was replaced by a completely cell-based non-animal test method in 2011. This was the culmination of a 10-year public awareness campaign waged by the Humane Society of the United States (2011). The key to success was public opinion, based on the fact that Botox has a cosmetic application, which is what brought it into public view. Millions of mice have thus been spared a cruel death. Apart from this rare example, industry is certainly guilty of animal abuse in the form of corporate inertia in the field of regulatory toxicology. The example of Botox is an incisive illustration that the biggest obstacle to the replacement of animal tests in industry is, often, not a lack of technology but a lack of will to either develop new methods or to adopt already approved non-animal methods (Menache 2012a).

A recent example of corporate inertia in industry was flagged by Dr Thomas Hartung, a former director of the European Centre for the Validation of Alternative Methods [ECVAM] (European Union Reference Laboratory for alternatives to animal testing [EURL-ECVAM] 2012). Hartung described as a 'missed opportunity' the fact that 400,000 rabbits are still being used worldwide each year as living test tubes although a recognised non-animal replacement method exists (Hartung 2015). The non-animal method has been available to industry since 2009 but continues to be ignored by large sectors of industry. This example illustrates once again the inability or lack of will by governments to enforce legislation concerning the replacement of animal experiments. Significantly, Hartung resigned from ECVAM in 2008, citing a lack of support by industry to develop alternatives to the use of animals. In addition, a continued lack of funding by the European Commission means that alternative methods successfully reviewed by ECVAM are required to wait in line to be processed by regulatory authorities

(AltTox 2008). Since the overall procedure of validation, peer review and regulatory acceptance can take up to seven years on average to complete, it is perhaps unsurprising that companies are not enthusiastic to embark on such projects and prefer to rely on animal data (Center for Alternatives to Animal Testing 2009). This sad situation is also counterproductive for innovative projects that could accelerate the replacement of animal use, since a state-of-the-art test method submitted for validation today may find itself already out of date when it finally becomes available after a period of seven long years (Bottini 2007).

Fundamental Research

Fundamental (or basic) research is defined by the OECD (1963) as:

> Experimental or theoretical work undertaken primarily to acquire new knowledge of phenomena and observable facts, without any particular application or use in view; It is usually undertaken by scientists who may set their own agenda and to a large extent organise their own work.

Although fundamental research is primarily curiosity driven, researchers will justify their use of animals by claiming some possible benefit for human health (Greek and Greek 2010). Indeed, most fundamental research involving animals would not receive funding otherwise, as most EU citizens (68 %) are opposed to the use of animals in curiosity driven research, according to the largest EC survey of its kind published in 2006 (Citizen's questionnaire on the revision of Directive 86/609/EEC on the protection of animals used for experimental and other scientific purposes—Question 22).

Fundamental research is de facto almost immune to the principle of 'replacement' (within the context of the 3Rs principle of 'replacement, reduction and refinement') embodied in Directive 2010/63/EU. Unlike regulatory toxicology, where there are usually clearly defined end points, fundamental research is hypothesis-driven, where the researcher may or may not obtain a result. Whereas animal use is still a legal requirement in the pharmaceutical and the chemical industry, there is no legal obligation to use animals in fundamental research. Provided that a researcher can justify the animal study within the context of the 3Rs and obtain the necessary funding, there is very little scope for replacement of animals in fundamental research as will be explained. Following are a few examples to illustrate this point.

Example 1. Mother-Infant Separation in Monkeys

Between 1957 and 1963, the US animal researcher Harry Harlow and his associates studied the effects of maternal deprivation in macaque monkeys (Harlow et al. 1965). In these experiments baby rhesus monkeys were removed from their mothers in order to observe the effects of partial and total social isolation. Some of the monkeys were kept in solitary confinement for up to 15 years. The motivation for these studies was the WHO *Maternal Care and Mental Health* report published in 1951, which set out the maternal deprivation hypothesis (Bowlby 1951). Harlow began his studies of behaviour of non-human primates in the 1940s. Initially the studies were largely observational and based on cognitive tasks. In the late 1940s, Harlow began surgically removing parts of the brain of his monkey subjects to see to what extent the brain damage impaired their cognitive and behavioural abilities. One such study is titled 'Discrimination learning by normal and brain operated monkeys' (Warren and Harlow 1952). Despite severe criticism of Harlow's work both by some of his peers and the animal protection community, maternal deprivation studies in monkeys continue to receive funding and ethical approval and have been published as recently as 2009 and 2010 (Law et al. 2009a, 2009b; Arabadzisz et al. 2010).

Example 2. Desensitization of the Glans Penis and Sexual Behaviour in Cats

In the 1960s, Dr Lester Aronson at the American Museum of Natural History conducted invasive research on the sexual behaviour of cats with a research grant from the National Institute of Child Health and Human Development (a member of the US National Institutes of Health, the principal government funding agency for medical research). A Freedom of Information Act request revealed that Aronson, together with his assistant Madeline Cooper, chronicled 15 years of experiments in which the two had mutilated cats in order to observe the effects on the behaviour of the animals (Singer 1998; Aronson and Cooper 1967). As with the example of Botox, it was once again public outcry and public opinion that put an end to these animal experiments, all of which had obtained ethical approval according to NIH guidelines.

The following, more recent examples, are intended to illustrate the point that not much has changed since the 1960s and that fundamental research involving severe animal suffering invariably obtains ethical approval because of a scientific culture that both encourages and rewards curiosity driven research.

Example 3. Foot Shock and Fear

A review published in 2015 entitled 'Electric foot shock stress: a useful tool in neuropsychiatric studies' sums up the 'usefulness' of the technique thus:

> foot shocks of varying intensity produce behavioral and neurochemical changes reflecting depression, anxiety, and post-traumatic stress disorder (PTSD) in humans. Animals generally do not habituate to foot shocks in comparison to other stressors, including loud noise, bright light, and hot and cold temperatures. (Bali et al. 2015).

Example 4. Sleep Deprivation and Manic Behaviour

A study published in 2008 demonstrated, according to the authors, that sleep deprivation or exposure to aggressive cage mates resulted in mice that show behaviour similar to that seen in people with manic bipolar disorder. According to the authors, this mouse model would be useful to study the efficacy of new antimanic and mood stabiliser drugs (Benedetti et al. 2008).

Example 5. Brain Recordings in Awake Behaving Monkeys

In this study published in 2015, two adult rhesus monkeys underwent surgery to prepare them for awake-fMRI experiments. Each animal was implanted with an MRI-compatible headpost secured to the skull with ceramic screws, plastic strips and bone cement (Ortiz-Rios et al. 2015). The monkeys were trained to lie in sphinx position in a specially adapted primate chair placed inside a double-walled acoustic chamber and were trained to wear headphone equipment. In addition, the animals were required to fix their vision on a red spot while waiting for a sound signal indicating that they needed to look to the left or the right. The monkeys were rewarded with a few drops of fruit juice only when they performed the task well enough.

Within the animal research community, the use of food and water deprivation is a common and accepted method as a means of motivating animals, particularly non-human primates, to perform repetitive cognitive tasks against their will (Prescott et al. 2010). Monkey experiments involving water deprivation were reported on German National Television in 2014, following an undercover investigation at a leading EU neuroscience laboratory (the Max Planck Institute for Biological Cybernetics in Tübingen, Germany). The Max Planck Society responded to the release of the film by commissioning an 'independent expert investigation' led by Professor Stefan Treue, Head of the German Primate Centre, who subsequently attested that the Institute's employees exercised great care in the treatment of the animals and that he could find no indication that the animals had been neglected (Max Planck Society 2014).

Animal Abuse in Light of Current Science

People today have a choice between purchasing cosmetics tested or not tested ('cruelty free') on animals. However, in the case of pharmaceutical drugs, there is no such choice since all medical products undergo animal testing by law. Similarly, proponents of fundamental research who use animals insist that human medical cures will not be possible without some animal experimentation. In the face of authoritative assertions made by respected scientists and professors, most members of society accept some animal research as being a 'necessary evil'. This theme is aptly summed up by a quote in the journal *Nature*:

> In the contentious world of animal research, one question surfaces time and again: how useful are animal experiments as a way to prepare for trials of medical treatments in humans? The issue is crucial, as public opinion is behind animal research only if it helps develop better drugs. Consequently, scientists defending animal experiments insist they are essential for safe clinical trials, whereas animal-rights activists vehemently maintain that they are useless (Giles 2006).

The public debate surrounding vivisection has traditionally been portrayed to the public as 'science versus animal rights' or even as 'scientists versus terrorists'. Until fairly recently, the issue of animal suffering was purely an ethical and moral one, summed up in the words of utilitarian philosopher Jeremy Bentham: 'The question is not, can they reason? Nor, can they talk? But, can they suffer?' (Bentham 1823). Powerful as these moral arguments may be, they cannot on their own convince society that humans should abandon medical progress for altruistic reasons. By the same token, the extension of racism and sexism to 'speciesism' (a term coined in 1970 by psychologist Richard Ryder), however logical in terms of moral philosophy, still falls short of the mark

(Ryder 1970). Just as racism and sexism represent the unlawful subjugation of one group by another, so 'speciesism' illegitimately imparts greater moral rights on humans compared with non-humans. This moral construct is frequently used by animal researchers to justify the infliction of animal suffering. If, in addition, however, there was a convincing scientific argument that animal-based research is largely useless and perhaps even counter-productive then we would have a very different debate on our hands.

Recent critiques of animal based research have begun to surface both from individual scientists and within the medical establishment itself. An editorial published in the British Medical Journal in June 2014 bluntly asks the question 'How predictive and productive is animal research?' (Godlee 2014) The editorial echoes an article that appears in the same publication, entitled 'Is animal research sufficiently evidence based to be a cornerstone of biomedical research?' (Pound 2014). Surprisingly, animal research has not been subjected to the rigors of evidence-based medicine. In contrast, human medicine is increasingly evidence-based as can be seen by the efforts of the Cochrane Collaboration, which conducts 'systematic reviews of primary research in human health care and health policy, and are internationally recognised as the highest standard in evidence-based health care resources' (Cochrane Collaboration n.d.).

Of the few systematic reviews that have been conducted to compare treatment outcomes in laboratory animals with outcomes in clinical trials, animal experiments demonstrate poor human clinical and toxicological utility (Knight 2007; Greek and Menache 2013). Equally bizarre is the fact that, while modern non-animal test methods are required to undergo a rigorous process of validation before they can be considered for regulatory approval, animal tests have never been the subject of a formal validation process as attested by the US FDA in 1998: 'Most of the animal tests we accept have never been validated. They evolved over the past 20 years and the FDA is comfortable with them' (O'Connor 1998). Validation is the process whereby the reliability and relevance of a procedure are established for a specific purpose (Balls and Clothier 2009).

While animal use is gradually declining in some sectors of regulatory toxicology, the opposite trend can be seen in academic institutions, where fundamental research is largely conducted. These trends are clearly documented in the UK (Home Office 2014). A total of 1,133,203 animals were used under the category 'fundamental biological research'. In addition 2,101,670 animals were used under the category 'breeding of Genetically Modified (GM) or Harmful Mutant (HM) animals'. In comparison, a total of 375,000 animals were used in regulatory toxicology. Based on these figures it is evident that the production of GM animals is the biggest contributor to the overall number of animals used in the UK in 2013, which stands at 4,017,758. The production of GM animals is responsible for many defective, dead or surplus animals and constitutes one of the worst forms of animal abuse in science today. Almost all GM animals are mice. Manipulation of their genes invariably does the animal more harm than good. Some GM mice will die before they are born, others will die shortly after birth due to defective lungs or cleft palate, which means they are unable to drink their mother's milk. Some GM mice are deliberately bred to have a 'harmful phenotype' which means that they will be physically, biochemically or mentally damaged. They will then be subjected to more suffering when they are used in further experiments (Stallwood 2013). According to official Swiss statistics, out of a total of 780,071 GM mice housed in animal laboratories, only 149,683 (19.2 %) were used in actual experiments during that year (Swiss Federal Food Safety and Veterinary Office 2014). Some scientists have called for efforts to reduce the enormous wastage of surplus GM animals but the animal research community as a whole appears to be slow to heed the call (International Society for Transgenic Technologies BLOG 2013).

The vast majority of GM animals are destined for fundamental research. Thus, if we combine the number of animals used in fundamental biological research and the number of GM animals used in breeding, we obtain a figure close to three million animals, which represents 75 % of all animals used in the UK in 2013. These figures clearly illustrate the increase in animal use in fundamental research, which should raise the question, where is the evidence that fundamental research, using animals, is effective in developing new drugs and new cures for people? In the 1970s, the researchers Comroe and Dripps (1976) conducted a landmark study to determine the relative contributions of fundamental and clinical research to important medical advances (Comroe 1976). In their published report they concluded that 62 % of key articles that led to advances were the result of fundamental research. The study by Comroe and Dripps is often quoted in support of increased funding for basic biomedical research (Pound et al. 2004). However, a subsequent review of the report by Grant and colleagues found that it was 'not repeatable, reliable, or valid and thus is an insufficient evidence base for increased expenditure on basic biomedical research' (Grant et al. 2003). More recently, other researchers have questioned the translation rate of fundamental research into clinically useful treatments. A study by Contopoulos-Ioannidis and colleagues looked at the translation rate of 25,000 fundamental research articles to see how many had led to a clinical application (Contopoulos-Ioannidis et al. 2003). Their study was further analysed by Crowley, who published the findings as follows:

> Of the 25,000 articles searched, about 500 (2 per cent) contained some potential claim to future applicability in humans, about 100 (0.4 per cent) resulted in a clinical trial, and, according to the authors, only 1 (0.004 per cent) led to the development of a clinically useful class of drugs (angiotensin-converting enzyme inhibitors) in the 30 years following their publication of the basic science finding (Crowley 2003).

What is equally intriguing is the fact that the development of this class of drugs did not depend on animal experiments. Rather, they were the result of rational drug design (Kellici et al. 2015).

The Current Ethical Review Process Is Complicit in Animal Abuse

Article 27 of Directive 2010/63/EU makes provision for the establishment of an Animal Welfare and Ethical Review Body [AWERB] to oversee institutional animal experiments. One of the tasks of the AWERB is 'to advise the staff on the application of the requirement of replacement, reduction and refinement and keep it informed of technical and scientific developments concerning the application of that requirement'.

Article 26 of the directive stipulates that the AWERB 'shall include at least the person or persons responsible for the welfare of the animals and, in the case of a user, a scientific member', as well as receiving input from a designated veterinarian. There is no official requirement to co-opt representatives from the public or independent scientific experts. This is an important omission in the directive as it may exclude public participation in the ethical review process. Although most AWERBs do contain an ethicist or a philosopher, these individuals are not a substitute for public representatives or independent experts who are knowledgeable on the use of replacements to animal experiments. In a best case scenario where an AWERB does contain a public representative or a member of an animal protection organisation, that individual will automatically be in a minority position and can expect to be systematically outvoted on major issues (Ashby 2012).

The current ethical review process is an almost watertight system for approval of any animal study proposal, not only because of the imbalance in the composition of the AWERB, but also because of the framework imposed by the directive. Once an animal researcher has adequately addressed the 3Rs, there is very little to stop an animal experiment from going ahead. As discussed above, the vast majority of experiments will be of a fundamental nature, for which there is rarely any scope for replacement.

What almost all proposals for fundamental research share is a common formula: the researcher will state that disease X affects a large proportion of the world's population; that there is currently no known cure for this disease; that his or her laboratory has developed an animal model of the disease; that the disease is complex and cannot be studied in simple cell culture; and that the disease must, therefore, be studied in a living animal. There is no scope within the 3Rs principle to question whether the animal model is relevant to the human genome (Greek et al. 2012). Fundamental research is of itself sufficient justification. To paraphrase the quote by Jeremy Bentham, 'The question is not, can the animal experiment be replaced? But, does it actually work?'

In ignoring current science the ethical review process is complicit in animal abuse. Few animal researchers are willing to engage in scientific debate with experts who consider the animal model to be invalid as a modality for predicting how a drug or a disease will affect human beings. Some of the most powerful criticisms of the animal model have recently been voiced by animal researchers. For example, Seok and colleagues published an article entitled 'Genomic responses in mouse models poorly mimic human inflammatory disease' (Seok et al. 2013). Another paper published in the journal Nature in 2014 clearly shows that mice and men are genetically far further apart than was previously thought. Although mice and humans share most of their genes, the way those genes are regulated is very different in the two species, thus calling into question the role that rodents play in medical research (Yue et al. 2014). These articles and others (for example 'Of Mice and Not Men: Differences between Mouse and Human Immunology') (Mestas and Hughes 2004) are highly significant for two reasons. First, it is the mouse that bears the brunt of animal abuse and suffering in science in terms of sheer numbers; and second, if the immune system of the mouse is not predictive of what happens in humans, then almost all mouse research becomes irrelevant since the immune system plays an absolutely key role in disease research, from vaccines to arthritis and from wound healing to multiple sclerosis.

In the competitive world of science, in order to survive one must 'publish or perish'. In this context, many animal researchers tend to put their careers well ahead of animal suffering. Thus, there is a tendency to increase the size of the test group (for example using 10 animals per group when 8 would suffice for statistical purposes). Scientific journals require that 'Experiments generating data that are essential to support any conclusion of the study must be performed more than once and must be repeated a sufficient number of times to demonstrate reproducibility' (The Journal of Experimental Medicine 2015). These instructions may lead researchers to repeat tests in triplicate, simply in order to increase the chance of publication of their study, even though a test in duplicate is the norm. This would not be an issue when dealing with test tube experiments. However, when the test in question involves living animals subjected to incarceration and invasive procedures, this clearly constitutes animal abuse in science from an animal welfare perspective and evokes the earlier quote by Giles (2006).

Conclusion: A paradigm Shift Is Needed to End Animal Abuse in Science

A strong connection has been found between domestic violence and animal abuse. This link is so well established that profilers routinely use animal cruelty reports in their assessment of criminals (for example, Animal Legal Defense Fund 2013; American Humane Association n.d. and American Society for the Prevention of Cruelty to Animals 2016). Acts of wanton cruelty towards animals are generally not tolerated in civil society. How much animal abuse in the name of science should civil society be prepared to tolerate? It is disturbing to see to what lengths some animal researchers will go in order to devise ways to induce stress, anxiety, depression, helplessness, aggression and even obsessive compulsive behaviour in their animal subjects (Senay 1966; McKinney and Bunney 1969; Dinsmoor et al. 1971; Bliss and Zwanziger 1966). The 'ingenuity' of the animal researcher is generally proportionate to the amount of physical and psychological animal suffering induced in the test subjects. Rats and mice, because of their convenient size, are most commonly used in specific behavioural tests, such as the despair test (or forced swim test) and the tail suspension test, to assess the efficacy of psychiatric drugs intended for human use (Menache 2012b).

Some researchers have openly expressed the moral conflict they face when using living animals, especially non-human primates in experiments (Barnes 1990). These researchers acknowledge the negative effects of family separation, isolation and boredom, as well as the pain and suffering inflicted on the animals during the experiments. Several studies have indicated that the chimpanzee has a sense of self and self-awareness

(Gallup 1970; Kaneko and Tomonaga 2011), which has led scientists, particularly behaviourists, to suggest that chimpanzees should be afforded special protection from pain, suffering and incarceration (Goodall 1987). In addition, studies of mice and rats, suggest that they too possess awareness of self and even subtle 'human' qualities associated with empathy and social joy (Panksepp 2007).

Animal abuse in science will continue for as long as society remains ignorant of the historical and legal foundations of animal experimentation. In addition to the ethical debate, there is a strong scientific case to be made against animal based research in an era of the human genome. The biggest obstacle to the replacement of animals in laboratories is not a lack of innovative technology. Rather, it is the logistical challenge of mass communicating a complex message to politicians and policy makers, most of whom do not have a background in the life sciences. Ultimately, this crucial debate will not go away until it is resolved in a transparent manner that embraces both societal norms and current scientific evidence.

References

Aird, W. C. (2011). Discovery of the cardiovascular system: from Galen to William Harvey. *Journal of Thromb Haemost, 9*(Suppl 1), 118–129.

AltTox (2008). *Thomas Hartung leaving ECVAM.* http://alttox.org/thomas-hartung-leaving-ecvam/. Accessed 25 August 2015.

American Humane Association (n.d.). *Facts about animal abuse & domestic violence.* http://www.americanhumane.org/interaction/support-the-bond/fact-sheets/animal-abuse-domestic-violence.html. Accessed 25 August 2015.

American Medical Association [AMA]: Board of Trustees (1946a). *Minutes of the May 1946 meeting, (ACHRE No. IND-072595-A), 156–157.* AMA Archive, Chicago, IL.

AMA: Board of Trustees (1946b). *Minutes of the 19 September 1946 meeting, AMA Archive, Chicago, Illinois (ACHRE No. IND-072595-A), 51–52.* AMA Archives, Chicago, IL.

Animal Legal Defense Fund (2013). *No boundaries for abusers: the link between cruelty to animals and violence toward humans.* http://aldf.org/resources/when-your-companion-animal-has-been-harmed/no-boundaries-for-abusers-the-link-between-cruelty-to-animals-and-violence-toward-humans/. Accessed 25 August 2015.

American Society for the Prevention of Cruelty to Animals (2016). *Domestic violence and animal cruelty.* https://www.aspca.org/fight-cruelty/report-animal-cruelty/domestic-violence-and-animal-cruelty. Accessed 25 August 2015.

Arabadzisz, D., Diaz-Heijtz, R., Knuesel, I., Weber, E., Pilloud, S., Dettling, A. C., et al. (2010). Primate early life stress leads to long-term mild hippocampal decreases in corticosteroid receptor expression. *Biol Psychiatry*, 67(11), 1106–1109.

Aronson, L. R., & Cooper, M. L. (1967). Penile spines of the domestic cat: their endocrine-behaviour relations. *Anat Rec*, 157(1), 71–78.

Ashby, M. & Menache, A. (2012). The composition of animal ethics committees needs to change. *BMJ, 345*, e7627.

Bali, A., & Jaggi, A. S. (2015). Electric foot shock stress: a useful tool in neuropsychiatric studies. *Rev Neurosci.* https://www.degruyter.com/view/j/revneuro.2015.26.issue-6/revneuro-2015-0015/revneuro-2015-0015.xml. doi: 10.1515/revneuro-2015-0015. [Epub ahead of print].

Balls, M., & Clothier, R. (2009). FRAME and the validation process. *Altern Lab Anim, 37*(6), 631–640.

Barnes, D. (1990, May 15–16). The use of nonhuman animals in psychobiological and behavioral research. In N.B. Natelson & M.J. Cohen (Eds.), *Proceedings from future medical research without the use of animals: facing the challenge.* Tel Aviv, Israel.

Benedetti, F., Fresi, F., Maccioni, P., & Smeraldi, E. (2008). Behavioural sensitization to repeated sleep deprivation in a mice model of mania. *Behav Brain Res, 187*(2), 221–227.

Bowlby, J. (1951). *Maternal care and mental health.* Geneva: World Health Organisation. http://apps.who.int/iris/handle/10665/40724. Accessed 25 August 2015.

Balcombe, J. P., Barnard, N. D., & Sandusky, C. (2004). Laboratory routines cause animal stress. *Contemp Top Lab Anim Sci, 43*(6), 42–51.

Bentham, J. (1823). *Introduction to the principles of morals and legislation.* 2nd edition. Chapter 17, footnote.

Bernard, C., & Greene, H.C. (1957). *An introduction to the study of experimental medicine.* New York: Dover Publications, Inc.

Bliss, E. L., & Zwanziger, J. (1966). Brain amines and emotional stress. *J Psychiatr Res., 4*, 189–198.

Bottini, A. A., Amcoff, P., & Hartung, T. (2007). Food for thought…on globalisation of alternative methods. *ALTEX, 24*, 255–261.

Center for Alternatives to Animal Testing (2009). *Evidence based toxicology* (powerpoint presentation page 10) John Hopkins University. http://www.opentox.org/data/documents/development/meeting/OTUS-CAAT. Accessed 25 August 2015.

Cochrane Collaboration (n.d.). *What is Cochrane evidence and how can it help you?* http://www.cochrane.org/. Accessed 25 August 2015.

Comroe, J. H., & Dripps, R. D. (1976). Scientific basis for the support of biomedical science. *Science, 192*(4235), 105–111.

Contopoulos-Ioannidis, D. G., Nitzani, E., & Ioannidis, J. P. (2003). Translation of highly promising basic science research into clinical applications. *Am J Med, 114*(6), 477–484.

Cox, F. E. G. (2002). History of human parasitology. *Clin Microbiol Rev, 15*(4), 595–612.

Crawford, A. Z., Patel, D. V., & McGhee, C. N. J. (2013). A brief history of corneal transplantation: From ancient to modern. *Oman J Ophthalmol, 6*(Suppl 1), S12–S17.

Crowley, W. F. Jr. (2003). Translation of basic research into useful treatments: how often does it occur? *Am J Med, 114*(6), pp. 503–505.

Dinsmoor, J. A., Bonbright, J. C. Jr., & Lilie, D. R. (1971). A controlled comparison of drug effects on escape from conditioned aversive stimulation ('anxiety') and from continuous shock. *Psychopharmacologia, 22*, 323–332.

European Commission (2013). *Seventh report on the statistics on the number of animals used for experimental and other scientific purposes in the member states of the European Union.* http://eur-lex.europa.eu/LexUriServ/LexUriServ.do?uri=COM:2013:0859:FIN:EN:PDF. Accessed 25 August 2015.

European Commission (2010). *Directive 2010/63/EU of the European Parliament and of the Council of 22 September 2010 on the protection of animals used for scientific purposes.* http://eur-lex.europa.eu/legal-content/EN/TXT/?uri=celex:32010L0063. Accessed 25 August 2015.

European Commission (2006). *Results of questionnaire for the general public on the revision of Directive 86/609/EEC on the protection of animals used for experimental and other scientific purposes.* http://ec.europa.eu/environment/chemicals/lab_animals/pdf/results_citizens.pdf. Accessed 25 August 2015.

European Economic Community (1986). *Council Directive of 24 November 1986 on the approximation of laws, regulations and administrative provisions of the Member States regarding the protection of animals used for experimental and other scientific purposes* (86/609/EEC). http://ec.europa.eu/food/fs/aw/aw_legislation/scientific/86-609-eec_en.pdf. Accessed 25 August 2015.

European Medicines Agency (2008). *Guideline on Repeated Dose Toxicity.* http://www.ema.europa.eu/docs/en_GB/document_library/Scientific_guideline/2009/09/WC500003103.pdf. Accessed 25 August 2015.

European Union Reference Laboratory for alternatives to animal testing [EURL-ECVAM] (2012). *European Union reference laboratory for alternatives to animal testing.* https://eurl-ecvam.jrc.ec.europa.eu/. Accessed 25 August 2015.

Gallup, G. G. Jr. (1970). Chimpanzees: self-recognition. *Science*, 167, 86–87.

Giles, J. (2006). Animal experiments under fire for poor design. *Nature, 444*, (7122), 981.

Godlee, F. (2014). How predictive and productive is animal research? *BMJ, 348*, g3719.

Goodall, J. (1987, May 17). A plea for the chimps. *New York Times Magazine*, pp. 108–110.

Grant, J., Green, L., & Mason, B. (2003). *From bedside to bench: Comroe and Dripps revisited.* London: Brunel University, Health Economics Research Group [HERG] (Research Report No 30).

Greek, R., & Greek, J. (2010). 'Is the use of sentient animals in basic research justifiable?. *Philos Ethics Humanit Med,* 5, 14.

Greek, R., & Menache, A. (2013). Systematic reviews of animal models: methodology versus epistemology. *Int J Med Sci, 10*(3), 206–221.

Greek, R., Menache, A., & Rice, M. (2012). Animal models in an era of personalized medicine. *Personalized Medicine, 9*(1), 47–64.

Greek, R., Pippus, A., Hansen L. A. (2012). The Nuremberg code subverts human health and safety by requiring animal modelling. *BMC Med Ethics, 13,* 16.

Gribaldo, L., Gennari, A., Blackburn, K., Clemedson, C., Deguercy, A., Meneguz, A., et al. (2005). *Acute toxicity.* http://ec.europa.eu/consumers/sectors/cosmetics/files/doc/antest/%285%29_chapter_3/1_acute_tox_en.pdf. Accessed 25 August 2015.

Harlow, H. F., Dodsworth, R. O., & Harlow, M. K. (1965). Total social isolation in monkeys. *Proc Natl Acad Sci, 54,* 90–97.

Hartung, T. (2015). The human whole blood pyrogen test – lessons learned in twenty years. *ALTEX, 32*(2), 79–100.

Home Office (2014). *Statistics of scientific procedures on living animals, Great Britain 2013.* https://www.gov.uk/government/statistics/statistics-of-scientific-procedures-on-living-animals-great-britain-2013. Accessed 25 August 2015.

Humane Society of the United States (2011). *Animal-free protocol developed for Botox.* http://www.humanesociety.org/news/press_releases/2011/06/allergan_botox_testing_062711.html. Accessed 25 August 2015.

International Society for Transgenic Technologies BLOG (2013). *Workshop report: animals bred, but not used in experiments.* http://transtechsociety.org/blog/?tag=surplus-animals. Accessed 25 August 2015.

Ivy, A. C. (1946) *Report on war crimes of a medical nature committed in Germany and elsewhere on German nationals and the nationals of occupied countries by the Nazi regime during World War II.* This report was not published, but it is available at the National Library of Medicine. A copy also exists in the AMA Archive (ACHRE No. DOD-063094-A). 1946.

Joutsivio, T. (1997). Vesalius and De humani corporis fabrica: Galen's errors and the change of anatomy in the sixteenth century. *Hippokrates (Helsinki),* pp. 98–112.

Kaneko, T., & Tomonaga, M. (2011). The perception of self-agency in chimpanzees (Pan troglodytes). *Proc Biol Sci, 278*(1725), 3694–3702.

Kellici, T. F., Tzakos, A. G., & Mavromoustakos, T. (2015). Rational drug design and synthesis of molecules targeting the angiotensin II Type 1 and Type 2 Receptors. *Molecules,* 20(3), 3868–3897.

Knight, A. (2007). Systematic reviews of animal experiments demonstrate poor human clinical and toxicological utility. *Altern Lab Anim, 35*(6), 641–659.

Lafollette, H., & Shanks, N. (1997). Animal experimentation: the legacy of Claude Bernard. *International Studies in the Philosophy of Science,* 8(1994)(3), 195–210. http://www.tandfonline.com/doi/abs/10.1080/02698599408573495.

Law, A. J., Pei, Q., Feldon, J., Pryce, C. R., & Harrison, P. J. (2009). Gene expression in the anterior cingulate cortex and amygdala of adolescent marmoset monkeys following parental separations in infancy. *Neuropsychopharmacology*, 12(6), 761–772.

Law, A. J., Pei, Q., Walker, M., Gordon-Andrews, H., Weickert, C. S., Feldon, J., et al. (2009). Early paternal deprivation in the marmoset monkey produces long-term changes in hippocampal expression of genes involved in synaptic plasticity and implicated in modd disorder. *Neuropsychopharmacology, 34*(6), 1381–1394.

Lee, W. M. (2003). Drug-induced hepatotoxicity. *N Engl J Med, 349*, 474–485.

Max Planck Society (2014). *Max Planck society statement dated 18 September*. http://www.mpg.de/8412572/statement. Accessed 25 August 2015.

McKinney, W.T. Jr., & Bunney, W.E. Jr. (1969). Animal model of depression. I. Review of evidence: implications for research. *Arch Gen Psychiatry*, 21, 240–248.

Menache, A. (2012a). Trends in animal use and replacement in the 'Three I's' of industry. *ATLA*, 40, 20–21.

Menache, A. (2012b). Are animal models relevant in modern psychiatry? *Psychiatric Times*, 29(3), 1–9.

Mestas, J. & Hughes, C. C. (2004). Of mice and not men: differences between mouse and human immunology, *J Immunol, 172*(5), 2731–2738.

O'Connor, A. (1998). *Office of science FDA* in personal communication to Andre Menache.

Organisation for Economic Co-operation and Development [OECD] (2015a). *Guidelines for the testing of chemicals*. http://www.oecd.org/chemicalsafety/testing/oecdguidelinesforthetestingofchemicals.htm (home page). Accessed 25 August 2015.

OECD (2015b). *Guidelines for the testing of chemicals: section 4*. http://www.oecd-ilibrary.org/docserver/download/9742301e.pdf?expires=1440697078&id=id&accname=guest&checksum=DD7FF73612DC8DAD84317246F0871261. Accessed 25 August 2015.

OECD (1963). *The measurement of scientific and technical activities: proposed standard practice for surveys of research and development*. Paris: Organisation for Economic Cooperation and Development.

Ortiz-Rios, M., Kusmierek, P., DeWitt, I., Archakov, D., Azevedo, F. A. C., Sams, M., et al. (2015). Functional MRI vocalization-processing network in the macaque brain. *Front Neurosci, 9*, 113.

Panksepp, J. (2007). Neuroevolutionary sources of laughter and social joy: modeling primal human laughter in laboratory rats. *Behav Brain Res, 182*, 231–244.

Pound, P. (2014). Is animal research sufficiently evidence based to be a cornerstone of biomedical research? *BMJ, 348*, g3387.

Pound, P., Ebrahim, S., Sandercock, P., Bracken, M. B., & Roberts, I. (2004). Where is the evidence that animal research benefits humans?. *BMJ*, 328(7438), 514–517.

Prescott, M. J., Brown, V. J., Flecknell, P. A., Gaffan, D., Garrod, K., Lemon, R. N., et al. (2010). Refinement of the use of food and fluid control as motivational tools for macaques used in behavioural neuroscience research: Report of a Working Group of the NC3Rs. *J Neu Meth, 193*(2), 167–188.

Russell, W. M. S., & Burch, R. L. (1959). *The principles of humane experimental technique.* Methuen.

Ryder, R. D. (1970). *About: Dr Richard D. Ryder.* http://www.62stockton.com/richard/index.html. Accessed 30 October 2015.

Select Committee on Animals in Scientific Procedures (2001). *Report.* http://www.publications.parliament.uk/pa/ld200102/ldselect/ldanimal/150/15004.htm#a4. Accessed 25 August 2015.

Senay, E.C. (1966). Toward an animal model of depression: a study of separation behavior in dogs. *J Psychiatr, 4*, 65–71.

Seok, J., Warren, S. H., Cuenca, A. G., Mindrinos, M. N., et al. (2013). Genomic responses in mouse models poorly mimic human inflammatory diseases. *Proc Natl Acad Sci USA, 110*(9), 3507–3512.

Shanks, N., Greek, R., & Greek J. (2009). Are animal models predictive for humans? *Philos Ethics Humanit Med, 4*, 2.

Singer, P. (1998). *Ethics into action.* Lanham, MD: Rowman and Littlefield Publishers, Inc., (page 55).

Stallwood, A. (2013). *Science corrupted.* Animal Aid. http://www.animalaid.org.uk/images/pdf/booklets/ScienceCorrupted.pdf. Accessed 25 August 2015.

Swiss Federal Food Safety and Veterinary Office (2014). http://www.blv.admin.ch/themen/tierschutz/00777/index.html?lang=en. Accessed 25 August 2015.

The Journal of Experimental Medicine (2015). *Instructions for authors.* http://jem.rupress.org/site/misc/ifora.xhtml. Accessed 25 August 2015.

United States Department of Agriculture (2013). *Animal Welfare Act.* http://www.aphis.usda.gov/wps/portal/aphis/ourfocus/animalwelfare. Accessed 25 August 2015.

US Food and Drug Administration (2010). International Conference on Harmonisation; Draft Guidance on M3(R2) Nonclinical Safety Studies for the Conduct of Human Clinical Trials and Marketing Authorization for Pharmaceuticals. *Fed Regist 73* (ed. HHSs), 51491–51492. http://www.fda.gov/ScienceResearch/SpecialTopics/RunningClinicalTrials/GuidancesInformationSheetsandNotices/ucm219488.htm. Accessed 25 August 2015.

Warren, J. M., & Harlow, H. F. (1952). Discrimination learning by normal ad brain operated monkeys. *J Genet Psychol, 81*(1), 45–52.

Watson, S. (2009). *Animal testing: issues and ethics.* New York: The Rosen Publishing Group, Inc.

World Medical Association (1964). *Declaration of Helsinki: ethical principles for medical research involving human subjects.* http://www.wma.net/en/30publications/10policies/b3/. Accessed 25 August 2015.

Yue, F., Cheng, Y., Breschi, A.,Vierstra, J., et al. (2014). A comparative encyclopaedia of DNA elements in the mouse genome. *Nature*, 515(7527), 355–364.

André Menache holds degrees in zoology and veterinary medicine. He is a Diplomate of the European College of Animal Welfare and Behavioural Medicine (subspeciality Animal Welfare Science, Ethics and Law) and has served on several animal research ethics committees both within and outside the European Union.

Part VI

The Abuse of Animals by Agents of the State

Harms to Police Dogs: Barking Up the Wrong Tree

Janine Janssen

I also saw the suspect putting his right arm with a large piece of wired glass stuck in it through the smashed window of the front door and subsequently put his head through the hole. I saw that he could see me and my leashed on surveillance dog. I heard him shouting: 'And you bugger off with that fucking dog!' I saw him throwing wired glass at my face (. . .). I felt very much threatened and feared for my life. Then I saw the suspect (. . .) with another piece of glass threatening my colleagues again. Because my colleagues were driven in a corner and had nowhere to go and the suspect continued making stabbing movements and continued to threaten them with the broken glass, I instructed the surveillance dog who was still on leash to attack the suspect. I saw my dog Rex biting the suspect in his right arm and the suspect pulling his arm back into the house again with force. Due to this, the surveillance dog, which weighs forty kilogram and which still had the suspect's arm in his grasp, was partly pulled through the smashed window of the front door (Naeyé 2005).

Introduction

Topics on the welfare of other than human animals (aothas) have taken a prominent place in the political and social debate in the Netherlands. Notable examples are the introduction of an animal police and the debate

J. Janssen (✉)
Avans University of Applied Sciences, 's-Hertogenbosch, The Netherlands
e-mail: janine.janssen@ziggo.nl

J. Maher et al. (eds.), *The Palgrave International Handbook of Animal Abuse Studies*, DOI 10.1057/978-1-137-43183-7_19

on the ban on unstunned slaughter of animals (Janssen 2014). Aothas that play an active part in law enforcement organisations run all sorts of risks affecting their welfare as is described in the passage above. The best known examples of people working with aothas in law enforcement are dog handlers and mounted police officers. Now and again there are pleas in the Dutch political media for harsher punishment for violence used against dogs and horses in the police service, often in the wake of a broader debate on violence used by members of the public against the police (Janssen 2013). However, the question to what extent police work has generally caused damage to aothas is never considered. In this chapter, I will focus on police dogs. What is known about the nature and the prevalence of abuse of and the harms caused to these aothas? And how is this abuse explained and responded to by policy makers?

In *Street-level Bureaucracy* in 1980, Lipsky demonstrated that there is a discrepancy between policymaking and the implementation. Although policy makers are quite capable of writing fantastic plans based on ideas derived from societal and political debate, their instructions will never be concrete enough to provide practitioners with a workable repertoire that fits in every imaginable scenario in everyday occurrences. This implies that the practitioners have to decide for themselves on how they are to carry out their tasks on a daily basis. They have a certain amount of discretionary power at their disposal. That freedom to partly carry out certain policies in accordance with their own views actually makes them policy makers as well. Lipsky, therefore, names them *street-level bureaucrats*. The question now is, if and how dog handlers as street-level bureaucrats give shape to their discretionary power when it comes to the well-being of police dogs, is welfare of aothas an issue for them or are the dogs in this respect barking up the wrong tree? I will try to respond to that question on the basis of a review of literature. Next to that I will use information from interviews with members of the police service. While I was preparing a publication about the first introduction of police dogs in the Netherlands, I came into contact with several dog handlers and other police officers interested in working with dogs (Janssen 2008). Since 2008 to date, I have conducted several informal interviews with dog handlers and other police officers interested in working with dogs from different parts of the Netherlands. Some of these conversations were more in depth than others. I have had in-depth conversations on several occasions with approximately five officers (Janssen 2008, 2013). In the first section, I will consider the literature on the nature and prevalence of abuse of police dogs. Next, I will discuss the way police officers use their discretionary power in order to guarantee the welfare of the dogs they are working with. I then turn to the impressions that I have gathered while interviewing the police officers. Finally, I will propose some lines for further research in order to fill in the gaps in our knowledge about abuse of police dogs.

Police Dogs in Politics, Literature and Research

Missing Link

Virtually, all the political parties in the Netherlands devote attention to welfare of aothas, and there is an animal rights party, the *Party for Animals* (Partij voor de Dieren), that promotes the interests of aothas in the Dutch parliament. In addition, there are numerous animal welfare organisations active with the aim to improve the welfare of aothas (for example, *Bird Protection* (Vogelbescherming) and the *Humane* Society (Dierenbescherming). A number of indicators of animal welfare and animal health have been laid down for policy purposes. However, the report *The State of the Animal* (De staat van het dier) (Leenstra et al. 2011) indicates that it is difficult to measure the status of animal welfare in the Netherlands. At the European level, measurement protocols are being developed to provide more of an insight into the welfare and health of animals, for example, protocols on when and how to measure blood pressure and heart rate. Currently, measuring protocols focus on *the animal environment.* Although a satisfactory living and working environment is important, it cannot guarantee an animal's welfare or health. The authors furthermore state that they focus on domestic animals that are directly subordinate to human animals. Police dogs, however, are not mentioned in the report. In a survey on the views on animal welfare in the Netherlands around a thousand respondents were questioned about the areas in which they had concerns about animal welfare. Nearly a third mentioned the bio-industry, about 20 % livestock transport, another 20 % the care of animals, 10 % cited cruelty to animals while 8 % of the respondents mentioned laboratory animals (Werkman et al. 2007). None mentioned the welfare of aothas active in law enforcement, not even under the category 'other'. In 2010, the *Council of Animal Affairs* in the Netherlands (Raad voor Dierenaangelegenheden, RDA) presented an agenda for the policies on animal welfare. One of the authors' recommendations was that the Dutch government should give an answer to the question of how it is justified that animals are kept in Dutch society. For which purposes and under what circumstances is it acceptable to keep them? In the report, there is no attention whatsoever for aothas, such as police dogs, that play a role in law enforcement. In sum, while the government as well as parliament spend considerable time discussing animal welfare, issues relating to aothas in the law and order sector rarely come up in these debates. How does that affect dog handlers? These *street-level bureaucrats* have to implement the policy on animal welfare within the discretionary power they are provided with, while that policy seems to be missing any specifics in relation to the welfare of police dogs. There is clearly a missing link.

Literature and Research on Police Dogs

The literature on police dogs can be categorised into three areas (Sanders 2006). First, there are manuals that handle aspects of training, domestication and care of these dogs. Police dogs have been used in the Netherlands since 1908 (Janssen 2008). As early as the beginning of the twentieth century, manuals on police dogs were published by and for dog lovers (Kessler 1909; Rothpletz 1910; Van der Mos 1910 and Hössen 1911). In the very beginning, mainly, the dogs themselves were assessed during training and inspections, while nowadays more emphasis is put on interaction and cooperation between dogs and their handlers. The second category focuses mainly on judicial aspects related to the use of police dogs. Naeyé (2005), for example, focuses on the ability and legal right of the Dutch police to use violence and force in relation to the use of surveillance dogs as weapons like truncheons and firearms (2005). From a legal perspective, the surveillance dog is considered to be a weapon more dangerous than a truncheon and less dangerous than a firearm. Internal protocols and guidelines for the deployment and guidance of dog handlers also fit into this second category of the literature on police dogs.

Third, there are publications commending the achievements and successes of police dogs highlighting them with considerable pride. Frequently, reports appear in police publications about the role of police dogs used, for instance, during the arrest of armed suspects or a tribute honouring a valued dog that has died. From around June 2008 through to October 2010, I collected approximately 120 press releases regarding other than human animals by the police of The Hague. About a fifth of these short articles were about the often considered to be heroic work of the police dog. In these articles the names of the dogs are mentioned and they are presented as loyal comrades like the famous TV-dog Lassie. There is a remarkable story about the parents of the 24-year-old Jeroen Dekkers who was murdered in 2004. The story was published in a popular women's magazine called *Linda* in March 2011.

After the violent death of their only son, the parents very much wanted to meet the sniffer dogs that had found their son; and so a meeting was arranged. During that poignant moment, it became apparent that one of the two dogs called Mouse was suffering from back trouble that was so severe that she had to retire. A new home had to be found to provide her with the peaceful retirement she deserved. The parents of Jeroen Dekkers took the dog into their home. 'Mouse is a living memory to our Jeroen', said Jeroen's father. 'They are irredeemably tied to each other although they never knew one another. When she dies we want to have her cremated and put her urn on Jeroen's grave. Till that day I give her a kiss every night before going to bed. Sleep well Mouse.' On 22 February 2012 the Dutch daily *de Volkskrant* reported on the death of Mouse: 'And now, a few weeks later, there is only an urn for Jeroen's parents Bert and Gerda in remembrance of Mouse. And in a little while the urn will have disappeared too and Bert and Gerda will then take Mouse to her last resting place: Jeroen's grave.'

Literature on the tasks of police dogs and their handlers is paradoxical.

Manuals on the training and care of police dogs certainly contain all sorts of advice of animal welfare as well as the emphasis on social relations between aothas and humans, but the aim of these texts is utilitarian. They are not about the aothas themselves but specifically about dogs as tools to be used in a certain type of police work, namely sniffer and/or surveillance work. The dogs are subordinate to humans and are meant to serve their masters or mistresses. That instrumental approach is also expressed in judicial publications that are particularly focused on regulations on the use of police dogs. Police dogs are regarded as objects such as weapons and strictly judicially they are objects and not legal persons. That approach is also apparent in the internal protocols that contain instruction on maintaining the welfare of dogs, such as the care and housing of the animals. They are more like manuals. In contrast, daily newspapers, weekly magazines and periodicals frequently write about police dogs as personalities rather than as instruments or objects. In literature on human-aotha relationships, the navigation between objectifying aothas and looking at them as individuals with a sense of compassion is referred to as the *constant paradox* (Herzog 1993; Arluke and Sanders 1996; Wilkie 2010).

Equally, the manner in which interaction with the public is discussed is paradoxical. In the texts in the second category, for example, guidelines on the deployment of dogs in relation to the legal right of the police to use violence, the frequency and the nature of injuries caused by a bite of a police dog are often discussed. In the third category, which is written in a more journalistic tone, attention is particularly focused on concrete meetings and interaction between police officers with their dogs and members of the public. Now and again pieces appear in research literature that give impressions of the interaction between police officers and civilians. There is one example of a survey in Australia on the use of drugs at parties. The researchers found that partygoers there managed to hide their drugs better when they suspected that sniffer dogs were about to be deployed and considered ways on how to avoid the dogs (Dunn and Degenhardt 2007). Nabben (2010) refers to a survey conducted in the Netherlands which showed that Dutch partygoers did not the least feel intimidated by the police and their dogs and continued to use drugs undisturbed. Regrettably, there is no consensus on how police dogs and their handlers should be deployed to have an adequate effect on members of the public. Although there is an increasing amount of social scientific literature on human-aotha relations available, remarkably little is written about the experience at work and the well-being of people and other animals that are active in law enforcement. Critical criminologist Cazaux states:'[i]nvestigations into the welfare of these aothas and the legitimacy of putting aothas to this use are issues that remain unexplored. What happens to the "K-9's" [police dogs] when they no longer live up to the requirements of the job or when they get hurt in practice?' (2001/2002, p. 149).

However, there is some literature on animals and the police that draws serious attention to animal welfare as well as human-animal relations. The ethnographic work by Sanders (2006) about the ins and outs of a so-called 'K9-unit' of the American police forces and the survey on the methods and procedures used by the American Animal Police by Arluke (2004) makes essential reading. The staff members of the Animal Police do not work *with* the aothas but are among other things responsible for tracking down and looking after neglected and maltreated aothas. But here in the Netherlands, in the social sciences, human-aotha relations in police work and the interaction with members of the public have never been systematically scrutinised. What very little is known about the working experience of aothas in the police force, I have frivolously tried to bring to light in a book I wrote on police dogs by incorporating 'interviews' with the dogs. Naturally, the form and the contents of these 'conversations' have escaped my mind, but by giving the dogs the opportunity to complain about specific risks in their work I have tried to draw attention to this subject. In one of the interviews, I have made police dog Nicky comment: '(W)e cannot escape the impression that some members of the public as well a particular group of police officers regard us merely as utilities and objects that can be written off. That I find very hard to digest' (Janssen 2008, p. 27). All in all we can conclude that literature on police dogs in general does not often uncover the nature and true prevalence of abuse of these creatures. The ways in which dog handlers can use their discretionary power, in order to take care of the welfare of the dogs they are working with, also seems to be neglected. Literature and research do not provide much answers.

Reality Check

Tasks for the Dogs and Discretionary Power for the Handler

Dogs were introduced in the Dutch police forces in 1908. A 100 years ago dogs were merely deployed as 'generalists' (Janssen 2008). Nowadays police dogs have become specialists. The *Department of Tracking- and Specialist Animals* (Afdeling Speur- en Specialistische Dieren) own dogs that are able to detect the smell of money, drugs, humans, drowned bodies, dead bodies, blood, combustible substances and explosives. A sniffer dog generally possesses just one speciality. Then there are dogs deployed for the so-called *Urban Search and Rescue* (USAR). They are used at the aftermath of disasters and/or accidents to track down people who have been buried or trapped. The deployment coordination of these animals takes place centrally. In addition, surveillance dogs have been placed with the 10 regional police forces. These dogs are used to track down objects or to accompany bailiffs. They can be deployed by the riot police during demonstrations or can be used to give assistance during the arrests of dangerous persons. They can be used at roadblocks, during evacuations and during house searches. These dogs are taken on surveillance and deployed at disturbances of the peace as a use of force. Furthermore, there are the so-called AOE-dogs that assist the *Arrest and Support Unit* (Arrestatie-en Ondersteuningseenheid). This unit comes into action in life-threatening cases: suicide threats, hostage situations and cases with suspects who carry fire arms.

Every day the police dogs and their handlers follow a schedule that regulates their effort and their availability. In such a schedule, so-called 'obligatory tasks' are laid down, such as giving assistance to the riot police, assisting in emergencies or surveillance activities, often during nighttime. Furthermore, there are obligatory training sessions for both the dogs and their handlers. In addition, the handlers and dogs are free to carry out various other activities on their own initiative and at their own discretion. Theoretically one could conclude that there is some discretionary power left. However, during the obligatory sessions, dog handlers sometimes unexpectedly have to deal with increasing external pressure when, for example, a mayor of a town requires reinforcements during a football match or a superior of an emergency room is forced to deploy surveillance units to deal with a sudden stream of incidents as a result of which it is team leaders rather than the dog handlers themselves who decide the nature of activities and lay down the conditions of the procedures of the activities. It raises the question of how dog handlers should be able to use their discretionary power benefiting the well-being of the dogs besides the activities they are entrusted with as mentioned above. I discovered from my inquiries since 2008 that in the Netherlands, there has been no research using systematic observations, differentiated according to the various qualities of the dogs.

Talking About Welfare

As mentioned above, after I finished my book on police dogs (Janssen 2008), I stayed in touch with dog handlers and since then I had several meetings with some of them to conduct unstructured interviews in an informal setting in order to obtain more insight into the welfare of police dogs. I found it difficult to open these meetings with questions about abuse because I sensed that that was a difficult topic. Therefore, I started by focussing on the positive aspects of welfare. In the job description of dog handlers, it states that the handler is responsible for the well-being and health of the dog in his or her care. However, I have never come across a clear definition or concrete guidelines on the actual well-being of police dogs including reactions towards abuse of dogs. Aspects of welfare often mentioned, were the length of a dog's working life and its life after its retirement I have come across frequently. Opinions about the length of the police dog's career vary. Many experts in the field feel that a retirement at 9 years of age is appropriate. There have been discussions about postponing the retirement of the dogs by a few years provided they are deployed for physical tasks that are less demanding. Some experts feel that it is irresponsible. It is the dog handlers who have the closest bond with their dogs, and therefore, theoretically, they are able to give better judgement on the physical and mental well-being of their cronies. It means, therefore, that dog handlers have a big say when it comes to assessing whether a dog should be deployed or not. The discretionary power of a dog handler, however, does not provide him with complete authority on a dog's deployment. Decisions are usually taken in consultation with a superior.

> That of course is only logical. When a sick dog is medically examined it is the dog handler who is best able to inform the vet about the dog's behaviour, whether the dog is frightened, how the dog's appetite is, what the nature is of its defecation or whether or not the dog has problems with walking. Only the handler is able to answer questions like that. Buying a dog, have it trained as well as calling in a vet, cost a lot of money and you can't just say I want a new one or I want the vet to have a look at him now. You have to talk that over with your superior (Janssen 2013, pp. 251–252).

The same applies to police dogs at the end of their career. Often dog handlers take their dogs that have 'retired' into their home: 'Of course there are limits. Because if you have already two dogs at home and another dog you work with in the force, taking in a fourth dog may be a little over the top. You make sure that a good home is found for the dog and they provide you with the opportunity to make that happen.' What is important is that a former police dog does not end up with a drugs dealer with the risk of that person getting the opportunity to have an insight in police detective work or that a dog may be put to use as a weapon.' I also interviewed an experienced policeman who in the past took charge of large-scale police operations. He told me the following: 'I myself have been in situations whereby the dog handlers and the riders prior to the operation made known that the animals that were to be deployed where physically not fully operational or that they expected problems because the animals lacked proper training. In such cases, we tried to find some lighter tasks for the respective animal and its handler. I also know of examples whereby the question whether or not a dog or horse could be used for a certain operation was carefully considered. In situations like that, for me the knowledge and experience of the handler was the deciding factor. On the arguments on the well-being of animals that are used by the police I have actually never been approached. My personal impression is that if the well-being of police dogs is at issue dog handlers generally use terms such as 'fitness' and 'feasibility' and apparently such terms fit in better with the robust police culture where expressions like 'what a poor dog or horse' are commented on as soft. However, apart from that, regrettably, I have heard very little about interaction between police dogs, dog handlers, supervisors and members of the public while police work was carried out, and thus, I have very little insight of what goes on. What is important to know is to what extent a dog handler is allowed, during a demonstration, to address a commander in charge to express his or her doubts whether or not a particular dog should be deployed from an animal welfare point of view and to what extent are superior officers receptive to such situations. Based on these observations I cannot give figures about the frequency of abuse. But these insights show that within the police service there is difference in opinion regarding what is acceptable regarding the well-being of the police dog. Therefore, I suppose, there is also variation in what police officers might consider to be abuse of the police dog. The same goes for ideas regarding motives for abuse and ways to react towards abuse.

The Constant Paradox

Fortunately, I can shed some light on these issues. Thus, I think I may have detected traces of the *constant paradox* that match perfectly with the theoretical ideas of Reus-Iain (1983) on *street* and *management cops.* According to Reus-Ianni *street cops* and *management cops* have their own police culture. Both cultures have each a different view on statistics and targets. Managers are focused on values and terms that are easily measurable such as 'productivity' and 'efficiency'. People in the workplace cannot always understand how gathering figures contributes to providing proper policing. Members of the police who informed me about the costs of keeping police dogs were mostly superior officers. In a way that is quite understandable because these officers are responsible for a balanced budget and are often faced with extensive costs for the purchase of dogs, food, equipment, medical care, transport and training. The dog handlers whom I talked to were conversant about the costs involved, but repeatedly stressed the necessity of sufficient spending on things like specific means of transport and adequate floor covering of the dog kennels that benefits the physical well-being of the dogs, in particular, when it concerns the sensitivity of hip joints and paws. It was only the handlers who provided this sort of clarification of required expenditure. But money as such was never a prominent subject in the conversations I had with the handlers. Most of the time we talked about the relationship that they had with their dogs. Spontaneously, they told me how long they had worked with their dog and what their dog's qualities were. Many told me about their dog's character: 'he really is a hard worker', 'she still is a bit playful.' or 'he is my best friend.' There was one example that made me realise that handlers regard their dogs as individual personalities: 'If you are aware that you are deployed with the riot police unit you must not only take into account that there may be some dogs that are nervous or have little experience. The dogs need to work as a team and you must make sure that you don't bring dogs along that don't get along with one another. It causes an unnecessary burden in your work' (Janssen 2013, p. 253). It is obviously important for a dog handler to have an amiable relationship with his or her dog. During the training and the exam each dog and its handler are tested as one unit. Officers who are deployed at a demonstration that threatens to get out of hand or members of an arrest- and support unit who are sent into a bank building with their dogs to catch hold of a raider need to count on their companions in such perilous situations. Furthermore, after work the handlers take their dog home where they have their own kennel. So, the dogs and their handlers spend many hours a day together both at work and at home. It is, therefore, obvious that dog handlers tend to emphasise the personal relationship they have with their animals. In the literature on human-animal relations, it is argued that the constant paradox is manifested in linguistic usage (Janssen 2013). A dog has no plug or a petrol tank but in some forces where there is a hierarchical system and thus considerable distance between those in the workplace and people at the top, there is the tendency to regard police dogs merely as tools. A striking example is a statement by an official saying that a dog that was ill needed to be 'repaired' by the vet. Another is a superior officer who wonders if his personnel are willing to work with smaller dogs, such as poodles. According to this superior, these dogs are not considered to be very 'masculine accessories'. That sort of language is not appreciated by the dog handlers who regard their dog as their best friend. According to Reus-Ianni (1983), there is a distinction between managers who are relatively ignorant of the daily practice on the street and police officers in the workplace causing the latter to feel alienated from their superiors. Some so-called *management cops* may in the past have had some experience as a police officer in a local precinct but by far not all the managers in the force have themselves ever worked with dogs. That may well be a contributory factor when there are feelings of alienation. Knowledge of possibilities and limitations in relation to the deployment of the dog are of essential importance in a dog handler's job. 'Dogs have sensitive paws and the paws' cushions are not suited for walking on hot tarmac or iron stairs with lots of little holes. Therefore, it is important that it is absolutely clear how practitioners should react when problems like that are likely to arise.'

Another interesting point in this context is the value of police dogs in the field of public relations. In many police forces, there is a sound awareness that these dogs are of advertising value. Articles regularly appear in police publication and in the world of public relations and communication canine charm offensives are put into use. Demonstrations to show the skilfulness and competence of the animals thoroughly impress a lot of members of the public both young and old. According to the dog handlers, however, the possibilities of using the dogs as public relations tools are limited. That argument can also be found in literature about police dogs:

> Some police departments can be faulted for seeing the public relations plusses that flow from canine use not just as an advantage, but as the primary purpose for the cop's existence! This is wrong. The police dog is not meant to be a public relations tool with which to awe small children and to be prepared through an endless stream of girl and boy scout and service club meetings and used every now and then for a touch of law enforcement work. Just the opposite. A department's canine unit must be an integral part of a well thought out, carefully conceived law enforcement program (Chapman 2009).

One dog handler told me once about a discussion he had with some colleagues of his and superior officers about the suggestion to give members of the public in a shopping area the opportunity to 'pet' some of the surveillance dogs but then when required to deploy those same dogs as a means of force. 'First to have it caressed and then to instruct it to attack is difficult for a dog to understand. It confuses the animal and it makes it feel insecure. The dog in question is very likely to hide behind its master.' From the public relations perspective it seemed a nice idea but according to the dog handlers the initiators failed to take a dog's psyche into consideration. My interviewee felt that in situations like this, his knowledge of dogs can be of fundamental importance when it comes to policy decisions on the use of police dogs. And so this *street-level bureaucrat* has become a policy maker himself.

Hierarchy

Up to now, I have linked my impressions of the *constant paradox* to the hierarchical gap between the handlers on the shop floor and their superiors partly inspired by the work of Reus-Ianni (1983). However, I am increasingly doubtful about the accuracy of the connection. In the summer of 2011 rumors that particularly dog handlers were put under a lot of pressure to switch to the just introduced animal police caused considerable consideration. The creation of that organisation was in process at that time, and the first 125 officers were to be placed with the animal police by September 2011. 'Of course those people are fond of animals but they often see dogs chiefly as a weapon or a tool. And yes, they care about animals but you can't expect these people with such a strong drive all of a sudden to take little kittens out of a tree', said Jos Hermans of the Union ANVP in the daily *Algemeen Dagblad* of Saturday, 2 July 2011. An aggrieved 'dog man' sent me a copy of that article. He thought it striking and disappointing that the union man made a distinction between working *with* animals and working *for* animals because it is assumed that people working with dogs see these animals particularly as instruments and the officers working for the animal police, on the other hand, are expected to dispose of their instrumental approach towards the dog, and above all, show compassion for the animal. On the one hand, the reaction of the angry handler fits in well with what I have written: someone who has a higher position in the police hierarchy lacks the knowledge of what the work of the dog handler really involves, but on the other hand, it is striking that a union man in particular described in his account the instrumental relation between a dog and its handler. It could possibly mean that the *constant paradox* cannot directly be linked to the hierarchical system in the police force. Because if the union man is right, the instrumental view on animals would also exist among dog handlers in the workplace. I am rather apprehensive to offer a firm conclusion at this stage, but it has raised a number of questions. First of all, we should ask ourselves, what is it that motivates police officers to decide to work with dogs. When I recall the conversations I had with the dog handlers, I had the impression that some of them liked nothing better in their career than working with dogs although some clearly seemed to see their work with animals more as an intermediate stage within the broad development of their career within the force. These people clearly had a different look on aothas. Christensen and Crank (2001) discuss the difference between officers who have had a rural background and those who have not. A rural background would, leaving rank and position aside, perhaps influence the way the handler experiences and appreciates his job with a police dog. Furthermore, we need to consider what sort of change of views on the role and position of the dog could occur during the developing career of a dog handler. Because, where is it stated that the various views on police dogs are set in stone? Why should a *hardliner* not be able to learn to build a social relationship with a dog and is it really impossible for a dog lover to become more receptive to a more concise approach with regard to police dogs?

Lines of Research for the (Near) Future

Nearly half a century ago, a member of The Hague City Council, Schuckinck Kool, who was known for his activist streak said the following: 'To abuse the relation based on mutual trust between parents and children is punishable by law while police dogs that are far more dependent than children are being exploited without any protest. As a protester I think it is fair of me to say that that is a really dirty trick' (Janssen 2008, p. 20). In the foregoing, I have tried to show that the question of how the deployment of dogs in police work might influence their wellbeing is hardly ever raised. Therefore, so little is known about the nature and frequency of abuse of these dogs. The same goes for explanations and reactions towards abuse. In that respect the dogs are indeed barking up the wrong tree. With reference to the arguments I have put on paper and inspired by the enthusiasm with which the dog handlers talked about their jobs I have four lines of research in mind. First of all, the well-being of police dogs should be thoroughly examined whereby the various tasks these dogs have to carry out are taken into consideration. Such an investigation would provide valuable input for the debate on the well-being of these aothas. Second, there should be an analysis of the implicit hypotheses and views on human-aothas relations in general and on the work involving aothas in particular, not only among policy makers but also among superior police officers, police practitioners such as dog handlers and members of public. Are we to assume that aothas and humans are equal or are aothas chiefly considered as subordinate to humans? Third, we should consider the possibility of developing a framework of standards, so-called 'check and balances', on the basis of which the well-being of aothas deployed by the police can be monitored in a transparent way. Fourth, it is of eminent importance to observe how interactions between dogs, their handlers, the superior officers and members of the public actually occur on the basis of observation studies. Only then we can get a clear view of how dog handlers use their discretionary power that is to the benefit of the well-being of aothas such as dogs.

References

Arluke, A. (2004). *Brute force. Animal police and the challenge of cruelty*. West Lafayette, Indiana: Purdue University Press.

Arluke, A., & Sanders, C. R. (1996). *Regarding animals*. Philadelphia: Temple University Press.

Cazaux, G. (2001/2002). *Anthropocentrism and speciesism regarding animals other than human animal in contemporary criminology. Analysing the concept 'Animal Abuse' in criminological sciences and in Belgian legislation regarding the protection and welfare of animals.* Ph.D dissertation. Ghent: University of Ghent, Faculty of Law.

Chapman, S. G. (2009). *Police dogs in North America.* Springfield: Charles C. Thomas Publisher.

Christensen, W., & Crank, J. P. (2001). Police work and culture in a non-urban setting: an ethnographical analysis. *Police Quarterly, 4*(1), 69–98.

Dunn, M., & Degenhardt, L. (2007). *NSW trends in Ecstacy and related drug markets 2006. Findings from the Ecstacy and related drug reporting system* (EDRS). *NDARC Technical Report 277.* Sydney: University of New South Wales, National Drug and Alcohol Research Centre.

Herzog, H. (1993). Human morality and animal research. *American Scholar, 62,* 337–349.

Hössen, Ch. F. (1911). *Verzorging, africhting en gebruik van den politiehond in de praktijk.* Ooltgensplaat: M. Breur & Zonen.

Janssen, J. (2008). *Hondenbaan. 100 jaar honden bij politie Haaglanden.* Den Haag: Politie Haaglanden.

Janssen, J. (2013). De mistige discretionaire ruimte van hondengeleiders. Over het onbekende dagelijkse werk van politiehonden en hun geleiders. In H. Moors & E. Bervoets (Eds.), *Frontlijnwerkers en het sleepnet van veiligheid: cases, patronen, analyse* (pp. 243–257). Den Haag: Boom Lemma.

Janssen, J. (2014). On the relationship between animal victimization and stigmatization of ethnic groups: the case of ritual slaughter. In T. Spapens, R. White, & M. Kluin (Eds.), *Environmental crime and its victims. Perspectives within green criminology* (pp. 205–217). Burlington: Ashgate.

Kessler, M. (1909). *De africhting van den politiehond, den ambulance- en den oorlogshond. Een beknopte handleiding.* Den Haag: Luctor et Emergo.

Leenstra, F. R., Neijenhuis, F., Hanekamp, W. J. A.,. Vermei, I. (2011). *De staat van het dier 2.* Wageningen: Wageningen UR Livestock Research.

Lipsky, M. (1980). *Street-level bureaucracy. Dilemmas of the individual in public services.* New York: Russel Sage Foundation.

Mos, H. A. van der. (1910). *Beknopte handleiding voor de opleiding van de hond ten dienste der politie en justitie.* Nijmegen.

Nabben, T. (2010). Cops and dogs against party drugs. In T. Decorte & J. Fountain (Eds.), *Pleasure, pain and profit. European perspectives on drugs.* Lengerich: Pabst Science Publishers.

Naeyé, J. (2005). *Niet zonder slag of stoot. De geweldsbevoegdheid en doorzettingskracht van de Nederlandse politie.* Zeist: Uitgeverij Kerkebosch.

RDA. (2010). *Agenda voor het dierbeleid. Morele vraagstukken en speerpunten voor het dierbeleid in Nederland. Een zienswijze van de Raad voor Dieraangelegenheden.*

Reus-Ianni, E. (1983). *Two cultures of policing. Street cops and management cops.* New Brunswick: Translation Books.

Rothpletz, J. P. A. (1910). *De politiehond, zijn dressuur, voeding, verzorging, huisvesting en dienst, beneevens eenige wenken bij het fokken en voor de behandeling van zieke honden*. Assen: N.V. StoomdrukkerijFloralia.

Sanders, C. (2006). The dog you deserve. ambivalence in the K-9 officer/patrol dog relationship. *Journal of Contemporary Ethnography, 35*(2), 148–172.

Werkman, W., Valk, M., & Leineweber, M. (2007). *Opvattingen over dierenwelzijn in Nederland. Verslag van eenpublieksenquête*. Amsterdam: Ergo.

Wilkie, Rh. M. (2010). *Livestock/deadstock: working with farm animals from birth to slaughter*. Philadelphia: Temple University Press.

Janine Janssen is a cultural anthropologist and criminologist with a special interest in the intersection between the study of multicultural society and green criminology. She is Head of Research of the Dutch police force's National Centre of Expertise for Honour-related Violence and is Professor of Violence in Dependency Relationships at the Avans University of Applied Sciences in the Netherlands.

Conservation and Invasive Alien Species: Violent Love

Krithika Srinivasan and Rajesh Kasturirangan

Introduction

Some alien invaders have to travel all the way from another planet while others need only journey from another part of Earth. 'Alien invader threatens Britain's native wildlife', warns a front page headline from a special edition of the UK Canal & River Trust's newsletter (WaterPatrol 2015). Describing the American crayfish as an 'aggressive predator' that can 'infiltrate' rivers and canals and 'cause the destruction of native populations', the newsletter seeks support from the public, for its invasive species control programme (WaterPatrol 2015, p. 1). Animals such as mink, terrapins, the Chinese mitten crab, killer shrimp, and zebra mussels, as well as plants such as the Japanese knotweed, giant hogweed, Himalayan balsam, and floating pennywort are some of the non-native invaders that are the targets of the Canal & River Trust's eradication programme (Canal and River Trust 2015).

K. Srinivasan (✉)
University of Edinburgh, Edinburgh, United Kingdom
e-mail: k.srinivasan@ed.ac.uk

R. Kasturirangan
Azim Premji University, Bangalore, India
e-mail: rajesh@rajeshkasturirangan.org

J. Maher et al. (eds.), *The Palgrave International Handbook of Animal Abuse Studies*, DOI 10.1057/978-1-137-43183-7_20

Prevalence

The UK Canal & River Trust's focus on protecting 'native' wildlife from 'a flood of invasive creatures' (WaterPatrol 2015, p. 2) echoes global anxieties about invasive alien species. While the discourse about the impacts of invasive alien species (IAS) is often framed around their impacts on 'native' species, the broader concern is the impact on biodiversity. The Convention on Biological Diversity (CBD) identifies IAS as one of the 'main direct drivers of biodiversity loss at the global level' and as a cross-cutting issue to be addressed by all of its thematic programmes (Convention on Biological Species 2015c). Article 8(h) of the CBD requires that 'Each Contracting Party shall, as far as possible and as appropriate: (h) Prevent the introduction of, control or eradicate those alien species which threaten ecosystems, habitats or species'(Convention on Biological Species 1993b). The International Union for Conservation of Nature (IUCN), one of the world's largest and best known conservation groups, similarly prioritises the control of IAS arguing that they 'represent the second most significant cause of species extinction worldwide after habitat destruction' (IUCN 2015).

In general, conservation action across the world and at various levels is devoting increasing attention to the control of animals and plants that are considered 'invasive alien'. Invasive alien organisms are also targeted by the private sector when financial profits are negatively impacted (for instance, the logging industry can be impacted by grey squirrels).

This international concern translates into extensive research and action into management of IAS across the world. The dispersed (across the public and private sectors) character of programmes to manage IAS and the conflation of the costs of management and impact make it difficult to determine accurately the numbers of organisms affected by these programmes. However, partial estimates of the expenditure and projected costs of IAS management offer a sense of the prevalence of the problem. Annual government spending in the UK on just quarantine and surveillance of IAS is estimated to be GBP £17.766 million (Williams et al. 2010). It is estimated that the annual costs of controlling IAS in just 12 countries to meet the Convention on Biological Diversity's Aichi 2020 targets will be USD $15,083.9 million (Turpie and Jurk 2012, p. 14). Globally, it is estimated that USD $73,421 million is required annually for the prevention and control of IAS to meet CBD targets (Turpie and Jurk 2012, p. 21).

This chapter examines the violence and abuse towards animals implicated in the control of IAS. In particular, we focus on the legitimisation and support of such violence in conservation discourse and practice. The social formation of conservation has the raison d'être of caring for and protecting nonhuman nature. This chapter asks how such violent practices are considered acceptable in the conservationist space of care, and even encouraged, as an ethical response to the presence of certain organisms in a region. The chapter first offers a brief overview of conservationist definitions, discourse, and practice relating to IAS. We then present the case of rabbits in Australia to illustrate the nature of the problematic practices that are entailed in the conservationist management of IAS. Following this, we draw on Michel Foucault's work on biopower (2003, 2008, 2009) to explain and respond to the complicated manners in which conservation becomes infused with discourses and practices of violence. In deploying the biopolitical analytical lens, the chapter demonstrates the role of collective ontologies such as ecosystem, biodiversity, and species in rendering invisible the individual organisms that are the targets of conservationist action on IAS. It argues that an ecocentric approach that focuses on the collectivity not only results in the intertwining of care and harm in conservation but also enables the juggling of competing agendas relating to human socio-economic interests, on the one hand, and the protection of nonhuman nature, on the other.

The chapter then further problematises the abusive management generated by the category of IAS. It does so by highlighting the socially constructed character of this category. By bringing together the biopolitical analysis with literatures in geography and environmental philosophy, we highlight the politically charged nature of the 'invasive alien' classification, thereby opening opportunities for contesting the resulting abuse. The chapter draws on material from intergovernmental conservation policy instruments such as the Convention on Biological Diversity and from documents generated by conservation groups in order to illustrate its arguments.

Defining and Managing Invasive Alien Species

The CBD describes invasive alien species as 'species whose introduction and/or spread outside their natural past or present distribution threatens biological diversity' (Convention on Biological Species 2015b). Alien species are defined in relation to '*native* species'. 'Native' refers to organisms that in 'a given territory...[have] been observed in the form of a naturally occurring and self-sustaining population in historical times' (Convention on Biological Species 2015a). By contrast, the term 'alien species' refers to those organisms whose presence in a particular geographical site is attributable to human intervention within a certain timescale; they are those species that have been introduced in a region, either deliberately or accidentally, by humans.

The term 'invasive' is added to 'alien' to refer to those species that are perceived as causing harm to pre-existing (native) plant and animal life in the area. Not all alien species are characterised as invasive; it is only when an organism is viewed as 'generating a negative impact on the local ecosystem and species' (IUCN 2015) and thereby threatening biodiversity as a whole that it is classified and dealt with as invasive.

Species can be introduced into an ecosystem in multiple ways; species introductions can be intentional, for example, when organisms are introduced in new regions for agricultural, horticultural, or recreational reasons. Or they can be accidental, for example, as a consequence of global (human) travel—whether marine, road or air—and trade. International trade and tourism are now major vectors of transmission (McNeely et al. 2001). Global shipping and the associated disposal of ballast water in particular has been a key route for the introduction of what are later seen as alien species. Indeed, it is recognised in conservation biology that many species that we take for granted as native today might have originally been introduced by marine travel which predates the discipline of natural history (Wonham 2006).

Three main criteria are used to define the *invasive alien* character of a particular species: (i) spatial scale; (ii) temporal scale; and (iii) threat to biodiversity. The threats posed by invasive organisms to biodiversity can be direct or indirect. Direct impacts stem from predation (for example, cats on birds), the spread of new diseases to which native organisms do not have resistance (for example, squirrel parapoxvirus which is carried by the grey squirrel but affects the red squirrel), competition for resources, and parasitism. Indirect impacts include those that result from habitat changes caused by the invasive species, indirect competition (for example, when invasive species attract an increased number of a common predator which then preys on native species), and alteration of local food chains and habitats. These impacts can be affected by the interaction of multiple invasions in the same region (Wonham 2006).

The arguments about the impacts of invasive species are often couched in economic terms. It is commonly argued that IAS cause damages worth nearly a trillion US dollars—as well as being the second biggest contributor to biodiversity loss after habitat destruction. The annual costs in the USA of invasive species are estimated at over USD $100 billion which includes costs of control (Convention on Biological Species 2015d). Here, the non-economic value of biodiversity as an intrinsic good is combined with economic assessments.

Conservation programmes for the control of IAS stem from anxieties about the effects of organisms that are introduced where they had not previously existed. Globally, a range of methods is deployed for the management of IAS (Wittenberg and Cock 2001). These methods can range from the prevention of the spread of invasives to eradication. Eradication more often than not involves techniques such as shooting, trapping, poisoning, burning, and the deliberate spread of disease. These techniques are inherently violent and cause significant suffering. Many of these management methods can, therefore, be described as abuse.

A Case Study: Rabbits in Australia

Rabbits were first introduced to Australia in 1788, primarily as food animals. They were released in the wild for hunting and sport in 1859, when the grazier Thomas Austin said 'the introduction of a few rabbits could do little harm and might provide a touch of home, in addition to a spot of hunting' (Department of Agriculture 2015). That touch of home turned out to be a two-handed grab, as rabbits spread all across Australia, feeding on native species of plants as well as agricultural crops. Here too, the human influence was paramount: rabbit populations exploded as woods and scrublands were replaced by farms growing crops that suited the rabbits. As European settlers sought to replicate their home environments in a new continent, rabbits made themselves comfortable as well.

Rabbits were soon reclassified as pests. A Royal Commission was established in 1901 to assess the situation (Crawford 2015). Soon after, an infamous 'rabbit-proof' fence was built to keep rabbits out but seems to have failed in its purpose (Crawford 2015). Since then, individual farmers as well as the government of Australia have used innumerable means to kill rabbits and prevent new populations from arising—methods including shooting, poisoning, trapping, biological control through disease, and warren ripping. The latter refers to the use of bulldozers to destroy rabbit warrens, essentially dismembering the trapped rabbits or burying them alive. Ripping is a particularly violent technique, so much so that a handbook produced by the Invasive Animal Cooperative Research Centre suggests (Sharp 2012, p. 2):

> It is more humane to perform ripping when rabbit numbers are at their lowest e.g., after drought, disease, warren fumigation or poison baiting or when they are not breeding. This means that lower numbers of rabbits will be killed by this relatively inhumane technique.

The suggestion that poisoning and fumigation are more humane alternatives highlights how violent ripping is.

The language of warfare, violence, control, and even hatred is endemic to the literature on invasive species. For example, the UK Canal & River Trust's newsletter has a section listing invasive species titled 'Have you spotted the eight we hate?' (WaterPatrol 2015, p. 3), while Blackburn et al. (2010, p. 228) warn that 'we are a long way from winning the war against IAS.' It is not just about language: most known forms of warfare—conventional, chemical and biological—have been used against invasive organisms, both to prevent damage to human interests and to protect biodiversity.

Other Invasive Alien Species

Rabbits are classified as vermin and invasive species in several parts of the world, including Britain, but they are hardly the only invasive species introduced by human beings. That list includes almost every animal genus[1] including crustaceans (for example, green crab), fish (for example, catfish), amphibians (for example, cane toad), reptiles (for example, brown tree snake), birds (for example, the Common Myna), and mammals (for example, red deer) (Invasive Species Specialist Group 2015).

The conservationist management of invasive species involves the use of many different kinds of techniques. Apart from prevention (of the spread of IAS), these include: mechanical control (shooting, trapping, digging out, and other mechanical means of killing); chemical control (insecticides, rodenticides and other poisoning agents); biological control (introduction of disease agents, parasites or predators that target the invasive organism); population control (through the introduction of sterile males or sterilising pathogens); habitat management (burning, grazing); and integrated pest management (involving all suitable methods) (Wonham 2006). The deployment of these management measures has not been unproblematic. For example, chemical control can affect non-target species while introduced predators can become invasive in their own right.[2] Moreover, these control measures raise fundamental ethical concerns relating to their impacts on the target organisms as the above example of rabbits in Australia showed. Shooting, trapping, poisoning, burning all have adverse welfare implications, as do disease/parasitic agents which can cause significant suffering before death. Many of these

[1] And many plants.

[2] For example, cane toads, introduced to control cane beetles in Australia, went onto become 'invasive'.

methods, including the use of snares or disease, result in long-drawn-out and painful deaths. The philosopher Freya Matthews refers to this as the 'anguish of wildlife ethics' (Mathews 2012).

Despite the implications for animal welfare, the disturbing aspects of invasive species control are usually viewed in conservation as 'an open question' (Wonham 2006, p. 317)—as ancillary to the broader goal of protecting biodiversity from invasive species. What's more, the abuse that is entailed in the control of invasive species enjoys a degree of public acceptance that other instances of animal abuse, for instance, in livestock production, would not. In general, there is public support for the control of IAS, including animals such as grey squirrels (in the UK) and rabbits (in multiple parts of the world). In the case of grey squirrels, even those who balk at the idea of killing wildlife and who are otherwise sympathetically inclined to these animals, give a nod to lethal control in the absence of alternatives (Warwick 2014).

It is useful to remember that the social formation of conservation emerged as a response to the human abuse and exploitation of nonhuman nature; the raison-d'être of conservation is to protect nonhuman nature from the harmful impacts of human activity (Meffe et al. 2006). It is, therefore, worth examining why a field that is concerned first and foremost with fostering the flourishing of nonhuman nature engages in activities that are directly harmful to it. To put it differently, what lies behind these materialisations of harm in this space of care?

The Biopolitics of Invasive Species Management

In addressing the above question, we argue that Michel Foucault's work on biopower and biopolitics (2008) offers a useful analytical lens to explain, understand, and critique the abuse of nonhuman animals that is embedded in conservation programmes that target IAS. While Foucault's original scholarship focused on the operation of power in purely human domains, his observations on the working of non-benign power in spaces of social change and care are pertinent for the examination of the conservationist space of care (e.g., Srinivasan 2014; Chrulew 2011), and more specifically, the conservationist management of invasive species.

Biopower, Harm, and Care

Foucault's writings and lectures on disciplinary, governmental, and biopolitical power are essentially concerned with forms of power that depart from the conventional schema of power as something that is associated with force and overt violence, as something that is resonant with the power of the sovereign to 'take life and let live' (Foucault 2008, p. 136). To Foucault, power in contemporary society can take multiple creative forms and be directed at promoting the *flourishing* of life. Characterising this as biopower or the power to 'make live and let die', Foucault (2003, p. 241) shows that many spaces of care and transformation from the eighteenth century onwards (such as the transition from monarchy to democracy) are characterised by mechanisms of power that are directed at regulating and fostering life—instead of ruling by threat of violence and death.

However, this focus does not necessarily imply the absence of harm. Indeed, the key insight in Foucault's scholarship lies in his teasing out of the intricate entanglement of *harm* with techniques of power that are aimed at *caring* for life. As Foucault, drawing on his observations of modern warfare argues, war (and the accompanying violence) is no longer waged in defence of the sovereign, but on 'behalf of the existence of everyone . . . in the name of life necessity' (Foucault 2008, p. 136), that is, for the welfare of society as a whole.

This insight has been used to investigate spaces of care such as the war on terror, international development, and even animal welfare (Srinivasan 2013; Dillon and Reid 2009; Li 2007). Instead of violence and harm being justified in the name of the sovereign, in the exercise of biopower, harm is portrayed as fundamental to the protection of life—but life at a larger scale, at the level of the population. In the exercise of biopower, individual members of society, or some groups in society, can be harmed and sacrificed in order to promote the well-being and flourishing of the larger population/collectivity (Gudmand-Hoyer and Lodrup 2009).

Thus, in the logics of biopower, individuals are not attributed much ethical significance; they are largely 'the instrument, relay, or condition for obtaining something at the level of the population' (Foucault 2009, p. 42). Furthermore, as Foucault writes, those individuals and groups who 'resist the regulation of the population, who try to elude the apparatus by which the population . . . subsists at an optimal level', can become the targets of violent management including 'exile, death and punishment' (Foucault 2009, p. 44). Biopower, the power of care, therefore is characterised by two key features: (i) a focus on the flourishing of life at the level of the population/collectivity; (ii) the entanglement of harm and care. It is these two features of Foucault's schematisation of biopower that are crucial for the analysis of the conservationist control of invasive alien species.

Fostering Biodiversity, Killing Invasives

The emphasis in conservationist discussions on IAS is on *caring* for nature and nonhuman life. The social formation of conservation is by no means comparable to other domains where the abuse and exploitation of nonhuman animals for human gain can be expected—for example, the meat, medical and recreational industries (Twine 2013; Pilkington 2010; Shukin 2009). Rather, conservation discourse and practice is primarily about care. However, as explained below, the Foucauldian analytical lens helps to identify the *biopolitical* character of conservationist care (Srinivasan 2014), For one, the social formation of conservation is directed at protecting life, but at the scale of collectivities such as populations, species, ecosystems and biodiversity (Callicott 2006). This is often described in environmental philosophy as ecocentrism (Sarkar 2012). Ecocentrism refers to the attribution of intrinsic value to aggregations or collectivities of nonhuman nature such as ecosystems, biotic communities, species, and populations (see also chapter on Legal and Illegal Theriocide for further discussion).[3] Indeed, when conservation biology was first established as a scholarly discipline, it was defined as follows (Soule 1986):

Conservation biology, a new stage in the application of science to conservation problems, addresses the biology of species, communities, and ecosystems that are perturbed, either directly or indirectly, by human activities or other agents.

This definition is striking in its omission of the individual organism. In the context of IAS, a similar emphasis on the larger collectivity prevails in the form of the goal of protecting the native ecosystem and global biodiversity from the impacts of the invasive organisms. This focus on promoting the collectivity results in conservation programmes that harmfully intervene on 'undesirable' elements of nonhuman nature—the invasive organisms. This emphasis on protecting 'biodiversity' is evident in the very definition of invasive species: 'an alien species whose introduction and/or spread threaten biological diversity' (Convention on Biological Species 2015a). Species that are the targets of control are viewed as undesirable members of the ecosystem/biodiversity and as such they are sacrificed. While an entire species may be labelled and targeted as invasive, the harm that is exercised is done so at the level of the *individual* organism, which experiences the harms of poisoning, shooting, trapping, burning, ripping, and other methods.

[3] By contrast, biocentrism refers to the attribution of intrinsic value to individual living organisms.

In other words, these interventions are enabled by the biopolitical side-lining of the well-being of individual organisms.[4]

This biopolitical emphasis on biodiversity as a whole and the concomitant marginalisation of the lives and well-being of individual organisms go along with the co-articulation of harm and care that is central to the conservationist management of IAS. The abuse that is entailed in the conservationist control of invasive organisms such as mink, rabbits, and grey squirrels *does not* have the objective of exploitation for meeting human self-interest. Rather, it is predicated on biopolitical rationalities of *care*, that is, care for the very object of abusive intervention—nonhuman life—at the level of biodiversity or the ecosystem. For example, grey squirrels are not targeted for violent management as IAS merely to meet narrowly defined human ends but because they are viewed as threatening red squirrels and biodiversity more generally.

It is this biopolitical co-articulation of harm and care, enabled by the ontological focus on the larger collectivity that permits the abusive control of some organisms labelled as invasive alien in a social formation that is primarily about protecting nonhuman nature. Indeed, the eradication of organisms labelled as invasive alien becomes an act of care. It is the immunitary logics peculiar to biopolitical power (Esposito 2008), that is, logics relating to protecting life from *a threat from within*, that allow for the abuse that is part and parcel of the management of IAS to remain acceptable in both conservationist and public imaginaries.

Win-win Solutions for the Anthropocene

The biopolitical focus on the larger collectivity not only allows for the rearticulation of the violent control of IAS as a manifestation of conservationist care, but also enables the juggling of competing interests: human and nonhuman. As discussed earlier, integral to the definition of alien species is that of human introduction. Only those organisms that are introduced to a region by human means are classified as alien. Indeed, it is widely acknowledged (Wonham 2006; McNeely et al. 2001) that the constant traffic of humans and human artefacts in an increasingly globalised world is a key factor in the emergence of invasive species as a threat from within to nonhuman nature broadly conceived. Despite this recognition of the solely human cause of the problem, measures that address the cause at its root—for

[4] For exceptions see newly emerging literatures on compassionate conservation (Ramp and Bekoff 2015; Paquet and Darimont 2010)

example, by deglobalising and by reducing the movement of people and human artefacts across the planet—remain politically unviable. At the same time, the push to protect nonhuman nature from the impacts of human actions has arguably never been as strong as it is in an era that has come to be referred to as the Anthropocene (Crutzen and Stoermer 2000).

In other words, as has been argued in other contexts (Srinivasan 2015), there is an ongoing tension between normative objectives relating to the protection of nonhuman nature, on the one hand, and the prevailing dominance of human interests, on the other. This tension is partly resolved through a biopolitical focus on the larger collectivity because it enables *win-win* interventions (such as the eradication of invasive species) that are directed at protecting nonhuman nature from the impacts of human activities, but that do not involve any significant curtailment of those very same human activities—such as global trade, tourism, or habitat use—that endanger nonhuman nature in the first place. The locus of responsibility is shifted from *human* activity to *nonhuman* activity and this shift is facilitated by the ontological focus on the larger collectivity—biodiversity/ecosystem. Thus, the competing goals of human interest and nonhuman well-being are simultaneously addressed.

In the case of IAS, grey squirrels in the UK, for example, the discourse about grey squirrels driving out red squirrels hides the human activities that lie at the root of the problem. Not only were grey squirrels introduced by humans, but it is habitat degradation because of human activity that makes red squirrels particularly vulnerable to the presence of grey squirrels. While grey squirrels are more adapted to human-modified conditions, red squirrels are already threatened by habitat destruction and fragmentation (The Forestry Commission UK 2015; Cooper 1997). Despite these multiple, intersecting, *human* causes that threaten the survival of red squirrels, the political unviability of bringing a halt to human-induced habitat degradation means that the eradication of grey squirrels becomes the win-win solution that simultaneously addresses the competing goals of protecting nonhuman nature (the red squirrels) and meeting human interests (competing uses of habitat).

The violence integral to the eradication of grey squirrels in order to protect red squirrels, however, becomes invisibilised by discourses of care that describe these interventions as necessary to protect red squirrels, so as to promote the flourishing of a larger collectivity: biodiversity. That the protection of red squirrels is a means to the end of protecting biodiversity is evident from the history of *red* squirrels in the UK. These animals were actively exterminated as pests in the early twentieth century (The Forestry Commission UK 2015), and it is only more recent conservationist concern about biodiversity loss that has resulted in programmes to protect them.

Thus, the firm focus of conservationist care on an ontological construct such as biodiversity not only allows for the overlooking of the harm embedded in the control of IAS, but also enables the juggling of competing normative goals relating to human interests and nature protection. The biopolitical analytical lens helps us understand how human interests can reign supreme even *within an attitude of care towards nonhuman life*. It is the deployment of collective ontologies such as biodiversity and ecosystem in caring for non-human nature that enables the eliding of the much tougher question of a hierarchy of interests, one in which the primacy of human interests can remain unquestioned.

Collectivist Ontologies and the Social Construction of Nature

It is useful to emphasise here these various concepts deployed and taken-for-granted in conservation—IAS, biodiversity, ecosystem—are manifestations of what political ecologists might refer to as the co-production of nature and society (Castree and Braun 2001). To put it differently, the classification of grey squirrels as invasive alien or the identification of 'biodiversity' as a relevant ontological concept are outcomes of the human imagination in general, and the scientific imagination more specifically. These concepts exemplify the social construction of nature, and as such, are inherently political (Braun 2009).

Take for example, the concept of biodiversity. It is defined as the 'the variability among living organisms from all sources . . . diversity within species, between species and of ecosystems' (Convention on Biological Species 1993a). This definition demonstrates the ontological nebulousness of the concept. Biodiversity does not refer to a fixed, tangible, element of nonhuman nature, but to the idea of variability or diversity—as perceived by humans. The variations that undergird the concept of biodiversity are approximations—there is no clear line that divides one species from another, or that demarcates where one ecosystem ends and another begins. Nonetheless, the social formation of conservation deploys this concept as a concrete category of nature which needs to be protected. Other commonly used concepts such as ecosystem are similarly contingent on the classificatory imagination. Given the globally interconnected character of nonhuman nature on the planet, the identification of the boundaries of a specific, regional ecosystem, for example, a forest ecosystem, are entirely bound up with the interests and priorities of the people doing this identification. Franklin (2015, p. 68) points out that the idea of ecosystem originally was put forward as an abstract conceptualisation of the 'relational nature' of life on the planet, but was later 'extrapolated and...mapped onto contiguous definable territorial units...for national estate management purposes'. To Franklin (2015, p. 68), this move exemplifies Alfred Whitehead's 'fallacy of misplaced concretism' in that 'a theoretical understanding of a system of connections' was wrongly extrapolated to 'territorially bounded spaces'.

The concept of IAS offers even more food for thought. Warren (2007) offers an excellent parsing of this concept. As discussed earlier, there are three criteria that go into the categorisation of an organism as invasive alien. The first is spatial scale, and has to do with area, location or region. Alien species are those that are found outside of 'their natural range of distribution' (IUCN 2015). The same animal elsewhere might be celebrated as 'native'. This 'natural' range is defined by examining the organism's presence/absence in a particular region at a particular point in time. For example, grey squirrels are considered alien to the UK because they were not present on the island before 1876 when they were introduced by humans (The Forestry Commission UK 2015).

Time or temporal scale is the second criterion. Native species are those that have been present in a region, without the aid of human introduction, since a particular time in the past. Rabbits are considered alien and invasive to Scotland because they were *not* there at the beginning of the current interglacial period and were introduced later on by humans. But they were present in Scotland in previous interglacial periods (Warren 2007). Nonetheless, they are categorised as 'alien' because a particular point in history is used as a cut-off date for these classificatory decisions. Indeed, organisms that are classified as 'native' need not necessarily have been present in a region all through the time period used as a cut-off. For example, red squirrels, an emblematic 'native' species in Scotland, went extinct in some parts of Scotland by the eighteenth century because of extensive habitat loss and were later *reintroduced* from Scandinavia and England (The Forestry Commission UK 2015).

Furthermore, the inherently partial and incomplete character of natural history records means that 'there is no reliable biological or ecological method that can distinguish between aliens and natives' (Peretti 1998, p. 185). The spatio-temporal criteria used to decide whether an organism is alien or native are ultimately a question of choice, and arguably, a political one. Particularly telling is the increasing use of geopolitical borders as spatial criteria for determining the 'alien' character of organisms. Conservation discourse (McNeely et al. 2001) refers to organisms that are 'alien' to the USA or India and recommends border control measures as key to the management of invasives, thereby conflating geopolitical borders with biophysical ones.

The third criterion is that of environmental harm and is used to make decisions about invasiveness (Sagoff 2005). An alien species is deemed invasive if it is perceived as causing harm: ecological or economic. Most calculations about the harm caused by invasive species refer to adverse effects, if any, they may have on human activities and the financial costs that results. Figures relating to the financial damages that can be attributed to invasive species usually include the costs of control (Sagoff 2009). These estimates of damages do not usually take into consideration services provided by invasive animals: for example, cats in controlling rodents, or zebra mussels in preventing eutrophication (Sagoff 2005).

With respect to the ecological harm that is attributed to invasive species, there is no fundamentally ecological criterion or 'fact of nature' that can be used to determine such harm. As conservation biologists themselves explain, 'the ecological impacts of introduced species are *inherently* neither bad nor good. Such judgments can only be made in the context of an explicit [human] value framework...or an economic bottom line (Wonham 2006, p. 295, emphasis as in original). Even if an invasive organism causes the extinction of another, native, organism, there is no 'truth' of nature that can be used as a criterion to judge whether this extinction constitutes a 'good' or a 'bad'. Extinctions have been part and parcel of the history of the planet. Value judgements about extinction or ecosystem change often rest on steady-state conceptions of nature and the biosphere at a particular point in time and space. However, the biosphere is in constant flux: some organisms dwindle or disappear, others emerge or become abundant. Indeed, it could be interpreted as a process of natural selection in which the more adaptable organism thrives (Gould 1997 in O'Brien 2006). Furthermore, as Sagoff (2009) argues, introduced species can also result in increased diversity by 'stimulating the evolution of new kinds of organisms'. He also points out the attribution of a *positive* value to variety (biodiversity) is itself fundamentally social.

The above points about the socially constructed character of widely accepted conservationist ontologies are not meant to deny the existence or moral value of nonhuman nature, or the gravity of the impacts of human activity on nonhuman life. Nor are they meant to deny the vulnerability of 'native' organisms that face new threats from new species that have been introduced by human movement. Rather, the aim is to emphasise that identification and control of some organisms as invasive alien, far from being based on some ecological truth, is fundamentally political. If the classification of certain organisms as invasive alien is contingent on spatial, temporal, and impact criteria that are selected by humans, then the taken-for-granted character of this classification, the assumption that it stems from a 'fact of nature' (Latour 2004), becomes questionable. This, in turn, renders problematic the biopolitical entanglement of harm and care that is central to the conservationist governance of IAS.

Conclusion

This chapter has examined the conservationist management of IAS. It has asked how a social formation that has as its founding goals the protection of nonhuman nature comes to engage in discourses and practices that cause violent harm to some elements of the very same nature. Using Michel Foucault's work on biopower as an analytical lens, it has argued that the conservationist focus on collectivities such as biodiversity/ecosystem and the associated ethical and ontological marginalisation of individual organisms result in the complex entanglement of harm and care that is seen in the management of invasive species. The emphasis on collectivities of nonhuman life such as biodiversity and the invisibilisation of individual organisms allows for the displacement of responsibility from the human to the nonhuman and the abusive control that results.

In other words, biopolitical rationalities and techniques facilitate the conflation of four distinct ethical issues that trouble debates around invasive species. These are: (i) the rights of native species and ecosystems vis-a-vis invasive species; (ii) the duties of humans who govern these interactions and make judgements about invasives; (iii) the responsibility of humans towards native ecosystems that are threatened by invasive species; (iv) the responsibility of humans towards invasive species that would not have colonised native ecosystems in the absence of human invasion of those ecosystems. The widespread acceptance of the violent eradication and control of invasive species suggests that these four issues are run together into one meta-response centred on the first of these four issues. This conflation is enabled by the biopolitical ontological and ethical focus on the larger collectivity and the concomitant invisibility of individuals which in turn allows for the violent control of some organisms.

The chapter also offered a problematisation of taken-for-granted concepts such as biodiversity and IAS which lie at the foundation of the abuse of some organisms. The socially constructed character of these concepts, we argued, destabilises the certainty with which harmful interventions are wielded against some organisms in order to protect ecosystems and biodiversity. This is not to imply that nonhuman nature, whether individual organisms, habitats or biodiversity as a whole, does not need protection from human activity. This is only to point to the problematic character of conservationist care that harms some forms of nonhuman life in order to protect nature at the scale of a larger collectivity from the consequences of human activity.

There is nothing intrinsically wrong in reasoning with and making decisions based on collectivist ontologies. It is inevitable when we lack knowledge about individuals or that knowledge is difficult or unethical to obtain. Also, in the case of conservation, collectivities such as habitats need to be protected in order to safeguard the individual organisms that live in the habitat.

However, a narrow focus on collectivities in the absence of safeguards for individuals can lead to naked displays of violent power. This is clear in the context of invasive species, and also in the human world. International relations are a case in point, where nations further their interests to the detriment of the citizens of other nations and strategic calculation can often trump individual rights. However, unlike discourse about the human world which often mixes several moral schema (for example, human rights which are focused on the individual, and group rights which are focused on collectivities based on nationality, race, culture, etc.), discourse about nonhuman nature in the conservation/biodiversity literature is overwhelmingly characterised by ecocentric moral schema and collectivist ontologies.

Privileging either the individual or the collectivity to the detriment of the other is not the only option available for conservationist decision-making. There are ethical accounts that connect the individual to the collectivity. In the case of IAS, liberal theories of citizenship (Donaldson and Kymlicka 2011), which have recently been developed in the context of nonhuman animals, are a possible alternative. Applying ideas from these theories would suggest that the privileges of the native populations are greater than those of 'alien' organisms but that does not mean that alien organisms can be treated as vermin and eradicated. Another possible body of literature that might be of use for conservationist decision-making about IAS pertains to the idea of multi-optic seeing (Kim 2015). In multi-optic approaches, the vulnerabilities of multiple organisms and groups are simultaneously and equally considered so as to avoid the dismissal of some vulnerabilities in order to protect others.

While these are some routes that offer opportunities for more careful and caring decision-making about IAS and nonhuman nature more broadly, the main point this chapter makes is with regard to the biopolitical character of existing approaches to invasive species. The recognition of the entanglement of harm and care in conservationist discourse and practice relating to invasive alien organisms, and a keen awareness of the social construction of taken-for-granted conservationist concepts, are key first steps towards a less violent and abusive relationship between the social formation of conservation and nonhuman life.

References

Blackburn, T. M., Pettorelli, N., Katzner, T., Gompper, M. E., Mock, K., Garner, T. W. J., et al. (2010). Dying for conservation: eradicating invasive alien species in the face of opposition. *Animal Conservation, 13*, 227–228.

Braun, B. (2009). Nature. In N. Castree, D. Demeritt, D. Liverman, & B. Rhoads (Eds.), *A companion to environmental geography* (pp. 19–36). Malden, Oxford, Chichester: Blackwell.

Callicott, J. B. (2006). Conservation values and ethics. In G. K. Meffe & C. R. Caroll (Eds.), *Principles of conservation biology* (pp. 111–135). Sunderland, MA: Sinauer Associates Inc.

Canal and River Trust. (2015). Invasive species—rogues' gallery. https://canalrivertrust.org.uk/news-and-views/features/Invasive-species-rogues-gallery. Accessed 7 January 2015.

Castree, N., & Braun, B. (Eds.). (2001). *Social nature: theory, practice and politics.* Malden and Oxford: Blackwell.

Chrulew, M. (2011). Managing love and death at the zoo: the biopolitics of endangered species preservation. *Australian Humanities Review, 50*, 137–157.

Convention on Biological Species. (1993a). Article 2: Use of Terms. https://www.cbd.int/convention/articles/default.shtml?a=cbd-02. Accessed 7 April 2015.

Convention on Biological Species. (1993b). Article 8: in-situ conservation. https://www.cbd.int/convention/articles/default.shtml?a=cbd-0. Accessed 7 January 2015.

Convention on Biological Species. (2015a). Glossary of terms. https://www.cbd.int/invasive/terms.shtml. Accessed 7 January 2015.

Convention on Biological Species. (2015b). What are invasive alien species? https://www.cbd.int/invasive/WhatareIAS.shtml. Accessed 2 July 2015.

Convention on Biological Species. (2015c). What's the Problem? *Convention on Biological Diversity.* https://www.cbd.int/invasive/problem.shtml. Accessed 7 January 2015.

Convention on Biological Species (2015d). Why does it matter? https://www.cbd.int/invasive/matter.shtml. Accessed 7 January 2015.

Cooper, M. (1997). Information and advisory note number 70: red squirrels. http://www.snh.org.uk/publications/on-line/advisorynotes/70/70.html. Accessed 7 April 2015.

Crawford, J. S. (2015). History of the state vermin barrier fences. http://pandora.nla.gov.au/pan/43156/20040709-0000/agspsrv34.agric.wa.gov.au/programs/app/barrier/history/Crawford_Rcommission.htm. Accessed 7 February 2015.

Crutzen, P. J., & Stoermer, E. F. (2000). 'The 'Anthropocene'. *Global Change Newsletter*, *41*, 17–18.

Department of Agriculture. (2015). History. *The State Barrier Fence of Western Australia.* http://pandora.nla.gov.au/pan/43156/20040709-0000/agspsrv34.agric.wa.gov.au/programs/app/barrier/history.htm. Accessed 7 February 2015.

Dillon, M., & Reid, J. (2009). *The liberal way of war: killing to make life live.* London & New York: Routledge.

Donaldson, S., & Kymlicka, W. (2011). *Zoopolis: A political theory of animal rights.* Oxford & New York: Oxford University Press.

Esposito, R. (2008). *Bios: Biopolitics and philosophy.* Minneapolis: University Of Minnesota Press.

Foucault, M. (2003). *Society must be defended: Lectures at the College de France 1975–1976.* New York: Picador.

Foucault, M. (2008). *The history of sexuality (Vol. 1): The will to knowledge.* Camberwell: Penguin Books.

Foucault, M. (2009) *Security, territory, population: Lectures at the College de France 1977–78.* Basingtoke: Palgrave Macmillan.

Franklin, A. (2015). Ecosystem and landscape: strategies for the Anthropocene. In M. Boyd, M. Chrulew, C. Degeling, A. Mrva-Montoya, F. Probyn-Rapsey, Savvides, N., et al. (Eds.), *Animals in the Anthropocene: critical perspectives on non-human futures* (pp. 63–87). Sydney: Sydney University Press.

Gudmand-Hoyer, M., & Lodrup, H. T. (2009). Liberal biopolitics reborn. *Foucault Studies*, *7*, 99–130.

Invasive Species Specialist Group. (2015). 100 of the world's worst invasive alien species. *Global Invasive Species Database.* http://www.issg.org/database/species/search.asp?st=100ss. Accessed 7 February 2015.

IUCN. (2015). Invasive species. *International Union for Conservation of Nature.* http://www.iucn.org/about/union/secretariat/offices/iucnmed/iucn_med_programme/species/invasive_species/. Accessed 7 January 2015.

Kim, C. J. (2015). *Dangerous crossings: race, species, and nature in a multicultural age.* Cambridge: Cambridge University Press.

Latour, B. (2004). *Politics of nature: how to bring the sciences into democracy.* Cambridge, MA: Harvard University Press.

Li, T. M. (2007) *The will to improve: governmentality, development and the practice of politics.* Durham & London: Duke University Press.

Mathews, F. (2012). The anguish of wildlife ethics. *New Formations*, *76*, 114–131.

McNeely, J. A., Mooney, H. A., Neville, P. S., & Waage, J. K. (Eds.) (2001) *Global strategy on invasive alien species.* Gland, Switzerland & Cambridge, UK: IUCN.

Meffe, G. K., Carroll, C. R., & Groom, M. J. (2006). What is conservation biology? In M. J. Groom, G. K. Meffe, & C. R. Carroll (Eds.), *Principles of conservation biology* (pp. 3–25). Sunderland, MA: Sinauer Associates Inc.

O'Brien, W. (2006). Exotic invasions, nativism, and ecological restoration: on the persistence of a contentious debate. *Ethics, Place & Environment, 9*(1), 63–77.

Paquet, P. C., & Darimont, C. T. (2010). Wildlife conservation and animal welfare: two sides of the same coin? *Animal Welfare, 19*(2), 177–190.

Peretti, J. H. (1998). Nativism and nature: rethinking biological invasion. *Environmental Values, 7*(2), 183–192.

Pilkington, E. (2010, February 25). Killer whale Tilikum to be spared after drowning trainer by ponytail. *Guardian*. http://www.guardian.co.uk/world/2010/feb/25/killer-whale-tilikum-drowned-trainer-hair. Accessed 16 August 2012.

Ramp, D., & Bekoff, M. (2015). Compassion as a practical and evolved ethic for conservation. *BioScience*. Advance Access, 1–5.

Sagoff, M. (2005) Do non-native species threaten the natural environment? *Journal of Agricultural and Environmental Ethics, 18*, 215–236.

Sagoff, M. (2009). Environmental harm: political not biological. *Journal of Agricultural and Environmental Ethics, 22*, 81–88.

Sarkar, S. (2012) *Environmental philosophy: from theory to practice*. Chichester: John Wiley & Sons.

Sharp, T. (2012). Standard operating procedure RAB006: rabbit warren destruction by ripping. Invasive Animals Cooperative Research Centre. http://www.pestsmart.org.au/wp-content/uploads/2013/08/RAB006_warren-ripping.pdf. Accessed 7 February 2015.

Shukin, N. (2009) *Animal capital: rendering life in biopolitical times*. Minneapolis: University of Minnesota Press.

Soule, M. (1986). What is conservation biology? *BioSocieties, 35*(11), 727–734.

Srinivasan, K. (2013). The biopolitics of animal being and welfare: Dog control and care in the UK and India. *Transactions of the Institute of British Geographers, 38*(1), 106–119.

Srinivasan, K. (2014). Caring for the collective: biopower and agential subjectification in wildlife conservation. *Environment and Planning D: Society and Space, 32*(3), 501–517.

Srinivasan, K. (2015). The welfare episteme: Street dog biopolitics in the Anthropocene. In M. Boyd, M. Chrulew, C. Degeling, A. Mrva-Montoya, F. Probyn-Rapsey, N. Savvides, et al. (Eds.), *Animals in the Anthropocene: critical perspectives on non-human futures* (pp. 201–220). Sydney: Sydney University Press.

The Forestry Commission UK. (2015). Red squirrel facts. *Forest Research*. http://www.forestry.gov.uk/fr/INFD-8C8BHC. Accessed 7 April 2015.

Turpie, J., & Jurk, C. (2012) *Costs of meeting Aichi Targets for 2020: target 9—invasive alien species*, Convention on Biological Diversity. https://www.cbd.int/doc/meetings/fin/hlpgar-sp-01/information/hlpgar-sp-01-aichitargets-05-en.pdf. Accessed 11 January 2016.

Twine, R. (2013). Animals on drugs: understanding the role of pharmaceutical companies in the animal-industrial complex. *Bioethical Inquiry, 10*, 505–514.

Warren, C. R. (2007). Perspectives on the 'alien' versus 'native' species debate: a critique of concepts, language and practice. *Progress in Human Geography, 31*(4), 427–446.

Warwick, H. (2014). Should we cull grey squirrels to save the native red? *The Guardian*. http://www.theguardian.com/commentisfree/2014/nov/28/cull-grey-squirrels-save-native-red. Accessed 7 March 2015.

WaterPatrol. (2015). Alien invader threatens Britain's native wildlife. Invasive species special. *WaterPatrol*.

Williams, F., Eschen, R., Harris, A., Djeddour, D., Pratt, C., Shaw, R. S., et al. (2010) *The economic costs of invasive non-native species on Great Britain*. CABI.

Wittenberg, R., & Cock, M. J. W. (Eds.) (2001). *Invasive alien species: a toolkit of best prevention and management practices*, Wallingford, Oxon: CAB International.

Wonham, M. (2006). Species invasions. 3rd edition. In M. J. Groom, G. K. Meffe, & C. R. Carroll (Eds.), *Principles of conservation biology* (pp. 293–331). Sunderland, MA: Sinauer Associates Inc.

Krithika Srinivasan is a lecturer in Human Geography at the University of Edinburgh. Her research and teaching interests lie at the intersection of geographies of nature, more-than-human geographies and animal studies, and post development politics.

Rajesh Kasturirangan is the co-coordinator of the Mind and Society initiative at Azim Premji University in Bangalore. He's a cognitive scientist and mathematician whose work spans mathematical models of language and perception and theories of well-being.

Legal and Illegal Theriocide of Trafficked Animals

Ragnhild Sollund

Introduction

The focus of this chapter is the fate of animals who are trafficked to Norway and seized at airports or in private homes. They are victims of the so-called 'wildlife trade' (WLT) that threatens a large number of species and results in unspeakable harm to and loss of animal lives; they are forcibly captured, abducted, trafficked, or killed on the spot, whether it be for the pet trade, trophy hunting, medicinal purposes, collecting, status, or innumerable other exploitations that humans can devise. (For more details concerning the WLT see Herrera and Hennessey 2007; Weston and Menon 2009; Wright et al. 2001; Santana et al. 2008; Gonzales 2003; Guzman et al. 2007; Herbig 2010; Sollund 2011, 2013a, 2015b; Wyatt 2009, 2011, 2013; Sollund and Maher 2015; Schneider 2012, in addition to reports made by the NGO, TRAFFIC[1]). The animals of concern in this chapter are those who have been trafficked alive as part of the pet trade.

WLT is regulated in the CITES convention. The convention has 181 member states. Trade is regulated according to a species' threat of extinction.

[1] http://www.traffic.org/ Traffic has published a vast amount of reports about WLT, I therefore direct readers to their website rather than list any of these here.

R. Sollund (✉)
University of Oslo, Oslo, Norway
e-mail: ragnhild.sollund@jus.uio.no

J. Maher et al. (eds.), *The Palgrave International Handbook of Animal Abuse Studies*, DOI 10.1057/978-1-137-43183-7_21

Species listed in Appendix I are threatened with extinction, and usually banned from trade. Species listed in Appendix II are vulnerable, and trade must be controlled in order to avoid utilization incompatible with their survival. Species listed in Appendix III are those of whom the trade is under surveillance upon demand from a country where it is vulnerable. CITES requires that the individual who is trafficked is accompanied by the necessary export (re-export) and import certificates (CITES n.d.).

Before I turn to the pet trade and trafficking, I will briefly discuss some relevant terminology. I begin with the word 'animal'. There are difficulties in applying this word because of its speciesism and othering effect; it creates a gulf between the human animal and animals other than humans (Derridá 2002), as if 'the others' were one category. The term 'nonhuman' is also sometimes used, but it implies the other animals are simply the negation of what it is to be human, which is also alienating. The term 'aota' for animals other than human animals has been suggested, but as I find it stylistically poor, and therefore, for lack of a better alternative, I will use the word 'animal' unless the species (or category) of the animal in question is of special interest or known.

This chapter is based on an ongoing research project[2] in three locations, Norway, Colombia, and Brazil, in which I am using a number of different methods including documentary analysis of approximately 50 Customs confiscation reports, in this case of seized animals.[3] Because the chapter is about how trafficking victims are killed after being seized by the authorities in Norway, I could refer to their deaths merely as 'animal killings,' yet the act of killing an individual of *any* animal species, whether willful or unintentional, is equally harmful for the victim whether he/she is human or nonhuman. As a remedy, Beirne (2014) offers the term theriocide for such acts.

> 'Theriocide' refers to those diverse human actions that cause the deaths of animals. Like the killing of one human by another (e.g., homicide, infanticide and femicide), theriocide may be socially acceptable or unacceptable, legal or illegal. It may be intentional or unintentional. It may involve active maltreatment or passive neglect. Theriocides may occur one-on-one, in small groups or

[2] I am grateful to The Norwegian Animal Protection Fund for contributing financially to the research project on which this chapter is based. The project is part of an EFFACE project, funded by the FP7, EC. See http://efface.eu/.

[3] I don't have the total overview of confiscation reports that may be included in penal cases yet. These are the ones provided to me directly from the Customs directorate.

> in large-scale social institutions. The numerous sites of theriocide include intensive rearing regimes, hunting, trafficking, vivisection, militarism, and climate change. (Beirne 2014, p. 55).

I accept his terminology, but I wish to point out that this term too may be othering because it suggests, like in the word 'animal', that all 'therios' belong to a single category, as if they were all the same. In addition, we are left, once again, with a distinction between two categories: the killing of a human by a human—homicide—as one kind of act and the killing of an animal by a human—theriocide—as another. If, however, one accepts that therios are as sentient as humans, then no matter by what method the acts of violence or killing are committed or whether against homo or therio, the harm committed is equal. In his definition of theriocide, Beirne clarifies the etymological origin of the word (2014, p. 55);

> It combines the ancient Greek θρίον (an animal other than a human) and the Latin cædere. θρίον, first, is a prosaic variant of θηρ, which seems originally to have meant a beast of prey. Later, θηρ was extended to other animals, probably including wild and domesticated animals and metaphorical monsters

Consequently; the animals referred to in the ancient greek *developed* to include not only beast of prey, domesticated animals, or metaphorical monsters, but *all those animals that are nonhuman*. Beirne also discusses which animal species could be included, without drawing a conclusion (p. 60). Thus, it remains unclear who comprises the category—is a bee included?—and therefore, the degree to which those who are usually encompassed in the animal category are sentient[4] and merit equal concern (Regan 1983). Because I hold that the animals discussed in this chapter *are* sentient, that is, they are 'subjects of their lives' (Regan 1983), perhaps, as Beirne (2014) suggests, the term 'murder' can encompass both the killing of an animal and the killing of a human. *Murder* could *equally* be referred as to murder independent on the species of the sentient victim, although Beirne's agenda is specifically to name the killing of *animals*, thus

[4] As this concept ('sentience') is usually understood, although one could, out of precaution, choose not to define this in terms of the senses and feelings humans are able to recognize and thereby acknowledge, and rather be open minded toward all nonhuman beings. For example, according to recent research, even plants are sentient and intelligent (Hance 2015). Accessed 11 August 2015 from http://www.theguardian.com/environment/radical-conservation/2015/aug/04/plants-intelligent-sentient-book-brilliant-green-internet?CMP=Share_AndroidApp_Gmail).

highlighting the seriousness of the harm and injustice involved for animals. As Beirne argues, the loss of a human life and the loss of an animal life are comparable; both human and nonhuman individuals share an interest in a *continued* life (Francione 2014). As I acknowledge that animals are sentient beings, I find it legitimate to refer to them as 'who' and as 'he/she' rather than 'it'.

'Wildlife' is another problematic term. In its anthropocentrism, it not only groups a large number of animal species in the same category but also fails to distinguish them from plants. 'Wildlife' further implies that these species are alien and threatening in some way to humans and that they represent a contrast to civilized, cultured humans and 'domesticated' animals put under human dominion, like nature and 'wilderness' may be regarded as alien and terrifying (Brisman and Rau 2009).

'Trafficking' in this chapter, describes both the legal and illegal trade in animals, as I see few differences between the two in terms of the harm to the victim, although illegal trafficking may result in more victims dying as the trade is then clandestine and the animals hidden, for example, in bottles, suitcases, and other containers. I use the term 'abduction' rather than 'poaching' to refer to forcibly removing someone from their familiar surroundings because the latter implies that killing/taking animals from their habitats is acceptable as long as it is done legally. 'Poaching' also assumes that animals are property (Sollund 2011), whether of a game park or the state.

A 'pet'[5] in this context is defined as an animal kept within a domestic setting where the main purpose of keeping him/her is for (human) personal interest, entertainment or companionship (Bush et al. 2014, p. 664). This definition does not necessarily imply that there is any bond of affection or any form of mutuality between the human and the 'pet' in question, for example, reptile owners may be more fascinated by their 'pets' than love them (Sollund 2013a).

I will begin with a brief overview of trafficking for the pet trade after which I contextualize it by discussing Norway's position vis-à-vis trafficking and the actions taken by officials based on findings from my own empirical findings of research into this matter. Next, I present my findings related to theriocide of trafficking victims followed by some philosophical thoughts on this matter.

[5] Elsewhere (Sollund 2011, p. 438) I argue that the word 'pet' implies affection, but it also has a devaluating connotation implying ownership over property, thus objectifying the animals who are there for humans who want or need a physical proximity to a nonhuman animal, which in turn benefits the human, e.g., children, who use the 'pet' in an instrumental way, for example the child is expected to learn to show care for others through having a pet.

The International Pet Trade

The transnational trafficking of pets is, together with habitat loss, a major threat to many species and is also known to have caused species extinction. This is the situation whether animals are trafficked illegally or legally:

> The legality of trade [of animals] does not guarantee its sustainability. By default, trade is legal unless a motion is successfully brought before CITES to demonstrate negative impacts. Therefore one can assume that there is legal trade that is damaging because of outdated conservation assessments or lack of motivation to bring the case before CITES (Busch et al. 2014, p. 673).

Reptiles and birds are the species most trafficked for the pet market and consequently the species that are most often seized in the EU and beyond elsewhere (van Uhm 2015). Parrots, of which millions have been trafficked in recent decades (Tella and Hiraldo 2014) are of particular concern, together with many of the reptile species that are trafficked which also are threatened with extinction (Natush and Lyons 2012). According to interviews with reptile keepers, reptiles provide great sources for fascination and are kept also as collector items (Sollund 2013a).

van Uhm (2015) states that seizures of live animal species in the illegal wildlife trade in the EU consist mainly of live reptiles (tortoises), followed by birds (parrots) and incidentally mammals (primates). An overview of major international seizures within the EU in 2013 revealed that 1,570 live reptiles were seized (TRAFFIC 2015). EU TWIX[6] seizures show that more than 30,000 live reptiles were confiscated in 2001–2010 in the EU (van Uhm 2015). Between 2000 and 2003, the EU imported 2.8 million wild CITES-approved birds (FAO 2011).

Reptiles are thus highly sought after as pets (or collector items) of whom many are trafficked from South East Asia, especially Indonesia, due to its biodiversity and lack of illegal wildlife trade (IWT) law enforcement (Lyons and Natush 2011). According to Lyons and Natush (2011), the pet trade in reptiles threatens many species that are suffering from drastic decline, among them tortoises and freshwater turtles. While reptiles trafficked to Norway may be purchased at Terraristika Hamm in Germany, an international reptile expo notorious for selling wild-caught reptiles, and reptile owners in Norway claim even reptiles sold in zoo shops in Denmark and Sweden appear to be wild caught (Sollund 2013a), their place of origin is hard to determine.

[6] European Union Trade in Wildlife Information eXchange database. http://www.eutwix.org/

Busch et al (2014), in a study of CITES records of animal trade, found that in 2006–2012, 56,792 birds, 6,310 reptiles and 1,226 mammals were trafficked legally (p. 670). Of the nonhuman animals to be abducted, birds (23 %) and reptiles (10 %) were most likely to have been abducted from their habitats, or to be the first generation of abducted parents. These numbers include CITES I-listed species, for example, yellow-naped parrots (amazon auropalliata), 88 of whom were abducted from Central and South America and trafficked to the US and Canada (Busch et al. 2014). Latin America and Southeast Asia are great source and import localities for the trade of animals also within a country's borders (for example, from the forest to urban areas) or between neighboring countries (Goyes 2015; Busch et al. 2014; Herrera and Hennessey 2007; Sollund and Maher 2015; Pires and Clark 2011).

The more desirable a species is for humans, the more at risk it is for trafficking. Tella and Hiraldo (2014; see also Pires and Clark 2011) found that a cross cultural preference for species of parrots that have certain characteristics—colorfulness, large size and speaking ability—increases these species' risk of extinction. African grey parrots, for example, which are trafficked mainly from Cameroon and the DR Congo for the pet market, are another species that is threatened because of their cognitive skills and ability to learn human language (Pepperberg 1999). This is understandable considering the numbers of trafficking victims: between 1994 and 2003 according to Wildlife Extra (2008), 350,000 African greys were traded legally, yet these numbers say nothing of the number of individuals dying in transit or the number of birds who are trafficked illegally.

The EU is a large market for the pet trade (Sollund and Maher 2015), despite its ban on wild-bird trade in 2007[7] which came as a result of the avian flu. The ban entailed reduced import to the EU, while export to the Middle East (for example, 753 falcons from Germany in 2006 on one occasion) and to South America increased (Busch et al. 2014). CITES expressed disappointment about the ban in wild-bird import to the EU (CITES 2007). The focus of CITES is as always on 'wildlife' as a natural resource that should continue to be exploited for human benefit (Sollund 2011); therefore, a fall in import of live birds may represent a disappointment because the birds remain 'unexploited resources'. The CITES website states that the global trade in wild birds has declined from an estimated 7.5 million birds a year in 1975

[7] On 11 January, 2007, the European Commission's Standing Committee on the Food Chain and Animal Health (SCOFCAH) unanimously adopted a permanent prohibition on the import of wild-caught birds into EU countries, effective 1 July 2007, in order to address the health threat posed by H5N1 avian influenza and other diseases (SSN 2007)

(when CITES came into effect) to about 1.5 million (CITES 2007). The lack of protection for individual animals offered by CITES is a point to which I return when discussing the fate of seized animals in Norway.

The animals who are seized may represent only the tip of the iceberg of the number of victims who are smuggled, abducted, killed and trafficked on a daily basis (Sollund 2013a). It is important to note that a great part of illegal wildlife trafficking will never be detected due to the clandestine character of the trade, and lack of priority by law enforcement agents worldwide which entails loads of animals go under the radar.

Mortality rates are shown to be high: up to 90 % of the parrots who are abducted die before they reach their end point (See Sollund 2015b, pp. 151–152 for further details). Some species handle the hardship of trafficking and captivity so badly they are referred to as 'cut off flowers', such as reptile species (Herbig 2010) and slow lories who are sold off cheaply because they die quickly in captivity (Busch et al. 2014, p. 665).

The Internet has become an important connection between buyers and sellers, not only of animal products, but also of live animals who are traded as pets (Lavorgna 2014, 2015; IFAW 2008; Izzo 2009). This is of concern not only because trafficking results in species extinction, but because of the abuse (and deaths) inherent in the trade (Busch et al. 2014; Sollund and Maher 2015).

Because birds and reptiles figure so prominently in the international literature concerning the pet trade and in seizure reports from customs in Norway, and are most frequently represented in my interview data also (see below), reptiles and birds as victims of trafficking will remain the main focus of the chapter.

Norway's Position in Relation to Pet Trafficking of Endangered Species

Norway and Iceland are the only countries in Europe where the possession of alien reptiles is illegal.[8] Norway joined CITES in 1976 and also bans the importation of alien 'exotic species' through a regulation under the Animal

[8] In Norway, exceptions are made for people with allergies who, because they are unable to keep more conventional pets such as cats, dogs and rabbits, can, upon application to the Food Safety Authority, be granted permission to keep a tortoise. These are thus regarded as legal, while other 'exotic' reptile species are regarded as illegal. There are also legal reptiles in zoos. It is open to debate whether human and nonhuman animals may be legal or illegal, for example, migration researchers will rather refer to migrants without the required documents as irregular than as illegal, as they claim humans cannot be illegal. The same should apply to nonhumans. Can anybody's life be legal or illegal, or is the animal rather forcefully misplaced? Is s/he only misplaced if this takes place by force as in the case of human and animal trafficking?

Welfare Act which was revised in 2009.[9] According to paragraph 1 of the Act, it is forbidden to import, sell, buy, give away, receive, or keep as domestic animals, companion animals, or otherwise in captivity alien (exotic) mammals, reptiles, toads, frogs, or salamanders. Therefore, reptiles are not openly for sale in Norway, whether on Norwegian Internet sites, at reptile fora or in other ways.

The legality of owning reptiles in Sweden and Denmark makes it possible for Norwegian reptile enthusiasts to buy a reptile in zoo shops there and traffic the animals to Norway (Sollund 2013a). Because Norway shares a long and porous border with Sweden and also borders Finland and Russia in the north, trafficking animals to Norway from these countries is fairly easy (Sollund 2013a), especially given the focus of Norwegian Customs is on drugs rather than on CITES, according to interview data (See also Runhovde 2015). For example; Customs have seizure targets for drugs but not for CITES which entail drugs are prioritized. Consequently, they concentrate on detecting drugs, e.g., when they search parcels sent to Norwegian from other countries, rather than animals or animal products.

When it comes to parrots, however, the situation is quite different. Parrots, although exotic, can be obtained relatively cheaply and easily on the website Finn.no. There is, in effect, no requirement in Norway that parrots for sale are not wild caught because there is no demand that owners document where their birds came from, birds must not be id chipped which could facilitate tracing their origin. Often on Finn.no, owners sell their birds after only owning them a short while (one to two years), indicating that parrots are often bought on impulse by people who are unaware of the demands of a parrot and the challenges involved in keeping one, for example, droppings, noise, difficult behavior (birds are often sold when they reach puberty at age 3 or 4 when they, like human teenagers, can be harder to handle). Even though there is no ban against possessing or selling parrots, it is, nonetheless, illegal to bring them to Norway without permission from the Norwegian Environment Agency which extends an import permit if CITES regulations are followed, that is, if the trafficker has an export permit from the state the bird is taken (all parrots are CITES listed).[10] The fact that breeding parrots and selling them is legal in Norway, however, puts caught wild birds in danger. Breeders often need fresh genes, and this need will continue to drive the wildlife trade despite claims of breeding facilities for wildlife, including zoos, that they are run in order to preserve species (Rodríguez and García 2008; Busch et al. 2014). In Norway, my data include several verdicts concerning bird traffickers who also

[9] https://lovdata.no/dokument/SF/forskrift/1976-11-20-3.

[10] https://lovdata.no/dokument/SF/forskrift/2002-11-15-1276.

run businesses breeding and selling parrots (see below). This may indicate their business is a means by which they launder wild caught birds, for example, owners may claim that they breed the birds, when in reality they are illegally trafficked to the country. Import of cheap wild caught birds may also sustain their business and provide an addition to their own parrot breeding if the results are insufficient.

Data/Methodology

The seizure reports, completed by Customs officers when animals (or any illegal goods) are seized at Norwegian borders, contain information about the animals, the location and circumstances for the seizure, in addition to information provided by the person carrying/sending animals about his/her intention behind the act and in general his/her explanation for it. I have traced several of the cases that have been produced by the prosecutor as a consequence of these confiscation reports through a number of phone calls to determine how they ended, that is, with a verdict (if the case was brought to trial). Most often, however, they end with a fine or are dismissed.

In addition, in Norway, I conducted 12 semi-structured individual and group interviews with people, who, because of their profession, e.g., as veterinarians, police and customs officers, have specific insight into the illegal wildlife trade. Groups comprised from three to six persons. In addition, I interviewed five offenders (reptile keepers). I also carried out manifold email exchanges and had numerous phone conversations with police, prosecutors and experts. I have conducted further 18 interviews from South America (14 from Colombia and four from Brazil) with veterinarians, wildlife experts, NGO staff, and environmental police.[11] Analysis of newspaper articles that are too many to detail here, on the subject, were also a part of my research.

---

[11] Secretaría ambiental de ambiente; Asociación de veterinaries de vida silvestre; TRAFFIC (Latin America) Fundación Proaves; Centro de recepción y rehabilitación de vida silvestre; ARIE Matão de Cosmópolis/ICMBio, Secretaría de Meio Ambiente do Sao Paolo, Corporación para el Desarrollo sostenible del Norte y oriente Amazónico; Secretaria Municipal do Verde e do Meio Ambiente—Sao Paulo; Ministerio de Ambiente y Desarrollo Sostenible; Policía Militar Ambiental—Sao Paulo; Entropika.

Persons in Colombia and Brazil who want to be credited for their participation in the project are Claudia Isabel Brievar Rico, Bernardo Ortíz von Halle, Javier Cifuentes, Márcia Gonçalves Rodrigues, Claudia Terdiman Schaalmann, Daniela Desgualdo, Wilfredo Pachón, Ricardo Gandara Crede, Claudia Rodríguez, Marcelo Robis Francisco Massaro and Angela Maldonado.

Interviews in Norway (17) were conducted by the author, while interviews in Colombia and Brazil (with the exception of one interview done by the author on SKYPE) were conducted by David Rodríguez Goyes, for which I am grateful.

I was also given access to the paperwork relating to a large number of penal cases which can only be superficially and selectively treated at this point as they far outnumber what can possibly be analyzed for this brief chapter (but see Sollund forthcoming). The penal cases include 87 cases coded as '2510: Illegal importation of alien wildlife species' (breach of Wildlife law §47) and 723 cases coded as '5901: Illegal importation/dealing with exotic species' §30 nr. 76 (breach of a regulation under the Animal Welfare Act) in STRASAK, the central penal case statistics of the police. These files include all from charges, police interrogations, fines, verdicts, photos, and so on; in short all material the police have gathered in relation to an offence.

Typical Cases: Reptile/Combination Cases and Parrot Trafficking

Findings indicate there are typically two different types of seizures of live animals in Norway; a repeated violation is trafficking parrots into the country, but the most frequently seized species are reptiles. Reptiles are seized at borders or in private homes. In most cases relating to parrots, these are attempted smuggling (traffickers not declaring the parrots to Customs) but some cases also include problematic paperwork when the necessary CITES permits are not in place, for example, more birds being brought into the country than the number that the permits allow. The number of individuals may vary; the most birds who were seized at once during the time I have conducted the research (between 2010–2015) was 25. On some occasions, and this is the case for a particular recidivist offender, he trafficked birds together with other contraband such as alcohol and tobacco. This indicates that his main motive for smuggling is profit, as both parrots and alcohol may be sold for a good price. Another typical type of offender featured in the confiscation reports is the tourist who purchases a tortoise at a local market while visiting Turkey or Greece and brings her/him home in the pocket or hand luggage to have the animal as a pet. Other typical penal cases in the material I studied are what I refer to as 'combination cases' in which a recidivist offender who is charged on numerous grounds, usually violent and drug offences, is also convicted of a breach of the wildlife law or violation of the regulation against the keeping of exotic species under the Animal Welfare Act because a reptile is found in his home during a police search.

In such combination cases, except when the main offence is another crime, the punishment for trafficking is usually very lenient—usually a fine or a brief suspended prison sentence. (The failure of such punishment in serving as a deterrent and in creating awareness will not be discussed in this chapter, but see Sollund and Maher 2015; Sollund 2013a, 2015b).

It is striking, however, that while the trafficker receives a small fine, the fate of the majority of the animals involved is death. Before I turn to this outcome, the logic behind it, the explanations for it and the species injustice thereby perpetuated, I will address briefly the abuses the animals suffer before they reach their endpoint.

Abuse Through Trafficking

Despite the legality and regulation of much animal trafficking, the ways in which animals are trafficked and the conditions in which they live are often characterized by abuse. I take my understanding of animal abuse from the definition laid out by Robert Agnew (1998, p. 179) and specified by Piers Beirne.

> [...] any act that contributes to the pain, suffering or death of an animal or that otherwise threatens its welfare. Animal abuse may be physical, psychological, or emotional; may involve active maltreatment or passive neglect or omission; and may be direct or indirect, intentional or unintentional. (Beirne 1999 p. 121).

Normally, when animals are taken from their habitats for the pet trade, or when they are bred for that purpose, there is no intention to abuse them. Unfortunately, abuse often occurs. As mentioned above, deaths are widespread among birds and reptiles, and the ways in which they die—from suffocation, starvation, dehydration, and shock and pain—are clearly causing them great harm and suffering. For example, one of our interviewees in South America described an incident in which locals were abducting and trafficking parrots. When they came upon a police control, and as they were near water, they simply submerged the cage with the birds to prevent them from screaming. It is unknown how many of the birds died as a result of this. Recently, in Indonesia, cockatoos were smuggled in bottles and only a few survived (Awford 2015). An interviewee from Colombia provided another example:

> For the birds they use PVC tubes where they stuff the birds, they are thus totally immobilized, they can traffic 1000 birds in this way, of which 10 to 15 percent may survive, which is sufficient to produce profit (Proaves, translated from Spanish).

Even if animals survive their abduction and transport, there is no guarantee that they will receive proper treatment—that is, be given adequate food and shelter, stimuli, company, room for exercise—once they reach their final destination. In South America, captured birds are often left to die of malnutrition because they can be easily replaced. In Norway, pet owners do not need to demonstrate to sellers that they are capable of giving an animal proper care and attention (Sollund 2013c). There is a requirement in the Norwegian Animal welfare act's § 6 about competence in animal keeping for those who shall take over an animal;[12] however, private owners selling or giving away their animals and the people who take them on are not controlled. So, for instance, traumatized birds, who are also fed with the wrong food, are victims of abuse because of the damage this does to their physical and mental health.

In the case of reptiles, transport often proves very harmful. They are often trafficked in boxes and sent from their habitat to Europe by mail/package service. As many originate in Indonesia, the journey is long and many die in transit or shortly after arriving (see Herbig 2010). In the numerous penal cases I examined that concern reptiles, photos and the description of how the reptiles are kept confirm that they endure less than ideal living conditions, such as being contained in small, bare glass boxes while in transit. This constitutes suffering because naturally many reptile species roam great distances and have needs in regards to physical movement and also the mental stimulation they get from finding food. In one case, the offenders explained to the police that they took over a boa snake for a friend, and it was evident from what they said that care for the animal was of low priority. Offenders pose in pictures with the snakes wrapped around their bodies, thus using them as artefacts to display some sort of status, perhaps related to masculinity ideals, rather than caring for the animals involved. Paradoxically, what may add to the inadequate care reptiles receive is the fact that because it is illegal to keep them in Norway, partly for animal welfare reasons, owners are hesitant to bring them to a veterinarian because they are afraid they will be reported, and when they do, veterinarians do not always provide adequate treatment because they lack experience, while others refuse to treat them entirely.

It must be emphasized though, that many reptile keepers care for their animals and try to provide living conditions for their pets which they find appropriate (interview data). Still, the question remains whether any 'wild'

[12] According to § 6, animal keepers must ensure animals are adequately taken care of, no children under 16 shall have an independent responsibility for an animal, and the animal keeper must not transfer the responsibility for the animal to someone for whom it is reason to believe will not treat the animal in a responsible way. https://lovdata.no/dokument/NL/lov/2009-06-19-97.

animal can live a good life in a cage or a glass box, deprived of the habitat in which he/she was born. Consequently, all unnatural keeping of reptiles and birds may be characterized as abusive to some degree, despite the good intentions of keepers.

State Theriocide

In the penal cases I have examined (coded as 5210, 4901, see above), the most frequent outcome of a case is that the animal, usually a reptile, is killed. Most often, the act of theriocide is committed by veterinarians from the Food Safety Authority (Mattilsynet).[13] While the Food Safety Authority takes care of the animals who are seized, the Norwegian Environment Agency will usually first be consulted in regards to what the Food Safety Authority shall do with the animals, when they may be CITES listed. The Norwegian Environment Agency is the largest agency under the Ministry of Climate and Environment; it is responsible for CITES in Norway and reports to the CITES authorities. It is also the formal owner of all confiscated wildlife in Norway. Staff working with CITES issues at the Norwegian Environment Agency are consequently the ones consulted also by customs (when animals are seized at a Norwegian entry point) in regards to the animals' CITES listing or by police (when animals are seized during house searches).

According to my data, the Norwegian Environment Agency staff has, on occasion endeavored to have the Kristiansand Zoo or Oslo Reptile Park adopt the seized animals. These institutions, however, will accept only those animals who are not already represented in their collections or of which they have few. Usually veterinarians are called upon to euthanize the animals. If, after consultation with the Norwegian Environment Agency, it is discovered that the animal is CITES I-listed, attempts may be made to save him/her. This may also happen if the animal is CITES II-listed, but usually such a listing is used as an argument for why they should be killed—that is, they are not sufficiently threatened (and thus not sufficiently valuable) to be saved.

Several of the penal cases and confiscation reports pertain to different parrot species, often African greys (Sollund and Maher 2015; Sollund 2013a, 2015b, forthcoming). While the species is attractive precisely because of the personality of its individuals, making them appealing pets, this is not reflected in the eyes of the authorities, who merely see the parrots as illegal

[13] The name *Mattilsynet* clearly shows that the most important role animals have in Norway is as *food*.

'goods' or as 'specimens' who are not worthy of preserving because they are still too numerous to be critically endangered. It appears, though, that more attempts are made to save parrots than, for example, boas.

One offender was convicted for smuggling 12 African greys on two separate occasions: four parrots in November 2010 and eight parrots in November 2011. According to my data, this offender had been convicted previously in Sweden for similar crimes. Following the 2010 seizure, the birds were all killed by the authorities. The verdict does not reveal what happened to the birds who were seized in 2011, but according to interview data, some were saved and others killed. That the fate of the victims in this case is not clarified in the verdict is an interesting point in itself. On August 12, 2014 another offender attempted to smuggle in six African greys via the ferry from Denmark to Kristiansand. The birds were killed at the order of the Norwegian Environment Agency. On March 30, 2014, 44 parrots, 36 for whom the trafficker had the necessary CITES permits, were brought in at Kristiansand by the ferry from Denmark. The other birds, one barnardius zonarios parrot and seven agapronis parrots were offered to Kristiansand Zoo, which rejected them. Consequently, these birds were also killed.

The files also contain other verdicts, fines and seizure reports concerning parrots, but there are no records presenting an overview of seized animals killed in Norway. The general impression I gleaned, confirmed by the Norwegian Environment Agency, is that a trafficked animal can consider himself/herself very lucky if he/she survives after being 'in the care of' Norwegian authorities.

The main reason for this systematic theriocide committed by Norwegian authorities is that there are no rescue facilities for seized animals in Norway. (The UK, Brazil and Colombia all have such rescue facilities. In Colombia and Brazil, they provide veterinary care, rehabilitation and when possible, repatriation [Sollund and Maher 2015].) Despite efforts made several years ago by the Norwegian Environment Agency to pressure Norwegian authorities to establish a rescue center (interview data), and despite recommendations from CITES in this regard, the lack of political will has meant that nothing has been done to establish rescue centers (interview data).

Not Seeing the Other

In order to discuss these crimes against trafficking victims from a philosophical perspective, I will approach the topic of how we perceive the other, but in a way different from the sociological discussion of othering, which implies the creation of a social and thus emotional distance (Baumann 1991;

Christie 1975). It is possible through processes of alienation to maintain a *social* distance to persons and animals we may be *physically* near to, which in turn may facilitate abuse and harm. For example, generally many people have more social distance to a pig, who is used as food, despite his/her abilities and degree of sentience, than to a dog who is regarded most often as a human companion, and thus in the western hemisphere, not regarded as edible and less likely to be abused, at least systemically (Vialle 1996; Sollund 2008). I will here, focus instead on what I understand to be the opposite—to truly *see* the other as your *next*—in the terms of Lévinas (Aarnes 1994), Berger (2009) and Derridá (2002). Bettino (2015) argues that according to Lévinas, it is in *seeing* the other's face, through recognizing the other that a moral responsibility toward the other arises:

> It is an interpretive, phenomenological description of the rise and repetition of the face-to-face encounter, or the intersubjective *relatio*n at its precognitive core; viz., being *called* by another and *responding* to that other. If precognitive experience, that is, *human sensibility*, can be characterized conceptually, then it must be described in what is most characteristic to it: a continuum of *sensibility and affectivity*, in other words, *sentience and emotion in their interconnection* (n.p.).

While Lévinas wrote about the human face-to-face encounter and the moral and ethical responsibility arising from it for the human other, Berger and Derridá are concerned about animals as the other—worthy of recognition and empathy. Berger (2009) describes the experience of meeting the eyes of caged animals in the zoo, and what position the animals are in the enclosures, prevents humans from seeing the animal:

> The zoo cannot but disappoint. The public purpose of zoos is to offer visitors the opportunity of looking at animals. Yet nowhere in a zoo can a stranger encounter the look of an animal. At the most, the animal's gaze flickers and passes on. They look sideways. They look blindly beyond. They scan mechanically. They have been immunized to encounter, because nothing can any more occupy a *central* place in their attention (p. 37).

Thus, the animal is *looked upon*, but he/she is not *seen*, and he/she is not perceived as anyone, as someone to whom the person looking can relate. Neither does the animal *see* under these conditions. Often the glance will be empty, resigned or purely desperate. He/she is deprived of her/him being her/him because she is forced into the denigrating position of being caged. Many animal owners, although unfortunately not all, *see* an animal when they relate personally to the other animal under their ownership (Sollund 2009). This is easier when the animal in question is not placed in a cage. A caged animal—a bird, for example—becomes a 'cage bird', and the bird (and the animal) are identified as a specific kind, through which the cage comes to define the bird and prevent the owner from seeing *who* the bird is. The bird and the cage, in other words, become one entity. An example of this is the pionus parrot who has been 'on display' for 16 years in a garden center in Oslo, as though he were just another plant adorning the space. This topic was highlighted in a recent verdict from Borgarting lagmannsrett [A Norwegian appeal court] (January 20, 2015) concerning trafficked and confiscated African grey parrots killed by the authorities in which the judges argued that because these birds were commonly held in cages as 'cage birds', they could not be encompassed under the Norwegian Wildlife Law because they could not survive in Norwegian nature. According to the court, in order for an animal to be considered 'wildlife', he/she had to be born in Norway or, at least, be capable of surviving in Norway without human intervention. Consequently, rather than being 'wild lives' that had been trafficked,/and the offence thus being breach of §47 of the Norwegian Wildlife law, they were considered 'illegal goods' that, according to the verdict from the first court instance in this case, had to be conficated in order to enforce the CITES convention. The outcome for the birds was not only that they were confiscated to set an example, but that they were killed as part of the regular procedure in Norway. So even though CITES should protect endangered animals, the application of the convention in court had the adverse effect, at least at individual level.

The main reason, however, why these trafficking victims are not seen in a way that engenders compassion is 'doxic speciesism' (Sollund 2012), which creates an effective barrier against seeing animals as our next of kin—as *our* other. When the Norwegian authorities repeatedly and continuously kill trafficking victims, they do so for practical reasons—they have nowhere to put them—but also because these 'animal others' are objectified and not valued and regarded as subjects with rights (Benton 1998).

Derridá (2002) criticizes those writers, including Lévinas, who have seen, analyzed and reflected on the animal, but who have never *been seen* by an animal (as he was seen naked by the cat): 'They have taken no account of the fact that the animal could look at them, and address them from down there from a wholly other origin' (p. 382). Derridá continues by saying that he and other philosophers have made of the animal a theorem, something seen (but not acknowledged) and not seeing (p. 383). In light of this, in order to *see* the other—the animal who is a sentient being with interests (Regan 1983)—one must acknowledge that oneself is also *seen*—the animal will also look at the human—and when they see each other, they are equals in that meeting. As long as the human being of this encounter continues to look *upon* the other being as 'an animal', he is prevented from seeing her. Using the word 'animal', unassuming as it is, has important implications because in this way man's self-given right and authority to name all those other beings with this categorically discriminating term also allows himself the right to abuse and kill them; they are 'merely' animals. The CITES convention, for example, further denigrates animals by referring to them as 'specimens'—one of a kind, rather than an individual, whose value and thereby right to protection lies only in the number of individuals who remain as part of any one particular species.

When reptiles and birds are killed by Norwegian veterinarians, whether as the executioners of the decisions made by the Environment Agency when CITES-listed species are confiscated, or when they make this decision themselves about animals who are not CITES listed, I doubt they *see* the animals. I doubt they appreciate the fear in their eyes and thereby understand that if they were to fare well, as animals should according to the Norwegian Animal welfare act, then authorities should not kill them (Francione 2014). The abyss created by the animals' 'animalism' (Derridá 2002) supposedly prevents them from being seen by the humans who are in charge of their fate. This abyss is a consequence of lack of species justice and individual animal rights (Benton 1998; Regan 1983).

Conclusion

Theriocide of trafficking victims in Norway is the ultimate act of abuse and violence these animals encounter; it is also the regular fate for animal trafficking victims in Norway. To acknowledge that animals, like humans, are sentient beings, a comparison between human and animal trafficking victims is necessary (Sollund 2013b). A similar treatment of women and children who are trafficking victims would rightfully be met by a general outcry and would be regarded as unlawful homicide and consequently severely punished. As humans who are trafficking victims may be subject to enslavement, abuse and harm, even death, so are animals, and as humans the animals dealt with in this chapter are sentient beings equally capable of suffering. When the trafficking victim is a nonhuman animal, the killing garners little reaction; it is state authorized and within the law. These acts of violence and theriocide would not be possible were it not for speciesism (Beirne 1999)—the overall denial of animals' vicitimization (Sollund 2015b), of their interests and the rights they should be accorded because they are sentient beings, like us (Regan 1983).

Usually, trafficked animals will be killed with what veterinarians regard as humane methods, a lethal injection, not unlike what several American states use when a human is executed. For many people, the death penalty for humans is appalling, even when the offender has committed horrible crimes. Likewise, the death sentence inflicted on innocent animals is morally reproachable. Animals, whether human or nonhuman, generally seek to uphold life. To be killed even without physical pain (but one must assume they feel fear in the handling) is counter to their interests and cannot be done under the rubric of *animal welfare*, as their road to wellbeing is forcefully cut off (Francione 2014). What this says about the veterinarians' role and ethical standard is another issue which deserves being pursued at another occasion. While doctors serving humans take the Hippocratic Oath promising to do the best for their patients (Skatvik 2015), this seems not to be the case for these veterinarians.

The increasing strength of the animal protection movement both in Norway and more broadly indicates that many humans feel they are *related* to animals; they *see* animals as a reflection of themselves when looking into their eyes and thereby feel empathy which guides their actions toward them in a compassionate way (Donovan 1996; Adams 1996). Within a green criminology framework (see Beirne and South 2007; Beirne 2007; Sollund 2015a), the theriocides committed in Norway that I have described should be highlighted like crimes themselves. Today, these theriocides are a state reaction against the *victims* of the trafficking crimes, while the *offenders* receive but very lenient reactions. Given the responses, the victims disappear, (Sollund 2015b), while the offenders are free to continue with their violent affairs.

References

Agnew, R. (1998). The causes of animal abuse: A social-psychological analysis. *Theoretical Criminology, 2*(2), 177–209.

Aarnes A. (1994). *Den annens humanisme. Emmanuel Levinas; Oversatt og med innledning, noter og et essay av Asbjørn Aarnes: Efterord om Bergson og Levinas av Hans Kolstad'* [The humanism of the other. Emmanuel Levinas; translated and with introduction, notes and an essay by Asbjørn Aarnes]. Aschehoug: Oslo.

Adams, C. J. (1996). Caring about suffering: A feminist exploration. In J. Josephine & C. Adams (Eds.) *Beyond animal rights: a feminist caring ethics for the treatment of animals* (pp. 170–197). New York: Continuim.

Awford, J. (2015, May 4). Bottled birds: How callous smugglers cram cockatoos into plastic bottles to get them through customs. *Daily Mail.* http://www.dailymail.co.uk/news/article-3067691/Smugglers-birds-plastic-bottles-customs.html. Accessed 22 July 2015.

Bauman, Z. (1991). *Modernity and the Holocaust.* Polity Press: Oxford.
Beirne, P. (1999). For a nonspeciesist criminology: animal abuse as an object of study. *Criminology*. 37(1), 117–148.
Beirne, P. (2007). Animal rights, animal abuse and green criminology. In P. Beirne & N. South (Eds.), *Issues in green criminology: confronting harms against environments, humanity and other animals* (pp. 55–87). Devon: Willan.
Beirne, P. (2014). Theriocide: naming animal killing. *International Journal for Crime, Justice and Social Democracy, 3*(2), 50–67.
Beirne, P., & South, N. (2007). Introduction: Approaching green criminology. In P. Beirne & N. South (Eds.), *Issues in green criminology: confronting harms against environments, humanity and other animals* (pp. xiii–xxii). Devon: Willan.
Benton, T. (1998). Rights and justice on a shared planet: More rights or new relations?. *Theoretical Criminology, 2*(2), 1490–175.
Berger, J. (2009) *Why look at animals?* Johannesburg: Penguin Books.
Bergo, B. (2015). Emmanuel Levinas. In E. N. Zalta (Ed.), *The Stanford Encyclopedia of philosophy*. http://plato.stanford.edu/archives/sum2015/entries/levinas/. Accessed 27 July 2015.
Brisman, A. & Rau, A. (2009). From fear of crime to fear of nature: the problem with permitting loaded, concealed firearms in national parks. *Golden Gate University Environmental Law Journal, 2*(2), 255–272.
Bush, E. R., Baker, S. E., & Macdonald, D. W. (2014). Global trade in exotic pets 2006–2012. *Conservation Biology*, 28(3), 663–676.
Busch, E. R., Baker, S. E., & Macdonald, D. W. (2014). Global trade in exotic pets 2006–2012. *Conservation Biology, 8*(3), 663–676.
Christie, N. (1975) *Hvor tett et samfunn?* [How densly knitted a society]. Oslo: Universitetsforlaget.
CITES (2007). EU ban on wildlife bird 'disappointing'. https://www.cites.org/eng/news/pr/2007/070111_EU_bird_ban.shtml. Accessed 15 July 2015.
CITES (n.d.). How CITES works. https://www.cites.org/eng/disc/how.php. Accessed 10 August 2015.
Derridá, J. (2002). The animal that therefore I am: more to follow. *Critical Inquiry, 28*(xx), 369–418.
Donovan, J. (1996). Attention to suffering: sympathy as a basis for ethical treatment of animals. In J. Josephine & C. Adams (Eds.) *Beyond animal rights: a feminist caring ethics for the treatment of animals* (pp. 147–170). New York: Continuim.
FAO (2011) *International trade in wild birds, and related bird movements (in Latin).*
Francione, G. L. (2014). Animal welfare and the moral value of nonhuman animals. *The animal turn* (pp. 57–73). Lunde: Pupendorf Institute.
Gonzales, J. A. (2003). Harvesting, local trade, and conservation of parrots in the Northeastern Peruvian Amazon. *Biological Conservation, 114*, 437–446.
Goyes, D. R. (2015). Denying the harms of animal abductions for biomedical research. In Sollund, R. (ed). *Green Harms and Crimes* (pp. 170–188). London: Palgrave Macmillan.

Guzmán, J. C. C., Saldaña, M. E. S., Grosselet, M., & Gamez, J. S. (2007) *The illegal parrot trade in Mexico: defenders of wildlife*. https://www.defenders.org/publications/the_illegal_parrot_trade_in_mexico.pdf. Accessed 25 June 2014.

Hance, J. (2015). Are plants intelligent? New book says yes. *The Guardian*. http://www.theguardian.com/environment/radical-conservation/2015/aug/04/plants-intelligent-sentient-book-brilliant-green-internet?CMP=Share_AndroidApp_Gmail). Accessed 11 August 2015.

Herbig, J. (2010). The illegal reptile trade as a form of conservation crime: a South African criminological investigation. In R. White (Ed.), *Global environmental harm: criminological perspectives* (pp. 110–132). Devon: Willan.

Herrera, M., & Hennessey, B. (2007). Quantifying the illegal parrot trade in Santa Cruz de la Sierra, Bolivia, with emphasis on threatened species. *Bird Conservation International, 17*, 295–300.

International fund for animal welfare [IFAW] (2008) *Killing with keystrokes: an investigation of the illegal wildlife trade on the worldwide web*. http://www.ifaw.org/sites/default/files/Killing%20with%20Keystrokes.pdf. Accessed 14 June 2011.

Izzo, J. B. (2009). PC pets for a price: Combating online and traditional wildlife crime through international harmonization and authoritative policies. *William and Mary Environmental Law and Policy Review, 34*(3), 965–997.

Lavorgna, A. (2014). Wildlife trafficking in the internet age. *Crime Science, 3*(1), 1–12.

Lavorgna, A. (2015). The social organization of pet trafficking in cyberspace. *European Journal on Criminal Policy and Research, 21*(3), 353–370.

Lyons, J. A., & Natusch, D. J. (2011). Wildlife laundering through breeding farms: illegal harvest, population declines and a means of regulating the trade of green pythons (Morelia viridis) from Indonesia. *Biological Conservation, 144*(12), 3073–3081.

Natusch, D. J., & Lyons, J. A. (2012). Exploited for pets: the harvest and trade of amphibians and reptiles from Indonesian New Guinea. *Biodiversity and Conservation, 21*(11), 2899–2911.

Pepperberg, I. (1999) *The Alex studies: Cognitive and communicative abilities of grey parrots*. Cambridge: Harvard University Press.

Pires, S., & Clarke, R. B. (2011). Are parrots CRAVED? An analysis of parrot poaching in Mexico. *Journal of Research in Crime and Delinquency, 49*(1), 122–146.

Regan, T. (1983). *The case for animal rights*. California: University of California Press.

Regan, T. (1999) *Djurens rättigheter: En filosofisk argumentation* [The case for animal rights]. trans. Britt-Marie Thieme Bokförlaget Nye Doxa, Falun.

Rodríguez, D. G. (2015). Denying the harms of animals in biomedical research. In R. A. Sollund (Ed.), *Green harms and crimes: critical criminology in a changing world* (pp. 170–189). London: Palgrave.

Rodríguez, N. J. M., & García, O. R (2008). Comercio de fauna silvestre en Colombia. *Revista Facultad Nacional de Agronomía—Medellín, 61*(2), 4618–4645.

Runhovde, S. R. (2015). Seizures of inconvenience? Policy, discretion and accidental discoveries in policing the illegal wildlife trade at the Norwegian border. *Crime, Law and Social Change, 64*(2), 177–192.

Schneider, J. L. (2008). Reducing the illicit trade in endangered wildlife: the market reduction approach. *Journal of Contemporary Criminal Justice*, 24(3), 274–295.

Skatvik, F. (2015). Den Hippokratiske Ed. I Store norske leksikon. https://snl.no/Den_hippokratiske_ed. Hentet 11. Accessed 1 August 2015.

Sollund, R. (2008). Causes for speciesism: difference, distance and denial. In R. Sollund (Ed.), *Global harms. Ecological crime and speciesism* (pp. 109–131). New York: Nova Science Publishers.

Sollund, R. A. (forthcoming). *The crimes of wildlife trafficking. Legally right or wrong - morally unjust.*. Farnham: Routledge

Sollund, R. A. (2009). Menneskers forhold til kjæledyr og andre dyr—et akseptabelt paradoks?' (Humans' relationship to pets and other animals: An acceptable paradox?) *Sosiologi i dag, 39*(4), 42–68.

Sollund, R. A. (2011). Expressions of speciesism: the effects of keeping companion animals on animal abuse, animal trafficking and species decline. *Crime, Law and Social Change, 55*(5), 437–451.

Sollund, R. A. (2012). Speciesism as doxic practice versus valuing difference and plurality. In R. Ellefsen, R. A. Sollund, G. Larsen (Eds.), *Eco-global crimes: contemporary problems and future challenges* (pp. 91–115). Farnham and Burlington: Ashgate Publishing.

Sollund, R. A. (2013a). Animal trafficking and trade: abuse and species injustice. In R. Walters, D. Westerhuis, T. Wyatt (Eds.), *Emerging issues in green criminology: exploring power, justice and harm* (pp. 72–92). London: Palgrave.

Sollund, R. A. (2013b). The victimization of women, children and non-human species through trafficking and trade: crimes understood through an eco-feminist perspective. In N. South & A. Brisman (Eds.), *Routledge international handbook of green criminology* (pp. 317–331). London: Routledge.

Sollund, R. A. (2013c). Selskapsdyr: Vennskap versus utnytting (Companion animals: Friendship versus exploitation). In R. A. Sollund, T. Tønnessen, G. Larsen (Eds.), *Hvem er villest i landet her? Menneskers råskap mot dyr og natur i antropocen, menneskets tidsalder* (pp. 245–271). Oslo: Spartacus SAP.

Sollund, R. A. (2015a). Introduction: critical green criminology: an agenda for change. In R. A. Sollund (Ed.), *Green harms and crimes: critical criminology in a changing world* (pp. 1–27). London: Palgrave.

Sollund, R. A. (2015b). The illegal wildlife trade from a Norwegian outlook: tendencies in practices and law enforcement. In R. A. Sollund (Ed.), *Green harms and crimes: critical criminology in a changing world* (pp. 147–170). London: Palgrave.

Sollund, R. A., & Maher, J. (2015). The illegal wildlife trade: a case study report on the illegal wildlife trade in the United Kingdom, Norway, Colombia and Brazil (A study compiled as part of the EFFACE project). University of Oslo and University of South Wales. http://efface.eu/sites/default/files/EFFACE_Illegal%20Wildlife%20Trade_revised.pdf. Accessed 10 August 2015.

Species Survival Network [SSN] (2007). Response to the EU Ban on Wild Bird Imports a statement by the species survival network. http://www.ssn.org/Documents/news_articles_EU_bird_ban_EN.htm. Accessed 24 November 2015.

Tella, J. L., & Hiraldo, F. (2014). Illegal and legal parrot trade shows a long-term, cross-cultural preference for the most attractive species increasing their risk of extinction. *PLOS one*. http://journals.plos.org/plosone/article?id=10.1371/journal.pone.0107546. Accessed 10 August 2015.

TRAFFIC. (2015). Briefing prepared by TRAFFIC for the European Commission. Accessed from http://ec.europa.eu/environment/cites/pdf/Overview%20significant%20seizures%202014.pdf.

van Uhm, D. P. (2015). Illegal wildlife trade to the EU and harms to the world. In T. Spapens, R. White, W. Huisman (Eds.), *Environmental crime and the World*. Farnham: Ashgate.

Vialles, N. (1994). Animal to edible (trans. J.A. Underwood). Cambridge: Cambridge University Press.

Weston, M. K., & Memon, M. A. (2009). The illegal parrot trade in Latin America and its consequences to parrot nutrition, health and conservation. *Bird Populations, 9*, 76–83.

Wildlife Extra (2008). African grey parrot numbers in steep decline due to wild bird trade. http://www.wildlifeextra.com/go/news/news-africangrey.html#cr. Accessed 14 July 2015.

Wright, T. F., Toft, C. A., Enkerlin-Hoeflich, E., Gonzalez-Elizondo, J., Albornoz, M., Rodríguez-Ferraro, A., et al. (2001). Nest poaching in neotropical parrots. *Conservation Biology, 15*(3), 710–720.

Wyatt, T. (2009). Exploring the organization in Russia Far East's illegal wildlife trade: two case studies of the illegal fur and illegal falcon trades. *Global Crime, 10*(1 and 2), 144–154.

Wyatt, T. (2011). Illegal raptor trade in the Russian Federation. *Contemporary Justice Review, 14*(2), 103–123.

Wyatt, T. (2013) *Wildlife trafficking: a deconstruction of the crime, the victims, and the offenders*. London: Palgrave Macmillan.

Zimmerman, M. E. (2003). The black market for wildlife: combating transnational organized crime in the illegal wildlife trade. *Vanderbilt Journal of Transnational Law IVOL, 36*, 1657–1699.

Ragnhild Sollund is a professor at the Department of criminology and sociology of law at the University of Oslo. She has done extensive research within migration studies, police racial profiling, and in recent years, green criminology. She is the editor of *Global Harms: Ecological Crime and Speciesism* (2008) and *Green Harms and Crimes: Critical Criminology in a Changing World* (2015); and co-editor of *Eco-global Crimes: Contemporary Problems and Future Challenges* (2008). She has over the past five years been doing research into wildlife crimes, including trafficking, and is partner to EFFACE; an EU funded project about environmental crimes.

Animals in War

Ryan Hediger

Introduction

Nonhuman animals (henceforth, 'animals') have been involved in human wars as long as there have been wars. Indeed, given the exceedingly long association between humans and dogs, it is likely that dogs performed informal defensive roles for human encampments before war even existed. Thus, human/animal partnerships likely predate war as such and are more fundamental than the waging of war. This point is underscored by primatologist Frans De Waal, for instance, in his book *The age of empathy.* There, he challenges what he calls the 'false origin myth' of human beings 'that our species has been waging war for as long as it has been around' (2009, p. 22). De Waal also asserts, 'Although archeological signs of individual murder go back hundreds of thousands of years, we lack similar evidence for warfare (such as graveyards with weapons embedded in a large number of skeletons) from before the agricultural revolution' (pp. 22–23). Instead of making some essentialist link between war and human nature, then, De Waal argues only 'that our species has a *potential* for warfare' and that 'our ancestors probably never waged war on a grand scale until they settled down and began to accumulate wealth by means of agriculture. This made attacks on other groups more profitable' (24–25, De Waal's emphasis). On this point, De Waal joins a

R. Hediger (✉)
English Department, Kent State University, Kent, Ohio, USA
e-mail: rhediger@kent.edu

J. Maher et al. (eds.), *The Palgrave International Handbook of Animal Abuse Studies,* DOI 10.1057/978-1-137-43183-7_22

host of scholars including Marc Bekoff, Jessica Pierce, Donna Haraway, and Jane Goodall—all of whom emphasize cooperation and sympathy as fundamental to human beings and to human relationships with other animals.

Timelines for these early events remain hard to ascertain, but the first agricultural revolution is generally dated to around 10,000 BCE, while the domestication of the dog is commonly dated a little earlier, at about 13,000 BCE, or 15,000 years ago (Clutton-Brock 1999, p. 54; Grandin 2009, p. 68). But, as I note in *Animals and war*, there is evidence for human association with wolves that reaches much further back, to 100,000 years ago or earlier, and it is not entirely clear when association became domestication (Clutton-Brock 1999, p. 3; Hediger 2013, pp. 3–4). If domestication is, in fact, older than we know now, it may predate not only war, but also human use of language. The character of the original domestication is itself also in dispute. One line of thinking holds that domestication was an act of human aggression (Clutton-Brock 1999, p. 31); another holds that domestication was a mutual enterprise, with wolves slowly becoming more comfortable around human encampments as they found nourishment at human waste dumps (Coppinger and Coppinger 2001, p. 57). Wolves and humans, in this second scenario, found common cause over time, making possible other human associations with domesticated animals such as the horse, the pig, and so on

These early stages importantly speak to the topic of this chapter. A strong case can be made that most participation of animals in human war itself constitutes abuse, even if the day-to-day treatment is comparatively benign. However, that view can seem to condemn human beings in a fundamental way, and I believe we should be careful not to do so too quickly. Instead, we can understand human use of animals in wars as deriving from human fallibility and misguided philosophies, issues which can be addressed better than some ostensibly essential human attribute. The use of animals in human wars is a grim subject. But a sense of the complexities of human prehistory and of the paradoxes and nuances of human feelings toward other animals in war can offer resources for improving the lives of humans and animals today by providing a ground for critique of contemporary practices, a point with which this chapter concludes.

That is partly because even in the often-horrible circumstances of modern and contemporary war, as millions of humans and animals have been condemned to miserable deaths, powerful sympathies have formed between humans and animals. Very often, as we shall see below, animal abuse in war derives not so much from direct, vicious human mistreatment, but from structures and scenarios that limit human abilities to help either themselves or animals. Thus, animals are victims of structural violence, which is at the heart of much abuse. Indeed, animals are often systematically abused alongside human soldiers, all of whom endured trying circumstances with poor nourishment, challenging travel and logistics, and a grave loss of agency as they become part of a large biopolitical organization that constitutes war as such. This point—that war is, by definition, about organized violence—means that structures and systems of order are also at the root of abuse in war. Thus, it is partly upon those structures that those of us who wish to shrink or end animal abuse in war should train our attention.

It is already clear from the above that the topic of animal abuse in war is vast. The range of animals that has been involved in war is itself extensive. Dogs were the first, then likely horses and so many more: elephants, donkeys, oxen, camels, mules, buffaloes, all generally as draft and transportation animals but also in other roles; birds as messengers and sometimes as weapons or mascots; wolves, panthers, bears, tigers, foxes, antelopes, goldfish, cats, and many more were used as mascots (Cooper 1983, p. 174); and many other smaller forms of life, including fleas, lice, mosquitos, the West Nile virus, bacteria, plague, bees, and more (on bees, see Moore and Kosut 2013). And some of the very largest animals have also been involved, including not only sea lions and dolphins, but killer whales (Axtell 2009). This list is not comprehensive, but it reiterates that this topic is much too large to treat exhaustively in an essay such as this, or even in an entire book. Bearing that fact in mind, this chapter addresses the topic by attending to significant examples, with sections focusing especially on the highly significant horse, then on the dog, before glancing at other animals as well. In each section, I underscore the prevalence, nature, and explanations of animal abuse in war. To some extent, I also treat responses to animal abuse in war in each section, and I then return to responses to conclude the chapter.

Horses: Prevalence, Nature, and Explanations

The use of horses in war reaches back from the present day almost to war's beginnings, though, again, it is difficult to be certain. The absolute origin of war remains somewhat unclear, perhaps permanently so, partly because determining it depends on patchy archeological evidence, and partly because it involves matters of definition. What exactly counts as war, and what constitutes evidence of its existence? Those important questions are beyond the scope of this essay (see Keegan 1993, pp. 79–136). For our purposes here, suffice it to recognize the rough congruence between the first domestication of the horse and some of the earliest agreed-upon wars. When was the horse domesticated? Again, it remains difficult to be sure. But briefly: In *War horse*,

DiMarco, drawing from Clutton-Brock, pushes the date of the domestication of the horse back in time to around 4000 BCE, considerably before the figure of 3000 to 2000 BCE that is often cited (2008, p. 2). But Anthony pushes the event even further back to around 5000 BCE. Anthony puts this development in the context of herding other animals, with the use of the horse enabling people to possess more cattle. Such changes, Anthony supposes, may themselves have inspired new conflicts among peoples as their relationship to territory, animals, and land shifted (2007, p. 222). It seems at least possible that the additional powers and facilities won by human partnerships with horses and other animals helped to intensify or even create warfare as such. In other words, the cooperative relationship between humans and horses paradoxically helped lead to the traumas and abuses that I explore in the remainder of this chapter.

Several attributes of horses bear on their domestication and use in war. As Sandra Swart notes in her history of the horse in South Africa, 'They were large enough to be useful, but small enough to be manageable. Most importantly, they were herd animals, sociable and used to living within a hierarchy that translated easily into a new hierarchy under human custodianship' (2010, p. 12). These horse attributes suggest a relatively smooth, relatively painless transition into domestication for the horse, perhaps, but again, ironically, that predisposition eventually exposed them to new dangers in war. Further, Swart notes that horse biology has additional attributes that make their experiences in war worse than might be guessed:

> as prey animals, they reveal illness only if they cannot avoid it. They do not vocalise pain in the same way that other animals close to human society—like dogs—do, so it is difficult to tell when a horse is ill, at least in the early stages.

Combine this fact with the character of their digestive system, which is a weakness of horse biology, and, as Swart writes, 'Simple indigestion can [...] mean death'. Swart further remarks that war tends to involve a set of conditions—'unusual fodder', unusual or unfamiliar weather, and so on—that can play on these weaknesses, causing discomfort at best and fatality at worst (2010, pp. 103–104). Further, horses' tendency not to respond audibly to suffering, Swart notes, often facilitates human use of spurs and whips to direct horse actions, under the misguided theory that a minimal response from a horse indicates that it does not suffer. Of course, they suffer—silently. Conditions of war, with their extreme exigency, lend themselves to more spurs, whips, and the like, meaning horses undergo intensified abuse as a consequence of their biological background.

Perhaps these factors were less significant in the early skirmishes, or small conflicts, that Anthony postulates at the origin of horse domestication, but as war became more and more systematized, conflicts intensified, distances traveled grew, and challenges were magnified. Techniques, strategies, tools —all hinged on the omnipresence of the horse in warfare. As DiMarco notes in the opening of his book, horses 'were a key to the success of Alexander the Great in the fourth century BC, and, likewise, were integral to British General Edmund Allenby's successful Palestine campaign in the same part of the world 2,200 years later' (2008, p. ix). DiMarco underscores the surprising fact that 'the similarities' of these forces 'were far greater than their differences' (2008, p. ix). To gain some sense of this history, I first offer a brief account of the evolution of roles for horses in war and then turn to more recent history, which presents a somewhat clearer picture of horse activities. Horses receive the fullest treatment in this chapter because they have been so essential to the history of war.

The specific roles horses performed in war shortly after domestication remain less clear, but indications of forms of their use grow increasingly certain in time. As Clutton-Brock notes, we find pictographs from modern-day Iraq with boxes attached to wheels or sleds that would be drawn by horses or oxen, dating to 3200–3100 BCE (1992, p. 68). And Keegan recognizes that in Ur, which is modern-day Iraq, there is clear evidence on The Standard of Ur of use of onagers—large donkeys—to pull four-wheeled carts in war by about 2500 BCE (1993, p. 157; also see DiMarco 2008, pp. 3, 5, figure, and see note 9, 361). These four-wheeled carts became two-wheeled chariots, which, along with horses, Keegan writes, 'were truly to revolutionize warmaking, above all by putting the rich and stable but sedentary valley civilizations at risk from the predators who hovered in the horse-breeding lands beyond' (1993, p. 136). DiMarco writes, 'The technology for the two-wheeled war chariot migrated in all directions [. . .]'. It became 'the standard of advanced military technology' and would remain so for 600 years (1993, p. 4). What did the horses experience in these scenarios? In the Middle East, a document for the training of horses by Kikkuli suggests thoughtful treatment of the animals. Their diet is described, and they 'were gently broken to the task of chariot driving' (DiMarco 2008, p. 5). We also know war exposed horses to injury. This is common sense, but it is also demonstrated by the development and use of armor. Whole elements of these cultures revolved around protecting horses exposed to danger in war, since often the horse was the most vulnerable component of their warring systems (DiMarco 2008, p. 6). The very usefulness and value of horses led to their grave vulnerability.

As cultures improved their understanding of working with and breeding horses, the animals became larger (DiMarco 2008, p. 8). Horse cultures also launched the history of ever-developing and evolving ensembles of tools, weapons, and animals, a process which persists to this day. From the war cart to the chariot, from the smaller to the larger horse, and from the bow and arrow to gunpowder, horses would remain crucial to these innovations and to the cultures organized around them. Because each advance was often duplicated by or answered by opposing forces (Keegan 1993, p. 175), horses have long been caught in the middle of complex scenarios, assemblages of humans, animals, tools, and cultures that no person exactly controlled.

As Keegan argues, the chariot would remain important for later groups, including the significant Assyrians in the Middle East. Keegan claims that 'the Assyrian army remained at heart a charioteering force' (1993, p. 172), but that, ironically, the Assyrians seemed to be responsible for the switch to cavalry, a change that led to their downfall (1993, p. 177). The Scythians were 'a horse people' (Keegan 1993, p. 177), and their success against the Assyrians signals the importance of the cavalry horse to subsequent events. For instance, the Persians and their opponents the Greeks relied deeply on riding horses, an approach in use up through the present day, to some extent, in Afghanistan and elsewhere. Keegan summarizes this reality deftly:

> the first Scythians [. . .] were harbingers of what was to be a repetitive cycle of raiding, despoliation, slave-taking, killing and, sometimes, conquest that was to afflict the outer edge of civilization—in the Middle East, in India, in China and in Europe—for 2000 years. These persistent attacks on the outer edge of civilization of course had profoundly transforming effects on its inner nature, to such an extent that we may regard the steppe nomads as one of the most significant—and baleful—forces in military history. The innocent agents of the harm they were to do were the descendants of the little, rough-coated ponies which man had been breeding and eating on the Volga only a few dozen generations before [. . .]. (1993, p. 178)

Of course, the horses were not the only 'agents'. Their importance derives partly from their intimate relationship with the human culture and technology of the steppe, a point made by many sources. In Kistler's words, the 'steppe peoples' personal and public lives revolved around their horses'. He notes that children learned to ride very young, that clothes and equipment were made from horses, that horses were altogether central to steppe life, a point also made clear repeatedly in Anthony's book (Anthony 2007; Kistler 2011, p. 121).

The cavalry, made powerful by the steppe inhabitants, became crucial to most of the remaining history of war, right up to the shocks of World War I, when new machinery and tactics radically curtailed the effectiveness of cavalry, even if horses remained important. The massive scale and character of more recent wars has resulted in much more direct forms of abuse and suffering for horses. Kistler writes, for instance, about Napoleon's campaign against Russia in 1812, calling it 'an utter disaster' (2011, p. 144). DiMarco notes that the French rode into Russia in summer with some 80,000 horses, but forage was not to be found. The French lost 8,000 horses in the first eight days, 'mostly from lack of care' (2008, p. 208). The French nonetheless made their way to Moscow in September, writes DiMarco, but facing winter, 'Napoleon decided to withdraw [. . .] and began one of the longest and most desperate retreats in military history'. One night 'the cold was so intense that 30,000 horses died', horses who then became meat for the starving soldiers (2008, p. 208). Kistler describes soldiers eating horse blood pudding, horse hearts and livers, and half-cooked horse meat of other kinds (2011, p. 145). In such scenarios, the many logistical exigencies and challenges of war cause more horse (and human) suffering than the actual fighting.

DiMarco aligns such episodes with larger issues in the nineteenth-century French cavalry. He writes that 'military horsemanship took a definite turn for the worse during the Napoleonic period due to the large size of the armies, the high number of casualties, and the constant warfare' (2008, p. 214). Riders received too little training, resulting in poorly treated horses, and exhaustion took its toll on men and animals both (2008, p. 214). Under such conditions, soldiers resisted in ways that often fell hard on the horses. DiMarco remarks how commonly the horses experienced saddle sores, and he notes efforts by some people to 'shirk duty by intentionally injuring their horse[s]' by placing 'stones or even tacks under the saddle to cause back sores and thus eliminate horse and rider from duty' (2008, p. 216).

Similar patterns emerged in the U.S. Civil War (1861–1865) where, Kistler reports, inexperienced and unknowing Union soldiers gravely harmed or crippled their horses by overworking or overfeeding them (2011, p. 164). Such systematized warfare has many vulnerable points that bear on horses. DiMarco, for instance, writes about corruption besetting the Union's efforts to buy horses for use in the war. One of his representative examples involved a purchase of 400 horses; 'five died within hours of the sale, and 300 others were smaller than the standard, lame, blind, or sick' (2008, p. 241). These animals would be particularly ill-suited to the challenges of war and all the more likely to suffer injury or death. Also, the perennial problem of horse feed in war plagued the Union. In one case, President Lincoln's order to attack could not be carried out because the unit's '19,000 draft horses were starving and only 3,700 were usable' (Kistler 2011, p. 167).

This was not an isolated incident. The brutality of this war deeply impacted the animals involved. In one sense, the U.S. Civil War became largely a contest over horses, and the participants knew it. Kistler writes that, later in the war, the success of the Union's program to gather horses eventually meant that they 'had horses to spare' (2011, p. 174). To prevent the Confederates from gaining on the Union advantage, then, exhausted animals were not rested as had been done before; they were simply executed by the North. Kistler describes Sheridan's Northern troops at one point, under pursuit from the Confederates, leaving some 2,000 dead horses over 100 miles of road (2011, p. 174). Dead horses were everywhere in the Civil War. DiMarco reports that 'as many as 50 % of the animals in service' in the American Civil War died (2008, p. 302).

As bad as the U.S. Civil War was for horses, the Boer War, or South African War (1899–1902), seems to have been worse. Swart reports the stunning facts of this conflict, 'widely regarded as proportionally the most devastating waste of horseflesh in military history up until that time'. Swart explains, 'On the British side, 326,073 horses and 51,399 mules died between October 1899 and May 1902, at the rate of 66.88 % and 35.37 % of the total head count' (2010, p. 104). Part of the problem was, as Swart describes, that traditional forms of cavalry, long familiar to British warmaking and war in general, were challenged in South Africa both by the ever-more refined use of guns and by the specific tactics of the Boers, who did not stand and face the British cavalry charge, but rather conducted more mobile, guerilla-style tactics that exposed the British and their horses.

This war, like episodes that would occur early in World War I, clarifies how much suffering and abuse in war derives from strategies and tactics. It also reveals the risks to animals from simple logistics, which are a fundamental challenge of war, especially in the increasingly global wars of the nineteenth, twentieth, and twenty-first centuries. It is not just that horses, humans, and other animals suffer in the theater of war due to foreign terrain and food, but that they must be brought to the theater in the first place. This can prove very challenging. Swart writes of British efforts to bring horses to South Africa, for instance. Conditions on the ships were often poor: 'Aeration was inadequate and the stalls were poorly designed, which made it difficult to muck out the decaying dung and excoriating urine. Occasionally, insufficient fodder was packed and horses simply starved to death' (2010, p. 108). She cites a specific example of a 39-day journey on which '25 horses had died of starvation, while three-quarters of the remaining horses were so weak that they were unfit for duty for two months' (2010,

p. 108). Again, this is merely one example of a much broader reality, one utterly replete with suffering and abuse.

As I argue in *Animals and war*, we tend to imagine the World Wars in terms of increasingly sophisticated machinery such as airplanes, tanks, machine guns, and so on. However, animals, and especially horses, were also crucial to the war effort—ironically, often precisely *because* of the use of other machinery (2013, p. 10). Keegan describes this scenario compellingly, noting that the planning efforts in Europe during war mobilization in 1914 hinged on the presence and function of rail:

> Once arrived, however, they found that the almost miraculous mobility conferred by rail movement evaporated. Face to face with each other, they were no better able to move or transport their supplies than Roman legions had been; forward of railhead, soldiers had to march, and the only means of provisioning them was by horse-drawn vehicles. Indeed, their lot was worse than that of the well-organized armies of former times, since contemporary artillery created a fire-zone several miles deep within which re-supply by horse was impossible.... (1993, pp. 307–308)

This problem was further intensified by the fact that modern war

> demanded an ever larger trans-shipment of munitions between railhead and guns, which could only be undertaken by horses. As a result, horse fodder became the single largest category of cargo unloaded, for example, at French ports for the British arm on the Western Front throughout the period 1914–18 (1993, p. 308).

This scenario also meant great competition among nations in obtaining horses. Kistler reports that 'Germany began World War I with 4.5 million horses, [....] far more than any other nation except Russia' (2011, p. 192). To make up their deficit, the Allies relied significantly on the American supply, but horses gathered in such numbers were nonetheless sorely neglected. DiMarco quotes a source that notes, for instance, that by October 1914 among the French, 'the best commands had lost 2/3 of their horses, of which half were lost from overriding' (2008, p. 327). The British regime of care also led horses to suffer:

> Of 256,000 horses lost by the British on the Western Front, only 58,000 died from enemy fire. Most died of the winter cold. Their provisions were so scarce that many horses died from eating their own blankets, choking to death on the buckles (Kistler 2011, p. 192).

It is a grim but characteristic irony that so many animals died of such basic causes when the animals were necessary partly because of advanced war technology.

Horses, in other words, were directly impacted by the massive scale of technological production. Again, in Keegan's account: 'the industry of the mass-production age, which rolled the steel and cast the engine-blocks by which transportation was revolutionized, also spewed out the shells and bullets that mass armies devoured in ever larger quantity. Rates of consumption increased exponentially' (1993, p. 309). He notes the vast difference between, for instance, 'Napoleon's artillery at Waterloo' with 246 guns firing 'about a hundred rounds each during a battle', and the massive scale of the battle of the Somme, 1 July 1916, when 'British artillery fired 1,000,000 rounds, a total weight of some 20,000 tons of metal and explosive' (1993, p. 309). Much of this materiel was moved by horses, and a great deal of the dying was also done by horses. In his book *An illustrated history of the First World War,* Keegan reports the proportion of horses to men in that effort as 1:3 (2001, p. 68). Cooper, in *Animals in war,* gives the figure of eight million for the number of horses that died in World War I (1983, p. 12).

Keegan notes that the problem of movement resurfaced in World War II, again in part due to the complex realities of technology and national strategy (1993, p. 308). He describes the German army as 'deficient in motor transport because the German engineering industry had to devote its resources to manufacturing tanks, aircraft and U-boats'. Thus, he writes, the Germans

> actually took into service more horses than it had done between 1914 and 1918—2,750,000 as opposed to 1,400,000; most died in service, as did the majority of the 3.5 million horses mobilized by the Red Army between 1941 and 1945. (1993, p. 308).

Evans reports that the Germans used 'at least 625,000 [horses] on the Eastern Front', and that some 180,000 of them died in the first winter. Evans quotes an observer who said of the horses, 'At times they are the last and only thing we can rely on. Thanks to them we made it through the winter, even if they died in their thousands from exhaustion, lack of fodder and their tremendous exertions' (2009, p. 200). The Soviet Union, reports *The Oxford companion to World War II,* lost 'two thirds of its 21 million horses' during the course of that conflict (Dear and Fort 2001).

The massive scale of activity in the World Wars exposed everyone—animals, soldiers, civilians at home, wild ecosystems—to grave harm and vast suffering in ways that can be, at least, instructive as we work to reduce and eliminate animal abuse in war in the future.

Dogs: Prevalence, Nature, and Explanations

The history of dogs in war is also extensive, much too long and detailed to receive anything like a comprehensive treatment here. I noted at the opening of this chapter that humans have had cooperative relationships with dogs for longer, most likely, than we have participated in war. It is thus logical that dogs would accompany humans through the early stages of war, and they have continued to play various roles up to the present day. For instance, in Vietnam, there were as many as 4,000 dogs who worked with U.S. troops (Burnam 2000, v). In the Persian Gulf War of 1990–1991, the U.S. involved 'between 118 and 125 canine soldiers', with no lost dogs (Alger and Alger 2013, p. 88). Discussion of several episodes below reveals many of the same scenarios of abuse addressed above with regard to horses. With dogs, as with other animals, much of the worst treatment results from structural violence, from biopolitics.

Predictably, the two World Wars involved a large number of dogs. As part of the preparation for World War II, tens of thousands of dogs were gathered in the USA (perhaps it is more accurate to say these dogs were sacrificed). As Lemish writes, 'there was no guarantee that the dogs would be returned to their owners at the conclusion of the hostilities' (1996, p. 44). Alger and Alger write that 'over 40,000 dogs' were initially contributed to the military by private owners (2013, p. 82). The number of dogs actually accepted for service, they note, was considerably smaller, at about 18,000 (2013, p. 82). As the dogs were brought together, they were tested for disease and temperament. If they could be cured of disease, they often would be, but some 'fifteen hundred dogs died or were destroyed due to physical impairments of disease, and another thousand were destroyed because of temperament' (Lemish 1996, p. 45). In other words, dogs that did not fit the military's strict standards were deemed killable. Those who survived these steps were 'placed in a quarantine kennel for twenty-one days' (Lemish 1996, p. 44). Dogs are very adaptable animals, generally, but these experiences were likely to be traumatic for many of them. And then, of course, there were the war activities themselves to come.

Initially, Lemish reports, many of the dogs used by the U.S. military in World War II were employed as beach patrols, intended to alert the U.S. to intruders, which were a real problem early in the U.S. involvement (1996, pp. 47–52). But as the war wore on and attention turned increasingly to the Pacific and to

Japan, an idea took shape to train attack dogs for use on Pacific islands. Instrumental to this effort, writes Lemish, was Walter B. Pandre, who advocated this project and then worked to execute it. Pandre, however, was difficult for the military and for the dogs. Lemish writes, 'Pandre, as part of the training, used electric shocks and bullwhips and even tied some dogs behind horses and dragged them along the beach or had them fight for food in the sand along the beaches' (1996, p. 56). While Pandre was criticized for the brutality of his methods, his presence helps to reveal again the fundamental problem of training dogs to perform wartime roles. As they become weaponized to perform tasks humans desire of them, they also often become dangerous, at least temporarily. This reality is exemplified, for instance, in the successful dog program of the U.S. military in Vietnam. Dogs there had to be treated carefully and often muzzled so that they did not overstep their prescribed roles. Burnam, a dog handler for the U.S. in the Vietnam War, calls the dogs 'lethal weapons', even as he extolls their effectiveness and his and other handlers' love for the animals (2000, p. 75).

Still, the example of Pandre offers one more insight: the dogs themselves find ways to resist the training regimes according to their own desires. Their agency is proved by the dogs' unpredictability in many cases, and by the fact that Pandre specifically was unable to train the dogs to function the way he wanted them to. Ultimately, it was Pandre himself whom the military would reject and even declare 'potentially dangerous' (Lemish 1996, p. 57).

Not all dog trainers in war efforts were of Pandre's disposition, though. As Frankel writes in *Foreign policy* (2014), British Lt. Col. Edwin Hautenville Richardson was a prime force in the twentieth-century British effort to make dogs effective in the military. Dogs' participation certainly led them to experience brutal injuries and other forms of abusive trauma, but Frankel notes that Richardson sought to improve the effectiveness of the dogs by underscoring the power and value of the affection between human and dog. I have referred to this paradox as the weaponization of love—in war, the natural affection between canines and humans ultimately functions as a weapon.

But, Frankel explains, Richardson's affection for dogs was genuine, and it was displayed in his training methods: 'there was never to be any cruelty or abuse used in training' (2014, p. 91). In 1920, Frankel notes, Richardson published a book about training British war dogs, and his methods were well ahead of his time. His 'progressive attitude toward dogs' and his 'compassionate treatment' of them 'are the models for dog handling today' (2014, p. 91). For Frankel, Richardson's

> success with his dogs had less to do with study than with his singular and natural understanding of the animals. He was convinced that dogs were sentient, feeling beings able to reason and act with a set of rudimentary morals.

Frankel goes on, 'Richardson's breakthrough achievement [. . .] was to place the psychology and morality of the animal at the center of his training method' (2014, p. 93).

These ideas are familiar to contemporary animal scholars—the notion that centering an inquiry upon an animal yields important results; the idea that animals can reason and act morally. This last point, for instance, is demonstrated and defended by biologist Marc Bekoff and philosopher Jessica Pierce in their book *Wild justice* (2009). A thoughtful, sensitive, well-informed person like Richardson, then, dramatizes the paradox of animals in war. His gentle training methods and his serious regard for dogs helped win them a place in the brutal and destructive enterprise of human war. Love, in that sense, even sincere love, can amount to a kind of abuse.

Human love for dogs can therefore be a heavy burden, a strange form of harm, something that is also true of the history of horses and other animals in war. This reality is exemplified by the famous participant in World War II, Chips. Chips was a mixed-breed dog who was awarded a Purple Heart and Silver Star, only to have them revoked because it was decided that dogs should not receive awards intended for people (Lemish 1996, p. 76). Lemish reports that, by the time the dog's fame had grown, Chips 'began to grow weary and skittish from constant artillery shellfire' (1996). His notoriety led him to demonstrate that battle fatigue in a notable event: meeting General Eisenhower. Lemish writes that when Eisenhower 'innocently tried to pet him—Chips promptly nipped the general's hand' (1996, p. 76). This should not surprise us today. Military dog specialists have increasingly recognized that individuals like Chips can develop post-traumatic stress disorder, much as humans do (Perry 2012; Alger and Alger 2013, pp. 96–97). Further, when the war had concluded and Chips was sent back to the U.S., it became clear that the 'toll of war wore heavily on the dog': He survived only a few months before his heart stopped, 'with his kidneys already failing' (Lemish 1996, p. 78).

The story of Chips reiterates some of the problems with designating animal abuse in war. From one perspective, and in light of what we now know about his life's trajectory—increasing war stress that impacted his behavior, his health, and ultimately his longevity—Chips's participation in the war amounts to abuse. However, he is celebrated in texts, and was celebrated at the time, for his apparently eager, seemingly natural participation in war activities right from the start. One story exists in a number of texts about Chips' early engagement in war. Lemish tells it this way: Chips and his handler John P. Rowell were patrolling a beach in Sicily in the early morning when 'what appeared to be a small grass-covered hut' proved in fact to be 'a camouflaged pillbox'. When a 'machine gun opened fire',

> Chips broke loose from Rowell, trailing his leash and running full-steam toward the hut. Moments later, the machine-gun fire stopped and an Italian soldier appeared with Chips slashing and biting at his arms and throat. Three soldiers followed with their arms raised in surrender.

But just a sentence after presenting this assured version of the story, Lemish recognizes the limits of our firm knowledge about this episode: 'What actually occurred in the pillbox is known only by the Italians and, of course, the dog' (1996, pp. 74–75). Nonetheless, Chips's fame grew later that night when he was reported to have alerted to 'ten Italian soldiers approaching on the road' (Lemish 1996, p. 75).

Chips's vigorous and seemingly voluntary participation was key to his designation as a hero dog. But how voluntary was Chips's behavior in this scenario? Kistler's account of this story differs significantly from Lemish's. Kistler writes that

> Rowell unleashed Chips and ordered him to attack. Chips charged, and was hit by several bullets, yet knocked one machine gun over, burning his hair on the hot barrel, then grabbed the gunner by the throat and ripped out his jugular. The other two Italians fled and were shot by American troops. (2011, pp. 28–29).

While the injuries to Chips are similar in both accounts, several points of emphasis in the stories differ, including just what exactly the dog did to the Italians and who really initiated the action in the first place—Chips or Rowell.

From these sources, it is therefore difficult to conclude when or if Chips's participation in the war effort becomes abuse. At issue is partly the nature/nurture question: to what extent is such protecting and attacking behavior natural, and to what extent is it motivated by human intervention? As I argue in the introduction to *Animals and war*, this set of questions quickly grows complex and vexed, and is finally beyond the scope of this chapter (2013, pp. 3–5 and passim).

Even if one believes Chips was an entirely willing participant in war, far too many unambivalent cases of abuse and violence toward dogs exist. For instance, after World War I concluded, Lemish writes,

> The French military, then possessing fifteen thousand dogs in its employ, destroyed the animals as its great war machine demobilized. The vast quantities of dogs used by the British, Germans, Italians, and Russians faced the same fate. The actual number will never be known since these events were never accurately recorded. (1996, p. 29).

Certainly, no dog volunteered to be 'destroyed'. The hazy uncertainty about the number of dogs killed in this way is part of what permits such events to occur. Indeed, Lemish makes a crucial point here that informs every element of this chapter and that impacts this topic more generally: We have too little information about the participation of animals in war. Thus, histories like Lemish's, and projects like the present book, help to inform the public about these events, raising animal abuse into the visible sphere, which often leads to improved conditions for the future. For instance, consider the change in U.S. military policy with regard to dogs. The U.S. canine program in Vietnam became notorious when, at the end of the hostilities, it classified the 4,000 or so participating dogs as 'equipment', leaving nearly all of them behind, in country. Burnam notes that this meant many of the dogs were either euthanized or eaten, according to local practices (2000, p. viii). But, spurred in part by the agitation and activism of U.S. veteran dog-handlers from Vietnam, the U.S. legally changed its policy in 2000, permitting dogs to be eligible for adoption after they complete their military service (McCombs 2000). Such changes offer hope for a better future.

Other Animals: Prevalence, Nature, and Explanations

To further suggest the range of animal participation in war, and to reinforce the central arguments above, this section presents several anecdotes about other animal participation in war, with particular attention to systematic, biopolitical forms of abuse.

Mules often underwent treatment much akin to that of horses, and it often resulted in systematic suffering and abuse. In the U.S. Civil War, for instance, mules were commonly used as transportation animals, but they frequently faced neglect. Animals were often poorly fed: 'More than 10,000 Union mules died of starvation', for instance (Kistler 2011, p. 290). And the mules were often poorly treated in other ways. Kistler reports that many of the mules who died 'were too young to work'. They were 'not strong or developed enough for the hard work of military life' (2011, p. 291). Many of these deceased animals became meat for the soldiers.

Camels saw similar experiences in many wars. In World War I, the Palestinians campaigned against the Turks under the direction of General Allenby, who employed 50,000 camels. 'Less than half survived that final year of World War I' (Kistler 2011, p. 280). Similarly, when 'the exiled ruler of Ethiopia, Haile Selassie, led a large force from Sudan to retake Ethiopia', he used 15,000 camels, only 50 of which survived; 'the rest died in the forced march' (Kistler 2011, p. 280). Modern war is rife with animals suffering and dying at such massive scales.

Or consider the case of pigeons, often used as messengers in war, a relationship that goes well back in time. In modern wars, pigeons remained useful. Kistler reports, for instance, that '96 % of messages sent by pigeon in World War I arrived in a timely fashion' (2011, p. 248). In World War II, the single year 1942 saw the British Royal Air Force use 'nearly 500,000 pigeons' (Kistler 2011, p. 251). Such vast involvement helped to inspire the celebration of a particularly effective individual bird, Winkie, the pigeon awarded the first Dickin Medal, a British prize that celebrates the acts of animals in war (Kistler 2011). Wartime pigeon success, however, led to countermeasures: 'Nazis used trained hawks to kill pigeons' (Kistler 2011, p. 254), and 'the British drafted peregrine falcons to catch and kill' Nazi pigeons (Kister 2011, p. 248). A more macabre recognition of pigeons' effectiveness came in another episode, when the Germans invaded Belgium in World War I. Kistler writes that 'Commander Denuit, the head of the Belgian Pigeon Service, could not allow the enemy to capture his 2,500 homing pigeons. With tears running down his face, he set fire to the base, burning the birds alive' (2011, p. 244). It was exactly their success that led to their gruesome demise. In a situation parallel to the fate of U.S. war dogs in Vietnam, who were first successful in their work and then abandoned as an entire population, pigeons have seen their status radically reversed. Kistler points out, 'Since the end of pigeons in military service, the bird species is viewed only as a bane to human societies, not a help' (2011, p. 258). They have thus become targets to extermination in a range of places, from the U.S. to South Africa and beyond. Abuse in this case typifies too much of the thinking connected to war, in which whole populations of humans and animals become expendable, killable, a logic that Lindseth describes as 'exterminism'. He suggests 'ecology' as an alternative model, in which shared lives and interdependence receive emphasis, a view congruent with the argument of this chapter (2013).

An End to the Use of Animals in War?

The history of animals in war is horrible, but it is also full of human decency and sympathy. Case after case of soldiers and civilians feeling pity for animals and taking special pains to look after them is reported in the literature, as described for instance by Leinonen (2013, p. 132 and passim), Alger and Alger (2013, p. 98), and Burnam (2000, p. 75 and passim), among many other examples. As I argue in *Animals and war*, then, this paradoxical reality presents a problem. Often, it is war itself, and its capacity to unravel practically every element of ordinary life, that is to blame for animal suffering. Often, in circumstances of war, common decency seems to disappear in behavior toward humans and animals alike, a point that has special resonance in questions of animal abuse because so many of the arguments in defense of animals are constructed based on parallels between humans and animals. When conduct toward other humans grows brutal, it is no surprise that animals often fall to the same fate. Even today, as humans rely more and more upon machinery in wartime, animals end up paying all sorts of costs, as demonstrated for example by Kinder in his essay on modern war and the zoo. Kinder shows how frequently zoo animals become victims of wars in novel ways. Some are simply killed under the premise of exigency: the nation can no longer afford to feed them in the lean times of war (2013, p. 57). Others become accidental victims of social disorder in various ways (2013, p. 55 and passim). Similarly, animals—often 'pigs and goats'—are used to test wartime surgical procedures and other treatments, which require that the animals first be injured by gunshots, chemical weapons, amputations, and so on, and then treated (Gala, Goodman, Murphy, Balsam 2012, p. 907 and passim).

Such scenarios suggest that preventing animal abuse in war may require preventing war altogether. Of course, that is a huge task. But one dimension of animal studies strikes me as especially promising in promoting a decline in war: the ability to denaturalize war, the theme with which I opened this essay. We can continue to expose war as an anomaly of human power with a comparatively short history—short, that is, in comparison to the age of our species and the age of mammal life and other life. Too often war is treated as a kind of fundamental truth, when in fact it is the exception to life on this planet. No other animal wages war in the same sense that modern humans do. Chimpanzees, for instance, have sometimes been accused of participating in war, but I find Pinker's critique of that idea convincing. He recognizes instances of chimpanzee on chimpanzee violence, but notes that such cases tend to happen when aggressors 'outnumber their victim by at least three to one' (2011, p. 38). Other cases of intraspecies violence—in bears, dolphins, and so on—tend to take a similar pattern. No other species wages war like modern humans do. Even early humans did not.

Recognizing this fact can have direct bearing on the way we write and think about animals and animal abuse, upsetting commonly accepted views. For instance, many writers on animals and war adopt a stance of inevitability about the subject that we can resist. Lemish, for example, though he writes with compassion and sensitivity regarding animals, and though he notes that he 'does not glorify combat' (1996, p. xii), nonetheless resists 'animal rights proponents' and others who would 'argue that the use of dogs by the military establishment is nothing more than exploitation' (x). He notes that 'a soldier does not create the conflict he is engaged in', and therefore resembles the dog and other animals (xi). While I agree with Lemish's point about soldiers, this fact can be used to conclude upon the unjustness of war for nearly all its participants. Even when human soldiers consent to involve themselves in a war effort (something animals do not do), rarely can soldiers be said to know exactly what such consent entails. From that perspective, there is no entirely rational embrace of war, either for human or nonhuman animals. Instead, war necessarily involves involuntary, non-rational decision-making. War requires a form of commitment or compulsion that places the military unit or organization above the value of the lives of participants. War is therefore inherently abusive.

But this reality of group effort can be turned to good effect. The conduct of war relies for its power and horror upon assemblages of tools, animals, cultures, impacting all of them and the environment more generally (Nixon 2011, pp. 199–232). While this complexity can make it difficult for an individual to resist war and its horrors, a culture that decides against war can turn those dynamics the other way around, making peacefulness the reality difficult to resist, using cooperation and group effort against war, and therefore against animal abuse in it.

References

Alger, J. M., & Alger, S. F. (2013). Canine soldiers, mascots, and stray dogs in U.S. wars. In R. Hediger (Ed.) *Animals and war: studies of Europe and North America* (pp. 77–104). Leiden: Brill.

Anthony, D. W. (2007). *The horse, the wheel, and language: how bronze-age riders from the Eurasian steppes shaped the modern world.* Princeton: Princeton University Press.

Axtell, M. (2009). Bioacoustical Warfare. *Minnesota Review, 73/74*, 205–218.

Bekoff, M., & Pierce, J. (2009). *Wild justice: the moral lives of animals*. Chicago: University of Chicago Press.

Burnam, J. C. (2000). *Dog tags of courage: the turmoil of war and the rewards of companionship*. Fort Bragg: Lost Coast.

Clutton-Brock, J. (1992). *Horse power: a history of the horse and the donkey in human societies*. Cambridge: Harvard University Press.

Clutton-Brock, J. (1999). *A natural history of domesticated mammals*. 2nd edition. Cambridge: Cambridge University Press.

Cooper, J. (1983, 2000). *Animals in war*. London: Corgi Books.

Coppinger, R., & Coppinger, L. (2001). *Dogs: a new understanding of canine origin, behavior, and evolution*. Chicago: University of Chicago Press.

De Waal, F. (2009). *The age of empathy: nature's lessons for a kinder society*. New York: Harmony.

Dear, I. C. B., & Foot, M. R. D. (Eds.). (2001). *The Oxford companion to World War II*. Oxford: Oxford University Press.

DiMarco, L. A. (2008). *War horse: a history of the military horse and rider*. Yardley: Westholme Publishing.

Evans, R. J. (2009). *The third Reich at war*. New York: Penguin Press.

Frankel, R. (2014, September/October). The dog whisperer: how a British colonel altered the battlefields of World War I, and why his crusade still resonates today. *Foreign Policy, 208*, 90–95.

Gala, S. G., Goodman, J. R., Murphy, M. P., & Balsam, M. J. (2012). Use of animals by Nato countries in military medical training exercises: an international survey. *Military Medicine, 177*(8). 907–910.

Grandin, T. (2009). *Animals make us human: creating the best life for animals*. New York: Mariner Books.

Hediger, R. (2013). Animals and war: introduction. In R. Hediger (Ed.), *Animals and war: studies of Europe and North America* (pp. 1–25). Leiden: Brill.

Keegan, J. (1993). *A history of warfare*. New York: Vintage Books.

Keegan, J. (2001). *An illustrated history of warfare*. New York: Vintage Books.

Kinder, J. (2013). Zoo animals and modern war: captive casualites, patriotic citizens, and good soldiers. In R. Hediger (Ed.), *Animals and war: studies of Europe and North America* (pp. 45–75). Leiden: Brill.

Kistler, J. M. (2011). *Animals in the military: from Hannibal's elephants to the dolphins of the U.S. Navy*. Santa Barbara, CA: ABC-CLIO.

Leinonen, R. -M. (2013). Finnish narratives of the horse in World War II. In R. Hediger (Ed.), *Animals and war: studies of Europe and North America* (pp. 123–150). Leiden: Brill.

Lemish, M. G. (1996). *War dogs: a history of loyalty and heroism*. Washington, DC: Brassey's.

Lindseth, B. (2013). Nuclear war, radioactive rats, and the ecology of exterminism. In R. Hediger (Ed.), *Animals and war: studies of Europe and North America* (pp. 151–174). Leiden: Brill.

McCombs, P. (2000, December 3). Dogs no longer forced to die for U.S. *The Star-Ledger*, Sunday, final edition, News, p. 32.

Moore, L. J., & Kosut, M. (2013). Bees, border and bombs: a social account of theorizing and Weaponizing bees. In R. Hediger (Ed.), *Animals and war: studies of Europe and North America* (pp. 29–43). Leiden: Brill.

Nixon, R. (2011). *Slow violence and the environmentalism of the poor*. Cambridge: Harvard University Press.

Perry, T. (2012, November 26). Military's dogs of war also suffer post-traumatic stress disorder. *Los Angeles Times*. http://articles.latimes.com/2012/nov/26/nation/la-na-military-dogs-20121126. Accessed 21 July 2015.

Pinker, S. (2011). *The better angels of our nature: why violence has declined*. New York: Viking.

Swart, S. (2010). *Riding high: horses, humans, and history in South Africa*. Johannesburg: Wits University Press.

Ryan Hediger is Associate Professor of English at Kent State University. He has published essays on a range of subjects, including military dogs in the US conflict in Vietnam (*Animal Studies Journal*); hunting, ethics, and violence in Hemingway's work (*The Hemingway Review*); and Werner Herzog's film *Grizzly Man* (*Interdisciplinary Studies in Literature and Environment*). He co–edited the volume of essays *Animals and Agency* (Brill 2009) and edited another volume of essays, Animals and War (Brill 2013). He is currently at work on a monograph, 'Homesickness: Posthumanism, Uncanny Eco-cosmopolitanism, and the Desire for Place in the U.S'.

Part VII

Interventions

Interventions with Animal Abuse Offenders

Maya Gupta, Lisa Lunghofer and Kenneth Shapiro

Introduction

"So how do we make them *stop*?"

This question is becoming increasingly prominent as attention to animal abuse increases, both among the public and within the criminal justice system. While holding animal abuse offenders accountable through incarceration or other punitive measures remains a frontrunner topic, closely related is the concern about what offenders may do once they leave incarceration. Particularly given the tendency for animal abuse cases to receive "slap on the wrist" sentences or at best lesser jail time than those sentenced for other violent crimes, incarceration may not be a complete solution for protecting animals from future harm. Additionally, research on connections between animal abuse and other violent and antisocial behavior (see National Link Coalition 2016) raises the question of whether those who harm animals may in general be more likely to commit other criminal acts. By preventing further violence, an effective intervention program could have greater impact on animal and human safety than incarceration alone. Finally, the principles of balanced and restorative justice emphasize not only offender accountability and community safety, but also the improvement of offender functioning. For these reasons,

M. Gupta (✉) · L. Lunghofer · K. Shapiro
Animals & Society Institute, Ann Arbor, Michigan, United States of America
email: dr.gupta@kittenpizza.com

J. Maher et al. (eds.), *The Palgrave International Handbook of Animal Abuse Studies*, DOI 10.1057/978-1-137-43183-7_23

interventions aimed at animal abuse offenders have potential as a component of both judicial and nonjudicial approaches to the problem of animal abuse.

However, despite efforts over the past two decades, there are still no proven effective methods for stopping abusive behavior[1] toward animals. We begin this chapter by reviewing the relatively short list of interventions currently in use for both juvenile and adult animal abuse offenders, then consider obstacles to intervention, and present our recommendations for addressing these obstacles and tailoring future intervention approaches.

A few notes on terminology and focus are in order before continuing:

- Throughout this chapter, we prefer "animal abuse offenders" or "individuals who have abused animals" rather than "animal abusers." The term "abuser" connotes characteristic and ongoing behavior—which may be true for some offenders, but not all. It could be argued that the term "offender" is similarly problematic, though we retain its use here.
- We also refer to the approaches discussed in this chapter collectively as "interventions" rather than "treatment" or "therapy," because not all of them are therapeutic in nature. Depending on a variety of factors, such as the motivations for the abuse, therapy (which is based on the premise of an underlying disorder) may not always be appropriate. For example, with an offender whose neglect of an animal stemmed primarily from ignorance of proper care, an educational approach may be most beneficial (see chapter on Animal Neglect herein). Alternately, for an offender who abused an animal in the context of domestic violence (for example, harming the animal to intimidate human members of the household) or for those whose abuse of the animal was motivated by power and control, educational or non-therapy group intervention programs may be indicated (see also Chapters "Physical Cruelty to Pets", "Animal Hoarding," and "Animal Sexual Assault"). A recurring theme in our work is making a thorough assessment of the animal abuse and matching the intervention to the offender's individual needs.
- As the authors of this chapter are based in the United States, our focus is on interventions developed and based primarily in North America. At this time, we are unaware of significant intervention efforts taking place in other areas, though this is likely to change as attention to this topic increases.
- Finally, a substantial caveat: As discussed throughout the chapter, lack of data presents a major challenge to this work—and to the field of animal abuse

[1] The focus of this chapter is on animal abuse defined as "non-accidental, socially unacceptable behavior that causes pain, suffering, or distress to and/or the death of an animal" (Ascione and Shapiro 2009, p. 570).

prevention/response as a whole. There is a dearth of empirical information regarding not only the efficacy and effectiveness of most of the animal abuse interventions currently in existence, but also about animal abuse itself: rates, etiologies, typologies, trajectories. We also struggle to compile such basic statistics as the proportion of animal abuse cases that reach the attention of the courts or other agencies, the percent of court cases that are prosecuted, the outcomes of those prosecutions, the ratio of dispositions that include intervention, the frequency of completion of interventions, the availability of practitioners willing and able to handle cases involving animal abuse, and so on. Consequently, at present this work relies heavily on anecdotal evidence, the experience of the authors and their colleagues, and application of theory from other fields. It is our hope (and a rallying cry throughout this chapter) that the multiple disciplines and agencies that "touch" upon this issue will collaborate to plug the gaps that exist in the knowledge base, paving the way for more empirically supported interventions and a more sophisticated approach overall to the topic of animal abuse.

Existing Interventions

In presenting interventions currently in use, we begin by reviewing those directed at adults and then move to those designed for children. However, it is always important to match the intervention to the developmental level of the individual, which may be either above or below his/her actual age.

Interventions with Adults

AniCare Adult. AniCare (Jory and Randour 1999) was the first published intervention for juvenile and adult animal abuse. Based on intimate justice theory as used in domestic violence interventions (Jory et al. 1997), AniCare in its original format emphasized helping offenders accept accountability for their behavior and challenge internalized beliefs that justify abuses of power. The recently published second edition (Shapiro and Henderson 2016) addresses a wider range of motivations for animal abuse and incorporates a broader range of theoretical approaches, including cognitive-behavioral, attachment, trauma-based, and psychodynamic. AniCare is not a manualized intervention, but instead guides clinicians in making a thorough assessment of the factors underlying animal abuse (severity, culpability, motivation/psychodynamics, attitudes/beliefs, emotional intelligence, family history, and mitigating circumstances) and choosing appropriate intervention tools based on that assessment. These may involve clarifying values and attitudes about animals and acquiring empathy and other interpersonal skills.

Adult Diversion Programs. In the criminal justice system, diversion provides an alternative for subgroups of offenders for whom the completion of community-based court requirements, such as an intervention program, may be equally or more successful in preventing recidivism (reoffending) than traditional prosecution and sentencing (Center for Health and Justice at TASC 2013). These offenders typically have the opportunity to have the offence removed from their record upon successful completion of the requirements. The advantage to the court is typically less cost and time compared with full prosecution of a case.

For which subgroup(s) of animal abuse offenders might diversion be appropriate? Data on animal cruelty crimes have been difficult to obtain systematically, though the FBI's recent inclusion of cruelty in its National Incident-Based Reporting System (NIBRS) database (Federal Bureau of Investigation 2016) holds much promise. However, agencies tasked with enforcement of animal protection laws and ordinances report that the majority of the violations they handle are relatively simple infractions that stem from ignorance of animal protection laws and/or proper care of animals, often in conjunction with lack of resources. If responding to these situations with an intervention focus (e.g., instilling better knowledge of animal care) eliminates the reasons for the harmful behavior, it may be an effective and welcome alternative for a significant subset of offenders whom courts may be unlikely to sentence to incarceration in large numbers.

Note that the description of a case as "relatively simple" does not imply that the animal victim(s) suffered less: for example, a dog left in a car on a warm day by an owner unaware of how quickly vehicles heat up might suffer more than a dog maliciously yet rapidly killed by a gunshot. However, it may be possible to intervene effectively in the former situation with a more straightforward, educationally-focused approach while still holding the offender accountable for the harm that resulted. At the same time, there may also be value in more intensive approaches as diversion options for low-level and/or first offenders whose behavior toward animals is fueled not primarily by ignorance, but also by attitudes toward animals/violence, psychopathology, or other factors potentially amenable to intervention.

At the time of this writing, diversion programs for adult animal abuse offenders exist in a handful of communities, usually offered through a partnership with a local humane society. For example, the Washington Humane Society offers educational programs about basic animal care to low-level offenders.

Common challenges among adult diversion programs include the variability of curricula used within or across sites and the lack of routinely collected outcome data to determine whether these programs actually prevent recidivism (National Institute of Corrections 2011). In response, the Animals & Society Institute (2016) has developed a diversion program curriculum that will soon be piloted in Pennsylvania. The program consists of three levels: a basic three-hour animal care class (Companion Animal Responsibility and Education); a 16-session (one- to two-hour sessions) Level II intervention, BARK (Behavior, Accountability, Respect, and Knowledge), which incorporates work on accountability, attitudes, and beliefs; and a Level III referral to individual AniCare treatment. A version of the program is also available for juveniles. One goal of the pilot implementation is to gather data on both immediate and longer-term effectiveness so that the model, if successful, can be used elsewhere.

Animal Welfare Courts. The idea of creating specialized courts for animal cruelty cases, similar to drug, mental health, and domestic violence courts, is receiving increasing attention. In general, the specialized court model emphasizes rehabilitative needs of offenders alongside punishment, and permits greater focus on the special circumstances that often surround these types of offenses (National Institute of Justice 2013).

Currently we are aware of only one animal welfare court, located in Pima County (Tucson), Arizona, although preliminary efforts to replicate the Pima County model are underway in New Mexico. Pima County's animal welfare court handles misdemeanor animal cruelty cases that are not referred to Superior Court; as of September 2013, the court had heard approximately 175 cases (McNamara 2013). Offenders may be referred either to an animal welfare education class or to the Animal Treatment Offender Program (A.T. O.P.; Lowther 2012). A.T.O.P. is based on the original AniCare Adult model with some added topics, such as sessions on stress management, anger control, and substance abuse in its relationship to animal abuse. Based on the results of an individualized intake assessment, participants complete 16-52 group sessions, with up to 15 participants per group. One-on-one sessions are added as needed.

Promote Animal Welfare Online Course (PAWedu). This online course costs $25 and consists of a series of 14 self-study lessons on animal care, such as failure to provide protection from the weather and failure to provide proper food and water (PAWedu 2016). Anger and anger control are also addressed. Successful completion of the course's final exam generates a certificate that can be used to satisfy court (e.g., diversion or probation) requirements. Although outcome data on PAWedu have not been published, the content and format of the course make it likely to be most appropriate for low-level offenders for whom lack of basic knowledge of animal care was the primary factor in the offense, and those who are capable of completing the self-study format.

Interventions for Animal Hoarding. Arluke et al. (see chapter on Animal Hoarding herein) discuss interventions in their chapter on animal hoarding, so we do not deal with them here. In general, it appears that animal hoarding is a complex psychological and behavioral phenomenon that requires a carefully coordinated, multi-systemic response (mental health, justice system, animal protection) to be effective against the typically high rate of recidivism (Frost et al. 2015).

Interventions with Children

AniCare Child. This handbook for practitioners (Shapiro et al. 2014) guides the clinician in making an assessment of the child's relationship with animals, including animal abuse both perpetrated and witnessed by the child. The assessment process considers key factors similar to those in the adult version of AniCare, adjusted for the child's age (6-16 years) and developmental level. Interventions draw from empirically supported treatments for other forms of childhood behavior problems. For example, a child who becomes frustrated and aggressive when his dog does not obey commands might be helped by the practitioner to complete a cognitive-behavioral problem-solving exercise involving:

- identifying the problem
- brainstorming options such as ignoring his dog's disobedience, trying to give his dog commands in a more appropriate way that may make him more likely to obey, or enrolling in obedience classes with the dog
- evaluating pros/cons of each option (for example, responses from children included: "If I ignore my dog, I will still feel annoyed, but if I go to an obedience class my dog will listen to me better. However, I'm not sure where to find an obedience class.")
- selecting an option (for example, responses included: "I think going to an obedience school is the best solution. My dog would learn a lot and I would too. I know a store that sells pet supplies in my neighborhood; they

might tell me where to find obedience classes. And I can call the humane society about classes. They probably would know.")
- evaluating outcomes (for example, responses included, "My dog and I learned a lot and I like my dog better now.")

Additional intervention techniques are suggested within the handbook for those children whose animal abuse is determined to result primarily from insufficient empathy (e.g., working on taking an animal's point of view) or from attachment problems (e.g., helping children who have failed to develop a secure bond with a parent avoid taking out the frustration of their own unmet needs on a companion animal).

Children and Animals Together (CAT). This Phoenix, Arizona-based program (Risley-Curtiss 2014) targets children ages 6-17 who have committed animal abuse. Children may be referred from any source: the justice system, child protection, community mental health, parents/ guardians, etc. (Risley-Curtiss, personal communication, May 27, 2016). Individualized in-home assessment is a priority to obtain details about the animal abuse behavior, determine the child's motivation for harming animals, and establish whether the child has been exposed to family violence. The intervention plan is based on the results of the assessment, and children with severe pathology may be referred for more intensive, therapeutic interventions. The core intervention component of the CAT program is 14 weekly sessions (16 hours total) at a local animal shelter, focusing on learning prosocial skills while interacting with animals. Based in a systems approach, the program emphasizes participation by care-givers and other family members, with the goal of maintaining and reinforcing progress outside the sessions.

Teaching Love and Compassion for Juvenile Offenders (jTLC). This Los Angeles, California-based program is an outgrowth of the Society for the Prevention of Cruelty to Animals Los Angeles (spcaLA) Teaching Love and Compassion (TLC) violence prevention program (spcaLA n.d.). Whereas the original TLC program is an in-school intervention for at-risk youth not specifically identified as abusive to animals, jTLC works with the Los Angeles court system to intervene with juvenile animal cruelty offenders ages 8-18. Juveniles who have previously been adjudicated for cruelty to animals, or who have a history of other violent offenses, are ineligible. Juveniles who have not engaged in animal abuse but who have engaged in bullying may be admitted to the program, as may those who have witnessed animal abuse and/or family violence. The program curriculum includes conflict resolution, empathy, coping strategies, animal care education, and working with shelter dogs.

Challenges and Strategies for Developing More Effective Interventions

We now turn to an analysis of the factors that have hindered the development of interventions for animal abuse—including the aforementioned, lack of data, but also extending to systemic challenges in intervention referrals, practitioner familiarity, and overall understanding of animal abuse. For each, we present recommendations and calls to action for overcoming the obstacles and laying the foundation for enhanced approaches to intervention.

Fixing the Referral Pipeline

In order to provide interventions to those who abuse animals, it is first necessary to find them. Animal abusers do not typically wear signs labeling themselves, nor do most share common distinguishing features that make them readily identifiable. Further, as with other violent behaviors and illegal activities, most people who harm animals do not self-refer for help: they do not wish to disclose the behavior, and/or do not see it as a problem. The most common ways in which the social service system encounters individuals who have abused animals, then, are:

- through referral from the courts
- in the case of minors, through referral by parents/guardians
- through discovery of animal abuse that was not part of the initial presenting problem or referral question

Beyond the challenges inherent in working with what is generally an unwilling population, each of these referral paths is riddled with speed bumps and a few possible potholes:

Court Referral. It is likely that the majority of cases of animal abuse never reach the courts. Animal abuse is often a clandestine act, and its victims can neither report the crime nor identify their abusers. Animal cruelty laws, while improving, remain weak compared to laws for other violent crimes. Enforcement of cruelty laws is chronically underpowered and underfunded. For those cases that do enter the justice system, charges may be dropped or never filed for many of these same reasons, which result in insufficient evidence to prove the case (Arluke and Luke 1997). Additionally, although the designation of special animal cruelty prosecutors is on the rise and there is also now at least one animal welfare court in operation, in many prosecutors' offices animal cruelty cases still fall toward the bottom of the priority list—below crimes that directly affect human victims. (The growing body of research linking animal abuse to interpersonal violence and other crimes [see National Link Coalition 2016 for an extensive bibliography] may, over time, serve to elevate the perceived importance of these cases.)

Assuming that a defendant is found to have committed the offense, there is no guarantee that s/he will receive intervention. In an analysis of cases handled by the Massachusetts Society for the Prevention of Cruelty to Animals between 1975 and 1996, only 10% of the 280 sentences included counseling (Arluke and Luke 1997). Currently, 32 states' laws specifically mention counseling for adults convicted of animal cruelty or juveniles adjudicated for cruelty (National District Attorneys Association 2013). In some cases, judges "may order" counseling, whereas others "shall consider" or "shall order" it. Some statutes address only certain types of cruelty, such as animal fighting, torture, or bestiality. Notable among the laws is their lack of consistency across states and even within states, such as counseling required for juveniles but not adults. Laws addressing psychological evaluation of offenders—which is an important tool in determining appropriate interventions—demonstrate similar inconsistency. Even in states where laws mention counseling, anecdotal evidence suggests that judges inconsistently order it. Possible reasons for this discrepancy include:

- the judge or attorneys are unfamiliar with the section of the law pertaining to intervention
- neither the prosecution nor the defense asks for intervention as part of the sentence
- the judge or attorneys do not believe intervention will be useful, either for this particular offender or in general
- the judge does not feel justified in ordering counseling due to a perceived lack of severity of the offense
- the offender may be unable or claim to be unable to bear the costs of mandated intervention, leading the judge to waive it

Given these challenges to court referred intervention, it may be premature to focus on simply increasing legislative provisions for animal abuse offenders. Rather, focusing on improving anticruelty laws, enforcement, and the overall justice system response to animal abuse may be a prerequisite though not necessarily easy task. From there, increasing justice system awareness of animal abuse interventions may be the appropriate next step—though hopefully in concurrence with greater progress in developing more empirically supported interventions to which the justice system may refer offenders and in increasing the number of practitioners willing to provide them (see next section). These supply and demand variables interrelate closely.

Parent/Guardian Referral. One problem with this referral path is that parents/guardians may be unaware of their child's abusive behavior toward animals, either due to the behavior occurring in secret (Dadds et al. 2004) or due to lack of adult supervision. Children may harm animals outside the home in less readily observable settings, such as neighborhood cats or wildlife. Some adults who do encounter animal abuse by children minimize the behavior (e.g., "boys will be boys") and are unlikely to refer a child for intervention in the absence of other problems. Conversely, others may be ashamed to disclose their child's animal abuse due to perceived social stigma. Community education regarding animal abuse and the importance of children's healthy relationships with animals may be a key strategy to evaluate as a means to increase awareness, understanding, and response by adults to childhood animal abuse.

Incidental Revelation. It is also possible that information about animal abuse may come to light while an individual is undergoing intervention for some other issue. If an individual proactively discloses animal abuse, a great deal hinges on the practitioners' response: do they dismiss the information, or proactively explore and address it? Alternately, animal abuse can be identified through routine screening questions with all clients, regardless of whether animal abuse is known to have occurred or is a focus of the intervention. Unfortunately, the widespread lack of practitioner familiarity with the topic of animal abuse, and with the relevance of information about clients' relationships with animals in general (see next section), means that such routine questions are seldom asked. Further, questions about behaviors and attitudes toward animals rarely appear on standard intake or assessment instruments used in clinical settings. Where they do, they typically do not explore the subject in depth. For example, the widely used Child Behavior Checklist (Achenbach and Rescorla 2001) only contains the two items: "Cruel to animals," which leaves the definition of cruelty open to the respondent, and "Fears certain animals, situations, or places, other than school (describe)." The only response choices available are "Not true," "Somewhat or sometimes true," and "very true or often true." Instruments designed for general clinical use with adults that include items about animals are even rarer. Yet existing instruments specifically designed to assess animal abuse and/or clients' relationships with animals are not commonly used in the majority of practice settings. Most such instruments have been designed for research, rather than clinical use. Further, most practices are limited in the amount of time available for assessment, which may make it impractical to add a dedicated questionnaire about animals to the intake packet for all clients.

Our recommendation is that standard intake procedures in all intervention settings include at a minimum one screening question about animals, with more detailed follow-up if the item is endorsed. On a domestic violence crisis helpline, for example—where the length of the call may be determined by how long the victim is safely able to remain on the phone—an advocate may simply ask, "Are you concerned about any pets or other animals?" Similarly, school counselors could ask if a child has or has ever had animals, if s/he has ever lost one, and if s/he ever harmed or saw someone else harm one.

Finally, practitioners may obtain information about animal abuse through third-party sources, such as interviews with family members, teacher reports, or presentence investigation reports. However, this can only occur if these sources themselves report and/or document the animal abuse, which may be unlikely for reasons similar to those described above. In general, though, practitioners are wise to obtain information from multiple sources where practical and ethical. In the case of socially undesirable and potentially illegal behaviors such as animal abuse, third-party sources may be more likely than the client to voluntarily disclose information about such behavior.

Developing Practitioner Familiarity

If, despite the above obstacles, an offender does receive a referral for intervention, or if information about animal abuse is revealed during intervention for some other issue, the next question is whether there is a practitioner competent to address the animal abuse. Although attention to human-animal relationships is growing within the social sciences and helping professions, most practitioners remain relatively unfamiliar with animal abuse or its potential significance. Signal et al. (2013) found that most psychologists reading descriptions of animal abuse by children did not identify the animal abuse as a primary intervention target unless the psychologists suggested a preliminary diagnosis of Conduct Disorder for the child.

This lack of awareness can be traced in large part to the relative absence of animal topics in the professional training of human services personnel. Harm to animals receives only brief treatment in the current edition of the *Diagnostic and Statistical Manual of Mental Disorders* (*DSM-V*; American Psychiatric Association 2013). The only *DSM* disorder for which cruelty to animals is a diagnostic criterion is Conduct Disorder, and then only since the 1987 revision (*DSM III-R*). Zoophilia (sexual arousal involving animals) that causes clinically significant distress or impairment in functioning is contained in the category Other Specified Paraphilic Disorder (see also chapter herein on Animal Sexual Abuse). However, if zoophilia does not cause distress or functional impairment, it is not treated as a disorder according to *DSM-V* criteria. There is no *DSM-V* distinction between individuals who act on the arousal by committing animal sexual assault (bestiality) and those who do not. The new diagnosis of Hoarding Disorder in *DSM-V* mentions animal hoarding as a potential special manifestation of hoarding, which may spur greater awareness on the topic in coming years. Although animal abuse has been observed in clinical practice in association with numerous other mental disorders, with initial research suggesting particular connections to personality disorders and substance use disorders (Gleyzer et al. 2002; Vaughn et al. 2009), it has not yet been established as a diagnostic feature of other disorders such as would merit inclusion in their *DSM* criteria sets. Further research examining potential patterns of association between animal abuse and mental disorders is greatly needed.

For now, the upshot of this lack of awareness is that many practitioners do not understand animal abuse and do not consider themselves competent to work with individuals who have abused animals. From the current authors' experiences leading trainings, it is clear that an additional subset of practitioners is unwilling to work with these individuals because of their own discomfort in hearing about animal abuse and/or distaste for working with individuals who have harmed animals. If an offender is referred (by a court, guardian, etc.) for evaluation or intervention and no one will take the case, this may serve to delegitimize animal abuse as a concern within the system and discourage future referrals. At the same time, if referrals for animal abuse evaluation/intervention are infrequent, there is little incentive for practitioners to become competent in handling these cases.

Perhaps the single most powerful change that could be made systematically is to integrate material on animal abuse and human-animal relationships into the standard training of human service professionals. While specialized courses on the human-animal violence connection and the human-animal bond are growing in popularity (Animals & Society Institute 2016), it seems equally if not more important to reach those practitioners and practitioners-in-training who do not already have a special interest in this topic and who would be unlikely to sign up for an elective course on it. If these practitioners come to recognize animal abuse as another form of violent behavior that may be also connected to other problematic behaviors and/or other pathology, developing their competency in animal abuse intervention could be as straightforward as educating them on determining how the animal abuse is connected to the client's other functioning and incorporating this information into the interventions they already provide.[2] Consequently, these practitioners may be more willing to take identified animal abuse cases, as well as to be proactive in addressing animal abuse when it is not the identified focus of an intervention.

If animal abuse diversion programs and/or specialized animal welfare courts are successfully replicated across the US, this too may solve part of the "referral pipeline problem" and result in greater access to intervention by offenders for whom it is appropriate. Another potential outgrowth of these initiatives is that they may drive interest among clinicians in becoming familiar with this area in order to take advantage of demand by the courts.

Selecting a Finer Paintbrush

When the present authors conduct training on animal abuse prevention/intervention and ask participants to describe the first image that comes into their heads when thinking of an "animal abuser," the most common response—particularly from lay audiences—is an adult man beating or kicking a companion animal, such as a cat or dog. Yet the preceding chapters of this book demonstrate that animal abuse is not a homogeneous phenomenon. Rather, animal abuse can take multiple forms, within and across such categories as physical, emotional and sexual abuse, and neglect; it can be direct or indirect, and proximal (in close contact with the victim) or distal; its victims can be companion, wild, or farmed animals; it can be perpetrated by males or females of any age. Further, humans inflict harm on animals for a variety of reasons: financial gain, ignorance, aggression, retaliation, species prejudice, thrill, peer pressure, status, cultural practice, and so on (see Kellert and Felthous 1985 and Vermeulen and Odendaal 1993, for a fuller review). These differing motivations for abuse may themselves differ by gender: previous research by Gupta (2008) used

[2] Nevertheless, we recommend that stopping the abusive behavior toward animals be explicitly addressed even when it is not the intervention goal, and that animal abuse not be treated as a mere indicator.

structural equation modeling to illustrate potentially different pathways to violence against animals for males and females.

It follows that just as there is no single "cure" for interpersonal violence, there is unlikely to be one uniform approach to intervention that works for everyone who has harmed animals. If a heterogeneous group of offenders receives a single intervention, even if that intervention works very well for some, its positive effect is likely to be difficult to detect amidst the outcome data from the whole group. Yet while programs such as AniCare emphasize using the results of individualized assessment to inform intervention strategy, such toolkit-style, non-manualized approaches lend themselves less readily to outcome evaluation. Considerable work is needed to further clarify potential subtypes of animal abuse offenders who may warrant differing intervention approaches, and to develop distinct intervention approaches that work optimally for each. However, this work requires access to large populations of offenders in research-oriented intervention settings, which (as discussed as part of the "referral pipeline problem") is not currently the norm.

A controversial but related question is whether all animal abuse offenders actually need intervention. Public opinion suggests that they do: Bailey et al., (2016) assessed undergraduate students' reactions to reading animal cruelty vignettes in which the species of animal victim, age of perpetrator, and location of crime (that is, in kennel or shelter) varied. Across all vignettes, the median response was "Strongly Agree" to the item, "The guilty person should have to complete psychological counseling or complete an anger management program." At the same time, participants also strongly agreed that all offenders should receive punishment. Psychosocial interventions remain unpopular with some prosecutors who see them as antithetical to offender accountability and punishment, or as minimizing the seriousness of crime. In our view, this argument perpetuates a false dichotomy between intervention and punishment, illustrated satirically in the song "Gee, Officer Krupke" from the classic musical *West Side Story* (Sondheim 1957): e.g., "This boy don't need a job, he needs a year in the pen"; "The trouble is he's crazy/The trouble is he drinks/The trouble is he's lazy/The trouble is he stinks."

However, it is still important to ask—through a lens informed by data rather than opinion—whether there is a subset of animal abuse offenders for whom it may not be possible to develop effective intervention, and for whom punishment or other approaches may consequently be more effective. Although the current state of research knowledge may not yet permit answering this question definitively, it should remain on the table. The presence of significant numbers of "incurable" offenders in outcome research is likely to have the same result as providing an intervention that is appropriate for only one subtype of offenders: unless it is possible to identify the subset or subtype and examine their outcomes separately from the group as a whole, we may erroneously conclude that the intervention does not work at all, especially in small samples with inadequate statistical power to detect true differences.

An opposite yet no less egregious mistake than the above false negative (type II error) is to conclude that an intervention works when it actually does not (type I error). As lamented throughout this chapter, data are limited in the area of animal abuse interventions, and it is not uncommon for interventions to be developed and advertised with scant evidence of effectiveness. With outcome research on animal abuse in its infancy compared to other intervention research, and at least partially due yet again to the difficulty of obtaining solid samples of animal abuse offenders thanks to challenges previously described, methodological weaknesses haunt much of the existing work. Comparison groups such as no-treatment controls are often absent: thus, even if substantial improvement is observed in those receiving the intervention, it is impossible to identify whether the change was due to the intervention or would have occurred regardless (e.g., natural improvement over time). Attitudes are often used as a proxy for behavior—e.g., reporting that intervention participants demonstrated improved scores on a measure of kind attitudes toward animals—but seminal work by LaPiere (1934) illustrates that questionnaire-based attitudinal measures do not always predict actions. When behavior is measured, it is rare to see it measured over lengthy follow-up intervals, providing no indication as to the lasting effect of the behavior change beyond the end of the intervention. Notwithstanding the challenges inherent in studying animal abuse interventions, it is time for the field to hold itself accountable to a higher standard.

Where Else Next?

Bridging the Prevention/Intervention Divide

While the interventions described earlier in this chapter focus on individuals who have already harmed animals, programs aimed at preventing violence toward animals and/or humans are becoming more widespread. It may be useful to consider prevention and intervention as a continuum rather than a dichotomy; for this purpose, the public health model of primary, secondary, and tertiary prevention (Clark and Leavell 1958) may be helpful. As applied to mental and behavioral health, primary prevention aims to prevent initial onset of a disorder; secondary prevention emphasizes early detection and treatment once a disorder exists, with the aim of healing or eliminating the disorder; and tertiary prevention focuses on reducing disability and preventing relapse associated with an established disorder.

One branch of primary prevention, universal primary prevention, refers to efforts directed at the general population (Mrazek and Haggerty 1994). Humane education programs are a notable example of such an effort, often delivered in school classrooms and focused on healthy attitudes toward animals, empathy, and care and responsibility for animals in the home. In a literature review of humane education programs, Arbour et al. (2009) note that despite the existence of over 2000 such programs currently operating in the US, there is scant research documenting the effects of teaching children about humane animal treatment and empathy building skills on their subsequent behavior toward animals. The Healing Species Violence Intervention and Compassion Education Program (Pearson 2011) is the only animal-oriented program of any kind to be included on the National Registry of Evidence-based Programs and Practices (NREPP), a project of the Substance Abuse and Mental Health Services Administration. Designed for children aged 9 to 14 and aimed at the development of prosocial behaviors through interacting with an instructor and a rescued dog, the program demonstrates reductions in aggressive and violent behavior compared with children who do not receive the program, as well as reductions in disciplinary referrals and beliefs that aggression is normal.

Primary prevention can also be "selective," that is, targeted at at-risk populations rather than the population as a whole, or "indicated," targeting those who already show some minimal symptoms of a disease. Programs working with youth deemed at risk for violence toward animals vary in duration and intensity. For example, through Forget-Me-Not Farm, a weekly after-school program, children from families and communities in which violence is prevalent, learn the responsible care of animals (Rathman 1999). An adult-oriented example of a primary prevention program is Pets for Life (The Humane Society of the United States 2014), which uses a community outreach model to assist with animal care in underserved communities where lack of resources and information may jeopardize companion animal welfare.

As applied to animal abuse, primary prevention efforts aimed at preventing the initial occurrence of animal abuse may be viewed as one end of a continuum, with diversion (secondary prevention) and other intervention programs (secondary/tertiary prevention) treated as prevention efforts on that same continuum. This perspective may provide a more cohesive and powerful approach to animal abuse than *post hoc* intervention alone. Connection is key: if primary prevention is the domain of different researchers and practitioners from those who research and implement after-the-fact interventions, and if the two groups do not share knowledge effectively, then the theoretical benefit of the prevention continuum is lost. Consider two graduate students, one of whom wants to enter the field of humane education to help children be kinder to animals but cannot fathom working with people who harm animals, and the other of whom wants to work in forensic settings with animal abuse offenders but has no interest in "normal" human behavior. Each is in a position to learn something from the work of the other, and they may even encounter some of the same individuals at different points in time—but if their paths never intersect, they may unwittingly be working at cross-purposes.

A Note on Animal-Assisted Interventions

Some of the interventions described in the early part of this chapter involve offenders working with animals, while others do not or at least do not explicitly prescribe it. Perhaps one of the most polarizing questions in the field of animal abuse interventions is whether individuals who have harmed animals should be allowed to have contact with them. Hotly debated forms of "contact" include future animal ownership (a proscription against which is often sought in court cases), community service at animal shelters, and animal-assisted interventions (including animal-assisted therapies).

On one hand, for ethical and safety reasons, interventions targeted at perpetrators of other forms of violence do not typically recommend contact with the victim (or with potential other victims) as part of the offender's rehabilitation: someone convicted of child abuse is unlikely to be sentenced to work at a children's home without public outrage, and couples therapy is controversial and largely eschewed in the field of domestic violence intervention. Animal abuse offender registries, similar to sex offender registries, have been implemented in a few counties and in one state (Tennessee) with the goal of protecting animals and the public by monitoring and restricting offenders' contact with animals.

On the other hand, animal-assisted interventions are growing greatly in popularity, with federal research funding now being directed at their development and dissemination (Eunice Kennedy Shriver National Institute of Child Health and Human Development 2012). The use of actual animals has promise as a potent means of teaching boundaries, empathy, prosocial behavior, and attachment skills. If interventions with animals can be delivered in a carefully structured, supervised setting that minimizes risk to the animal while allowing the offender to practice developing more positive relationships and behaviors with animals, perhaps these serve as a valuable step toward offenders eventually interacting with animals in less supervised settings. (A major challenge of "no animal contact" orders in sentencing is that they are very difficult to enforce, given the general lack of enforcement resources for animal protection and the ease for most people of obtaining access to animals. We therefore adopt the assumption that individuals who have abused animals are likely to have opportunities to interact with and/or acquire animals again in future without the supervision, or perhaps even the knowledge, of the justice/intervention system.)

As with all human-animal interaction programs, including animal-assisted therapies, we emphasize the importance of considering the safety and well-being of the animal rather than solely the potential benefit to the human participant. In an appeal to parsimony, we also challenge animal-assisted interventions for animal abuse to demonstrate that they do in fact provide unique benefits to offenders that could not be achieved without the presence of the animal in the intervention.

Conclusion

The preceding serves as a review of currently available interventions for animal abuse offenders, whether those offenders are identified through the court system, through adult referral of a juvenile, or through incidental revelation of animal abuse in an intervention focused on another problem. Although promising programs exist, access to demonstrated effective interventions for both children and adults is clearly not yet available in most areas of the country. In painting a picture of why this is so, it is important not simply to fault the interventions themselves but to adopt a systemic view of factors at all levels that impede the development and dissemination of more effective services. It is our hope that this analysis will serve to spur initiatives in both research and policy that seek to overcome these obstacles. While it may be difficult to be patient, especially when the original question "So how do we make them stop?" becomes the more insistent "So why haven't you made them stop yet?," we believe that careful attention to these tasks that lie ahead in the field of animal abuse interventions is energy well invested toward safer and more compassionate communities for all.

References

Achenbach, T. M., & Rescorla, L. A. (2001). *Manual for the ASEBA school-age forms and profiles*. Burlington, VT: University of Vermont, Research Center for Children, Youth, and Families.

American Psychiatric Association. (2013). *Diagnostic and statistical manual of mental disorders*. 5th edition. Arlington, VA: American Psychiatric Publishing.

Animals & Society Institute (2016). *Human-Animal Studies courses*. http://www.animalsandsociety.org/human-animal-studies/courses/. Accessed 27 May 2016.

Animals & Society Institute (2016). *Jail diversion programs for animal abuse offenders* (PowerPoint slides). Ann Arbor, MI: Author.

Arbour, R., Signal, T., & Taylor, N. (2009). Teaching kindness: the promise of humane education. *Society & Animals, 17*(2), 136–148.

Arluke, A. & Luke, C. (1997). Physical cruelty toward animals in Massachusetts, 1975–1996. *Society & Animals, 5*, 195–205.

Ascione, F. R., & Shapiro, K. (2009). People and animals, kindness and cruelty: Research directions and policy implications. *Journal of Social Issues, 65*(3), 569–589.

Bailey, S. K. T., Sims, V. K., & Chin, M. G. (2016). Predictors of views about punishing animal abuse. *Anthrozoös, 29*(1), 21–33.

The Center for Health and Justice at TASC (2013). *No entry: A national survey of criminal justice diversion programs and initiatives*. Chicago: Author.

Clark, E. G., & Leavell, H. R. (1958). Levels of application of preventive medicine. In H. R. Leavell & E. G. Clark (Eds.), *Preventive medicine for the doctor in his community: An epidemiologic approach* (2nd edition, pp. 13–39). New York: McGraw-Hill.

Dadds, M. R., Whiting, C., Bunn, P., Fraser, J., & Charlson, J. (2004). Measurement of cruelty in children: The Cruelty to Animals Inventory. *Journal of Abnormal Child Psychology, 32*, 321–334.

Eunice Kennedy Shriver National Institute of Child Health and Human Development (2012). Processes in social and affective development: Human-Animal Interaction (HAI) research. https://www.nichd.nih.gov/about/org/der/branches/cdbb/programs/psad/hai/pages/overview.aspx. Accessed 27 May 2016.

Federal Bureau of Investigation. (2016, February 1). Tracking animal cruelty: FBI collecting data on crimes against animals. https://www.fbi.gov/news/stories/2016/february/tracking-animal-cruelty/tracking-animal-cruelty. Accessed 27 May 2016.

Frost, R. O., Patronek, G., Arluke, A., & Steketee, G. (2015). The hoarding of animals: An update. *Psychiatric Times, 32*(4), 1-5.

Gleyzer, R., Felthous, A. R., & Holzer, C. E. (2002). Animal cruelty and psychiatric disorders. *Journal of the American Academy of Psychiatry and Law, 30*, 257–265.

Gupta, M. (2008). Functional links between intimate partner violence and animal abuse: Personality features and representations of aggression. *Society and Animals, 16*(3), 223–242.

The Humane Society of the United States (2014). *Pets for life: An in-depth community understanding*. http://www.humanesociety.org/assets/pdfs/pets/pets-for-life/pfl-report-0214.pdf. Accessed 2 January 2016.

Jory, B., Anderson, D., & Greer, C. (1997). Intimate justice: Confronting issues of accountability, respect, and freedom in treatment for abuse and violence. *Journal of Marital and Family Therapy, 23*(4), 399–419.

Jory, B., & Randour, M. L. (1999). *The AniCare model of treatment for animal abuse*. Washington Grove: MD: PSYETA.

Kellert, S. R., & Felthous, A. R. (1985). Childhood cruelty toward animals among criminals and non-criminals. *Human Relations, 38*, 1113–1129.

LaPiere, R. T. (1934). Attitudes vs. actions. *Social Forces, 13*(2), 230–237.

Lowther, D. (2012). *Perception Counseling Animal Treatment Offender Program: Stopping animal cruelty*. Unpublished manuscript.

Lunghofer, L. (2015). Social responses to animal maltreatment offenders: Cruelty and sexual abuse. In L. Levitt, T. Grisso, G. Patronek (Eds.) *Animal maltreatment: Forensic mental health issues and evaluations* (pp. 251–286). Oxford: Oxford University Press.

McNamara, P. (2013). Animal Welfare court responds to special kind of crime. *Arizona Daily Star*. http://tucson.com/news/local/animal-welfare-court-responds-to-special-kind-of-crime/article_73478df1-23f8-5622-89ec-0cf954f68f7b.html. Accessed 2 January 2016.

Mrazek, P.J., & Haggerty, R.J. (Eds.). (1994). *Reducing risks for mental disorders: Frontiers for preventive intervention research*. Washington, DC: National Academy Press.

National District Attorneys Association. (2013). *Counseling laws for convicted animal abusers*. http://www.animalsandsociety.org/wp-content/uploads/2015/01/Counseling-Laws-for-Convicted-Animal-Abusers-February-2013.pdf. Accessed 2 January 2016.

National Institute of Corrections (2011). *Measuring what matters: Outcome and performance measures for the pretrial services field*. http://nicic.gov/library/025172. Accessed 10 June 2016.

National Institute of Justice (2013). *Specialized courts*. http://www.nij.gov/topics/courts/pages/specialized-courts.aspx. Accessed 2 January 2016.

National Link Coalition (2016). *Bibliography of the link between animal abuse, domestic violence, child abuse and elder abuse*. http://animaltherapy.net/animal-abuse-human-violence/bibliography/. Accessed 9 June 2016.

Pawedu (2016). Animal welfare education for animal cruelty offenders. http://pawedu.com/. Accessed 2 January 2016.

Pearson, W. J. (2011). The healing species: Animal-assisted character education for improving student behavior. *Journal of Youth Development: Bridging Research and Practice, 6*(1), 4–5.

Rathmann, C. (1999). Forget Me Not Farm: Teaching gentleness with gardens and animals to children from violent homes and communities. In F.R. Ascione & P.

Arkow (Eds.), *Child abuse, domestic violence, and animal abuse: Linking the circles of compassion for prevention and intervention* (pp. 393–409). West Lafayette, IN: Purdue University Press.

Risley-Curtiss, C. (2014). *Children and Animals Together Assessment and Intervention Program.* Unpublished manuscript, School of Social Work, Arizona State University, Phoenix, AZ.

Shapiro, K., & Henderson, A. J. Z. (2016). *The identification, assessment, and treatment of adults who abuse animals: The AniCare approach.* New York: Springer.

Shapiro, K., Randour, M. L., Krinsk, S., & Wolf, J. L. (2014). *The assessment and treatment of children who abuse animals: The AniCare child approach.* New York: Springer.

Signal, T., Ghea, V., Taylor, N., & Acutt, D. (2013). When do psychologists pay attention to children harming animals? *Human-Animal Interaction Bulletin, 1*(2), 82–97.

Society for the Prevention of Cruelty to Animals Los Angeles (n.d.). *jTLC: Teaching love and compassion for juvenile offenders.* Los Angeles, CA: Author.

Sondheim, S. (Lyricist) (1957). *Gee, Officer Krupke.* http://www.westsidestory.com/site/level2/lyrics/krupke.html. Accessed 2 January 2016.

Vaughn, M. G., Fu, Q., DeLisi, M., Beaver, K., Perron, B., Terrell, K., et al. (2009). Correlates of cruelty to animals in the United States: Results from the National Epidemiologic Survey on Alcohol and Related Conditions. *Journal of Psychiatric Research, 43,* 1213–1218.

Vermeulen, H., & Odendaal, J. (1993). Proposed typology of companion animal abuse. *Anthrozoös, 6,* 248–257.

Maya Gupta, Ph.D. earned her bachelor's degree from Columbia University and her master's and doctoral degrees in clinical psychology from the University of Georgia, with a predoctoral internship in the Psychology Service at the United States Penitentiary, Atlanta. Her work focuses on connections between animal cruelty and interpersonal violence, particularly family violence, and on using this knowledge to improve coordinated community response to violence in all forms. Her leadership in the field of human-animal relationships includes previous roles as Executive Director of the Animals & Society Institute and as Executive Director of the Ahimsa House domestic violence safe haven program for animals. She currently serves as Training Director of the American Psychological Association's Section on Human-Animal Interaction, on the Steering Committee of the National Link Coalition, on the Animal Cruelty Advisory Council of the Association of Prosecuting Attorneys, as an adjunct faculty member in the Master's Program in Anthrozoology at Canisius College, and as an instructor for the Veterinary Forensic Sciences program at the University of Florida.

Lisa Lunghofer, Ph.D. is the Director of Human-Animal Programs for the Animals & Society Institute. She has a PhD in social policy, an MA in psychology, and 20 years of experience developing and leading programs in the human service and criminal justice fields. As a consultant in both for-profit and nonprofit organizations, she has worked extensively in the areas of violence prevention, juvenile justice, and mental health. Since 2009, she has worked closely with a variety of animal-related programs throughout the country, helping them to develop logic models, write successful grant proposals, develop evaluation plans, craft marketing materials, and identify and track outcomes. She also volunteers with Lucky Dog Animal Rescue in Washington, DC.

Kenneth Shapiro, Ph.D. received his BA in History and Literature from Harvard University and his PhD in Clinical and Personality Psychology from Duke. He is cofounder of the Animals & Society Institute and one of its predecessor organizations, Psychologists for the Ethical treatment of Animals. He is founder and editor of *Society and Animals: Journal of Human-Animal Studies*; co-founder and co-editor of *Journal of Applied Animal Welfare Science*; and editor of the *Brill Human-Animal Studies* book series. His most recent book is *The Identification, Assessment, and Treatment of Adults Who Abuse Animals: The AniCare Approach* (2016), published by Springer (http://www.animalsandsociety.org/helping-animals-and-people/anicare/).

Author Index

J. Maher et al. (eds.), *The Palgrave International Handbook of Animal Abuse Studies*, DOI 10.1057/978-1-137-43183-7

N

O

P

Y

Z

Subject Index

J. Maher et al. (eds.), *The Palgrave International Handbook of Animal Abuse Studies*, DOI 10.1057/978-1-137-43183-7

B

D

E

F

CPSIA information can be obtained
at www.ICGtesting.com
Printed in the USA
BVOW06*0800020817
490914BV00014B/34/P

9 781137 43182